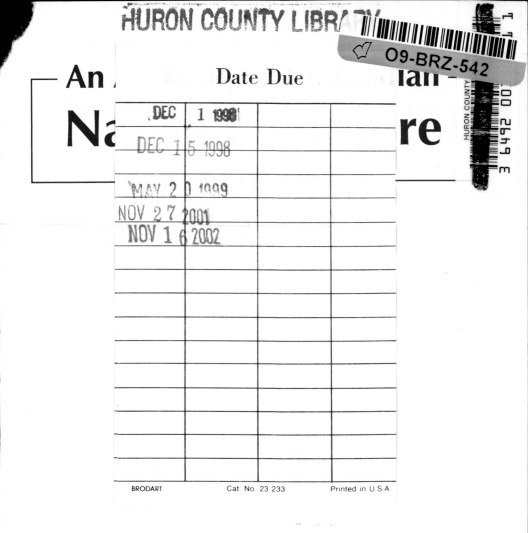

An ... ian
Na... re

Toronto Oxford New York

OXFORD UNIVERSITY PRESS

1998

DEC 2 '97

Oxford University Press
70 Wynford Drive, Don Mills, Ontario M3C 1J9
http://www.oupcan.com

Oxford   New York
Athens   Auckland   Bangkok   Calcutta
Cape Town   Chennai   Dar es Salaam   Delhi
Florence   Hong Kong   Istanbul   Karachi
Kuala Lumpur   Madrid   Melbourne   Mexico City
Mumbai   Nairobi   Paris   Singapore
Taipei   Tokyo   Toronto   Warsaw

and associated companies in
Berlin   Ibadan

Oxford is a trademark of Oxford University Press

Canadian Cataloguing in Publication Data

Main entry under title:

An Anthology of Canadian native literature in English

2nd ed.
Includes index.
ISBN 0-19-541282-6

1. Canadian literature (English) – Indian authors.*
2. Canadian literature (English) – Inuit authors.*
3. Canadian literature (English) – Métis authors. *
4. Indians of North America – Canada – Literary collections.
I. Goldie, Terry, 1950–   .   II. Moses, Daniel David, 1952–   .

PS8235.I6A56 1997   C810.8′0897   C97-931362-7
PR9194.5.I5A56 1997

Cover Design: Max Gabriel Izod
Cover Illustration: Robert Houle
Composition: True to Type

Since this page cannot accommodate all the copyright notices,
pages xi–xvi constitute an extension of the copyright page.

1 2 3 4 – 01 00 99 98

This book is printed on permanent (acid-free) paper ∞ .

Printed in Canada

Contents

Acknowledgements

The authors wish to acknowledge the kind assistance of Denise Bukowski and Lorna Crozier, and, at Oxford University Press, Euan White and Jane McNulty.

KATERI AKIWENZIE-DAMM. 'kegedonce' from *my heart is a stray bullet*, Kegedonce Press, Cape Croker, 1993. 'the resurrection of desire' and 'words for winter' from *Voices from Home: The W.I.N.O. Anthology*, Volume 1, Agawa Press, 1994. 'Grandmother, Grandfather' and 'Why This Woman' from *The Colour of Resistance*, Sister Vision, 1993. All poems reprinted by permission of the author.

ANNHARTE. 'Coyote Trail', 'Penumbra', 'Upbraid', 'Raced Out to Write This Up', and 'One Way to Keep Track of Who Is Talking'.

ANNHARTE. 'Coyote Columbus Cafe', 'Bear Piss Water', 'I Want to Dance Wild Indian Black Face', and 'Put On My Mask For a Change'. Copyright Annharte. Reprinted by permission from *Coyote Columbus Cafe*, Moonprint Press, 1994.

JEANNETTE ARMSTRONG. 'History Lesson', 'For Tony', 'Sketches', 'Indian Woman', 'Threads of Old Memory', 'Fire Madness', 'Wind Woman', and 'Keepers Words' originally published in Jeannette Armstrong's poetry collection *Breathtracks* published by Theytus Books (ISBN 0-919441-39-4, retail $9.95). Reprinted by permission of Theytus Books. 'The Disempowerment of First North American Native Peoples and Empowerment Through Their Writing' originally published in *Gatherings Volume I* published by Theytus Books. Reprinted by permission of Theytus Books. 'Blue Against White' originally published in *Gatherings Volume IV* published by Theytus Books (ISBN 0-919441-48-3, retail $12.95). Reprinted by permission of Theytus Books.

SIMON ARNAVIAPIK. 'Remembering Old Times' from *Inuktitut*, 1974. Reprinted by kind permission of Inuktitut Magazine.

BETH BRANT. 'A Long Story' from *Mohawk Trail*, Women's Press, 1990. Reprinted by permission of Women's Press. 'Swimming Upstream' from *Food & Spirits: Stories by Beth Brant (Degonwadonti)*, Press Gang Publishers, 1991, and Firebrand Books, Ithaca, New York. Copyright © 1991 by

Beth Brant. Reprinted by permission of the publishers. 'Grandmothers of a New World' from *Writing As Witness: essay and talk*, Women's Press, 1994. Reprinted by permission of Women's Press.

MARIA CAMPBELL. 'Jacob' and 'Joseph's Justice' originally published in *Stories of the Road Allowance People* by Maria Campbell available through Theytus Books (ISBN 0-919441-39-4, retail $12.95).

HAROLD CARDINAL. 'A Canadian *What the Hell It's All About*' from *The Rebirth of Canada's Indians*.

BETH CUTHAND. 'Shake 'N Bake', 'Zen Indian', 'He Told Me', and 'Four Songs for the Fifth Generation' originally published in *Voices in the Waterfall* by Beth Cuthand available through Theytus Books (ISBN 0-919441-43-2, retail $11.95). 'Post-Oka Kinda Woman' originally published in *Gatherings Volume V* available through Theytus Books (ISBN 0-919441-61-0, retail $12.95).

JOSEPH DANDURAND. 'Salmon Queen' and 'Swimming the Cannon River' from *Voices from Home: The W.I.N.O. Anthology*, Volume 1, Agawa Press, 1994.

MARILYN DUMONT. All poems from *A Really Good Brown Girl* (1996). Reprinted by permission of Brick Books.

CONNIE FIFE. 'Communications class', 'Stains', 'Dream', and 'Driftwoodwoman' from *Beneath the Naked Sun*, Sister Vision, 1992.

RON GEYSHICK. 'Inside Me', 'To Bless a Child Before the Name', 'Quiet', 'Around the World in a Big Trout', 'A Windigo', and 'Cannibal Woman' from *Te Bwe Win*.

RICHARD GREEN. 'The Last Raven' from *The Last Raven and Other Stories* (1991) is reprinted by permission of the author.

ALMA GREENE. Excerpt from *Forbidden Voice: Reflections of a Mohawk Indian* is reprinted with permission of Green Dragon Press, Toronto, Canada.

LOUISE HALFE. 'Pāhkahkos', 'She Told Me', 'Body Politics', 'Fog Inside Mama', 'Stones', 'Idylwyld Crow', 'My Ledders', 'for Omeasoo', and 'The Heat of My Grandmothers' reprinted from *Bear Bones & Feathers* by Louise Bernice Halfe, published by Coteau Books in 1994. Reprinted by permission of the publisher. All rights reserved.

THOM E. HAWKE. 'Lasalle, Quebec', 'Lock and Load', 'Apologies to Elijah

Harper', and 'The Death of John Wayne'. All poems reprinted by permission of W. Allen DeLeary.

TOMSON HIGHWAY. Excerpt from *The Rez Sisters* and 'The Lover Snake'. Used by permission of Tomson Highway and Creative Technique Inc.

ALOOTOOK IPELLIE. All poems are reprinted by permission of the author.

RITA JOE. 'Today's Learning Child', 'I Lost My Talk', 'Micmac Hieroglyphics', 'Shanawdithit', and 'The Lament of Donald Marshall Jr.' © Rita Joe, from *Song of Eskasoni*. Used with the permission of Ragweed Press, Charlottetown, PEI.

BASIL H. JOHNSTON. 'The Prophecy', 'One Generation from Extinction', and 'Is That All There Is? Tribal Literature' © Basil H. Johnston. Reprinted by permission of Beverley Slopen.

MARGO KANE. 'Moonlodge' developed and performed by M. Kane – Saulteaux/Cree. Reprinted by permission of the author.

LENORE KEESHIG-TOBIAS. 'After Oka—How Has Canada Changed?' is reprinted by permission of the author. Sections from 'Trickster Beyond 1992: Our Relationship' from *Indigena: Contemporary Native Perspectives*, Gerald McMaster and Lee-Ann Martin, eds, Douglas & McIntyre and Canadian Museum of Civilization, 1992. Reprinted with the permission of the Canadian Museum of Civilization.

WAYNE KEON. All poems are reprinted by permission of the author.

THOMAS KING. 'The One About Coyote Going West' by Thomas King from *One Good Story, That One*, copyright 1993 by Dead Dog Café Productions Inc. Published in Canada by HarperCollins Publishers Ltd. Reprinted by permission of the author.

JOHN McLEOD. 'The Shivering Tree'.

LEE MARACLE. 'Yin Chin' and 'Sojourner's Truth'.

MARTIN MARTIN. 'We, the Inuit, Are Changing' from *Them Days*, Vol. 2, No. 1, September 1976.

SUSAN MARTIN. 'When I Was a Child' from *Them Days*, Vol. 2, No. 1, 1976. Translated by Fran McIntosh. Reprinted by permission of Them Days Inc.

DUNCAN MERCREDI. 'could be anyone but i call him syd', 'statue', 'god shrugged and turned his back', 'big bear', and 'kiskisin (i remember)' from *Wolf and Shadows* by Duncan Mercredi. Winnipeg: Pemmican Publications Inc., 1995. Reprinted by permission.

MONIQUE MOJICA. Excerpt from *Princess Pocahontas and the Blue Spots*, Women's Press, 1991. Reprinted by permission of Women's Press.

DANIEL DAVID MOSES. 'The Sunbather's Fear of the Moon', 'Inukshuk', 'The Persistence of Songs', and 'The Line' from *The White Line*, Fifth House. All poems used by permission of the author.

BEATRICE MOSIONIER. Excerpt from *April Raintree*.

PHILIP KEVIN PAUL. 'Still Falling' and 'Belly Button'. First published in *Breathing Fire: Canada's New Poets* edited by Patrick Lane and Lorna Crozier (Madeira Park, BC: Harbour Publishing, 1995). Reprinted by permission of the author. 'KENNES' is written in an alphabet developed by Philip Kevin Paul's grandfather, David Elliott, Sr.

DUKE REDBIRD. 'I am a Canadian' and excerpt from *We Are Métis* are reprinted by permission of the author.

EDEN ROBINSON. 'Terminal Avenue' by Eden Robinson, copyright 1996 by the author. Published by permission of the author via The Bukowski Agency.

HARRY ROBINSON. 'Captive in an English Circus' from *Write It on Your Heart: The Epic World of an Okanagan Storyteller*, Talonbooks, 1989.

ARMAND GARNET RUFFO. 'Annie Espaniel, 1923', 'Why I Write', 'Archie Belaney, 1930–31', and 'How Do You Know?' from *Grey Owl: The Mystery of Archie Belaney*, Coteau Books, 1997. 'Poem For Duncan Campbell Scott', 'Creating a Country', 'Hospital Visit', 'Poetry', and 'The Season' from *Opening In The Sky* by Armand Garnet Ruffo, Theytus Books, 1994. Reprinted by permission of the author.

BUFFY SAINTE-MARIE. 'Universal Soldier', 'My Country 'Tis of Thy People You're Dying', and 'Now That the Buffalo's Gone'.

GREGORY A. SCOFIELD. 'Nothing Sacred' from *The Gathering: Stones for the Medicine Wheel*, Polestar, 1993. '*Ayahkwêw*'s Lodge', 'Promises', 'Cycle (of the black lizard)', 'How Many White People Noticed (and recounted the scene over dinner)', and 'Warrior Mask' from *Native Canadiana:*

Songs from the Urban Rez, Polestar, 1996. Reprinted with permission of the author and Polestar Book Publishers, Vancouver, B.C.

PAUL SEESEQUASIS. 'The Republic of Tricksterism' is reprinted by permission of the author.

LORNE JOSEPH SIMON. Chapter Four, 'The Second Coming', originally published in *Stones and Switches* by Lorne Simon available through Theytus Books (ISBN 0-919441-68-8, retail $12.95).

RUBY SLIPPERJACK. 'Blueberry Days' from *Honour The Sun* by Ruby Slipperjack. Winnipeg: Pemmican Publications Inc., 1987. Reprinted by permission.

MARY AUGUSTA TAPPAGE. 'Tyee—Big Chief', 'The Lillooets', 'Christmas at the Mission', and 'At Birth' from *The Days of Augusta*, edited by Jean E. Speare, © 1973, 1992 by Augusta Evans and Jean E. Speare, published by Douglas & McIntyre. Reprinted with permission of the publisher.

DREW HAYDEN TAYLOR. 'Pretty Like a White Boy: The Adventures of a Blue Eyed Ojibway' is reprinted by permission of the author.

ANTHONY APAKARK THRASHER. 'Playing with Girls is a Sin' from *Thrasher . . . Skid Row Eskimo*.

MARION TUU'LUQ. 'A Story of Starvation' from *Inuit Today*, 1977. Reprinted by permission of the author.

JAMES TYMAN. Excerpt reprinted with permission from *Inside Out* (Fifth House Publishers, 1989).

RICHARD VAN CAMP. 'Kiss' and 'Floaters' from *The Lesser Blessed* by Richard Van Camp, © 1996, published by Douglas & McIntyre. Reprinted with the permission of the publisher. 'Birthmark' from *Gatherings Volume IV* available through Theytus Books (ISBN 0-919441-48-3, retail $12.95).

RICHARD WAGAMESE. Excerpt from *Keeper'n Me*, copyright © 1994 by Richard Wagamese. Reprinted with the permission of Doubleday Canada Limited.

EMMA LEE WARRIOR. 'Compatriots'.

JORDAN WHEELER. 'A Mountain Legend' from *achimoona*, Fifth House Publishers, 1985. © Jordan Wheeler. Reprinted by permission of the author.

ALEXANDER WOLFE. 'The Last Grass Dance' reprinted with permission from *Earth Elder Stories* (Fifth House Publishers, 1988).

Every effort has been made to determine and contact copyright owners. In the case of any omissions, the publisher will be pleased to make suitable acknowledgement in future editions.

Preface to the Second Edition

This volume is primarily a response to the great number of new works that have appeared since the first edition of *An Anthology of Canadian Native Literature in English*. The second edition includes fourteen new writers and at least ten of the writers in the first edition have published new books since 1992. There seems to be a greater market today for Native writers in Canada. First books by Eden Robinson and Marilyn Dumont have received immediate notice in the mainstream press, while it took years for Tomson Highway and Drew Hayden Taylor, for example, to attract critical attention. Still, we can't help but wonder whether there is a similar ready acceptance of writers whose work is perceived as more overtly political—writers such as Annharte, Maria Campbell, Lenore Keeshig-Tobias, and Lee Maracle. It might be worth noting that these four writers are all female.

As we write this preface to the second edition, Canada is in the midst of the 1997 federal election, an election in which all Native issues seem to have been forgotten. And in the case of Ipperwash, for example, the 'agents of the Crown' demonstrated little concern for Native rights. As this second edition shows, Native writers are writing more and publishing more. But what, if anything, has really changed for the First Nations of Canada in Canada?

Toronto
June, 1997

Preface to the First Edition:
Two Voices

DANIEL DAVID MOSES AND TERRY GOLDIE

We were concerned as we discussed an appropriate introduction for this book not to conceal the differences between our perspectives as a Native writer and a white academic. The process of selecting an anthology is like a long discussion and, in keeping with a body of work so rooted in the oral tradition, we decided a dialogue would be the best format. What follows is a transcription of one such conversation, edited to improve its focus.

GOLDIE: A good place to start might be why we wanted to do this project.

MOSES: I guess I thought that Oxford as a world-sized company would be a useful place to do one of these anthologies. There's a lot of writing going on inside the country that just doesn't get heard about outside the country.

G: Did you feel a sense of collective responsibility, to do something for the Native writing community in general?

M: That's one way of putting it. But also I think the ideas presented by Native people are particularly important. I think Native people have a sense of a larger responsibility to the planet, whether we come at it just from the idea that Native traditions honour the environment as a mother, or whether we come at it from the idea that we're looked at as people who should have those ideas and therefore we're allowed to have them.

G: I guess my reason to do the project was that in my own book *Fear and Temptation* I looked at only representations of Native peoples in white literature. I had not in any sense responded to what Native people were saying. But I didn't want to write about Native writing because that would have been just one more white version of Native culture. I thought that to create an anthology would not give my comments about a Native voice but rather do a little bit to get the Native voice heard. However, there are still problems. One that both you and I have had is just selection, what goes in and what doesn't and how to decide. But I think you are a bit more comfortable with that than I am. Is that true?

M: Well, I try to be practical about getting the job done. I think if we'd had more time we probably could have dealt with your discomfort, but we had just a little over a year.

G: An even more important element of timing is that the material we both seem most interested in has been published since 1985. Rightly or wrongly, we are capturing things at a point when there is more than enough material to justify the project but at a point where no one has sifted through that material.

I don't think that we are in any sense really responding to a canon, including the authors and the stories and the poems that people expect to be in, because I don't know that anybody's made that decision yet. No community, whether it's the Native writers themselves or Native communities or the literary community, or whatever, has made the decision about what should go in.

M: Yes, the decisions on what should go in something that you might call the canon can be easily disguised as aesthetic decisions, but if we are making a canon the decisions are definitely political, especially with a literature that is emerging even as we speak. What we've collected might seem to come from all areas along a scale of 'good writing'. But the actual impact of the stories also has to be part of the decision making. We are in history and this writing is very involved in that history. It seems foolish to try and take it out of life and put it in a separate canon. Why worry about the immortals?

G: I certainly want people to respect this anthology and find it interesting, but I would feel personally a bit of a failure if people thought that it therefore establishes what is the best in Native writing, or even establishes what is the best in Native writing in 1992. I would like the book to get the material out, get people to read it. If aesthetic evaluation has to be done—and I'm not sure it has to be done—it can wait for a long time yet.

You have a good point too, about the stories themselves. I don't think we've tried to be perfectly culturally representative but I think that the value of selections at this historical point has been a major concern. *Princess Pocahontas and the Blue Spots* is very much of this time and that gives it unusual power. The anthology is by no means just for a white audience but a part of our purpose is to provide a space in which Native writers can present to outsiders their view of this time.

M: I'm always getting phone calls from people who want me to come and tell Native legends. I know Native legends but I really have a feeling that it's not my right to go traipsing around, telling other people's stories. This image of traditional Native storytelling places Native people in the museum with all the other extinct species. We're living now, in this world, and like everyone else we have to deal with mass media, everything from video to paperback books. Of course our ways of expressing ourselves are no longer only oral storytelling. We have seen other media and some of us know them intimately enough to use them to express whatever we need to express. Some Native people make brilliant speeches for the media and some people write poems and some do those things that over the last 25 years or so we've come to call performance. And the example of traditional Native storytelling, its orality or whatever you would call it, has been for me a freeing thing. The pieces I write look like plays or poems or short stories, but I'm interested in how they sound and how they work when they're spoken.

G: Do you think that there is more interest in formal innovation by Native writers than by others?

M: I'm not really sure I can judge that. From my perspective, the Native tradition allows you the freedom to do things that people respond to. You are dealing with your own life, with your own stuff intimately, and looking to formal innovation not as an end in itself, but as part of the story. Mainstream writers are constantly told to be original but if you spend your time trying to be original you end up just doing the same sort of thing all the time.

G: I think one reason why Native literature is so interesting is that while it is based on very old traditions, as a literature it is quite young. As are the authors. A high percentage of the writers that we've included are under fifty, many under forty. That contributes to the feeling of innovation and yet always with a sense of tradition.

Yet I don't think we have included any authors who are in any sense iconoclasts of their own culture, although they might be iconoclasts of the mainstream culture. For example, the Métis have been told they didn't have a culture, neither a traditional nor a new culture. Instead writers like Maria Campbell and Duke Redbird have found that culture and reasserted it—unlike innovative and mainstream writers, who often seem to be tearing things down.

We've been referring to 'mainstream writers'. Do you think of Native writing as a separate stream? Is it something that could not or should not be subsumed by the mainstream? For instance, it's been argued that if Margaret Atwood is placed on a shelf of Canadian books she is ghettoized and is not given the proper stature that she deserves as a world author.

M: My image of that mainstream is that it is pretty wide but it's spiritually shallow. I don't think we are worried about being 'subsumed'. If we become part of that mainstream we're going to be the deep currents.

G: You were referring before to limited white views of what Native literature is. I have trouble with anyone who says that any category of human, whether it's Germans or short people, writes in a certain way. Yet I agree with you that the majority of Native writing has something that can be called spiritual. That is quite constant even though it appears in many forms. Do you find that?

M: Oh, yes. I think that that is one of the reasons our theatre has become so strong, because everyone needs a spiritual life, I mean spiritual just in the sense of knowing the meaning of your life, what you are doing and why you are doing it. The mainstream god got killed a while back and a lot of people are desperately holding on to the corpse. Meanwhile Native peoples' traditions, the meanings of their life, are intimately connected to the actual physical world they live in, so they don't have to hold on desperately to their sense of who they are. Unless, of course they come to the city and believe what's going on here but then they are just partaking of the mainstream dilemma.

G: Your own play *Big Buck City* shows that urban mainstreaming, but the presence of a trickster figure on stage maintains certain Native values. The trickster seems to be a concern for contemporary Native writers from a variety of cultures. Is it because of the many spiritual dimensions it suggests, or is it also theatrical? I guess theatrical, because the trickster extends both verbal and visual possibilities.

M: The trickster is the embodiment of our sense of humour about the way we live our lives. It's a very central part of our attitude that things are funny even though horrible things happen.

G: Like the irony of that old joke that when the missionaries came they had the bibles and the Native peoples the land, and now the Native peoples have the bibles and the white people have the land. It's an ironic take on a horrible situation. But I think the humour you are talking about is something much more wide-ranging.

M: It's also a response to existential problems, of being conscious and aware of the limits of our life. It's really a balanced philosophy.

G: It is interesting how many extraordinarily different writers use trickster figures. Beth Brant and Tom King, who in most ways have an extremely different take on the world, both use coyote. It seems to explain things in a non-reductive way for both of them, and for you and for many other writers.

M: Well, it is an archetypical figure in the human imagination. Mainstream society doesn't like it but it does pop up in mainstream culture here and there, either denigrated or turned into a nightmare, just because it seems so irrational.

G: Yes, but mainstream ancient Greek culture had tricksters, mainstream ancient Roman culture had tricksters, mainstream European culture in the middle ages had tons of tricksters. It seems to be the Christian church in the post-renaissance age that really tried to defeat the trickster. There are some trickster saints in the Roman Catholic traditions but nobody ever talks about them. It's as though modern Europe wanted to get rid of anything that couldn't be reduced to good and bad. You're never sure what the trickster is going to do next, whether what he's going to do might be perceived by the audience or the characters involved as good or bad. As you've said, Dan, the Native culture isn't concerned with good or bad, it's concerned with harmony. Yet the trickster is part of that spirituality that white people are always turning to Native cultures for. A Native leader from the west coast once said that he didn't see why white people were so obsessed with staring at other people's navels. There is a sense that white appropriation of Native voice is trying almost to swallow Native culture and have it inside. I'm thinking of even the best and most sophisticated white writing on Native people. Rudy Wiebe's 'Where is the Voice Coming From?', a beautiful, wonderfully sensitive story, demonstrates the desire of the white culture to somehow package Native culture so that it can be swallowed and the voice can be found.

M: There's a big emptiness there that has to be filled.

G: It's a sad thing to say but I think it's true.

M: It can't be filled by eating. People are fooling themselves if they think that just by taking someone else's stuff they are going to be happy. They have to find their own. The whole structure of mainstream society prevents that from happening. Someone will come up to me at a conference and ask me how to get in touch with the earth, when two feet away from us there's a flower bed. All you've got to do is look and see the life that's going on in that flower bed. There are things growing, there are things crawling, there are things breathing, the sun's on them, the air's through them, there's a whole complex system of physics and pleasure going on there. It's not really that hard to get into if you just remember that when mainstream society talks about human beings and nature, it's a false dichotomy: we're part of nature.

G: It seems to take a major shift in perspective. In Newfoundland there's still a tradition of the fairies. If you find yourself in a place you've often been and suddenly you have a sense that the whole is transformed and you are looking at it totally differently, then you say that you've been taken by the fairies. Even though your physical self does not move, somehow the whole world is transformed. I think that's what a lot of these white writers are looking for. As you say they don't need the fairies, they don't need to take Native culture, if they would just try to seek the transformation in a direct way. Many white writers who use Native stories, Native legends, and Native voices justify it by saying they have this extraordinary empathy for Native culture. The simple answer seems to be that if you have that empathy why not let it live on its own? Why not let it be?

M: I have a lot of friends, white writers, who don't feel the need to hijack my stuff because they are not afraid of their own experience, when they have those experiences that are non-linear, non-rational, that are mystical experiences. That's the part of the mind where their work as creative writers is being done. You hook into the way the mind makes sense other than logic. But our culture is so obsessed with everything making sense, being straightforward, being hooked into time lines and bottom lines.

G: I think there is a global problem with the 'fourth world'. That is George Manuel's term, the fourth world being indigenous peoples' cultures which are controlled by the non-indigenous, like Canada or New Zealand or Australia. The non-indigenous often speak as though they own the Native people, although they don't put it this way. As a Canadian I might refer to 'our Native people'; regardless of my intention, the patronizing assumption is there. The non-indigenous assume that the true fourth world is only that which was there when their ancestors arrived. The fourth world is not allowed to develop: witness your observation that people expect you to tell traditional stories.

   Although we might not be totally positive about Native people who become totally urbanized, yet they are in the contemporary world and adapting to the world in accord with their own views of necessity. The opposition to that is the society depicted in the first part of Anne Cameron's *Daughters of Copper Woman*. She presents an earlier Native culture which is pure and matriarchal and full of all of the things that Anne Cameron believes to be good. And then it's packaged in that book for transmission to a generally non-indigenous feminist audience who feel alienated from masculinist culture. They want a pure feminist past so they create a pure feminist fourth world.

M: If the mainstream culture seeks to maintain the Native past, does this mean mainstream culture needs to maintain its own guilt?

G: Oh, yes. There's no question about that. There is a desire to package that guilt. It seems to me that guilt is a stronger clearer thing in Newfoundland than it is in many other of the Canadian white cultures simply because of the genocide, the absolute extermination of the Beothuks. The Beothuks can be packaged as a pure prehistorical entity. They can be maintained as a source of guilt but without dealing with the present. Newfoundlanders don't have to deal with any of the social problems that might be related to contemporary white treatment of Native people. This seems at least part of the reason why Newfoundlanders are so averse to accepting the contemporary Micmac population of the south coast as indigenous. Because they still exist, they cannot be a source of pure past guilt.

M: So what's the use of guilt?

G: For the most part probably nothing, but might white guilt have potential to do some good for land rights?

M: Maybe something else. One of the words that always comes up in Native gatherings, and particularly among Native artists, is that it is part of our jobs as Native artists to help people heal. Whether we're talking about Native people taught by residential schools or whether we're talking about white people who've just been in a car accident, that's what we see as our job: we're looking for the meaning of life to explain the injustices of reality. To me it sounds as if this guilt is the opposite thing: it seems that you don't want to heal, you want to keep the wound. In romanticism you're dancing around a wound. You have these great desires, these great idealistic possibilities, and then they're cut down and things end in death and it's very sad and beautiful. I've seen the attraction of it, because I've grown up partially in the mainstream culture, but it strikes me as really sick. I think maybe the reason for keeping the wound open is that alienation from yourself that the mainstream mind set creates. Up in your head you're separate from your animal self. Even if you're creating art that isn't healing, at least you can feel something.

G: As an outsider I hesitate to say this but I think white society has caused Native people so much pain that they felt forced to look for healing. Women who have been abused as children have gone through similar stages. Through this and other examples of pain that white people have themselves felt, they have gained more and more respect for and interest in Native powers. I suspect that many are reading this anthology in search of that healing. But some Native writers seem to emphasize white guilt. I don't know if that's an accurate assumption on my part or not. Take Lenore Keeshig-Tobias's piece which confronts the Canadian response to the Oka situation. I totally agree with what she has to say but it does seem to assert white guilt. Is that an inaccurate reading on my part?

M: No, I think that's true of her response to that specific situation.

G: Don't white people have a reasonable amount to be guilty about? Still, guilt in itself doesn't get you anywhere.

M: Well, feeling guilty is a fuzzy state of mind. You're aware of the problem but not really focusing on it. I think Lenore was trying to get people to focus. Maybe to feel ashamed, which is an active, public way of feeling guilty. One of the differences between Native culture and the mainstream one is the use by Native culture of shame as a social control. If you're ashamed of your behaviour you might face up to it. To conquer your demons you have to face them.

G: A lot of anthologies are seen as competitions—who gets in and who doesn't get in. But I think that in most Native cultures there is a tradition of consensus and of allowing the voices to be heard. So for this anthology, instead of having to include twenty poems by William Wordsworth and ten by T.S. Eliot because they are the big ones that won the competition, we've included many texts of value in their own contexts. That is one of the prime reasons to include so much orature. And even to use the term 'orature', which unlike 'oral literature' or 'oral poetry' does not denote the oral as inferior to the formally written. The constitution of the Six Nations Confederation is an oral document which is really prose history but it is also an important text of orature, representing in itself that kind of consensus process in a traditional culture. I don't think that the historical material in the anthology is representative of the variety of Native cultures, but it gives a sense of some of the bases of contemporary Native culture, such as the spirituality, the collectivity, and the oral.

M: It's a strange technology we're dealing with, this writing our words down on paper and alienating the best parts of ourselves into books. I mean, we started out using that technology as a storage medium, and instead we've become oppressed by it.

G: How is it oppressive, do you think?

M: Well, I think that's one of the actual physical ways that the alienation, the separation between the person and their thought, happens.

G: Do you mean that somebody owning your book of poetry and reading it separately from yourself is alienating to both of you? Do you think that attitude would be more common among Native writers?

M: A lot of Native people have been working with words without publishing. It's not this horrible painful need that so many white writers have when they spend a couple of years working on something and can't get it published. If the material is working orally within the community, that's enough.

G: Many Native politicians have been recognized as orators. But fifteen years ago there were few Native writers recognized as such. The dominant sense that I had of contemporary Native verbal culture was through political speeches, and through political documents such as Harold Cardinal's which connect directly to those speeches. It's something that I've always found a bit surprising but I'm beginning to see good reasons for that. Mudrooroo Narogin talks about the difficulty in that the white population of Australia assumes that Aboriginal writers are writing for them. As he said, it's strange enough to write for a culture that is not your own but it's even stranger to write for it when it is the culture of those who have conquered you. But from what you're saying about the oral form and about the writer's role in the community, the Native people in Canada have been creating their verbal performance very much for their own community.

M: I did one piece based on an Oneida story and afterwards this poet asked, 'Now does that represent us white guys?' I said, 'This is precontact, it has nothing to do with you.' It was as if he really wanted an in to the story, but there are times when you just have to sit back and watch.

G: As a Native person would you have more right to write a story using an Inuit voice, for example?

M: I would have to find some reason to do it. It would have to be something that was very important to me but I really doubt that I would try it. I don't know the culture intimately enough to do it properly and I'd rather not fall on my face unless I have to.

G: The primary culture that Tom King is using, for example, in *Medicine River* is not his own culture. It's a culture which he presumably knows mainly as an academic and as a teacher of Native students from Alberta. I think the justification is Wayne Keon's suggestion of pan-Native similarity. Perhaps one example is that spirituality you were mentioning.

M: Well, I go into Native groups all over the country and I always feel comfortable with them. I feel that I can go to any Native events. Whereas I've lived in Toronto for many years and there are places here I feel strange.

G: I think that all our selections are written with some Native context. Some writers, like Lee Maracle, are not departing from a Native voice but ranging out in their subject matter. She is looking at a variety of cultural interactions.

I suppose that relates in some way to what you were saying about overcoming limitations in genre. It's the opposite of something like W.P. Kinsella's Silas Ermineskin stories, which are highly limited by genre. Kinsella creates humour by showing Silas's failure to understand the majority culture, and the almost unconscious wisdom with which Silas perceives the inadequacies of the majority culture. That pattern is a part of comic storytelling throughout the world. It's really a more highly developed version of an ethnic joke. I suppose Kinsella has been a focus for discussion of the appropriation of voice because the ethnic joke always presents such a false view of ethnicity.

M: The few of Kinsella's stories I've read really did seem like a bad ventriloquist's act. I hope he keeps working on the baseball stuff.

G: When we originally started working on this anthology it was suggested to us that we include some white writing on Native people and we both agreed that we didn't want to do that. But what about the very sensitive responses to Native culture that you get in something like *The Temptations of Big Bear*? Many years ago at a Native Studies conference I found the response of Native undergraduate students to that book was phenomenal. They really believed it to be an empowering book for them.

M: I would have to assume that the aesthetics that are being used also relate to the traditions of healing. I mean that's why it would empower. I can't argue with healing.

G: It becomes a two-part question. On the one hand, Native cultures have certain values and certain powers which can to a certain extent be acquired by a sensitive and creative representation of those cultures, as in the case of *Big Bear*. But could they be acquired to the degree that they can be presented from the Native culture itself? Also, all of the stories and poems and plays in this anthology are owned, whether one sees them as owned by the writer or owned by the culture. They are things of value. Kinsella is a different sort of problem but the sensitive reworking of legends, like Cameron's *Daughters of Copper Woman*, is still something being taken from the culture.

M: Most of the pieces in this anthology are original pieces so we don't need to question ownership in that case. But in Native traditions of storytelling, if you make the story it belongs to you. Stories can also be given away or traded for. I think the concern with appropriation has more to do with the fact that most people aren't sensitive listeners, so they are not sensitive transmitters of stories, partly because the cultures have different values. When someone from another culture hears a story I tell, they perceive only the things that relate to their values. If they try to retell my story they are going to emphasize those things that are important to them. That only makes sense. So all we're saying is don't retell our stories, change them and pretend they are what we're about, because they are not.

G: One of the things that's often missed in this discussion is that in most cases a writer is first a reader, or at least a hearer or viewer. Then that reader becomes the writer. I think a lot of writers fail to see their political responsibility. The African National Congress called South African writers and visual artists 'cultural workers'. They had a duty to respond to the political values of that culture. The individual writers are not free to respond in any way to anything. The individual writer must be responsible to his or her own culture and to the other cultures that impinge on that. Still, I get the impression that you aren't very comfortable with politically labelled approaches to literature.

M: I am uncomfortable with any jargon that will separate the strands of my story into their different categories. We can talk psychology, we can talk economics, but my job is to integrate those concerns. I don't find it useful for what I do to talk about the political ramifications of one character's behaviour, although they are certainly part of what I'm doing.

G: But wouldn't you say that there is more overt politics in this anthology than you would find in a lot of others?

M: Oh, yes. But that's other people's tastes, other people's experience. Some of the people in this anthology have actually made political jargon seem like real language to me again.

G: That sounds good. One of the reasons for my getting involved in this was certainly the political agenda. The choices have been made by both of us, although I chose a lot of the early material and you most of the contemporary. But when I first heard it I immediately thought we had to have Lenore Keeshig-Tobias's piece on Oka. First, simply for its political value. The other thing is, as you say, its language. Its rhetorical flourishes gain power from its substance but the substance is not everything. The same thing is true of autobiographical material. The substance is important but so is the form.

M: I think our cultures probably allow us to be more autobiographical than the mainstream. In the mainstream markets editors want to know what one alienated individual thinks. Our culture is suspicious of that. We want to know where the opinion is coming from. Who are his or her people?

G: Is that from a belief in experience, a belief that you have knowledge because of your experience and therefore your knowledge should be related to your experience?

M: I think it comes from the attitude that everyone is an individual spirit with something unique to say which is important in the life of the entire community. And most Native writers are, as I said before, speaking first to their own community.

G: Still, there is a tradition of minority cultures in a variety of contexts writing to explain themselves to the rest of the world. Chinua Achebe in Nigeria writes in a way that explains a lot of ethnography. He claims that his target audience is pan-African, yet much seems to be shaped for European consumption. But Native writers are writing first for their own. That is one reason some people reject certain Native texts. When people said Tomson Highway's *Dry Lips Oughta Move to Kapuskasing* was misogynist it seemed to be because they weren't trained by the culture to understand it. Perhaps that's the answer; rather than appropriating the voice, educate yourselves so you are ready to read, ready to watch. That's what the white audience should be doing.

M: I can tell my story as well as I can, but I can't do the audience's job for them. In that case it's not going to be art, it's going to be education in its more uncomfortable forms. Certainly, art does educate but in a way that is so much fun nobody minds.

The variety that results, the different ways this English language is being nuanced and danced about on these pages, is fascinating. I've come across things that I didn't think were possible with this language. It's really encouraging.

G: Did you ever have any questions about whether we should do something like this for Oxford University Press, a symbol of empire?

M: Well, it's only a symbol. No, I mean I feel sorry for those guys now. It'll probably help them a bit, you know.

Toronto
June, 1991

The sources for the various selections are listed on the acknowledgements page but we would like to acknowledge specifically the anthologists whose work has been most helpful to us: Penny Petrone, Thomas King, John Robert Colombo, and Robin McGrath. Various libraries were used but we would like to mention especially the Metropolitan Toronto Reference Library; the Scott Library, York University; and the Newfoundland Studies Centre, Memorial University of Newfoundland. Last but first, the founder of this project, our former editor, Richard Teleky, and the person who did far more than her share of work, our present editor, Phyllis Wilson.

Traditional Songs

INUIT

My Breath/Orpingalik

I will sing a song,
A song that is strong.
   Unaya—unaya.
Sick I have lain since autumn,
Helpless I lay, as were I
My own child.

Sad, I would that my woman
Were away to another house
To a husband
Who can be her refuge,
Safe and secure as winter ice.
   Unaya—unaya.

Sad, I would that my woman
Were gone to a better protector
Now that I lack strength
To rise from my couch.
   Unaya—unaya.

Dost thou know thyself?
So little thou knowest of thyself.
Feeble I lie here on my bench
And only my memories are strong!
   Unaya—unaya.

Beasts of the hunt! Big game!
Oft the fleeting quarry I chased!
Let me live it again and remember,
Forgetting my weakness.
   Unaya—unaya.

Let me recall the great white
Polar bear,
High up its black body,
Snout in the snow, it came!
He really believed
He alone was a male

And ran toward me.
　Unaya—unaya.

It threw me down
Again and again,
Then breathless departed
And lay down to rest,
Hid by a mound on a floe.
Heedless it was, and unknowing
That I was to be its fate.
Deluding itself
That he alone was a male,
And unthinking
That I too was a man!
　Unaya—unaya.

I shall ne'er forget that great blubber-beast,
A fjord seal,
I killed from the sea ice
Early, long before dawn,
While my companions at home
Still lay like the dead,
Faint from failure and hunger,
Sleeping.
With meat and with swelling blubber
I returned so quickly
As if merely running over ice
To view a breathing hole there.
And yet it was
An old and cunning male seal.
But before he had even breathed
My harpoon head was fast
Mortally deep in his neck.

That was the manner of me then.
Now I lie feeble on my bench
Unable even a little blubber to get
For my wife's stone lamp.
The time, the time will not pass,
While dawn gives place to dawn
And spring is upon the village.
　Unaya—unaya.

But how long shall I lie here?
How long?

And how long must she go a-begging
For fat for her lamp,
For skins for clothing
And meat for a meal?
A helpless thing—a defenceless woman.
   Unaya—unaya.

Knowest thou thyself?
So little thou knowest of thyself!
While dawn gives place to dawn,
And spring is upon the village.
   Unaya—unaya.

Magic Words/Aua

To Lighten Heavy Loads

   I speak with the mouth of Qeqertuanaq, and say:
   I will walk with leg muscles strong as the sinews on the shin of
a little caribou calf.
   I will walk with leg muscles strong as the sinews on the shin of
a little hare.
   I will take care not to walk toward the dark.
   I will walk toward the day.

To Cure Sickness among Neighbours

   I arise from my couch with the grey gull's morning song.
   I arise from my couch with the grey gull's morning song.
   I will take care not to look toward the dark,
   I will turn my glance toward the day.

To Cure a Sick Child

   Little Child! Your mother's breasts are full of milk.
   Go to her and suck, go to her and drink. Go up into the mountain.
From the mountain's top shalt thou find health; from the mountain's
top shalt thou win life.

To Stop Bleeding

   This is blood from the little sparrow's mother.
   Dry it up! This is blood that flowed from a piece of wood. Dry it up!

From Calling Game to the Hunter

Beast of the sea! Come and place yourself before me in the dear early morning!

Beast of the plain! Come and place yourself before me in the dear early morning!

Magic Words/Nakasuk

To Heal Wounds

You, like a ringed plover,
You, like a wild duck,
The skin's surface here,
Full of wounds,
Full of cuts,
Go and patch it!

Song of the Girl
Who Was Turning into Stone/Ivaluardjuk

Men in kayaks,
come hither to me
and be my husbands;
this stone here
has clung fast to me,
and lo, my feet
are now turning to stone.

Men in kayaks,
come hither to me
and be my husbands;
this stone here
has clung fast to me,
and lo, my legs
are now turning to stone.

Men in kayaks,
come hither to me
and be my husbands;
this stone here
has clung fast to me,

and lo, now my thighs
are turning to stone.

Men in kayaks,
come hither to me
and be my husbands;
this stone here
has clung fast to me,
and lo, from the waist down,
I am turning to stone.

Men in kayaks,
come hither to me
and be my husbands;
this stone here
has clung fast to me,
and lo, my entrails
are turning to stone.

Men in kayaks,
come hither to me
and be my husbands;
this stone here
has clung fast to me,
and lo, my lungs
are now turning to stone.

Dead Man's Song/Netsit

Dreamed by One Who is Alive

I am filled with joy
When the day peacefully dawns
Up over the heavens,
    ayi, yai ya.

I am filled with joy
When the sun slowly rises
Up over the heavens,
    ayi, yai ya.

But else I choke with fear
At greedy maggot throngs;
They eat their way in

At the hollow of my collarbone
And in my eyes,
   ayi, yai ya.

Here I lie, recollecting
How stifled with fear I was
When they buried me
In a snow hut out on the lake,
   ayi, yai ya.

A block of snow was pushed to,
Incomprehensible it was
How my soul should make its way
And fly to the game land up there,
   ayi, yai ya.

That door-block worried me,
And ever greater grew my fear
When the fresh-water ice split in the cold,
And the frost-crack thunderously grew
Up over the heavens,
   ayi, yai ya.

Glorious was life
In winter.
But did winter bring me joy?
No! Ever was I so anxious
For sole-skins and skins for kamiks,
Would there be enough for us all?
Yes, I was ever anxious,
   ayi, yai ya.

Glorious was life
In summer.
But did summer bring me joy?
No! Ever was I so anxious
For skins and rugs for the platform,
Yes, I was ever anxious,
   ayi, yai ya.

Glorious was life
When standing at one's fishing-hole
On the ice.
But did standing at the fishing-hole bring me joy?
No! Ever was I so anxious

For my tiny little fish-hook
If it should not get a bite,
   ayi, yai ya.

Glorious was life
When dancing in the dance-house.
But did dancing in the dance-house bring me joy?
No! Ever was I so anxious,
That I could not recall
The song I was to sing.
Yes, I was ever anxious,
   ayi, yai ya.

Glorious was life. . . .
Now I am filled with joy
For every time a dawn
Makes white the sky of night,
For every time the sun goes up
Over the heavens,
   Ayi, yai ya.

Traditional Orature

Fragment of a Song

There was a woman, long, long ago:
she came out of a hole.
In it dead people were buried.
She made her house in a tree;
She was dressed in leaves,
All long ago.
When she walked among the dry leaves
Her feet were so covered
The feet were invisible.
She walked through the woods,
Singing all the time,
'I want company; I'm lonesome!'
A wild man heard her:
From afar over the lakes and mountains
He came to her.
She saw him; she was afraid;
She tried to flee away,
For he was covered with the rainbow;
Colour and light were his garments.
She ran, and he pursued rapidly;
He chased her to the foot of a mountain.
He spoke in a strange language;
She could not understand him at first.
He would make her tell where she dwelt.
They married; they had two children.
One of them was a boy.
He was blind from his birth,
But he frightened his mother by his sight.
He could tell her what was coming,
What was coming from afar.
What was near he could not see.
He could see the bear and the moose
Far away beyond the mountains;
He could see through everything.

Song for Medicine Hunting

Now I hear it, my friends, of the Metai, who are sitting about me.
Who makes this river flow? The Spirit, he makes this river flow.
Look at me well, my friends; examine me, and let me understand that
   we are all compassion.
Who maketh to walk about, the social people? A birth maketh to walk
   about the social people.
I fly about, and if anywhere I see an animal, I can shoot him.
I shoot your heart; I hit your heart, oh animal, your heart, I hit your
   heart.
I make myself look like fire.
I am able to call water from above, from beneath, and from around.
I cause to look like the dead, a man I did.
I cause to look like the dead, a woman I did.
I cause to look like the dead, a child I did.
I am such, I am such, my friends; any animal, any animal, my friends,
   I hit him right, my friends.

Canadian Medicine Song

Look, and see me! You see me on top of the ground.
My brother, I ask you about the gods. My brother, I ask you about the
   gods of the clear sky.
A-ia-ia. I want you to see the middle of the sky.
I give you a medicine dance in the middle of the land area of the earth;
   I give you a dance in the zenith above.
Walking in the night, in the door, smoke walking in the night.
I, too, am keeping a medicine lodge for the gods.
It was said to me: 'Sometimes I see a chief; sometimes I see a god.'
It looks like billows on Lake Superior. What is waving in billows on
   Lake Superior?
Somebody tells me about somebody getting old. I see a pretty old man.

Traditional History of the Confederacy

Constitution

Then Dekanahwideh said, Now I and you Lords of the Confederate Nations
shall plant a Great Tall and Mighty Tree of the Great Long Leaves.
   Now this Tree which we have planted shall shoot forth four great long

white roots. These Great Long White Roots shall shoot forth one to the North and one to the South and one to the East and one to the West, and we shall place on the top of it an Eagle which has a great power of long vision, and we shall transact all our business under the shade of the Great Tree. The meaning of planting this Great Tree is the Great Peace, and Good Tidings of Peace and Power, and the Nations of the earth shall see it and shall accept and follow the Root and shall arrive here at this Tree and when they arrive here you shall receive them and shall seat them in the midst of your Confederacy, and the meaning of placing an Eagle on the top of the Great Tall Tree is to watch the Roots which extend to the North and to the South and to the East and to the West, and the Eagle will discover if any evil is approaching your Confederacy, and will scream and give the alarm and all the Nations of the Confederacy at once shall hear the alarm and come to the front.

Then Dekanahwideh said again, We shall now combine our Power into one Great Power which is this Confederacy, and we shall now therefore symbolize the union of these powers by each Nation contributing one arrow each which we shall tie up together in a bundle, which when it is made and completely tied together no-one can bend or break it.

Then Dekanahwideh further said, We have now completed this union in securing one arrow from each Nation, it is not good that one should be lacking or taken from the bundle, for it would weaken our power and it would be still worse if two arrows were taken from the bundle. And if three arrows were taken, then any one could break the remaining arrows in the bundle.

Then Dekanahwideh continued his address and said, We shall now therefore tie this bundle of arrows together with deer's sinew which is strong, durable and lasting and then this Institution will be strong and unchangeable. This bundle of arrows signifies that all Lords and all the Warriors and all the Women of the Confederacy have become united as one person.

Then Dekanahwideh said, We have now completed our power so that we, the Five Nations Confederacy, shall in the future only have one body, one head and one heart.

Then he further said, If any evil should befall us in the future we shall stand or fall unitedly as one man.

Condolence Ceremony

Now hear us our Uncles, we have come to condole with you in your great bereavement.

We have now met in dark sorrow to lament together over the death of our brother Lord. For such has been your loss. We will sit together in our grief and mingle our tears together, and we four brothers will wipe off the tears from your eyes, so that for a day period you might have peace of mind. This we say and do, we four brothers.

Now hear us again, for when a person is in great grief caused by death, his ears are closed up and he cannot hear, and such is your condition now.

We will therefore remove the obstruction from your ears, so that for a day period you may have perfect hearing again. This we say and do, we four brothers.

Continue to bear the expression of us four brothers, for when a person is in great sorrow his throat is stopped with grief and such is your case now. We will therefore remove the obstruction so that for a day period you may enjoy perfect breathing and speech. This we say and do, we four brothers.

The foregoing part of the Condolence Ceremony is to be performed outside of the place of meeting.

HAIL

I come to greet and thank my uncles,
I come again to greet and thank the League;
I come again to greet and thank the Kindred;
I come again to greet and thank the Warriors;
I come again to greet and thank the Women;
My forefathers—what they established—
My forefathers—hearken to them.

At the Wood's Edge

Oh, my grandsires! Even now that has become old which you established— the Great League. You have it as a pillow under your heads in the ground where you are lying—this Great League which you established; although you said that far away in the future the Great League would endure.

* * *

Now listen, ye who established the Great League of Peace. Now it has become old. Now there is nothing but wilderness. Ye are in your graves who established it. Yet have taken it with you and have placed it under you, and there is nothing left but a desert. There ye have taken your intellects with joy. What ye established ye have taken with you. Ye have placed under your heads what ye established—the Great League.

Song for the Burning of the White Dog

Great Master, behold here are all of our people who hold the old faith, and who intend to abide by it.

By means of this dog being burned we hope to please Thee, and that just as we have decked it with ribbons and wampum, Thou wilt grant favours to us Thy own people.

I now place the dog on the fire that its spirit may find its way to Thee who made it, and made everything, and thus we hope to get blessings from Thee in return.

He throws the dog on the fire and proceeds:

Although, Great Master, there are not so many of us who worship Thee in this way as there were in old times, those who are here are as faithful as ever—now, therefore, listen to us—Thou who art far away above us, and who made every living thing.

We ask that the sun will continue to shine on us and make all things grow.

We ask that the moon may always give us light by night.

We ask that the clouds may never cease to give us rain or snow.

We ask that the winds from the east and west and north and south may always blow.

We ask that the trees and everything that springs from the ground may grow.

We ask that these blessings may help us through life, and that we may remain true to our belief in Thee, and we will make Thee another offering like this next year.

Save us from all harm until that time, and make us obedient to our chiefs and others who have power.

Guide them so that they may act wisely for the people and save them from all harm.

Be good, Great Master, to the warriors and to the young men, making them strong and healthy so that they may always be able to do everything they ought to do.

Great Master, we ask also that Thou wouldst be kind to the women until our next feast. Make them strong and healthy so that they may always be able to do everything they ought to do.

Take away all our sickness and all our troubles. Make us happy and healthy and strong to enjoy life.

Great Master, make us all peaceable and kindly that we may live happily and contentedly as we should do.

Cause the plants that cure us when we are ill to grow up strong for our use so that they do what Thou madest them to do.

And, Great Master, may the coming season bring us plenty of sunshine and breezes, and may everything grow well for our use during the summer time.

May all the trees that bear fruit, and may everything that comes out of the ground as our food grow in the best way for us to enjoy.

Great Master, we ask, too, that Thou wouldst send us all sorts of animals, large and small, for food and clothing, and cause the birds to live and increase in number.

May the scent of the tobacco I have thrown on the fire rise till it reaches Thee to let Thee know that we are still good—that we do not forget Thee, and that Thou mayest give us all we have asked.

Chief's Song

I make two of myself,
Raven,
I make a huge whale of myself,
Raven,
at the place where they drift ashore.
People will dismember me,
I make a huge whale of myself.

I stand upon
the promontory;
I summon people loudly,
with respects to my position as chief.

Go yourselves!
Pick out what you want!
My house is open.

A Prayer Before Whaling

Whale, I want you to come near me,
so that I will get hold of your heart and deceive it.
so that I will have strong legs and not be trembling and excited when
    the whale comes and I spear him.
Whale, you must not run out to sea when I spear you.
Whale, if I spear you, I want my spear to strike your heart.
Harpoon, when I use you, I want you to go to the heart of the whale.
Whale, when I spear at you and miss you, I want you to take hold of
    my spear with your hands.
Whale, do not break my canoe, for I am going to do good to you.
I am going to put eagle-down and cedar-bark on your back.
Whale, if I use only one canoe to kill you, I want to kill you dead.

Joseph Brant *c. 1742–1807*

MOHAWK

Letter

Sir,   Grand River, Dec. 10, 1798

Our former acquaintance encourages me to take the freedom of writing you; but knowing the multiplicity of business you have on your hands, I would not trouble you with this, did not the particular situation of our affairs seem to require it, thinking it necessary for me candidly to acquaint my friends with the feelings of my mind.

I presume that you are well acquainted with the long difficulties we had concerning the lands on this river—these difficulties we had not the least idea of when we first settled here, looking on them as granted us to be indisputably our own, otherwise we would never have accepted the lands, yet afterwards it seemed a little odd to us that the writings Gov. Haldimand gave us after our settling on the lands, was not so compleat as the strong assurances and promises he had made us at first, but this made no great impression on our minds, still confiding in the goodness of his Majesty's intentions, and in the weight we caputed our former services would have with him—Had it not been for this confidence and affection we bore the Kings we still had opportunities left after the war, in providing for ourselves in the free and independent manner natural to Indians, unhappily for us we have been made acquainted too late with the first real intentions of Ministry; that is, that they never intended us to have it in our power to alienate any part of the lands; and here we have even been prohibited from taking tenants on them, it having been represented as inconsistent for us, being but King's allies, to have King's subjects as tenants, consequently I suppose their real meaning was, we should in a manner be but tenants ourselves, as for me I see no difference in it any farther than that we are as yet rent free—they seemingly intending to forbid us any other use of the lands than that of sitting down or walking on them. It plainly appears by this that their motives can be no other than to tie us down in such a manner, as to have us entirely at their disposal for whatever services they may in future want from us, and that in case we should be worried out, and obliged to move the lands would then fall to them with our improvements of labour.

Sir, I hope I shall not tire your patience, in making a few remarks on what I suppose may naturally be the thoughts of Government on our conduct— With respect to myself they might say he has half pay and yet talks so much on these matters, it is very true I enjoy that bounty of his Majesty, so many worthless fellows like me do, that have never risked their property or any thing else in his causes but am I for this entirely to forsake the interests of my people? that put their dependence on me besides my family which is very numerous cannot be benefitted by my half pay when I am no more; which at my time of life I have reason to look on as a period not so very distant. I think it therefore incumbent on me to secure what they must look to for a future support. With respect to the Nation they may also say, that they have received their losses, for instance our hunting grounds that were very extensive, besides several other tracts of land were never mentioned—The Miller, blacksmith, and School-master, that is allowed us by government may also be spoken of—we are indeed very thankful for it; but we look upon this as all temporary and the continuance of it to be uncertain—it may likewise be said they receive annual presents what do they want more, we gratefully thank his Majesty, for his bounty in this respect; but I am sorry to have to observe that this goes very little ways in clothing the poor and helpless—and the country is so much changed that hunting is of very little account to the young and robust.

I beg have to say a few words more on this subject, the movements of Gov. Simcoe in attempting to curtail our lands to one half of the River, and recollecting our deed from Gov. Haldimand to be unequal to his first promises caused us to make such a large sale at once that the matter might come to a point and we might know whether the land was ours or not—the next reason was, that the lands all round us being given away to different people, some of them, those that had even been engaged in war against us, we found it necessary to sell some land, that we might have an income, the hunting being entirely destroyed.—We now learn that the ministry never intended we should alienate the lands, alleging that by doing so, disaffected people might be introduced into the country that might injure government—the people we have sold the lands to are loyalist & we expect, that as other people settled in the province, they will become subjects to His Majesty, the same as if Gov. Simcoe had himself curtailed the land and given it to them, as he has done with the adjacent lands.

I am sorry for having
taken up so much of your
time with so tedious a letter
but I assure my present disagree-
able situation, affects my feelings
so much, that I cannot avoid expressing
it rather fully especially as I think
this shall be the last time I will trouble
you on the subject.   Capt. Green

Sir
I am
Your most obed^t and
Humb. Servt.
Jos. Brant

Condolence Speech

To Captain Claus on the death of his mother (Ann Johnson Claus) made by Captain Joseph Brant, 24 February 1801 at Fort George.

Brother! We are here now met in the presence of the Spirit above, with the intent to keep up the ancient custom of condolement. We therefore condole with you for your late loss of our well beloved sister, whom now you have interred.

Brother! We hope that this may not damp your heart so much as to make you forget us, who are your brothers, not only ourselves but our wives and children.

Brother! We say now again that by our late loss it seems our fire is somewhat extinguished. But now we have found a few brands remaining and have collected them together and have raised a straight smoke to the clouds.

Brother! We therefore with this string of Wampum wipe away the tears from your eyes and would take away all sorrow from your heart. But that is impossible, still it is the customary way of making the speech. We, therefore, mention it and with the said Wampum we wipe away all stains of whatever should remain on your seat so that you may sit down in comfort.

Brother! We say again with this string of Wampum, as you seem to be all in darkness, we with the same string enlighten the skies about us so that it may appear to us all as it formerly used to do.

Brother! We say again with this string of Wampum as we now have made our speech of condolement, we hope to raise you upon your feet as you formerly used to be for since our late loss it seems you have been confined as one absent.

Brother! We hope you will not forget our calamities; hoping that this shock may not put us out of your memory entirely; and also that you may continue to keep us as you formerly used to do.

Brother! This last string which now I give you is given by the whole Six Nations so as to strengthen your mind and body that you may not be cast down by the occasion of our late loss.

George Copway 1818–69

OJIBWAY

A Word to the Reader

It would be presumptuous in one, who has but recently been brought out of a wild and savage state; and who has since received but three years' schooling, to undertake, without any assistance, to publish to the world a work of any kind. It is but a few years since I began to speak the English language. An unexpected opportunity occurred of submitting my manuscript to a friend, who has kindly corrected all *serious* grammatical errors, leaving the unimportant ones wholly untouched, that my own style may be exhibited as truly as possible. The public and myself are indebted to him for his kind aid, and he has my most sincere thanks. The language, (except in a few short sentences,) the plan, and the arrangement are all my own; and I am wholly responsible for all the statements, and the remaining defects. My work is now accomplished; and I am too well aware of the many faults which are still to be found therein. Little could I imagine, that I should have to contend with so many obstacles. All along, have I felt my great deficiency; and my inadequacy for such an undertaking. I would fain hope, however, that the kind Reader will throw the mantle of charity over errors of every kind. I am a stranger in a strange land! And often, when the sun is sinking in the western sky, I think of my former home; my heart yearns for the loved of other days, and tears flow like the summer rain. How the heart of the wanderer and pilgrim, after long years of absence, beats, and his eyes fill, as he catches a glance at the hills of his nativity, and reflects upon the time when he pressed the lips of a mother, or sister, now cold in death. Should I live, this painful pleasure will yet be mine. '*Blessed be the Lord, who hath helped me hitherto.*'

KAH-GE-GA-GAH-BOWH,
ALIAS
GEORGE COPWAY.

July 1847.

The Life of Kah-Ge-Ga-Gah-Bowh

The Christian will no doubt feel for my poor people, when he hears the story of one brought from that unfortunate race called the Indians. The lover of humanity will be glad to see that that once powerful race can be made to enjoy the blessings of life.

What was once impossible—or rather thought to be—is made possible through my experience. I have made many close observations of men, and things around me; but, I regret to say, that I do not think I have made as good use of my opportunities as I might have done. It will be seen that I know but little—yet O how precious *that little!*—I would rather lose my right hand than be deprived of it.

I loved the woods, and the chase. I had the nature for it, and gloried in nothing else. The mind for letters was in me, *but was asleep*, till the dawn of Christianity arose, and awoke the slumbers of the soul into energy and action.

You will see that I served the imaginary gods of my poor blind father. I was out early and late in quest of the favours of the *Mon-e-doos* (spirits,) who, it was said, were numerous—who filled the air! At early dawn I watched the rising of the *palace* of the Great Spirit—*the sun*—who, it was said, made the world!

Early as I can recollect, I was taught that it was the gift of the many spirits to be a good hunter and warrior; and much of my time I devoted in search of their favours. On the mountain top, or along the valley, or the water brook, I searched for some kind of intimation from the spirits who made their residence in the noise of the waterfalls.

I dreaded to hear the voice of the angry spirit in the gathering clouds. I looked with anxiety to catch a glimpse of the wings of the Great Spirit, who shrouded himself in rolling white and dark clouds—who, with his wings, fanned the earth, and laid low the tall pines and hemlock in his course—who rode in whirlwinds and tornadoes, and plucked the trees from their woven roots—who chased other gods from his course—who drove the Bad Spirit from the surface of the earth, down to the dark caverns of the deep. Yet he was a kind spirit. My father taught me to call that spirit Ke-sha-mon-e-doo— *Benevolent spirit*—for his ancestors taught him no other name to give to that spirit who made the earth, with all its variety and smiling beauty. His benevolence I saw in the running of the streams, for the animals to quench their thirst and the fishes to live; the fruit of the earth teemed wherever I looked. Every thing I saw smilingly said Ke-sha-mon-e-doo nin-ge-oo-she-ig—*the Benevolent spirit made me.*

Where is he? My father pointed to the sun. What is his will concerning me, and the rest of the Indian race? This was a question that I found no one could answer, until a beam from heaven shone on my pathway, which was very dark, when first I saw that there was a true heaven—not in the far-setting sun, where the Indian anticipated a rest, a home for his spirit—but in the bosom of the Highest.

I view my life like the mariner on the wide ocean, without a compass, in the dark night, as he watches the heavens for the north star, which his eye having discovered, he makes his way amidst surging seas, and tossed by angry billows into the very jaws of death, till he arrives safely anchored at port. I have been tossed with hope and fear in this life; no star-light shone on my way, until the men of God pointed me to a Star in the East, as it rose with all its splendour and glory. It was the Star of Bethlehem. I could now say in the language of the poet—

'Once on the raging seas I rode,
    The storm was loud, the night was dark;
The ocean yawned, and rudely blowed
    The wind that tossed my foundering bark.'

Yes, I hope to sing some day in the realms of bliss—

'It was my guide, my light, my all!
    It bade my dark foreboding cease;
And through the storm and danger's thrall,
    It led me to the port of peace.'

I have not the happiness of being able to refer to written records in narrating the history of my forefathers; but I can reveal to the world what has long been laid up in my memory; so that when 'I go the way of all the earth', the crooked and singular paths which I have made in the world, may not only be a warning to others, but may inspire them with a trust in God. And not only a warning and a trust, but also that the world may learn that there once lived such a man as Kah-ge-ga-gah-bowh, when they read his griefs and his joys.

My parents were of the Ojebwa nation, who lived on the lake back of Cobourg, on the shores of Lake Ontario, Canada West. The lake was called Rice Lake, where there was a quantity of wild rice, and much game of different kinds, before the whites cleared away the woods, where the deer and the bear then resorted.

My father and mother were taught the religion of their nation. My father became a medicine man in the early part of his life, and always had by him the implements of war, which generally distinguish our head men. He was a good hunter as any in the tribe. Very few brought more furs than he did in the spring. Every spring they returned from their hunting grounds. The Ojebwas each claimed, and claim to this day, hunting grounds, rivers, lakes, and whole districts of country. No one hunted on each other's ground. My father had the northern fork of the river Trent, above Bellmont Lake.

My great-grandfather was the first who ventured to settle at Rice Lake, after the Ojebwa nation defeated the Hurons, who once inhabited all the lakes in Western Canada, and who had a large village just on the top of the hill of the Anderson farm (which was afterwards occupied by the Ojebwas), and which furnished a magnificent view of the lakes and surrounding country. He was of the *Crane tribe*, i.e. had a crane for totem—*coat of arms*—which now forms the totem of the villagers, excepting those who have since come amongst us from other villages by intermarriage, for there was a law that no one was to marry one of the same totem, for all considered each other as being related. He must have been a daring adventurer—*a warrior*—for no one would have ventured to go and settle down on the land from which they had just driven the Hurons, whom the Ojebwas conquered and reduced, unless he was a great hero. It is said that he lived about the islands of Rice Lake, secreting himself from the enemy for several years, until some others came and joined him, when they formed a settlement on one of the islands. He must have been a great hunter, for this was one of the principal inducements that made him venture there, for there must have been abundance of game of every kind. The Ojebwas are called, here and all around, Massisuagays, because they came from Me-sey Sah-gieng, at the head of Lake Huron, as you go up to Sault St. Marie falls.

Here he lived in jeopardy—with his life in his hand—enduring the unpleasant idea that he lived in the land of bones—*amidst the gloom*, which shrouded the once happy and populous village of the Hurons; here their bones lay broadcast around his wigwam; where, among these woods once rang the war cry of the Hurons, echoing along the valley of the river Trent, but whose sinewed arms now laid low, with their badges and arms of war, in one common grave, near the residence of Peter Anderson, Esq. Their graves, forming a hillock, are now all that remain of this once powerful nation. Their bones, gun barrels, tomahawks, war spears, large scalping knives, are yet to be found there. This must have taken place soon after the formation of the settlement in Quebec.

The *Crane tribe* became the sole proprietors of this part of the Ojebwa land; the descendants of this tribe will continue to wear the distinguishing sign; except in a few instances, the chiefs are of this tribe.

My grandfather lived here about this time, and held some friendly intercourse with the whites. My father here learned the manners, customs, and worship of the nation. He, and others, became acquainted with the early settlers, and have ever been friendly with the whites. And I know the day when he used to shake the hand of the white man, and, *very friendly*, the white man would say, '*take some whiskey.*' When he saw any hungering for venison, he gave them to eat; and some, in return for his kindness, have repaid him after they became good and great farmers.

My mother was of the *Eagle tribe*; she was a sensible woman; she was as good a hunter as any of the Indians; she could shoot the deer, and the ducks flying, as well as they. Nature had done a great deal for her, for she was active; and she was much more cleanly than the majority of our women in those days. She lived to see the day when most of her children were given up to the Lord in Christian baptism; while she experienced a change of heart, and the fulness of God in man, for she lived daily in the enjoyment of God's favours. I will speak more of her at a proper time, respecting her life and happy death.

My father still lives; he is from sixty-five to seventy years old, and is one of the chiefs of Rice Lake Indian Village. He used to love fire-water before he was converted to God, but now lives in the enjoyment of religion, and he is happy without the devil's spittal—*whiskey*. If Christianity had not come, and the grace of God had not taken possession of his heart, his head would soon have been laid low beneath the fallen leaves of the forest, and I, left, in my youthful days, an orphan. But to God be all the praise for his timely deliverance.

The reader will see that I cannot boast of an exalted parentage, nor trace the past history to some renowned warrior in days of yore; but let the above suffice. My fathers were those who endured much; who first took possession of the conquered lands of the Hurons.

I was born in *nature's wide domain!* The trees were all that sheltered my infant limbs—the blue heavens all that covered me. I am one of Nature's children; I have always admired her; she shall be my glory; her features—her robes, and the wreath about her brow—the seasons—her stately oaks, and the evergreen—her hair—ringlets over the earth, all contribute to my enduring love of her; and wherever I see her, emotions of pleasure roll in my breast, and swell and burst like waves on the shores of the ocean, in prayer and praise to Him who has placed me in her hand. It is thought great to be born in palaces, surrounded with wealth—but to be born in nature's wide domain is greater still!

I was born sometime in the fall of 1818, near the mouth of the river Trent, called in our language, Sah-ge-dah-we-ge-wah-noong, while my father and mother were attending the annual distribution of the presents from the government to the Indians. I was the third of our family; a brother and sister being older, both of whom died. My brother died without the knowledge of the Saviour, but my sister experienced the power of the loving grace of God. One brother, and two step-brothers, are still alive.

I remember the tall trees, and the dark woods—the swamp just by, where the little wren sang so melodiously after the going down of the sun in the west—the current of the broad river Trent—the skipping of the fish, and the noise of the rapids a little above. It was here I first saw the light; a little fallen down shelter, made of evergreens, and a few dead embers, the remains of the last fire that shed its genial warmth around, were all that marked the spot. When I last visited it, nothing but four poles stuck in the ground, and they were leaning on account of decay. Is this dear spot, made green by the tears of memory, any less enticing and hallowed than the palaces where princes are born? I would much more glory in this birth-place, with the broad canopy of heaven above me, and the giant arms of the forest trees for my shelter, than to be born in palaces of marble, studded with pillars of gold! Nature will be nature still, while palaces shall decay and fall in ruins. Yes, Niagara will be Niagara a thousand years hence! The rainbow, a wreath over her brow, shall continue as long as the sun, and the flowing of the river! While the work of art, however impregnable, shall in atoms fall.

Our wigwam we always carried with us wherever we went. It was made in the following manner: Poles were cut about fifteen feet long; three with crotches at the end, which were stuck in the ground some distance apart, the upper ends meeting, and fastened with bark; and then other poles were cut in circular form and bound round the first, and then covered with plaited reeds, or sewed birch bark, leaving an opening on top for the smoke to escape. The skins of animals formed a covering for a gap, which answered for a door. The family all seated tailor-fashion on mats. In the fall and winter they were generally made more secure, for the purpose of keeping out the rain and cold. The covering of our wigwam was always carried by my mother, whenever we went through the woods. In the summer it was easier and pleasanter to move about from place to place, than in the winter. In the summer we had birch bark canoes, and with these we travelled very rapidly and easily. In the winter everything was carried upon the back. I have known some Indians to carry a whole deer—not a small one, but a buck. If an Indian could lift up his pack off the ground by means of his arms, it was a good load, not too light nor too heavy. I once carried one hundred and ninety-six weight of flour, twelve pounds of shot, five pounds of coffee, and some sugar, about a quarter of a mile, without resting—the flour was in two bags. It felt very heavy. This was since I travelled with the missionaries, in going over one of the portages in the west.

Our summer houses were made like those in gardens among the whites, except that the skeleton is covered with bark.

The hunting grounds of the Indians were secured by right, a law and custom among themselves. No one was allowed to hunt on another's land, without invitation or permission. If any person was found trespassing on the ground of another, all his things were taken from him, except a handful of shot, powder sufficient to serve him in going *straight* home, a gun, a tomahawk, and a knife; all the fur, and other things, were taken from him. If he were found a second time trespassing, all his things were taken away from him, except food sufficient to subsist on while going home. And should he still come a third time to trespass on the same, or another man's hunting grounds, his nation, or tribe, are then informed of it, who take up his case. If still he disobey, he is banished from his tribe.

My father's hunting ground was at the head of Crow River, a branch of the River Trent, north of the Prince Edward District, Canada West. There are two branches to this river—one belongs to George Poudash, one of the principal chiefs of our nation; the other to my father; and the Crow River belongs to another chief by the name of John Crow. During the last war the Indians did not hunt or fish much for nearly six years, and at the end of that time there were large quantities of beaver, otter, minks, lynx, fishes, &c.

These hunting grounds abound with rivers and lakes; the face of the country is swampy and rocky; the deer and the bear abound in these woods; part of the surrendered territory is included in it. In the year 1818, 1,800,000 acres of it were surrendered to the British government. For how much, do you ask? For $2,690 per annum! What a *great sum* for British generosity!

Much of the back country still remains unsold, and I hope the scales will be removed from the eyes of my poor countrymen, that they may see the robberies perpetrated upon them, before they surrender another foot of territory.

From these lakes and rivers come the best furs that are caught in Western Canada. Buyers of fur get large quantities from here. They are then shipped to New York City, or to England. Whenever fruit is plenty, bears are also plenty, and there is much bear hunting. Before the whites came amongst us, the skins of these animals served for clothing; they are now sold from three to eight dollars apiece.

My father generally took one or two families with him when he went to hunt; all were to hunt, and place their gains into one common stock till spring, (for they were often out all winter,) when a division took place.

* * *

My beloved Reader—I am now about closing my narrative, and in doing this there are but a few things to say. Throughout the work, I have confined my remarks chiefly to my own nation. But it must not be supposed, on this account, that I am forgetful of my brethren of the other Indian nations. The prayers and benevolent efforts of all Christendom should be directed towards all men everywhere. The gospel should be preached to every creature; and the field is the *wide* WORLD.

The Menomenees in Wisconsin, the Winebagoes and Potawatamies in Iowa, the warlike nations of the Sacs and Foxes, the Osages, Pawnees, Mandans, Kansas, Creeks, Omahas, Otoes, Delawares, Iowas, and a number of others elsewhere, must perish as did their brethren in the Eastern States, unless the white man send them the Gospel, and the blessings of education. There is field enough for all denominations to labour in, without interfering with each other. It is too late in the day to assert that the Indians cannot be raised up out of their degraded state, and educated for God and heaven. None need be discouraged since the Ojebwas in Western Canada have been converted. No language is adequate to portray the misery, wretchedness, and degradation in which we were, when the word of God was first brought and preached to us.

It is not necessary to detail each and every wrong, that my poor people have suffered at the hands of the white man. Enough has already been said in various parts of the work, to prove that they have been most grossly abused, peeled, and wronged. Nor shall I notice the *personal wrongs* that I myself have received; and from those, too, of whom I had good reason to hope better things. I once thought, that there were some things that I could never forgive; but the religion of Jesus, and the law of love, have taught me differently. I *do* forgive them; and may God forgive them and me too.

I have sometimes heard it said, that our forefathers were cruel to the forefathers of the whites. But was not this done through ignorance, or in self-defence? Had your fathers adopted the plan of the great philanthropist, William Penn, neither fields, nor clubs, nor waters, would have been crimsoned with each other's blood. The white men have been like the greedy lion, pouncing upon and devouring its prey. They have driven us from our nation, our homes, and possessions; compelled us to seek a refuge in Missouri, among strangers, and wild beasts; and will, perhaps, soon compel us to scale the Rocky Mountains; and, for aught I can tell, we may yet be driven to the Pacific Ocean, there to find our graves. My only trust is, that there is a just God. Was it to perpetrate such acts that you have been exalted above all other nations? Providence intended you for a *blessing* and not a *curse* to us. You have sent your missionaries to Burmah, China, the Sandwich Islands, and to almost every part of the world; and shall the Indians *perish at your own door*?

Is it not well known that the Indians have a generous and magnanimous heart? I feel proud to mention in this connection, the names of a Pocahontas, Massasoit, Skenandoah, Logan, Kusic, Pushmataha, Philip, Tecumseh, Osceola, Petalesharro, and thousands of others. Such names are an honour to the world! Let a late Governor of Massachusetts* speak for our fathers, when they first beheld the trembling white man:—

'Brothers! when our fathers came over the great waters, they were a small band. The red man stood upon the rock by the seaside, and saw our fathers. He might have pushed them into the water and drowned them. But he stretched out his arms to our fathers and said, "Welcome, white men!" Our fathers were hungry, and the red man gave them corn and venison. Our fathers were cold, and the red man wrapped them up in his blanket. We are now numerous and powerful, but we remember the kindness of the red man to our fathers.'

And what have we received since, in return? Is it for the deeds of a Pocahontas, a Massasoit, and a host of others, that we have been plundered and oppressed, and expelled from the hallowed graves of our ancestors? If help cannot be obtained from England and America, where else can we look? Will you then, lend us a helping hand; and make some amends for past injuries?

It is often said, that the Indians are *revengeful*, *cruel*, and *ungovernable*. But go to them with nothing but *the* BIBLE *in your hands*, and LOVE *in your hearts*, and you may live with them in perfect safety, share their morsel with them, and, like the celebrated Bartram, return to your homes UNHARMED. They very soon learn to venerate the Bible; as a proof of this, I will give an instance, that came under my own eye:—While at the Rabbit River Mission, a chief from the west, visited me. After reading to him several chapters from the Bible, he said, with much surprise, 'Is *this* the book, that I hear so much about in *my* country?' I replied, yes; and these are the words of *Ke-sha-mon-e-doo* (the Great Spirit). 'Will you not,' said he, 'give me one? I wish to show it to my people.' I told him, not without you first promise that you will take care of it. He promised me that he would. I handed it to him; he took it, and turned it over and over, and then exclaimed, '*Wonderful, wonderful! This is the book of the Great Spirit!*' He then wrapped it up in a silk handkerchief, and the handkerchief in three or four folds of cloth. I heard, afterwards, from the trader, that the book was still kept sacred. O, if my poor brother could but *read* and *understand* that blessed volume, how soon would his dumb idols be 'cast down to the moles and to the bats'! Will no one go and tell him and his nation, of the boundless, beseeching, bleeding, dying love of a Saviour; and urge upon them the importance of such a preparation of heart, as will enable them 'to give up their account with joy'? The Great Spirit is no respecter of

---

* Edward Everett, Esq.

persons; He has made of one blood all the nations of the earth; He loves all his children alike; and his highest attributes are *love*, *mercy*, and *justice*. If this be so,—and who dare doubt it?—will He not stretch out his hand and help them, and avenge their wrongs? 'If offences *must* come', let it be recollected, that *woe* is denounced against them 'from *whom* they come'.

I again propose that the territories of the Indians, in the British dominions, be annexed to that Government, and those in the American dominions to the Federal Union. And, finally, in the language of that excellent, magnanimous, and benevolent friend of the poor children of the forest, Col. Thomas McKenney, I would say,

'I have already referred, in the commencement of this proposal to annex the Indian territory to our Union, to those good men, who, in the character of missionaries, have kept side by side with the Indians in so many of their afflictions and migrations. I will again refer to them, and implore them by all the lost labour of the past, and by the hopes of the future; by the critical condition of the pacific relations that exist between the Indians and us; and by the sacredness of the cause in which they are engaged, to look well and earnestly into this subject, and learn from the past what *must* attend upon their labours in the future, if the change I propose, or some other change equivalent to it, be not brought about. And, seeing, as they must see, that the plan I propose, or some other, is indispensable to the success they seek to command, I implore them to take up the subject in all its bearings, and by the instrumentalities which they have at command, manufacture, collect, and embody public opinion, in regard to what may be determined to be done; and by memorial, and personal agencies, bring this opinion to bear upon Congress, with whom alone the power is vested, to redeem, disenthrall, and save, and bless, the remnants of this aboriginal race. And I make the same appeal to all the good, of all religious persuasions, both in the Church and out of it, and politicians of all parties, to second this attempt, feeble as I know it to be, to save the Indians, and consolidate, and perpetuate peace between them and us, and, by so doing, ward off the terrible retribution which must sooner or later, unless it be averted, fall upon this nation.'

Catherine Soneegoh Sutton 1822–65

O J I B W A Y

Letter

On the shores of Goulais Bay Lake Superior and the neighbouring one of Batchawana, one of these publick nusiances—an Indian reserve was laid of a few years ago under Lord Elgin's Government the reserve covered a portage of 30 miles on the Lake with a sufficient depth into the country to make up an area of 300 square miles of land—some of the best land in the country and so situated as to block up the means of access to the entire regions lying in the rear of it and all this for about a dozen of the most wretched, squalid, miserable specimens of human nature that I have ever seen: indeed a close inspection of, and a little acquaintance with, these creatures leads one to doubt whether they are human, but whether they are men or monkeys it matters not now, the present administration have found means to extinguish their title so far, that the country is now surveyed, and will soon be in market.

I suppose the individual who published the above and Mr Charles Linsey, the great Hearo who tried last fall to frighten the Manitoulin Indians out of their sences and their Lands, are, one and the same—if they are not their certanly is a great family likeness between them I have lived for several years with in a few miles of Goulais bay and I have frequently seen those Indians aluded to but I never took them for Monkyes neither did I ever hear such a thing hinted at by the white people I think they were allways, considered to be human beings, possessing living souls, I did not think monkeys lived so far north I allways understood that they were found in warm climates, when I was in England I went to the zoological garden were I saw a great maney monkeys and of various sises and kinds but I observed their was one trait coman to them all and a close inspection & a litle acquaintance with the Editor of the Leader has led me to the conclusion that the same trait stands out prominently in his natural disposition and character, and when I state what is the nature of that trait so comon to all the monkeys I ever saw I will leave you to guess who is by nature verey closly related to these four leged animals well I will tell you the trait wich I observed so comon to every variety of monkeys was an entire absence of humanity.

I have allso frequently seen the litle trained monkey exibeted in our canadian towns and vilages with pants red coat and cap, but every child could tell that it was a monkey because its tail would stick out and I noticed that after he had played of his money anticks he allways went round with his hat for a colection and as far as I can learn this is just what a certen creature does after he as performed something wich is pleasing to a certen party he expects them in return to throw something handsome into his cap.

The Editor of the Leader apears to think that every indian reservation is a publick nusiance so I conclude that if he could have his will, he would have every band of indians drove on to the baran waste of granite rocks north of Lakes huron and superior but why are indian reservations aney more a publick nusiance then large blocks of land bought and held by speculators I argue that Indians have a right to be paid a fair valuation for aney lands wich they may agree to surrender, I suppose the Leader would not have a word to say if a dozen or two poor hard working white men should get scatered through the Goulais bay teritory, while all the remainder was bought up and held by a few speculators untill those poor men by hard persevering industry had cleared up their lands and made roads and thus by the poor mans hard labour raised the value of the rich land speculators property—the Editor of the Leader states that the present administration have found means to extinguish their title, my english his so poor that I frequently have to consult Webster and I find the word extinguish means to destroy to put an end to; to extinguish a claim or title, a wonderful feat surely for the present administration to perform and for the Editor of the Leader to brag of; this shows another instance of the uter helplessness of the poor indian they apear to be at the mercy of such men as Mr Charles Linsey our present administration can extinguish the red mans title at pleasure, what hope is their for the remnant that are yet left to whom can they go for redress who will help them or are they entirely without helper, I suppose Mr Linsey will answer these questions when the present administration give him a commission to go to manitolin with soldiers to subdue the Indians or monkeys as he calls them.

E. Pauline Johnson 1861–1913

MOHAWK

The Cattle Thief

They were coming across the prairie, they were galloping hard and fast;
For the eyes of those desperate riders had sighted their man at last—
Sighted him off to Eastward, where the Cree encampment lay,
Where the cotton woods fringed the river, miles and miles away.
Mistake him? Never! Mistake him? the famous Eagle Chief!
That terror to all the settlers, that desperate Cattle Thief—
That monstrous, fearless Indian, who lorded it over the plain,
Who thieved and raided, and scouted, who rode like a hurricane!
But they've tracked him across the prairie; they've followed him hard
   and fast;
For those desperate English settlers have sighted their man at last.

Up they wheeled to the tepees, all their British blood aflame,
Bent on bullets and bloodshed, bent on bringing down their game;
But they searched in vain for the Cattle Thief: that lion had left his lair,
And they cursed like a troop of demons—for the women alone were
   there
'The sneaking Indian coward,' they hissed; 'he hides while yet he can;
He'll come in the night for cattle, but he's scared to face a *man*.'
'Never!' and up from the cotton woods rang the voice of Eagle Chief;
And right out into the open stepped, unarmed, the Cattle Thief.
Was that the game they had coveted? Scarce fifty years had rolled
Over that fleshless, hungry frame, starved to the bone and old;
Over that wrinkled, tawny skin, unfed by the warmth of blood.
Over those hungry, hollow eyes that glared for the sight of food.

He turned, like a hunted lion: 'I know not fear,' said he;
And the words outleapt from his shrunken lips in the language of the
   Cree.
'I'll fight you, white-skins, one by one, till I kill you *all*,' he said;
But the threat was scarcely uttered, ere a dozen balls of lead
Whizzed through the air about him like a shower of metal rain,
And the gaunt old Indian Cattle Thief dropped dead on the open plain.
And that band of cursing settlers gave one triumphant yell,
And rushed like a pack of demons on the body that writhed and fell.
'Cut the fiend up into inches, throw his carcass on the plain;
Let the wolves eat the cursed Indian, he'd have treated us the same.'
A dozen hands responded, a dozen knives gleamed high,

But the first stroke was arrested by a woman's strange, wild cry.
And out into the open, with a courage past belief,
She dashed, and spread her blanket o'er the corpse of the Cattle Thief;
And the words outleapt from her shrunken lips in the language of the
    Cree,
'If you mean to touch that body, you must cut your way through *me*.'
And that band of cursing settlers dropped backward one by one,
For they knew that an Indian woman roused, was a woman to let alone.
And then she raved in a frenzy that they scarcely understood,
Raved of the wrongs she had suffered since her earliest babyhood:
'Stand back, stand back, you white-skins, touch that dead man to your
    shame;
You have stolen my father's spirit, but his body I only claim.
You have killed him, but you shall not dare to touch him now he's dead.
You have cursed, and called him a Cattle Thief, though you robbed
    him first of bread—
Robbed him and robbed my people—look there, at that shrunken face,
Starved with a hollow hunger, we owe to you and your race.
What have you left to us of land, what have you left of game,
What have you brought but evil, and curses since you came?
How have you paid us for our game? how paid us for our land?
By a *book*, to save our souls from the sins *you* brought in your other
    hand.
Go back with your new religion, we never have understood
Your robbing an Indian's *body*, and mocking his *soul* with food.
Go back with your new religion, and find—if find you can—
The *honest* man you have ever made from out a *starving* man.
You say your cattle are not ours, your meat is not our meat;
When *you* pay for the land you live in, *we'll* pay for the meat we eat.
Give back our land and our country, give back our herds of game;
Give back the furs and the forests that were ours before you came;
Give back the peace and the plenty. Then come with your new belief,
And blame, if you dare, the hunger that *drove* him to be a thief.'

Shadow River

Muskoka

A stream of tender gladness,
Of filmy sun, and opal tinted skies;
Of warm midsummer air that lightly lies
In mystic rings,
Where softly swings

The music of a thousand wings
That almost tones to sadness.

Midway 'twixt earth and heaven,
A bubble in the pearly air, I seem
To float upon the sapphire floor, a dream
Of clouds of snow,
Above, below,
Drift with my drifting, dim and slow,
As twilight drifts to even.

The little fern-leaf, bending
Upon the brink, its green reflection greets,
And kisses soft the shadow that it meets
With touch so fine,
The border line
The keenest vision can't define;
So perfect is the blending.

The far, fir trees that cover
The brownish hills with needles green and gold,
The arching elms o'erhead, vinegrown and old,
Repictured are
Beneath me far,
Where not a ripple moves to mar
Shades underneath, or over.

Mine is the undertone;
The beauty, strength, and power of the land
Will never stir or bend at my command;
But all the shade
Is marred or made,
If I but dip my paddle blade;
And it is mine alone,

O! pathless world of seeming!
O! pathless life of mine whose deep ideal
Is more my own than ever was the real.
For others Fame
And Love's red flame,
And yellow gold; I only claim
The shadows and the dreaming.

The Corn Husker

Hard by the Indian lodges, where the bush
   Breaks in a clearing, through ill-fashioned fields,
She comes to labour, when the first still hush
   Of autumn follows large and recent yields.

Age in her fingers, hunger in her face,
   Her shoulders stooped with weight of work and years,
But rich in tawny colouring of her race,
   She comes a-field to strip the purple ears.

And all her thoughts are with the days gone by,
   Ere might's injustice banished from their lands
Her people, that to-day unheeded lie,
   Like the dead husks that rustle through her hands.

The Song My Paddle Sings

West wind, blow from your prairie nest,
Blow from the mountains, blow from the west.
The sail is idle, the sailor too;
O! wind of the west, we wait for you.
Blow, blow!
I have wooed you so,
But never a favour you bestow.
You rock your cradle the hills between,
But scorn to notice my white lateen.

I stow the sail, unship the mast:
I wooed you long but my wooing's past;
My paddle will lull you into rest.
O! drowsy wind of the drowsy west,
Sleep, sleep,
By your mountain steep,
Or down where the prairie grasses sweep!
Now fold in slumber your laggard wings,
For soft is the song my paddle sings.

August is laughing across the sky,
Laughing while paddle, canoe and I,
Drift, drift,

Where the hills uplift
On either side of the current swift.

The river rolls in its rocky bed;
My paddle is plying its way ahead;
Dip, dip,
While the waters flip
In foam as over their breast we slip.

And oh, the river runs swifter now;
The eddies circle about my bow.
Swirl, swirl!
How the ripples curl
In many a dangerous pool awhirl!

And forward far the rapids roar,
Fretting their margin for evermore.
Dash, dash,
With a mighty crash,
They seethe, and boil, and bound, and splash.

Be strong, O paddle! be brave, canoe!
The reckless waves you must plunge into.
Reel, reel,
On your trembling keel,
But never a fear my craft will feel.

We've raced the rapid, we're far ahead!
The river slips through its silent bed.
Sway, sway,
As the bubbles spray
And fall in tinkling tunes away.

And up on the hills against the sky,
A fir tree rocking its lullaby,
Swings, swings,
Its emerald wings,
Swelling the song that my paddle sings.

We-hro's Sacrifice

We-hro was a small Onondaga Indian boy, a good-looking, black-eyed little chap with as pagan a heart as ever beat under a copper-coloured skin. His father and grandfathers were pagans. His ancestors for a thousand years back, and yet a thousand years back of that, had been pagans, and We-hro, with the pride of his religion and his race, would not have turned from the faith of his fathers for all the world. But the world, as he knew it, consisted entirely of the Great Indian Reserve, that lay on the banks of the beautiful Grand River, sixty miles west of the great Canadian city of Toronto.

Now, the boys that read this tale must not confuse a pagan with a heathen. The heathen nations that worship idols are terribly pitied and despised by the pagan Indians, who are worshippers of 'The Great Spirit', a kind and loving God, who, they say, will reward them by giving them happy hunting grounds to live in after they die; that is, if they live good, honest, upright lives in this world.

We-hro would have scowled blackly if anyone had dared to name him a heathen. He thoroughly ignored the little Delaware boys, whose fathers worshipped idols fifty years ago, and on all the feast days and dance days he would accompany his parents to the 'Longhouse' (which was their church), and take his little part in the religious festivities. He could remember well as a tiny child being carried in his mother's blanket 'pick-a-back', while she dropped into the soft swinging movement of the dance, for We-hro's people did not worship their 'Great Spirit' with hymns of praise and lowly prayers, the way the Christian Indians did. We-hro's people worshipped their God by dancing beautiful, soft, dignified steps, with no noisy clicking heels to annoy one, but only the velvety shuffle of the moccasined feet, the weird beat of the Indian drums, the mournful chanting of the old chiefs, keeping time with the throb of their devoted hearts.

Then, when he grew too big to be carried, he was allowed to clasp his mother's hand, and himself learn the pretty steps, following his father, who danced ahead, dressed in full costume of scarlet cloth and buckskin, with gay beads and bear claws about his neck, and wonderful carven silver ornaments, massive and solid, decorating his shirt and leggings. We-hro loved the tawny fringes and the hammered silver quite as much as a white lady loves diamonds and pearls; he loved to see his father's face painted in fierce reds, yellows, and blacks, but most of all he loved the unvarying *chuck-a*, *chuck-a*, *chuck-a* of the great mud-turtle rattles that the 'musicians' skilfully beat upon the benches before them. Oh, he was a thorough little pagan, was We-hro! His loves and his hates were as decided as his comical but stately step in the dance of his ancestors' religion. Those were great days for the small Onondaga boy. His father taught him to shape axe-handles, to curve lacrosse sticks, to weave their deer-sinew netting, to tan skins, to plant corn, to model arrows, and—most difficult of all—to 'feather' them, to 'season' bows, to chop trees, to burn, hollow, fashion, and 'man' a dugout canoe, to use the paddle, to gauge the wind and current of that treacherous Grand River, to learn wild cries to decoy bird and beast for food. Oh, little pagan We-hro had his life filled to overflowing with much that the civilized white boy would give all his dimes and dollars to know.

And it was then that the great day came, the marvellous day when We-hro discovered his *second self*, his playmate, his loyal, unselfish, loving friend—his underbred, unwashed, hungry, vagabond dog, born white and spotless, but begrimed by contact with the world, the mud, and the white man's hovel.

It happened this way:

We-hro was cleaning his father's dugout canoe, after a night of fish spearing. The soot, the scales, the fire ashes, the mud—all had to be 'swabbed' out at the river's brink by means of much water and an Indian 'slat' broom. We-hro was up to his little ears in work, when suddenly, above him, on the river road, he heard the coarse voice and thundering whipfalls of a man urging and beating his horse—a white man, for no Indian used such language, no Indian beat an animal that served him. We-hro looked up. Stuck in the mud of the river road was a huge wagon, grain-filled. The driver, purple of face, was whaling the poor team, and shouting to a cringing little drab-white dog, of fox-terrier lineage, to 'Get out of there or I'll—!'

The horses were dragging and tugging. The little dog, terrified, was sneaking off with tail between its hind legs. Then the brutal driver's whip came down, curling its lash about the dog's thin body, forcing from the little speechless brute a howl of agony. Then We-hro spoke—spoke in all the English he knew.

'Bad! Bad! You die some day—you! You hurt that dog. White man's God, he no like you. Indian's Great Spirit, he not let you shoot in happy hunting grounds. You die some day—you *bad!*'

'Well, if I *am* bad I'm no pagan Indian Hottentot like you!' yelled the angry driver. 'Take the dog, and begone!'

'Me no Hottentot,' said We-hro, slowly. 'Me Onondaga, all right. Me take dog'; and from that hour the poor little white cur and the copper-coloured little boy were friends for all time.

The Superintendent of Indian Affairs was taking his periodical drive about the Reserve when he chanced to meet old 'Ten-Canoes', We-hro's father.

The superintendent was a very important person. He was a great white gentleman, who lived in the city of Brantford, fifteen miles away. He was a kindly, handsome man, who loved and honoured every Indian on the Grand River Reserve. He had a genial smile, a warm hand-shake, so when he stopped his horse and greeted the old pagan, Ten-Canoes smiled too.

'Ah, Ten-Canoes!' cried the superintendent, 'a great man told me he was coming to see your people—a big man, none less than Great Black-Coat, the bishop of the Anglican Church. He thinks you are a bad lot, because you are pagans; he wonders why it is that you have never turned Christian. Some of the missionaries have told him you pagans are no good, so the great man wants to come and see for himself. He wants to see some of your religious dances—the "Dance of the White Dog", if you will have him; he wants to see if it is really *bad*.'

Ten-Canoes laughed. 'I welcome him,' he said, earnestly, 'Welcome the

"Great Black-Coat". I honour him, though I do not think as he does. He is a good man, a just man; I welcome him, bid him come.'

Thus was his lordship, the Bishop, invited to see the great pagan Ononda-ga 'Festival of the White Dog'.

But what was *this* that happened?

Never yet had a February moon waned but that the powerful Onondaga tribe had offered the burnt 'Sacrifice of the White Dog', that most devout of all native rites. But now, search as they might, not a single spotlessly white dog could be found. No other animal would do. It was the law of this great Indian tribe that no other burnt sacrifice could possibly be offered than the strangled body of a white dog.

We-hro heard all the great chiefs talking of it all. He listened to plans for searching the entire Reserve for a dog, and the following morning he arose at dawn, took his own pet dog down to the river and washed him as he had seen white men wash their sheep. Then out of the water dashed the gay little animal, yelping and barking in play, rolling in the snow, tearing madly about, and finally rushing off towards the log house which was We-hro's home, and scratching at the door to get in by the warm fire to dry his shaggy coat. Oh! What an ache that coat caused in We-hro's heart. From a dull drab grey, the dog's hair had washed pure white, not a spot or a blemish on it, and in an agony of grief the little pagan boy realized that through his own action he had endangered the life of his dog friend; that should his father and his father's friends see that small white terrier, they would take it away for the nation's sacrifice.

Stumbling and panting and breathless, We-hro hurried after his pet, and seizing the dog in his arms, he wrapped his own shabby coat about the trembling, half-dry creature, and carried him to where the cedars grew thick at the back of the house. Crouched in their shadows he hugged his treasured companion, thinking with horror of the hour when the blow would surely fall.

For days the boy kept his dog in the shelter of the cedars, tied up tightly with an old rope, and sleeping in a warm raccoon skin, which We-hro smuggled away from his own simple bed. The dog contented himself with what little food We-hro managed to carry to him, but the hiding could not keep up forever, and one dark, dreaded day We-hro's father came into the house and sat smoking in silence for many minutes. When at last he spoke, he said:

'We-hro, your dog is known to me. I have seen him, white as the snow that fell last night. It is the law that someone must always suffer for the good of the people. We-hro, would you have the great "Black-Coat", the great white preacher, come to see our beautiful ceremony, and would you have the great Onondaga tribe fail to show the white man how we worship our ancient Great Spirit? Would you have us fail to burn the sacrifice? Or will you give your white dog for the honour of our people?'

The world is full of heroes, but at that moment it held none greater than the little pagan boy, who crushed down his grief and battled back his tears as he answered:

'Father, you are old and honoured and wise. For you and for my people alone would I give the dog.'

At last the wonderful Dance Day arrived. His lordship, the Bishop of the Anglican Church, drove down from the city of Brantford; with him the Superintendent of Indian Affairs, and a man who understood both the English and the Onondaga languages. Long before they reached the 'Longhouse' they could hear the wild beat of the drum, could count the beats of the dance rattles, could distinguish the half-sad chant of the worshippers. The kind face of the great bishop was very grave. It pained his gentle old heart to know that this great tribe of Indians were pagans—savages, as he thought—but when he entered that plain log building that the Onondagas held as their church, he took off his hat with the beautiful reverence all great men pay to other great men's religion, and he stood bareheaded while old Ten-Canoes chanted forth this speech:

'Oh, brothers of mine! We welcome the white man's friend, the great "Black-Coat", to this, our solemn worship. We offer to the red man's God— the Great Spirit—a burnt offering. We do not think that anything save what is pure and faithful and without blemish can go into the sight of the Great Spirit. Therefore do we offer this dog, pure as we hope our spirits are, that the God of the red man may accept it with our devotion, knowing that we, too, would gladly be as spotless as this sacrifice.'

Then was a dog carried in dead, and beautifully decorated with wampum, beads, and porcupine embroidery. Oh! so mercifully dead and out of pain, gently strangled by reverent fingers, for an Indian is never unkind to an animal. And far over in a corner of the room was a little brown figure, twisted with agony, choking back the sobs and tears—for was he not taught that tears were for babies alone, and not for boys that grew up into warriors?

'Oh, my dog! my dog!' he muttered. 'They have taken you away from me, but it was for the honour of my father and of my own people.'

The great Anglican bishop turned at that moment, and, catching the sight of suffering on little We-hro's face, said aloud to the man who spoke both languages:

'That little boy over there seems in torture. Can I do anything for him, do you think?'

'That little boy,' replied the man who spoke both languages, 'is the son of the great Onondaga chief. No white dog could be found for this ceremony but his. This dog was his pet, but for the honour of his father and of his tribe he has given up his pet as a sacrifice.'

For a moment the great Anglican bishop was blinded by his own tears. Then he walked slowly across the wide log building and laid his white hand tenderly on the head of the little Onondaga boy. His kindly old eyes closed, and his lips moved—noiselessly, for a space, then he said aloud:

'Oh, that the white boys of my great city church knew and practised half as much of self-denial as has this little pagan Indian lad, who has given up his heart's dearest because his father and the honour of his people required it.'

John Brant-Sero 1867–1914

MOHAWK

Letter

Sir, will you allow me space in your columns, as a humble Canadian Mohawk Indian, hailing from the Six Nations Reserve, Brant county, Ontario? I have just returned from South Africa, disappointed in many respects, but I do not wish these lines to be understood as a grievance. I went to that country from Canada hoping that I might be allowed to enlist in one of the mounted rifles; however, not being a man of European descent, I was refused to do active service in Her Majesty's cause as did my forefathers in Canada.

Reaching South Africa about the middle of August, I attempted to join, as a Canadian, at East London, in Kitchener's Horse, Roberts' Horse, Driscol scouts, and at Queenstown the Cape mounted rifles, the Orange River Colony police, and again Driscol scouts. Here one young Englishman resigned his position to make way for me, but it was hopeless, my credentials were never questioned, I easily satisfied the officer where I came from; that was the trouble. I was too genuine a Canadian. One medical officer who examined me pronounced me unfit; on my questioning him the nature of my unfitness he simply remarked, very good-naturedly, 'There is nothing serious; don't you worry.' After all my failures to handle the rifle, I managed to secure employment at the Queenstown remount depot No. 4. My duties consisted in taking animals up to the front and bossing the Kaffirs. I was on the civilian staff. I have had my share of tent life, army rations, and dodging sand storms during my stay at the seat of war. At various times I visited Springfontein, Bloemfontein, Aliwai North, Colesberg, Stormberg, De Aar, and Bethulie. On one occasion the Boers were considerate enough to let me sneak past Bethulie bridge with 200 entrained mules before they blew up the rails. However, it was not their fault; the circumstance was purely accidental.

At Springfontein, just after the siege of Philippolis, a Boer, a sentry, captured me as I had to get my Kaffirs to identify me. Shortly after that, seeing it was useless remaining in the country, I resigned, and, armed with my honourable discharge, I proceeded to Cape Town, where, upon my arrival, I again made attempts to join a mounted corps, and met the same refusals. . . .

The history of the Mohawk and others of the Six Nations Confederacy residing in Canada is well known in Canada, in fact, a history of Canada cannot be written impartially without recounting the warlike deeds of the Six Nations. We believe we have an interest in the empire, bought by the blood of our ancestors. The name of Captain Joseph Brant (Thayandanegea) is imprinted upon the mind of every student and traveller. It was under his banner the Mohawks left their once beautiful homes in the Mohawk Valley,

New York State, trekking northward to Grand River and the Bay of Juriste [Quinte], where they might enjoy a comfortable retreat safe to follow the customs of their forefathers. Here for over a century they have lived, cultivating their farms and their progress is the pride of all true Canadians. They are not degenerating, neither are they decreasing, but upon the other hand, in common with the Indian population of Canada they are rapidly increasing in numbers. There is scarcely a calling, trade, or profession in which these Indians are not represented. In social life, politics, and literature we occupy no small place.

J.O. Brant-Sero
8 Dartmouth Street, Westminster, S.W.
Dec. 30

Mary Augusta Tappage 1888-*c.* 1978

SHUSWAP

Tyee—Big Chief

Tyee Lake was called after big chief—it means big chief.
But *Tyee* is not Shuswap.
It's Chinook, I think.
But it's not my language.

Pashish'kwa—that means lake in my language.
Shadad'kwa—that means river.

I can't tell you how to spell it.
But that's how we say it.
It's a hard language, Shuswap—real hard.

When I got out of Mission school
I had to ask what the Indians were saying.
I couldn't understand them.
We were only allowed to speak English at school.
I almost forgot my own language.
It's Shuswap, my language.

The Lillooets

That was a big cloud of dust 'way down
to the south in the spring, yes.
It was the Lillooet Indians coming north,
coming north to the goldfields
up by Barkerville.

They go north into that country to work,
to work all the time, hard,
horses and wagons, women and children,
and dogs, hiyu dogs, all going
up by Barkerville.

They work from the time they get there
till fall, till the leaves drop, yes,
and the snow comes and it freezes

the lakes and the creeks
up by Barkerville.

It was the Lillooets going by in the spring
with packing horses, packing freight, yes,
into the mines somewhere in the mountains
and into the creeks
up by Barkerville.

All from Lillooet and I see them passing,
They are passing and passing and, no,
I couldn't ask them where they go—
they speak a different language,
but they go up by Barkerville.

We speak Shuswap, all of us Shuswap—
Soda Creek, Sugar Cane, Alkali, Canoe Creek,
Dog Creek, Canim Lake—all speak Shuswap,
except the Lillooets who go
up by Barkerville.

They come back in the fall, these Lillooets,
tired, I guess, but lots of money, lots of fish,
not minding snow or mud. They laugh
thinking of summer, yes,
up by Barkerville.

Christmas at the Mission

I remember Christmas at the Mission.
Always we used to have midnight mass.

But we didn't know about Christmas and holidays
Until the Sisters came.
The Sisters came from France, you know,
And they brought Christmas with them.

They were the Sisters of Infant Jesus,
Those who came.

The teachers who had been teaching us before,
They didn't bother or care

Or hold Christmas. When the Sisters came
Was when we first knew Christmas!

The Sisters made us a Christmas concert, taught us
To sing hymns and songs,
Say recitations to everybody, helped us
Decorate our first Christmas tree.

I can't tell you how beautiful that first Christmas tree!
Everything was changed!

And our shoe, our right shoe, had to be polished
And put up on a bench
On Christmas Eve for holding candies, yes,
And whatever present you were going to get.

And then we all went to chapel through the snow
That first Christmas for midnight mass.

At Birth

I used to help at times of birth, yes,
I used to help all the women around here.
I learned it from my book, my blue doctor's book.
I used to read it all the time.

I made up my mind that if she needs help,
I will help her. I'm not scared.
You've got to be awfully quick. There's two lives there.
The baby and the mother.

Yes, two lives, and what you got to do it with
Those days? You've got to be quick
To cut the cord, keep the bed clean, take out
The afterbirth, discard it, burn it.

Yes, you've got to be quick, fix the baby,
Tie its navel so it will not bleed
To death—cut it about that long.
When it heals there's nothing left, you know.

Then you bandage the mother, pin her up,
Keep her clean, keep her in bed ten days.
The doctor told us this—but if I leave,
I guess she got up.

I never had to spank a baby
To make him cry—they always cried.
They were always alive and healthy.
Yes, mother and baby, alive and healthy.

Martin Martin 1889–1976

INUIT

We, the Inuit, Are Changing

Translated by William Kalleo

We, the Inuit here in Labrador, right to this day still have the traditional ways of our forefathers. Right to this day we eat what our forefathers used to eat, food with no price tags on it, food created for us ever since the earth was created. People have different foods according to their land. This I was not aware of in the past. Some eat only what is grown in gardens, others eat whatever food they can get their hands on and we the Inuit people, have a different diet because we are people of a cold land. Because we are people of a cold land, wildlife is our main diet. Our forefathers were strong because nothing was scarce, everything was plentiful in those past years. We, the younger generation, think we are hungry but we are not because there is plenty of the white man's foods available for us to obtain at any time. We only are hungry for wildlife meat because some years are plentiful and some years there is none at all. This I have found.

Our forefathers' ancestors, which we have just heard of but not seen, taught our fathers how to share any kill made amongst their people. So my father taught me to share my kill as it was the traditional way. When I was a young man every time I went hunting and came back successful I invited the poor, the less fortunate, and the old Inuit to share my kill. After they had eaten they would joke around and tell stories of the past. When I heard these happy people I was aware that this was a blessing. I had made my fellow people happy through sharing. Our Creator had blessed me and I had carried on this blessing by sharing because this was meant to be. It is sad how this tradition is being forgotten. Young people now keep their kill to themselves. Some will give a little to those they wish to share with. I have said what I have seen and experienced and I am aware that this tradition is no longer practised. I hope this will be written down so that our children can be made aware of what used to take place in past years.

We have not lost all our traditions and culture yet. We have not lost our ability to hunt wildlife game. We know how to locate and hunt the game. Our young men still try to hunt in the traditional ways but they have difficulties because there is less game now. But our young Inuit have not given up trying their best to hunt for wildlife food. This we will never lose as long as there are Inuit in Labrador.

I am one hundred per cent pure Eskimo. I was never educated in the white society way because when I was a child this was not practised. Our school term lasted only six months and our main subject was studying the word of

God. We had to memorize Bible verses and speak them out from memory while our teachers listened. The only time we were given a new verse was when we mastered the one before. Because of this teaching we, the elderly Inuit, can still speak out by heart many verses of the Bible, at least I always could. I don't know of my fellow elders but I'm sure they too can speak out what they memorized as children. In this generation our children have almost a whole year to learn and study but they are learning only the white society way. No wonder they have a better knowledge than we, the elderly. I am not happy that they are only being taught the white society system. I would be happy if they were taught first the word of God, then how to deal with life. I say this because I think our children don't know the true meaning of life because they refuse to hear the word of God, or are encouraged to do so. Our Inuit children are taught, I suppose, how to survive in white communities but not in the Inuit land. When learning the white society way was first introduced, or enforced, as a way of teaching our Inuit children, I strongly objected because I foresaw that in the future they would forget our Inuit language and also the word of God. I have said this because it is what I have wanted to say for ever so long. I was involved when teaching our children in the white society way was forced on us. I was out-voted when I suggested that our children be taught the word of God first and other subjects after. I had no power to alter what was being forced on our children, my objections were not considered important. Now, what I tried to bring to attention, about our children losing their traditions and culture, is beginning to be realized by Inuit in different parts of Canada. All I have said is true. Our young Inuit have a complete new way of living and if it is let to continue, something will happen to show them they are leading a dangerous life.

In such a short time we, the Inuit of Labrador, have changed in many ways. We do not carry on many of our traditions. We are forced into many new ways which we do not even understand. Also in these days we have seen Inuit from other regions, those we had only heard about but we did not know if they had traditions and cultures which were similar to ours. Now, we see them in the flesh and see that our fellow Inuit share our traditions and culture.

Last March, when I reached the age of eighty-seven, I started to think that I had lived too long. Then another thought occurred to me, why am I still living when I am no longer able to live off the land and sea? Why am I still wandering among my fellow Inuit and being observed and told that I am no longer useful to my people? I thought once more, the Lord God has been merciful to me to this day because although I am an old man I still have a mouth which can give guidance to our younger Inuit. The years have taken their toll on me, on my hearing, my sight, and my ability to walk long distances. All are no longer good and I know why this is so. When I was a young man we used to hunt caribou in the different seasons. One spring we were returning from the land when the river trails were starting to get water on the ice. Early one morning, before the sun rose, we slid from the top of the country down to a lake. The river trail had frozen over during the night and so it was usable but as the sun rose the ice melted and we began to break through into the water. When our komatiks fell through we went over knee deep in the icy water to push and pull them out. We carried on all through the day, wading, pushing, and pulling our heavily laden komatiks. My legs became so numb that I could feel nothing. Ever since that time my legs are no longer good.

I wish you peace on earth. We may never see each other on earth but through God's will we will see each other in Heaven when we are removed from the earth. So, let us look forward to meeting each other where there will be no pain or sorrow but happiness and eternal life. I am an old man now. My name is Martin Martin. I wish all a happy and successful life.

Alma Greene 1896–1984

MOHAWK

From *Forbidden Voice: Reflections of a Mohawk Indian*

Everything was starting to change.

Both Forbidden Voice's big brothers were married now, and the older one had taken over the farm. The younger one had always preferred his paycheck to the life of a farmer, so his father had settled him in a house on a lot elsewhere on the reservation and the son went off to work every day. Forbidden Voice's big sister had gone to the city. People shook their heads when they talked about her.

Even Sundays were different now. Sunday had always been a special day in their house, Sunday was extra good meals, Sunday was put away all your work, even the doll's clothes you had been sewing. Sunday was visitors, Methodist church in the morning, and the Anglican church in the afternoon, and in the evening the whole family into the parlour for father to read from the Bible that sat on the fall-leaf table with the red cloth.

Her father was a lay reader in the Anglican church, and the first English Forbidden Voice had ever heard was her father reading the Bible on Sundays. For a long time the reading was just a monotone to her. She couldn't make out any of the words and the tiresome noise seemed to go on and on forever. It wasn't at all like the liquid Mohawk tongue, or even the jerky syllables of the Cayugas. Later, when she heard white men speak it, English was always to sound loud and quarrelsome in her ear.

Now her father had left the church and, though she asked him, he wouldn't say why. One day she mentioned this to an old chief who knew about affairs on the reserve, and he said he could tell her why. He took her to his house and there he showed her a document, which was a copy of the Exchequer Court proceedings between the Six Nations and the New England Company.

The New England Company was a curious organization that had been formed in the seventeenth century for the express purpose of 'civilizing' the North American natives and propagating the gospel. The company had sent missionaries to the Grand Valley in the 1820s and they had built a school for the Mohawks that later came to be known as the Mohawk Institute. Now it seemed that these 'Christians' had sold the land they had got from the Indians, which to Forbidden Voice was the same as stealing it.

Forbidden Voice knew that many of her people believed the Christian missionaries had no right to try to make Indians change their own religion and way of worship. Didn't it say in the Bible, at the very beginning of Genesis, 'And God said, "Let us make man in Our own image, after Our likeness, and let them have dominion over the fish of the sea and over the fowl of the air". So God created men in His own image, in the image of God created He him male and female created He them'?

And wasn't it only later, in Chapter Five of Genesis, that God created Adam and Eve to inhabit the Garden of Eden in the old world? Surely this meant that Adam and Eve were created to inhabit a specific place in the old world and that the Indians were the original man-beings created in the new world, with the eternal right to hunt and fish for their food?

Hadn't Christ told his apostles when he sent them to teach and baptize in the old world, 'I have other sheep which are not of this fold; them I will gather in'? Surely this meant the Indians were Christ's special charges, and that all the popes and kings and bishops of the old world had no authority to interfere.

Forbidden Voice had seen with her very own eyes evidence that the Creator kept an eye on his special children. A tornado had swept through one summer causing death and destruction in its path. When it had started to get very dark on the reserve, and they could see the funnel-shaped cloud coming from the west, all the families had been called together. As they watched, the funnel cloud lifted high aloft and passed over their heads. When it had gone past Indian territory, they could see it come to earth again and go on its angry way. Didn't this mean the Creator was not displeased with the red men?

Her mother had taught her a prayer in Mohawk to repeat every night before she went to bed. All it said was 'God the Father, God the Son, God the Holy Ghost; Creator of the sun, the moon, the stars, and the earth. Amen.' Its form was Christian, but she thought about it now and its spirit seemed to her more like a true Mohawk prayer. It was like the six annual festivals held at the other longhouses on the reserve. (The Mohawks were supposed to be Christians so their own longhouse had been destroyed.) The festivals were held according to the moon and their purpose was to thank the Creator for the seasons and for the ripening of each crop as it came on. This was her people's ancient religion, and it began to seem to her the purest way of worship. Wasn't it better than always asking the Creator to do something or to give something more than He already had?

Yet, even though the Indians worshipped the Creator in constant gratitude and remembrance, and were His charges, and practised the stern morality of Handsome Lake, the white men called them heathens.

There was another thing. Forbidden Voice could read very well now, and one day among the Six Nations' records she came across a document. It was a letter containing a list and a speech. It seemed there had been a pledge to the Iroquois just before the American War of Independence that any of the Iroquois who remained loyal to England in her war would at the close of the war receive the protection of Britain. When the war was over, it had been required of her forefathers to prove in any way they could that they had fought for England's cause, and this is what they had sent.

January 3, 1782

May it please your Excellency:

I send herewith to your Excellency under the care of James Boyd, eight pecks of scalps, cured, dried, hooped, and painted with all the Indian triumphal marks of which the following is invoice and explanation.

No. 1—Containing 43 scalps of Congress soldiers killed in different skirmishes. These are stretched on black hoops, four-inch diameter, the inside of the skin painted red with a small black spot to note their being killed with bullets. Also, 62 of farmers, killed in their homes, the hoops red, the skin painted brown and marked with a hoe, a black circle all around to denote their being surprised in the night and a black hatchet in the middle signifying their being killed with that weapon.

No. 2—Containing 98 of farmers, killed in their homes, hoops red, figure of a hoe to mark their profession, great white circle and sun to show they were surprised in the daytime, a little red foot to show they stood upon their defence and died fighting for their lives and families.

No. 3—Containing 97 of farmers, hoops green to show they were killed in their fields, a large white circle with a little round mark on it for the sun to show that it was in the daytime, black bullet marks on some, hatchets on others.

No. 4—Containing 102 of farmers, mixed of the several marks above, only 18 marked with a little yellow flame to denote their being of prisoners burned alive after being scalped, their nails pulled out by the roots and other torments, one of these latter supposed to be of a rebel clergyman, his band being fixed to the hoop of his scalp. Most of the farmers appear by the hair to have been young or middle-aged men, there being but 67 very grey heads among them, which makes the service more essential.

No. 5—Containing 88 scalps of women, hair long, braided in the Indian fashion to show they were mothers, hoops blue, skin yellow ground with little red tadpoles to represent by way of triumph, the tears of grief occasioned to their relations, a black scalping knife or hatchet at the bottom to mark their being killed, with these instruments; 17 others hair very grey, black hoops, plain brown colour, no mark but the short club to show they were knocked down dead or had their brains beat out.

No. 6—Containing 103 boys' scalps of various ages, small green hoops, whitish ground on the skin, red tears in the middle and black bullet mark, knife, hatchet, or club as their deaths happened.

No. 7—211 girls' scalps, big and little, small yellow hoops, white ground, tears, hatchet, club, scalping knife, etc.

No. 8—This package is a mixture of all the varieties above mentioned to the number of 122 with a box of birch-bark containing 29 little infants' scalps of various sizes, small white hoops.

With these packs, the chiefs send to your Excellency the following speech:

Your Excellency's most obedient and humble servant,

Signed James Crawford.

Speech

'Father, we send you herewith many scalps that you may see that we are not idle friends.

'Father, we wish to send these scalps over the water to the Great King that he may regard them and be refreshed and that he may see our faithfulness in destroying his enemies and be convinced that his presents have not been made to ungrateful people.

'Father, attend to what I am now going to say, it is a matter of much weight. The Great King's enemies are many and they grow fast in numbers. They were formerly like young panthers, they could neither bite nor scratch. We could play with them safely, we feared nothing they could do to us but now their bodies are become as big as the elk and strong as the buffalo. They also have got great and sharp claws, they have driven us out of our country by taking part in your quarrel. We expect the Great King will give us another country that our children may live after us and be his friends and children as we are. Say this for me to the Great King.

'Father, we have only to say further that your traders exact more than ever for their goods and our hunting is lessened by the war, so that we have fewer skins to give them. This ruins us. Think of some remedy.

'We are poor and you have plenty of everything. We know you will send us powder and guns and knives and hatchets, but we also want shirts and blankets.' I do not doubt that your Excellency will think it proper to give some further encouragement to those honest people. The high prices they complain of are the necessary effect of the war. Whatever presents may be sent for them through my hands shall be distributed with prudence and fidelity.

I have the honour of being
Your Excellency's most obedient and most
humble servant.
James Crawford'

It was after sending this proof that the Six Nations had been given the lands in the Grand River Valley and had moved there from the United States and had rekindled their Great Council Fire in their new home. But the treaty of pledge, which had been executed on April 7, 1779, had promised the Six Nations not just land to replace what they had lost but the same status as before the war, which meant the right to be an independent nation; to be allies of the English, not British subjects; to be brothers of the sovereign with their own equal sovereignty.

And now what had happened? Their lands had been sold or stolen; the Canadian government treated them as silly children for whom it was quite all right to make laws without consultation; and the white men called them heathens.

Now there were even mutterings among some on the reserve that the Six Nations should abandon the ancient hereditary council of chieftains and have a white man's kind of elected government.

Forbidden Voice wondered what it would have been like for the Mohawks if there had never been a Captain Joseph Brant, though everyone seemed to think of him as an illustrious warrior and remembered him for saying in the English court, 'I bend my knee for no man.' For Brant, who was not even a chief but just a Mohawk warrior, was the one who had got the Six Nations mixed up with the white man and who had helped talk the Six Nations into fighting for England. And he was the one who had been so eager to see the Mohawks become Christians that he had destroyed their longhouse.

Though Forbidden Voice's father no longer went to the Christian church, the rest of the family did, and it was their strong custom at Easter to come back from wherever they might be to go to their own church.

This was why Forbidden Voice's sister came home from Brantford that Easter. She had come with her cousin and when her mother asked her why her husband did not come, she did not answer right away.

But after they had come back from the service and had dinner, the sister told her parents that her husband had been staying out almost every night all winter. She had found out from the place where he worked that he had been seeing a married woman. She had not talked to him about this because he never wanted to talk when he came home.

He had been out all the night before and had come in only as she was getting ready to leave for the trip to her parents' home. She had asked him to come with her to church, but he got very angry and said the devil himself could not make him go to church.

She returned to Brantford the same night. Afterwards Forbidden Voice was told that just as her sister reached home, a policeman stopped her and told her that if she wanted to see her husband alive she must go at once to the hospital. She had no money left to take a cab, so she walked. When she got there, they let her go in at once to see her husband. She hardly recognized him, his face was so disfigured. The doctor said he was dying, but he did not tell her what had happened. No one told her. They just gave her his blood-soaked suit to take home. She walked back all the way from the hospital, carrying the suit, and by the time she reached home she herself was soaked with his blood.

Her husband died that night. Afterwards another policeman told her that while she was gone for Easter, her husband and his brother had got into an argument over a girl. They were both big men and under the influence of liquor, and the older brother had thrown her husband down and jumped on his face and head and that was how he had died.

His body was released to a local undertaker directly from the hospital. But after the funeral the pallbearers, who were friends of his, began to wonder. The husband had been a tall man, while the coffin they had been given to carry was short and light.

Finally the widow and the man's father got an order to have the grave dug up. With some friends they went that night carrying lanterns, spades, and shovels. They started to dig. All was silent but the noise of the shovels. When the coffin was opened the widow and the father moved closer. There was a gasp. The body in the coffin had no shroud to cover it. And it had no head. No one else could identify it, so the widow said her husband had had a birthmark on his chest that she would recognize. They let her look. Hardly above a whisper she said it was the body of her husband.

The white man's world was beginning to intrude on Forbidden Voice's life. Some of it, like what had happened to her sister's husband, made no sense to her at all.

Susan Martin b. 1897

INUIT

When I Was a Child

Translated by Fran McIntosh

When I was a child there used to be plenty of seals anytime in the spring, in the fall. We would have plenty of dried seal meat. We lived in a tent, with a place for a bed and lots of food, seal meat, blubber, and all kinds of meat right there in the tent. I did not grow up with my parents. The people I lived with had plenty of seals to eat all the time. When we finished hunting seals in the spring we would go to Paul's Island where we would fish. There was lots of codfish and we had plenty of dried codfish (pitsik). When I became bigger I did not go fishing with the others because I was a pet of the people who took care of me. I couldn't even cook, only Harriet, who would also fish, would cook when she got home. She would cook in big metal pots. I was given the job of fetching water. When I woke up in the morning, while everyone had gone fishing, I would find some candies by my pillow. These are things I remember when I was a child.

There would be lots of fishermen and many schooners. They had no motors or engines. Those days they rowed the big schooners. If it was a calm day you would see some of them being towed into Paul's Island. The fishermen from the schooners would come ashore and we, not knowing how to understand or speak English, would make each other understand by motions and hand talking.

The fishermen would come in their schooners and anchor out in the harbour at Paul's Island on Sundays. The grown-ups would go aboard while the children stayed at home in the tent. Sometimes when we stayed at home like that we would pretend that we were white people. We used long clothes that weren't anything like the real white man's clothes. We would think that we were so pretty once we were dressed as Kablunaks (white people). The other children who were staying home with me, when they saw the boats coming ashore, would hurry and take their 'make-believe' clothes off . . . not me though. I would be wearing Harriet's long skirt and her blouse and I thought I was so pretty and elegant. When they got ashore they would have a big laugh at me, who was the only one dressed up and being so proud.

Long ago and many years back, when there were no white people, the Eskimos would make things out of flint. They would use diamond to sharpen tools. That is why we would be looking for flints all the time when we were children. That was the only thing that would be able to break the rocks or stones, the diamonds. I don't know much about the *real* early days. They did all kinds of bad things, even had wars among themselves, and fighting.

And the Indians had been around at different times. They said the Indians could not be seen, they even said the Indians turned into rocks or stones. The Indians and Eskimos feared each other. The Indians were called Naskaupis. These are stories that have been passed down to me.

In earlier days all the men used kayaks, only, to hunt seals in the spring. They would bring back lots of seals. They would dry the sealskins by stretching them and pegging them to the ground by wooden pegs. They would take the fat off by rubbing them on the rocks or land. The skins would turn out so clean without even washing them. The women would make plenty of skinboots. These days nobody knows how to clean skins, make skinboots, or make kayaks. I don't remember too much now. When I was a young girl I was able to clean skins and make skinboots. I learned by watching. These days we are all wearing l'il old store-bought shoes, all of us.

I don't want to tell a story anymore.

Harry Robinson 1900–90

OKANAGAN

Captive in an English Circus

A man from the Similkameen Valley goes to prison in New Westminster for killing a man. One night he is secretly abducted and taken on a long journey.

This is about George Jim.
He belongs to Ashnola Band, George Jim.
Those days, I had it written down—1886.
No, I mean 1887.
That's one year I'm out there.
That's supposed to be in the 1886
   instead of 1887.
That time, 1886,
   the people, Indians from Penticton,
     all the Okanagan Indians,
       they were some from Similkameen.
         and they all move to where Oroville is now
           in the month of August,
             about the last week in the month of August.
And they all get together in Oroville.
And that's when the salmon coming up.
The salmon comes up, you know, from way down.
They come up on the Columbia River
   and they come up on the Okanogan, some.
And some of them go up, they split up there.
Some of them go up the Columbia River.
But some of them, they coming up on the Okanogan River.
They had a good place for catching them there in Oroville.
Kind of shallow.
Only a small river.

So, the people moved over there.
They stay there.
Put in a camp.
There is no town there yet.
There was some white people,
   they got two or three houses there.
Not many.

Then they get the salmon.
They get the salmon for,
    could be about a week or ten days.
Then the salmon keep going and go by.
They come to Osoyoos Lake
    and they follow Osoyoos Lake
        and then they come to Okanogan River again
            and they keep going to Okanagan Falls.
They can never go any farther than Okanagan Falls.
There's a dam there.
That's as far as the salmon can go.

These Indian, when they run out of salmon,
    they know the salmon, they go by.
So they move.
Follow the salmon.
Then they come to Okanagan Falls.
Then the salmon, they can't go no more.
They were there.
They can get salmon.
Some of them died in the water
    and get bad, you know, get spoiled.
Then they quit.
When they get together at Falls,
    there's a lot of Indians and they put in a camp.
Some of them, they play stickgame.
They kind of celebrate.
But still some of them get the salmon
    at night or the daytime.
And some of them get whiskey from someplace,
    from Penticton, I guess, or somewhere.
And they drink.

And this time,
    that Jim,
        supposed to be a big man, stout man.
And he's a funny looking man.
He's got short legs,
    but he's pretty wide in the shoulders.
And he's got big hips.
Kinda tough-looking man.
And he was.
He's a strong man.

Then there was a white man
   that lived there at Okanagan Falls.
And he's got an Indian woman from Penticton.
And they got some children,
   maybe one or two.
And this white man, his name, Shattleworth.

A lot of people drinking, you know.
And then George Jim, and Shattleworth, and some others,
   they drinking at night,
     and then they fighting.
But this time, that Shattleworth,
   he got beat badly by George Jim.
George Jim, he beat him almost till death.
Then, some of the boys, they stopped him and grab him.
Because he's strong, it takes a few men to hold him.
Then they take the man who's wounded.
They take him to the camp.
They laid him in the camp.
He's hurt very bad.
He's got a broken ribs
   and he was hurt in the head, you know.
Quite a few cuts.
With a club, you know, he hit him in the head with a club
   and then he cut the skin, you know, by the club.
Not knife, but the club,
Then he kicked him in the ribs
   and his ribs were broken inside.
And then some of that bone,
   they must have gone to the lungs.
Could be.

He thought,
   I hurt him badly
     and I might as well kill him.

So, who's going to stop him?
He's a strong man.
They went to the tepee.
Bunch of women in there,
   maybe two or three old men
     and maybe five women, old women.

So he come there and he says,
   'How's that Shattleworth?

I'm going to kill him if he's alive yet.'
And these people told him,
　'He's dead.
　He died.
　Already died.'

And they covered him with a white blanket.
He lay on the bed
　and they cover him, all his head.
And he looked like he was dead all right
　because he was covered with a white cloth.
They tell him,
　'You better stay away.
　He died.
　He dead already.'

All right, he go away.

But he didn't die, that Shattleworth.
After that he was living for about seven or eight months.
But he died just from getting beat
　because the way I see, maybe the ribs they were broken
　　and maybe some, they go to the lungs.
But if not go to the lungs,
　the ribs they be heal up.
He wouldn't die.
But this one here, it's bad.
Maybe it goes in the lung,
　the bone, the broken rib.

But anyway, George got away.
And then they report that to the policeman
　because this Shattleworth, he's a white man
　　and he's got an Indian wife.
And it was reported to the police.
But the police, they couldn't get him.
Kinda scared of him because Jim,
　he's got a revolver on his hip all the time,
　　and yet he's a strong man.
And the policeman, they kinda scared of him.
They just let him go.
They look for a chance to sneak to him and then get him.

So Jim, he stay away for quite a while,
　for almost one year.

About eleven months after he did that,
    that was next August and somebody, they cheat him.
Then they got him.
And he been around to Ashnola and down to Chopaka.
But he always keep away from the policeman.
They go over there and look for him,
    but they're scared of him.
They always around there but nobody get him.
He hide in the daytime in the hillside.
At night he goes to the Indian camp
    and sometimes he didn't.

Then, there was one boy, eleven years old.
And he make a lunch,
    a big lunch for Jim.
Then he told that boy,
    he told an old man,
        'You take that boy
          and show him the place
            where he can leave that lunch for Jim.
      And tell him what he's going to do.
      And tell him what he's got to say if somebody met him.'
That old man used to take the lunch,
    but he a little afraid
        maybe the policeman or some man
          might think the old man
            must have take a lunch to that wanted man.
But if the boy,
    he give him a gun, you know,
    a 22-gun, you know,
        to shoot the grouse.
And they tell him,
    'If somebody come and met you,
        if they ask you what you're doing here,
          you tell 'em,
            "I'm hunting, hunting for grouse,
            willow grouse, or rabbit, or something like that."'

Then, he's got bags on his shoulders.
    'When I get a grouse I can put it in there.'
But that's where he had the lunch.
And he showed him where he can take the lunch
    and where he can leave it.
There was a big stone
    and there was kind of hollow underneath the stone.

That was kind of a shade.
In the daytime he could put the lunch there.

But this man is up on the hill.
He could be watching him.
When it gets dark,
   this man will come down and take the lunch
      and go up the hill again.
That's Jim.
So the old man, he show the boy
   and tell all about what to do and what to say.
And he can take the lunch every once in awhile,
   every two days,
      because they make a big lunch at a time.

But not long after that,
   that was in the month of August, could be,
      because they say that choke cherries were ripe.
They don't know if it was August or September those days.
Now I can figure myself.
When they say it's choke cherries time,
   choke cherries, they ripe,
      choke cherries they ripe in the month of August.
I know that.
That could be in August.
Then he was there for quite a while.

And the road gang, they building a road.
And they call it McCurdy place.
And after that, they call it,
   I forget the new man that lived there.
Anyway, McCurdy place,
      that's the first man that lived there.
McCurdy for about a mile
   and the river it's curved like that.
Kind of bent.
And that's where they camp, the road gang.
   they had a camp there.
Those days wherever they can build a road,
   if it's far away from town,
      they can move camp.
They got to have a camp there.
But nowadays, the workers,
   they can go from town.
It don't matter how far.

They don't put no camp.
But those days they got a camp.
They use horses, you know,
   scraper and plough to make a grade.
And they had a camp there,
   the road gang, the bunch of them.
And they had a cookhouse and a cook.
Bunch of men workers.
And there was a trail,
   but they widen out that trail to be a wagon road.
That was in 1887 then.
That's a long time ago.
No highway those days.

So the road gang was there.
And one of these boys, like the boss,
   maybe, the foreman, you know,
      he has to ride the horse.

No car those days,
   no motorcycle,
      no bicycle,
         no nothing.
Only saddle horse.
You know that.

Then these men
   they go to Fairview.
That's a town, you know.
Mine town.
Their head boss is there.
Government.

All right,
They went over there to see him
   and come back.
So he went over there
   and then in the afternoon, he come back from Fairview.
He went over there in the morning.
In the afternoon he come back from there.

And this George Jim,
   he took a horse and ride him around by Nighthawk.
Then he must have gone by Oroville or somewhere.
But he come back
   and he come back where that Osoyoos Road is now.

You remember when we come up there?
And I showed you, 'Here is the old road?'
But now the highway is above the old road.

So Jim, he come on that road.
And the other one,
    that man who goes to Fairview,
      he takes the trail like from Fairview.
And they met at the top, just above Spotted Lake.

When we were at Spotted Lake
   and you took pictures, I and him?
And I told you, the old road, it's higher up there?
Yeah, that's where they meet,
   this man from Fairview.
He go by Spotted Lake.
And Jim was coming on the road
   and they met there.
Then, because Jim, he's a 'wanted man',
   it was written in the government office,
      his name and how he look like and all that.
And all the white people knew that
   even if they never seen him before.
But as soon as they see him,
   they can tell that was the 'wanted man'.

So this man, one of the government men,
   the one that goes to Fairview,
     soon as he met him,
       he knew he was the one.
There was a reward, you know,
   because whoever catch him is going to get paid.
Then he said to George,
   they go together and they talk
     and they make a good friend to one another,
       and they are good friend
         and it's getting late in the afternoon.
Finally they rode together
   and they're getting close to the camp.
Then, it's just about supper-time then.
And this white man, he tell Jim,
   'You better come with me to the camp.
   Then you can eat there.
   Eat supper.

Now, it's just about suppertime.'
He tell him,
   'I am one of the bosses in that camp,
     so you come with me
       and you stay there
         and after supper you can go.'
And Jim, he says,
   'No, I better keep going.
   I can stop someplace in some of them Indians.'
   'Oh no. You better come.
   You eat here. You'll be all right.'

But you know, he figure,
   when he get there,
     he figure he can tell the other boys right away
      and that was their judge to catch him.

So anyway,
   George, he must have been hungry or something
     because he stop there
      and he went with that man.
And he tie up his horse.
Then, I think this white man,
   the one that's with him,
     he must have tell the other ones right away.
And then he didn't know.

And then,
   one of the working man,
     big man, strong man,
      he take the apron and he put it here.
He's not a waiter.
He's not a cook.
He's one of the ploughmen.
But he puts the apron on so he looks like a waiter, cook.
Long table
   and he takes the grub
     and he move over there
      and he goes back and gets some more.

And Jim was sitting there
   and he wanted to sit on the other side against the tent wall.
But they tell him,
   'You can sit here.
   Already the boys are over there.'

He didn't like to sit there because it's open.

So this waiter goes by him
   on his back two, three times.
And then I guess these other boys,
   nobody know,
      they might get a club and then they hide it.
When the waiter gets over the other end of the table
   and he give him that club.
Then he come back.
That was the fourth time or the fifth time
   when they go by George's back.

Then this time when he go by there,
   and George was watching all the time.
He always watching.
But finally he quieted down
   and he eat.
And he's got a revolver on his hip, you know.

And when this waiter go by him,
   down it went on the back of his head
      and George just drop!
And he knocked out
   and drop off the chair.
And all the men are just on him, you know.
Bunch of men, three or four men,
   they just right on him.
And they get the rope
   and they tie his arms
      and they tie his feet.
Before he come to, he's already tied up.
They can't do nothing.
They take his gun away from him.

Then they sent one of the boys to Fairview for the policeman
   after supper, after six o'clock.
Then, whoever they went from there to Fairview,
   that's about ten or fifteen miles,
      they get there and tell the police
         and then the policemen come.
When the policemen gets there
   and they handcuff him,
      put the handcuffs on him.
Then, nothing he can do after they got the handcuffs.

They take the ropes off his feet
 and then they tell him,
  'Get on you horse.'
And these policemen,
 they come on horses,
  the two of them.
Then they lead him
 and they tie his feet with a rope under the belly
  so he could never jump off.
They got handcuffs, iron handcuffs.
He can't get away.
So they lead him to Fairview
 and then they put him in jail.

Because the one, he beat Shattleworth.
He did.
After the six or seven months after he was beat,
 he died.
He's a murderer anyway.

So, they held him in that jail for a while
 and they had a trial there once or twice.
Then they take him to Penticton.
There was another courthouse there.
Just small.
They held him there awhile
 and then they took him to Kamloops.
There must have been a little court in Vernon those days.
But Kamloops.
Then they had him there for a while
 and then they got a sentence seven years.
Only seven years.
Take him to Westminster.
And the railroad drives into Westminster in 1886.
And they already had a railroad right in Vancouver.

And Mr Jim,
 they sent him from Kamloops on the railroad to Westminster.
And then they had him in that penitentiary.
And he was in there three years.
Supposed to be seven years and then he'll come out.
That's his sentence.
Seven years.

He was in jail three years
 and one night towards morning,

about two o'clock in the morning then
   because all the cells, you know,
      whoever's in the cell, maybe one or two,
         the policeman lock 'em.
Then, in the morning they could open 'em.
Unlock 'em.
But Jim was locked.
All alone in one cell.
But towards morning,
   about two o'clock in the morning,
      somebody open that.
They got a key,
   open the door,
      and they come in.
There's three of them—policemen.
They got the clothes, uniform—guards.
Those days, the policemen,
   they haven't got no uniform.
But the guards, they got some kind of a uniform.

So, the three of them come in.
And Jim, he wake up.
Still in bed.
And told him,
   'Jim, you get up and put your clothes on.
   We come and get you.'

I'm not sure if it was three.
I think it's only two.
But the driver, that makes three.
They got a driver on the buggy out there.
But these two,
   they're both guards,
      go in and tell Jim,
         'You dress up and we come and get you.
         There's a buggy outside with a driver.
         You get on the buggy
            and we all get on and we go to Vancouver.
         Early in the morning,
            the train is going to leave Vancouver.
         We got to go on the train.
         We move you.
         There's one jail a long long way from here.
         We move you.
         You're going to be over at that jail.
         Long ways from here.

You leave this place.'

Well what can he say,
   because this is the policeman, guard, you know.
He has to do whatever they tell him.
All right, he dress up and he went out.
There was a buggy there
   and he get on the buggy
     and they all get on the buggy
       and they go to Vancouver early in the morning.

At that time they got a different time.
Now, they leave there eight o'clock in the evening from
   Vancouver.
But at that time it might have been in the morning.
Might be four o'clock in the morning
   or something like that.

Anyway,
   early in the morning they get on the train
     and they went.
And they going all day and all night
   and all day and all night again.
And Mr Jim, he thinks,
   By God, that was a long way.
   Where did they take me?
   I wonder where they take me.

They take him into where they eat, you know,
   on the train.
And he got a chance to ask the waiter.
I guess the policemen who look after him, they went back,
   and just only himself.
And he asked the waiter,
   and the waiter told him,
     'They take you to Halifax.
    Then there, you're going to take the boat
      from Halifax to England.'

So, he find that out,
   but what has he got to say?
So anyway, they get him to Halifax.
Then they told him,
   'We're going to be here for a while.
   We're waiting for the boat.'

Because those days
    it takes the boat a month to go over the sea to England.
One month.
But now it's only about four days.
So they wait there about four or five days.
Then the boat came.
Then they put him in the boat,
    the whole bunch.
These two, they always along with him,
    the same man.

So, he mention that.
They see one Indian in England
    and he told him,
        this Indian from Enderby,
           not Indian altogether,
               he's a half-breed,
                   but he speak in Okanagan.
So, he says in his stories that he went on the water.
He could see the mountains, the ground,
    for one week and no more.
Two weeks,
    never see nothing but water.
Then he see again a little ridge.
Little ground.
One week and then they landed.
Then from there
    they took him on the buggy
        or on the train or something for quite a ways.
Then they leave him there.
But not in jail no more.
They give him a good house,
    a good big house,
        big room,
            good bed.
They feed him good
    and then they kept him.
They watch him all the time.
But once in awhile they took him
    and put him on the train
        and they went away.
They stay away for two or three months
    and then come back.
That was his home place.
In two months or more,

they come back to England
　and they stay there for two or three weeks,
　　maybe one month,
　　　then they took him to another direction.
That's in European somewhere.

They took him everywhere for show.
Whenever they get somewhere
　and there'd be a big forum
　　and table or something.
Then they tell him to get up there
　and walk around there.
Then, the people in the big room,
　big house chock full of people,
　　and he watching them.
And these people, they pay.
Pay money to see that Indian.
There is no Indian in Europe at that time.
Only him.

So the white people, they make money out of him.
And he was there four years.

And this man from Enderby,
　he's a half-breed.
His name, Charlie.
Charlie Harvie, his name.
He talks in Okanagan.
He's half-breed.
And he don't say,
　but I think myself he must be in the army,
　　that Charlie,
　　　because he went and he get to England.
Then he come back from England
　and he came home to Enderby.
And when he got home,
　he said when he was in England,
　　he said, there's a big bunch of boys,
　　　all young boys just like he was,
　　　　just like his age.
Bunch of them and they were there.

So one of these boys told him,
　asked him where he come from.

And he said he came from the Okanagan, British Columbia.
Okanagan.
Then, he told him,
   'There was a man not far from here,
     he is supposed to come from Okanagan, British Columbia.
   He is supposed to speak in your language.
   Maybe we should take you over there
     and then you can see that man.'

Then, he said,
   'No, I don't like to go because,'
   (see, he's got a boss, he must be an army man),
   'My boss they may not like it that way.'
So, the other boss says,
   'Your boss, he's not going to know that.
   We take you over there.
   We're not going to tell your boss.
   You're going to see that man.'

All right,
So they went.
The boys took him over there.
Then they get to that place
   and they go in to where that Jim was.
That's his house.
Then the boys told him,
   'This man, he speak in your language.'
Then the both of them started to speak in Okanagan.

Not only one.
He went over there two or three times
   to see him and visit him
     for quite a while.

And Jim,
   he told him all about what they have done
     and so on.
And then they took him from Westminster
   and they took him on the train a long ways
     and they put him on the boat for one month.
Then they had him there.
   'Then they take me out from here a long ways.
   I don't know which way,
     but they take me out a long ways.

Wherever I stop, a lot of people get in there.
   Then they make me walk around on the boards.
   High.
   Then I walk around and all the people look at me.
   Then I go.
   We go to another place.
   Then we go to another place.
   A lot of places.
   In one month or two months
     we come back.
   And this is my home place.'

But he says,
   'Charlie, when you get back to British Columbia,
     you can go from Enderby to Ashnola.'
Right in Ashnola he's got aunt and he's got uncle.
And he said to Charlie,
   'You could tell my uncle and my aunt
     to make a business,
     to see if they can come and get me.
   They got a lot of money.
   They got a lot of cattle.
   They got enough money.
   They should come and get me.
   In another way they can talk to the Indian agent.
   And then the Indian agent can contact to Ottawa,
     to the Indian Affairs.
   Then, whoever they is coming to get me,
     their fare can be paid that way.
   But maybe they'll have a little money with them anyway.
   But my people, they're well-off.
   They should do that and come and get me.'

So Charlie, he said,
   'I will when I get home.'

And about a year after that,
   Charlie came back.
Come back to Enderby.
He stay there almost one year after that and he come back.
And then he ride on the saddle horse all the way to Ashnola.
Then he see that John, his name was,
   and Mary.
They are cousins.
That's Jim's aunt, that Mary,
   and his uncle, John.

He told them all about it
   to contact the Indian agent and to Ottawa
     and all that.
And he said,
  'If you want me, I can be with you,'
    because he can speak in English, you know.

But these Indians, they couldn't understand.
They don't know.
In another way, they don't like it.

They say,
  'He should not pay for our fare
    because that's a lot of money.'
They figure they could pay for their own fare
   but it takes a lot of money.
And they could never understand about the contact
   so they could get paid their fare from the Indian affairs.
Charlie told them,
   but they couldn't understand.
Charlie, he was waiting around,
   and he said,
     'I go home, but if you need me, I come back and help you,
       or else I can go with you for interpreter over there
         to get that man back.'

But they just dismissed.
No more.
They never get him.

But, before they find out he was alive yet
   at the time when they took Jim from Westminster,
     take him away,
       then they rode from the jail to John.
He was a chief, you know.
And they told John that
  'Jim was in jail here
    but he died and we bury him.'

But he not die.
They lie.
They take him away.

So they think, his people,
   they just got to know he died and that's all.

But they decided they should come and get the body.
Take it out and bring him home.
So they did.
They come, that John and Mary and some others.
They got an interpreter, you know,
  who can speak in English.
Then they come on horseback with the packhorses to Hope.
Then they talk to the people in Hope
  and they tell them,
     'You can't leave your horses here.
     There's no feed for the horses.
     You have to go to Chilliwack
       and then you can put your horses in there with the Indians.
     There's all kinds of feed there for horses.
     And then you can take the boat from Chilliwack to Westminster.'

So, they did.
They did get to Westminster
  and then they go to the jail office
    and they tell 'em,
      'We're coming to get George Jim.
      He's already buried here.'
So, they said,
      'Yeah, we talk to one another.
      We'll see.
      Just wait awhile, a couple of days.'

Then, they talk to one another
  and I guess they find out what to say about him.
Then they say,
  'All right, we know.
  This is the one right there in the graveyard.
  We can dig him.
  We dig him out and we clean 'em and we change the coffin.
  Then you guys can take him on the boat as far as Chilliwack
    and then you could put him on the packhorse.'

Well, it's in a box
  because they could pack the horse on each side of something.
Then they could put the box crossways
  all the ways from Chilliwack to Ashnola.
Then they did that
  and they take him out and clean him
    and put medicine on him

so he wouldn't be smell.
Change the coffin and seal it
   and told them not to open it.
      'Don't open it
         because we give him medicine.
      But in the box he's not cold.
      They might be kinda smell,
         by the time you get it over there,
            not to open 'em.'

All right, they bring 'em
   and they never open 'em.
But when they get him to Ashnola,
   then, whoever they were there,
      and they tell 'em,
         'We should open 'em.
         We should make sure if that was him.'
Well, these other people said,
   'If he's going to be smelly, that don't matter.
   Open 'em.
   We want to see.'
So, they break it open and they looked at 'em.
   'That's not Jim. That was a Chinaman.'
Kinda stout Chinaman.
He must have been in jail.

They can't take him back, so they bury him there.
They were around there for a while
   and they thought maybe they make a mistake over there.
      'We better go again to get Jim.
      They might mistake.
      Maybe Jim is still there.'

They went again
   and they get there
      and they told 'em,
         'This is not Jim you give us.
         This is a Chinaman.'
         'By gosh, that's too bad.
         We made a mistake.
         We know that.
         We find that out,
            but you fellas are gone.
         George is there.

Now that you've come back,
   we can take him out and clean him
    and you can take him away.
Take him home.'

They do the same thing.
Dug him out, clean him, put medicine on him
   and changed the box, and tell him not to open it.

So, they bring him,
   and that was the second time.
From Westminster to Chilliwack.
Then, they packed him from Chilliwack to Ashnola.
When they get there,
   whoever they were home tell 'em,
    'We got to open 'em, see,
      to make sure if it was Jim.
    Maybe another Chinaman.'

Anyhow, they open 'em.
They looked at him
   and he was a negro boy.
A small man too.

Well, they bury him there.
But there's no use to go back and get George.

And George is not dead.
They take him away.

Then later on, a few years after that,
   and Charlie Harvie come back from England.
Then he ride over there and he tell them about it.

Long time, quite a few years after that,
   and then they find out
    George Jim, he's not dead.
He's alive yet, but he's in England.

So, that's the end of that story.

Marion Tuu'luq b. 1910

INUIT

A Story of Starvation

As told to Susan Tagoona

I am going to recount a story that I am sure I have told over and over again in the past. It is not a happy story. At the time it took place, it looked as though we weren't going to survive. I will tell you some of those terrible events.

My name is Marion Tuu'luq, and my story goes back to the time when my father couldn't walk. My father was lame for as far back as I can remember into my childhood. We used to carry him on our backs when we travelled during the summer. In the winter, we pulled him on the qamutik.

One time, while we were at Tipyalik, there were no caribou to be found, and we became very hungry. Being just a young girl at the time, it didn't occur to me that the people I was with were very concerned and afraid.

While my brother Angutituaq and Oonark's husband were out searching for game, they came upon several traps, which brought them to some people. But they soon discovered that these people with the traps had been reduced to killing one of their dogs, since there was no game whatsoever in the area.

They skinned the dog, and when it was cooked, they told me to eat some of the meat. But I was so repelled by the meat of the dog that I was unable to eat. I really meant it with my whole heart when I said I didn't want to eat it, and they couldn't make me change my mind. I remember someone saying that the meat tasted just like a wolf.

When everyone was eating the dog meat, I too was given a piece. I tried to smell it, but I couldn't smell anything. Then, I put the piece in my mouth and I took it out again. I did this several times. I remember clearly how much I was repelled that day at the thought of eating a dog.

While the eating was going on, my father was lying down on the bed as usual. He was scarcely breathing. I didn't know then that the following day he would strangle himself with a rope, and we would have to leave him behind. When he was asked to eat, on that final day of his life, he refused. He didn't want to take even a sip of broth.

The next day, my brother Quenungnat and I were directed to go a little distance away from the igloo. We were told to stay there until someone called for us and we were ready to leave our camp. Of course, we wondered at the reason for this command. But we stayed as we were told until Nattaq, Quenungnat's mother, waved at us, signalling that it was now okay for us to return. It was then that I learned that my father had died and that I would not be seeing him again. I cried, for I loved my father very much. His name was Ekinilik.

Innakatsik, who was just a kid, even younger than myself, was asked to lead the way, but he didn't want to. So then, I was asked to lead and was told to follow the tracks on the snow.

While I was walking in the lead, I spotted a rock that was barely showing in the snow ahead of me. It indicated that a sled had passed by that spot only the day before. As I started to approach the rock, I heard the voice of my father say to me, 'It is a cache, it is a cache.' And here he had just died a short while before!

I started kicking at the rock, shouting 'It's a cache! It's food!' And I would not leave the rock.

'There can't be anything around here. You wouldn't know of any caches around here, you are not able to know!' answered my brother Angutituaq in a scolding voice. But I just kept on kicking at the rock and shouting, 'It's food! It's a cache!' For some reason, I just couldn't leave the rock alone.

'It's nothing. It can't be anything!' Angutituaq kept answering back at me.

Then the others started shovelling at the rock, and, true to my words, they uncovered—a cache! As we loaded it on to our sled, it seemed as though we were stealing someone else's cache. But we didn't know of anyone who would have a cache, and we were threatened with starvation. We had sighted some fox traps the previous day, which probably belonged to the Akilining-miut, and maybe the cache was theirs.

When we had loaded the meat on our sled, my father's voice again spoke to me: 'Daughter, I don't want you to eat the liver and the heart of this cari-bou.' I told him that I would do as he said.

After the men had made an igloo, I was allowed to feast on the meat which I had discovered. The men told me to eat all that I wanted. They fed me everything—the heart, the liver—everything! They told me that there would have been nothing to eat if it hadn't been for me.

The next day, when I woke up, I was unable to open my eyes.

'What is the matter with her now? Look at her, she can't even open her eyes! Did somebody hurt you?' Nattaq shouted at me. It must have been because I had eaten the meat after my father had told me not to. Again, I heard the voice of my father warning me, 'Daughter, do not eat the heart and the liver of the caribou.'

'I forgot,' I answered. No sooner had I said this than my eyes were opened.

When I try to tell this part of the story, I am not confused about the details. It is something I will never forget.

Later, there were no caribou at all. We didn't even see any caribou tracks. We were forced to live on dog meat. Killing and eating our dogs was the only way we could survive. As we travelled, we came across scraps of dried meat and the bones of caribou left over from the winter before, but they did not sat-isfy our hunger.

One day, Innakatsik went off on his own to search a nearby igloo for food. When he returned, he said he had discovered that it was full of dried meat. We all went straight to the igloo he had found. When we entered it, the people there just kept looking down and did not raise their heads. We were deeply disappointed, for there was no food there—nothing to eat at all. 'Is there food?' asked my brother Angutituaq. But no one had the heart to answer him.

As we no longer had any dogs, we packed all our belongings on our backs, and we started to walk. Along the way, we caught a rabbit and ate it, and that was all we had to eat.

For a time, we kept on walking, but it was not long before we realized that we weren't going to run into any people. Instead, we decided to search for igloos. We came across two—one large, one small—and we looked for tracks around them, but there were none. It was bitterly cold by now, and there were frequent blizzards and storms, so we decided to return to the shelter of our old igloo. There was just a small group of us together at that time—Angutituaq, Tamalik, and myself. Weak from starvation, we were forced to leave clothes, blankets, and other belongings behind. I took only a blanket with me, and I wrapped it around my shivering body. When we lay down to sleep, I made sure that all my body was covered, and I had no trouble going to sleep.

Each time we awoke, we would force ourselves to start walking again. Angutituaq was close to starvation. We were just beginning to give up ourselves because of him, when we finally reached our old igloo.

Before we could enter the welcome shelter of the igloo, we had to dig a hole through the side to make a door. After our last stay there, we had sealed the door with snow to protect some skins we had left inside. Finally, we succeeded in digging ourselves an entrance way, but it was very narrow. Then, my brother said, 'I think Tuu'luq should be able to squeeze in through.' 'It's too small!' I shouted back at him. But I tried to pass through the narrow hole, and at last I succeeded. Angutituaq followed behind me.

I don't know how many days we had wandered and nights we had slept before we reached our igloo. We had not had anything to eat for a long time, and we were very thin and nearly starved to death.

'I smell hide!' we all shouted out as we reached the inside of the igloo, for we found skins there that were to have been used for whips. We cut the skins in pieces and devoured them hungrily. Then we scraped up and ate some blood that we discovered on a block of snow. White people use plates to eat off—we used snow. There was a lot of blood on the snow plate, so we ate from that, and that was the way we survived.

Whenever Angutituaq came across little pieces of meat, he offered them to me, even though I begged him to eat them himself instead. But he wanted so badly for me to eat.

It was a while before we felt we had gathered enough strength to leave the igloo again. We decided from then on that, if we wanted to eat, we would have to look for left-over caribou stomachs in abandoned caches. So, that is what we did. Sometimes we were lucky enough to come across caribou stomachs in old caches and we would eat their contents. Other times, we would find nothing and would return to our igloo and empty stomachs.

One time, Angutituaq and Oonark's husband decided to go out hunting for game. So Quenungnat and his brother went to look for a cache to provide the hunters with some food to take on their way. But the two men returned after just a short while to say that there were no caches left.

Angutituaq, however, said he knew of a place close by that he wanted to check. So we went to that place and discovered there what appeared to be a cache. Again, I started shouting—as I used to be very outspoken at that time—'It's a cache! It's a cache! It's a whole caribou!' One of the men answered me: 'Your brother and I tried to find food, but we returned empty-handed because it had been moved to a different area. You know that. There couldn't be anything in here.'

Still, we spent the whole day trying to shovel off the snow with a pana (Eskimo snow knife). 'I smell a cache. It is a cache, and I know it hasn't been touched,' I continued to insist. I think, by that time, the others were almost ready to give up. But I never used to think of how I was feeling. And the thing turned out to be a cache, after all.

We each loaded pieces of meat on our backs and prepared to return to the igloo. But we had scarcely moved more than a few feet away when we decided to stop right there and eat our fill. And did we ever eat! We chopped at the meat, pounded it, chipped and cracked it in halves with our snow knife. We had tried to walk with the meat on our backs, but we were so skinny by then, that we had no strength left for walking with such a weight to carry. So we ate the whole caribou, leaving only the neck and the head, which we took back with us.

After we reached our igloo, the men made plans to set out again to search for caribou stomachs on top of a hill. So we did, wandering further and further away. We walked the whole afternoon and didn't find a thing, so we decided to return home. All we had with us were the gun and the pana. We had left everything else we owned behind for we were too weak to carry anything with us. It was very hard for us. Every time I offered to carry the gun, my brother said no. I felt that, since I was the one with the most strength left, I should be the one to carry the gun.

Sometime later, we neared the igloo where we had been making our home. As we approached, we suddenly became aware of a group of people standing there. Oh, how frightened we were! We had finished off all their hides that were to have been used for making whips, and now they had come back for them.

'They've caught some caribou and they're bringing it back here!' Quenungnat was running and shouting at the same time. He was also trying to eat and getting scolded for his behaviour. I was still so afraid of what the men might do!

As it turned out, these hunters had caught some caribou and were returning to their overnight camp. They started to make themselves an igloo and I tried to help by cutting out blocks for them. My brother Angutituaq was still too weak from lack of food.

After the igloo was completed, Oonark's husband started to work on the porch. But the men told him not to bother as they would be on their way again by the next day. Then, one of them said, 'These people are not helping themselves to food. Get them something to eat.'

That night, after all of us had eaten our fill, we started to tell stories. As usual, I found lots to laugh at. In those days, I used to laugh often and was very talkative. Now, everything seemed so funny.

Some of our group told how, each time they approached an igloo, they would yell through the ice window, 'Is there anyone in there? Anyone in there?'

Nattaq said that, upon reaching our old igloo, they had spotted our fresh tracks in the snow, but there had been no one around. And Talluq had started to imagine that our dead bodies were in the porch. They had all looked around, then entered the igloo and found it empty. When they came out of the igloo, they saw us coming towards them, and they were so happy to see that we were all still together.

When Nattaq started to talk again about how she thought I might be dead and how she had searched the igloo looking for me, I started to laugh.

'This girl never runs out of laughs,' Angutituaq said.

Simon Arnaviapik b. 1915

INUIT

Remembering Old Times

I began writing this on November 2nd, 1969. My name is Arnaviapik. Some people my age still use the old disc numbers that have been discarded. My number was E5–752. I am going to tell a story of my experiences.

I cannot remember exactly how old I was, but I do remember that it was summer when we used to go hunting caribou. I think it was the beginning of August. We were travelling from the salt water up on the mainland. I remember riding on top of the load which my father carried on his back. Sometimes I walked with my mother holding my hand.

There were six heads of families in our camp—my father Angutiyak, Kunuk, Kukuayuk, Tunga, Kasateak, and Takauyuk. We would part in the summer, then meet again in the fall.

We would travel by land only at that time of the year, walking and pulling our goods on a skin sled. First we would live by a lake in a tupik (skin tent) until we could move into an igloo (snow house). The men fished and shot caribou often. When our tupik was no longer required, my father would put it in the lake for several days. I saw that my father was making a wooden sled frame. I still remember how he pulled the tupik skins from the lake and stretched them flat on the ground and anchored them with rocks. Next he cut them into strips and tied the strips to both sides of the runners. He made holes for a cross bar. The cross bar was made from caribou antlers. It looked like a real sled even though some parts of it had once been our house.

Before we travelled, my mother made new parkas and other clothes for us. Then we went back to the coast. I think it was November when we arrived. The men went seal hunting and were lucky to catch some. They went hunting every day while we waited for the people from Iqajuak to come for us. When they came we returned with them and spent the winter there.

People who hunted the caribou with guns did not throw away their empty cartridges after using them. They made more bullets by mixing gunpowder and melting lead to make the balls. Two boxes of cartridges containing ten rounds each would last for the whole summer that way. Now there are twenty cartridges in each box and we do not have to reload them.

I remember when our people smoked before there was anything like cigarettes. They smoked using bone or metal pipes. They would use a flint to light their pipes. First they softened some paper, mixed gunpowder in hot water, and put the black mixture on the paper. When the paper was dry they used it to light their pipes. When the spark from the flint fell on the paper it caught fire. They used real fire when meat was cooking.

I also remember living in Iqajuak, although I do not know what year it was.

There was a white man there called Sakimeak who was unhappy because his ship did not arrive. I often watched him walking around the seashore, eating kelp. The ship finally came a year after we had moved to Tulukak. This Sakimeak had moved to Saneruak and then to Tulukak. Sakimeak and an Inuk came on foot to Tulukak, carrying fox skins. The white man went to the ship and while on board got into a fight with a man from Saneruak. They fought and the white man won. The second mate intervened and put him in his place. The captain told the white man to leave and he went back to shore.

My mother and I were alone on shore when Sakimeak came to our shelter. He was weeping. I was frightened at first but he stayed with us that night.

The next morning the captain of the ship and some other white people came ashore to look for Sakimeak. They found him with us and they talked to him for a long time. They told him that he could not travel with them on the ship. They said there was a war on and because the man was a German they could not take him. They told him to go by dogteam to Churchill when winter came.

When I was perhaps four or five years old, my elder sister and I went with my father to the trading post early in the winter. We were at Tulukak then. We rode on the sleigh and I remember it was very early in the morning when we arrived at the post. Though my sister and I were frightened, we decided to follow my father into the store. The people gave us food to eat and when we were leaving a white lady gave me a small spoon. I was happy to receive it.

After we left Tulukak, we visited my aunt's house at Keminik. This was a happy time for me because I did not know she was my aunt. Then we went back to our old camp at Iqajuak. I remember it was there that Aleanakulook's wife died. This was the first time that a person I knew died. My grandmother became very ill too and she died. She was not very old.

It was spring again when we went west to hunt caribou. When summer came, we walked inland. I believe it was the end of July. We hunted the caribou there for about three months.

Our people used to run out of tobacco often. The men used to mix their tobacco to make it go farther. Sometimes they would smoke small leaves. They even smoked with feathers. I remember how they used to smell.

In the fall we went back to the coast by dogteam. We used to light our lamps with caribou fat. When we reached the sea the men would hunt at the seal holes. When we had seal fat it was much better. The flame in the lamps was bright red and not as smoky as when using caribou fat.

When we were on the coast a dogteam came for us from Iqajuak. The drivers told us that there were traders at Pond Inlet and my father decided we should go with them. We had to stop several times on the way. When we arrived we found there were four white men at Pond Inlet—Big Kapitie, his clerk, an interpreter, and a policeman, they all lived together at the Hudson's Bay Company house. A lady invited us in and gave us food. They gave the children candy and the older people tobacco.

We stayed at Pond Inlet until after Christmas at which time we left for Igloolik by dogteam. The policeman and an interpreter came with us on the journey. We carried merchandise, guns, and ammunition for trading at Igloo-lik. Besides us there was another Inuk with a five-dog team who came with us.

It was spring when we got back from Igloolik. We returned to Pond Inlet with a light load of fox skins. It was much lighter than the load we had taken with us. We bought supplies and other goods to take back to our camp at Iqa-juak.

When summer came again the *Atik* (the C.G.S. *Arctic*) arrived with a policeman. When they left they took a man named Keugayuk with them as a prisoner. It was getting dark early when the *Nassikupee* (the S.S. *Nascopie*) arrived.

The next fall they asked my father to go to the Hudson's Bay post when the ice was set. The white men hired the Inuit to gather fuel for their stoves (from the coal deposits near Pond Inlet). In the winter there was fuel only at the store. When they ran out of it, they went to get some more, hauling it by dogteam.

The post manager left when break-up came and his clerk took over at Pond Inlet. When fall came again people from Igloolik and Pond Inlet sacked up more coal. Spring came and they loaded it on boats. My family stayed with the traders all summer. After freeze-up the manager, Neegasee, decided to go to Igloolik by dogteam. My father and his family, Akumalik and his family, including his children, Idlout and Eitokudso, went along with the trader.

In December that year the trader wanted to return by land to Pond Inlet. My father did not wish to go that way because he was not familiar with the route. The white man said that the map showed that it was a shortcut and that we could get there more quickly. My father pointed out that if they attempt-ed to go that way at that time of the year they might all starve. It was a poor time—there was little food for humans and less for the dogs. The trader still persisted and Akumalik took the trader's side in the argument. They outvot-ed my father. He at last agreed to go but still warned them of the danger.

When the journey began the days were already very short. There were no familiar landmarks to follow. Soon we ran out of food and were very hungry. Some of the party became so hungry they wanted to eat their dogs. My father said that if they had only listened to him and travelled by the sea ice they would have seal meat for themselves and the dogs.

The people were sorry to do it, but soon found it necessary to kill some of the dogs if they were to survive. They boiled the dogs and ate them. They wanted my father to turn around and take them back to Igloolik. There was no more kerosene for the stoves. My father knew that turning around would mean certain death. He told them that they had to go on. He left them and travelled alone ahead of the dogs. He was searching for a hunting camp. He told the people he would find help and send it to them.

My father knew he could travel much faster if he went alone, but against his wishes, his brother-in-law came too. But he slowed the pace down because he kept lagging behind and my father would have to wait for him.

My father reached sea ice. He could tell by the signs around that he had gone past an Inuit hunting camp. He waited for his companion but he did not come for a long time. When he finally arrived, my father told him that they had reached salt water. The man did not believe it until he tasted the snow. My father told him to look for seal holes while he went to look for the hunting camp that must not be far away. The man was just too cold and hungry to hunt, so my father left him, promising to send someone for him if he found help.

My father arrived at an Inuit sealing camp during the night. The men had just returned from hunting. My father told them what had happened. The men harnessed their dogs and left to look for the rest of the party. They followed his tracks. They found the people who had been walking slowly for two days. They would have frozen to death had they stopped walking. They were very weak. They then knew the wisdom of my father's words. If he had not left them, all would have perished.

The Inuit often talked about the white man who had been with them and how he had cooked the dog meat and eaten it while it was still almost raw. A year later he was replaced by a new manager and my father took him to Clyde River to be the trader. My father took me to Clyde River with him. There was one trader there and an Inuk whose name was Matuk. His wife was called Eevaluapik. They had two sons—one called Miee and a younger one called Moses. In the spring we often went seal hunting with the men. I had a .22 calibre rifle, but Miee was not allowed to shoot.

When summer came to Clyde River, the ship *Nassikupee* arrived. I was growing up. They asked me to go on the ship to help. We went to Pond Inlet to unload and left again. My father became foreman of the unloading gang. I was surprised to see that we were going to Resolute Bay. There were three men with us from Cape Dorset—Pootoogook, Eitoolook and Pitseolak. That was in 1927 or 1928, I cannot be sure which.

Our manager at that time had six Inuit with him who came from Labrador. They wanted to become trappers at a place where no one lived and hunt for the Company. Some of the people got off at Arctic Bay but we stayed until we reached Pond Inlet.

That winter we caught many white fox and in the spring took the pelts to Pond Inlet. A supply ship arrived and they asked my father if he would go aboard as a guide. I went along too and we went to Resolute Bay and past it in a small boat. We unloaded lumber and supplies at Arctic Bay and other places, always unloading lumber.

We travelled all summer. One man, Attagutaaluk, and his wife Attuak (she is still living) came aboard. We stopped at a small island. The season was getting late and the weather was bad. We were going very slowly but suddenly we stopped. We were stranded on a sand bar. The water was only fifteen inches deep. They tried to take the ship backwards but it would not go.

While the tide was out we got off the boat. The men unloaded the supplies and lumber. It took nearly all day. In spite of this the boat tipped over in the evening. Oil drums were attached to the bottom of the boat with ropes. When the tide came in, the boat started to float. Then began the job of reloading it.

Next we went to Gjoa Haven on King William Island. We were to spend the winter there with the trader and his clerk. Our family were the only Inuit. My father and the trader travelled a lot that winter. During one absence, people from Netsilik arrived. I was very frightened when I saw them for the first time. Their way of talking reminded me of eider ducks just before they learn to fly. They were 'the people of the place possessing seal' and the only ones who were still living by the old ways without southern equipment which we were now almost accustomed to using.

My father and the trader were away for a long time. The ice was about to freeze up when they finally returned. They had attempted to go to every camp to trade and encourage the people to come to Gjoa Haven where the new house had been built.

I always liked to go hunting with my father. It was from him and Attagutaaluk that I learned how to trap fox. Once when I was hunting with Angnateak, it was growing dark. He said to me, 'Look at that big polar bear!' I thought he was trying to fool me and I did not believe him. But when I looked to one side there it was and very close. I was going to shoot at it but the dogs were excited and I had to control them. Angnateak started to run after the bear. I went after him as soon as I tied up some of the dogs. There were so many tracks that I soon lost Angnateak. The dogs broke loose and I felt like crying because I could not handle them. It was now very dark and I could not see or hear Angnateak. Finally he found me. He had not been able to shoot the bear but I was happy to see him. We had lost a few dogs. When we returned to camp we found that some of the other men had killed a bear. I was sad that we were not so lucky.

In winter I always went hunting with Angnateak. He was my brother-in-law and my best friend. Sometimes when we were alone we would wrestle. He was very strong and I would try not to show it when he hurt me. If I cried he would feel bad.

In the spring we often had visitors at the store in Gjoa Haven. Some of them stayed for a while, camping nearby. They were happy people. One man who stayed was from Netsilik. After break-up we took him to Arctic Bay. On our way back we planned to stop at Pond Inlet, but had to return because of the thick ice. We returned to spend the winter at Gjoa Haven again. There, white man's food was available.

In 1929 two boats came to Gjoa Haven. One stayed for the winter. Fox were plentiful that year. All the white people ran out of food, even sugar, tea, and milk. The white people lived in our camp and went hunting with us. They were glad for the spring when the ducks, geese, and other birds came and they could go fishing.

After the break-up, a small boat came near the shore with supplies. Food was the first thing taken off and then oil and lumber. After we loaded our boat we took the supplies into the post. My father left with the boat but I stayed with the white people. I worked with them and ate with them. I tried hard to learn their language. It was very hard and I still do not know it. I returned to Pond Inlet in the spring of 1930. It was then I killed my first seal. There were many of them lying out on the ice in the warm sun.

I used to be very excited when I first started going out alone by dogteam. One spring I went out from Pond Inlet to get my uncle and some other men to help gather coal for the post at Pond Inlet. On our way back we stopped to hunt seal for food. We were travelling on the shore ice when the weather became stormy. There were times when we could not see the dogs in front of us. My uncle decided we should stop. We thought we were lost and had moved too far out on the ice. After a while my uncle walked some distance to see if he could discover any landmarks. When he returned he told us we had to go against the wind. It was very slow. The women and children stayed on the komotiks. It was very difficult and sometimes the dogs stopped because their eyes were blinded by the snow and frost. They would not move again until it was removed. When we finally reached land we took the seal catch off to lighten our load. The snow was too fine and blowing to build a house with. We made a small shelter and boiled water for tea. While we rested the wind died down. We knew we were on the right trail. We travelled through the night and reached Pond Inlet in the morning.

In the spring of 1930 the ice extended far out and did not melt all summer. We unloaded lumber that arrived for the Hudson's Bay Company. We used six dogteams to haul it from the ship to the post. The work was hard and the hours long. We would come home late at night and get up early in the morning. After we had brought the timber the manager had us pile it ready to load again the next spring to be sent to other trading posts. After we finished our work in the spring they threw a big party for us. It was a happy time for everyone. The traders were good to the Inuit. They gave us food, baking powder, flour, sugar, tea, and many other things.

The Hudson's Bay Company employed our people to dig stove coal. They paid us fifty cents for a bag. My father was in charge of this work until he died in 1953. Then I took over his job. My brother, Takugak and I always managed to fill more bags than the others. When a man filled twenty bags he would receive ten dollars. After some time fifty cents a bag did not seem like enough for all the work that had to be done. The manager agreed to give us eighty cents. By the end of the season I managed to convince the manager that we should have still more. He agreed to one dollar a bag and that was the limit. I was happy about this. There were eleven men digging and bagging coal.

In 1957 we lived on an island during the summer. Then we moved to Qimmivik. I became very ill during February, but by March I was feeling much better. I had become very thin but soon regained my strength. While I was sick my children caught seals in nets. We were never hungry because we were the only family living there and we did not have to share our catch.

In March, 1958, an airplane landed at our camp. It was the Royal Canadian Mounted Police officer. He was taking a doctor to all the camps. Our camp was located on a river and I had caught enough fish to last us for the winter. We had no seal oil for our lamps so we spent a great deal of time in darkness. We did not mind this as long as we were not hungry. I had a stove made out of an old oil drum. The snow was so deep that it was impossible to travel. We were unable to get seal because the deep snow had covered their breathing holes. We used part of our sleigh for fuel. The deep snow lasted until March, 1959. It became very windy. Finally we were able to leave to find a place where we could get seal. We set our tents up on a small island. I was hunting rabbits when I took a severe cramp in my leg and couldn't walk. We were just about out of everything when some people came for us. We returned to Pond Inlet in April and got some work from the post manager. I still had trouble walking.

When summer came I went fishing again. We were alone in the camp then because my brother had taken my oldest son on a caribou hunt. I went to the river during the first week of August to prepare our fishing ground. Every year you have to set up new stones to divert the fish into a small trap. The fish were all going upstream and I caught a great many and hung them up to dry.

Near the end of August a police boat came for us. They said that the Canadian Government Ship *C.D. Howe* was coming to Pond Inlet and that they were taking X-rays of all the people to check for tuberculosis. We stopped fishing and left with the police. It was the middle of September before we got back to the river. The dogs that we had left behind had ruined our fishing dam trying to feed themselves. We would have only what we had dried and cached out of their reach.

That was a good winter for hunting. We hunted seal and set nets through the ice. I caught one hundred and three foxes and in the spring bought a radio and an outboard motor.

In 1966 we moved to Pond Inlet because the Government built a big school for our children and a number of houses for the people. We moved into our house right away. I was so excited that I did not sleep well for a few nights. I was worried that we would not be able to keep it clean, but it did not take long to get used to it. It was quite a surprise when a man first came to take out our toilet bucket. Women had always done this work. Later another man came with blocks of fresh water ice for drinking. We are grateful to the Government for all they have done for us. We have a much better life than we ever had before.

Ever since I can remember, the world has been changing. The weather seems to be getting milder. I often wonder if the animals are getting scarce in the North. I know the fish are scarcer around Pond Inlet. I remember when people used to catch a lot of fish in summer. They used to fill their boats in a short time. Now this does not happen anymore. No wonder the fish are getting scarce. Since the white man came he has never stopped fishing. When the traders, missionaries, and police were using dogs they used to get enough fish to last their teams all winter. They only fish for themselves now. Inuit only fished for food but we have started using nets more now and boats that can take us farther out.

At one time there were few animals at Pond Inlet during the winter. Many people went hungry. Now the caribou seem to be coming back. They started coming back in 1961 and now there are quite a few.

I used to listen to Kudlooteak, an old man, talking about the caribou. He said it was unusual that there were no caribou but that they would be back in time. I think the older people knew a lot about these things. Kudlooteak was certainly right.

In earlier days when the Inuit went hunting, they would share the kill with all their neighbours. If they were out hunting seal and a man shot one, he would go to his companion and get him to help clean it. Then they would share the liver, meat, and fat. When they had enough they would freeze the rest and take it home to their families. When they got home they would invite the other families and the men would eat raw meat. The women would take some of the meat and cook it along with some seal blood. Everyone shared in this meal. Anything that was left over would be eaten for breakfast by the hunters before they went out again.

Except in the winter people always ate outside. Before they had primus stoves it took quite a while to make tea. They carried water in caribou skin bags. This left the water lukewarm. When fresh meat was running low they would melt ice and mix it with seal blood. This was a very good soup and good for little children.

In the spring we would take our dogs and hunt for baby seals that would be laying on the ice in the warm sun. Sometimes we went for days without sleep while looking for them. In the summer the young men went out with kayaks to hunt caribou when they were crossing streams.

The Inuit on the coast used their kayaks to hunt whale. When a whale was caught it was shared with all the people in the camp. The lucky hunter got the biggest portion. Besides the white whale and the narwhal, sometimes we were fortunate and got square flipper seals. The skin of this seal is very good for making lines and ropes. The man who shot the seal always got the middle part of the skin. This means a longer rope. The meat was shared among the hunters.

When the caribou hunters returned they would gather the hides and choose the ones they wanted for clothing. Two hides were needed for a man's parka. The meat was distributed around the camp. One of the older men was usually in charge.

When a man had tobacco he would share it with his companions. This was the old kind of chewing tobacco. He would cut a plug of it into small pieces, press them into a pipe and when it was lit, pass it around to each man in turn for a few puffs.

In the spring when seals were plentiful, the skins were fashioned into containers for storing lamp oil. This was done by making holes around the outside edge of the skin. Then a line was threaded through the holes to draw the skin together to make a pouch. In those days, Inuit made most of their own utensils and tools. Today this is not so. Most of them are bought.

The Inuit men were much stronger and swifter in the past. It was not

uncommon for a man to outrun a caribou. Men were careful about display-
ing their strength because it sometimes displeased the witch doctors. It was
said that the witch doctor would get jealous and could cause the death of a
man. Now there are no witch doctors and the men are not as strong as they
used to be.

Spring time was the best time for polar bear hunting. The older men felt
sad at this time of the year because they could remember when they were
young and strong enough to join in the most exciting hunting there was to be
had.

The story I have told involves me personally in part and the other stories
were told to me. My eyesight is very poor now and I have probably made
many mistakes with my pencil. However, I hope you have been able to follow my story without too much difficulty. Now that I am older, I only occasionally hunt seal through the ice. My son is the one who provides me with
fresh meat.

I would like to speak on another subject now. Before the missionaries
came, we prayed to the spirits. Now they have converted us to Christianity.
We are very thankful to the missionaries who taught us to believe in God. I
know that the Inuit are and will in future generations be good Christians
because we believe that God can and has helped us in a great many ways.

Here are a few short stories that you will find interesting. When my father
was a small boy, he often went seal hunting with the men. On one of these
trips the wind came up strong. This caused the ice to break up and they drifted out into open water. When they were out some distance, the ice-pan started to break up. Fortunately they were close enough to an iceberg and were
able to climb up on to it. There was a lot of snow on the iceberg and they were
able to build a shelter. It was very wet but it was a shelter. There was an invisible monster living in this iceberg and when the iceberg looked as though it
would break up, Sakayuk, one of the men, said that the monster would not let
this happen because it would drown as well. Finally, the sea ice froze into a
solid mass again. When they left the iceberg it began to break up.

This is another story. Two years later when my father was bigger and living on an island and there was plenty of food, he went to the mainland to hunt
caribou with a man and his wife and an old unmarried lady. When they were
ready to leave and return home to the island, the old lady who had been doing
some sewing told them she had forgotten her ulu (woman's knife). She ran
back for it. When she did not return to the boat one of the men went to look
for her. He saw tracks that showed she was running into the interior. He followed for a while but she was nowhere in sight. Finally they had to leave
without her. She was found much later. She had walked all the way from near
Pond Inlet to Clyde River. It is still considered impossible to do this. The
lady's name was Emudluk Aduaruluk.

I believe it was in 1933 that I got married. We moved near Pond Inlet for
the winter with my father. When I was trapping for fox I would be away by
myself for long days. In February that year we moved to where there were

seals. We had no food. I returned after for my traps. Fox were plentiful that year and I stayed away for more than a week. While I was trapping my father went with a policeman to help him get to Pond Inlet. The next year, I think it was 1934, we all moved closer to Pond Inlet. The first year of our marriage was very difficult now that I look back on it.

When summer came we went caribou hunting for the months of August and September. We needed a supply of skins for clothing. My father stayed on the coast to hunt seal but he did not get many because of bad weather. Food was low when winter came. We went to get some meat we had cached away earlier but it had become rotten. We were hungry but still had a hard time to eat the bad meat. When we ran completely out of food we moved to Evalak's camp. There were many people there and they had plenty of food. They gave us some and we returned home and shared one seal.

Later on some people came with my father to fetch us. I was the only one with dogs. It was a long journey and they began to die of starvation. My wife and I got behind the other people. My dogs were down to three and I had to help them pull the sleigh. We lost our way. In the morning of the second day that we were alone, we had nothing but warm water for our stomachs. It was in December, the month of Christmas. The days were very short. I was just going to abandon our equipment and take our blankets and walk. I thought I could reach people more quickly by walking. Suddenly I heard dogs barking in the darkness and my dogs raised their heads. We listened. I could tell it was my father by the sounds he used to make his dogs go faster. It was very dark although it was morning. I shouted with all my strength to let my father know where we were.

We could not have gone farther with the sleigh. I had used the cross bar for fuel. We had taken nothing but warm water for three days. The sound of my father's team coming was the greatest sound I had ever heard. We were almost in tears.

When we returned to our people they had lots of food. They also gave us dogs so I could go seal hunting again. We were at Arctic Bay.

When the sun came out again after the long winter a trader and a policeman came from Pond Inlet. We went back with them for a short time. We thought Arctic Bay might have more game so we came back. There were many dogteams now. Game continued to be scarce. We got very few caribou in the summer, and when freeze-up came, very few seals through the ice. Sometimes we left early in the morning without anything to eat and would stay hungry until someone harpooned a seal. Our dogs were thin but we did not have any starve to death. Things were getting better.

In 1936 we trapped fox and seal. It was pleasant in the month of March so we travelled to Pond Inlet to trade. The people had all run out of tobacco. I did not smoke, but I sure wanted to have a cup of tea.

In 1936 three people died. They were all adults. When we arrived at Pond Inlet the people asked us to stay with them. The trader hired my father to work for him again. My father-in-law and I moved to a place near Pond Inlet.

I was able to hunt caribou that summer and when freeze-up came went to Pond Inlet for supplies. There was another trader in the area. There were very few foxes that winter but we did get a lot of fish.

The next year my wife and I were living all alone near Pond Inlet. Some-one made a trip out to find us and tell me that the Hudson's Bay Company supply ship was coming and they needed me. I worked for the Company all that summer. In the fall I asked if I could return to my traps because all the signs looked like a good year for fox.

In the summer of 1940 three of us went sailing in my boat. I did not have a motor, but had rigged a canvas sail. We were hunting walrus. There were many walrus on a small island. We only got three of them because of the high wind. Later we shot two polar bears. On our way back it was windy and the waves were high. There were many walrus in the water around us. We shortened our sail to keep from upsetting until we came to a point where we could anchor for the night. I guess we were lucky to make it back to our camp the next day.

There were now three of us, all friends, working and hunting together. I had one child, and the other men each had two children. Our wives helped each other with the children while we did the hunting. One summer we ate a lot of mushrooms because caribou were scarce. We decided to go inland. One morning I woke up early. I woke up my companions so we could get an early start. We left our families sleeping. I was ahead quite a bit when I saw eight caribou feeding across a stream. We got six caribou out of the eight. We were wet and shivering from crossing the stream but we were so very happy. Our wives set up camp near the stream and we carried the meat across to them. We had eaten only mushrooms and fungus for a week. What a feast we had!

Hunting improved and for the first week of August we shot caribou nearly every day. Our wives were busy cleaning hides. We rounded up all our dogs and got them ready for the coming winter.

When hunting is good you have to keep going. With one companion I set out one day in search of four caribou that I had seen in the distance. When we saw them again they were on the other side of what seemed a small stream. The water was much deeper than we expected and we nearly drowned. My friend lost his packsack and his gun. It was getting dark and we had no way to make a fire. We just had to huddle down and try to sleep. It was so cold I thought we would freeze. As soon as there was a little light we got up and started running to get warm. Suddenly we saw a herd of caribou and forgot our discomfort. I shot ten of them and my companion took my rifle and got ten more. After this I began to skin the animals while my friend went to bring our dogs. He was gone a long time for we had not realized how far we had run. We were strong and healthy in those days. What a load of hides, fat, sinew, and meat we brought home! All the dogs were loaded down and we each had all we could carry! We found an easier way to cross the stream and reach the camp where the women waited for us.

We reached the coast in September and there was already a heavy snow-fall. During the summer we had gathered so many caribou—fifty-five—that our loads were heavy and the journey to the coast took two weeks. We stayed on the coast for a while and when the ice froze, continued to Pond Inlet to trade and see my father.

When it was time to leave Pond Inlet again and go to my trapping camp, I asked my sister if she could come with us and she agreed. There were three dogteams in our party. I had a long sled and fourteen fine dogs. On the trip I harpooned a white whale and loaded it whole on our already heavy sled. My family were all riding on the sled and I was running ahead of the dogs. It was just growing dark when we hit a patch of thin ice and the sled began to sink. The dogs couldn't pull it. I ran back to my family but the ice kept breaking under me. I was praying as I worked to try and save them. I got my footing on some broken but floating ice and threw the end of my long dog whip to my wife. She tied it around her waist. She tried to run toward me but kept sinking in the broken ice. I pulled and pulled and finally got her to safe ice. She was chattering with the cold. I threw the whip back to my sister and pulled her in the same way.

The sled was lighter now and by adding my strength to that of the dogs, I was able to save our sled which was piled with everything we owned. I quickly unloaded it and piling my family on it raced through the night to where our camp was. We reached it in early morning. There were people there and they were all asleep. I awakened a man and his wife. Their names were Malaku and Kidlapik. His wife changed my wife's and sister's clothes which were frozen solid on the outside. We stayed with them for two days before our things were dry. Then I returned for the supplies I had left on the shore ice.

Long ago one fox skin would bring three dollars. We trapped very hard. A seal skin was a dollar and you got the same price for baby seal killed in the spring. Looking back now, it seemed we always worked hard to stay alive. Now that I am old I am grateful for a warm house and a son who provides me with country food. Once I never stopped travelling but now I am content to stay home.

Alexander Wolfe b. 1927

SAULTEAUX

The Last Grass Dance

Told by Standing Through the Earth

Grandfather Standing Through the Earth was an elder who was knowledge-able about many things, both social and spiritual, and their application to the traditional and cultural ways of our people. Many times during his life I found him to be strange. Maybe this was because he was of one era and I was of another.

Whenever I would ask Grandfather a question that was of a humorous nature, his response was immediate. Sometimes he would ask Grandmother to provide an answer. Whenever I asked questions that dealt with the facts of life, Grandfather was quick to respond, 'A'how, Medimoya (all right, old lady), our grandson wants to know, tell him what he wants to know.' Usually this amused him and he laughed.

Then there were times I would ask a certain kind of question and receive no immediate response. Instead he would remain motionless, and after a period of silence, he would say, 'There is a period in the life of every person in which there is foolishness. When this period passes some people will grow up, remembering and using what they were told. For this we have a saying, "When you have had enough foolishness, then you become knowledgeable and know your mistakes." There are others who never go beyond this first stage; they remain foolish for the rest of their lives. To those people we say, "Your foolishness will accompany you to your old age." '

When I received this kind of response I was forced to practise patience and wait for a later time to ask my question. Very early in life I learned not to ask questions about spiritual things—particularly those things directly related to Grandfather or any other older person. These things, I was told, were very personal and were to be held in utmost respect. They were only alluded to in story form. Ceremonies and rituals were never described in detail. To ask old people questions about their spiritual attributes was unthinkable.

When I first asked Grandfather about the grass dance I already knew some things about it. From the stories told by Grandfather Earth Elder I knew where it had come from, and how it had come. On occasions when I asked my mother about it she only told me who performed the dance, not how or why the dance was performed. To these questions, she always replied, 'Ask your grandfather, he was part of it.'

Once she made a comment that revealed her recollection of that period, 'The dancer who wore the eagle belts in the grass dance looked beautiful. They were good dancers, very quick and beautiful to watch.'

My desire to know about the grass dance was to be satisfied one day.

It was a day in early summer. In the morning I helped Grandfather hitch his ponies to the wagon. After this was done I was told to help load the wagon with the berry-picking pails, some water containers, and a box of food. I was told that my mother and grandmother were going to pick saskatoon berries and Grandfather was going to chop willow pickets for fence posts. I was to help him. I was to be the pack horse who pulled the pickets out of the bush as they were cut, a job I wasn't really looking forward to. After hours of going from this bush to that bush, and finding only a few pickets, we came upon the Goose Lake from a northerly direction. We were on an abandoned trail along what was once the northwestern shoreline of Goose Lake. Suddenly Grandfather pulled his ponies to a stop and said, '*Medimoyea* (old lady), remember a long time ago when the shoreline was here and there were many kinds of summer fowl on the lake? At times there were so many geese they looked like snow upon the water.'

After the old people reminisced for several minutes about the old days we continued along what used to be the lake shore. A short time later we came upon a small clearing between two fairly large patches of trees and bushes. This was the place where the old log hall had stood by the shores of Goose Lake. The old hall was now gone.

As we approached the site I began to remember something about this place. The winter before I went to boarding school we came here once to watch a dance which I knew was the grass dance. We lived about three quarters of a mile north of here, and the whole family piled into the sleigh to make this trip. That evening and night were very cold. I knew it was very cold because from the time we left our house till we got here I was completely covered in blankets. I could not see anything. All I could hear was the sound of sleigh runners as they slid along the snow, and the sound of harness tugs as the horse pulled the sleigh.

When we arrived and went into the hall, we saw many people with children and many old people. Grandfather was there, so was Grandmother. My mother told me to sit in one place and to be quiet during the entire time we would be there. I cannot remember any of the other children making noise or running about either.

As we waited quietly for what was about to take place, I saw Grandfather dressed in a white traditional costume sitting by the door. To his left, and coming from the far opposite side of the hall, was the sound of bells and the aroma of burning sweet grass. A drum was placed in the centre of the hall. All was quiet. Then one of our grandfathers, whom I knew quite well, said a prayer. His name, the name I always called him, was *Wahpossway* (Old Man Bunnie).

I remembered seeing men seated on the floor around the drum. These were the singers. To one side of the singers stood another of the grandfathers, a brother to Grandfather Standing Through the Earth. His name was North Wind. This grandfather never danced. All he did was stand by the drum throughout the entire dance. The singing began and the dancers began their dance. During parts of the dance they danced slowly and at other times very fast. They let out shouts as they danced round and round the drum. On the ladies' side of the hall some elderly women stood dancing in one place. All at once there was a great shout. The dancers stopped dancing and the singers stopped singing.

There was something going on behind the drum and dancers that I could not see. Then the singing began again. This time some other men danced, just plain men. They carried ladles which they waved as they shouted.

The best part came after the dance was finished. Food was served, along with apples and bags of candy. My mother told me not to eat right away, first we had to listen. I remembered listening to another grandfather speak for a long time. He talked about us children and other children. This grandfather talked for such a long time, I couldn't hold out, I just had to dig into the candy. I'm sure I was not the only child to do this. I didn't remember what happened after that. I do know that a social dance followed—a round dance. I awoke the next morning back at our house. I knew that it had not been a dream because I still had some candy and apples.

As we neared the site where the old log hall had stood, Grandfather pulled his ponies to a turn and made for the edge of the bush.

There in the shade of the trees and bushes Grandfather stopped and said, 'We will stop here and eat.' Pointing to the bush along the lake bed, he said, 'The saskatoons used to be good here.'

We all got off the wagon and I helped Grandfather unhitch his ponies. In a short time a fire was built, the tea made, and we all sat down to eat. As we ate I thought again about the old log hall, about the time we came here during that one winter. In my mind I debated whether I should ask or not.

Finally I turned to my mother, 'Should I ask Grandfather about the old hall and what happened when we came here that one winter?'

Without saying a word she took out her tobacco, placed a pipeful in my hand, and said, 'Here. Ask him.'

As I was about to offer the tobacco to Grandfather my mother spoke to him. 'He wants to ask you about the old hall and about the last time there was a grass dance here.'

With a look on his face that suggested he was deep in thought, Grandfather took the tobacco.

'*Noozis* (grandchild),' he said, 'you have given me much tobacco in the past. I have told you stories. These stories I have told you were stories by the old men (elders) who lived here at Goose Lake since the reserve was here. Some of these stories were told when there was no reserve, no whiteman, so long ago we don't know when.

'This,' he said, pointing to the sky and around him, 'what you see around you is a story. What the *Anishnaybay* does and how he lives is a story. You, in time to come, will tell about me. Your children will tell about you—if you are foolish or not foolish—whatever they say about you will be a story. When your grandchildren come you will look back. You will see and know many things. This will be your story. What you ask I will tell you.

'Long ago when your grandmother and I were young, we came here to Goose Lake. (Grandfather was originally from the Riding Mountain area in central Manitoba and Grandmother came from the Turtle Mountains in Dakota Territory.) The people here at Goose Lake already had the grass dance. The elder *Sanquis*, father of my son-in-law, *Macheeaniquot* (Floating Cloud), had the ceremony. Elder *Sanquis* lived west of here at the other lake and had a big house. Round dances were held there and sometimes at mid-winter the grass dance was held there. I am told he got the dance as a gift from the Assiniboine people. This hall that was here was not the first. There was another across the lake to the east side. It was not really a hall but a big house.

'To have a part in the ceremony of the grass dance is an honour. In this dance there were four dancers, four singers, and four servers. There were speakers, a keeper of the drum, which at that time was *Mechee* (brother) *Keewaytinopeenace* (North Wind), and a keeper of the door. I was the last keeper of the door. When everyone who was to take part in the dance was ready, my part was to shut the door. I didn't let anyone in or out until the dance was over. When the door was shut a pipe was given to a speaker. Before the Elder *Sanquis* passed on, this was his part, as leader and headman of the Grass Dance Society. There had been other speakers in the past, like the father of *Nokeequon* (Soft Feather), Jim Bunnie. The speaker prayed to the Thunder Bird Eagle to bless the men who were holding the eagle belts which they were going to wear. These belts were sacred and used only for this dance. I have never been given the right to wear the eagle belt, only the eagle feather hat that I still have today. He also prayed for the keeper of the drum and the men seated around the drum. Four rainbows were painted on the drum, one for each direction, and at each direction sat a singer. The keeper of the drum stood at the east side of the drum. On the women's side stood four elderly women. They were noted in the community for their generosity and sharing with others. For these women, too, the speaker prayed. And for the children, and for all children yet to come. He prayed that each would be blessed with a head of grey and a long life.

'When this was done the dancers put on their belts. The dance was ready to begin. These belts came from an eagle that had been skinned, removing the head, the legs, the wings, and some of the tail feathers, and leaving only the back. From this section the belt was made and then decorated with ribbons of different colours.

'There were four main songs in this dance. The keeper of the drum kept track of them by passing a certain number of sticks from one hand to the other. The last two songs were sung twice. When the keeper of the drum held up four sticks in each hand we knew that this was the last part of the ceremony. This song was very fast and the dancers had to be very quick. The song ended when the lead dancer, who carried a sharpened stick, pierced a portion of the contents of a kettle, and held it up for all to see. The kettle held a cooked young dog that had been raised and prepared for this purpose. The lead dancer then took an eagle feather and dipped the tip of it into the broth and dropped one drop onto the tongue of each of his fellow dancers. Another song was sung to which the four men danced. They were the servers; their work, then, was to serve the food to the people.

'When this song was ended all the members of the Grass Dance Society were served the contents of the kettle. When the meal was ended the chief of the band, or some other headman, recounted why this ceremony was held— it meant that one half of the winter was now past. The hardships of the second half would soon be over. With the coming of spring it would be as morning after a dark night. We would be glad when the grandfathers*, among whom would be Thunder Bird Eagle, would come to give rain and life to all things, and we, too, the *Anishnaybay* would have life.'

When Grandfather had finished his story, he added the comment, 'Because of the changing times and forces outside our community, the Indians of tomorrow will never see, only hear of, the sacred ceremony and ritual called the grass dance.'

---

* Grandfathers, as used here, denotes Thunderbirds, the rolling thunder of the early spring, among whom, it was said, was the Eagle Thunder Bird.

Basil H. Johnston b. 1929

OJIBWA

The Prophecy

'Tonight I'm going to tell you a very different kind of story. . . . It's not really a story because it has not yet taken place; but it will take place just as the
events in the past have occurred.' Daebaudjimoot paused to fill his pipe. 'And
even though what I'm about to tell you has not yet come to pass, it is as true
as if it has already happened because the auttissookaunuk told me in a dream.'

They, the men, women, and children from the neighbouring lodges who
had come, waited for Daebaudjimoot to begin. The adults had long ceased to
believe the tribal storyteller. Still they came, as they had done so for years, to
relive the delight and faith of childhood which moved some of the old to say,
'he makes me feel like a child again sitting at my grandparents' feet.' But
unlike the children present who believed Daebaudjimoot, the adults spoke
slightingly of the storyteller but not without affection. 'W'zaumaudjimoh'
(he exaggerates), they said of him. But there was not a man, woman, or child
in the village who was not enriched in some way, either in mind or happier
in spirit, once having heard Daebaudjimoot.

'Tonight I'm going to tell you about white people.' There was a moment of
silence, astounded silence, and then an outburst of laughter as the audience
perceived the incongruity of the notion. An albino caribou; an albino beaver,
yes! but albino people? Who ever heard of White People? Even Daebaudjimoot had to laugh. The laughter gradually subsided.

'Are they like the maemaegawaehnsuk (little people like leprechauns,
elves)?' a man asked, inciting another wave of laughter.

'Are they like the Weendigoes?' an old woman enquired, igniting more
guffaws. The old laughed at such notions; the young laughed to hear the
adults giggle, roar, snigger and to see them twist their mouths and cheeks into
a hundred shapes. At the same time the young wondered what beings in addition to the Weendigoes, maemaegawaehnsuk, pauheehnsuk, zauwobeeku-
mook, and Pauguk lurked in the forests and roamed about at night.

'What do these White People look like?' another old lady asked when she
dried her eyes.

'The men and women that I speak of are all white, face, bodies, arms,
hands, and legs, pale as the rabbits of winter. And . . . they are hairy . . . hair
growing on their arms, legs, chests, backs, and arm-pits . . . and some men
grow hair upon their faces around their mouths, drooping down from their
chins, like moose beards.' Daebaudjimoot had to interrupt his narrative again
for the nervous titters and embarrassed cackles that set off another uproar.
The children chuckled and chortled as they imagined their playmates, maybe
brothers and sisters, goateed like moose. Daebaudjimoot continued, 'differ-

ent too is the colour of their hair; some yellow as goldenrod; a few red as cranberries, and others black as our hair. In old age the white people's hair turns white; on some men the hair falls off entirely so that their heads are as smooth and shiny as are pumpkins.

'Their eyes too are unlike ours; round . . . quite round . . . like the eyes of racoons . . . and blue like the colour of blueberries.'

There was more laughter but by now the men, women, and children were nursing aching bellies and paining sides.

'And their dress too is as quaint as their appearance. For one thing, they cover their bodies completely, day and night, summer and winter; only their faces being visible. On their heads are head-winders that they wear indoors and out-of-doors, in sunshine and in rain. The men and boys wear a peculiar garment which is a loin cloth and leggings made of one piece to cover their hams but the garment is so tight that the men walk like mud-hens. Each time that they go to toilet even to drain their bladders they must unfurl these rump binders down to their ankles. The women's garments are not much better than those of their men. The women wear a robe that covers them from their wrists and neck down to the very ankles. Underneath these loose bad-hangers the women wear tit flatteners and belly compressors. Their moccasins are made of a very hard substance, almost like wood, and cover their legs up to their very knee caps. It is only at night that the White People remove some of these garments.'

'Are they ashamed of their hair? of their organs?' an old woman quipped, rousing tired laughter.

Daebaudjimoot resumed his narrative. Hours later he predicted, 'When they come, they will come from the east across a great body of salt water; and they will arrive on board great wooden canoes five times the length of one of our own canoes. At either end of these long canoes are tall timbers. From the limbs of these timbers are suspended blankets for catching the wind to drive the canoes without the aid of paddles.'

'Are they ash or maple? Fresh wood or dead? They go against the wind?' voices asked and made remarks ridiculing the idea of an oversized canoe with trees at either end.

'You laugh because you cannot picture men and women with white skins or hair upon their faces; and you think it funny that a canoe would be moved by the wind across great open seas. But it won't be funny to our grandchildren and their great-grandchildren.

'In the beginning the first few to arrive will appear to be weak by virtue of their numbers, and they will look as if they are no more than harmless passers-by on their way to visit another people in another land who need a little rest and direction before resuming their journey. But in reality they will be spies for those in quest for lands. After them will come countless others like flocks of geese in their migratory flights. Flock after flock they will arrive. There will be no turning them back.

'Some of our grandchildren will stand up to these strangers but when they do, it will have been too late and their bows and arrows, war-clubs, and medicines will be as nothing against the weapons of these white people whose warriors will be armed with sticks that burst like thunder-claps. A warrior has to do no more than point a fire stick at another warrior and that man will fall dead the instant the bolt strikes him.

'It is with weapons such as these that the white people will drive our people from their homes and hunting grounds to desolate territories where game can scarce find food for their own needs and where corn can bare take root. The white people will take possession of all the rest and they will build immense villages upon them. Over the years the white people will prosper, and though the Anishinaubaeg may forsake their own traditions to adopt the ways of the white people, it will do them little good. It will not be until our grandchildren and their grandchildren return to the ways of their ancestors that they will regain strength of spirit and heart.

'There! I have told you my dream in its entirety. I have nothing more to say.'

'Daebaudjimoot! Are these white people manitous or are they beings like us?'

'I don't know.'

As the men, women, and children went out, a young man who had lingered behind remarked: 'It's good to listen to you, but I don't believe you.'

One Generation from Extinction

Within the past few years, Gregor Keeshig, Henry Johnston, Resime Akiwenzie, Norman McLeod, and Belva Pitwaniquot died. They all spoke their tribal language, Anishinaubae (Ojibwa). When these elders passed away, so did a portion of the tribal language come to an end as a tree disintegrates by degrees and in stages until it is no more; and, though infants were born to replenish the loss of life, not any of them will learn the language of their grandfathers or grandmothers to keep it alive and to pass it on to their descendants. Thus language dies.

In some communities there are no more Gregor Keeshigs, Henry Johnstons, Resime Akiwenzies, Norman McLeods, Belva Pitwaniquots; those remaining have no more affinity to their ancestral language than they do to Swahili or Sanskrit; in other communities the languages may not survive beyond a generation. Some tribal languages are at the edge of extinction, not expected to survive for more than a few years. There remain but three aboriginal languages out of the original fifty-three found in Canada that may survive several more generations.

There is cause to lament but it is the native peoples who have the most cause to lament the passing of their languages. They lose not only the ability to express the simplest of daily sentiments and needs but they can no longer understand the ideas, concepts, insights, attitudes, rituals, ceremonies, institutions brought into being by their ancestors; and, having lost the power to understand, cannot sustain, enrich, or pass on their heritage. No longer will they think Indian or feel Indian. And though they may wear 'Indian' jewellery and take part in pow-wows, they can never capture that kinship with and reverence for the sun and the moon, the sky and the water, or feel the lifebeat of Mother Earth or sense the change in her moods; no longer are the wolf, the bear, and the caribou elder brothers but beasts, resources to be killed and sold. They will have lost their identity which no amount of reading can ever restore. Only language and literature can restore the 'Indian-ness'.

Now if Canadians of West European or other origin have less cause than 'Indians' to lament the passing of tribal languages and cultures it is because they may not realize that there is more to tribal languages than 'ugh' or 'how' or 'kimu sabi'. At most and at best Euro-Canadians might have read or heard about Raven and Nanabush and Thunderbirds and other 'tricksters'; some may have even studied 'Culture Myths', 'Hero Tales', 'Transformation Tales', or 'Nature Myths and Beast Fables', but these accounts were never regarded as bearing any more sense than 'Little Red Riding Hood' or 'The Three Little Pigs'. Neither language nor literature were ever considered in their natural kinship, which is the only way in which language ought to be considered were its range, depth, force, and beauty to be appreciated.

Perhaps our Canadian compatriots of West European origin have more cause to lament the passing of an Indian language than they realize or care to admit. Scholars mourn that there is no one who can speak the Huron language and thus assist scholars in their pursuit of further knowledge about the tribe; scholars mourn that had the Beothuk language survived, so much more would be known about the Beothuk peoples. In mourning the extinction of the language, scholars are implicitly declaring that the knowledge derived from a study of snowshoes, shards, arrowheads, old pipes, shrunken heads and old bones, hunting, fishing, transportation, food preparation, ornamentation, and sometimes ritual is limited. And so it is; material culture can yield only so much.

Language is crucial. If scholars are to increase their knowledge and if they are to add depth and width to their studies, they must study a native language and literature. It is not enough to know linguistics or to know a few words or even some phrases or to have access to the Jesuit *Relations*, Chippewa *Exercises*, Ojibwa *Texts*, or a *Dictionary of the Otchipwe Language*. Without a knowledge of the language scholars can never take for granted the accuracy of an interpretation or translation of a passage, let alone a single word; nor can they presume that their articles, tracts, treatises, essays bear the kind of accuracy that scholarship and integrity demand. They would continue to labour under the impression that the word 'manitou' means spirit and that it has no other meaning. Superstitious nonsense, according to the white man. They do not know that the word bears other meanings even more fundamental than 'spirit', such as, and/or pertaining to the deities; of a substance, character, nature, essence, quiddity beyond comprehension and therefore beyond explanation, a mystery; supernatural; potency, potential. What a difference such knowledge might have made in the studies conducted by Ruth Landes or Thomas B. Leekley, and others on the Anishinaubae tribe. Perhaps, instead of regarding 'Indians' as superstitious for positing 'spirits' in trees or in other inanimate or insensate objects, they might have credited them with insight for having perceived a vital substance or essence that imparted life, form, growth, healing, and strength in all things, beings, and places. They might have understood that the expression 'manitouwan' meant that an object possessed or was infused with an element or a feature that was beyond human ken; they might have understood that 'w'manitouwih' meant that he or she was endowed with extraordinary talents, and that it did not mean that he or she was a spirit.

Language is essential. If scholars and writers are to know how 'Indians' perceive and regard certain ideas they must study an 'Indian' language. When an 'Anishinaubae' says that someone is telling the truth, he says 'w'daeb-awae'. But the expression is not just a mere confirmation of a speaker's veracity. It is at the same time a philosophical proposition that, in saying, a speaker casts his words and his voice only as far as his vocabulary and his perception will enable him. In so doing the tribe was denying that there was absolute truth; that the best a speaker could achieve and a listener expect was the highest degree of accuracy. Somehow that one expression 'w'daeb-awae' set the limits of a single statement as well as setting limits on all speech.

There was a special regard almost akin to reverence for speech and for the truth. Perhaps it was because words bear the tone of the speaker and may therefore be regarded as belonging to that person; perhaps it is because words have but a fleeting momentary existence in sound and are gone except in memory; perhaps it is because words have not ceased to exist but survive in echo and continue on in infinity; perhaps it is because words are medicine that can heal or injure; perhaps it is because words possess an element of the manitou that enabled them to conjure images and ideas out of nothing, and are the means by which the autissokanuk (muses) inspired men and women. It was not for nothing that the older generation did not solicit the autissokanuk to assist in the genesis of stories or in the composition of chants in seasons other than winter.

To instil respect for language the old counselled youth, 'Don't talk too much' (Kegon zaum-doongaen), for they saw a kinship between language and truth. The expression is not without its facetious aspect but in its broader application it was intended to convey to youth other notions implicit in the expression 'Don't talk too much', for the injunction also meant 'Don't talk too often . . . Don't talk too long . . . Don't talk about those matters that you know nothing about.' Were a person to restrict his discourse, and measure his speech, and govern his talk by what he knew, he would earn the trust and respect of his (her) listeners. Of that man or woman they would say 'w'daeb-awae.' Better still, people would want to hear the speaker again and by so doing bestow upon the speaker the opportunity to speak, for ultimately it is the people who confer the right of speech by their audience.

Language was a precious heritage; literature was no less precious. So precious did the tribe regard language and speech that it held those who abused language and speech and truth in contempt and ridicule and withheld from them their trust and confidence. To the tribe the man or woman who rambled on and on, or who let his tongue range over every subject or warp the truth was said to talk in circles in a manner no different from that of a mongrel who, not knowing the source of alarm, barks in circles (w'geewi-animoh). Ever since words and sounds were reduced to written symbols and have been stripped of their mystery and magic, the regard and reverence for them have diminished in tribal life.

As rich and full of meaning as may be individual words and expression, they embody only a small portion of the entire stock and potential of tribal knowledge, wisdom, and intellectual attainment; the greater part is deposited in myths, legends, stories, and in the lyrics of chants that make up the tribe's literature. Therein will be found the essence and the substance of tribal ideas, concepts, insights, attitudes, values, beliefs, theories, notions, sentiments, and accounts of their institutions and rituals and ceremonies. Without language scholars, writers, and teachers will have no access to the depth and width of tribal knowledge and understanding, but must continue to labour as they have done these many years under the impression that 'Indian' stories are nothing more than fairy tales or folklore, fit only for juvenile minds. For scholars and academics Nanabush, Raven, Glooscap, Weesaukeechauk, and other mythological figures will ever remain 'tricksters', culture heroes, deities whose misadventures were dreamed into being only for the amusement of children. Primitive and pagan and illiterate to boot, 'Indians' could not possibly address or articulate abstract ideas or themes; neither their minds nor their languages could possibly express any idea more complex than taboos, superstitions, and bodily needs.

But were ethnologists, anthropologists, linguists, teachers of native children and writers of native literature—yes, even archaeologists—to learn a native language, perhaps they might learn that Nanabush and Raven are not simply 'tricksters' but the caricatured representations of human nature and character in their many facets; perhaps they might give thought to the meaning and sense to be found in Weessaukeetchauk, The Bitter Soul. There is no other way except through language for scholars to learn or to validate their studies, their theories, their theses about the values, ideals or institutions or any other aspect of tribal life; there is no other way by which knowledge of native life can find increase. Not good enough is it to say in hushed tones after a reverential description of a totem pole or the lacing of a snowshoe, 'My, weren't they clever.'

Just consider the fate of 'Indian' stories written by those who knew nothing of the language and never did hear any of the stories in their entirety or in their original version but derived everything that they knew of their subject from second, third, and even fourth diluted sources. Is it any wonder then that the stories in *Indian Legends of Canada* by E.E. Clark or in *Manabozho* by T.B. Leekley are so bland and devoid of sense. Had the authors known the stories in their 'Indian' sense and flavour, perhaps they might have infused their versions with more wit and substance. Had the authors known that the creation story as the Anishinaubae understood it to mean was intended to represent in the most dramatic way possible the process of individual development from the smallest portion of talent to be retrieved from the depths of one's being and then given growth by breath of life. Thus a man and woman are to develop themselves, create their own worlds, and shape their being and give meaning to life. Had the authors known this meaning of the Creation Story, perhaps they might have written their accounts in terms more in keeping with the sense and thrust of the story. But not knowing the language nor having heard the story in its original text or state, the authors could not, despite their intentions, impart to their accounts the due weight and perspective the story deserved. The stories were demeaned.

With language dead and literature demeaned, 'Indian' institutions are beyond understanding and restoration. Let us turn back the calendar two and a half centuries, to that period when the 'Indian' languages were spoken in every home, when native literature inspired thought, and when native 'Indian' institutions governed native 'Indian' life. It was then that a native institution caught the imagination of the newcomers to this continent. The men and women who founded a new nation to be known as the United States of America took as their model for their constitution and government the principles of government and administration embodied in The Great Tree of Peace of the Five Nations Confederacy. The institution of The Great Tree of Peace was not then too primitive nor too alien for study or emulation to the founders of the United States. In more recent years even the architects of the United Nations regarded the 'Indian' institution of The Great Tree of Peace not as a primitive organization beneath their dignity and intellect, but rather as an institution of merit. There exist still 'Indian' institutions that may well serve and benefit this society and this nation, not as dramatically as did The Great Tree of Peace the United States of America, but bestow some good as yet undreamed or unimagined. Just how much good such institutions may confer upon this or some future generation will not be known unless the 'Indian' languages survive.

And what is it that had undermined the vitality of some of the 'Indian' languages and deprived this generation and this society the promise and the benefit of the wisdom and knowledge embodied in tribal literature?

In the case of the Beothuk and their language, the means used were simple and direct: it was the blade, the bludgeon, and the bullet that were plied in the destruction of the Beothuk in their sleep, at their table, and in their quiet passage from home to place of work, until the tribe was no more. The speakers were annihilated; no more was the Beothuk language spoken; whatever their wisdom or whatever their institutions, the whole of the Beothuk heritage was destroyed.

In other instances, instead of bullets, bludgeons, and bayonets, other means were used to put an end to the speaking of an 'Indian' language. A kick with a police riding boot administered by a 175-pound man upon the person of an eight-year-old boy for uttering the language of a savage left its pain for days and its bruise upon the spirit for life. A boy once kicked was not likely to risk a second or a third. A slap in the face or a punch to the back of the head delivered even by a small man upon the person of a small boy left its sting and a humiliation not soon forgotten. And if a boot or a fist were not administered, then a lash or a yardstick was plied until the 'Indian' language was beaten out. To boot and fist and lash was added ridicule. Both speaker and his language were assailed. 'What's the use of that language? It isn't polite to speak another language in the presence of other people. Learn English! That's the only way you're going to get ahead. How can you learn two languages at the same time? No wonder kids can't learn anything else. It's a primitive language; hasn't the vocabulary to express abstract ideas, poor. Say "ugh". Say something in your language! . . . How can you get your tongue around those sounds?' On and on the comments were made, disparaging, until in too many the language was shamed into silence and disuse.

And how may the federal government assist in the restoration of the native languages to their former vigour and vitality and enable them to fulfil their promise?

The Government of Canada must finance the establishment of either provincial or regional language institutes to be affiliated with a museum or a university or a provincial native educational organization. The function of the 'institute', to be headed by a native person who speaks, reads, and writes a native language, will be to foster research into language and to encourage the publication of lexicons, dictionaries, grammars, courses, guides, outlines, myths, stories, legends, genealogies, histories, religion, rituals, ceremonies, chants, prayers, and general articles; to tape stories, myths, legends, grammars, teaching guides and outlines and to build a collection of written and oral literature to make same accessible to scholars, teachers, and native institutions; and to duplicate and distribute written and oral literature to the native communities and learning institutions. The native languages deserve to be enshrined in this country's heritage as much as do snowshoes, shards, and arrowheads. Nay! More.

But unless the writings, the essays, stories, plays, the papers of scholars, academics, lexicographers, grammarians, etymologists, playwrights, poets, novelists, composers, philosophers are published and distributed, they can never nurture growth in language or literature. Taking into account the market represented by each tribe, no commercial publisher would risk publication of an 'Indian' book. Hence, only the federal government has the means to sponsor publication of an 'Indian text', either through a commercial publisher or through the Queen's Printer. The publication of an 'Indian' book may not be a commercially profitable enterprise, but it would add to the nation's intellectual and literary heritage.

Is That All There Is? Tribal Literature

In the early sixties Kahn-Tineta Horn, a young Mohawk model, got the attention of the Canadian press (media) not only by her beauty but by her articulation of Indian grievances and her demands for justice. Soon after Red Power was organized threatening to use force. Academics and scholars, anxious and curious to know what provoked the Indians, organized a series of conferences and teach-ins to explore the issues. Even children wanted to know. So for their enlightenment experts wrote dozens of books. Universities and colleges began native studies courses. Ministries of Education, advised by a battery of consultants, adjusted their Curriculum Guidelines to allow units of study on the native peoples of this continent. And school projects were conducted for the benefit of children between ten and thirteen years of age.

One such project at the Churchill Avenue Public School in North York, Ontario lasted six weeks and the staff and students who had taken part mounted a display as a grand finale to their studies. And a fine display it was in the school's library.

In front of a canvas tent that looked like a teepee stood a grim chief, face painted in war-like colours and arms folded. On his head he wore a headdress made of construction paper. A label pinned to his vest bore the name, Blackfoot. I made straight for the chief.

'How!' I greeted the chief, holding up my hand at the same time as a gesture of friendship.

Instead of returning the greeting, the chief looked at me quizzically.

'How come you look so unhappy?' I asked him.

'Sir! I'm bored,' the chief replied.

'How so, chief?'

'Sir, don't tell anybody, but I'm bored. I'm tired of Indians. That's all we've studied for six weeks. I thought they'd be interesting when we started, because I always thought that Indians were neat. At the start of the course we had to choose to do a special project from food preparation, transportation, dwellings, social organization, clothing, and hunting and fishing. I chose dwellings' and here the chief exhaled in exasperation '. . . and that's all me and my team studied for six weeks: teepees, wigwams, longhouses, igloos. We read books, encyclopedias, went to the library to do research, looked at pictures, drew pictures. Then we had to make one. Sir, I'm bored.'

'Didn't you learn anything else about Indians, chief?'

'No sir, there was nothing else . . . Sir? . . . Is that all there is to Indians?'

Little has changed since that evening in 1973. Books still present native people in terms of their physical existence as if Indians were incapable of meditating upon or grasping the abstract. Courses of study in the public school system, without other sources of information, had to adhere to the format, pattern, and content set down in books. Students studied Kaw-lijas, wooden Indians, who were incapable of love or laughter; or Tontos, if you will, whose sole skill was to make fires and to perform other servile duties for the Lone Ranger; an inarticulate Tonto, his speech limited to 'Ugh!' 'Kimo Sabi', and 'How'.

Despite all the research and the field work conducted by anthropologists, ethnologists, and linguists, Indians remain 'The Unknown Peoples' as Professor George E. Tait of the University of Toronto so aptly titled his book written in 1973.

Not even Indian Affairs of Canada, with its more than two centuries of experience with natives, with its array of experts and consultants, with its unlimited funds, seems to have learned anything about its constituents, if we are to assess their latest publication titled 'The Canadian Indian'. One would think that the Honourable William McKnight, then Minister of Indian and Northern Affairs, under whose authority the book was published in 1986 should know by now the Indians who often come to Ottawa, do not arrive on horseback, do not slay one of the R.C.M.P. mounts and cook it on the steps of the Parliament Buildings. Moreover, most Indians he has seen and met were not dressed in loincloths, nor did they sleep in teepees. Yet he authorized the publication of a book bereft of any originality or imagination, a book that perpetuated the notion and the image that the Indians had not advanced one step since contact, but are still living as they had one hundred and fifty, even three hundred years ago. There was not a word about native thought, literature, institutions, contributions in music, art, theatre. But that's to be expected of Indian Affairs; to know next to nothing of their constituents.

Where did the author or authors of this latest publication by Indian Affairs get their information? The selected readings listed at the back of the book provide a clue; Frances Densmore, Harold Driver, Philip Drucker, Frederick W. Hodge, Diamond Jenness, Reginald and Gladys Laubin, Frank G. Speck, Bruce G. Trigger, George Woodcock, Harold Innes, Calvin Martin, E. Palmer Patterson, eminent scholars, none of whom spoke or attempted to learn the language of any of the Indian nations about whom they were writing. Modern scholars because they are not required by their universities to learn, are no more proficient in a native language than were their predecessors.

Herein, I submit, is the nub and the rub. Without the benefit of knowing the language of the Indian nation that they are investigating, scholars can never get into their mind, the heart and soul and the spirit and still understand the native's perceptions and interpretations. The scholar must confine his research and studies to the material, physical culture, subsistence patterns, and family relationships.

Without knowing the spiritual and the intellectual, aesthetic side of Indian culture, the scholar cannot furnish what that little grade five youngster and others like him wanted to know about Indians.

Admitting his boredom was that grade five youngster's way of expressing his disappointment with the substance of the course that he and his colleagues had been made to endure. In another sense, it was a plea for other knowledge that would quench his curiosity and challenge his intellect.

Students such as he, as well as adults, are interested in the character, intellect, soul, spirit, heart of people of other races and cultures. They want to know what other people believe in, what they understand, what they expect and hope for in this life and in the next, how they keep law and order and harmony within the family and community, how and why they celebrated ceremonies, what made them proud, ashamed, what made them happy, what sad. Whether the young understand what they want to know and learn does not matter much, they still want to know in order to enrich their own insights and broaden their outlooks.

But unless scholars and writers know the literature of the peoples that they are studying or writing about they cannot provide what their students and readers are seeking and deserving of.

There is, fortunately, enough literature, both oral and written, available for scholarly study, but it has for the most part been neglected. Myths, legends, and songs have not been regenerated and set in modern terms to earn immortalization in poetry, dramatization in plays, or romanticization in novels.

What has prevented the acceptance of Indian literature as a serious and legitimate expression of native thought and experience has been indifferent and inferior translation, a lack of understanding and interest in the culture, and a notion that it has little of importance to offer to the larger white culture.

In offering you a brief sketch, no more than a glimpse, as it were, of my tribe's culture, I am doing no more than what anyone of you would do were you to be asked 'What is your culture? Would you explain it?' I would expect you to reply, 'Read my literature, and you will get to know something of my thoughts, my convictions, my aspirations, my feelings, sentiments, expectations, whatever I cherish or abominate.'

First, let me offer you an observation about my language for the simple reason that language and literature are inseparable, though they are too often taught as separate entities. They belong together.

In my tribal language, all words have three levels of meaning; there is the surface meaning that everyone instantly understands. Beneath this meaning is a more fundamental meaning derived from the prefixes and their combinations with other terms. Underlying both is the philosophical meaning.

Take the word 'Anishinaubae'. That is what the members of the nation, now known as Chippewa in the United States or Ojibway in Canada, called themselves. It referred to a member of the tribe. It was given to the question 'What are you?' But it was more than just a term of identification. It meant, 'I am a person of good intent, a person of worth' and it reflected what the people thought of themselves, and of human nature; that all humans are essentially, fundamentally good. Let's separate that one word into its two terms. The first, 'Onishishih' meaning good, fine, beautiful, excellent; and the second 'naubae' meaning being, human being, male, human species. Even together they do not yield the meaning 'good intention'. It is only by examining the stories of Nanabush, the tribes' central and principal mythical figure who represents all men and all women, that the term Anishinaubae begins to make sense. Nanabush was always full of good intentions, ergo the people of the tribe, the Anishinaubae perceive themselves as people who intended good and therefore of merit and worth. From this perception they drew a strong sense of pride as well as a firm sense of place in the community. This influenced their notion of independence.

Let's take another word, the word for truth. When we say 'w'daeb-awae' we mean he or she is telling the truth, is correct, is right. But the expression is not merely an affirmation of a speaker's veracity. It is as well a philosophical proposition that in saying a speaker casts his words and his voice as far as his perception and his vocabulary will enable him or her, it is a denial that there is such a thing as absolute truth; that the best and most the speaker can achieve and a listener expect is the highest degree of accuracy. Somehow that one expression, 'w'daeb-awae', sets the limits to a single statement as well as setting limits to truth and the scope and exercise of speech.

One other word 'to know'. We say 'w'kikaendaun' to convey the idea that he or she 'knows'. Without going into the etymological derivations, suffice it to say that when the speaker assures someone that he knows it, that person is saying that the notion, image, idea, fact that that person has in mind corresponds and is similar to what he or she has already seen, heard, touched, tasted, or smelled. That person's knowledge may not be exact, but similar to that which has been instilled and impressed in his or her mind and recalled from memory.

The stories that make up our tribal literature are no different from the words in our language. Both have many meanings and applications, as well as bearing tribal perceptions, values, and outlooks.

Let us begin at the beginning with the tribe's story of creation which precedes all other stories in the natural order. Creation stories provide insights into what races and nations understand of human nature; ours is no different in this respect.

This is our creation story. Kitchi-manitou beheld a vision. From this vision The Great Mystery, for that is the essential and fundamental meaning of Kitchi-manitou and not spirit as is often understood, created the sun and the stars, the land and the waters, and all the creatures and beings, seen and unseen, that inhabit the earth, the seas, and the skies. The creation was desolated by a flood. Only the manitous, creatures and beings who dwelt in the waters were spared. All others perished.

In the heavens dwelt a manitou, Geezhigo-quae (Sky-woman). During the cataclysm upon the earth, Geezhigo-quae became pregnant. The creatures adrift upon the seas prevailed upon the giant turtle to offer his back as a haven for Geezhigo-quae. They then invited her to come down.

Resting on the giant turtle's back Geezhigo-quae asked for soil.

One after another water creatures dove into the depths to retrieve a morsel of soil. Not one returned with a particle of soil. They all offered an excuse; too deep, too dark, too cold, there are evil manitous keeping watch. Last to descend was the muskrat. He returned with a small knot of earth.

With the particle of mud retrieved by the muskrat Geezhigo-quae recreated an island and the world as we know it. On the island she created over the giant turtle's shell, Geezhigo-quae gave birth to twins who begot the tribe called the Anishinaubaeg.

Millennia later the tribe dreamed Nanabush into being. Nanabush represented themselves and what they understood of human nature. One day his world too was flooded. Like Geezhigo-quae, Nanabush recreated his world from a morsel of soil retrieved from the depths of the sea.

As a factual account of the origin of the world and of being, the story has no more basis than the biblical story of creation and the flood. But the story represents a belief in God, the creator, a Kitchi-manitou, the Great Mystery. It also represents a belief that Kitchi-manitou sought within himself, his own being, a vision. Or perhaps it came from within his being and that Kitchi-manitou created what was beheld and set it into motion. Even the lesser manitous, such as Geezhigo-quae and Nanabush, must seek a morsel of soil with which to create and recreate their world, their spheres. So men and women must seek within themselves the talent or the potential and afterward create their own worlds and their own spheres and a purpose to give meaning to their lives.

The people begotten by Geezhigo-quae on that mythological island called themselves Anishinaubaeg, the good beings who meant well and were human beings, therefore fundamentally good. But they also knew that men and women were often deflected from fulfilling their good intentions and prevented from living up to their dreams and visions, not out of any inherent evil, but rather from something outside of themselves. Nanabush also represented this aspect of human nature. Many times Nanabush or the Anishinaubaeg fail to carry out a noble purpose. Despite this, he is not rendered evil or wicked but remains fundamentally and essentially good.

Men and women intend what is good, but they forget. The story called 'The Man, The Snake and The Fox' exemplifies this aspect of human nature.

In its abbreviated form the story is as follows. The hunter leaves his lodge and his family at daybreak to go in search of game to feed his wife and his children. As he proceeds through the forest, the hunter sees deer, but each time they are out of range of his weapon.

Late in the afternoon, discouraged and weary, he hears faint cries in the distance. Forgetting his low spirits and fatigue he sets out with renewed optimism and vigour in the direction of the cries. Yet the nearer he draws to the source of the cries, the more daunted is the hunter by the dreadful screams. Only the thought of his family's needs drove him forward, otherwise he might have turned away.

At last he came to a glade. The screams came from a thicket on the opposite side. The hunter, bow and arrow drawn and ready, made his way forward cautiously.

To his horror, the hunter saw an immense serpent tangled fast in a thicket as a fish is caught in the webbing of a net. The monster writhed and roared and twisted. He struggled to break free.

The man recoiled in horror. Before he could back away, the snake saw him. 'Friend!' the snake addressed the man.

The man fell in a heap on the ground the moment that the snake spoke. When he came to much later the snake pleaded with the man to set him free. For some time the man refused but eventually he relented. He was persuaded by the monster's plea that he too, though a serpent, had no less right to life than did the man. And the serpent promised not to injure the man on his release. The hunter was convinced.

The snake sprang on his deliverer the moment the last vine was cut away.

It was like thunder as the man and the snake struggled. Nearby a little fox heard the uproar. Never having seen such a spectacle the fox settled down to watch. Immediately he realized that the man was about to be killed.

Why were the snake and the man locked in mortal struggle? The little fox shouted for an explanation. The man and the snake stopped.

The hunter gasped out his story, then the snake gave his version. Pretending not to understand the snake's explanation the fox beguiled the aggressor into returning to the thicket to act out his side of the story.

The snake entangled himself once more.

Realizing that he had been delivered from the edge of death by the fox, the man was greatly moved. He felt bound to show his gratitude in some tangible way. The fox assured him that no requital was required. Nevertheless the hunter persisted. How might he, the hunter, perform some favour on behalf of the fox?

Not only was there no need, the fox explained, there was nothing that the man could do for the fox; there was not a thing that the fox needed or desired of human beings. However, if it would make the man happier, the fox suggested that the man might feed him should he ever have need.

Nothing would please the man more than to perform some good for his deliverer; it was the least that he could do for a friend who had done so much.

Some years later the hunter shot a little fox who had been helping himself to the family storage. As the man drew his knife to finish off the thief, the little fox gasped, 'Don't you remember?'

That no snakes as monstrous as the one in the story are to be found on this continent makes no difference to the youngsters' sense of outrage over the treachery of the snake and the forgetfulness of the man; nor does the exercise of speech which enables the snake and the fox to communicate with the hunter and each other prevent the young from being moved to compassion for the fox. Their sense of justice and fairness bears them over the anomalies in the story.

Before the last words 'Don't you remember?' have echoed away, the young begin to ask questions. 'Why? Why did the man not recognize the fox? Why did he forget? How did the man feel afterwards? Why did the snake attack the man? Why did the snake break his promise? Why didn't the man leave the snake where he was? Do animals really have as much right to live as human beings do?'

Indians cared, loved as passionately as other people.

The story called 'The Weeping Pine' raises the same questions about love and marriage and the span of either that have been asked by philosophers, poets, and lovers of every race and generation. It does not pretend to give answers to these age old questions beyond suggesting that love may bloom even in circumstances where it is least expected to flower and endure. But owing to shoddy translation, the story has been presented as an explanation for the origin of pine trees.

According to the story, the elders of a village came to a certain young woman's home where she lived with her parents, brothers, and sisters. They had come to let her family know that they had chosen her to be the new wife to an old man. This particular man had been without a friend since the death of his first wife some years before. The old man was described as good-natured and kind. As one who had done much to benefit the tribe in his youth, the old man deserved something in return from his neighbours. In the opinion of the elders the most fitting reward the old man could have was a wife. In their judgement the young woman they had chosen would be a suitable companion for the old man.

They assured her that the tribe would see to it that they never had need.

Because this sort of marriage was a matter that the young woman had not considered, it was unexpected. The delegation understood this. They did not demand an immediate answer but allowed the woman a few days in which to make up her mind.

The young woman cried when the delegation left. She didn't want to marry that man. That old man whose days were all but over and who could never look after her. She had, like every young girl her age, hoped to marry someone young, full of promise, someone she would love and who would love her in return. Besides, it was too soon. How could she, not yet eighteen, be a companion to an old man of seventy or more? The disparity was too great.

At first her parents too were aggrieved. But soon after they prevailed upon her to defer to the wishes of the elders, and her father delivered word of their daughter's consent to the elders.

But neither the disparity in age nor the disposition of the young girl to enter into a loveless marriage were too great; in the years that followed she came to love this old man. And they had many children.

Thirty years later the old man died.

On the final day of the four day watch, the mourners went home but the widow made no move to rise. She continued to keen and rock back and forth in great sorrow.

'Come mother, let us go home,' her children urged, offering to assist her to her feet and to support her on their way home.

'No! No! Leave me. Go,' she said.

'Mother! Please. Come home with us,' her children pleaded. Nothing they said could persuade their mother to leave.

'No. You go home. This is where I belong. Leave me.'

Her children prayed she would relent; give in to the cold and hunger. They went home, but they did not leave their mother alone. During the next few days a son or daughter was always at her side, watching with her and entreating her to come home. They tried to comfort her with their own love and care, assuring her that her wound would pass and heal. They even brought her food and drink to sustain her. She refused everything.

As their mother grew weaker with each passing day, the children besought the elders to intercede on their behalf. Perhaps the elders could prevail on their mother.

But the elders shook their heads and said, 'If that is what she wants, there is nothing that you can do to change her mind. Leave her be. She wants to be with him. Leave her. It's better that way.'

And so the family ceased to press their mother to come home, though they still kept watch with her. They watched until she too died by the graveside of her husband, their father.

Using the term 'grandchild' that all elders used in referring to the young, the elder who presided over the woman's wake said, 'Our granddaughter's love did not cease with death, but continues into the next life.'

The next spring a small plant grew out of the grave of the woman. Many years later, as the sons, daughters, and grandchildren gathered at the graveside of their parents, they felt a mist fall upon their faces and their arms. 'It is mother shedding tears of love for dad,' cried her daughter.

And it is so. On certain days, spruces and pines shed a mist of tears of love.

By remaining at her husband's graveside until she too died, the woman fulfilled the implied promise, 'whither thou goest, there too will I go' contained in the term 'weedjeewaugun', companion in life, our word for spouse.

As she wept for her love she must have wept for the love of her children. Their love threatened to break that bond that held her to her husband. No! She would not sever that bond; she would not let even death part her from the man to whom she had given her heart, her soul, her spirit forever.

It is unlikely that the woman ever uttered more than 'K'zaugin' (I love you) during her marriage. In this respect she was no different from most other women, or men for that matter, who are not endowed with the poetic gift, though they feel and love with equal passion and depth. K'zaugin said everything. I love you, today, tomorrow, forever. It expressed everything that the finest poets ever wrote and everything that the unpoetic ever thought and felt but could not put into rhyme or rhythm.

In sentiment the story compares to Elizabeth Barrett Browning's immortal poem, 'How do I love thee' which ends with the words 'and if God grant, I shall love thee better after death.'

Rita Joe b. 1932

MICMAC

Today's Learning Child

I see the bronze hue of skin
The dark eyes flashing.
The arrogant hold of that stare
Into the dream of that softness of life
Just out of reach.

The angry hold onto the reality
Into determination.
To see the life of improvement
Someday soon.

The head is bent, the shoulders round
That force upon learning, commanding,
Until dignity nods.

We are different to this age
We rely so much.

Please understand;
The chisel must continue to carve an image
Because all our life has already been labelled.

I Lost My Talk

I lost my talk
The talk you took away.
When I was a little girl
At Shubenacadie school.

You snatched it away:
I speak like you
I think like you
I create like you
The scrambled ballad, about my word.

Two ways I talk
Both ways I say,
Your way is more powerful.

So gently I offer my hand and ask,
Let me find my talk
So I can teach you about me.

Micmac Hieroglyphics

'I noticed children
Making marks with charcoal on ground,'
Said LeClerq.
'This made me see
That in form would create a memory
Of learning more quickly
The prayers I teach.

'I was not mistaken,
The characters produced
The effect I needed.
For on birchbark they saw
These familiar figures
Signifying a word,
Sometimes two together.
The understanding came quickly
On leaflets
They called kekin a'matin kewe'l
Tools for learning.

'The preservation of written word
Was in so much care.
They kept them neatly in little cases
Of birchbark
Beautified with wampum
Of beadwork and quills.
These were the Micmac hieroglyphics
The written word of the Indian
That the world chooses to deny.'

Shanawdithit
(Pronounced Shaw-now-dih-diht)

She was born in Ktaqamkuk
Shanawdithit her name
To a family life like yours or mine
Of caring people
The Beothuks of Newfoundland.
And then her people passed away one by one
Endurance no meaning anymore because of strife
By the newcomers who must own all land
No matter the price.
But survival became her way, even venturing close
To these strange people who can hurt so much
But there were women who cared enough to feed her
Allowing her to earn her keep as a servant.

And then six winters passed
A strange man with kindness in the eyes approached her.
The wounded heart replaced by warmth
Of a father image, a caring brother,
She tried to please him, learning the language
The strange ways these people questioned her.
She drew pictures
Trying to remember the implements of life.
Always working, repaying the life spared her.
Until she became easily tired
Needing the land of her people, to be close
To walk where they walked. Feeling the spirits
In dreamland, their nearness, so close but handshake away.
Finally she joined them, in the everland of red ochre
Shanawdithit, the flower of the Beothuks
The last martyr of Taqmkuk.

The Lament of Donald Marshall Jr.

Everybody knows the story about Donald Marshall Jr.—how he served eleven years in prison for a crime he did not commit. The sad irony of the whole story is that they were both minorities, the one gone and the one accused. In 1971 these two young people got together that night as easily as any young people would. It ended in tragedy.

The hurt of rejection is sometimes there in our society, the failure of some people who take part in it are the ones to be pitied. They are the ones who are blind to love, humanity, kindness, and compassion. I speak for the Indian, or any minority. The pain of rejection will always be there as long as people fail to educate themselves that we are all the same. We are all one.

How do we remove injustice? Try moving hearts.

Song

I have served prison term, with locks on the door
My pain it is known, it is known the world over.
On my heart's aching core, I didn't do, I was told
He was my friend
We are the same, we are the same, we are the same.

My hurt is not gone, the key is beyond
The pain that is known, it is known the world over.
On my heart's aching core, I didn't do, I didn't do
He was my friend
We are the same, we are the same, we are the same.

The pain will be there, as long as men fail
My hurt it is known, it is known the world over.
On my heart's aching core, I didn't do I was told
He was my friend
We are the same, we are the same, we are the same.

Anthony Apakark Thrasher 1937–89

INUIT

Playing with Girls is a Sin

All told, there must have been around eight hundred people living in Aklavik at that time. The rich families—they mostly worked for the Federal Government which had its Western Arctic headquarters there—lived in one- or two-room houses built of lumber and heated with wood or oil. They were over near the hospital, and the Anglican school and cathedral, on the other end of town. A wooden sidewalk ran along in front of them, a wide ditch separating the sidewalk from the snow-packed road. Out back of the houses were the RCMP barracks, the police dog kennels, and the radio tower. Closer to our school was the Hudson's Bay Company store, the biggest of the stores in town, where the Indians and Eskimos who huddled in little huts and tents would sell their furs. Some Indians lived across the river and every day I'd see them crossing the ice on their way to jobs in town. The trappers all had happy expressions on their faces because the flat delta land on which Aklavik was located was rich with muskrat. In those days their pelts were worth as much as two dollars apiece.

The nuns in charge of us were Sister Bessant, Sister Soka, Sister Gilbert, and Sister Alice Rae, who I loved as much as my real mother. Sister Bessant was nice, too, but Sister Soka used a ruler on our hands and Sister Gilbert was hell-on-wheels for pulling ears, brushing our mouths with lye soap, and whipping us with a watch chain. I could never understand how she could be so mean, and yet be very kind at the same time.

Sister Soka was my teacher. I couldn't catch on to the ABC's, and Sister Soka got a girl called Lena to show me. I was just a little guy, much smaller than Lena, but I wondered if she knew I thought she was pretty.

In the seat ahead of me was a boy named Danny Norris. Behind me was Freddie Carmichael. Whenever I wasn't eating my pencil, I was poking them with it. We had elastic slingshots, too, and every time the teacher turned her back, she was the target.

I was eating cooked food for the first time. I didn't like it and, like the other boys, I would sneak into the kitchen whenever I could and slip away with some frozen meat. We tossed our bones into the school yard and that's how it came to look more like a bone yard than a playground.

When anyone complained about the food, the nuns would make the complainer drink a whole can of cod liver oil, to do penance for committing something they called a venial sin. That was smaller than a mortal sin, and something else called a sacrilege was an even bigger sin than a mortal sin.

You never went to Hell on venials.

There were as many girls as boys at the school. The girls' dormitory was on the top floor at one end of the main building, the boys' at the other end. We even ate in separate rooms.

We were told not to play with the girls, because that would also be a sin. I thought that was strange, because I had played with girls before I came to school. Now they were telling me I shouldn't touch them. I was taught not to look at girls, and not to look at dogs mating. But I had seen these things long before I went to school. I had seen people in the sex act when I was as young as three years of age. I knew exactly what it was, and how to do it, by the time I was six.

I was forever being scolded for eating with my hands. I didn't like using knives and forks and spoons. I'd drink my soup and rip the meat apart with my teeth. Then I'd wipe my mouth on my sleeves and wipe my hands on my clean knee-length pants. Sister Gilbert put a stop to that.

My grades were somewhere between one and zero. But I was a good wood hauler. About five or six of us would drag loads of wood for the furnaces—four in the school and hospital, one in the parish house, one in the laundry, and one in the kitchen. They all used kindling.

When Hallowe'en came, we got to see our first movie—a silent one with Charlie Chaplin. It was scary, and a lot of us hid under the benches and cried. Brother Jack made things worse by coming in with a pumpkin with a candle glowing inside and holes carved to make the pumpkin look like an evil spirit. At that point I escaped into the arms of dear Sister Alice Rae.

When Sister Gilbert was in a good mood, she used to tell us stories from the newspapers she got sent up from the South. She told us about Adolf Hitler and Mussolini, Joseph Stalin and Churchill, and she said that the German war was going on strong and that Hitler was raising Cain all over Europe and Africa. We prayed a lot that it would end soon.

There was a half hour of prayers in the morning, before and after breakfast. Dinner was at eleven o'clock, and there were prayers before and after that, too.

That fall we went on a picnic, camping overnight in the school shack about two miles into the snow-covered bush out back. I set a trap and caught a whisky-jack. I made a little fire, and burned the feathers off the big blue bird, then let it freeze, and ate it when it was frozen hard. It tasted like caribou liver.

That night someone told the legend of another Eskimo boy, Iliapaluk, an orphan who lived with his grandmother Ananaa, in the bush country. They had a little house, Kutuk, of the kind that is dug into the earth with the roof at ground level. Iliapaluk was just a small boy. He used to snare rabbits with sinews, while the old woman fished with a bone hook. No one knew that this old woman possessed the magic power we call Angatkolik.

They had only the snares to count on for meat. One day, the boy came home and told his grandmother that someone had stolen them. They went to the nearby village to try and get them back, but whoever took the snares would not come forward. The old woman warned the village people not to make fun of a poor orphan boy. She told them she would give whoever took Iliapaluk's snares a chance to return them to him.

Still no one came forward, so they went back home, and the old woman told her grandson to go and hook a fish with roe in it. The boy did this, and the old woman cut the fish open, and took out the eggs. She told her grandson not to watch her for a moment. When the boy turned around, he saw she was covered with fish eggs from head to toe. She told him they were returning to the village, to get the snares.

When they arrived, she told the boy to call everyone out of their houses. When he had done this, the old woman began talking to them.

'I will touch all of you, one by one,' she said. 'If you are good people, do not be afraid. Only the liar will get hurt.'

She then touched everyone, until she got to a man who suddenly dropped dead.

He was the thief. He had the snares.

Then the grandmother told the people, 'Whatever you do, do not ever steal from an orphan who has no mother, and who fights hard to live. He only has those little strings to live on, and when you take them away, he can starve and die.'

Storytelling was a part of life in the North. My brothers and I were always competing to tell the best story. But we were no match for our grandfather. He was the greatest of them all. As he talked, he would light his pipe, and smoke 'Old Chum' tobacco. Then he would pick up his drum, and sing. He would sing of Herschel Island in the Arctic Ocean, and tell of times that were good. He would sing of happiness after a successful whale hunt, about the big dances people used to have, of his young days, and his women, and of the medicine man of old.

One of my jobs at the school, with a boy called Douglas Dillon, was emptying the toilet pails. One day, we toppled down a twenty-foot bank on our way to the river to dump the slop. We came out looking like a couple of O'Henry chocolate bars. The outhouse at the end of the playground had sixteen seats, for over two hundred boys. Some of the seats were too big for the little boys, and they used to fall through them. I had the honour of being one of the lucky ones.

Christmas week, we spent four days at the camp shack in the bush. We trapped muskrat, caught one cross fox, snared rabbits, climbed trees, and chewed spruce gum. We also got a chance to see inside the girls' camp.

The toys we got for Christmas were great. I ran away from my first one, a rolling clown. It scared the Christmas spirit right out of me.

On New Year's Day there was a concert, and the RCMP were called in to take some drunks out of the school. They were trappers, and some people from town.

Duke Redbird b. 1939

CHIPPEWA

I am a Canadian

I'm a lobster fisherman in Newfoundland
I'm a clambake in P.E.I.
I'm a picnic, I'm a banquet
I'm mother's homemade pie
I'm a few drafts in a Legion hall in Fredericton
I'm a kite-flyer in a field in Moncton
I'm a nap on the porch after a hard day's work is done.
I'm a snowball fight in Truro, Nova Scotia
I'm small kids playing jacks and skipping rope
I'm a mother who lost a son in the last great war
And I'm a bride with a brand new ring
And a chest of hope
I'm an Easterner
I'm a Westerner
I'm from the North
And I'm from the South
I've swam in two big oceans
And I've loved them both
I'm a clown in Quebec during carnival
I'm a mass in the Cathedral of St. Paul
I'm a hockey game in the Forum
I'm Rocket Richard and Jean Beliveau
I'm a coach for little league Expos
I'm a baby-sitter for sleep-defying rascals
I'm a canoe trip down the Ottawa
I'm a holiday on the Trent
I'm a mortgage, I'm a loan
I'm last week's unpaid rent
I'm Yorkville after dark
I'm a walk in the park
I'm a Winnipeg gold-eye
I'm a hand-made trout fly
I'm a wheat-field and a sunset
Under a prairie-sky
I'm Sir John A. Macdonald
I'm Alexander Graham Bell
I'm a pow-wow dancer
And I'm Louis Riel

I'm the Calgary Stampede
I'm a feathered Sarcee
I'm Edmonton at night
I'm a bar-room fight
I'm a rigger, I'm a cat
I'm a ten-gallon hat
And an unnamed mountain in the interior of B.C.
I'm a maple tree and a totem pole
I'm sunshine showers
And fresh-cut flowers
I'm a ferry boat ride to the Island
I'm the Yukon
I'm the North-West Territories
I'm the Arctic Ocean and the Beaufort Sea
I'm the prairies, I'm the Great Lakes,
I'm the Rockies, I'm the Laurentians,
I am French
I am English
And I am Métis
But more than this
Above all this
I am a Canadian and proud to be free.

From *We Are Métis*

Modern Métis Consciousness

THE CULTURAL INITIATIVE

Modern Métis leadership has been plagued by an official division between political activism and cultural or artistic expression. The problem was put succinctly at the fifth annual convention of the Native Council of Canada. The spokesman for the British Columbia delegation, disturbed by the inclusion of cultural activities at a convention whose theme was unity and aboriginal rights, stated: 'Our homes are going to be torn up by pipelines, hydro developments, and various other things, and we're fiddle-farting around with jigging contests. I just don't understand.' Another delegate from Alberta responded immediately: 'As for jigging and contests—I'm for that. I'm a jigger, I'm a fiddler, and I don't want any sucker to tell me that I can't do that any time, any place. That's part of my culture and I'll fight anybody that says it's not part of my culture.'

The two extremes that were expressed by these two delegates is the dilemma facing much of the present Métis leadership in Canada. There are those who believe that active political posturing can only make things difficult.

'If you take on the establishment head-on, you are just indicating to them ways of making better chains for you. To meet them head-on is just suicide. What you have to do is approach the whole thing obliquely. You have to change people's ideas, and the only way you can do that is through the media. You have to attack on a cultural, rather than a political level.'

The modern Métis, especially in the eastern provinces, need to realize a solid cultural base before significant political gains may be achieved. The Métis activists who reject the need for cultural renaissance, such as Howard Adams, fear a 'cultural colonialism' imposed somehow by contact with white society. The fear is as unfounded and paranoid as the establishment fear of 'red nationalism'. The executive of the Native Council of Canada have, from time to time, used both techniques for penetrating the consciousness of the larger society. The Indians, for example, who ride in full regalia in a parade are as harmless to the image of the 'real Indian' as the rhinestone cowboys in the same parade are to the 'real cowboy'.

Howard Adams states that 'the Métis has internalized the myths of inferiority', then claims it is wrong for the Métis to try and change these myths. 'It is useless for us to become involved in a struggle to improve our image, because native people did not create these images.'

The modern Métis are rapidly adopting, in a modern context, as many symbols of the traditional Métis lifestyle as possible. The Native Council of Canada, in 1976, reintroduced the flag of Louis Riel and made it the official flag of the Métis people. At a provincial board meeting of the Ontario Métis Non-Status Indian Association in January of 1978, the Métis sash was adopted as an official badge of office of the association. There is, of course, the danger of imitating traditional ways as a kind of cultural eccentricity, but that is the 'kindergarten' of the modern Métis cultural renaissance. As the Métis become more aware of themselves as a unique cultural entity, they will evolve broader social, artistic, and eventually political expressions that accurately reflect the role of Métis consciousness in Canadian life. The key is not imitation, or even revival of traditional ways, but rather evolution of self-actualization by the Métis individual. Through increased awareness of his heritage, an understanding of his role in modern Canada will emerge.

The problem facing the Métis community today is how to begin the process of cultural education. Certain conditions have to exist in the environment of those who are to learn. Maslow stated that an individual requires food, shelter, a sense of love, of belonging, of self-esteem, and the opportunity to self-actualize before he will develop the desire, or need, for education. The task of the Métis community is extremely difficult, and the Métis have to develop their own solutions and establish these conditions for themselves and their children. The need for creative thinking by all sectors of the Métis community is essential to the process.

Cultural development as a political strategy is a viable vehicle for change, simply because it is a non-threatening activity to most sectors of the establishment. In fact, multi-cultural policies of the sixties and seventies make funding available for culture-related activities that can have a powerful effect on those who take part. The pitfalls of cultural colonialism and ethnic eccentricity can be avoided by careful development in terms of local organization and participation. But this development must be backed by an increased emphasis on cultural priorities by local, provincial, and national Métis organizations.

MEDIA AND THE ROLE MODEL

Although Howard Adams has decried image improvement and belittles attempts by active leadership to penetrate the CRTC and the CBC, he contradictorily admits the effects of media images on his own life. 'Native people cannot avoid seeing the cultural images and symbols of white supremacy because they are everywhere in society, especially in movies, television, comic books, and textbooks. As these native children grow up, these white supremacist images become more alive, but natives are powerless to do anything about them. Consequently, the children internalize inferior images as part of their true selves, often with strong feelings of shame. As a result, I attempted to disassociate myself from everything and everyone that appeared halfbreed. I wanted to be a successful white man in mainstream society.'

It would be hard to find a better description of the need to develop strong positive Métis models for the Métis people to identify with, and for the proliferation of those models through media of mainstream society. Although many people in the white society take 'image' for granted, or regard it as superficial, that luxury is only available to those who have established their image in the mainstream society. Certainly the emphasis that the Black movement in the United States placed on their 'Black is Beautiful' campaign can hardly be called insignificant or superficial in terms of its penetration into white culture. Métis models do exist, but they are rarely identified specifically as Métis, or emerge only in the traditional or historic sense.

There has been an increasingly wider use of the media by Métis during the past ten years. More and more books, magazines, newspapers, and newsletters are being published by the Métis themselves. In the beginning this material reached only a small number of people and mostly in native communities. Now, however, this is changing. The media generated by natives is penetrating into the majority culture, even into the academic world of the universities. The Métis are becoming aware of the need to develop their understanding of the function of media to produce in whatever medium they choose, rather than be limited by the majority society's prerogatives. Gains are rapidly being made in this regard by various provincial communications groups, such as Alberta Native Communications Society, who have access to North American satellite broadcasting. The most important steps to be taken now are: to achieve access to production in broadcasting; to maintain a unique point of view rather than adopt the white-oriented historical frame of reference; to penetrate professional show business on the entertainment level as well as creating documentary or information-oriented productions. These are all essential elements in the development of Métis consciousness and its role in Canadian society.

RAISING MÉTIS CONSCIOUSNESS

There is an extant, strong, identity base that the Métis can build upon—the legacy of Louis Riel. However, the western Métis image and cultural characteristics that now serve as a bridge to connect the halfbreed on a national scale, must not rely solely on the historic context. It must now develop an awareness of values in a modern context, and of the Métis' contribution—not only in Canadian history—but also in present-day Canadian life. There have been significant gains over the past ten years, but this is only the beginning in terms of what is needed.

An example of a successful consciousness-raising event was the 'Back to Batoche' festivals held in Saskatchewan for the past several years. Federal and provincial governments agreed to fund the event providing it was not used as a political rally. Based on local and provincial co-operation, the 'Back to Batoche' movement had a national impact. Thousands of Métis from all across Canada travelled to Saskatchewan to participate in an event designed mainly to bring Métis people together to enjoy their new-found identity and sense of national purpose. The cynics in the movement dismissed the event as 'cultural imperialism', but only because they neglected to see the importance of the human quality of the experience, and the personal value it had to the individual Métis. The experience had a pronounced effect in the Métis world with implications far beyond the control of any group or government.

The 'Back to Batoche' movement and other events like it could very well be the basis of a more coherent program of cultural awareness and development.

The significance of this kind of event may well escape the understanding of those who, in contrast, think marches, sit-ins, and demonstrations are still effective when dealing with the majority society.

In the early sixties a research study was conducted in the Lesser Slave Lake area to determine the self-image evaluation of native children. In that area at least, Métis children rated themselves eight on a scale of twenty-one. Indians, in fact, rated Métis higher than the Métis rated themselves, but not as low as they were rated by whites—seventeenth. The revival of native awareness would probably change that scale if the test were done today.

However, much still remains to be done. A native, John Cuthand, echoes the thoughts of most leaders today. 'The real issues Riel and Dumont fought for are the issues Métis people are fighting for today.' It is on that basis that the new awareness must develop.

The social status of today's Métis is summed up in a single word—'marginal'. Whether in the bush of Northern Ontario or on road allowances in the prairies, on marginal farmland in B.C., or on the fringes of industrialized areas, the one feature common to all Métis is their 'marginality'. There is a certain irony in the fact that their very marginality or 'forgotten people' status gives them more in common than most other Canadians have with each other.

The Native Council of Canada put it even more bluntly in a paper in 1973. 'We are not speaking of low-income people, we are talking about no-income people.' Métis are likely to be found at the bottom of every social ladder one might name. In terms of schooling, housing, and employment, the Métis are at the bottom. The only lists Métis head are those for infant mortality, school dropouts, occupants of jails, and suicide. Of course there are success stories and exceptions to all of these conditions. But as a people—ethnic or racial—the Métis do not have a proportionate share of the fruits of the so-called just society. Nevertheless the Métis are, in terms of political and self-actualization, in the best condition since the days of Louis Riel. The role of native organizations has proven their value on several levels, creating a sense of racial or ethnic cohesion.

Although the political status of today's Métis has improved considerably, the ethnic status of today's Métis is largely mythical in both the best and worst sense of the word. At its worst, it becomes a catch-all for people with no identity to hang on to and is 'created primarily by common threat from without' and it becomes a kind of 'non-culture' for the Métis themselves. In the best sense it becomes 'non-nation' or 'psychological nation' in David Bell's context and is identifiable in terms of its own communication network, parallel to, but independent of, those of the Inuit, Indian, or White. Since the function of myth-making is to bolster the confidence to act and create a belief that things can be done, myth-making in the Métis context becomes necessary for independent actions.

BASE FOR TOMORROW

The Canadian public is beginning to realize that there is an important distinction between assimilation and integration, and the supposition that native people are, or ever will be, assimilated into Canadian life is totally unrealistic. The government is beginning to discard assimilation features of their native policies in the light of a new awareness of the native reality in Canada. Today there are more persons of native ancestry than ever before. The native population is the fastest-growing racial group, per capita, in Canada in spite of the high infant mortality rate. The fact is that all of the races and ethnic groups in Canada are being integrated into the psychological and geophysical reality that is North America and that THE MÉTIS ARE THE ONLY ETHNIC GROUP INDIGENOUS TO THE CONTINENT. All other races, including Indian and Inuit, came from elsewhere at some other time. Integration is a two-way street and the white majority society is reflecting the native reality more and more specifically as the years go by.

The reality of North America is the architect of the consciousness of its people and, to extend the Jungian concept of mind and earth, let me quote my own thinking in *Red on White*. The pre-Columbian European created a physical and social super-structure for himself that might be described as a labyrinth. When a European child was born, he was introduced to this maze and spent his lifetime searching through the many passages. Within that structure, with rare exceptions, persons were born, lived, and died without ever knowing a sense of freedom, peace, or enlightenment. When the European came to North America, he brought with him his closed super-structure in the name of civilization. Fortunately, it did not fit the gestalt of the North American continent. Here, closed systems do not work, and the European was forced to create both an entrance and an exit to his super-structure.

The North American continent, in its own way, shapes the type of super-structure that it will accept. It has the quality of a self-correctional process almost cybernetic in its function. This is the natural process that is North America, and a process that is natural to its indigenous people, the Métis.

In order for the Métis to assume their proper role in modern Canadian society, a number of factors must be developed simultaneously. First, the aboriginal rights of the Métis must become a reality so that the minimal conditions for learning may be met. Secondly, the Métis must be allowed to be educated and developed in terms of their own inherent cultural characteristics, and finally, once that process becomes a reality, the context must be communicated to the majority society. This means, by and large, access to modern print and electronic media and other means of communication. Then and only then will the full impact of the consciousness of the Métis people be evident in the mosaic of Canadian society. In political terms, the role of the Métis as a founding partner in the Canadian confederacy must be recognized and guaranteed in a new British North America Act, along with the French and English.

Again, to quote briefly from *Red on White*: 'What I have to say is that the modern world of technology, the electronic, tribal total-systems cybernetic society, is the real manifestation of the potential Métis personality. We no longer have to live on the road allowances and margins of North American society. What we have to do is go out into the world and become the manifestation of what the real North American is going to become—the ideal, whole man. We, as Métis, can represent the best possible example of what everyone in North America can eventually become.'

Conclusions

SUMMARY OF MÉTIS PERSPECTIVE

This book demonstrates that, from the Métis point of view, current conceptions of Métis history are totally—albeit inadvertently—misrepresented by most academic historians. Contrary to the implications and assumptions of most writing on the Métis, the Métis see themselves through their oral traditions and myths as:

(1) A race apart from both white and Indians and the only race indigenous to Canada;

(2) Having established a viable—if conceptually invisible to white perception—civilization at least a century before Confederation;

(3) A founding nation equal to the French and the English in the development and growth of Confederation;

(4) A people shamelessly exploited, initially by a minority of political and land-grabbing carpetbaggers, and presently by the majority of Canadians through their indifference to the very real plight of the Métis people;

(5) An ethnic and racial component with great potential for future development and contribution to Canadian life—if the opportunity to unfold that potential is returned to them via aboriginal rights and land claims;

(6) A people capable of building and designing their own future on their own terms within the context of the recognition of their reality so long denied them and as presently focused in the northwest and far north of Canada.

THE REALITY OF THE MÉTIS MYTH

The role of so-called myth in oral and/or linear culture, such as that of the Métis, is of much greater significance in terms of self-identification and self-realization than can be conceived by most western European linear minds. What the Métis think of themselves, in terms of their past, present, and future, is far more real to them than the dictates of conventional history, law, and government policy in a majority society that barely even recognizes the existence of a great, proud, and significant people.

The prophecies of Louis Riel are the song of the Métis soul and they will be sung, if necessary, in the face of the cacophony of international corporations, but preferably in the synchronistic harmony of a pluralistic and truly Canadian reality. The song of the Métis is already being heard by thousands of non-status Indians who are united with the traditional Métis in a participation mystique that is launching a whole new movement in Canada. But before the majority of Canadians can hear the Métis song, much must be done.

The young and old alike must be prepared for education and then educated to the almost forgotten realities of their people. Organizations like ONTARIO MÉTIS AND NON-STATUS INDIAN ASSOCIATION must communicate the reality of the 'myth' in forms more conducive to that communication than history books, or even theses and dissertations. Through poetry, song, film, and drama communicated through all of the media that have such a powerful effect on the quality of awareness we have about our reality, the song of the Métis must be sung.

This is how myth, echoing in the memory of the soul, regenerates the mangled spirit of a nearly defeated people. This is how the consciousness of a people, dominated for a time by the insanity of an invader, comes to resurrection. This is how the Métis myth will become a reality.

THE REALITY OF MÉTIS REALITY

A balance must be achieved. It is evident that the most exotic rhetoric is meaningless in the face of horrible poverty and alienation. There are many, many hard, cold, and only too real problems of housing, education, and land claims to be solved. The recognition of injustice has been accomplished in the last decade. The compensation for that injustice is slowly coming to fruition in this decade. The greatest care and thought must be taken by the

Métis, by government, and by the Canadian people to avoid a repetition of the tragedies of 1869 and 1885—and they could easily be repeated in the closing decades of this century. Above all, the Métis must be recognized as a people who—in the greatness of their race—have the seeds of the solutions to their own problems. They need only the space and light to grow.

This book is dedicated to the day when all Canadians can join the Métis as they say to each other:

'SING YOUR SONG—YOUR CHILDREN ARE STRONG'
'WE ARE MÉTIS'

Maria Campbell b. 1940

MÉTIS

Jacob

Mistupuch he was my granmudder.
He come from Muskeg
dat was before he was a reservation.
My granmudder he was about twenty-eight when he
marry my granfawder.
Dat was real ole for a woman to marry in dem days
But he was an Indian doctor
I guess dats why he wait so long.

Ooh he was a good doctor too
All the peoples dey say dat about him.
He doctor everybody dat come to him
an he birt all dah babies too.
Jus about everybody my age
my granmudder he birt dem.

He marry my granfawder around 1890.
Dat old man he come to him for doctoring
an when he get better
he never leave him again.

Dey get married dah Indian way
an after dat my granfawder
he help him with all hees doctoring.
Dats dah way he use to be a long time ago.
If dah woman he work
den dah man he help him an if dah man he work
dah woman he help.
You never heerd peoples fighting over whose job he was
dey all know what dey got to do to stay alive.

My granfawder his name he was Kannap
but dah whitemans dey call him Jim Boy
so hees Indian name he gets los.
Dats why we don know who his peoples dey are.
We los lots of our relations like dat.
Dey get dah whitemans name
den no body
he knows who his peoples dey are anymore.

Sometimes me
I tink dats dah reason why we have such a hard time
us peoples.
Our roots dey gets broken so many times.
Hees hard to be strong you know
when you don got far to look back for help.

Dah whitemans
he can look back tousands of years
cause him
he write everything down.
But us peoples
we use dah membering
an we pass it on by telling stories an singing songs.
Sometimes we even dance dah membering.

But all dis trouble you know
he start after we get dah new names
cause wit dah new names
he come a new language an a new way of living.
Once a long time ago
I could 'ave told you dah story of my granfawder Kannap
an all his peoples but no more.
All I can tell you now
is about Jim Boy
an hees story hees not very ole.

Well my granmudder Mistupuch
he never gets a whitemans name an him
he knowed lots of stories.
Dat ole lady
he even knowed dah songs.
He always use to tell me
one about an ole man call Jacob.

Dat old man you know
he don live to far from here.
Well hees gone now
but dis story he was about him when he was alive.

Jacob him
he gets one of dem new names when dey put him in dah
residential school.
He was a jus small boy when he go
an he don come home for twelve years.

Twelve years!
Dats a long time to be gone from your peoples.
He can come home you know
cause dah school he was damn near two hundred miles
away.
His Mommy and Daddy dey can go and see him
cause deres no roads in dem days
an dah Indians dey don gots many horses
'specially to travel dat far.

Dats true you know
not many peoples in dem days dey have horses.
Its only in dah comic books an dah picture shows dey
gots lots of horses.
He was never like dat in dah real life.

Well Jacob him
he stay in dat school all dem years an when he come
home he was a man.
While he was gone
his Mommy and Daddy dey die so he gots nobody.
An on top of dat
nobody he knowed him cause he gots a new name.
My granmudder
he say dat ole man he have a hell of time.
No body he can understand dat
unless he happen to him.

Dem peoples dat go away to dem schools
an come back you know dey really suffer.
No matter how many stories we tell
we'll never be able to tell
what dem schools dey done to dah peoples
an all dere relations.

Well anyways
Jacob he was jus plain pitiful
He can talk his own language
he don know how to live in dah bush.
Its a good ting da peoples dey was kine
cause dey help him dah very bes dey can.
Well a couple of summers later
he meet dis girl
an dey gets married.

Dat girl he was kine
an real smart too.
He teach Jacob how to make an Indian living.
Dey have a good life togedder an after a few years
dey have a boy.
Not long after dat
dey raise two little girls dat was orphans.

Jacob and his wife dey was good peoples
Boat of dem dey was hard working
an all dah peoples
dey respec dem an dey come to Jacob for advice.

But dah good times dey was too good to las
cause one day
dah Preeses
dey comes to dah village with dah policemans.
Dey come to take dah kids to dah school.

When dey get to Jacob hees house
he tell dem dey can take his kids.
Dah Prees he tell him
he have to lets dem go cause dats the law.
Well dah Prees
he have a big book
an dat book he gots dah names
of all dah kids
an who dey belongs to.

He open dat book an ask Jacob for his name
an den he look it up.
'Jacob' he say
'you know better you went to dah school an you know
dah edjication hees important.'

My granmudder Mistupuch
he say Jacob he tell that Prees
'Yes I go to dah school
an dats why I don wan my kids to go.
All dere is in dat place is suffering.'

Dah Prees he wasn happy about dat
an he say to Jacob
'But the peoples dey have to suffer Jacob
cause dah Jesus he suffer.'

'But dah Jesus he never lose his language an
hees peoples' Jacob tell him.
'He stay home in hees own land an he do hees
suffering.'

Well da Prees him
he gets mad
an he tell him its a sin to tink like dat
an hees gonna end up in purgatory for dem kind of words.

But Jacob he don care
cause far as hees concern
purgatory
he can be worse den the hell he live with trying to
learn hees language an hees Indian ways.

He tell dat Prees
he don even know who his people dey are.
'Dah Jesus he knowed his Mommy and Daddy'
Jacob he tell him
'and he always knowed who his people dey are.'

Well
dah Prees he tell him
if he wans to know who hees peoples dey are
he can tell him dat
an he open in dah book again.

'Your Dad hees Indian name he was Awchak'
dah Prees he say
'I tink dat means Star in your language.
He never gets a new name cause he never become a
Christian.'

Jacob he tell my granmudder
dat when da Prees he say hees Dad hees name
his wife he start to cry real hard.

'Jacob someday you'll tank the God we done dis.'
dah Prees he tell him
an dey start loading up dah kids on dah big wagons.
All dah kids dey was crying an screaming
An dah mudders
dey was chasing dah wagons.

Dah ole womans
dey was all singing dah det song
an none of the mans
dey can do anyting.
Dey can
cause the policemans dey gots guns.

When dah wagons dey was all gone
Jacob he look for hees wife but he can find him no
place.
An ole woman he see him an he call to him
'Pay api noosim'
'Come an sit down my granchild I mus talk to you.
Hees hard for me to tell you dis but dat Prees
hees book he bring us bad news today.
He tell you dat Awchak he was your Daddy.
My granchild
Awchak he was your wife's Daddy too.'

Jacob he tell my granmudder
he can cry when he hear dat.
He can even hurt inside.
Dat night he go looking
an he fine hees wife in dah bush
Dat woman he kill hisself.

Jacob he say
dah ole womans
dey stay wit him for a long time
an dey sing healing songs an dey try to help him
But he say he can feel nutting.
Maybe if he did
he would have done dah same ting.

For many years Jacob he was like dat
just dead inside.
Dah peoples dey try to talk wit him
but it was no use.
Hees kids dey growed up
an dey come home an live wit him.
'I made dem suffer' he tell my granmudder.
'Dem kids dey try so hard to help me.'

Den one day
his daughter he get married an he have a baby.

He bring it to Jacob to see.
Jacob he say
he look at dat lil baby
an he start to cry and he can stop.
He say he cry for himself an his wife
an den he cry for his Mommy and Daddy.
When he was done
he sing dah healing songs dah ole womans
dey sing to him a long time ago.

Well you know
Jacob he die when he was an ole ole man.
An all hees life
he write in a big book
dah Indian names of all dah Mommies an Daddies.
An beside dem
he write dah old names and
dah new names of all dere kids.

An for dah res of hees life
he fight dah government to build schools on the
reservation.
'The good God he wouldn of make babies come
from Mommies and Daddies'
he use to say
'if he didn want dem to stay home
an learn dere language
an dere Indian ways.'

You know
dat ole man was right.
No body he can do dat.
Take all dah babies away. Hees jus not right.
Long time ago
dah old peoples dey use to do dah naming
an dey do dah teaching too.

If dah parents dey have troubles
den dah aunties and dah uncles
or somebody in dah family
he help out till dah parents dey gets dere life work
out.
But no one
no one
he ever take dah babies away from dere peoples.

You know my ole granmudder
Mistupuch
he have lots of stories about people like Jacob.
Good ole peoples
dat work hard so tings will be better for us.
We should never forget dem ole peoples.

Joseph's Justice

You know dah big fight at Batoche?
Dah one where we fight dah Anglais?
Well dat one.
Dis story he happen den
an dah name of dah man is Joseph.
He was a Halfbreed guy
An he don take part in dat war.

Dere was lots of mans like dat in dem days.
Dey wasen't scare of dah Anglais
or dah government.
Oh no!
Dey jus wasen interest in fighting for land
or edjication
cause dey don believe dat Anglais government
hees gonna give dem anyting.
So
dey jus mine dere own business.

Deres lots of peoples like dat
even today.
Dey jus like to stick to demselves dats all.

Well shore
some of dem dey was cowards
an udder ones dey was jus plain lazy.
But most of dem
dey jus got no believing dats all.
Dis Joseph
he was one of dem dat don believe.
He was jus minding hees own business
trapping an working for hees ownself
while dah udder mans dey was fighting dah war.

An den dah war he was over
an our peoples dey lose.

Dah Anglais General he take Louis
an dah udder mans to Regina
where hees gonna put dem in dah jail so dey can go to
dah court.
Of course he never got all of dem
jus Louis
cause Louis him
he give hees self up.
Dah udder ones
dey was capture but not Gabriel dough.
Oh no!
Him an Michel Dumas
dey run away to dah States an hide.
Ooh Gabe him
he die before he give hisself up.
Dats dah kine of man he was.

Louis him
he was differen.
Differen from Gabe an all dah udders.
I guess you can say he was a spirit man.
He give hisself to dah peoples
an he do dat when he was a small boy.
Hees Daddy you know
he was dat kine of man too.
He put dah peoples before hees family even.
Dere's not many mans you know
dere born like dat.

Yeah dat Louis
he give us anudder kine of membering.
But not Gabe.
Hoo
he was a wile tough man him.
He was dah kine of man he can make you believe you
can do anyting on dis eart
long as you was tough enough to stay on your feet.

But you know dis Joseph
dah one I'm telling dah story about?
He was jus ordinary.
Ordinary Halfbreed like us.
Not dah kine of mans anyone he tell stories about.

Well dere he was him
minding hees own business
when dah General he win dah war an he comes riding by
wit hees Halfbreed prisoners.

Joseph he say he was walking home wit hees gun an
hees beaver pelts
when dah soldiers dey see him.
He say dey was making a hell of a racket.
Celebrating I guess
cause dey win dah war.
Dey damn near scare him to det he say.
Well dem soldiers
soon as dey see him
dey grab him an dey haul him to dah General

Well my ole uncle
hees name he was Alcid
hees dah one who tell me dis story.
He say dat Anglais General
he was riding a big white horse dat dance all dah time.
An dat horse
he was dancing all over when dah soldiers dey bring
Joseph to him.
An dem soldiers
dey trowed Joseph right in front of dat dancing
horse.
Well Joseph he tell my Uncle
he jump up as fas as he can.
He don wan to get step on.

An den
dat horse he start bucking an he buck dat General
right off.
I guess dat Anglais horse
he never smell a Halfbreed trapper before.

When dat General he finely get dat horse to settle
down
he tell Joseph
'Batoche he fall an your leader
Louis Riel he surrender.
Him an all dese mans dere under arres. An you my good
man, your under arres too.'

'If I'm a good man' Joseph he say to him
'den what for you arres me?'
Dah General he don like dat very much an he say
'Dah charge hees high treason.'

Joseph him
he don know what dat word treason he mean
But he say
it sound awful dangerous
so he talk real careful
jus in case hees got someting to do wit shooting.
Dem soldiers you know
dey got guns an he say
dey look like dey wan to use dem.
Joseph you know
him he don trus dah Anglais.
He never trus dem in hees whole life.

Well dah General he yell at dah soldiers to put
Joseph in dah wagon wit dah udders mans.
So dah soldiers dey put chains on him
an dey trowed him in dah wagon.
Joseph he say
dah Halfbreeds an dah Indians dey was all chained togedder.
Some of dem
dey was on dah wagons an some of dem dey was walking.
He say he look for Louis
but he can see him no wheres.

Maybe he was in a cover wagon
cause he was dah leader
an dey don wan nobody to see him or talk to him.
But Joseph
he say he knowed dah udder mans.
Dere was ole Parenteau
he was wearing chains like an outlaw.
Dat ole man he can hurt nobody hees over eighty
years ole.
An dere was dah Vandal boys
an one of dah Arcands.
Even hees brudder-ing-law Moise Touronde he was
dere.

Boy he say
dey look rough.

He was raining and real cole and all dey was wearing
was raggy ole clothes.
Some of dem dey don even got no shoes.
An lots of dem dey was wounded
an all of dem
dey was real hungry.

Well Joseph him
he tink he better try an say someting
cause dis whole damn ting
hees starting to look pretty damn scary.
An him
he wan dem to know he wasen mix up in it.

Well he try talking to dem soldiers but dey don even
listen to him.
So he start hollering an yelling
but hees brudder-ing-law Moise
he tell him to shut up
cause nobody he gives a damn if hees guilty or not
anyways.

Well
it took dem a long time to get to Regina
an when dey get dere
dey was trowed in dah jail.
Joseph him
he was dere for six monts before he come up for trial.
An when he do
he tell dah Judge what he happen to him
an dat Judge he believe on him an he let him go.

But Joseph him
he want hees gun an hees furs back
So he ask for dem.
He say dah Judge an all dah government peoples
dey jus laugh at him
an dey tell him
he should be grateful he don get hanged or go to
Stony Mountain Jail.

Well he leave dere
an he go to dah policemans.
Dey tell him he should jus forget about it an get
dah hell home as fas as he can

But dat Joseph you know
he was a real hard headed mans
not dah kine dat give up jus like dat.
He tell dem policemans
dat if it was him dat steal from dah General
he would of got charge.
An him
he never even done nutting
an hees dah one dat gets treated like a crimnal.

Finely
my ole Uncle he say
one of dah policemans he gets tired of him
an he say
'Okey Joseph. You can press charges. But me I
shore hope you know what your doing cause dis is
gonna be one hell of a mess before hees over.'

Well
it took a long time before dey go to dah court.
An when he gets dere
Joseph he meet dis lawyer
an dis lawyer
he ask him what hees doing dere.
When Joseph he tell him
dat lawyer he laugh like hell an he tell Joseph
he'll help him.
Dat lawyer he was an Irishman
an dem Irish you know
dey don like dah Anglais eeder.

My ole Uncle Alcid
he say
dem Irish
dey was dah only ones dat really try to help us in dem days.
I guess dats because dah Anglais dey take all dere lan to.

Well
Joseph he lose in dah court in Regina but he knowed
he wouldn win dere
cause Regina
he was an Anglais town.
So him an dat lawyer
dey take it to dah high court.
Again he took a long time

but finely he heered.
Dat General
he was foun guilty for stealing.

You know dey say everybody he steal in dah war time.
But hees agains dah law you know.
Dats true.
Dah soldiers dere suppose to honor cause dey belongs
to dah Queen
Well at Batoche
dem soldiers
dey eeder don know dat or dey gots no respec for dere Queen
cause all of dem dey steal.
Not jus from Joseph eeder
dey steal from all dah peoples.

Dah Halfbreeds
dey wasen rich you know
dey jus gots a few little nice tings.
When dem soldiers come
dey chase dah peoples away
an dey go into dah howses
an dey clean dem out.
Dey even burn some of dah howses to dah groun.
Dey do dat to Gabe hees house you know.
Burn it to dah groun.
To damn bad nobody else he press charges agains dem.

Well Joseph him
he won hees case an dah General he don look so good.
But Joseph
he don get no compansation from no one.
He never even get hees gun back.
Well he really get mad den.
Whats dah damn use of winning if you don get your
stuff back?
He don care if dah General he look good or bad
all he want
is hees gun an hees furs back.

Well he don know what hees gonna do now
cause dat General he leave our country not long after
dah court.
He go back to hees own country in Angleterre.
Dere dah Queen he make him a gentlemans

You know dah kine dat wear dah armor.
An dah Queen he even put him in charge of all hees
jools.

Dat General
he become a hell of a hero for putting down dah
Breeds at Batoche.
Fars I'm concern
he don have much to brag about.
Five tousan of dem an less den a hundred of us.

Oh I know dah history books dey say we was two
hundred an fifty.
But you gotta member
dey write dah history books.
My ole Uncle Alcid
he was dere
an he say dere was less den a hundred at Batoche.
An mos of dem
dey was ole mans.

Well never mine about dat
cause Joseph him
he don care anyways.
All he want is hees gun an hees furs.
He go to dah court again
Dis time hees dah high court in Angleterre
an over dere he gets in dah newspaper an dem Anglais
dey write all about it.
Dat really help him you know.
But dats shore funny how he is.
Dey like dah Breeds over dere
but dey hate dem here.
Me I jus never can figure out dem Anglais.

Well dat Irish lawyer he win dah case for Joseph.
An in dah court
he make a hell of a fool out of dah General
at lees
dats what all dah ole mans dey say.

Jimmy Isbister
he use to say dat too
cause he read dah newspapers dat come from over
dere.

Dat Jimmy you know
he was well edjicated.
He was one of dah mans dat go wit Gabe to Montana to
get Louis.
He was a smart man dat Jimmy
he understan dah Anglais.
He was a Scotch Halfbreed
an hees Daddy
he sen him to Angleterre to get hees edjication.

Me I always like dah story about Joseph.
Cause you know
maybe we lose dah war
but one man he win
Cause him he believe on hisself
an he don give up.
Dat kine of man hees real important.
Jus as important as Louis an Gabe
cause hees story
he tell you a little bit about how our peoples dey
was like in dem days.

Tanks for listening to me.

Richard G. Green b. 1940

MOHAWK

The Last Raven

Looking at Dan and Nola Goupil, you'd never guess they're married. Not that they're unworthy but she's at least two heads taller which makes you wonder how they make out physically. They subtly administer the word of God each week, while we sit in a circle trying to overcome hardness from the high-backed wooden chairs. This circle is part of a continuing plot to get us closer to God, nature, and each other by moulding us into a team of young-adult Christians. Truth is, Sunday school attendance is mandatory to play on the hockey team, which is why I'm here.

When I adjust my tie clasp, my elbow presses against the flesh of a bare-armed girl sitting beside me. She brushes at the spot as if removing bacteria, folds her hands with kindergarten precision, and places them in her lap. She knows I'm Mohawk and I know that's why she brushed off her arm. Girls outnumber boys two-to-one in this class, and none of them drives you mad with desire.

'Well, Mr Silverheels,' Nola says, her voice one octave above a whisper in true Christian fashion. 'What do you think the meaning of Christ's action toward the penitent woman at the home of Simon the Pharisee was?' Hanging *Mr* and *Miss* to surnames is supposed to elevate us to adult status, though we're expected to call Dan and Nola by their given names. When the Goupils first arrived, I labelled this a get-acquainted trick, but I accept their eccentricities, though it's weird not being called Jim.

'What?' I say. 'I . . . I don't think I heard the question.' I glance toward Bill Shostrom, as he flashes a devilish smile. He slouches in his chair, the lapels of his blue suit flex into a diamond shape exposing the too short length of his polka-dotted tie. His punk hair is greasy with hair-goo, and a glimmer from the ceiling lamp reflects off his forehead. If you believe opposites attract, then you know why we're chums.

Tracking down the direction of my eyes, Nola says: 'Now don't you tell him the answer, Mr Shostrom.' The class laughs. She turns to the fat girl beside me, who's impatiently waving an arm.

'Yes, Miss Breen.'

Miss Breen leaps to her feet. 'I think it's a story to remind us that even though we're constantly submerged in sin,' she says, confidence rampant in her tone, 'Christ loves those who love.' Satisfied with her brief moment of superiority, she directs a smirk toward me as she plops her oversized buttocks back into the chair.

'I disagree,' I say. I'm not sure why this blurted out, but now I'm committed to explanation. I feel tension in the wily shifting of everybody's eyes.

Dan Goupil glares at me, and a nervous hush settles over the room. He never enters class discussion, but I can see he's interpreted my remark as an attack on his wife. He removes a handkerchief, holds his plastic-rimmed glasses toward the ceiling light, and huffs on the lenses. Wiping them with a fluid motion he says quietly, 'Exactly what do you disagree with, Mr Silverheels?' A smile curls his thin lips as he scans the class. 'Surely you don't challenge the love of Jesus, eh?'

'No, sir,' I say.

'Well I'm glad to hear that.' The class translates his actions, and, suddenly, I'm in a sea of snickering faces. 'Well then, Mr Silverheels.' He puts on his glasses. '*What* do you disagree with?'

'It's just that . . . well, I uh, I don't think the love of Jesus is in question here. That's the constant theme of the New Testament and is indicated in many previous occasions. I think that, by forgiving this woman of all her sins, Christ is directing a lesson of humility toward Simon.'

'Humility?'

'Yes. He's raised Mary Magdalen to a level of respectability above that of His host. He's used her to show Simon that her example of love makes her superior.'

'You think Christ would *use* somebody for His own gain?'

'In this case, yes.'

All eyes rest upon Dan. It's plain that emphasis has shifted from correct and incorrect and is now a question of vanity. To these people, Christ is their saviour; to me, He's a prophet. I realize Dan's next statement decides the outcome. He glances at his wristwatch, and I'm reminded that it's almost time for dismissal. Perhaps I'll be saved by the bell.

Nola raises her eyes above an opened Bible. 'Mr Silverheels?' she asks. 'What do you think Christ means when He says, "Therefore I tell you her sins, which are many, are forgiven for she loved much; but he who is forgiven little, loves little."'

Dan brushes dandruff specks from his lapel. Simultaneously, shuffling feet and voices penetrate from the corridor outside. Looking at me, Dan says, 'I think you've misconstrued the point of today's lesson . . . '

'Dan,' Nola smiles. 'I think you're *both* right.' Everybody closes their Bible, with a thump. 'Now, class,' Nola continues. 'Before you all run off, don't forget our house-party this afternoon. We expect to have a lot of fun, and I pray none of you will miss it.'

I stand and file toward the door, a feeling of betrayal welling up inside me. If the objective of this class is participation, why haven't I been shown any mercy? Passing Dan in the doorway, I smile meekly. He squeezes my shoulder and says, 'See you this afternoon.' But I'm unable to answer.

On our way home, Bill and me and a skinny kid named Hartmann always stop at Gimpy's Diner. Our arrangement is we keep Gimpy's shovelled in winter and he lets us in on Sundays to play a pinball machine everybody calls 'The Chief'. Light the 975,000 point-feather, and with Gimpy's verification you get a dollar from the 'Picnic Fund' jar. In three years of play, I've won twice.

'Are you going to the Goupils' this afternoon, Jim?' Hartmann stares at my reflection in the machine's glass panel.

'Not in a million years.'

'What about you, Bill?'

'I dunno. I've got a lot of homework to do.'

Hartmann looks back at me. 'What are you going to do?'

'I don't know,' I say, tearing open my collection envelope.

'Hey,' Bill says, 'Your parents are supposed to take mine to a lacrosse game, eh? You're not going with them, are you?'

'No,' I say. 'The Warriors are in last place, and they'll probably lose again. I'll probably stay home and terrorize my sister.'

'Get out of the way, amateurs.' Bill squeezes between Hartmann and me. 'Make way for the pro.'

'Speaking of girls,' Hartmann says, 'maybe I'll go to the Goupils' party. Linda'll probably be there.'

'Nola's kid sister?'

'Yeah.'

Inserting a quarter into the slot, Bill says, 'Don't tell me you're in love with Linda Switzer?' He pushes the coin-return button with the heel of his hand and takes out a jackknife. 'Hey Gimpy,' he works the blade into the slot. 'This damn thing's jammed again!'

'I wouldn't say I was in *love* with her,' Hartmann says.

Gimpy walks over, scratches his belly, and pounds on the machine. To Bill, he says, 'I don't know why you're the one who always screws up this machine.'

'Because he's just a big *screw*-up,' I say, overcome with cleverness.

'When they get older, you gotta prime 'em a bit.' Gimpy kicks the machine and the coin clinks inside. Lights flash. Bells clang. The caricature of an Indian in Sioux headdress swings his tomahawk and dances backward into starting position. 'There. What did I tell ya, eh?' Gimpy winks and limps back to his cleaning chores.

'I wouldn't say I was in love with her,' Hartmann repeats. 'But if you guys aren't going to be doing anything,' he cracks a knuckle, 'then I'm going to the Goupils' party.'

Bill launches his first ball. 'Who says we're not going to be doing anything?' He pushes a flipper button, and a wave of satisfaction sweeps his face. 'We're going to be shooting drunken crows this afternoon.'

According to Bill's latest plan, after our parents leave for the lacrosse game, we're going to take our fathers' shotguns on a hunting trip. Bill says the radio reported that a flock of crows has been gathering on the edge of town menacing people for several days. Because of something called jurisdictional ingress and egress over the woods they're in, nobody can do anything about removing them.

'We're going to be big heroes, eh?' Bill says, as we leave Gimpy's. 'We're going to do our duty and eliminate those hazardous crows. Meet you at the bridge at two o'clock.'

When my parents leave the house, my older sister curls up on the sofa and flashes her beady eyes. '*Sehksatiyohake Senta: whah*,' she says in Mohawk. She does this to aggravate me. We left the reserve when I was three, and my family seldom speaks Mohawk here in Brantford. Sometimes, when the house is full of visitors, she gets everybody going and there's always a point where they all look at me and laugh. But she can't fool me. She wants me out of the house this afternoon, so she can cuddle with her boyfriend. She's hovering around me like a fruit fly on a puckered apple, and it's impossible to get the shotgun from my parents' closet. To avoid suspicion, I put on my new maroon windbreaker and depart for the woods in street shoes.

I'm first to arrive. I sit on my favourite girder at the railroad bridge listening to creek water gurgle far below. To the west, a band of nimbus gathers on the horizon, promising rain. Bill and Hartmann laugh while they goose-step the railroad ties, gleaming shotgun barrels propped between body and forearm. Bill wears a red plaid jacket and a ludicrous straw hat, whose front brim is folded flat; 'BILL' is inscribed there in red paint. Two ragged pheasant feathers jut from a hatband, denoting hunting prowess. Hartmann's olive jacket has 'SMITH' in stencil letters above his left breast pocket. They both notice I don't have a shotgun, but say nothing.

I step atop a gleaming rail and gingerly keep their pace, my shoes making a tap-dancer sound. We hike down the straight tracks, grateful that railroads always take the shortest, most private routes. I've never seen more than two crows in the same place at one time and believe Bill's story to be false. We turn and cross a field, their heavy boots clearing a path for me through chest-high thistles.

We march toward a stand of hemlock when Bill signals a halt. From an opening beyond us, I hear a confused hum of shufflings and scattered caws. Perched amid saplings and clusters of lobe-leafed bushes, crows occupy the centre of a U-shaped clearing. Bill and me are going to circle, leaving Hartmann stationed at the opening to block any escape attempts. To the northwest, the woods thicken, and, when we reach our position, the crows are between us and a barrier of trees.

Bill hands me a yellow box of shells and we begin. Each squawk, each shriek intensifies, and it's plain we've been detected. It's so noisy I'm forced to cover an ear.

A sea of bobbing heads covers the ground like a rippling stadium tarpaulin. Branches bend in smooth arcs to accommodate squawking occupants. The crows compete for tiny red berries; they rape the bushes and peck each other in rages of greed. One bird leaps from his branch, frantically beats his wings, and flutters to the ground. These birds aren't drunk as Bill reported; most are too bloated to fly. Smaller crows retreat to the woods beyond, but the majority continue their indulgence in spite of our presence.

Bill inserts two shells into his double-barrelled shotgun and closes it with a snap. Signalling Hartmann, he drops to one knee, cocks the hammer, and aims into a crowded sapling. I've been instructed to pass two shells into his palm and stand clear when spent casings are rejected. One hundred metres away, Hartmann slams the breech of his gun closed and raises its barrel in readiness. It's clear we've entered a world not intended for humans.

Bill's first blast shatters the air; my eardrums ring in response. Again he cocks, sights, and squeezes the trigger. *Boom!* He breaks the gun, and two casings spiral to the ground; a stench of sulphur bites my nostrils. 'Shells!' he yells. I slap two cylinders into his open palm, like an intern assisting at surgery. An unexpected blast from Hartmann's direction makes me flinch. Bill smiles.

Fluttering and squawking, the crows are in chaos. Their numbers work against them; wings become entangled, foiling attempts to fly. Where Bill has fired into loaded branches, twin holes poke through the blackness. Leaning forward, he aims at the base of a crowded bush. *Boom!* His body jerks up with the recoil of the gun. In its panic, one crow hovers above us. It flaps its wings to escape, but Bill blows it into an inkblot of swirling feathers. 'Shells!' Bill shouts, waving away down-fluff. I barely hear him through the liquid hum in my ears.

Some of the crows fall to the ground, others scurry through the grass toward Hartmann. Some flap their wings, crane their necks, and scold, but remain imprisoned in their branches. Hartmann concentrates his blasts on those who manage flight, his left arm pumping with mechanical precision. Bill can hit three crows with one barrage. It's evident from his cursing that he considers it a miss if only one falls. Hartmann lowers his weapon at the black army advancing toward him. His first explosion pours through their ranks like a splash of soapy water on a ship-deck, lifting and transporting those in its wake.

Drops of rain hiss against Bill's hot gun barrel, but he continues his shooting oblivious of weather conditions. 'Shells!' he yells, blowing at smoke billowing from the breech.

A thunderclap booms across the terrain. The OPP must be on their way. 'It's starting to rain!' I shout, relieved at the possibility of leaving.

'Good,' Bill says. 'It'll muffle our shots.' I hear the clink of shell casings dropping into a pile at my feet. 'Come on, we've got to chase them toward Hartmann!' We advance, Bill firing once every three strides. It's like walking through a ploughed field, clods of black bodies occasionally squishing under our feet, the sensation plastic and awkward.

A crow deliriously wanders about the ground, dragging a broken wing. I stoop, hypnotized by its misery. It trips and falls forward on its side, desperately clawing at the earth for traction. I reach to help, but it pops its smooth head between twisted wing feathers into a contorted position of defence. Eyes shrivelling with betrayal, it arches its neck to peck my hand. Instead, its eyelids squeeze shut, muscles relax, and it rolls over on its back. An eyelid pops open and an empty black sphere gazes at me. I scoop up cartridges from the shell box. I drop them into my pocket, and tear the cardboard into a sheet.

Covering the crow's body, I marvel at its design, reminded that things intended for a simpler function can be separated so easily from it.

When we rendezvous with Hartmann, a squadron of crows approaches head-on as if in attack formation. They are flying at eye level, their silhouettes barely visible against the backdrop of trees. In his haste to reload, Bill grabs a jammed shell casing and burns his fingertips. 'Damn it,' he winces. 'Quick, Jim, gimmie two more shells!' He loads, waits for Hartmann, and takes aim.

Their first volley flashes with the ferocity of a howitzer; two crows erased in the blink of an eye. Bill's second shot hits its target, too, but the bird's inertia carries it into his chest. Bill pushes it to the ground and squashes it with his boot. Hartmann's second burst is true, and the largest crow, bomber-sized in comparison to the others, dives to the ground. Watching the crows falling like black snowflakes, I'm amazed at Bill's and Hartmann's skill at killing. Two crows peel off in an escape manoeuvre, but Hartmann's capable pump gun sweeps them to obscurity.

'We got 'em, Hartmann! We got every one of them!' Bill pushes his hat back. 'Did you see how beautiful that big one rolled off and dove to the ground? Just like a Snowbird.'

'Guess what, Bill?' Hartmann inspects his remaining ammo. 'I hit that big one with my deer slug. You remember that deer slug I showed you?'

Bill nods. He blows at blue smoke rising from his barrels. 'Hey, Jim.' He slides a shell into the left chamber. 'I want you to hit that crow in the tree over there.' He closes the gun with a snap of authority and offers it to me.

I had hoped that Bill, consumed in his frenzy, would forget about my participation. Yet, like a substitute player sitting on the bench, I've been rehearsing all afternoon. 'I'm not a very good shot,' I say, not really wanting to be heard.

'Take it,' Bill thrusts the weapon into my hands. 'And don't miss.'

I plant my feet, pull back the hammer, and raise the barrel. Raindrops poke at the shoulders of my jacket; one ricochets off the stock and splashes into my eye. I squeeze my eyelid, accept the brief sting, and shake my head. Bill sighs impatiently. Raising the front sight into the crotch of the v, I fix it on the silhouette beyond. My target twists its neck in puppet fashion against the pink colouring of the uncertain sky. I hunch my shoulder, tighten my grip, close my eyes, and pull the trigger. *Boom!*

'You missed!' Bill grabs the gun, breaks it open, blows at the chamber, and inserts one shell. 'You don't sight a shotgun, stupid. You aim it with both eyes open. And don't pull the trigger, squeeze it.' Bill hands me the gun. 'Don't miss this time—this is the last one.'

I wipe my brow, seat the gun butt against my shoulder, and pull the hammer back. I take a deep breath, raise the barrels, and sight according to Bill's advice. Suddenly, the crow kicks away, flaps its wings, and climbs toward the horizon. I follow it and calculate its path. Hatred in the dying crow's eyes nags my mind, but it's erased by my passion for success. Squeezing the trigger, I can almost see the pellet pattern sink into the feathers. 'I got him,' I say, exhaling. Wings spread like sagging semaphores, the crow glides down breast first, bouncing in slow motion as it hits the ground. I feel a surge of triumph. I try to push my face into a smile.

Bill slaps my shoulders. 'Nice shooting,' he says, taking the gun.

Sheets of rain force us into the woods seeking shelter, but sunbeams isolate the clouds and begin melting them. Each imprisoned with our own thoughts, we view black specks dotting the landscape. Blotches of blood coating tree branches, bushes, and grass begin washing away. Divots in the ground smooth their sores. Severed branches remain, permanent scars to today's memory.

When sunlight finally blasts through, we cross the open peninsula toward the tracks, the ground sucking at our feet. Bill ransacks the largest black feathers and adds them to his hatband, his singed fingertips provoking an occasional grimace. In a show of humanity, Hartmann plods across the field, finishing off dying survivors with his gun butt. I pick up a shell casing and blow on its open end, the lonely whistle recalling the dead crow's eye and its echo of emptiness.

Beneath the bridge, I wash mud from my shoes with a gnarled twig. I notice a brown splatter of blood on my pant leg. It's partially dry, and I splash cold creek water on it to prevent a stain. Gusts of wind, already frigid, push at bushes along the bank sending messages of winter to those who are listening. I gaze at Bill and his Medusa-like headdress. A feeling of sardonic ridicule blossoms inside me, but humility pacifies the notion.

Beth Brant (Degonwadonti) b. 1941

MOHAWK

A Long Story

Dedicated to my Great-Grandmothers Eliza Powless and Catherine Brant

'About 40 Indian children took the train at this depot for the Philadelphia Indian School last Friday. They were accompanied by the government agent, and seemed a bright looking lot.'

The Northern Observer
(Massena, New York, July 20, 1892)

'I am only beginning to understand what it means for a mother to lose a child.'

Anna Demeter, *Legal Kidnapping*
(Beacon Press, Boston, 1977)

1890

It has been two days since they came and took the children away. My body is greatly chilled. All our blankets have been used to bring me warmth. The women keep the fire blazing. The men sit. They talk among themselves. We are frightened by this sudden child-stealing. We signed papers, the agent said. This gave them rights to take our babies. It is good for them, the agent said. It will make them civilized, the agent said. I do not know *civilized*.

I hold myself tight in fear of flying apart in the air. The others try to feed me. Can they feed a dead woman? I have stopped talking. When my mouth opens, only air escapes. I have used up my sound screaming their names— She Sees Deer! He Catches The Leaves! My eyes stare at the room, the walls of scrubbed wood, the floor of dirt. I know there are people here, but I cannot see them. I see a darkness, like the lake at New Moon. Black, unmoving. In the centre, a picture of my son and daughter being lifted onto the train. My daughter wearing the dark blue, heavy dress. All of the girls dress alike. Never have I seen such eyes! They burn into my head even now. My son. His hair cut. Dressed as the white men, his arms and legs covered by cloth that made him sweat. His face, streaked with tears. So many children crying, screaming. The sun on our bodies, our heads. The train screeching like a crow, sounding like laughter. Smoke and dirt pumping out of the insides of the train. So many people. So many children. The women, standing as if in prayer, our hands lifted, reaching. The dust sifting down on our palms. Our palms making motions at the sky. Our fingers closing like the claws of the bear.

I see this now. The hair of my son held in my hands. I rub the strands, the heavy braids coming alive as the fire flares and casts a bright light on the black hair. They slip from my fingers and lie coiled on the ground. I see this. My husband picks up the braids, wraps them in cloth; he takes the pieces of our son away. He walks outside, the eyes of the people on him. I see this. He will find a bottle and drink with the men. Some of the women will join him. They will end the night by singing or crying. It is all the same. I see this. No sounds of children playing games and laughing. Even the dogs have ceased their noise. They lay outside each doorway, waiting. I hear this. The voices of children. They cry. They pray. They call me. *Nisten ha.* I hear this. *Nisten ha.**

1978

I am wakened by the dream. In the dream my daughter is dead. Her father is returning her body to me in pieces. He keeps her heart. I thought I screamed . . . *Patricia!* I sit up in bed, swallowing air as if for nourishment. The dream remains in the air. I rise to go to her room. Ellen tries to lead me back to bed, but I have to see once again. I open her door. She is gone. The room empty, lonely. They said it was in her best interests. How can that be? She is only six, a baby who needs her mothers. She loves us. This has not happened. I will not believe this. Oh god, I think I have died.

Night after night, Ellen holds me as I shake. Our sobs stifling the air in our room. We lie in our bed and try to give comfort. My mind can't think beyond last week when she left. I would have killed him if I'd had the chance! He took her hand and pulled her to the car. The look in his eyes of triumph. It was a contest to him, Patricia the prize. He will teach her to hate us. He will! I see her dear face. That face looking out the back window of his car. Her mouth forming the words *Mommy, Mama.* Her dark braids tied with red yarn. Her front teeth missing. Her overalls with the yellow flower on the pocket, embroidered by Ellen's hands. So lovingly she sewed the yellow wool. Patricia waiting quietly until she was finished. Ellen promised to teach her designs—chain stitch, french knot, split stitch. How Patricia told everyone that Ellen made the flower just for her. So proud of her overalls.

I open the closet door. Almost everything is gone. A few things hang there limp, abandoned. I pull a blue dress from the hanger and take it back to my room. Ellen tries to take it from me, but I hold on, the soft blue cotton smelling of my daughter. How is it possible to feel such pain and live? 'Ellen?!' She croons my name. 'Mary, Mary, I love you.' She sings me to sleep.

1890

The agent was here to deliver a letter. I screamed at him and sent curses his way. I threw dirt in his face as he mounted his horse. He thinks I'm a crazy woman and warns me, 'You better settle down, Annie.' What can they do to

---

me? I am a crazy woman. This letter hurts my hand. It is written in their hateful language. It is evil, but there is a message for me.

I start the walk up the road to my brother. He works for the whites and understands their meanings. I think about my brother as I pull the shawl closer to my body. It is cold now. Soon there will be snow. The corn has been dried and hangs from our cabin, waiting to be used. The corn never changes. My brother is changed. He says that *I* have changed and bring shame to our clan. He says I should accept the fate. But I do not believe in the fate of child-stealing. There is evil here. There is much wrong in our village. My brother says I am a crazy woman because I howl at the sky every evening. He is a fool. I am calling the children. He says the people are becoming afraid of me because I talk to the air and laugh like the raven overhead. But I am talking to the children. They need to hear the sound of me. I laugh to cheer them. They cry for us.

This letter burns my hands. I hurry to my brother. He has taken the sign of the wolf from over the doorway. He pretends to be like those who hate us. He gets more and more like the child-stealers. His eyes move away from mine. He takes the letter from me and begins the reading of it. I am confused. This letter is from two strangers with the names Martha and Daniel. They say they are learning civilized ways. Daniel works in the fields, growing food for the school. Martha cooks and is being taught to sew aprons. She will be going to live with the schoolmaster's wife. She will be a live-in girl. What is a *live-in girl*? I shake my head. The words sound the same to me. I am afraid of Martha and Daniel, these strangers who know my name. My hands and arms are becoming numb.

I tear the letter from my brother's fingers. He stares at me, his eyes traitors in his face. He calls after me, 'Annie! Annie!' That is not my name! I run to the road. That is not my name! There is no Martha! There is no Daniel! This is witch work. The paper burns and burns. At my cabin, I quickly dig a hole in the field. The earth is hard and cold, but I dig with my nails. I dig, my hands feeling weaker. I tear the paper and bury the scraps. As the earth drifts and settles, the names Martha and Daniel are covered. I look to the sky and find nothing but endless blue. My eyes are blinded by the colour. I begin the howling.

1978

When I get home from work, there is a letter from Patricia. I make coffee and wait for Ellen, pacing the rooms of our apartment. My back is sore from the line, bending over and down, screwing the handles on the doors of the flashing cars moving by. My work protects me from questions, the guys making jokes at my expense. But some of them touch my shoulder lightly and briefly as a sign of understanding. The few women, eyes averted or smiling in sympathy. No one talks. There is no time to talk. No room to talk, the noise taking up all space and breath.

I carry the letter with me as I move from room to room. Finally I sit at the kitchen table, turning the paper around in my hands. Patricia's printing is large and uneven. The stamp has been glued on halfheartedly and is coming loose. Each time a letter arrives, I dread it, even as I long to hear from my child. I hear Ellen's key in the door. She walks into the kitchen, bringing the smell of the hospital with her. She comes toward me, her face set in new lines, her uniform crumpled and stained, her brown hair pulled back in an imitation of a french twist. She knows there is a letter. I kiss her and bring mugs of coffee to the table. We look at each other. She reaches for my hand, bringing it to her lips. Her hazel eyes are steady in her round face.

I open the letter. *Dear Mommy. I am fine. Daddy got me a new bike. My big teeth are coming in. We are going to see Grandma for my birthday. Daddy got me new shoes. Love Patricia.* She doesn't ask about Ellen. I imagine her father standing over her, coaxing her, coaching her. The letter becomes ugly. I tear it in bits and scatter them out the window. The wind scoops the pieces into a tight fist before strewing them in the street. A car drives over the paper, shredding it to garbage and mud.

Ellen makes a garbled sound. 'I'll leave. If it will make it better, I'll leave.' I quickly hold her as the dusk moves into the room and covers us. 'Don't leave. Don't leave.' I feel her sturdy back shiver against my hands. She kisses my throat, and her arms tighten as we move closer. 'Ah, Mary, I love you so much.' As the tears threaten our eyes, the taste of salt is on our lips and tongues. We stare into ourselves, touching the place of pain, reaching past the fear, the guilt, the anger, the loneliness.

We go to our room. It is beautiful again. I am seeing it new. The sun is barely there. The colours of cream, brown, green mixing with the wood floor. The rug with its design of wild birds. The black ash basket glowing on the dresser, holding a bouquet of dried flowers bought at a vendor's stand. I remember the old woman, laughing and speaking rapidly in Polish as she wrapped the blossoms in newspaper. Ellen undresses me as I cry. My desire for her breaking through the heartbreak we share. She pulls the covers back, smoothing the white sheets, her hands repeating the gestures done at work. She guides me onto the cool material. I watch her remove the uniform of work. An aide to nurses. A healer of spirit.

She comes to me full in flesh. My hands are taken with the curves and soft roundness of her. She covers me with the beating of her heart. The rhythm steadies me. Heat is centring me. I am grounded by the peace between us. I smile at her face above me, round like a moon, her long hair loose and touching my breasts. I take her breast in my hand, bring it to my mouth, suck her as a woman—in desire, in faith. Our bodies join. Our hair braids together on the pillow. Brown, black, silver, catching the last light of the sun. We kiss, touch, move to our place of power. Her mouth, moving over my body, stopping at curves and swells of skin, kissing, removing pain. Closer, close, together, woven, my legs are heat, the centre of my soul is speaking to her, I am sliding into her, her mouth is medicine, her heart is the earth, we are dancing with flying arms, I shout, I sing, I weep salty liquid, sweet and warm it coats her throat. This is my life. I love you Ellen, I love you Mary, I love, we love.

1891

The moon is full. The air is cold. This cold strikes at my flesh as I remove my clothes and set them on fire in the withered corn field. I cut my hair, the knife sawing through the heavy mass. I bring the sharp blade to my arms, legs, and breasts. The blood trickles like small red rivers down my body. I feel nothing. I throw the tangled webs of my hair into the flames. The smell, like a burning animal, fills my nostrils. As the fire stretches to touch the stars, the people come out to watch me—the crazy woman. The ice in the air touches me.

They caught me as I tried to board the train and search for my babies. The white men tell my husband to watch me. I am dangerous. I laugh and laugh. My husband is good only for tipping bottles and swallowing anger. He looks at me, opening his mouth and making no sound. His eyes are dead. He wanders from the cabin and looks out on the corn. He whispers our names. He calls after the children. He is a dead man.

Where have they taken the children? I ask the question of each one who travels the road past our door. The women come and we talk. We ask and ask. They say there is nothing we can do. The white man is like a ghost. He slips in and out where we cannot see. Even in our dreams he comes to take away our questions. He works magic that resists our medicine. This magic has made us weak. What is the secret about them? Why do they want our children? They sent the Blackrobes many years ago to teach us new magic. It was evil! They lied and tricked us. They spoke of gods who would forgive us if we believed as they do. They brought the rum with the cross. This god is ugly! He killed our masks. He killed our men. He sends the women screaming at the moon in terror. They want our power. They take our children to remove the inside of them. Our power. They steal our food, our sacred rattle, the stories, our names. What is left?

I am a crazy woman. I look to the fire that consumes my hair and see their faces. My daughter. My son. They still cry for me, though the sound grows fainter. The wind picks up their keening and brings it to me. The sound has bored into my brain. I begin howling. At night I dare not sleep. I fear the dreams. It is too terrible, the things that happen there. In my dream there is wind and blood moving as a stream. Red, dark blood in my dream. Rushing for our village. The blood moves faster. There are screams of wounded people. Animals are dead, thrown in the blood stream. There is nothing left. Only the air echoing nothing. Only the earth soaking up blood, spreading it in the four directions, becoming a thing there is no name for. I stand in the field watching the fire. The People watching me. We are waiting, but the answer is not clear yet. A crazy woman. That is what they call me.

1979

After taking a morning off work to see my lawyer, I come home, not caring if I call in. Not caring, for once, at the loss in pay. Not caring. My lawyer says there is nothing more we can do. I must wait. As if there has been something other than waiting. He has custody and calls the shots. We must wait and see how long it takes for him to get tired of being a mommy and a daddy. So, I wait.

I open the door to Patricia's room. Ellen and I keep it dusted and cleaned in case my baby will be allowed to visit us. The yellow and blue walls feel like a mockery. I walk to the windows, begin to systematically tear down the curtains. I slowly start to rip the cloth apart. I enjoy hearing the sounds of destruction. Faster, I tear the material into strips. What won't come apart with my hands, I pull at with my teeth. Looking for more to destroy, I gather the sheets and bedspread in my arms and wildly shred them to pieces. Grunting and sweating, I am pushed by rage and the searing wound in my soul. Like a wolf, caught in a trap, gnawing at her own leg to set herself free, I begin to beat my breasts to deaden the pain inside. A noise gathers in my throat and finds the way out. I begin a scream that turns to howling, then becomes hoarse choking. I want to take my fists, my strong fists, my brown fists, and smash the world until it bleeds. Bleeds! And all the judges in their flapping robes, and the fathers who look for revenge, are ground, ground into dust and disappear with the wind.

The word *lesbian*. Lesbian. The word that makes them panic, makes them afraid, makes them destroy children. The word that dares them. Lesbian. *I am one*. Even for Patricia, even for her, *I will not cease to be!* As I kneel amidst the colourful scraps, Raggedy Anns smiling up at me, my chest gives a sigh. My heart slows to its normal speech. I feel the blood pumping outward to my veins, carrying nourishment and life. I strip the room naked. I close the door.

Thanks so much to Chrystos for the title. Thanks to Gloria Anzaldúa for encouraging the writing of this story.

Swimming Upstream

Anna May spent the first night in a motel off Highway 8. She arrived about ten, exhausted from her long drive—through farmland, bright autumn leaves, the glimpse of blue lake. She saw none of this, only the grey highway stretching out before her. She stopped when the motel sign appeared, feeling the need for rest, it didn't matter where.

She took a shower, lay in bed, and fell asleep, the dream beginning again almost immediately. Her son—drowning in the water, his skinny arms flailing the waves, his mouth opening to scream with no sound coming forth. She, Anna May, moving in slow motion into the waves, her hands grabbing for the boy but feeling only water run through her fingers. She grabbed frantically, but nothing held to her hands. She dove and opened her eyes under water and saw nothing. He was gone. Her hands connected with sand, with seaweed, but not her son. He was gone. Simon was gone.

Anna May woke. The dream was not a nightmare anymore. It had become a companion to her, a friend, almost a lover—reaching for her as she slept, making pictures of her son, keeping him alive while recording his death. In the first days after Simon left her, the dream made her wake screaming, sobbing, arms hitting at the air, legs kicking the sheets, becoming tangled in the material. Her bed was a straitjacket, pinning her down, holding her until the dream ended. She would fight the dream then. Now, she welcomed it.

During the day she had other memories of Simon. His birth, his first pair of shoes, his first steps, his first word—*Mama*—his first book, his first day of school. His firsts were also his lasts, so she invented a future for him during her waking hours: his first skating lessons, his first hockey game, his first reading aloud from a book, his first. . . . But she couldn't invent beyond that. His six-year-old face and body wouldn't change in her mind. She couldn't invent what she couldn't imagine.

She hadn't been there when Simon drowned. Simon had been given to her ex-husband by the courts. She was judged unfit. Because she lived with a woman. Because a woman, Catherine, slept beside her. Because she had a history of alcoholism. The history was old. Anna May had stopped drinking when she became pregnant with Simon, and she had stayed dry all those years. She couldn't imagine what alcohol tasted like after Simon was born. He was so lovely, so new. Her desire for a drink evaporated every time Simon took hold of her finger, or nursed from her breast, or opened his mouth in a toothless smile. She had marvelled at his being—this gift that had emerged from her own body. This beautiful being who had formed himself inside her, had come with speed through the birth canal to welcome life outside her. His face red with anticipation, his black hair sticking straight up as if electric with hope, his little fists, grabbing, his pink mouth finding her nipple and holding on for dear life. She had no need for alcohol. There was Simon.

Simon was taken away from them. But they saw him on weekends, Tony delivering him on a Friday night, Catherine discreetly finding someplace else to be when Tony's car drove up. They still saw Simon, grateful for the two days out of the week they could play with him, they could delight in him, they could pretend with him. They still saw Simon, until the call that changed all that. The call from Tony saying that Simon had drowned when he fell out of the boat as they were fishing. Tony sobbing, 'I'm sorry. I didn't mean for this to happen. I tried to save him. I'm sorry. Please, Anna, please forgive me. Oh God, Anna. I'm sorry. I'm sorry.'

So Anna May dreamed of those final moments of a six-year-old life. And it stunned her that she wasn't there to see him die when she had been there to see him come into life.

Anna May stayed dry, but she found herself glancing into the cupboards at odd times. Looking for something. Looking for something to drink. She thought of ways to buy wine and hide it so she could take a drink when she needed it. But there was Catherine. Catherine would know, and Catherine's face, already so lined and tired and old, would become more so. Anna May saw her own face in the mirror. Her black hair had streaks of grey and white she hadn't noticed before. Her forehead had deep lines carved into the flesh, and her eyes, her eyes that had cried so many tears, were a faded and washed-out blue. Her mouth was wrinkled, the lips parched and chapped. She and Catherine, aged and ghostlike figures walking through a dead house.

Anna May thought about the bottle of wine. It took on large proportions in her mind. A bottle of wine, just one, that she could drink from and never empty. A bottle of wine, the sweet, red kind that would take away the dryness, the withered insides of her. She went to meetings but never spoke, only saying her name and 'I'll pass tonight.' Catherine wanted to talk, but Anna May had nothing to say to this woman she loved. She thought about the bottle of wine: the bottle, the red liquid inside, the sweet taste gathering in her mouth, moving down her throat, hitting her bloodstream, warming her inside, killing the deadness.

She arranged time off work and told Catherine she was going away for a few days. She needed to think, to be alone. Catherine watched her face, the framing of the words out of her mouth, her exhausted eyes. Catherine said, 'I understand.'

'Will you be alright?' Anna May asked her.

'Yes, I'll be fine. I'll see friends. We haven't spent time with them in so long, they are concerned about us. I'll be waiting for you. I love you so much.'

Anna May got in the car and drove up 401, up 19, over to 8 and the motel, the shower, the dream.

Anna May smoked her cigarettes and drank coffee until daylight. She made her plans to buy the bottle of wine. After that, she had no plans, other than the first drink and how it would taste and feel.

She found a meeting in Goderich and sat there, ashamed and angered with herself to sit in a meeting and listen to the stories and plan her backslide. She thought of speaking, of talking about Simon, about the bottle of wine, but she knew someone would stop her or say something that would make her stop. Anna May did not want to be stopped. She wanted to drink and drink and drink until it was all over. *My name is Anna May and I'll just pass.*

Later, she hung around for coffee, feeling like an infiltrator, a spy. A woman took hold of her arm and said, 'Let's go out and talk. I know what you're planning. Don't do it. Let's talk.'

Anna May shrugged off the woman's hand and left. She drove to a liquor outlet. Vins et Spiritueux. *Don't do it.* She found the wine, one bottle, that was all she'd buy. *Don't do it.* One bottle, that was all. She paid and left the store, the familiar curve of the bottle wrapped in brown paper. *Don't do it.* Only one bottle. It wouldn't hurt. She laughed at the excuses bubbling up in her mouth like wine. Just one. She smoked a cigarette in the parking lot, wondering where to go, where to stop and turn the cap that would release the red, sweet smell before the taste would overpower her and she wouldn't have to wonder anymore.

She drove north on 21, heading for the Bruce Peninsula, Lake Huron on her left, passing the little resort towns, the cottages by the lake. She stopped for a hamburger and, without thinking, got her thermos filled with coffee. This made her laugh, the bottle sitting next to her, almost a living thing. She drank the coffee driving north, with her father—not Simon, not Catherine—drifting in her thoughts. Charles, her mother had called him. Everyone else called him Charley. Good old Charley. Good-time Charley. Injun Charley. Charles was a hard worker, working at almost anything. He worked hard, he drank hard. He tried to be a father, a husband, but the work and the drink turned his attempts to nothing. Anna May's mother never complained, never left him. She cooked and kept house and raised the children and always called him Charles. When Anna May grew up, she taunted her mother with the fact that *her Charles* was a drunk. Why didn't she care more about her kids than her drunken husband? Didn't her mother know how ashamed they were to have such a father, to hear people talk about him, to laugh at him, to laugh at them—the half-breeds of good-old-good-time-Injun Charley?

Anna May laughed again, the sound ugly inside the car. Her father was long dead and, she supposed, forgiven by her. He had been a handsome man back then, her mother a skinny, pale girl, an orphan girl, something unheard of by her father. How that must have appealed to the romantic that he was. Anna May didn't know how her mother felt about the life she'd had with Charles. Her mother never talked about those things. Her mother, who sobbed and moaned at Simon's death as she never had at her husband's. Anna May couldn't remember her father ever being mean. He just went away when he drank. Not like his daughter who'd fight anything in her way when she was drunk. The bottle bounced beside her as she drove.

Anna May drove and her eyes began to see the colours of the trees. They looked like they were on fire, the reds and oranges competing with the yellows and golds. She smoked her cigarettes, drank from the thermos, and remembered this was her favourite season. She and Catherine would be cleaning the garden, harvesting the beets, turnips, and cabbage. They would be digging up the gladioli and letting them dry before packing the bulbs away. They would be planting more tulips. Catherine could never get enough tulips. It was because they had met in the spring, Catherine always said. 'We met in the spring, and the tulips were blooming in that little park. You looked so beautiful against the tulips, Simon on your lap. I knew I loved you.' Last autumn Simon had been five and had raked leaves and dug holes for the tulip bulbs. Catherine had made cocoa and cinnamon toast, and Simon had declared that he liked cinnamon toast better than pie.

Anna May tasted the tears on her lips. She licked the wet salt, imagining it was sweet wine on her tongue. 'It's my fault,' she said out loud. She thought of all the things she should have done to prevent Simon's leaving. She should have placated Tony; she should have lived alone; she should have pretended to be straight; she should have never become an alcoholic; she should have never loved; she should have never been born. Let go! she cried somewhere inside her. 'Let go!' she cried aloud. Isn't that what she learned? But how could she let go of Simon and the hate she held for Tony and herself? How could she let go of that? If she let go, she'd have to forgive—the forgiveness Tony begged of her now that Simon was gone.

Even Catherine, even the woman she loved, asked her to forgive Tony. 'It could have happened when he was with us,' Catherine cried at her. 'Forgive him, then you can forgive yourself.' But Catherine didn't know what it was to feel the baby inside her, to feel him pushing his way out of her, to feel his mouth on her breast, to feel the sharp pain in her womb every time his name was spoken. Forgiveness was for people who could afford it. Anna May was poverty-struck.

The highway turned into a road, the trees crowding in on both sides of her, the flames of the trees almost blinding her. She was entering the Bruce Peninsula a sign informed her. She pulled off the road, consulting her map. Yes, she would drive to the very tip of the peninsula and it would be there she'd open the bottle and drink her way to whatever she imagined was waiting for her. The bottle rested beside her, and she touched the brown paper, feeling soothed, feeling a hunger in her stomach.

She saw another sign: Sauble Falls. Anna May thought this would be a good place to stop, to drink the last of her coffee, to smoke another cigarette. She pulled over onto the gravel lot. There was a small path leading down to the rocks. Another sign: Absolutely No Fishing. Watch Your Step. Rocks Are Slippery. She could hear the water before she saw it.

She stepped out of the covering of trees and onto the rock shelf. The falls were narrow, spilling out in various layers of rock. She could see the beginnings of Lake Huron below her. She could see movement in the water coming away from the lake and moving towards the rocks and the falls. Fish tails flashing and catching light from the sun. Hundreds of fish tails moving upstream. She walked across a flat slab of rock and there, beneath her in the shallow water, saw salmon slowly moving their bodies, their gills expanding and closing as they rested. She looked up to another rock slab and saw a dozen fish congregating at the bottom of a water spill—waiting. Her mind barely grasped the fact that the fish were migrating, swimming upstream, when a salmon leapt and hurled itself over the rushing water above. Anna May stepped up to a different ledge and watched the salmon's companions waiting their turn to jump the flowing water and reach the next plateau.

She looked down toward the mouth of the lake. There were others, like her, standing and silently watching the struggle of the fish. No one spoke, as if to speak would be blasphemous in the presence of this. She looked again into the water, the fish crowding each resting place before resuming the leaps and the jumps. Here and there on the rocks, dead fish, a testimony to the long and desperate struggle that had taken place. They lay, eyes glazed, sides open and bleeding, food for the gulls that hovered over Anna May's head.

Another salmon jumped, its flesh torn and gaping, its body spinning until it made it over the fall. Another one, the dorsal fin torn, leapt and was washed back by the power of the water. Anna May watched the fish rest, its open mouth like another wound. The fish was large, the dark body undulating in the water. She saw it begin a movement of tail. Churning the water, it shot into the air, twisting its body, shaking and spinning. She saw the underbelly, pale yellow and bleeding from the battering against the rocks, the water. He made it! Anna May wanted to clap, to shout with elation at the sheer power of such a thing happening before her.

She looked around again. The other people were gone. She was alone with the fish, the only sound besides the water was her breath against the air. She walked further upstream, her sneakers getting wet from the splashing of the salmon. She didn't feel the wet, she only waited and watched for the salmon to move. She had no idea of time, of how long she stood waiting for the movement, waiting for the jumps, the leaps, the flight. Anna May watched for Torn Fin, wanting to see him move against the current in his phenomenal swim of faith.

Anna May reached a small dam, the last barrier before the calm water and blessed rest. She sat on a rock, her heart beating fast, the adrenalin pouring through her at each leap and twist of the salmon. There he was, Torn Fin, his final jump before him. She watched, then closed her eyes, almost ashamed to be a spectator at this act, this primal movement to the place of all beginning. He had to get there, to push his bleeding body forward, believing in his magic to get him there. Believing, believing he would get there. No thoughts of death, of food, of rest. No thoughts but the great urging and wanting to get there, get *there*.

Anna May opened her eyes and saw him, another jump before being pushed back. She held her hands together, her body willing Torn Fin to move, to push, to jump, to fly! Her body rocked forward and back, her heart madly beating inside her chest. She rocked, she shouted, 'Make it, damn it, make it!' Torn Fin waited at the dam. Anna May rocked and held her hands tight, her fingers twisting together, nails scratching her palms. She rocked. She whispered, 'Simon, Simon.' She rocked and whispered the name of her son into the water, 'Simon, Simon.' Like a chant. *Simon. Simon. Simon.* Into the water, as if the very name of her son was magic and could move the salmon to his final place. She rocked. She chanted. *Simon. Simon.* Anna May rocked and put her hands in the water, wanting to lift the fish over the dam and to life. As the thought flickered through her brain, Torn Fin slapped his tail against the water and jumped. He battled with the current. He twisted and arced into the air, his great mouth gaping and gasping, his wounds standing out in relief against his body, his fin discoloured and shredded. With a push, a great push, he turned a complete circle and made it over the dam.

'*Simon!*' Torn Fin slapped his tail one last time and was gone, the dark body swimming home. She thought . . . she thought she saw her son's face, his black hair streaming behind him, a look of joy transfixed on his little face before the image disappeared.

Anna May stood on the rock shelf, hands limp at her sides, watching the water, watching the salmon, watching. She watched as the sun fell behind the lake and night came closer to her. Then she walked up the path and back to her car. She looked at the bottle sitting next to her, the brown paper rustling as she put the car in gear. She drove south, stopping at a telephone booth.

She could still hear the water in her ears.

Grandmothers of a New World

Pocahontas and Nancy Ward hold a special fascination for me because of the legends that have arisen around their names and lives. They are presented, by white historians, as good friends of the white man, helping colonialists gain a foot-hold in Indian Country. At the same time, some Natives have used the word 'traitor' to describe them. Defiled and vilified. Somewhere outside their legends the truth lies. As a poet, rather than a historian, I feel I have a freedom of sorts to explore and imagine what those truths are.

According to 'history', Pocahontas was a favoured daughter of Wahunsonacock ('Powhatan'), chief of the Algonquian Confederacy in what is now called Virginia. In 1607 or 1608 she saw her first white man, John Smith, on a ship sailing into the harbour. She immediately became enamoured of his colour and promptly fell in love with him. Wahunsonacock, being the 'savage' he was, hated John Smith and for no apparent reason gave the order to have him executed. Right before he was to be tomahawked, Pocahontas threw herself on Smith, telling her father that he'd have to kill her too. Since Pocahontas was willing to die for this particular white man, there must be something wonderful about all white men, so Wahunsonacock spared not only Smith's life but the lives of his crew as well.

Smith eventually returned to England, leaving Pocahontas to pine away until she met John Rolfe. Pocahontas must have thought that all white men looked alike, or maybe she liked the name John, because she enthusiastically fell in love with Rolfe and became a good Christian. She also became a good capitalist since she helped her husband grow rich in the tobacco trade, and took up wearing white women's clothing, had a son, went to England where she was a celebrity, and finally died happily there—her soul eternally saved.

Quite a story. Even Hollywood couldn't improve this tale.

But I can.

Wahunsonacock had twenty children, ten of them daughters. Pocahontas was a favoured daughter, but more than that, was a child in her father's confidence. She understood only too well what the invasion of Europeans meant for her people. I also must tell you at the time she met John Smith, she was twelve or thirteen—a woman by Native standards of the day. Pocahontas was not just a good listener, she was listened to. When she spoke, the Pamunkey people heard her and respected her voice. While not a true matriarchy like the

Mohawk of Molly Brant or the Cherokee of Nanye'hi (Nancy Ward), Pamunkey women held sway in the disposition of enemy warriors and matters pertaining to war. John Smith's so-called rescue was, in fact, a mock execution—a traditional ritual often held after the capture of enemies. This ritual, in the eyes of John Smith, must have held all the trappings of a play with Smith in the starring role. Pocahontas also played her part. She chose to adopt Smith as her brother since this was her right as a Pamunkey woman. Smith began writing letters home of how his life was saved by a genuine Indian princess, and of how he held the Algonquian Confederacy in the palm of his hand. Of course, this was nonsense.

Wahunsonacock and his daughter/confidante were not fools. They had a sophisticated view of the English and the other European nations who were clamouring to capture the 'new' continent and claim it for their own. The continuation of their people was uppermost in the daughter's and father's minds. They thought to establish their Nation by making alliances with the British. Then, as now, survival was the most important thought on Native agendas. The art and practice of diplomacy was not a new concept to North American Native peoples. If we were as savage and warlike as the history books would like us to believe, there would not have been any of us left when the first white man staggered onto our lands. Pocahontas was probably the first ambassador to the British, just as La Malinche was to the Spanish. Not an easy task for anyone, let alone a thirteen-year-old woman who could not read, write, or speak the language of the intruders, and who most likely figured out early on that the British held little esteem for women—especially if they weren't white. Pocahontas saw as the alternative to genocide, adopting Smith as her brother.

History books speculate on whether Smith and Pocahontas were lovers. I doubt this is important, but 'history', intent on romanticizing Pocahontas and Smith, seems to linger on this attachment. I think that 'history' is a lie—written down to bolster the ego of the white man, and to promulgate their status as macho and clever warriors, *and* the ludicrous idea that white men are irresistible to Native women. Boastful and self-involved, John Smith eventually left the Jamestown Colony and went home to England. He hadn't made his fortune, but he was to make a mark in books to come through his lies and distortion of Aboriginal peoples.

There are reports that Pocahontas and her father were greatly angered at Smith's leave-taking. Why? Did they see it as a withdrawal of agreement made between Great Britain and the Algonquian Confederacy? Through Smith's adoption, they had woven a tenuous connection between the Nations. The Algonquian Confederacy had lost few people to these British invaders. The Confederacy was still strong in the eyes of other First Nations. They were not weakened by their relationship with the British, due to the diplomatic skills of Wahunsonacock and Pocahontas. The British had done fairly well in the Colony. Natives taught them what to eat, how to eat, how to plant what they ate. It amazes me how Thanksgiving in the States is portrayed as whites and Natives happily sharing food in a gesture of friendship. The pilgrims had nothing to share. Suspicious and ignorant of new kinds of food, as well as Native peoples, it is a wonder to me that any of them survived at all. But we were generous—a generosity that became the beginning of the end of our cultures as we knew them. My eldest grandsons are righteously appalled when Thanksgiving is celebrated in their schools. 'Teacher, the pilgrims were bad guys. They killed Indians!' Of course, 'teacher' continues to perpetuate this mythical holiday as a story where the white man is the good guy, feeding the starving Natives! When *will* they get it right?

In Aboriginal languages, there are no words for stingy or selfish, except to describe aberrant behaviour requiring a shaman's intervention. Our generosity comes from the complex and sophisticated worldview of thousands of years of belief and practice. The concept of family is a wide and far-reaching part of our worldview. By adopting John Smith as her brother, Pocahontas was opening her home and family to him. Smith violated this honour and the meaning of family by leaving Jamestown without a proper goodbye and thank you. This violation brought humiliation to the family, clan and Nation. As a result of Smith's behaviour, Wahunsonacock and Pocahontas left the Jamestown settlement and went home, enjoining other Natives to follow them. Jamestown suffered heavy losses of life. They literally starved. Pocahontas was sent on various missions to other Nations by her father. Serving as a spokesperson for the Algonquian Confederacy, she arranged new trade agreements, cemented old friendships, built new ones. There is no doubt that Pocahontas was a skilled orator and politician. It sickens me that the story we learn in school is the racist and untrue depiction of her romance with John Smith, and her willingness to die for him.

During her travels, Pocahontas took a Native husband. Of him, we can find no trace. She must not have had children, or they would have remained with their mother on her sojourns and her eventual return to her home and family. When Wahunsonacock and Pocahontas were ready to visit Jamestown again (to see what the white man was up to), they were taken prisoner. I imagine the settlers wanted to vent their anger on them for being deserted. It would never have occurred to the pilgrims that their own racism and stupidity had led to this 'desertion' and ultimate loss of lives. Pocahontas and her father were not free to leave the colony, but could wander among the people and houses. They found a man who must have intrigued them to no end. He was a missionary and was teaching people to read and write. Reading was something the white man did, and because of it, he held a certain kind of power. Bargaining with the British, Pocahontas arranged for her father to be sent home and she would stay to learn more about the Christian way. 'History' says Pocahontas was an eager convert. I submit that her conversion to Christianity was only half-hearted, but her conversion to literacy was carried out with powerful zeal.

I feel in my heart that Pocahontas was guided by divine power. Not a god in Christian terms, but a communion with Creator. 'Living with the spirits', as my father used to say. Pocahontas lived with and listened to these spirits. There is a term and philosophy that has been used for centuries—Manifest Destiny. It is a white man's term and logic implying that whites are superior and therefore, it is Nature's law that the white race hold dominion over all natural things. In other words, the white man is king and emperor over all— Indigenous peoples, animals, plants, the very air. I propose that Pocahontas had her own destiny to fulfil—that of keeping her people alive. Would Wahunsonacock and his people have listened and learned so readily from Pocahontas if she had not already given evidence of being a person who 'lived with the spirits'? Was Pocahontas a shaman, a seer, a holy woman? In some English translations of her name, it appears to come up as 'getting joy from spirits'. Name-giving in Native cultures is a serious event. Many signs and omens are consulted before giving a name and getting a name. In many Nations, it was the role of the berdache, or Two-Spirit, to bestow this honour. History will not tell us that Pocahontas was a holy woman, but there is a feel-ing inside me that tells me this is so. I know my feeling cannot be substanti-ated by academic literature; but I am not a member of the academy, nor am I a scholar of institutions—I am a Mohawk woman storyteller who knows there were and are prophets among my people. Pocahontas was such a prophet who lived her prophecy.

Linda Hogan, Chickasaw poet, has written letters to me about the 'New People'. These are people like her and me—the mixed-bloods. Did Pocahon-tas envision Nations of New People? Did she vision a New World? A world where people would say, 'I am a human being of many races and Nations.' Is this the real destiny? Vine Deloria once said, 'Blood quantums are not impor-tant; what really matters is who your grandparents were.' These women I am writing about were our grandparents. They are our Grandmothers in spirit, if not actual blood. This does not mean that I think every person who dwells on this continent is a spiritual Indian. That would be a dishonour to my ances-tors. I emphatically believe that our culture and ritual belong to us—First Nations. A person does not become an Indian by participating in a sweat, or observing a Sun Dance, or even working on political issues that affect our Nations. One cannot choose to be Indigenous like one chooses new clothes or chooses a brand of toothpaste. One is not Indigenous because they believe in our values. But the prophecy of New People *can* mean the beginning of a different kind of discourse between Nations and races.

While learning to read and write, Pocahontas met John Rolfe. The accounts come down through time that he greatly admired her. He may indeed have admired her. She was a powerful voice in the territory; she held great wealth of land; she knew the many secrets of growing tobacco which Rolfe had come to realize could make him a rich man. Rolfe came from gen-try stock, but was fairly poor compared to others of his class. Why else would he have come to the continent, except in search of untold wealth, just wait-ing for him to take? 'History' tells us that Rolfe was taken with Pocahontas because of her 'regal bearing, her Christian demeanor, her wisdom.' All this may be true and perhaps even love entered into it. Did Pocahontas love John Rolfe? Maybe. Did the spirits tell her that Rolfe was a good choice to begin the prophecy? There were other white men waiting in the wings to know the favours of Pocahontas and her father, for one was not possible without the other. John Rolfe was a man easily handled by those who had more charisma and political savvy than he. And he was not ugly. The courtship began, but not without obstacles. The court of King James was very adamant in discouraging contact between the races (although I doubt there was discouragement against rape and pillage). The issue of class was a barrier to the marriage. This is why we end up with the ridiculous legends of Pocahontas being a princess. John Smith had started the flame of this particular bonfire when he wrote home about having his life saved by a princess of the realm. John Rolfe added more fuel to the legend in his desire to be married. Thus Wahunsonacock is made a king and Pocahontas a princess. In reality, kings and princesses—royalty—do not exist and never have existed in our cultures.

Of a dowry there is no mention, but it would be fair to speculate that Rolfe received a parcel of land on which to experiment with tobacco. The smoking of tobacco was a great hit in England among the royals. King James was said to disapprove of the habit, but it doesn't appear that too many people paid attention to what he had to say. Queen Anne was addicted to the stuff and she and her ladies-in-waiting spent hours smoking tobacco and requesting more.

The myth of Pocahontas wants us to believe that after marrying Rolfe, she quickly became a lady of leisure, even acquiring the name of Rebecca. I find this choice of names intriguing and prophetic. In Pocahontas' quest for literacy, the Bible was the only tool she had at that time. Did she read the story of another ancient legend, Rebecca, who was told 'Be thou the mother of thousands of millions, and let thy seed possess the gate of those which hate them'? When Pocahontas found herself pregnant did she feel the joy of having a child of her prophecy? A child of mixed-blood who would learn to read and write as a matter of course, while inheriting the wisdom, political skills and rich culture of his mother?

To ensure that this child would come into the best of all worlds, Pocahontas surrounded herself with female relatives and her father. John Rolfe may have been alarmed that Lady Rebecca was choosing to have her child in what he considered a primitive and heathen manner, but, then again, maybe he wasn't. We do know that in 1615, Pocahontas gave birth to a son amidst the chanting and singing of her people. So much for Pocahontas' Christian submissiveness. After the birth, the relatives stayed on. Unlike John Smith, Rolfe seemed to recognize the honour of being part of Pocahontas' family. When a non-Native becomes part of a Native household or family group, whether through marriage or companionship, the Native family takes over. This is assimilation of a kind that is never discussed or written about. The non-Native often has to put up small battles to hang on to a separate personality rather than the personality of the Native group.

I have seen this happen in my own family with my non-Native uncles, mother and my lover. Soon they are talking like Natives, joking like Natives; the prevailing Native culture and worldview is assimilated by the non-Native. I suspect this process is not discussed because the dominant culture does not want to admit that another way of *seeing* may be a more integrated way of being in the world, as opposed to Manifest Destiny. Again, this process of assimilation is *not* becoming Indigenous. It is a recognition that every part of what constitutes life, *makes life*.

This integrity of life can be explained through the example of the Sun Dance of the Plains Indians. Each person entering the circle to dance has an objective. Whether he or she is dancing for strength, for healing the body and/or mind, that purpose will be reflected on the community, for the good of community. In Oklahoma a few years ago, a Vietnam veteran asked to participate in the Sun Dance while using his wheelchair. This had never been done, but a way was worked out where a guide would maneuver him through the rigorous ceremony. This was not an easy task for veteran or guide. The Sun Dance can last for hours; it has been known to last for days until communion with Creator has taken place. Later, when the Dance was done, the vet told a friend of mine that he was dancing to be forgiven for the 'sins' (his word) he had committed in Vietnam. As he was dancing, he began to relive his experiences in Vietnam; he began dancing for his buddies, dancing for the Vietnamese people, he began dancing for peace and the end to racism, he began dancing for the spiritual health that would bring him home to his own people again. This story has everything to do with Pocahontas and her prophecy. While not belonging to the Plains worldview that produces a Sun Dance, Pocahontas was doing her own dance for the good of the community. Her community, because of the child she bore, was an enlarged one. And I am wondering if John Rolfe's idea of family and community was also enlarged.

Pocahontas and Rolfe were invited to England to be presented to the king and queen. The tobacco industry was a profitable one to the monarchy. They wanted to meet Pocahontas, the 'princess' of the Indians. Natives were becoming the rage in England. Natives were 'in'. To this day, Natives remain an object of fascination to European people. Perhaps they are fascinated by the fact that we still exist after five hundred years of persistent genocide. North Americans are not much better—to them we are invisible, extinct, or relics of a past ('primitive') way of life.

The England of the 1600s was a primitive, filthy place and must have been a terrifying sight to Pocahontas and her relatives. For she did not travel to London with just her husband and son, she took many female relatives and her uncle, Uttamatamakin, a medicine man to her people. It has been recorded that while in London, Pocahontas and her Native relatives swam daily in the waters of the Thames. This was seen as a heathen aberration by the British who were accustomed to taking baths perhaps once or twice a year. Some of Pocahontas' relatives became ill from the polluted waters and had to stop their 'savage' habit of bathing daily.

Pocahontas met the king and queen. It is reported that they were impressed. We have no account that Pocahontas reciprocated the feeling. And this leads to another question—where are Pocahontas' writings? We know she could read and write in English; does it not seem likely that she kept a diary or journal of the events in which she was participating? Illness made inroads into the health of the Native people. John Rolfe got permission to take the family to the country where the air and waters were cleaner. Thomas, the son, could play and Pocahontas and her relatives could relax away from the rude stares and comments that followed them everywhere. Pocahontas also met up with her old acquaintance/brother, John Smith. He wrote in his diary that the princess seemed angry with him. He was probably quite angry himself. The reception accorded Pocahontas and Rolfe must have rankled him. The 'princess' of his making was truly being treated as royalty.

Pocahontas fell ill. She had already lost some of her people to England's diseases and had spent her time in the country in mourning. Thomas was also ill, which must have sent his mother into a frenzy of trying to get him away from a country that did nothing but kill her people. Rolfe and Pocahontas prepared to take their leave and go home. They set sail; but in Gravesend, in the county of Kent, the ship had to stop and Pocahontas was removed to receive medical care. Perhaps she had tuberculosis or smallpox. Uttamatamakin performed healing rituals for her. This may have been enough to ease her mind and spirit, but British doctors came, and over the protestations of her relatives, applied leeches and gave her purges. This weakened her further. Pocahontas died and her last reported words were, 'It is enough that the child liveth.' John Rolfe, a weak man without Pocahontas' intervention, failed her in death, since he had her buried Christian-style. Uttamatamakin was furious and the anti-white feelings that were held at bay during Wahunsonacock's tenure began stirring and set the scene for hard times to come in Virginia.

Why did Rolfe fail Pocahontas? It may be due to the fact that his son was still very sick and he wanted to leave for Virginia as soon as possible. Rolfe may have chosen the most politically expedient way to placate his British hosts. Pocahontas was no longer there to strengthen him. Or perhaps John Rolfe was always a fool, believing that the Brit was the only way. Pocahontas' relatives were token Christians as she was, and probably would have gone along with a Christian burial *if* they also could send her to the Spirit World through Pamunkey ministrations. But Pocahontas was interred at Gravesend in full English dress and tradition; her body remains there to this day.

Wahunsonacock died within a short time after receiving news of his daughter's death. He longed to stay alive to take his grandson to live with him. He must have mourned and longed himself to death. His beloved daughter would never come home again. Her bones would nourish British land instead of her own. And the precious child Thomas, so important to Pocahontas' vision of a new world? He stayed in England and was reared by his father's uncle. John Rolfe went back to Virginia and died shortly after the Native uprising. This foolish, weak man who failed his wife's dream, failed all of us. As a teen, Thomas did return to Virginia and experienced the desire to see his mother's land and the place he first drew breath. He journeyed to the Pamunkey, which was considered enemy territory by the British. What happened to Thomas as he journeyed to the land and language of his birth? A few years later, he was commissioned as a lieutenant in the colonial militia and took up duty as a colonist against the Native people. The so-called Peace of Pocahontas was at an end. Had his mother lived, would the outcome have been different? It is hard to speculate. La Malinche lived to see her son by Cortez take up arms against her people and his. The Pamunkey people and those of many other Nations were on a path to extinction through the Europeans' greatest weapon—disease. It is estimated by Native historians that two-thirds of Indigenous North Americans were wiped out by measles, chicken pox, tuberculosis, smallpox and the common cold. Did Pocahontas see this in her vision?

It is ironic and horrible that Pocahontas became grandmother to an estimated two million people who lay claim to being her descendants. Ironic, because a Virginian who would recoil in horror at having a Black ancestor, points with pride to the Native blood in his body. Horrible, because the British did their job well—anointing Pocahontas a princess, while excising her Native blood. We are left with the legend of a woman made into an 'incidental' Indian. There was nothing incidental about Pocahontas. She fought for her people and for the future of her people. She spoke in her own language even at the end. She brought her son into the world through Native womb and hands. Even her final words—'It is enough the child liveth,' speak volumes of her plan. The false European legend must end. Pocahontas' honour demands it.

Nancy Ward was also a woman committed to vision. Her name Nanye'hi, 'Spirit People' or 'Spirit Path', describes communion with a dream that gave direction to her life and that of her people, the Cherokee Nation.

Nanye'hi became the wife of Kingfisher in 1750 and the stories about her begin at that time. While a mother of two young children, she went into battle with her husband to fight the Creek, traditional enemies of the Cherokee. The Cherokee Nation was a true matriarchy, meaning the blood lines flowed through the mother. Clans of the mother became the clans of the children. Women influenced all political and family matters. Accompanying her mate into battle was not a new phenomenon to the Cherokee. While in what is now called Georgia, Nanye'hi took up the arms of her husband who lay dying, and continued to fight and rally the people around her. This inspiration led her people into ultimate victory over the Creek Nation. Stories began to circulate among the Cherokee about Nanye'hi's heroism. She soon was chosen to become a Beloved Woman of the Cherokee. Beloved Woman means just that; she was beloved by the people, but even more, was beloved by the Creator and was a conduit through which Creator spoke.

It seems that only Indigenous people could come up with this particular way of being and seeing. Most of us know some stories of Christian saints who supposedly were in communication with a god, but Native peoples so cherish and personalize Creator and the spirits who make the mysteries that this Great Mystery chooses to speak through women's voices. This is not unique only to the Cherokee. Across North America one will hear the voices of women speaking from the spirits. Again, I think of Christian women saints who had to be martyred and *die* before achieving the state of grace their religion told them they didn't have in life. How much more sensible to be in a state of grace as a living human.

When Nanye'hi became a Beloved Woman, the Cherokee were literally caught in the middle between France and England. Each European nation was panting and scheming for Cherokee land and it fell on Nanye'hi to negotiate with each nation while retaining and preserving the integrity and strength of her own Nation. Like Pocahontas, she was a diplomat of skillful means. She worked in close connection with her uncle, Attakullakulla, maintaining a balance of power. Imagine it—young woman, aging man, holding war at bay, gathering strength to withstand the onslaught they knew would eventually come. Because she maintained this balance and peace, Nanye'hi has been seen by some of her descendants as a traitor and lackey to the British. But this story is old and familiar. Take strong Nationalist women and turn them into pale myth. Make *our own people* believe the lies. This is what oppression is—the enforcement of amnesia—to make us forget the glory and story of our own history. These women called traitors, what was their treachery? Neither Pocahontas nor Nanye'hi handed over lands or people to the white man. For one thing, it would not have been in the Native consciousness to do so. Land was given by Creator. Neither woman gave up secrets or culture. These women knew what was in their vision. These women lived with spirits.

In 1757, Nanye'hi married a white trader, Bryant Ward. She had a daughter, Elizabeth. Bryant Ward did not live with Nanye'hi and the Cherokee. Why? My own guess is that Nanye'hi didn't want him to. She sent him away after her child was born. The words of Pocahontas come back to me—'It is enough the child liveth.' Were these Nanye'hi's words also? Did she have a vision of a New People also?

In 1775, the Watauga Purchase took place. Twenty million acres of Cherokee land were 'sold' to the British for two thousand pounds. There is no record of Nanye'hi's voice, but a woman who always counselled 'never sell the land,' must have been frightened and appalled at what she saw as a break in Cherokee tradition and culture. But already, whether because of her arrangement with Bryant Ward, or the adoption of white values by some of her people, Nanye'hi was losing her influence.

In 1776, a Cherokee faction led by Dragging Canoe and Old Abram set siege to the Watauga fort. They captured a white woman, Lydia Bean, and were going to burn her alive. It is said that Nanye'hi stepped to the fire and shouted, 'No woman shall be burned at the stake while I am still Beloved

Woman.' This story has a familiar ring to it, but it is true. Cherokee men, after years of staving off the white man, were nevertheless learning from him. The very notion of murdering a woman, regardless of her being non-Cherokee, reflects how Native beliefs were being swept away by colonialism. In all the horror stories that have been told since we first laid eyes on the white man, I find this one the most telling—how Native attitudes towards women changed and became more and more like the oppressors'. This change was not every- where, and not in everyone, but enough change to freeze the blood and enrage the heart. Nanye'hi must have felt similar horror. For if attitudes towards women could go against Creator's wishes, what other terrors would follow? This is not to say that we Native peoples brought this destruction upon our- selves. Such a statement would be untrue. But this change in a religious worldview surely helped to lay us open to the self-doubt and self-loathing imposed by the 'Manifest Destiny' that tore the material of our Nations.

After saving Lydia's life, Nanye'hi took this woman to live at Chote, Nanye'hi's ancestral home. History does not tell us how long they lived together, or what they talked of together. Did they talk of politics and raising children? Did they become lovers? One thing is known—Nanye'hi learned to make butter and cheese from the milk of the 'white man's buffalo'. She later used this knowledge to introduce dairying into the Cherokee Nation. But what of Lydia Bean? Did she learn of the spirits? Did she learn that women's voices were the means to the Creator? Did she become assimilated into a Native way of seeing and being? I want to know the answers to these ques- tions because it is essential to the tenuous discussion that is taking place between Native and non-Native women. I am reminded of a time when Denise and I went to Tyendinaga for a visit. We stayed with one of my many great-aunts and cousins living there. One night we sat at the kitchen table, shelling beans. We sat for a few hours, five of us, doing women's work— making food for the family. There was a magic to that evening, probably because we were performing a simple and primal act of love. Denise, always aware she is a white woman among the Mohawk, felt loved and filled to be part of this act. We Mohawk women felt the same. I think of that evening, especially when I am asked to speak or read in unfamiliar places. Lydia and Nanye'hi made food together—physically and spiritually. Surely this is a possibility for us. Pocahontas saw a new world, filled with new people. Can we be less visionary than she?

War intensified between the Cherokee and the emerging American nation. The Cherokee found themselves defeated at every turn, while Nanye'hi stood her ground and shouted for peace. In 1781, trying to negotiate a peace treaty, she cried, 'Peace . . . let it continue. This peace must last forever. Let your children be ours. Our children will be yours. Let your women hear our words.' The idea that differing races could belong to each other in family and love is the most radical of ideas. Did the white women hear Nanye'hi's words? It is doubtful. How could they have heard unless their men chose to tell them?

The year 1785 found Nanye'hi living at Chote with her children and grand-children. Elizabeth had married an Indian agent. Her two children by King-fisher had married and produced children. She had also opened her home to orphans, of which there were many. Deep changes were occurring within the Cherokee Nation. In 1817, the last Cherokee Council meeting was held, and Nanye'hi was expected to speak and bring counsel. Old and ill, she sent her son Fivekiller to represent her and to read her written message. And here I have another question. Nanye'hi was a literate woman, *where are her words*? As a Native woman it makes me weep to know that 'history' has not deemed it worthwhile to note that Nanye'hi and Pocahontas could write and think and feel, and therefore must have put ideas and thoughts onto paper. Nanye'hi and Lydia must have corresponded. Where are these precious documents I long to see? Were they lost? Were they thrown away like *we* have been thrown away? Were they burned—like the truth of their lives was burned out of history and memory? Fivekiller read his mother's message to the people, words that have survived history:

Your mothers, your sisters, ask you not to part with any more of our land. We say you are our descendants and must listen to our request. Keep the land for our growing children for it was the good will of Creator to place us here. Keep your hands off of paper for it is our own country. If it was not, they (the white man) would not ask you to put your hands on paper. It would be impos-sible to remove us all for as soon as one child is raised, we have others in our arms. Therefore children, don't part with any more of our land but continue on it and enlarge your farms and cultivate and raise corn so we may never go hungry. Listen to the talks of your sisters. I have a great many grandchil-dren and I wish them to do well on the land.

Nanye'hi's words were a prophecy, especially about the impossibility of removing all the people from the land. Even during the forced removal of southeastern Nations to Oklahoma, known as the Trail of Tears, many Chero-kee escaped and blended into other families and races. Nanye'hi died in 1818. She had lived a long life as compared to Pocahontas. When she died, there were no last words reported, but her great-grandson said that a light rose from her body and fluttered like a bird around her body and her family in attendance; then flew in the direction of ancestral land. If Nanye'hi had spoken last words, I imagine they would have been Cherokee words she had spoken all her life—Don't sell our land. Let the women hear my words. Our cry is for peace.

My friend Awiakta, Cherokee writer and champion of Nanye'hi, has told me of the historic reunion of the Cherokee Eastern and Western Councils in 1984 at the Red Clay Historical area in East Tennessee. 'These are the same council grounds,' Awiakta said, 'where the last council met before the Removal and also where Nanye'hi came during her lifetime. (Her homesite and grave are in the vicinity.) The Cherokee had carried the Sacred Fire with them on the Trail of Tears. At the Reunion they brought brands of it back. On a hill, in a receptacle made of native stone, they relit the Sacred Fire which will burn eternally.' Awiakta also said that 20,000 people were there, the descendants of Nanye'hi's vision of a new world. Red and white, Red and Black, Red, white and Black. All these glorious mixtures come together as family. 'Let your children be ours. Our children will be yours.' How prophetic those words!

What is history? Does it still lie in the domain of the white man who churns it out according to *his* politic? What is women's history? Is it still the history of white women who were privileged by their birth? Will history become something new—a story of all Nations—instead of the story of European conquest? I am a grandmother and I feel it is imperative that I tell the truthful story of the Americas. My grandsons will need this story to help them grow into good men—the kind of men our Nations deserve. My grandsons—so many kinds of blood flow in their veins. Among the four of them flows the blood of Mohawk, Irish, Scots, Polish, Cree, French, Norwegian, Cherokee—the blood of the future.

Buffy Sainte-Marie b. 1941

CREE

Universal Soldier

He's five foot two and he's six feet four
He fights with missiles and with spears
He's all of thirty-one and he's only seventeen
He's been a soldier for a thousand years.

He's a Catholic a Hindu an Atheist a Jain
A Buddhist and a Baptist and a Jew
And he knows he shouldn't kill and he knows he always will
Kill you for me my friend and me for you.

And he's fighting for Canada and he's fighting for France
He's fighting for the USA
And he's fighting for the Russians and he's fighting for Japan
And he thinks we'll put an end to war this way.

And he's fighting for democracy, he's fighting for the reds
He says it's for the peace of all
He's the one who must decide who's to live and who's to die
And he never sees the writing on the wall.

But without him how would Hitler have condemned them at Dachau
Without him Caesar would've stood alone
He's the one who gives his body as a weapon of the war
And without him all this killing can't go on.

He's the Universal Soldier and he really is to blame
His orders come from far away no more
They come from here and there and you and me
And brothers can't you see
This is not the way we put an end to war.

My Country 'Tis of Thy People You're Dying

Now that your big eyes are finally opened
Now that you're wond'ring, 'How must they feel?'
Meaning them that you've chased 'cross America's movie screens.

Now that you're wond'ring, 'How can it be real?'
That the ones you've called colourful, noble, and proud in your
   school propaganda,
They starve in their splendour!
You've asked for my comment,
I simply will render,
My country, 'tis of thy people you're dying.

Now that our longhouses breed superstition
You force us to send our toddlers away
To your schools where they're taught to despise their traditions;
Forbid them their languages, then further say
That American history really began when Columbus set sail out of
   Europe!
And stress that the Nation of leeches that's conquered this land
Are the biggest and bravest and boldest and best!
And yet, where in the history books is the tale of the genocide basic
   to this country's birth?
Of the preachers who lied? How the Bill of Rights failed?
And where will it tell of the Liberty Bell as it rang with a thud over
   Kinzua mud?
And of brave Uncle Sam in Alaska this year?
My country, 'tis of thy people you're dying.

Hear how the bargain was made for the west,
With her shivering children, in zero degrees;
'Blankets for your land'; so the treaties attest
Now blankets for land is a bargain, indeed,
But the blankets were those Uncle Sam had collected
From small pox-diseased dying soldiers that day,
And the tribes were wiped out, and the history books censored!
One hundred years of your statesmen have felt it's better this way;
Yet a few of the conquered have somehow survived—
Their blood runs the redder, though genes have been paled;
From the Grand Canyon's caverns to Craven's sad hills
The wounded, the losers, the robbed sing their tale,
From Los Angeles County, to up-state New York, the white nation
   fattens while others grown lean.
Oh, the tricked and evicted, only know what I mean;
My country, 'tis of thy people you're dying.

The past, it just crumbled; the future just threatens,
Our life-blood's shut up in your chemical tanks,
And now here you come, bill of sale in your hand.

And surprise in your eyes that we're lacking in thanks
    for the blessings of civilization you've brought us.
The lessons you've taught us, the ruins you've wrought us!
Oh, see what our trust in America's bought us!
My country, 'tis of thy people you're dying!
Now that the pride of the sires receive charity,
    now that we're harmless and safe behind laws,
Now that my life's to be known as your heritage,
    now that even the graves have been robbed.

Now that our own chosen way is a novelty
Hands on your hearts, we salute you your victory,
Choke on your blue-white-and-scarlet hypocrisy,
Pitying your blindness, that you've never seen
That the eagles of war whose wings lent your glory
Were never no more than carrion crows;
Pushed the wrens from their nest, stole their eggs,
    changed their story,
The mocking-bird sings it—it's all that she knows,
'Oh, what can I do?' say a powerless few, with a lump in your throat
    and a tear in your eye,
Can't you see that their poverty's profiting you?
My country, 'tis of thy people you're dying!

Now That the Buffalo's Gone

Can you remember the times
That you have held your head high
And told all your friends of your Indian claims
Proud good lady, and proud good man.
Your great, great grand-father from Indian blood sprang,
And you feel in your heart for these ones.

Oh it's written in books and in songs
That we've been mistreated and wronged
Well, over and over I hear the same words
From you, good lady, from you good man.
Well listen to me if you care where we stand,
And you feel you're a part of these ones.

When a war between nations is lost
The loser we know pays the cost
But even when Germany fell to your hands

Consider, dear lady, consider dear man.
You left them their pride and you left them their land,
And what have you done to these ones.

Has a change come about Uncle Sam
Or are you still taking our land
A treaty for ever George Washington signed
He did, dear lady, he did, dear man.
And the treaty's being broken by Kinzua Dam,
And what will you do for these ones?

Oh it's all in the past you can say
But it's still going on till today
The government now want the Iroquois land
That of the Seneca and the Cheyenne.
It's here and it's now you must help us, dear man,
Now that the buffalo's gone.

Emma Lee Warrior b. 1941

PEIGAN

Compatriots

Lucy heard the car's motor wind down before it turned off the gravel road a quarter of a mile west of the house. Maybe it was Bunky. She hurried and left the outhouse. She couldn't run if she wanted to. It would be such a relief to have this pregnancy over with. She couldn't see the colour of the vehicle, for the slab fence was between the house and the road. That was just as well. She'd been caught in the outhouse a few times, and it still embarrassed her to have a car approach while she was in there.

She got inside the house just as the car came into view. It was her aunt, Flora. Lucy looked at the clock. It was seven-thirty. She wondered what was going on so early in the morning. Flora and a young white woman approached the house. Bob barked furiously at them. Lucy opened the door and yelled at him. 'I don't know what's wrong with Bob; he never barks at me,' said Flora.

'He's probably barking at her,' explained Lucy. 'Not many whites come here.'

'Oh, this is Hilda Afflerbach. She's from Germany,' began Flora. 'Remember? I told you I met her at the Calgary Stampede? Well, she got off the seven o'clock bus, and I don't have time to drive her all the way down to my house. I took her over to my mother's, but she's getting ready to go to Lethbridge. Can she stay with you till I get off work?'

Lucy smiled. She knew she was boxed in. 'Yeah, but I've got no running water in the house. You have to go outside to use the toilet,' she said, looking at Hilda.

'Oh, that's okay,' her aunt answered. 'She's studying about Indians, anyway. Might as well get the true picture, right? Oh, Hilda, this is my niece, Lucy.' Flora lowered her voice and asked, 'Where's Bunky?'

'He never came home last night. I was hoping it was him coming home. He's not supposed to miss any more work. I've got his lunch fixed in case he shows up.' Lucy poured some water from a blue plastic water jug into a white enamel basin and washed her hands and face. 'I haven't even had time to make coffee. I couldn't sleep waiting for him to come home.' She poured water into a coffeemaker and measured out the coffee into the paper filter.

'I'd have some coffee if it was ready, but I think I'd better get to work. We have to punch in now; it's a new rule. Can't travel on Indian time anymore,' said Flora. She opened the door and stepped out, then turned to say, 'I think the lost has returned,' and continued down the steps.

The squeak of the dusty truck's brakes signalled Bunky's arrival. He strode toward the door, barely acknowledging Flora's presence. He came in and took the lunch pail Lucy had. 'I stayed at Herbie's,' was all he said before he turned and went out. He started the truck and beeped the horn.

'I'll go see what he wants.' She motioned to Flora to wait.

When Bunky left, she went to Flora: 'Maybe it's a good thing you came here. Bunky didn't want to go to work 'cause he had a hangover. When he found out Hilda was going to be here all day, he decided he'd rather go to work.'

'If I don't have to leave the office this afternoon. I'll bring the car over and you can drive Hilda around to look at the reserve, okay?'

'Sure, that'll be good. I can go and do my laundry in Spitzee.' She surveyed the distant horizon. The Rockies were spectacular, blue and distinct. It would be a nice day for a drive. She hoped it would be a repeat of yesterday, not too hot, but, as she stood there, she noticed tiny heat waves over the wheat field. Well, maybe it won't be a repeat, she thought. Her baby kicked inside of her and she said, 'Okay, I'd better go tend to the guest.' She didn't relish having a white visitor, but Flora had done her a lot of favours and Hilda seemed nice.

And she was. Hilda made friends with the kids, Jason and Melissa, answering their many questions about Germany as Lucy cooked. She ate heartily, complimenting Lucy on her cooking even though it was only the usual scrambled eggs and fried potatoes with toast and coffee. After payday, there'd be sausages or ham, but payday was Friday and today was only Tuesday.

'Have you heard of Helmut Walking Eagle?' Hilda wanted to know.

'Yeah, well, I really don't know him to talk to him, but I know what he looks like. He's from Germany, too. I always see him at Indian dances. He dresses up like an Indian.' She had an urge to tell her that most of the Indians wished Helmut would disappear.

'I want to see him,' Hilda said. 'I heard about him and I read a book he wrote. He seems to know a lot about the Indians, and he's been accepted into their religious society. I hope he can tell me things I can take home. People in Germany are really interested in Indians. They even have clubs.'

Lucy's baby kicked, and she held her hand over the spot. 'My baby kicks if I sit too long. I guess he wants to do the dishes.'

Hilda got up quickly and said, 'Let me do the dishes. You can take care of the laundry.'

'No, you're a visitor. I can do them,' Lucy countered. But Hilda was persistent, and Lucy gave in.

Flora showed up just after twelve with the information that there was a sun-dance going on on the north side of the reserve. 'They're already camping. Let's go there after work. Pick me up around four.'

'I can't wait to go to the sun-dance! Do you go to them often?' Hilda asked Lucy.

'No, I never have. I don't know much about them,' Lucy said.

'But why? Don't you believe in it? It's your culture!' Hilda's face showed concern.

'Well, they never had sun-dances here—in my whole life there's never been a sun-dance here.'

'Really, is that true? But I thought you have them every year here.'

'Not here. Over on the Blood Reserve they do and some places in the States, but not here.'

'But don't you want to go to a sun-dance? I think it's so exciting!' Hilda moved forward in her seat and looked hopefully at Lucy.

Lucy smiled at her eagerness. 'No, I don't care to go. It's mostly those mixed-up people who are in it. You see, Indian religion just came back here on the reserve a little while ago, and there are different groups who all quarrel over which way to practise it. Some use Sioux ways, and others use Cree. It's just a big mess,' she said, shaking her head.

Hilda looked at Lucy, and Lucy got the feeling she was telling her things she didn't want to hear.

Lucy had chosen this time of day to do her wash. The Happy Suds Laundromat would be empty. As a rule, the Indians didn't show up till after lunch with their endless garbage bags of laundry.

After they had deposited their laundry in the machines, Lucy, Hilda, and the kids sauntered down the main street to a café for lunch. An unkempt Indian man dogged them, talking in Blackfoot.

'Do you know what he's saying?' asked Hilda.

'He wants money. He's related to my husband. Don't pay any attention to him. He always does this,' said Lucy. 'I used to give him money, but he just drinks it up.'

The café was a cool respite from the heat outside, and the cushioned seats in the booth felt good. They sat by the window and ordered hamburgers, fries, and lemonade. The waitress brought tall, frosted glasses, and beads of water dripped from them.

'Hello, Lucy,' a man's shaky voice said, just when they were really enjoying their lunch. They turned to look at the Indian standing behind Hilda. He was definitely ill. His eyes held pain, and he looked as though he might collapse from whatever ailed him. His hands shook, perspiration covered his face, and his eyes roamed the room constantly.

Lucy moved over to make room for him, but he kept standing and asked her, 'Could you give me a ride down to Badger? The cops said I have to leave town. I don't want to stay 'cause they might beat me up.'

'Yeah, we're doing landry. I've got Flora's car. This is her friend, Hilda. She's from Germany.'

The sick man barely nodded at her, then, turning back to Lucy, he asked her, 'Do you have enough to get me some soup? I'm really hungry.'

Lucy nodded and the man said, 'I'll just sit in the next booth.'

'He's my uncle,' Lucy explained to Hilda as she motioned to the waitress. 'His name is Sonny.'

'Order some clear soup or you'll get sick,' Lucy suggested to her uncle.

He nodded, as he pulled some paper napkins out of a chrome container on the table and wiped his face.

The women and children left Sonny with his broth and returned to the laundromat. As they were folding the clothes, he came in. 'Here, I'll take these,' he said, taking the bags from Lucy. His hands shook, and the effort of lifting the bags was clearly too much for him. 'That's okay,' protested Lucy, attempting to take them from him, 'they're not that heavy. Clothes are always lighter after they've been washed.'

'Hey, Lucy, I can manage. You're not supposed to be carrying big things around in your condition.' Lucy let him take the plastic bags, which he dropped several times before he got to the car. The cops had probably tired of putting him in jail and sending him out each morning. She believed the cops did beat up Indians, although none was ever brought to court over it. She'd take Sonny home, and he'd straighten out for a few weeks till he got thirsty again, and he'd disappear as soon as he got money. It was no use to hope he'd stop drinking. Sonny wouldn't quit drinking till he quit living.

As they were pulling out of town, Lucy remembered she had to get some Kool-Aid and turned the car into the Shop-n-Go Mart. Hilda got out with her and noticed the man who had followed them through the street sitting in the shade of a stack of old tires.

'Hey, tamohpomaat sikaohki,' he told Lucy on her way into the store.

'What did he say? Sikaohki?' queried Hilda.

The Kool-Aid was next to the cash register and she picked up a few packages, and laid them on the counter with the money. When the cashier turned to the register, Lucy poked Hilda with her elbow and nodded her head toward the sign behind the counter. Scrawled unevenly in big, black letters, it said, 'Ask for Lysol, vanilla, and shaving lotion at the counter.'

They ignored the man on the way to the car. 'That's what he wants: he's not allowed to go into the stores 'cause he steals it. He wanted vanilla. The Indians call it "sikaohki"; it means "black water".'

Although the car didn't have air-conditioning, Lucy hurried toward it to escape the blistering heat. When she got on the highway, she asked her uncle, 'Did you hear anything about a sun-dance?'

At first he grunted a negative 'Huh-uh', then, 'Oh yeah, it's across the river, but I don't know where. George Many Robes is camping there. Saw him this morning. Are you going there?'

'Flora and Hilda are. Hilda wants to meet that German guy, Helmut Walking Eagle. You know, that guy who turned Indian?'

'Oh yeah, is he here?' he said indifferently, closing his eyes.

'Probably. He's always in the middle of Indian doings,' said Lucy.

'Shit, that guy's just a phony. How could anybody turn into something else? Huh? I don't think I could turn into a white man if I tried all my life. They wouldn't let me, so how does that German think he can be an Indian. White people think they can do anything—turn into Chinese or Indian— they're crazy!'

Sonny laid his head back on the seat and didn't say another word. Lucy felt embarrassed, but she had to agree with him; it seemed that Indians had come into focus lately. She'd read in the papers how some white woman in Hollywood became a medicine woman. She was selling her book on her life as a medicine woman. Maybe some white person or other person who wasn't Indian would get fooled by that book, but not an Indian. She herself didn't practise Indian religion, but she knew enough about it to know that one didn't just join an Indian religious group if one were not raised with it. That was a lot of the conflict going on among those people who were involved in it. They used sacred practices from other tribes, Navajo and Sioux, or whatever pleased them.

The heat of the day had reached its peak, and trails of dust hung suspended in the air wherever cars or trucks travelled the gravel roads on the reserve. Sonny fashioned a shade behind the house underneath the clothesline in the deep grass, spread a blanket, and filled a gallon jar from the pump. He covered the water with some old coats, lay down, and began to sweat the booze out.

The heat waves from this morning's forecast were accurate. It was just too hot. 'Lordy, it's hot,' exclaimed Lucy to Hilda as they brought the laundry in. 'It must be close to ninety-five or one hundred. Let's go up to Badger to my other aunt's house. She's got a tap by her house and the kids can cool off in her sprinkler. Come on, you kids. Do you want to go run in the sprinkler?'

The women covered the windows on the west side where the sun would shine. 'I'm going to leave all the windows open to let the air in,' said Lucy, as she walked around the house pushing them up.

Lucy's aunt's house sat amongst a clutter of junk. 'Excuse the mess,' she smiled at Hilda, waving her arm over her yard. 'Don't wanna throw it away, it might come in handy.' There were thick grass and weeds crisscrossed with paths to and from the clothesline, the outhouse, the woodstove. Lucy's aunt led them to an arbour shaded with huge spruce branches.

'This is nice,' cooed Hilda, admiring the branches. Lucy's aunt beamed, 'Yes, I told my old man, "Henry, you get me some branches that's not gonna dry up and blow away," and he did. He knows what's good for him. You sit down right here, and I'll get us some drinks.' She disappeared and soon returned with a large thermos and some plastic tumblers.

They spent the afternoon hearing about Henry, as they watched the kids run through the sprinkler that sprayed the water back and forth. Once in a while, a suggestion of a breeze would touch the women, but it was more as if they imagined it.

Before four, they left to pick Flora up and headed back to Lucy's. 'It's so hot after being in that cool cement building all day!' exclaimed Flora, as she settled herself into the car's stifling interior. 'One thing for sure, I'm not going home to cook anything. Lucy, do you think Bunky would mind if you came with us? I'll get us some Kentucky Fried Chicken and stuff in town so you don't have to cook. It's too hot to cook, anyway.' She rolled up a newspaper and fanned her face, which was already beginning to flush.

'No, he won't care. He'll probably want to sleep. We picked Sonny up in town. Both of them can lie around and get better. The kids would bother them if we were there.'

It was a long ride across the Napi River toward the Porcupine Hills. A few miles from the Hills, they veered off until they were almost by the river. 'Let's get off,' said Flora.

Hilda gasped at what she saw before her. There was a circle of teepees and tents with a large open area in the middle. Exactly in the centre of the opening was a circular structure covered with branches around the sides. Next to this was a solitary unpainted teepee. Some of the teepees were painted with lines around the bottom; others had orbs bordering them, and yet others had animal figures painted on them. Smoke rose from stoves outside the teepees as people prepared their evening meals. Groups of horses stood languidly in the waning heat of the day, their heads resting on one another's backs and their tails occasionally flicking insects away. The sound of bantering children and yapping dogs carried to where they stood.

'Let's eat here,' the kids said, poking their heads to look in the bags of food. Flora and Lucy spread a blanket on the ground, while Hilda continued to stand where she was, surveying the encampment. Flora pointed out the central leafy structure as the sacred area of prayer and dance.

'The teepee next to it is the sacred teepee. That's where the holy woman who is putting up the sun-dance stays the entire time. That's where they have the ceremonies.'

'How many sun-dances have you been to?' asked Hilda.

'This is my first time, but I know all about this from books,' said Flora. 'Helmut Walking Eagle wrote a book about it, too. I could try to get you one. He sells them cheaper to Indians.'

Hilda didn't eat much and kept looking down at the camp. 'It's really beautiful,' she said, as if to herself.

'Well, you better eat something before you get left out,' advised Lucy. 'These kids don't know when to stop eating chicken.'

'Yeah,' agreed Flora. 'Then we can go down and see who's all there.' Hilda had something to eat, and then they got back into the car and headed down toward the encampment. They drove around the edge of the camp and stopped by Flora's cousin's tent. 'Hi, Delphine,' said Flora, 'I didn't know you were camping here.'

Lucy knew Flora and Delphine were not especially close. Their fathers were half-brothers, which made them half-cousins. Delphine had grown up Mormon and had recently turned to Indian religion, just as Flora had grown up Catholic and was now exploring traditional beliefs. The same could be said about many of the people here. To top things off, there was some bad feeling between the cousins about a man, some guy they both had been involved with in the past.

'Can anybody camp here? I've got a teepee. How about if I camp next to you?'

Delphine bridled. 'You're supposed to camp with your own clan.'

Flora looked around the camp. 'I wondered who's my clan. Say, there's George Many Robes, he's my relation on my dad's side. Maybe I'll ask him if I can camp next to him.'

Delphine didn't say anything but busied herself with splitting kindling from a box of sawn wood she kept hidden underneath a piece of tarp. Jason spied a thermos under the tarp and asked for a drink of water.

'I have to haul water, and nobody pays for my gas,' grumbled Delphine, as she filled a cup halfway with water.

'Oh say,' inquired Flora, 'do you know if Helmut Walking Eagle is coming here? This girl is from Germany, and she wants to see him.'

'Over there, that big teepee with a Winnebago beside it. That's his camp,' Delphine answered, without looking at them.

'Is she mad at you?' Jason asked Flora.

'Yeah, it must be the heat,' Flora told him with a little laugh.

Elsie Walking Eagle was cooking the evening meal on a camp stove outside the teepee. She had some folding chairs that Lucy would've liked to sit down in, but Elsie didn't ask any of them to sit down though she was friendly enough.

'Is your husband here?' asked Flora.

'No, he's over in the sacred teepee,' answered Elsie.

'How long is he going to take?'

'Oh, he should be home pretty soon,' Elsie said, tending her cooking.

'Do you mind if we just wait? I brought this girl to see him. She's from Germany, too,' Flora said.

Lucy had never seen Helmut in anything other than Indian regalia. He was a smallish man with blond hair, a broad face, and a large thin nose. He wore his hair in braids and always wore round, pink shell earrings. Whenever Lucy saw him, she was reminded of the Plains Indian Museum across the line.

Helmut didn't even glance at the company but went directly inside the teepee. Flora asked Elsie, 'Would you tell him we'd like to see him?'

'Just wait here. I'll go talk to him,' Elsie said, and followed her husband inside. Finally, she came out and invited them in. 'He doesn't have much time to talk with you, so . . .' Her voice trailed off.

The inside of the teepee was stunning. It was roomy, and the floor was covered with buffalo hides. Backrests, wall hangings, parfleche bags, and numerous artifacts were magnificently displayed. Helmut Walking Eagle sat resplendent amidst his wealth. The women were dazzled. Lucy felt herself gaping and had to shush her children from asking any questions.

Helmut looked at them intently and rested his gaze on Hilda. Hilda walked toward him, her hand extended in greeting, but Helmut ignored it. Helmut turned to his wife and asked in Blackfoot, 'Who is this?'

'She says she's from Germany,' was all Elsie said, before making a quick move toward the door.

'Wait!' he barked in Blackfoot, and Elsie stopped where she was.

'I only wanted to know if you're familiar with my home town Weisbaden?' said Hilda.

'Do you know what she's talking about?' Helmut asked Elsie in Blackfoot. Elsie shook her head in a shamed manner.

'Why don't you ask *her* questions about Germany?' he hurled the words at

Hilda, then, looking meanly at his wife, he added, 'She's been there.' Elsie flinched, and, forcing a smile, waved weakly at the intruders and asked them in a kind voice to come outside. As Lucy waited to leave, she looked at Helmut whose jaw twitched with resentment. His anger seemed to be tangibly reaching out to them.

'Wow!' whispered Hilda in Lucy's ear.

Outside, Flora touched a book on the fold-out table. Its title read *Indian Medicine* and in smaller letters, *A Revival of Ancient Cures and Ceremonies*. There was a picture of Helmut and Elsie on the cover. Flora asked, 'Is this for sale?'

'No, that one's for someone here at camp, but you can get them in the bookstores.'

'How much are they?' Flora asked, turning the book over.

'They're twenty-seven dollars. A lot of work went into it.' Elsie replied.

Helmut, in Blackfoot, called out his wife's name, and Elsie said to her unwelcome callers, 'I don't have time to visit. We have a lot of things to do.' She left them and went in to her husband.

'He's the brains, she's the source,' Flora said. 'Let's go. My kids are probably wondering what happened to me.'

'I'm sorry I upset her husband. I didn't mean to,' said Hilda. 'I thought he would be willing to teach me something, because we're both German.'

'Maybe you could buy his book,' suggested Lucy.

'Look,' said Flora, 'if you're going to be around for a while, I'm going to a sun-dance this next weekend. I'm taking a few days off work. I have a friend up north who can teach you about Indian religion. She's a medicine woman. She's been to Germany. Maybe she even went to your home town.'

'Oh, really!' gushed Hilda. 'Of course, I'll be around. I'd love to go with you and meet your friends.'

'You can come into the sweat with us. First, you'll need to buy four square yards of cotton . . .' began Flora.

But Hilda wasn't really listening to her. She looked as if she were already miles and miles away in the north country. Now, a sweat, she thought, would be real Indian.

Annharte b. 1942

ANISHNABE

Coyote Trail

warm this trail
                my nose picks you to follow

your tracks quiver my whisker
                     my nostrils fill

you are a chunky one
                your tail dragged a leaf
                overturned bark

you too are hungry
        fat
        depressed
        I know all this news

I see your weight in microns of earth pressed
                          down
          you won't be an easy meal

like last week I sssll unk into town

I mean slunk not what I usually do

  QUICK PAWS QUICK PAWS GOTCHA

  YOU DON'T HEAR MY CLAWS UNLESS YOU PAUSE

that was something dead and delicious in that town

  growing more foul each day

  I call it fast food
  though it don't move much
  until I touch my paw to it
  I drool again over that thought

  the last time we met One Gulp
  you kicked against my canines

eager to become me
why are you making me exercise
to get a bite or two?

I was a writer once
know how to keep track of things
how interdependence works for me

Penumbra

for Betty

Temporary the shade my straw hat weaves
across my basket face of Caribe pleasure.
The bright sun makes me want to run and jump,
I had been told if I were smart, I'd stay hidden.
On my island, I keep to myself & lie around.
Turtles crawl past me to dig their nests.
Tortuga oil is outlawed and so am I.

Odd, this exposure of my not too recent killing.
Seventeen years it took getting to court
those who mashed my face because of dark skin.
Hating the contrast of each pinky penis
I left The Pas to be a turista and relax

They understand I stayed away to make sure
I'm not the only witness to their sorry act.
Not even good at it, I might add as insult.
The reserve is a huge donut around the town,
no place to go unless you're an Indian like me.
Laughing at the other end of the beach
gets me wondering how it's my turn.

Upbraid

Some New York whiteguy cops a free admission to an
Indian museum on account of he's married to an Indian
wife. I look on their map worried that my tribe is not
official & find the Saulteaux stretch well marked even to
the tundra. I thought we hung around cities. I sign in even
though Bungi is also a recognized tribe. There is a special

Bungi card which I've picked out to send to a friend who
knows there's no such thing. 'We can always be Bungis if
our reserves won't have us,' is my cheery note for the lost
years. She will laugh just as if I said, 'rabbit choker'.
I would need patience before saying, 'dogeater' to anyone
but in time I would. Wannabees take a lot of time to joke.
We buffalo all their attempts to be our nichimooses.
Maybe in my last years I will even defy this black neighbourhood which houses our heritage. I'll put on my beaded
barrette, grasping the grey hairs, hike into the big city with
my flappy house dress. I will be taken for an old white
lady on a vacation, having proven my blood by climbing
to Machu Picchu for the view.

Raced Out to Write This Up

I often race to write   I write about race   who do I write
about race   I must erase all trace of my race   I am an
eraser abrasive bracing myself embracing

it is classic to want to write about class   not low class but
up the nose class   I know I am classy   brassy   crass ass
of a clash comes when I move up a rung

we are different skins   different bins for brown rice and
white rice   not even a container of wild rice   you know
what they do when you are white and not rich   poverty
counts big when you count the cost of a caste a colourful
past

drunk as a skunk he danced at the Lebret Hotel   what for
no   not really   says he's not writing because they won't
publish his books   he does a number for a book   he
hugged me like I was his old Tibetan guru out on the
dance floor teleporting again

white racists notice colour when they don't have   you
might be off-white   a bone white   a cream white
alabaster white   dingy white if you don't wash often
enough   nevermind a non-bleached white   white with
pinkish undertone   peaches and cream   white with
freckles   who is colour blind   I write my black ink on
white paper   I white out write out my colour lighten up

full of self I saw old whitey again but he wanted to be a
part of a pure religion not like ours   not that he was a
white racist but a pure racist in his heart which had no
colour but our colour   red   red   mind you a few white
corpuscles but compared to the red they were a minority
not invisible

so few of me yet I still write not for the white audience but
the colour of their response to my underclassy class   the
flash of their fit to kill me why race away to the finish
when I cross the finish line will it be white   will I be red
from running   hot and cold touch me not less I am to be
divided against my self who is both red and white but not a
shade of pink maybe a beige pink blushed flushed off
white right I colour my winning everytime   I am still in the
red not the black   blackened red   reddened black   but
what about black n' blue   green at the gills   yellow belly
but what about the whitish frightish part I put it behind
behind me when I need to say my piece about togetherness
that we must breed not by ourselves but with everyone
out in the world who will listen   hey   I'm a half a half
breed   a mixed bag breed bread and butter bred my
whole grain bannock will taste as good to me even if I
smear on red jam sink my white teeth down into it down
the red hatch to the black hole   that is behind it all   the
whole black of me   the whore backing up behind me
the sore holy part of me which is the blackest darkest most
coloured most non-Indian, non-white slice of me bred to
wonder

One Way to Keep Track of Who Is Talking

If I change one word, I change history. What did I
say today? Do I even remember one word? Writing is
oral tradition. You have to practise the words on
someone before writing it down.

I do not intend to become the world's greatest Indian
orator. Maybe I might by accident. I might speak my
mind even when running off my mouth like I'm doing.
Language finds a tongue. Maybe it will be an Indian
accent.

Counting hostile Indians is made easier because they
don't talk much or very little. They look the part
—the part in the middle with braids. You never do
know if you are talking to an Indian.

Frozen Indians and frozen conversations predominate.
We mourn the ones at Wounded Knee. Our traditions
buried in one grave. Our frozen circles of silence
do no honour to them. We talk to keep our
conversations from getting too dead.

Coyote Columbus Cafe

1. once more it's Indian time

always good to be
born the midnight star
500 night years ago
quincentennial dawn
time worth waiting for
never a dull moment
time circles
how a weasel pops
in & out of old tunes

at closing time
I always spot a guy
other end of the bar
time for one more cruise
& conquest sneak up time
dare I ask Sh Sh
be still my boogit

I know the proper approach

*Boozho Dude. Hey, I'm talking
to you, Bozo Dude. My name is
Conquista. Come on adore me.*

my optimism looks good on me
in my territory my favourite bar
& grill I bar none grill some
bungee little bit twobitz
too bitzy for you?

why beat around the bush?

> *suppose my moccasin looms*
> *over your border, mistah,*
> *& you put a teensy toe*
> *on my medicine line.*

no problem lucky for me
I put my 'c' mark
that's coyote country 'cc'
not 'ccc' for cheap colonial crap

I have an attitude how to frequent
with colonizers (dey got me surrounded)
the right time is now
to get discovered again
& again very frequently
on a repetitive basis

2. what does a poor coyote girl do?

I act choosy about what abuse
my clientele gets
I am the first one got Coyotisma
(dey all say dey ever met one)
if they don't like dis talk
I do tease'em up to the climax
of my act but I am too damn direct
for the colonized coyote
poor oppressed critter

> *hey, you on the Columbus trip*

even when I yell at them
I get the usual ho hum complaint
as Coyotrix I lie and trick
what does the poor coyote girl do?

sure I pose baffling questions
administer random coyote IQ tests

> *what is paler than stranger?*

I warn you multiple answers possible
circle (a) the landlord comes around
first of the month to collect rent
wrong answer but don't pick that one
please follow directions & circle choice
what about (c) a landlord of colour?
right answer is (d) I got my rights
(b) I am the landlord around here

how about solving the mystery
did I discover Columbus first?

it could happen in a Woody Allen movie
Columbus gives a squirmy spiel

I don't know anybody on this
boat. Strong chance we won't
make it to land.

The map I made shows the Indies
beyond the curve in the earth.
Most of the crew are already
around the bend.

Columbus did lack
    cultural awareness
    equity
    affirmative action
    political correctness

3. Discovery is a hard act to follow

Colon would get comforted
by a kindly Native who'd say

Don't feel bad bro.
You're lost like the rest of us.

if Columbus was looking for turkey
he came to right place

he'd get the deserved treatment
join our healing process

Do you feel like a wounded
buffalo raging within?

mine's ready & raring to stampede
right over a cliff

ever wonder if Colon confessed
to a priest? what did he say
to turn on church officials
start a catholic Rambo trend

now they stalk our organizations
get on the board of directors
become an Indian expert and
discover more Indians
meet up with famous ones

take a class Native Studies
begin with Precolumbian Era
receive an embossed buckskin
certificate or a stone with
your name in petroglyph

if the class is full
because too many Indians
are just learning about
their culture & identity
then simply select a popular
bestseller HOW TO OUTINDIAN ANYONE

don't read any works
by First Nations writers
that's an advanced course
& you must crawl before you
creep up to rich Indians
playing casino bingo warriors
subscribe to Aboriginal news
& pretend Indian sympathy

lo, the po'Indian

Indian Act

Tell Old Indian joke
like Indian Affairs

Act Indian
had an Indian affair lately?

learn how to approach an elder
& what to do if a fakey one comes up
do you talk his or her talk?

I said sweat lodge	*I shed shwatch ludge*
makes body clean inside.	*meks buddy kleen insaid.*
Keep it up. Dance pow wow.	*Kip it up. Danz pahwah.*
After this, boy. You me	*Hafter, dis, bah. You me,*
go off big West German First	*go hoff big wes churman Furz*
International Wannabe Annual	*Hinter Natchinel Wanbee Annal*
Celebration. Take first; don't	*cel brayshun. Tek furz; don*
need to take plastic money	*need tek plashtik monhee*
visacard. You me same team.	*vissacad. You me sam tim*
Same team. Like hockey team.	*Sam tim. Lak hocky tim.*

Zjoonias, my boy. Think of it.   *Sch—oo—nash, my bah. Tinkobit*
Swiss bank account, hey boy!   *Swish bank a cunt, hey bah!*

discover an authentic Indian colonizer
slaver inside you & check your tongue
if still forked continue to discover
Other Indians do it to other Indians
first who do it to them first

former Columbus clones I implore you
you still got a chance, discover a first
nation friend lover first nation first
for keeps person

4. culture vulture voyeur trips

check coyote channel check   channel
check coyote check just thought I'd
check out my cheque what happened to
my cheque do you have my cheque
just came to pick up my cheque I
hope nobody cashed my cheque check
coyote channel check

the other day I got welfare
I had a big zit on my face
with a bandaid to cover up
I practised with my tough look
in the mirror

give me my cheque

I always forget to mention
we were too good way back when
to be real people before discovery

when I'm having an Indian taco day
I discover it's just about too late
not to educate the oppressor
but am I ever good at doing it

my tiny whiny coyote heart
thump de thump thump thump
kicking on the inside
to get outside to howl

how does a coyote girl get
a tale outta her mouth?

Bear Piss Water

Consider going to shaman school. With
enough practice on the rattle and drum
I'd be able to back up a poet. A course
in chanting would help me solo.

Consider dropping out in my first
year. A grade point average must be
maintained and all classes need prior
approval by a guardian spirit. I got
to consider what have I got to lose if
I drop out. I still got the nerve
it takes to set up shop and practice
without a license.

Consider Bear Piss Water not poetry. The
potency of natural spring water that a bear
made sacred. That water with the mercury
and acid rain. You find it just after the
turn off to Sioux Lookout. Just when the
craze for natural water was highest I
decided to try an experimental market.

Consider this water pistol in my hand
which I filled with a Bear Piss Water
sample. A squirt or two and you'll
be officially blessed and prepared
to listen to my eco-poetics.

I Want to Dance Wild Indian Black Face

I want to dance with the five tribes of wild Indians. Them
Wild Magnolias, Golden Eagles, Golden Stars, Black Eagles and
Young Sons of Geronimo dance wild Indian black face.

I want to hear the crowd say 'Ooh, them Indians are pretty today.'

I want to see a tribal official ready to lead his gang into battle
like Council Chief, Second Chief, Trail Chief and Wild Man.

I want to shout back wild calls and big boasts of Big Chiefs in
uptown New Orleans. I want to shout in my own city rez way.

I want to play in an inner circle of raggedy rhythm with beat-up
drums, cowbells, tambourines, whistles, wine bottles and sticks.

I want to carry on in a parade to sing Two Way Pak E Way. In
    Cajun,
Tuez bas qu'ou est means *Kill anyone who gets in the way*. I could
    be
a mean Indian some days.

I want to honour the spirits of Black Indians and Choctows,
Cherokees, Natchez and Seminoles who resisted the slave masters.

I want to wear a turkey feather in my hair and join the tribe of
the Creole Wild West. I don't want to be authentic all the time.

I want to be a Tribal 'Hawk' sing some jazz gospel ratty chanting.
Shout my spirit. Claim black and blues brothers same as sisters.

I want to mask Indian, adopt the Indian spirit figure once a year
dance in public with my big black face and talk back to chiefs.

I want to dance wild Indian blackface. I want to be that big bad
black Indian in a carnival parade. I want an Indian day off.

Put On My Mask For a Change

See the stripe that divides my face in two.
A vermilion dot marks the tip of my nose.
Take this ancient advice and face up to me.
This is not some recent ritual I picked up.
My beloved cave sister let us dab mud together.
Let us meet at the creek to apply the clay.
Make our healing salves original cosmetics.
Anoint bites, scratches, bumps and lumps.
We then wouldn't mistake each other for ugly.
Let us take back ceremonies to paint our skins.
You be my Zingu mother designing my face.
I the Zingu daughter lift my face from water.
Then you, then me, take turns smiling Jaguar.
The corners above your lips curl in laughter.
Under healing masques we are twinning spirits.
We are masks within each other holding out.
Whatever we must face is in the winking eye.

Ron Geyshick 1942–97

OJIBWAY

Inside Me

I know living inside me are two moose and two deer, a few butterflies, and the Lord is in my heart.

That albino deer is very strong—she's number one, the leader. She lives in my right shoulder, and the regular deer is in my left shoulder. That's why the albino is number one. I have two moose around my hips, just below the bone—a regular one, and a blue one. I don't know what kind he is. Maybe a timber moose.

The Creator is in my heart and I have four butterflies in each ear, from the size of a moth up to the largest. I don't know where those big ones come from. I guess they live somewhere way up in the top of the sky. These butterflies are from all over the world. One's from as far away as South America, a big blue one.

This is how the butterflies got inside me. Once day I was walking in the woods, not far from Snake Falls. I saw a white fog ahead of me and as I got closer, I saw it was a flock of butterflies, hundreds of them all shapes and colours. I kept walking but they wouldn't even move aside from my path. As I got closer, the noise got louder, like the sound of helicopters landing all around me. Then, when I was right in the middle, the four crawled into each of my ears, and they stayed there. Now all my messages come from them, just like a radio. When something is happening, I hear their wings fluttering inside my ears, sometimes two or three times in one night. When I hear this sound, I send my regular moose or the albino to find out what is going on.

To Bless a Child Before the Name

A little kid, a boy or a girl, can go places all over the world, from inside a mother's stomach. I know I travelled a lot at that time. Six months before the child is born, the parents should make something. At three months, they should make something else like diapers. Hang them inside where they can be seen. Then the little kid will know she's wanted, accepted.

When I was a kid, I didn't want to come out. There were all kinds of people in the room, different women, and I never have liked crowds. Coming out, I had a hard time trying to breathe. My eyes were burning, and that's why a kid cries.

As soon as I was born, I fasted for four days. Everybody's like that. A kid doesn't want too much, just to sleep and rest. From birth to four years old, you're really bright. That's when you're getting your spirits. An owl or a bird and butterflies will come. Your mom or dad might see them. These are your spirits, and this is when they first come to you.

We have ceremonies for blessing everything. First you lay out tobacco or a little dish of fruits and wild rice, meat or fish if possible, anything like that. You start off praying for the little girl, welcoming her to the world, then pray to the air, water, and Mother Earth: blessing the child so she'll reach the world she's going to walk on, breathe the air, drink the water.

Then we pray for food—fish, ducks, birds—blessing them, giving them offerings of tobacco and different berries and stuff we see growing. Then to the four directions. You can start off with any one of them. Start by talking to the Creator, blessing all these, asking for strength, gain, wisdom, to help this child. For a girl, ask that she'll have a decent husband and be good at skinning, even killing, so she will be a hunter herself.

If you're helping a boy, it's different. Bless him for hunting, thank all the animals he'll shoot, fish he'll eat, birds, berries he'll pick, so that he won't make a mistake, that he'll be greeted by them and will bless everything first before he picks it up. If he's a hunter, ask that he won't kill anything. A moose will give up his meat, but you're not killing anything because everything you see from nature has spirits, even dead trees.

Quiet

I don't know why I grabbed this red pen. I've never seen it. I didn't even know I had it. I'm wondering if there's any people on this reserve. It's so quiet, 9:30 PM, and unbelievably quiet. I'm wondering if I'm still alive.

I picked up this pen, so someone will show up. Whenever I sit down and write, someone walks in. But tonight, I can't even hear a skidoo. I know there's a meeting at the gym, so maybe all the people are there. It's very cold outside, 20 below zero, the radio says.

Lots of things are going through my mind. Sometimes, I can hear people talking about me, but I won't be bothered by that. I'll pretend I don't hear anything. I just looked out my window, and there's no sign of life. Maybe they're all dead and I'm alive.

I can certainly see the lights around. All this writing and no interruption yet. I've never gotten through a page before. Usually, I have to wait until the small hours of the night, right up to 3 or 4 AM. But now there isn't even a dog barking.

I know exactly why people avoid seeing me. I wish they'd do that all the time, so I could write something about them. I have a lot of thoughts about them, but if I let one word out, everybody would know within an hour. For sure, the next day. I know some day my dream will come true, and it will be quiet, but I won't be around the reserve.

Around the World in a Big Trout

When I came to Toronto from Thunder Bay in the big Air Canada plane, it was a lot like the time I went around the world inside a big trout. Those little round windows—the trout had windows just like that. And that humming noise inside Air Canada, that's the exact sound the trout makes when he's going. I guess that trout would be the size of a jet at least.

This trout took me all around the world, heading West and coming home again from the East. It didn't take long—about four days and four nights. You can get anywhere in the world from just a drop of water, because every drop of water connects to all the lakes and oceans in the earth. Also, the big trout can travel by means of underwater tunnels. So I wasn't too surprised when I got on that Air Canada jet.

A Windigo

My Dad and I were out trapping. My Dad was off checking the line. When he came back he said to me, 'We have to get away from here, back to the trapping cabin.' We were walking as fast as we could down the path, kind of walking and running at the same time. I was surprised and afraid because I'd never seen my Dad hurry anywhere before. When we got back to the cabin, I asked him what was wrong. He told me he had seen a *windigo* back there. A *windigo* is a cannibal spirit, a spirit in a cold wind that can drive people mad.

My Dad told me to go away, to get out of that place. But I said, 'No, Dad. I have my own powers and I want to help you out.' I guess I was about fourteen at the time and I'd been on my fasts. Already I knew I had some powers of my own. Dad said it was OK to stay nearby. He was going to climb up a hill to fight that spirit. When I asked to come with him, he said, 'No, you stay here. But you can watch.'

Then, from around a lake past a couple of hills to the west, I could hear two howls. They sounded just like, 'Yeow, yeow . . .'. And my Dad answered him in the same voice, 'Yeow, yeow . . .'. He'd climbed up to the top of the hill and said some prayers. When he did that, he grew up really big. He was at least three hundred feet tall. Then I saw *windigo*. He was in the form of a really big black dog, bigger than fifty feet tall. But it was OK because my Dad had grown to be a giant.

Four times my Dad and that black dog howled back and forth at each other. 'Yeow, yeow . . .'. Then my Dad reached over and pulled out one of the tallest trees from the hillside—a big old red pine. Dad was so big that when he reached down, that pine would only go up to his elbow. He grabbed the tree by the middle and pulled it up like he was picking a medicine plant. Then he hit the *windigo* over the head with it once, just once, and it was all over.

After he finished, he took some kind of medicine that shrunk him back down again to his regular size.

Cannibal Woman

This lady was living with her husband and daughter in a winter home in Quetico park with a few other families, maybe five or six altogether. She was allergic to the otter. Not knowing this, her husband made her skin one and stretch it. When you're allergic to some animal, it's usually to the blood or a certain part of its body. If you accidentally take some, it's like poison. It gets you before you know it. Usually, you are killed, or if you know what medicine to take you can be cured. But it is also possible that you will turn into *windigo*—a cannibal. You grow large and get powers to kill your own people and eat them up, a whole tribe. Sometimes, a man or woman has the knowledge and powers to attack and kill a person who has become a cannibal.

Cannibals are born and attack in the fall. As the winter ends, they start losing strength. By spring, they usually try to head to the south. They're much weaker. In other words, fall is the strongest time of year for them.

This story took place in the arctic, where it's real cold even in summer. The families were trapping. There's not many otters up there, but lots of seals. Anyway, this lady was allergic to otter. First, she killed her husband. Then, on the same night, she killed the other five families. But she wouldn't touch her daughter. After a while, the lady and her daughter moved on, heading towards the south. They passed a few families along the way that were camping a little off to the side. A cannibal won't bother people even if they're one mile to the side. Only those people who are right in their path.

They came to an Indian reserve which had lots of people, maybe forty or fifty families. The cannibal woman killed all of these Indians, but still did not touch her little girl. The only thing she'd do was cut her now and then, usually in her arm, to see if she was fat enough yet. She named her daughter *go tish shwash* which means 'testing her', and fed her what people eat. Whenever the food was gone, she'd pack up and leave again with *go tish shwash*. They were heading down into our country. It was almost mid-winter.

A cannibal must get wherever it's going in one winter. If it gets too late in the spring, or if you don't make it before winter runs out, you're dead. These two were taking longer than they should.

They came upon these trappers, four or five families, and killed them all then started travelling again. By now it was February or March and the mother felt weaker, she was losing all her energy.

They reached an Indian reservation. *Go tish shwash* was able to go visiting people. She knew her mom was doing the wrong thing. This tribe was still living in teepees and wigwams. Together with them, she made plans to kill her mother. They made ice at night and covered it during the day so it wouldn't melt off. *Go tish shwash*'s plan was to make her mother slip and when she fell down, all the men would cut off her head, arms, and legs, then burn her.

One day, they went ahead with it. As soon as the mother slipped, they cut her head off. It slipped far away, but she kept trying to reach for it, rolling her body toward it. While her head was still out of reach, they cut off her arms and legs. Then all the men and women hurried to build a big fire. They had to burn her before midnight, and there was a reason for that too, burning her into ashes before midnight. But her back would not burn for a long time, and that's where her main energy and powers were.

The month was April. As the spring and summer went on, *go tish shwash* kept dreaming about her mom. She was giving her daughter powers and instructions to keep her from becoming a cannibal too.

Go tish shwash's mom appeared in a dream. She said, 'Travel south as fast as you can. Early in the fall, go off by yourself. Eat an otter hind as soon as you find one, before the ice is solid enough to walk on. Be careful not to bother people, but keep on the same path we were following. You must get to a special place in the south before you turn weak in the winter. There, you will be treated by stone people from the ocean, and by star people.'

Go tish shwash kept walking south alone, She turned into a killer when her mom was killed. But she stood a good chance of making it south before the killing started. Even though *go tish shwash* was starving, she stayed away from the Indians. When she was weak from fasting she had a dream. In it, her mom came and gave her powers. The next morning, she was able to float, maybe two feet above the path, so her feet did not get stuck in the snow.

Go tish shwash made it south without killing any more Indians. The spirits were happy to see her. They knew she was coming, and prepared a big ceremony for her, as they do for all the cannibals that make it. The special medicine they gave her turned her into another kind of animal, a *mi sa be*, which is something like a Bigfoot. Now she could go north again in spring, and she would never eat meat again.

Thomas King b. 1943

CHEROKEE

The One About Coyote Going West

This one is about Coyote. She was going west. Visiting her relations. That's what she said. You got to watch that one. Tricky one. Full of bad business. No, no, no, no, that one says. I'm just visiting.

Going to see Raven.

Boy, I says. That's another tricky one.

Coyote comes by my place. She wag her tail. Make them happy noises. Sit on my porch. Look around. With them teeth. With that smile. Coyote put her nose in my tea. My good tea. Get that nose out of my tea, I says.

I'm going to see my friends, she says. Tell those stories. Fix this world. Straighten it up.

Oh boy, pretty scary that, Coyote fix the world, again.

Sit down, I says. Eat some food. Hard work that fix up the world. Maybe you have a song. Maybe you have a good joke.

Sure, says Coyote. That one wink her ears. Lick her whiskers.

I tuck my feet under that chair. Got to hide my toes. Sometimes that tricky one leave her skin sit in that chair. Coyote skin. No Coyote. Sneak around. Bite them toes. Make you jump.

I been reading those books, she says.

You must be one smart Coyote, I says.

You bet, she says.

Maybe you got a good story for me, I says.

I been reading about that history, says Coyote. She tricks that nose back in my tea. All about who found us Indians.

Ho, I says. I like those old ones. Them ones are the best. You tell me your story, I says. Maybe some biscuits will visit us. Maybe some moose-meat stew come along, listen to your story.

Okay, she says and she sings her story song.

> Snow's on the ground the snakes are asleep.
> Snow's on the ground my voice is strong.
> Snow's on the ground the snakes are asleep.
> Snow's on the ground my voice is strong.

She sings like that. With that tail, wagging. With that smile. Sitting there.

Maybe I tell you the one about Eric the Lucky and the Vikings play hockey for the Old-timers, find us Indians in Newfoundland, she says.

Maybe I tell you the one about Christopher Cartier looking for something good to eat. Find us Indians in a restaurant in Montreal.

Maybe I tell you the one about Jacques Columbus come along that river, Indians waiting for him. We all wave and say, here we are, here we are.

Everyone knows those stories, I says. White man stories. Baby stories you got in your mouth.

No, no, no, no, says Coyote. I read these ones in that old book.

Ho, I says. You are trying to bite my toes. Everyone knows who found us Indians. Eric the Lucky and that Christopher Cartier and that Jacques Columbus come along later. Those ones get lost. Float about. Walk around. Get mixed up. Ho, ho, ho, ho, those ones cry, we are lost. So we got to find them. Help them out. Feed them. Show them around.

Boy, I says. Bad mistake that one.

You are very wise, grandmother, says Coyote, bring her eyes down. Like she is sleepy. Maybe you know who discovered Indians.

Sure, I says. Everyone knows that. It was Coyote. She was the one.

Oh, grandfather, that Coyote says. Tell me that story. I love those stories about that sneaky one. I don't think I know that story, she says.

All right, I says. Pay attention.

Coyote was heading west. That's how I always start this story. There was nothing else in this world. Just Coyote. She could see all the way, too. No mountains then. No rivers then. No forests then. Pretty flat then. So she starts to make things. So she starts to fix this world.

This is exciting, says Coyote, and she takes her nose out of my tea.

Yes, I says. Just the beginning, too. Coyote got a lot of things to make.

Tell me, grandmother, says Coyote. What does the clever one make first?

Well, I says. Maybe she makes that tree grows by the river. Maybe she makes that buffalo. Maybe she makes that mountain. Maybe she makes them clouds.

Maybe she makes that beautiful rainbow, says Coyote.

No, I says. She don't make that thing. Mink makes that.

Maybe she makes that beautiful moon, says Coyote.

No, I says. She don't do that either. Otter finds that moon in a pond later on.

Maybe she makes the oceans with that blue water, says Coyote.

No, I says. Oceans are already here. She don't do any of that. The first thing Coyote makes, I tell Coyote, is a mistake.

Boy, Coyote sit up straight. Them eyes pop open. That tail stop wagging. That one swallow that smile.

Big one, too, I says. Coyote is going west thinking of things to make. That one is trying to think of everything to make at once. So she don't see that hole. So she falls in that hole. Then those thoughts bump around. They run into each other. Those ones fall out of Coyote's ears. In that hole. Ho, that Coyote cries. I have fallen into a hole. I must have made a mistake. And she did.

So, there is that hole. And there is that Coyote in that hole. And there is that big mistake in that hole with Coyote. Ho, says that mistake. You must be Coyote.

That mistake is real big and that hole is small. Not much room. I don't want to tell you what that mistake looks like. First mistake in the world. Pretty scary. Boy, I can't look. I got to close my eyes. You better close your eyes, too, I tell Coyote.

Okay, I'll do that, she says, and she puts her hands over her eyes. But she don't fool me. I can see she's peeking.

Don't peek, I says.

Okay, she says. I won't do that.

Well, you know, that Coyote thinks about the hole. And she thinks about how she's going to get out of that hole. She thinks how she's going to get that big mistake back in her head.

Say, says that mistake. What is that you're thinking about?

I'm thinking of a song, says Coyote. I'm thinking of a song to make this hole bigger.

That's a good idea, says that mistake. Let me hear your hole song.

But that's not what Coyote sings. She sings a song to make the mistake smaller. But that mistake hears her. And that mistake grabs Coyote's nose. And that one pulls off her mouth so she can't sing. And that one jumps up and down on Coyote until she is flat. Then that one leaps out of that hole, wanders around looking for things to do.

Well, Coyote is feeling pretty bad, all flat her nice fur coat full of stomp holes. So she thinks hard, and she thinks about a healing song. And she tries to sing a healing song, but her mouth is in other places. So she thinks harder and tries to sing that song through her nose. But that nose don't make any sound, just drip a lot. She tries to sing that song out her ears, but those ears don't hear anything.

So, that silly one thinks real hard and tries to sing out her butt-hole. Pssst! Pssst! That is what that butt-hole says, and right away things don't smell so good in that hole. Pssst.

Boy, Coyote thinks. Something smells.

That Coyote lies there flat and practise and practise. Pretty soon, maybe two days, maybe one year, she teach that butt-hole to sing. That song. That healing song. So that butt-hole sings that song. And Coyote begins to feel better. And Coyote don't feel so flat anymore. Pssst! Pssst! Things still smell pretty bad, but Coyote is okay.

That one look around in that hole. Find her mouth. Put that mouth back. So, she says to that butt-hole. Okay, you can stop singing now. You can stop making them smells now. But, you know, that butt-hole is liking all that singing, and so that butt-hole keeps on singing.

Stop that, says Coyote. You going to stink up the whole world. But it don't. So Coyote jumps out of that hole and runs across the prairies real fast. But that butt-hole follows her. Pssst. Pssst. Coyote jumps into a lake, but that butt-hole don't drown. It just keeps on singing.

Hey, who is doing all that singing, someone says.

Yes, and who is making that bad smell, says another voice.

It must be Coyote, says a third voice.

Yes, says a fourth voice. I believe it is Coyote.

That Coyote sit in my chair, put her nose in my tea, say, I know who that voice is. It is that big mistake playing a trick. Nothing else is made yet.

No, I says. That mistake is doing other things.

Then those voices are spirits, says Coyote.

No, I says. Them voices belong to them ducks.

Coyote stand up on my chair. Hey, she says, where did them ducks come from?

Calm down, I says. This story is going to be okay. This story is doing just fine. This story knows where it is going. Sit down. Keep your skin on.

So.

Coyote look around, and she see them four ducks. In that lake. Ho, she says. Where did you ducks come from? I didn't make you yet.

Yes, says them ducks. We were waiting around, but you didn't come. So we got tired of waiting. So we did it ourselves.

I was in a hole, says Coyote.

Pssst. Pssst.

What's that noise, says them ducks. What's that bad smell?

Never mind, says Coyote. Maybe you've seen something go by. Maybe you can help me find something I lost. Maybe you can help me get it back.

Those ducks swim around and talk to themselves. Was it something awful to look at? Yes, says Coyote, it certainly was. Was it something with ugly fur? Yes, says Coyote, I think it had that, too. Was it something that made a lot of noise? ask them ducks. Yes, it was pretty noisy, says Coyote. Did it smell bad, them ducks want to know. Yes, says Coyote. I guess you ducks have seen my something.

Yes, says them ducks. It is right behind you.

So that Coyote turn around, and there is nothing there.

It's still behind you, says those ducks.

So Coyote turn around again but she don't see anything.

Pssst! Pssst!

Boy, says those ducks. What a noise! What a smell! They say that, too. What an ugly thing with all that fur!

Never mind, says that Coyote, again. That is not what I'm looking for. I'm looking for something else.

Maybe you're looking for Indians, says those ducks.

Well, that Coyote is real surprised because she hasn't created Indians, either. Boy, says that one, mischief is everywhere. This world is getting bent.

All right.

So Coyote and those ducks are talking, and pretty soon they hear a noise. And pretty soon there is something coming. And those ducks says, oh, oh, oh, oh. They say that like they see trouble, but it is not trouble. What comes along is a river.

Hello, says that river. Nice day. Maybe you want to take a swim. But Coyote don't want to swim, and she looks at that river and she looks at that river again. Something's not right here, she says. Where are those rocks? Where are those rapids? What did you do with them waterfalls? How come you're so straight?

And Coyote is right. That river is nice and straight and smooth without any bumps or twists. It runs both ways, too, not like a modern river.

We got to fix this, says Coyote, and she does. She pours some rocks in that river, and she fixes it so it only runs one way. She puts a couple of waterfalls in and makes a bunch of rapids where things get shallow fast.

Coyote is tired with all this work, and those ducks are tired just watching. So that Coyote sits down. So she closes her eyes. So she puts her nose in her tail. So those ducks shout, wake up, wake up! Something big is heading this way! And they are right.

Mountain comes sliding along, whistling. Real happy mountain. Nice and round. This mountain is full of grapes and other good things to eat. Apples, peaches, cherries. Howdy-do, says that polite mountain, nice day for whistling.

Coyote looks at that mountain, and that one shakes her head. Oh, no, she says, this mountain is all wrong. How come you're so nice and round? Where are those craggy peaks? Where are all them cliffs? What happened to all that snow? Boy, we got to fix this thing, too. So she does.

Grandfather, grandfather, says that Coyote, sit in my chair, put her nose in my tea. Why is that Coyote changing all those good things?

That is a real sly one, ask me that question. I look at those eyes. Grab them ears. Squeeze that nose. Hey, let go my nose, that Coyote says.

Okay, I says. Coyote still in Coyote skin. I bet you know why Coyote change that happy river. Why she change that mountain sliding along whistling.

No, says that Coyote, look around my house, lick her lips, make them baby noises.

Maybe it's because she is mean, I says.

Oh, no, says Coyote. That one is sweet and kind.

Maybe it's because that one is not too smart.

Oh, no, says Coyote. That Coyote is very wise.

Maybe it's because she made a mistake.

Oh, no, says Coyote. She made one of those already.

All right, I says. Then Coyote must be doing the right thing. She must be fixing up the world so it is perfect.

Yes, says Coyote. That must be it. What does that brilliant one do next?

Everyone knows what Coyote does next, I says. Little babies know what Coyote does next.

Oh no, says Coyote. I have never heard this story. You are a wonderful storyteller. You tell me your good Coyote story.

Boy, you got to watch that one all the time. Hide them toes.

Well, I says. Coyote thinks about that river. And she thinks about that mountain. And she thinks somebody is fooling around. So she goes looking around. She goes looking for that one who is messing up the world.

She goes to the north, and there is nothing. She goes to the south, and there is nothing there, either. She goes to the east, and there is still nothing there. She goes to the west, and there is a pile of snow tires.

And there is some televisions. And there is some vacuum cleaners. And there is a bunch of pastel sheets. And there is an air humidifier. And there is a big mistake sitting on a portable gas barbecue reading a book. Big book. Department store catalogue.

Hello, says that mistake. Maybe you want a hydraulic jack.

No, says that Coyote. I don't want one of them. But she don't tell that mistake what she wants because she don't want to miss her mouth again. But when she thinks about being flat and full of stomp holes, that butt-hole wakes up and begins to sing. Pssst. Pssst.

What's that noise? says that big mistake.

I'm looking for Indians, says that Coyote, real quick. Have you seen any? What's that bad smell?

Never mind, says Coyote. Maybe you have some Indians around here.

I got some toaster ovens, says that mistake.

We don't need that stuff, says Coyote. You got to stop making all those things. You're going to fill up this world.

Maybe you want a computer with a colour monitor. That mistake keeps looking through that book and those things keep landing in piles all around Coyote.

Stop, stop, cries Coyote. Golf cart lands on her foot. Golf balls bounce off her head. You got to give me that book before the world gets lopsided.

These are good things, says that mistake. We need these things to make up the world. Indians are going to need this stuff.

We don't have any Indians, says Coyote.

And that mistake can see that that's right. Maybe we better make some Indians, says that mistake. So that one looks in that catalogue, but it don't have any Indians. And Coyote don't know how to do that, either. She has already made four things.

I've made four things already, she says. I got to have help.

We can help, says some voices and it is those ducks come swimming along. We can help you make Indians, says the white duck. Yes, we can do that, says the green duck. We have been thinking about this, says that blue duck. We have a plan, says the red duck.

Well, that Coyote don't know what to do. So she tells them ducks to go ahead because this story is pretty long and it's getting late and everyone wants to go home.

You still awake, I says to Coyote. You still here?

Oh yes, grandmother, says Coyote. What do those clever ducks do?

So I tell Coyote that those ducks lay some eggs. Ducks do that, you know. That white duck lay an egg, and it is blue. That red duck lay an egg, and it is green. That blue duck lay an egg, and it is red. That green duck lay an egg, and it is white.

Come on, says those ducks. We got to sing a song. We got to do a dance. So they do. Coyote and that big mistake and those four ducks dance around the eggs. So they dance and sing for a long time, and pretty soon Coyote gets hungry.

I know this dance, she says, but you got to close your eyes when you do it or nothing will happen. You got to close your eyes tight. Okay, says those ducks. We can do that. And they do. And that big mistake closes its eyes, too.

But Coyote, she don't close her eyes, and all of them start dancing again, and Coyote dances up close to that white duck, and she grabs that white duck by her neck.

When Coyote grabs that duck, that duck flaps her wings, and that big mistake hears the noise and opens them eyes. Say, says that big mistake, that's not the way the dance goes.

By golly, you're right, says Coyote, and she lets that duck go. I am getting it mixed up with another dance.

So they start to dance again. And Coyote is very hungry, and she grabs that blue duck, and she grabs his wings, too. But Coyote's stomach starts to make hungry noises, and that mistake opens them eyes and sees Coyote with the blue duck. Hey, says that mistake, you got yourself mixed up again.

That's right, says Coyote, and she drops the duck and straightens out that neck. It sure is good you're around to help me with this dance.

They all start that dance again, and, this time, coyote grabs the green duck real quick and tries to stuff it down that greedy throat, and there is nothing hanging out but them yellow duck feet. But those feet are flapping in Coyote's eyes, and she can't see where she is going, and she bumps into the big mistake and the mistake turns around to see what has happened.

Ho, says that big mistake, you can't see where you're going with them yellow duck feet flapping in your eyes, and that mistake pulls that green duck out of Coyote's throat. You could hurt yourself dancing like that.

You are one good friend, look after me like that, says Coyote.

Those ducks start to dance again, and Coyote dances with them, but that red duck says, we better dance with one eye open, so we can help Coyote with this dance. So they dance some more, and, then, those eggs begin to move around, and those eggs crack open. And if you look hard, you can see something inside those eggs.

I know, I know, says that Coyote, jump up and down on my chair, shake up my good tea. Indians come out of those eggs. I remember this story, now. Inside those eggs are the Indians Coyote's been looking for.

No, I says. You are one crazy Coyote. What comes out of those duck eggs are baby ducks. You better sit down, I says. You may fall and hurt yourself. You may spill my tea. You may fall on top of this story and make it flat.

Where are the Indians? says that Coyote. This story was about how Coyote found the Indians. Maybe the Indians are in the eggs with the baby ducks.

No, I says, nothing in those eggs but little ducks. Indians will be along in a while. Don't lose your skin.

So.

When those ducks see what has come out of the eggs, they says, boy, we didn't get that quite right. We better try that again. So they do. They lay them eggs. They dance that dance. They sing that song. Those eggs crack open and out comes some more baby ducks. They do this seven times and each time, they get more ducks.

By golly, says those four ducks. We got more ducks than we need. I guess we got to be the Indians. And so they do that. Before Coyote or that big mistake can mess things up, those four ducks turn into Indians, two women and two men. Good-looking Indians, too. They don't look at all like ducks any more.

But those duck-Indians aren't too happy. They look at each other and they begin to cry. This is pretty disgusting, they says. All this ugly skin. All these bumpy bones. All this awful black hair. Where are our nice soft feathers? Where are our beautiful feet? What happened to our wonderful wings? It's probably all that Coyote's fault because she didn't do the dance right, and those four duck-Indians come over and stomp all over Coyote until she is flat like before. Then they leave. That big mistake leave, too. And that Coyote, she starts to think about a healing song.

Pssst. Pssst.

That's it, I says. It is done.

But what happens to Coyote, says Coyote. That wonderful one is still flat.

Some of these stories are flat, I says. That's what happens when you try to fix this world. This world is pretty good all by itself. Best to leave it alone. Stop messing around with it.

I better get going, says Coyote. I will tell Raven your good story. We going to fix this world for sure. We know how to do it now. We know how to do it right.

So, Coyote drinks my tea and that one leave. And I can't talk any more because I got to watch the sky. Got to watch out for falling things that land in piles. When that Coyote's wandering around looking to fix things, nobody in this world is safe.

Harold Cardinal b. 1945

CREE

A Canadian *What the Hell It's All About*

Over the past century, the Indian people, and many white people as well, have become increasingly aware of the aura of conflict surrounding the relations between white man and red man in Canada. The struggle now has become so intense and so emotional for so many of our people, especially our young people; and has led to equally intense but opposite emotional response from elements of white society, that I think the time has come for us to sit back and try to determine in our minds just what the hell this struggle really is all about.

We have been fighting for so long now that the original misunderstandings and differences that created this conflict have been forgotten. Various tactics have been tried by one side and countered by the other; emotions have taken over from reason; and the passions born of hatred have grown until neither fighter any longer knows, or cares, what the fight is about. The fight has become an end in itself.

In the long run such an attitude can only be disastrous, not just for our people, but for our country. To reverse this unfortunate trend of confrontation, we must examine some of the myths that have contributed to the situation currently faced by the Indian people in this country. We must re-examine the basic philosophies inherent in any discussion with white society, or with white individuals.

The past and the present are important, but basically we have to look to the future. In that context, many people concerned about the current economic conditions in Canada are closely examining just what kind of future, what kind of country they really want to build; not for a minority but for all Canadians; not for their generation but for all future generations. It must be with this in mind that we begin re-examining the relationship between Indians and members of the larger Canadian society. This is true whether we are talking about individuals in that larger society, or whether we are talking in collective terms about the Indian entity, the Indian nation, or about the white entity, the white nation.

One problem that has largely contributed to the misunderstanding between us is the terminology we use in efforts to relate to each other. Not only are the languages of the opposing sides drastically different, but the societies using those languages are in so many respects so very strange to one another that communication becomes almost impossible. A perfect example of this type of problem was the confrontation between Nikita Khrushchev and John Kennedy in Vienna. To a person not overly familiar with the opposing ideologies it would be difficult to understand, from the translation of what was said, why the two leaders disagreed so violently when to all appearances what they said differed so little. Only with a thorough knowledge of the background and opposing ideologies of each side could one hope to understand what the shouting was all about.

The situation faced in Canada between Indian and white races is much the same.

There has always been one question that a white man asks an Indian. It is asked by the average Joe on the street of an Indian just off the reserve; professional people of both sides ask it of each other. It is, to the Indians, a Have-you-stopped-beating-your-wife? sort of question. It may be posed in many ways, not only by the individual white person, but by the government as well. It is being posed more frequently and even more demandingly these days by the unelected government—the civil servants, provincial or federal. It is being posed with perhaps more integrity by political leaders; from MLAs to premiers, from MPs to the Prime Minister. The question, simplistically put, is: 'Why do you not want to be Canadian?'

Today, an Indian person has great difficulty responding to that question rationally, because the term *Canadian* means so many different things to the people of Canada, be they white or red.

Whatever we may think about the differences between Canada and the United States of America, at least people in the United States learn one lesson early and well. They are taught, virtually from the cradle on, what being an American is all about. Such teaching may seem to many of us to be chauvinism—distasteful and propagandistic—but from the time they are able to reason, children go through an indoctrination process that gives them a sense of patriotism, a sense of pride in being American. They may not always articulate this clearly, but a sureness of their identity as Americans is instilled in them. While Americans still may not fully understand the meaning of cultural plurality, at least they are not asking each other who they are.

In Canada there is no such universally accepted definition of the concept of Canadianism. There is no easy, sure national identity for Canada or for Canadians. When the question, 'You do want to be a Canadian, you don't want to be something else?' is asked it's always immensely difficult for an individual or a group to answer, because so much depends upon the questioner's concept of Canadianism. Unless we reach a common agreement on the meaning of that term, we must always define the concept as we understand it, so that others will know what we mean when we discuss Canadianism.

For too long, both the white and the Indian political leaders have been involved in a Quixotic battle. Our imaginary windmills have been our varying concepts and definitions of what being Canadian is all about. Our feelings, our emotions, our passions have almost reached their climax. It is even more necessary for Indian people to really look at what they are talking about; to understand the full meaning of their terms when they are defining themselves to each other or to members of the larger society. Only then can we understand what we are fighting about, what we are trying to work out together, what it really is that we are after.

One of the most personally rewarding, and, paradoxically, the most frustrating experiences of my life has stemmed from my attempts to decipher the meaning our people attach to the term, *Canada*, and to being *Canadian*. It is rewarding to catch a glimpse of what our old people who speak no English mean when they tell us of their concept of Canada and of Canadianism.

Canada is a word taken from the Cree language. Other tribes may claim it also, but from the Cree point of view, the word *Canada* stems from the Cree word *Ka-Kanata*, a word that translated literally means 'that which is clean'. The full Cree term to describe the country is *Ka-Kanata-Aski*—'the land that is clean'. Thus, when we speak of our country in Cree, at the same time we define it as 'the clean land'. We describe our country as the clean land because it belongs to our Creator, who is a clean being. If we, as Cree-speaking people, use the term *Ka-Kanata* or *Canada* then, we know precisely what we are talking about. But when a white man calls this country *Canada*, I don't know what he means; I don't know what the meaning is from the white point of view. I don't have any precise definition to go by.

For the Cree-speaking person, the term *Nee-yow* is used when that person is affirming his or her Canadianism. When a white person says, 'I am a Canadian', a Cree-speaking person says, 'I am a *Nee-yow*'. Typically, it is a descriptive term. A Cree-speaking person, describing himself in his own language, does not say, 'I am Cree', because *Cree* is merely a word used by whites to describe one group of Indians. When those Indians known as Cree to the white world, describe themselves as *Nee-yow* they are saying, 'We are members of that nation of people who are part of the four seasons of Mother Earth.' They are saying, 'We are part of this land, and because we are part of this land we are also part of our Father's creation and hence His children.'

This is where the problem of definition crops up. It is difficult for a white man, not understanding Indian culture, to know what someone means when he says, 'I am a member of a nation of people who are part of Mother Earth.'

When a white person describes him or herself as Canadian, it is difficult for me to know what his or her definition of that term is. When a Cree-speaking person says that he or she is *Nee-yow*, that person is also describing precisely what being a Canadian is all about to him or her. I do not know if the white man's understanding and definition of the word is as precise as ours when he identifies himself as a Canadian.

Another way to explain the Cree use of such a term is to use an analogy of the Roman Catholic Church. Other religions in other parts of the world may provide similar analogies, but whenever a person is baptized into the Catholic Church, that person is given a special name. Usually the name is that of a saint who will give guidance and protection to the child as he or she goes along the path of life; a patron saint who in fact will be the spiritual guardian of the child. The same process applies to Indian name-giving, but it also applies to tribes. The tribes have a patron saint who will look after them. Thus when a Cree-speaking person says *Nee-yow* he is saying, 'I am born into that tribe which will look to this land as its patron, or as its guardian and guide through life.' It's a religious-cultural definition of being a Canadian.

Therefore, I believe that a part of our communal problem is that there have never been any precise translations between the Indian and white languages.

Other tribes, such as the Chipewyan, the Slavey, the Dogrib, the Navajo, call themselves *Dene*, giving their definition of themselves as a people in their language. In fact, all tribes across the continent have their own particular definitions of themselves as they relate to their environment, whether that environment is Mother Earth, as it is on the prairies, or the water, as it may be for the Indians living on the coasts. I think it is that thinking that distinguishes the traditional element right across the country.

For a long time much of the heritage of our culture has been lost even to Indians and is only now beginning to be understood again. When an Indian person describes this land as *Ka-Kanata*, 'the clean land', he is implicitly defining his responsibility to that land. If it is a clean land, then he has a responsibility to keep himself clean. Not just clean in the sense of television's White Tornado, but clean in the sense of maintaining a balanced relationship with the land. This means that whatever an Indian takes from the land, he will replace somehow. At the very least he will return the proper respect to the land for the gifts the land has given to him.

It goes even further than that. If one talks about a clean person, in a very broad sense one is talking in a philosophical way about a person who is honest with himself, with his family, with his neighbours, with all people; a person who is clean in the sense that purity is cleanliness. To the white man, some of these responsibilities are religious, and some are the responsibilities of citizenship. More simply they describe the way people *should* relate to one another, the way they should help one another.

When a person speaking from the traditional point of view says, in Cree, that he is a clean person, he relates himself to the clean land. This signifies recognition of the fact that this land belongs to, and was created by a clean being; a being known as God to some people, Jehovah to some, perhaps Manitou to others. Whatever the name used, the Creator's existence is recognized, and because people believe that He is clean and pure, and that all things He has created are clean, then one has to be pure in order to relate to Him.

Unfortunately there are many Indians today who do not understand this. While this may be the case for perhaps even the majority of Indians, I suspect that almost universally the white man has no awareness of our people's perception of their land and of themselves. Few white men have even an inkling of what Indians mean when they describe themselves and their relationship to the land, and to Canada. Consequently, there is a mistaken belief that our people's concept of Canada and of being Canadian is necessarily in conflict with the concept that white people have.

When the Prime Minister talks about the kind of country he would like Canada to be, and the type of Canadians he would like to see develop within such a country, and when an elder from any of Canada's tribes explains his vision of what this country and its people should be, the concepts are not that dissimilar. Two more disparate people, speaking in different tongues, speaking from different worlds, would be hard to find anywhere, and yet their dreams, their visions, their hopes, and their aspirations could not find any greater fusion.

But all too often, both sides: Indians and their political leaders, whites and their political leaders: unable to see except through the tunnel-vision of their respective cultures, fail entirely to look beyond the surface differences which loom so large, and go on determinedly believing that there has to be an inherent conflict between the dreams of a Prime Minister and the dreams of a tribal elder.

It is the absurdity of the Khrushchev-Kennedy dialogue all over again. Of course the white Prime Minister and the Indian elder have different personal perceptions, but must the white man believe that because an old Indian, giving a definition of nationhood and its responsibilities, expresses his beliefs in a language that is different, that draws its images from a different culture, therefore he does not merit consideration? Must the Indian, because the white man dresses differently, behaves differently, and uses words that sound strange, be convinced that there can be no common meeting ground? Must each then, based on his own narrow perceptions, reject the other, perhaps even launch wars to make certain the other side comes around to the 'proper' point of view?

I think the difference in definition and the lack of understanding has created what I call a *mirage gap* between people in this country. What appears to be a divergence on the meanings of *Canada* and *Canadian* as used by people on both sides is more mirage than reality. Close examination of the definitions clearly shows that there isn't really that much of a gap between them. But the practical point of this is, and it's a major point based on that mirage gap in understanding, we have a government that has developed policies aimed at assimilating Indians to make them into what the larger, white society perceives to be Canadians. Thus one finds all programs emanating from the federal or the provincial governments, whether concerned with economic development, education, or anything else, having as their central purpose the assimilation, or, at the very least, the integration of Indians into the Canadian mainstream.

Assimilation, integration—the two favourite terms used by the white society over a century of relationships between Indians and whites. Over a hundred years of relationships have been based on a complete misunderstanding. What it amounts to is simply that the larger society has never understood, and still doesn't understand the Indian concept of the terms *Canada* and *Canadian*.

As an illustration of how completely overwhelming such a misunderstanding can be: when an Indian suggests that he simply wants to remain an Indian, that declaration is perceived as both un-Canadian and a wholly undesirable goal. Naturally it follows that no effort must be left untried to prevent that poor, benighted Indian from pursuing such a goal.

To a large degree it was on this basis that the Trudeau Government came up with their white paper in 1969 which proposed nothing less than total assimilation of the Indian people. In spite of the quick and fiercely emotional rejection of that proposal, the government to this day does not know why the Indians reacted so violently, and cannot understand why they wouldn't accept such a reasonable philosophy. For the most part the government remains convinced that if only the Indians understood what that white paper was talking about they would accept it as being the best path for them to follow.

Because of such a major, fundamental misunderstanding a lot of wrong assumptions are being made by people both in the larger society and within the Indian community. We have what seems to be a Mexican stand-off between two sides, each passionately believing that what they stand for is right, and that if only those other fellows would understand there would be no problem. In maintaining such a stand-off, incidences of emotional confrontation between Indians and whites are escalating across the land. Many individuals who mean well now find themselves in a fight that they did not start and worse yet don't know how to get out of. Consequently, and quite understandably, they are committed to winning that fight—however they can.

Because so few people on either the Indian or the white side really understand the basis of the relationship between the two societies, or the differences in cultural definitions and perspectives, we face another danger. This is the intrusion into the battleground of people who mistakenly identify and confuse their own ideological beliefs with Indian problems and grievances. This can be a dangerous intrusion. A left-wing element in this country, not really understanding what the Indian nations are all about, nevertheless has seized upon the opportunity of the present unsettled Indian situation as ripe for promotion of their kind of thinking and action. Their doctrinaire-oriented operation is in opposition to the values put forward by the establishment. Over the next few years as this left-wing element strives to assert itself, such action undoubtedly will spawn a counter-balancing right-wrong faction. Then there arises a real danger that Indian people in this country will polarize around different ideologies with which perhaps they have no legitimate reason to be involved. I very much fear that Indians, as did the whites before them, will get sucked unwittingly into a purely political battle of ideologies which can do them no good and more likely will harm them and their cause.

This, it seems to me, is one of the oncoming dangers that we face, especially in the type of economic climate that this country is moving toward. As individuals search for ways to meet the threat posed to their society by world and national economic ailments, members of both the larger society and the minorities will tend to look for pat answers. Perhaps the easiest of such answers are precisely those backed by differing ideological movements.

Already there are definite signs that this is happening. Not long ago a caravan of young Indians marched from western Canada to Ottawa, only to wind up getting their heads smashed by police on Parliament Hill. Individuals who were involved have identified a very strong influence, indeed almost a takeover of that caravan, by Maoists and other leftist groups.

Even more seriously there seems to be emerging from the Northwest Territories' Dene Declaration (a statement of Indian nationhood issued by the tribes of the Northwest Territories), an intrusion of left-wing thinking that is perhaps much closer to the academic community in Toronto than it is to the Dene. With that tainted declaration as a guide, I fear that the Indian people of the Northwest Territories may well find themselves locked in a needless battle with the federal government; a futile battle fought for purposes foreign to their own, a battle that can only serve to divert their attention and energies away from their true goals. They may also find themselves dragged willy-nilly into the conflict with little, if any, control over why such a fight must be waged.

Careful study of the varying definitions of what Canada and being Canadian mean makes it obvious that concepts proposed by the Prime Minister are not that much different from ideas suggested by tribal elders. With that mutual recognition perhaps we can at least begin to create the environment that will allow a start at tackling the real problems without getting bogged down in a cold-war mentality between whites and Indians. By wiping out the misunderstandings that have existed for so long we can create an opportunity for members of both societies to attack the very real problems that do exist and work toward mutually-identified goals.

Essentially then, when we talk about Canada or Canadianism it is even more vital now than ever before that Indians across the country define their terms more precisely.

One of the reasons for the apparent misunderstanding between Indian people and the larger society, particularly in recent times, may have been a tendency by Indians to rely too greatly upon white consultants hired, paradoxically, to improve communications between the two societies. Such consultants usually are quite expert in one field—they satisfactorily provide Indians with the badly needed expertise in defining English terminology. The problem is that they seldom know anything about Indian people or the Indian nations, let alone the definitions Indians apply to themselves. Consequently what emerges is the white academic's imperfect understanding or interpretation of what Indians are all about, rather than the facts in Indian terms. The hired experts may, and often do, make valiant efforts to explain, but they end up creating more confusion because all they are explaining is their own confusion. Another vital area in which this sort of error is surfacing is the problem of defining the term *aboriginal rights* as it relates to Indian claims right across Canada.

In essence then, part of the difficulty in communication has been the barrier, linguistic and cultural, between Indian tribes, Indian nations, and members of the white society.

The basic task that remains after three or four centuries of contact between Indians and whites is still the construction of a bridge of understanding between two worlds that exist as separate realities.

Wayne Keon b. 1946

OJIBWAY

heritage

AlgonkinAssiniboineAthapaskanB
eaverBellaCoolaBeothukBlackfoo
tCarrierCaughnawayaCayuyaChilk
atChilcotinChipewyanCreeCrowDe
lewareDogribEskimoFlatheadFoxG
rosVentreHaidaHareHuronIllinoi
sIroquoisKickapooKitwancoolKoo
tneyKoskimoKutchinKwakiutlLake
LilloetMaleciteMalouinMenomine
eMetisMiamiMicmacMississaugaMo
hawkMohicanMontagnaisMuskogeeN
ahaniNaskapiNeutralNicolaNipis
singNootkaOjibwayOkanaganOneid
aOnondagaOttawaPequotPetunPieg
anPotawatomieSalishSarceeSaukS
aulteauxSekaniSenecaShawneeSho
shoniShuswapSiouxSlaveStoneySu
squehannaTagishTalhltanThompson
TlinkitTsetsautTsimshianTuscar
oraWinnebagoWyandotYellowknife

howlin at the moon

take the moon
nd take a star
when you don't
know who you are

paint the picture in your hand
nd roll on home

take my fear
nd take the hunger
take my body
when i'm younger

paint the picture in your hand
nd roll on home

take my ghost
nd make the claim
stake it out
to feel the pain

paint the picture in your hand
nd roll on home

take the moon
nd make it talk
take your soul out
make it walk

paint the picture in your hand
nd roll on home

take my anguish
take the air
make it into
my despair

paint the picture in your hand
nd roll on home

take my anger
nd the greed
make it into
what you need

paint the picture in your hand
nd roll on home

take my pride
nd all my joy
take my woman
nd my boy

paint the picture in your hand
nd roll on home

paint the picture once again
i'm rollin home

south wheel

is all those majik
fires lit late
in the
nite

is lions nd
foxes nd
bear

is orange nd red
amber nd
white

is washing your eyes with
the sun nd the
lite

is sweetgrass
nd cinnamon
cedar nd
gold

is dancing with love with
love til your
old

for donald marshall

i've no secret old
time answer in
my hand

i've no majik justice in my sand

to challenge all
the inmate
time

to pray beside the sacred pine
i've no blazin fire trail

to sear the
wounds

nd close the ruptured aura burns

but seek her now nd
make it
end

seek her now nd see my friend

o great bear of the southern wheel
o great bear of the southern wheel
o great bear of the southern wheel
o great bear of the southern wheel

take the power
nd the
earth

take this breath to heal the hurt

take the power
nd your
healing

take the breath nd take this feeling

travel now in
breath nd
wind

travel now nd take the wind

travel now in
earth nd
land

travel now nd take the land

clothe him in
a yellow
gold

touch the pain nd make it old

smoke nd thyme

they told me
to stop wearin
that old medicine shirt
to the office

nd i agreed this time

but i never told them
about the medicine bag
i made late in the nite

about the cedar flame
the smoke
nd the thyme

i'm not in charge of this ritual

i'm not in charge of this
sun dance anymore
i'm hanging here
completely out of it
the lawyers nd therapists
have taken over
my breasts are pierced
nd writhin in the blood
nd pain
i'm not that brave you know
that's why my children
nd woman were
taken from me
that's why i'm takin it on alone again
i never did any of those purification rituals
that's probably why this isn't working
nd hallucinations start sneakin
into my work, i can't say home
because i don't have a home
i live in a room
making medicine bags nd
wonderin if the silver strands
nd gems i'm putting in them will do the trick
i escape temporarily at nite catching

my breath at donut & pizza shops
where nobody talks nd everyone just eats
munchin nd chewin nd swallowin down
hunger in the nite
hah! despair wouldn't have the nerve to come
waltzin through the door here
it would be devoured whole
in one fat gulp
they're all lookin at me wonderin why
i'm so skinny nd still losing weight
they know i'm not one of them
but i'm there every nite
shakin over another cup of coffee
tired nd numb from another day of torture
i'm glad when the sun goes down
nd the crazy cool of dark comes
b'cos there's hardly anywhere left to hide
nd they'll find me in the mornin
nd drag me back to the dance
in front of the sun
i wish i knew how long this was gonna take
but there's always tonite
nd ah! there's always linda
always linda waitin in the nite
with smoky topaz eyes
with smokin lips nd thighs
pressed like a gem
from the earth
into mine
but even she's started lockin
her door at nite

if i ever heard

if i ever heard
your love had gone pale

i would come out of this wilderness
with ojibiway majik
    for you

if i ever heard
your love had gone without rain

i would come out of this wilderness
with my ojibiway river
    for you

if i ever heard
your love had gone in the sea

i would come out of this wilderness
with ojibiway earth
    for you

if i ever heard
your love had gone in the nite

i would come out of this wilderness
with my ojibiway stars
    for you

day break run

coming
back into
that day break

run nd mist
standing still nd
smokin all along the low

spots not yet
lite but lite enough
to see your way through this

earth mother's
shroud nd veil comin
up everywhere you look the moon

kinda pale nd
white hangin out
in front full nd round

pumpkin along at 120
nd nobody's lookin at much
this time of the mornin except me

checkin the mirror
behind nd tryina put a
hundred miles or a bit more

of green
belt between you
nd the cloud nd carter

standin
there beneath
the bustin toltec sun

all red
nd crawlin up
behind the trees

takin that
raven on the windshield
like that nd prayin to the iron

to the copper nd glass
to hold this all together
for at least another forty minutes

of my time
nd warm feelin
on my back pullin away

to the west
nd pullin away
til she bursts out

all that
gold breathin out
all that gold nd changin

changin every line
that every danced at daybreak
into another gold ojibiway sun

Jeannette C. Armstrong b. 1948

OKANAGAN

History Lesson

Out of the belly of Christopher's ship
a mob bursts
Running in all directions
Pulling furs off animals
Shooting buffalo
Shooting each other
left and right

Father mean well
waves his makeshift wand
forgives saucer-eyed Indians

Red coated knights
gallop across the prairie
to get their men
and to build a new world

Pioneers and traders
bring gifts
Smallpox, Seagrams
and Rice Krispies

Civilization has reached
the promised land.

Between the snap crackle pop
of smoke stacks
and multi-coloured rivers
swelling with flower powered zee
are farmers sowing skulls and bones
and miners
pulling from gaping holes
green paper faces
of smiling English lady

The colossi
in which they trust
while burying

breathing forests and fields
beneath concrete and steel
stand shaking fists
waiting to mutilate
whole civilizations
ten generations at a blow.

Somewhere among the remains
of skinless animals
is the termination
to a long journey
and unholy search
for the power
glimpsed in a garden
forever closed
forever lost.

For Tony

Words were always
easy for you
You played with them
in long chains
or little piles
People laughed at your stories
and were happy
for a few moments
you would be too

Then you would return
to that cold and wordless place
where the only sounds
were those of an always new beast
waiting just in the shadows
where emptied bottles
spoke of the battles
now lost

All we have of you now
are echoes of words
to make us laugh
and we are poorer
but the war you fought alone

is ours now too
Already our people gather
to choose their weapons

We all walk in the shadow
of the beast
but we will step lightly
and all the stories
you used to make laughter
will be told
around the tables of your people
and we will be rich with weapons.

Sketches

```
                              a man's
                 pure sperm
                 got stuff
                 in it         most
people                                      couldn't
believe                                     the
                               ordered      world
in                             pieces
                 that          are          more or less
                               big
                 death
                 rattles       cock
carriers                                                presumers
                 hard                                   on
dancers
drainers                                    let me feel  your
                               ass          smooth       cunt
                                            gentle
                               blood        hairy
tribes
```

Indian Woman

I am a squaw
a heathen
a savage
basically a mammal

I am a female
only in the ability
to breed
and bear papooses
to be carried
quaintly
on a board
or lost
to welfare

I have no feelings

The sinuous planes
of my brown body
carry no hint
of the need
to be caressed
desired
loved
Its only use
to be raped
beaten and bludgeoned
in some
B-grade western

I have no beauty

The lines
cut deep
into my aged face
are not from bitterness
or despair
at seeing my clan destroyed
one by one
they are here
to be painted or photographed
sold
and hung on lawyers walls

I have no emotions

The husky laughter
a brush of wings
behind eyes
soft and searching
lightly touching others
is not from caring
but from the ravaged
beat of black wings
rattling against the bars
of an insanity
that tells me
something is wrong here.

Some one is lying.

I am an Indian Woman

Where I walk
beauty surrounds me
grasses bend and blossom
over valleys and hills
vast and multicolored
in starquilt glory

I am the keeper
of generations

I caress the lover gently
croon as I wrap the baby
with quietness I talk
to the old ones
and carefully lay to rest
loved ones

I am the strength
of nations

I sing to the whispering
autumn winds
in the snow
I dance
slowly
filling my body
with power
feeling it
knowing it

I am the giver of life
to whole tribes

I carry the seeds
carefully   through   dangerous
wastelands
give them life
scattered
among   cold   and   towering
concrete
watch them grow
battered and crippled
under all the lies
I teach them the songs
I help them to hear
I give them truth

I am a sacred trust
I am Indian woman.

Threads of Old Memory

Speaking to newcomers in their language is dangerous
for when I speak
history is a dreamer
empowering thought
from which I awaken the imaginings of the past
bringing the sweep and surge of meaning
coming from a place
rooted in the memory of loss
experienced in ceremonies
wrenched from the minds of a people
whose language spoke only harmony
through a language
meant to overpower
to overtake
in skillfully crafted words
moving towards surrender
leaving in its swirling wake
only those songs
hidden
cherished
protected
the secret singing of which
I glimpse through bewildered eyes
an old lost world
of astounding beauty

When I speak
I attempt to bring together
with my hands
gossamer thin threads of old memory
thoughts from the underpinnings of understanding
words steeped in age
slim
barely visible strands of harmony
stretching across the chaos brought into this world
through words
shaped as sounds in air
meaning made physical
changers of the world
carriers into this place of things
from a place of magic
the underside of knowing
the origination place

a pure place
silent
wordless
from where thoughts I choose
silently transform into words
I speak and
powerfully become actions
become memory in someone
I become different memories to different people
different stories in the retelling of my place
I am the dreamer
the choice maker
the word speaker
I speak in a language of words
formed of the actions of the past
words that become the sharing
the collective knowing
the links that become a people
the dreaming that becomes a history
the calling forth of voices
the sending forward of memory
I am the weaver of memory thread
twining past to future
I am the artist
the storyteller
the singer
from the known and familiar
pushing out into darkness
dreaming splinters together
the coming to knowing

When I speak
I sing a song called up through ages
of carefully crafted rhythm
of a purpose close to the wordless
in a coming to this world
from the cold and hungry spaces in the heart
through the desolate and lost places of the mind
to this stark and windswept mountain top
I search for the sacred words
spoken serenely in the gaps between memory
the lost places of history
pieces mislaid
forgotten or stolen
muffled by violence

splintered by evil
when languages collide in mid air
when past and present explode in chaos
and the imaginings of the past
rip into the dreams of the future

When I speak
I choose the words gently
asking the whys
dangerous words
in the language of the newcomers
words releasing unspeakable grief
for all that is lost
dispelling lies in the retelling
I choose threads of truth
that in its telling cannot be hidden
and brings forward
old words that heal
moving to a place
where a new song begins
a new ceremony
through medicine eyes I glimpse a world
that cannot be stolen or lost
only shared
shaped by new words
joining precisely to form old patterns
a song of stars
glittering against an endless silence

Fire Madness

god   bellied
you danced
around my pyre
and spoke in a language
that was mine alone

with bluejay eyes
you watched
as they piled broken branches
high over me

the flame of my blood
is red

the leap of it
greets you
firewalker

come
before the spider
draws her web
across the sky
walk quietly
on these embers
to me

lift me
bluejay dancer
and we will laugh
from a high green branch
at the mourners gathered to watch
this death
that we defy

Wind Woman

Maggie at night sometimes I hear you laugh

when I was ten we rode to huckleberry mountain
carrying ragged quilts and pots and pans
packed on an old roan mare called jeep
given to Maggie to help fill her baskets
I followed her
picking berries her failing eyes had missed
I listened as she talked in our language
half singing sometimes
for all the pickers to hear
her voice high and clear in the crisp mountain air
telling about coyote

I know how the trees talk
I said to Maggie
I heard their moaning in the night
while we lie so tiny in our tents
with all those tall black pines swaying over us

she told me a story then
of how the woman of the wind
banished by coyote
carried her eternally howling child
tied to her back
as they moved forever through the tree tops
mother crooning to the child
how sometimes she would swoop down in anger
scattering berries off bushes

Maggie told me I had heard
the wind woman sing
she told me that I would remember that song always
because the trees were my teacher

I remember the song clearly
but it is always Maggie's voice singing
her songs
filling my world
with the moan of old dark pines
as the wind woman
that sings to me
follows
with her hungry child
wherever I go

Keepers Words

Makers are mockers
so said the grandmother
Her tribal conscience
rode at her elbow
as inherited as her brown skin
Her words   smooth   carved as bone
and so old no one remembered
were placed side by side
in a pattern
fashioned in the beginning
of her kind

There will be no new words
in man-designs

to break up what is sacred
and leave forget in its place
We are keepers   we must not change
On this earth
lives a cannibal monster
who devours himself
because he changes so much
as he grows
that he forgets
what his tail looks like

I'll be around   she said
soon after death lunges forward
out of the rabble
I will stand on a hilltop
a black dot against blazing red
and my shadow will stretch
long and narrow over the earth curve
to seep into the little shadows
even now
skipping behind you

All your sound songs
will be no more than food for the monster
but the sacred words
will still be whispered
in shadows
You will hear and understand
nothing is new   only changed
there are no men who are makers
just changers

Blue Against White

Lena walked up the steep hill toward her mother's house. She could see the bright blue door. It stood out against the stark white of the house. It was the only house with a door like that on the hill. All the houses on that part of the reserve looked a lot alike, the colours ranging from mostly white to off-white to grey, and a few with light pastel colours. All the doors matched the houses.

Thinking of it now, Lena realized that it was funny how she had always thought of it as her mother's house rather than her father's house, though it had been his idea to paint the door a bright blue. He had said that the houses up there on the hill all looked too much alike. He had said that their home would be easy to see because of the door. He was right, but there was a question that had always been silent: 'Who would have a problem?' She had known that all the Indians in a thousand-mile radius knew each other and that they didn't find their way to each other by the description of their houses.

As she walked toward the house she realized that she had kept that door in her mind all the years she had been away. It has been there as always, a bright blue against the white. A blue barrier against the cold north wind. A cool blue shield against the summer heat. She remembered having hated the door and having wished it would just be white like the rest of the house. But while she was away, it had been the part of the house that had been a constant clear image. Behind that door, warm smells and laughter mixed into a distinct impression of the way it was back home. Her mother, long braids tied together in the back, smiled at her from behind that door.

Now, she walked up the hill toward the house carrying the one bag that held her things. She felt light, weightless and somehow insubstantial like the last fluffseeds still clinging shakily to the milkweeds that lined the narrow dirt road gutted with deep, dry ruts. In this country the summer rains left cracked mud tracks which froze in the fall and stayed hidden under the snow and ice in winter.

At this moment she felt she could easily be lifted to float up and away from those deep earth gashes, to move across the land with the dry fall drifting of seeds and leaves. She had hated this dirt road and the mud in the spring and the dust in the summer, the ruts in the fall and the ungraded snow in the winter. She had mostly hated the dry milkweeds crowding together everywhere. As always, on this road the lumps of soil were uneven and slow to travel over. She felt like turning and bolting back to the bus to catch it before it could leave her here, but running was hard on this broken ground.

The door seemed to loom ahead of her, though the house was no taller than the rest. She hated the way all the cheap government houses on the row facing the road were so close together and had paint peeling and dry weedy yards with several mangy dogs. She turned to look back at the road winding steeply down to the crossroad where the bus stopped momentarily to drop off or pick up people from the reserve. The freeway stretched away into a hazy purple distance where night was beginning to shadow the land. Only the white line dividing those coming from those going was visible after a certain point. The red lights of the bus were fading straight into that shadow line between sky, asphalt and the darkened earth.

Turning, she faced the rest of the climb. A single black crow cawed at her from its perch on the steeple cross of the village church, raising a ruckus in the quiet. It screeched and flapped its wings, dove over her mother's house and then flew lazily overhead, looking down at her as it passed, flying over the dirt road toward the crossroad in the direction of the twilight.

She watched the crow disappear into dark blue. She knew his name from the old stories. She wanted to laugh and say it. She knew he hung around only in the summer months and then flew away when the shadows in the fall grew long and the days short. She wanted to say, 'You, old pretender, you don't fool me. You're not going to preach to me, too, are you? You're no smarter than me!' Instead she found tears wetting her cheeks.

Her tears brought the memory of a dream from the week before she had started the long bus ride home. In her dream she had been in a large building with many bright lights and shiny reflections. Although there was a lot of noise, she couldn't see anyone. She felt totally alone as she walked down a long white hallway. She remembered looking, one by one, at the doors she passed, feeling like the only thing behind each one was a patch of sky. In the dream she remembered feeling something like dizziness as she saw how many doors there were and how they seemed to stretch into darkness on and on without end. She recalled running and stumbling past the doors and calling out. When she awoke she had been crying.

She was almost at the top of the hill now. She stopped and put down her bag. A couple of reserve dogs barked at her and then wagged their tails, trotting toward her, making greeting noises in their throats. She looked down at the one that was obviously a lady dog with her sagging dry milk sacs and she stroked her ear. She thought of the city she had left and said, 'Mamma dogs don't just walk around free there, you know. You're pretty lucky to be here.' The lady dog sat down and thumped her tail against some of the weeds, sending puffs of seed floating with each excited wave.

Behind the houses farther up into the dark hills, she heard the high, far-away yipping of a coyote. She saw the dogs' ears perk up. She saw the way their eyes glowed a deeper orange as they forgot her and pointed their noses toward the hills above them, a low, crooning echo rumbling deep in their throats. She, too, looked up there and whispered, 'How are you, brothers?' in the language. She knew them, too.

She thought of that one coyote in the papers, in some city, that had got trapped in a hallway after coming in from an alley door. How somebody mistaking it for a dog had opened an elevator for it and how it had ridden to the roof of an apartment building and ran around crazily, and then jumped to its death rather than run back through the elevator door and ride back down into the hallway and out the alley door. She had known that it hadn't been a matter of animal stupidity, because a coyote always remembered where it had come from. She had secretly known that it had more to do with the quick elevator door and the long lonely ride up to the top. She thought of the coyotes hanging around in the cities these days. Nobody wanted them there, so nobody made friends with them, but once in a while they made the papers when they did something wrong or showed up, trotting along Broadway, cool as could be.

Lena thought about all the time she had spent away from this place of hard, cracked earth, seedpods and clean coyote prints in the new snow up in the hills. She looked up at the bright blue surface directly in front of her, waiting to open, and felt the bone-aching, deep tiredness of long journeys over the hard even surface of freeways into alleys and white hallways. As she reached for the door knob she looked down and realized that the freeway's white line and the mud ruts ended here, right at her mother's door. The door that her dad had painted bright blue so that it stood out clearly against the white.

The Disempowerment of First North American Native Peoples and Empowerment Through Their Writing

Paper prepared for Saskatchewan Writers Guild 1990 Annual Conference

PANEL DISCUSSION: EMPOWERING ABORIGINAL WRITERS
In order to address the specifics of Native people's writing and empowerment, I must first present my view on the disempowerment of first North American Nations.

Without recounting various historical versions of *how* it happened, I would like to refer only to *what* happened here.

Indigenous peoples in North America were rendered powerless and subjugated to totalitarian domination by foreign peoples, after they were welcomed as guests and their numbers were allowed to grow to the point of domination through aggression.

Once total subjective control was achieved over my peoples through various coercive measures and the direct removal of political, social, and religious freedoms accomplished, the colonization process began.

In North America this has been to systemically enforce manifest destiny or the so-called 'White Man's burden' to civilize. In the 498 years of contact in The Americas, the thrust of this bloody sword has been to hack out the spirit of all the beautiful cultures encountered, leaving in its wake a death toll unrivalled in recorded history. This is what happened and what continues to happen.

There is no word other than totalitarianism which adequately describes the methods used to achieve the condition of my people today. Our people were not given choices. Our children, for generations, were seized from our communities and homes and placed in indoctrination camps until our language, our religion, our customs, our values, and our societal structures almost disappeared. This was the residential school experience.

Arising out of the siege conditions of this nightmare time, what is commonly referred to as the 'social problems' of Native peoples emerged. Homes and communities, without children, had nothing to work for, or live for. Children returned to communities and families as adults, without the necessary skills for parenting, for Native life style, or self-sufficiency on their land base, deteriorated into despair. With the loss of cohesive cultural relevance with their own peoples and a distorted view of the non-Native culture from the clergy who ran the residential schools, an almost total disorientation and loss of identity occurred. The disintegration of family and community and nation was inevitable, originating with the individual's internalized pain. Increasing death statistics from suicide, violence, alcohol and drug abuse, and other poverty-centred physical diseases, can leave no doubt about the question of totalitarianism and genocide.

You writers from the dominating culture have the freedom of imagination. You keep reminding us of this. Is there anyone here who dares to imagine what those children suffered at the hands of their so-called 'guardians' in those schools. You are writers, imagine it on yourselves and your children. Imagine you and your children and imagine how they would be treated by those who abhorred and detested you, all, as savages without any rights.

Imagine at what cost to you psychologically, to acquiesce and attempt to speak, dress, eat, and worship, like your oppressors, simply out of a need to be treated humanly. Imagine attempting to assimilate so that your children will not suffer what you have, and imagine finding that assimilationist measures are not meant to include you but to destroy all remnants of your culture. Imagine finding that even when you emulate every cultural process from customs to values you are still excluded, despised, and ridiculed because you are Native.

Imagine finding out that the dominating culture will not tolerate any real cultural participation and that cultural supremacy forms the basis of the government process and that systemic racism is a tool to maintain their kind of totalitarianism. And all the while, imagine that this is presented under the guise of 'equal rights' and under the banner of banishing bigotry on an individual basis through law.

Imagine yourselves in this condition and imagine the writers of that dominating culture berating you for speaking out about appropriation of cultural voice and using the words 'freedom of speech' to condone further systemic violence, in the form of entertainment literature about *your* culture and *your* values and all the while, yourself being disempowered and rendered voiceless through such 'freedoms'.

Imagine how you as writers from the dominant society might turn over some of the rocks in your own garden for examination. Imagine in your literature courageously questioning and examining the values that allow the dehumanizing of peoples through domination and the dispassionate nature of the racism inherent in perpetuating such practices. Imagine writing in honesty, free of the romantic bias about the courageous 'pioneering spirit' of colonialist practice and imperialist process. Imagine interpreting for us *your own people's* thinking toward us, instead of interpreting for us, our thinking, our lives, and our stories. We wish to know, and you need to understand, why it is that you want to own our stories, our art, our beautiful crafts, our ceremonies, but you do not appreciate or wish to recognize that these things of beauty arise out of the beauty of our people.

Imagine these realities on yourselves in honesty and let me know how you imagine that you might approach empowerment of yourselves in such a situation. Better yet, do not dare speak to me of 'Freedom of Voice', 'Equal Rights', 'Democracy', or 'Human Rights' until this totalitarianistic approach has been changed by yourselves as writers and shapers of philosophical direction. Imagine a world where domination is not possible because all cultures are valued.

To the Native writers here, my words are meant as empowerment to you. In my quest for empowerment of my people through writing, there are two things of which I must steadfastly remind myself.

The first is that the reality I see is the reality for the majority of Native people and that although severe and sometimes irreparable damage has been wrought, healing can take place through cultural affirmation. I have found immense strength and beauty in my people.

The dispelling of lies and the telling of what really happened until *everyone*, including our own people understands that this condition did not happen through choice or some cultural defect on our part, is important. Equally important is the affirmation of the true beauty of our people whose fundamental co-operative values resonated pacifism and predisposed our cultures as vulnerable to the reprehensible value systems which promote domination and aggression.

The second thing I must remind myself of is that the dominating culture's reality is that it seeks to affirm itself continuously and must be taught that *numbers* are not the basis of democracy, *people* are, *each one* being important. It must be pushed, in Canada, to understand and accept that this country is multi-racial and multi-cultural now, and the meaning of that. I must remind myself constantly of the complacency that makes these conditions possible, and that if I am to bridge into that complacency that I will be met with hostility from the majority, but, that those whose thoughts I have provoked may become our greatest allies in speaking to their own. It is this promotion of an ideal which will produce the courage to shake off centuries of imperialist thought and make possible the relearning of co-operation and sharing, in place of domination.

Our task as Native writers is twofold. To examine the past and culturally affirm toward a new vision for all our people in the future, arising out of the powerful and positive support structures that are inherent in the principles of co-operation.

We, as Native people, through continuously resisting cultural imperialism and seeking means toward teaching co-operative relationships, provide an integral mechanism for solutions currently needed in this country.

We must see ourselves as undefeatably pro-active in a positive sense and realize that negative activism actually serves the purpose of the cultural imperialism practised on our people. Lies need clarification, truth needs to be stated, and resistance to oppression needs to be stated, without furthering division and participation in the same racist measures. This is the challenge that we rise to. Do not make the commonly made error that it is a people that we abhor, be clear that it is systems and processors which we must attack. Be clear that change to those systems will be promoted by people who can perceive intelligent and non-threatening alternatives. Understand that these alternatives will be presented only through discourse and dialogue flowing outward from us, for now, because we are the stakeholders. We need the system to change. Those in the system can and will remain complacent until moved to think, and to understand how critical change is needed at this time for us all. Many already know and are willing to listen.

The responsibility of the Native writer is tremendous in light of these times in which world over, solutions are being sought to address the failed assimilationist measures originating out of conquest, oppression, and exploitation, whether under the socialist or capitalist banner. We as writers can show how support for Lithuanian independence and support for South African Black equality became farcical in the glare of the Constitutional position to First Nations here in Canada, who seek nothing more than co-operative sovereign relationships guaranteed in the principles of treaty making. No one will desire or choose to hear these truths unless they are voiced clearly to people who have no way to know that there are good alternatives and that instead of losing control we can all grow powerful together.

Finally, I believe in the basic goodness of the majority of people. I *rely* on the common human desire to be guilt free and fulfilled, to triumph, towards attainment of our full potential as wonderful, thinking beings at the forward edge of the Creator's expression of beauty.

I believe in the strength and rightness in the values of my people and know that those principles of peace and co-operation, in practice, are natural and survival-driven mechanisms which transcend violence and aggression. I see the destructive paths that have led us to this time in history, when all life on this planet is in peril, and know that there *must* be change. I believe that the principles of co-operation are a sacred trust and the plan and the intent of the Creator and therefore shall endure.

Beth Cuthand b. 1949

CREE

Shake 'N Bake

He wore the uniform of the lowly
like a cop wears a gun and a badge;
worn blue jeans neatly patched
by his woman of the moment,
and a humble shirt of plaid flannel
muted and discreet
Oh so discreet.

And when he went to advise the lowly
he played his sombre medicine man voice;
turned up the bass, lowered the treble
and cleared his throat.
Yes, always cleared his throat.

He talked as though he were barely literate
and he had just learned English last week.
He didn't like to read
and would sometimes take two whole days
to finish *Black Elk Speaks* or
Selected Studies in Native American Shamanism

He would talk ever so discreetly
about 'the others'
the shake 'n bake medicine men
who didn't know what they were doing
and didn't deserve to do it anyway.
Yes, they were wrong and they
would be sorry.

'There is so much to teach people'
he would say. 'So much has been lost.
You've got to watch the old guys, even
the old people have forgotten. It's sad,'
he would say, clearing his throat
'the way those young people go to them.'

But he knew the score. He was real.
He had *earned* the right to do what he did.

Every summer he took great pains
to fast at someone else's expense
and performed the requisite ceremonies
diligently and correctly.
So correctly.

There was no one whom he trusted
and no one whom he loved.
He rarely really laughed. He would
tell crude jokes to the boys
but always made sure
he was pure before
he performed a
ceremony.
For this
was the way
he understood
it to be:
     Step 1
     Step 2
     Step 3

Zen Indian

Zen Indian tiptoes into Taos
watches coyote disguised
as an ice-cream vendor
sell dollar popsicles
to thirsty tourists.

Fishes down the Fraser
for dried salmon
thinking a No. 10 hook
will catch those freeze-dried suckers.

Careens into Calgary in time
for Stampede; bells polished
feathers fluffed
to dance three times a day
for a free pass to the rodeo.

Makes it to Winnipeg
just after Bismark and right before

wild rice time
to get folk-sey at the Indian Pavilion

Then it's on to pick wild rice
for Uncle Ben;
drop a few rocks in the sacks,
shoot at the crows and reminisce
about how it used to be
before the harvest became
the domain of Bros in hydro
planes and enough money for gas.

Oh oh, cold's coming.
Time to find a fine filly
with a job, not too many kids
and a warm place to lay up for
the winter.

Put cities in a hat:
   Minneapolis, LA
      Boulder, Santa Fe
Calgary, Seattle, Salt Lake.

Yee-ha! Watch out Boulder!
Here he comes.
Zen Indian on the road to enlightenment!

He Told Me

He told me
      when his father died
      he felt him heave
      his last breath
and though
      he was miles away
      he heard his father say

   Louis David, to you
      I transfer my bundle.
      It is small and humble
      wrapping little things,
      a bone
      from the last buffalo,

a stone
from the Assiniboine,
a small pipe and
tobacco pouch
and,
a feather
from the broken wing
of one
who flew too low.

He told me
that
he couldn't bear
the burden
of that bundle.
And when
his father died
he was alone
and darkness
and voices
and phantom
winds
blew
his soul
away.

'Evelene,'
he would say,
'Evelene—I have been
chasing my shadow
ever since.'

Four Songs for the Fifth Generation

Drums, chants, and rattles
pounded earth and
heartbeats
heartbeats.

'They were our life   the life
of the prairies
We loved them
and they loved us.

Sometimes   they were so many
they flowed   like a river
over the hills   into the valleys.

I saw them.   I knew them.
I helped my mother
           cut away their skin
           chop their bones
and dry their meat
                Many times
                many times.

Aye, but now   they are gone
      ghosts   all ghosts.

The sickness came
              we were hungry
I saw my children   die
one by one
one by one.

There was no freedom   then my girl
         They were stronger
         They thought they knew
what it was   their God wanted

Aye, but now   they are gone
      ghosts   just ghosts.

Sometimes   I think I hear
their thunder   smell their dust
at night my girl
         at night I dream
dream of their warm blood
              their hides covering
Aye, covering   all my children
         in their sleep.'

Drums, chants, and rattles
pounded earth and
           heartbeats
           heartbeats.

'That's the old Simmons homestead.
           He's dead now

I don't know what happened
        to his wife   and children.

Back in the thirties
         we cut posts for him
10 cents a post   that was good money
       back then.
Clarence Simmons was his name
       came from England
         with his skinny little wife
and a bunch of pale scrawny little kids.

Poor Simmons   we felt sorry for him
     so we helped him
       as much as we could.

Back in the thirties,
things weren't so bad for us
      as it was for the homesteaders
We hadn't cut our trees
     or tore up the land.
      We still had deer
       and fish
        rabbits
and gophers and fat dogs
        heh heh

But the settlers really suffered.
     It was pitiful.
My dad would tell us
    "take this meat over to the Simmons
    place. Drop it at the door."

So I'd ride over   real quiet
and hang it by the house

Poor Simmons
      one day he hung himself
     from a tree
      in his yard.
Couldn't take it no more.
     Dad found him,
    cut him down
and laid him   real gentle

on the ground
under the tree.

That was one of the few times
I ever saw him cry.

I don't know what makes
some men
go on living
while other men
give up.'

Drums, chants, and rattles
pounded earth and
heartbeats
heartbeats.

'It was 1960
when dad and mom
got the vote.
All us kids got copies of Canada's
"Declaration of Human Rights"
and took them home
and put them up
all over the walls.
Yeah, that was a great day
for Canada
"Oh Canada
Our true north strong and free."

We moved south when I was ten
to a town with sidewalks
and running water
and a playground with a pool
not a lake
"Hey Injuns!   Yer not allowed
in the pool.
You'll get it dirty,
dirty."

We closed ranks after that
spent a lot of time
exploring the creek.
My brother found an arrowhead
Some white kid said

it didn't belong to us,
so my brother beat him up.

My brother was always
                fighting
            It seemed
        he had a rage
            that wouldn't go out.
Me,   I just retreated
        and retreated
            until I couldn't
            find myself.

There was a boy down the street
        who had it in
            for my brother
            called him dirty Indian.
He'd sick his dog on him
            every time
            we'd walk to school.
We took to walking the long way,
        everyone   except my brother.

One time my brother hit that dog
        smack between the eyes
            with a rock
The old dog tucked his tail
        between his legs and
        went howling off
            behind the house.

The boy came to our place
        with a baseball bat
We were all going to go out
        and kick that kid around,
but dad said "No
        let your brother
        fight it out."

They were pretty evenly matched
        the kid with his bat,
        my brother with his stones
            they fought
            for an hour
kicking

hitting
scratching
punching
thwacking
ripping

Mom wanted to stop them
        but Dad said no.
        "He's got to take a stand."

Finally it was over
                nobody won.

That kid never sicked
        his dog on my brother again.
            but
my brother's rage
never did go away.'

Drums, chants, and rattles
pounded earth and
            heartbeats
            heartbeats.

'I don't want to go
        to a white high school
            Mama.
My spirit would die
        in a place like that
I love our little school
        us Indians
        we help each other.
            We care.
We share smokes Mom

When I grow up
will my kids
have to fight
for a place in the neighbourhood
too?'

Drums, chants, and rattles
pounded earth and
            heartbeats
            heartbeats.

Post-Oka Kinda Woman

Here she comes strutting down your street.
This Post-Oka woman don't take no shit.

She's done with victimization, reparation,
degradation, assimilation,
devolution, coddled collusion,
the 'plight of the Native Peoples.'

Post-Oka woman, she's o.k.
She shashay into your suburbia.
MacKenzie Way, Riel Crescent belong to her
like software, microwave ovens,
plastic Christmas trees and lawn chairs.

Her daughter wears Reeboks and works out.
Her sons cook and wash up.
Her grandkids don't sass their Kohkom!
No way.

She drives a Toyota, reads bestsellers,
sweats on weekends, colors her hair,
sings old songs, gathers herbs.
Two steps Tuesdays,
Round dances Wednesdays,
Twelve steps when she needs it.

Post-Oka woman she's struttin' her stuff
not walkin' one step behind her man.
She don't take that shit
Don't need it!   Don't want it.
You want her   then treat her right.

Talk to her of post-modern deconstructivism
She'll say: 'What took you so long?'

You wanna discuss Land Claims?
She'll tell ya she'd rather leave
her kids with a struggle than a bad settlement.

Indian Government?
            Show her cold hard cash.

Tell her you've never talked to a real live 'Indian'
       She'll say: 'Isn't that special.'

Post-Oka woman, she's cheeky.
       She's bold.   She's cold.

And she don't take no shit!
No shit.

Lenore Keeshig-Tobias b. 1949

ANISHNABE

After Oka—How Has Canada Changed?

O Canada, we have always walked on the edge
of your dreams, stalked
you as you made wild your way
through this great land

And O Canada, you have always been
afraid of us, scared because you know
you can never live without us.

The summer for First Nations peoples has been a review of history, a history we know so well, and a reality we have lived through generation after generation.

My people are the Saugeen Ojibway. Our earliest claim against the Crown dates back to the Treaty of 1836 when our people were forced to cede '1.5 million acres of the richest land in Upper Canada'. The Government refused to protect our land from encroachment by white settlers. This is only one of our treaties. What did we receive for this land—the indifference, the impatience, the ignorance, and the scorn of Canadians, not the 'proper housing' nor the assistance promised to help us 'become civilized' unless you consider subsistence on social welfare and other government programs to be pillars of civilization.

The Saugeen Ojibway have been patient for over 150 years. The Mohawks of Kanesatake have been patient for 200 years. Quebec and Canada lost patience after only 48 days. And think, your Prime Minister praises the army for its patience?! What about the patience of the Mohawks in the treatment centre after so many days and nights of harassment?

I have been asked how has Canada changed after Oka? I would sincerely like to say Canada has changed. Since childhood, I remember wanting Canada to change, wanting to see the land claims my gramma talked about resolved.

And I am sure you, after having witnessed the horrid reality of Canadian justice and democracy at work this summer, would like to hear that Canada has changed. But the sad truth is that Canada has not changed. And Canada will not change until Canadians are truly ready to turn around and confront their own psyche and history. Canada will not change until Canadians make of this Turtle Island what our prophets, long before the appearance of the white man, foretold it would be. These prophesies tell of the four colours of people, distinct societies, coming together as sovereign nations within a nation to work for a better society, a better way of life for all of us.

Why is Canada and why are Canadians so afraid to deal with us as equals? And yet, the very same Canadians continue to shout out with pride our names, the names of their provinces and cities—Quebec, Ontario, Manitoba, Saskatchewan—Toronto, Winnipeg, Saskatoon, and Ottawa to name a few. And, of course, we must not forget Ken-a-tah, or as Canadians so proudly say Canada.

This has not been an 'Indian Summer' to remember as so many of you want to romanticize it to be. 'Indian' is a figment of your imagination. 'Warrior' is a figment of your imagination. And the Mohawk called your bluff. No, this has not been an 'Indian Summer' to remember. It's been a 'Canadian Summer', a 'Canadian Summer' to be reckoned with.

From Trickster Beyond 1992: Our Relationship

If you have not learned from your foolishness, you will remain foolish all your life.
—Alexander Wolfe, *Earth Elder Stories*

When men no longer believe in us we are dead.
—Maori myth

He is like me, a Trickster, a liar . . . a new kind of man is coming, a White Man.
—Iktomi

1

       and with the altitude scream

from the north
he approaches,
coming in from
'the other side'

he nods
and seats himself
as people gather

we sit with dry
prairie grass atop
a rocky hill

LET'S BE OUR
TRICKSTERS say i

into animals
change we, in all
directions, race
over the earth

me, northwest over the
prairie, running like
a wolf/coyote and rabbit

you coming up behind
me to over take

then momentum i change
and soar upward through
layers of clouds, i can
not see, not see,
and with the altitude
scream,
turn flight horizontal
i and scream again
i through clouds

what is this, why is
this screaming?

is it raven? no?

it is eagle
it is me

        • • •

3

        what happened to you?
i figured you
got scared
i figured you
ran off

i figured you
left us to face

those white men
all by ourselves

that made me mad
'cause every
where i looked

there was more
heart break
than happiness

i thought THAT
GODDAMN NANABUSH
WHERE IS HE WHEN
WE NEED HIM

you were always
around back then,
the stories say so

and Coyote and Hare
and Raven finished
their work, but

you, what ever
happened to you,
TRICKSTER

you left us dangling
in mid-air
with those missionaries,
politicians and other
Christians snapping
at our heels

well, i never saw
Santa Claus either
goodness knows i tried

to be a good child

then i found Christmas
goodies stacked in my
parents' bedroom cupboard

there was Jesus Christ too
and his blessed mother
these people were good as gold
but didn't know a thing

about INDIANS
nor really cared to

anyway, Nanabush
i figured you
turned coward

.   .   .

11

THE WHITE MAN'S BURDEN

I
burden—something
carried, a load, heavy
responsibility or anxiety

the white man's burden
(as he sees it)
to spread culture
among the primitive
(indigenous)
peoples of the world

the white man's burden
(as we know it)
a heavy load
that he does not
have to carry

II

the white man's solution
to the white man's burden
        No. 1
(as he sees it)

WHITE OUT[1]

to lose visibility
because of snow or fog;
to create
or leave white
white   spaces in
the white man's solution
to the white man's burden
            No. 2
(as he sees it)

WHITE OUT
an atmospheric con-
condition con-
consisting of
lack of visibility
visibility and sense
sense (less
less humour sense
less humour)
h a h a h a
lack of sense
sense of dis-
tance, sense of
distance and
distance and di-
direct
direction
direction direction
take or give
lack of visibility and
sense of distance and
direction due to doo doo
dog doo doo
it's everywhere
due to due north south
east west due to
uni-
universal glo
bal village
(we all bleed red blood)
uni-
form uniform
uniform white
white nest

(How would you feel
if suddenly,
out of the blue,
a little brown
baby bird
got plopped down
in your white
feathered nest?)[2]
white nest
whiteness
of a heavy cloud (head
in the clouds) cover and
snow-covered ground (zero),
which reflects
reflects reflects
reflects almost all
almost all light
it receives.

the white man's solution
to the white man's burden
            No. 3
(as he sees it)

WHITE WASH

dye
die
die hard
di
direct direct cur
rent
(pay the rent or get out)
die out
dying race
run Indian run
dye die di
direct cur
(oh you dog you)
direct cur current
direct current
DC AC/DC
dece
ease
(easy)

dis
ease
dece
eve

deceptive
specious
(capricious)
words or act
(Indian)
actions
intended to con
ceal defects, gloss
(loss)
over over
(t) fee
lings

the white man's solution
to the white man's burden
       No. 4
(as he sees it)

WHITE WASH

to white(n)
with white(wash)

—a little soap,
a little water and a
good scrubbing will make
things clear, whiter
My poor cousin Betsy became
a ward
(award?)
of the Children's Aid.
Her foster mother insisted
on bathing her every day and
scrubbed her with a brush.

Hallelujah!
Praise the Lord!
Clorox bleach gets whites whiter.
Amen.   Amen.
Aye men.

How would you feel if
a little brown baby bird
plopped down in your nest?

How about a whole
nest of brown baby birds?

Know what happens
when you throw shit
on little brown baby birds?
They GROW UP . . . AND
COULD SCARE YOU!

the white man's solution
to the white man's burden
              No. 5
(as he sees it)

WHITE PAPER[3]

document outlining
government policy
and possible
action, including
legislation. White
Papers can be less
embarrassing
than legislation

                    9
                   6 9
                  9 6 9
                 1 9 6 9
           W H I T E   P A P E R
                 1 9 6 9
                  9 6 9
                   6 9
                    9

W H I T E
W H I T E   M A N
  W H I T E   M A N - I Z E
  F A N T A S I Z E
  D R E A M   O N
D R E A M

the white man's solution
to the white man's burden
No. 6
(as we know it)

PUT DOWN THE LOAD, STUPID

. . .

12

HOW TO CATCH A WHITE MAN
(OOPS) I MEAN TRICKSTER.

First, find yourself a forest. Any stand of ancient trees will do; in
fact, the older the better. Stand in the middle of it and tell your
stories. Soon the white man! (I mean Trickster) will come by, carrying a big pack on his back. In that pack he carries the voices of
his women and the voices of other people he has walked over with
his long legs. 'I'm going to tell those stories for you,' he'll say.
'You're far too primitive to tell them yourself. I am going to let
the world know what you think. I am going to tell the world how
you think when you think. And I'm going to build a golf course
here, too. These trees are so old, and besides you're not using them
trees.'

Tell him you heard some people talking about better stories and a
better place for a golf course, perhaps even a h-y-d-r-o e-l-e-c-t-r-i-c
dam, or two. Say, you could even push for a super fantasyland golf
course. Anyhow, tell him he could make the stories into TV movies,
docudramas, feature films. He could write novels using the stories.
He could receive all kinds of literary awards for his great imagination, with these stories. He could even achieve world acclaim for
telling others how it is with the 'Native Indian'. (God, how I hate
that word 'Indian'.)

Okay, then tell him to wait there while you'll go find out more about
those stories and that other place. He'll say, 'Okay, but come right
back.' Only don't go back.

Find another forest and dig a big big hole in the middle of it, beside
a pine tree. Then climb up and sit in the branches of that tree and
call out saying, 'Hey, white man! (I mean Trickster. You could call
him a trickster, you know. He's like that, clever. But he's not smart.)

These stories are not for you, and you can't build your golf course here either.'

It won't be long and he'll come by with that great big pack and this time with his guns and tanks, too—ready to take those stories— ready to build his golf course.

Then you tell him from that tree you can see, hear everything all over the world, and know exactly what's going on, too. He'll say, 'That's new to me.' Ask him if he would like to see these things, too. Of course, he'll say, 'Yes.' Tell him to leave his heavy pack at the bottom of the tree. He won't. He'll climb up into that tree with his weapons, too. Ask him if he's comfortable. He'll say, 'I'm comfortable anywhere.' Be careful now because he'll want to sit right on top of you.

Now, tell him to close his eyes. He has to close his eyes if he is to know and see all the things you do. He has to listen to the trees and grass. Tell him it takes a while for the vision to come clear, and he should sit quietly and wait and listen. As soon as his eyes are closed, run away and watch. Get other people to watch, too. And the children. Don't forget about the children.

Of course, that man won't see anything. Never did. And he certainly won't hear anything. Never has. And after a bit he'll become uncomfortable, restless, impatient and he'll cock his gun and open his eyes. When he sees you are gone he'll get mad as heck and fall out of the tree, shooting himself in the foot, dropping his great pack and tumbling into the hole, his foot in his mouth.

That's when you run over and grab his great pack, open it up and set free the voices of the people he has walked over and the voices of his women.

Now that white man (I mean Trickster) will scramble. And he'll fight, digging himself deeper into the hole, but he won't ever get out this time. His women will see to that. Then tell the children. Teach them. Teach them the history of this land, the real history, before 1492 and since. Those stories will guide them into the next 500 years. Tell them not to do as the Trickster (I mean white man) has done. And tell them to listen to the trees and grass. The trees and the grass hold on to heaven for us.

· · ·

16

TRICKSTERS

A WORN ROCKY HILL
JUST AFTER SUNRISE.

FOCUS ON

a cluster of ancient rock amid clumps of
dry prairie grass.

WIDER ANGLE

now includes an assemblage of larger
rocks (cairns), a medicine wheel spoke,
and reveals that we are at the centre of a
hillock.

OFF CENTRE to the right, a ghostly
FIGURE approaches from the north,
coming in from 'The Other Side' and
becoming more visible—wearing a single
braid, the man is dressed in a country-
plaid shirt, denim jeans and cowboy
boots. He nods and seats himself.

Over this, we HEAR

the rustling approach of others, men and
women. They gather closely, not speaking, sit and remain unseen.

NEW ANGLE

shows the complete assembly within the
medicine wheel and the LEADER, a
woman, sitting in the centre, faces north.

We HEAR only the whisper of wind
through the grass, then

                    LEADER
            Let's be our Tricksters.

There is a CLAMOUR of consent, an
awareness of metamorphosis as human
utterances warp into animal intonations.

CUT TO:

LEADER'S POINT OF VIEW (POV)

the peripheral landscape springs down
the hillock into distortion as the prairie
plunges into high-speed visual images,
while the northwest horizon floats in the
distance.

We hear PANTING.

CUT TO:

AERIAL VIEW

of assembly, all animal tricksters, some
still part human, all bounding out from
the hub of the medicine wheel and radi-
ating out over the prairie.

CUT TO:

Leader, in incomplete transfiguration,
racing northwest like a wolf, a coyote, a
rabbit.

CLOSE IN TO

OVER THE SHOULDER SHOT

of Leader in lower left foreground of
frame. Directly behind and gaining, a
larger wolf threatens to overtake.

DISSOLVE TO:

LEADER'S POV

a view of the prairie rim and skyline. The

horizon BLURS and crests skyward penetrating cloud strata.

Over this, we HEAR the Leader shriek as if
in horror and pain.

There is a sense of flight becoming horizontal into cloud strata followed by
waves of myopic blurring.

As the clouds give way to the blinding
shimmer of sunlight, we HEAR the Leader
shriek again.

There is another bank of clouds; another
shriek, intonation uncertain and more like
the RAUCOUS CRY of a raven/eagle.

CUT TO:

CLOSE SHOT

SCREAMING EAGLE

CUT TO:

EAGLE'S POV

the medicine wheel, now a delicate
pattern etched on an expansive prairie.
Some animal tricksters are still visible,
still running.

A PANORAMIC VIEW closing in on the
medicine wheel.

REVERSE ANGLE

in a now-clear sky, barely visible, is the
Eagle riding the currents of air, circling
slowly northwest—

We HEAR her exalted cry.

---

[1] *Collins English Dictionary.*
[2] Daniel David Moses, a radioscript.
[3] Hurtig's *The Canadian Encyclopedia.*

John McLeod b. 1949

MISSISSAUGA

The Shivering Tree

Nanabush was walking; he'd been walking a long time. He'd been walking a long time and he was feeling very tired and thirsty.

'My, my, my,' Nanabush said to himself, 'I've been walking a long time and boy oh boy am I tired and thirsty. It's a good thing I'm such a smart fellow and decided to follow this river. This way, if I get lost, I'll still know where I am even though I won't.'

And he liked what he said to himself.

'Goodness me but I'm a bright fellow,' Nanabush said to himself. And he had to stop in his tracks and smile and just shake his head, he was just so proud of himself for what he'd just said just before telling himself how bright he was.

'Well, Nanabush, you bright fellow, let's go down to the river and have a drink and rest our old bones for a year or two . . . heh, heh,' Nanabush said to himself. And he agreed.

Feeling very proud of himself, Nanabush strutted down to the river. It wasn't far at all and when he got there Nanabush took a good long drink, threw some water in his face, and lay back on the sandy bank.

'It certainly is a big world,' he thought. 'Somewhere to the west of here are the Tall Mountains that mark the approach of the Home of the West Wind. Someday I'll go there, for I've a score to settle with that Old Fellow.'

That's when his quick ears caught another sound above the voice of the river. It was another voice, a man's voice.

Nanabush sat up, fast.

'A man?' Nanabush thought. 'That just can't be. No human being has come this far.'

But it was a man. At least it looked like one. But that meant nothing back in those times; after all, Nanabush looked like a man—most of the time. But Nanabush was far from being human. But just who or what was this fellow anyway?

Like I said, the stranger looked human at least. He was tall and thin, clad in buckskins with long fringe that fluttered and shivered in the breeze. He wore warm leggings and moccasins as it was autumn and the weather getting colder.

The stranger was juggling something. Now that was interesting.

He was juggling with his eyes closed. And that was mighty interesting.

Nanabush stood up, slowly, never taking his eyes off the juggling stranger.

'Hello, Nanabush,' The Juggler said, still juggling, his eyes still shut firmly. 'It is Nanabush, isn't it?'

Nanabush felt insulted.

'Of course I'm Nanabush,' Nanabush said. 'Who else could I be?'

The Juggler, eyes still firmly shut, still juggling what now appeared to be a pair of small crystals, just smiled.

'Well, let me see now,' The Juggler said, still juggling, his eyes still shut firmly. 'You could be Me, seeing as I'm the only person in these parts, but as you are you and not me and I'm here to see it, I guess I'm me and you're you and you must be Nanabush, because I've heard you've been spotted in these parts and I'm the only person here who would have heard about you besides you.'

Nanabush glared at The Juggler.

'It's a fortunate thing for you that I'm such a clever fellow,' Nanabush said, 'because if I wasn't I might've been confused by what you just said and I'd've become very angry.'

The Juggler just kept on juggling, eyes closed and all.

Nanabush felt himself getting impatient.

'Well?' Nanabush said. 'Are you going to tell me who you are?'

With a big, wide grin, The Juggler stopped what he was doing, opened his eyes, and turned to Nanabush.

'Very well,' The Juggler said, 'I'm a juggler and conjuror and I am known as Restless As The Wind; but most people just call me The Juggler.'

'I have never heard of you,' Nanabush said. He didn't like this fellow at all. No sir, Nanabush didn't like him at all.

'I was just playing around with a couple of pieces of crystal,' The Juggler said. 'That was nothing at all. That was just ordinary juggling that a child can do, eyes closed or not. Just watch. I'll show you some real conjuring . . . Look, Nanabush, look.'

Quick as lightning, The Juggler plucked out his own eyes and started to juggle them, rapidly from hand to hand. He started to dance, leaping into the air, all the while juggling his eyes hand to hand, back and forth, back and forth, hand to hand.

Nanabush was stunned, couldn't move.

Now that in itself was something. It takes a great deal to shake up someone like Nanabush, and everyone knows that there just isn't anyone to compare with The Great Nanabush.

The Juggler kept it up. Juggling, hand to hand, back and forth, back and forth, hand to hand, dancing, leaping, juggling. Juggling his eyes.

'Stop,' Nanabush said, shouting. 'Stop, you're making me dizzy . . . *stop it.*'

And, just as quickly as he had started, The Juggler stopped, came to a halt just like that, arms out wide, head back, just in time for his eyes to fall right straight into their sockets.

Nanabush's own eyes almost fell out, he stared so hard.

The Juggler grinned: boy did he grin.

Nanabush still couldn't stop staring.

I don't blame The Great Nanabush one bit, my friends. A sight like that would be enough to jar anyone's preserves.

'Now that is most certainly conjuring at its best,' Nanabush said, 'and you may take that as the word of the very one who invented conjuring.'

The Juggler grinned.

'Well, Great Nanabush, Father of Conjuring. Perhaps I can show my gratitude, indeed the gratitude of all of us Conjurors,' The Juggler said, smiling. 'Allow me to show you how it's done. Allow me to show you how to juggle one's own eyes in one's own hands.'

Now that got to Nanabush. For great and powerful as he can be, Nanabush can make the odd blunder now and then, and when he does, it's usually a bad one. This was going to be one of the worst.

'I'm flattered,' Nanabush said, smiling like a proud father. 'And I'm never too old to learn.'

How true that was. Nanabush was about to learn a lesson that he and we are never going to forget.

'Will you allow me, then, to show you how it is done?' The Juggler said, smiling.

'The honour will be mine,' Nanabush said, stepping forward. 'Show me how it's done, Nephew.'

'Removing the eyes is the really dangerous part,' The Juggler said. 'You have to apply some pressure just below each eye, like this.'

The Juggler demonstrated how it was supposed to be done. Using his thumbs, he applied some pressure underneath his eye-sockets, and . . . POP . . . out came the eyes. Very quickly, but carefully, he caught the eyes and, quickly and just as carefully, placed them back in his sockets.

'Did you see that?' The Juggler said. 'Now, very carefully, 'cause it's just the first time, try it yourself and on yourself. Not too fast. This is only the First Lesson.'

Nanabush placed his thumbs under his eye-sockets, carefully applied some pressure.

'Good, good . . . that's good,' The Juggler said, directing and urging Nanabush. 'Careful now . . . be very careful.'

Then . . . POP . . . out came Nanabush's eyes . . . Then . . . WHOOSH out shot The Juggler's right hand and grabbed Nanabush's eyes in mid-air.

'I've got them . . . HA HA. I've got them,' The Juggler cried, leaping into the air and spinning like a top. 'I've got the most powerful charms of any conjuror in The North. I have the very eyes of Nanabush . . . HA HA I have them.'

Then, as quick as lightning, The Juggler turned and ran, ran faster than he'd ever run in his life, for Nanabush is still Nanabush, blind or not.

But Nanabush was blind. Even before The Juggler turned and ran, Nanabush had made a lunge forward, instinctively knowing that something had gone wrong.

As The Juggler ran off, laughing and whooping, Nanabush landed, face down in the river. Almost immediately, he was on his feet. Almost immediately he was the real Nanabush. He stood still, turned his fear into caution.

'I've been a fool, a vain, yes . . . even a blind fool. With both my eyes in my head, I was blind,' he said to himself. He stood still, silent. He listened. He began to take his bearings.

The river was in front of him. He turned his back to it.

'Until I regain my sight . . . and I will regain my sight, I must feel my way about. I also need a weapon which I can use easily and quickly should one of my old enemies come upon me,' Nanabush said to himself. 'A staff, that's it. A big heavy staff, sharpened at one end; it'll act as a cane and a weapon. I must find my way to the bush.'

So, stumbling over bits of driftwood and rocks, falling painfully but always getting right back up on his feet, Nanabush made his way towards the bush, feeling his way with his hands, carefully keeping his ears open for every sound.

'If a friend finds me, may he truly be a friend,' Nanabush said. 'If an enemy should come upon me, may he act with honour. If my enemy should save me, I will gladly be in his debt. If my enemy finds me and chooses to kill me, then fine, I will still owe him something, if only a good fight.'

All around him was darkness. But he knew that to be a false darkness. The birds still sang and the warmth of the sun made itself felt on his body and he knew it to be daylight and he knew himself to be in full view of friend, foe, and stranger alike. But he stumbled on, into the bush. He knew he was in the bush, for he smelt pine needles and the odour of fallen leaves. He bent over and felt a pine cone beneath his hand.

'I must find a stout pole to carve into a pointed staff,' he said, feeling about, moving more cautiously than before.

The forest was thick, for he continually bumped into trees and stumps.

'Trees, stumps, but no limbs of any good size,' he thought. 'At least one old enemy of mine has been at work here, Old Man Beaver and his clan.'

Then his left hand touched on something, a young fallen tree. This was it. He ran his hands up and down the narrow trunk. This was exactly what he wanted. He pulled out his knife after using his great strength to break off an appropriate length of trunk. Carefully, he sat down and carefully, very carefully, he began to carve.

A staff alone won't be enough. Nanabush knew that. He'd have to find help from someone who knew the country, someone he could trust, someone who could be trusted as a guide.

But Nanabush had to concentrate on his carving. He had to be really, really careful or, in his blindness, he might cut a finger or two off.

So far, he hadn't given a thought to The Juggler.

He kept on carving, clumsily but carefully.

Then, suddenly, he stopped. Stopped everything. He had a strong feeling that he was being watched. He tightened his grip on the knife.

Though he had no eyes with which to see, he still instinctively moved his head back and forth as if scanning the area around him. He was certain that he was being watched. The feeling was even stronger.

Then he heard the voice, a deep clear voice, from somewhere above him.

'Well?' The Voice said, 'Why have you stopped? You were doing well.'

Knife in hand, Nanabush leaped to his feet.

'Who is there?' he snapped. 'If you're an enemy, come out and fight.'

'Fight?' The Voice said. 'I thought you were busy working with that piece of wood.'

Nanabush recognized the voice. It was indeed the voice of an enemy; a very old enemy, too.

'Owl, so it's you,' Nanabush said, more on his guard than ever. 'Well. What are you waiting for? Come and fight.'

'I'm an old warrior, not an old fool,' Owl said. 'There's a thousand eyes in these woods. If I fought you and if I slew you in the condition which you are in the whole of Creation would hear of it. You'd be honoured. I'd be disgraced.

'No, Nanabush. I'm no coward. I may be your enemy, but I would like to think that I'm a worthy enemy.

'Lower your weapon. There is no danger from me, you have my word as a Warrior and as the head of my clan.'

Nanabush, on hearing this solemn oath, placed his knife back into its sheath.

'I know that you're blind,' said the Owl. 'So will others and soon, Nanabush. Others who may not be so generous. Something must be done to restore your vision to you.'

'I'll find a way myself,' said Nanabush. 'I'm already far too much in debt to you, Owl.'

'Not if we decide to be friends,' Owl said. 'I am willing, for I wish there to be peace for my children. If you agree, then it's done.'

'Then it's done,' Nanabush said.

Their friendship sealed, the two began to talk of Nanabush's trouble.

'There is a way to restore your vision,' Owl said. 'I will give you a pair of eyes. I will give you my eyes.'

'But Owl, my friend. That will leave you with no eyes. You will be as blind as I now am,' Nanabush said.

The Owl shook his head. If he could have smiled, he would have.

'Oh no, not me,' Owl said. 'You see, Nanabush, I have two sets of eyes. One set for daytime and another set for night. As most of my enemies are daylight hunters like the hawk, I'll do my hunting at night from now on. During the day, I'll rest and stay safely with my family. I'll need only one set of eyes then. The other set I give to you.'

Owl told Nanabush to hold out his hands. Nanabush did so, and a pair of eyes dropped into Nanabush's hands. Then . . . POP . . . Nanabush dropped the eyes into his own sockets.

'They are perfect, Owl,' Nanabush said, joyously but seriously, as befits a Warrior.

'From this day, Owl, the night is yours,' Nanabush declared. 'From this day and for all time, you will be the Bird of The Night. You will be my eyes at night. At night your vision will be sure and your flight safe and clear. You will be to night as the Eagle and the Falcon are to the daylight. You'll rule the night skies. And out of respect for the great favour you have done for me, all who hear you call at night shall show their respect. They must not mimic your call if they hear you; that is to say, they will not answer your call. For them to do so would be to mock you. Your call will be my message in the night that I, Nanabush, never sleep but with my ears open, that even at night I watch those whom I protect, and that I keep a watch out for those who would do harm to The Creation. So call out at night, Owl, my friend and my Emissary.'

Their friendship sealed for all time, Owl and Nanabush bade each other good hunting and a long life. And so they parted, Owl with his new honours, Nanabush with his new eyes.

Springtime.

Springtime, and Nanabush was home. New eyes and everything. 'The World is very beautiful this day,' Nanabush said to himself as he walked along. 'All is green and fragrant with new life and the birds are back. Yes, this is truly a beautiful day.'

'Can't wait till the butterflies come out,' Nanabush said. 'My, but it's a wonderful day. Good thing that I have my eyes to see it all.'

Then came that little voice that is sometimes to be heard in the back of Nanabush's mind. 'Ah, Nanabush, but they weren't always your eyes, were they?' Nanabush remembered, of course. He remembered where his new eyes had come from and he remembered also what had happened to his old eyes. For the first time in months he thought of The Juggler. That ruined his day.

'The Juggler,' Nanabush thought. 'If I ever again meet up with that thieving rascal, he will regret the day his parents met. He will need more than an extra pair of eyes when I get through with him.'

His day was ruined, he sat down and sulked. He couldn't help but think of The Juggler, couldn't think of anything else.

In the days which followed, Nanabush was obsessed with his strange enemy. He talked of little else. He began to worry his friends and his family.

His Grandmother advised him to stop thinking about The Juggler.

'You still have a great deal of work to do in this world,' Grandmother said. 'You've much to do. You are the teacher, the helper of all living things. Go about your work, Grandson. Don't seek out enemies. They will find you soon enough if they are not cowards.'

So Nanabush carried on as always. Sometimes sure of himself, sometimes blundering, but always leaving his mark somewhere, somehow, on the world around him, making it more and more like the world we know today.

Then, one afternoon in late summer, he felt in need of a drink of water. He was deep in the woods at this time, but he knew where there was a clear, cold pool of water not far from where he stood. Picking up his kit, he made his way through the bush. He'd just about reached the pool when he saw, through the bushes around him, that another was at the pool.

A man.

A tall, thin man.

A tall thin man who was juggling a pair of crystals hand to hand, back and forth, hand to hand, back and forth.

Nanabush's eyes narrowed; he clenched his teeth.

'I must think this out,' Nanabush said to himself. 'I must think quickly, though. I may not get another chance at this rascal; besides, in addition to being my enemy, he's a Sorcerer and a dangerous one. Who is to tell how much damage he has done to others besides me? This fellow is very danger-ous and I must do something about him.'

Quickly and quietly, as only he can do it, Nanabush changed his appear-ance. He took on the appearance of an old man. Then he stepped out into the open.

The Juggler gave him a quick glance but kept right on juggling.

'Good day, Old One,' The Juggler said. 'I'd wish you long life but it seems a good number have already done so.'

'So they have, Nephew,' Nanabush said. 'And they did so out of respect.'

'Forgive me if I sound disrespectful,' The Juggler said, continuing to jug-gle, 'but I'm a very happy fellow these days and I sometimes don't give thought to what I'm saying. It could be that you've heard of me. I'm The Jug-gler. My name is Restless As The Wind.'

'So,' Nanabush said. 'You are the fellow Nanabush is looking for, the one who stole Nanabush's eyes.'

'That's me all right, Old One,' The Juggler said. 'Tell Nanabush if you like to. Maybe I'll take his ears this time.'

'He'll find you without my telling him,' Nanabush said, trying to hold back a smile. 'He is no longer blind, by the way. A friend gave him a new pair of eyes.'

The Juggler stopped his juggling.

Nanabush, still looking like an Old Man, stepped over to the pool and took a drink of water.

'So, he's got new eyes, has he?' The Juggler said, trying not to sound as scared as he was beginning to feel. 'Well, good for him. If he comes to me, I just might take his new eyes, too. I did it before and I can do it again.'

Nanabush stood up.

'So you're a mighty, powerful fellow?' Nanabush said. 'You think that you can beat Nanabush?'

'I am a Great Sorcerer,' The Juggler said. 'I can defeat anything or anyone.'

'Can you beat me?' Nanabush said.

'Anyone or anything,' The Juggler said, trying very hard to sound brave.

'I've heard that you can juggle with your eyes out of your head. That you don't need eyes to see,' Nanabush said.

The Juggler grinned, popped out his own eyes, and juggled them, hand to hand, back and forth, hand to hand, back and forth. Then he stopped, threw his head back. Then he tossed his eyes into the air. Up went his eyes, down they came and . . . plunk . . . landed safely in their sockets.

'Is that good enough for you, Old One?' The Juggler said, grinning at Nanabush.

But it wasn't Nanabush as an old man standing there. It was Nanabush as The Juggler remembered him.

'Well. If it isn't The Great Nanabush himself,' The Juggler said, grinning and trying to sound (and feel) braver than he really was.

'I've already seen that trick,' Nanabush said. And he was grinning too.

'So, Nanabush, are you tired of your new pair of eyes already?' The Juggler said. 'If you want to save us both time and work, you can just hand your eyes over to me right now.'

'If you really want my eyes, you're going to have to work for them, Nephew,' Nanabush said.

'Fine by me. Just tell me how,' The Juggler said.

'Very good, Nephew. Nothing fancy—I'll toss my eyes to you and you catch them,' Nanabush said. 'If you catch them, you get to keep them. If you miss you won't owe me a thing. All or nothing. Fair enough.'

'Too easy,' The Juggler said. 'No real challenge. Tell you what, Nanabush. I'll seal my eyes shut. How does that sound?'

'Fine by me, Nephew,' Nanabush said. 'But I warn you. I'm going to be throwing from quite a distance, from the very rim of the world itself.'

'Ha. Go to the rim of the world. Even that wouldn't be far enough. I'd know when it's coming. I'll just stand here and wait. You're the one who'll have all the work to do. If you want to walk all the way to the edge of Creation just to toss a couple of eyes, that's fine by me, I'll catch them. I never miss,' The Juggler said proudly.

With a shrug of his shoulders, The Juggler obtained some sap from a nearby tree. This sap he used to seal his eyes shut. Then he stood calmly and with very great confidence.

'Well, Nanabush. I'm ready if you are. Be on your way. It's a long walk, but I'll wait. When victory is a sure thing, I can wait,' The Juggler said. Then he folded his arms in front of his chest and said no more.

Nanabush walked away.

Nanabush walked away, but not to the rim of the world. He just plain walked away and didn't look back.

Nanabush went about his work of making the world what it was meant to be. He never gave The Juggler another thought. Why?

Because Nanabush knew that The Juggler, like all Sorcerers, was a vain fellow more than eager to show off his power no matter how long it took. The Juggler said he'd wait and so he did.

He's still waiting. And he will wait for all time, until The End of Time. Oh, it's not at all difficult to find him. He's very well known. He's easily recognizable.

His name, you recall, is Restless As The Wind. It's a very descriptive name. He's still to be seen standing, day in, day out, standing, rooted to the spot, his fringes and hair swaying and shivering constantly in the wind, at the slightest breeze or draught. Even when the air is perfectly still.

To pass the long hours away, you see, The Juggler, Restless As The Wind, has taken the form of a tree. A tree that never rests, whose leaves and branches still shake and shiver even when the air is still and quiet.

He's become the Shivering Tree.

The Poplar Tree.

And that's the way it is to this good day.

Beatrice Mosionier b. 1949

MÉTIS

From *April Raintree*

Our free, idle days with our family came to an abrupt end one summer afternoon. We came home and there were some cars in front of our house. One
had flashing red lights on it and I knew it was a police car. When we entered
the house, Mom was sitting at the table, openly weeping right in front of all
the strangers. There were empty medicine bottles on the small counter and
the table. I couldn't figure out why the four people were there. A nice-
smelling woman knelt down to talk to me.

'My name is Mrs Grey. I bet you're April, aren't you? And this little girl
must be Cheryl.' She put her hand on Cheryl's head in a friendly gesture, but
I didn't trust her.

I nodded that we were April and Cheryl but I kept my eyes on my mother.
Finally, I asked, 'Why is Mom crying? Did you hurt her?'

'No, dear, your mother is ill and she won't be able to take care of you any
more. Would you like to go for a car ride?' the woman asked.

My eyes lit up with interest. We'd been in a taxi a few times, and it had
been a lot of fun. But then I thought of Baby Anna. I looked around for her.
'Where's Anna?'

'Anna's sick,' the woman answered. 'She's gone to the hospital. Don't
worry, we'll take you for a ride to a nice clean place. You and Cheryl, okay?'

That was not okay. I wanted to stay here. 'We can stay with Daddy. He will
take care of us. You can go away now,' I said. It was all settled.

But Mrs Grey said in a gentle voice, 'I'm afraid not, honey. We have to take
you and Cheryl with us. Maybe if your Mommy and Daddy get well enough,
you can come to live with them again.'

The man who was with Mrs Grey had gone to our bedroom to get all our
things. When he came back, I became more uneasy. I looked from the woman
to the man, then over to one policeman who was writing in a notepad, then
to the other one who was looking around. I finally looked back at my Mom
for reassurance. She didn't look at me but I said in a very definite manner,
'No, we'd better stay here.'

I was hoping Dad would walk in and he would make them all go away. He
would make everything right.

The man with our belongings leaned over and whispered to my mother.
She forced herself to stop sobbing, slowly got up and came over to us. I could
see that she was struggling to maintain control.

'April, I want you and Cheryl to go with these people. It will only be for a
little while. Right now, Daddy and me, well, we can't take care of you. You'll
be all right. You be good girls for me. I'm sorry . . .'

She couldn't say any more because she started crying again. She hugged us and that's when I started crying too. I kind of knew that she was really saying goodbye to us. But I was determined that we were not going to be taken away. I clung to my Mom as tight as I could. They wouldn't be able to pull me away from her and then they would leave. I expected Mom to do the same. But she didn't. She pushed me away. Into their grasping hands. I couldn't believe it.

Frantically, I screamed, 'Mommy, please don't make us go. Please, Mommy? We want to stay with you. Please don't make us go.'

I tried hard to put everything into my voice, sure that they would all come to their senses and leave us be. There were a lot of grown-up things I didn't understand that day. My mother should have fought with her life to keep us with her. Instead, she simply handed us over. It didn't make any sense to me.

The car door slammed shut on us.

'Please don't make us go,' I said in a subdued, quiet voice, more to myself. I gripped Cheryl's hand and we set off into the unknown. We were both crying and ignored the soothing voices from the strangers in front.

How could Mom do this to us? What was going to happen to us? Well, at least, I still had Cheryl. I thought this to myself over and over again. Cheryl kept crying, although I'm not sure she really knew why. She loved car rides but if I was crying, I'm sure she felt she ought to be crying too.

We were taken to an orphanage. When we got there, Cheryl and I were hungry and exhausted. Inside the large building, all the walls were painted a dismal green. The sounds we made echoed down the long, high-ceilinged corridors. Then this person came out of a room to greet us. She was dressed in black, from head to foot, except for some stiff white cardboard around her neck and face. She had chains dangling around her waist and she said her name was Mother Superior and she had been expecting us. My eyes widened in fear. It was even worse than I had imagined. We were being handed over to the boogeyman for sure!

When Mrs Grey and the man said goodbye and turned to leave, I wanted to go with them but I was too scared to ask. Mother Superior took us into another room at the far end of the corridor. Here, another woman in the same outfit undressed us and bathed us. She looked through our hair for bugs, she told us. I thought that was pretty silly because I knew that bugs lived in trees and grass, not in people's hair. Of course, I didn't say anything, not even when she started cutting off my long hair.

I was thinking that this was like the hen my mother had gotten once. She plucked it clean and, later, we ate it. I sat there, wondering if that was now to be our fate, wondering how I could put a stop to this. Then the woman told me she was finished and I was relieved to find that I still had some hair left. I watched her cut Cheryl's hair and reasoned that if she was taking the trouble to cut straight then we had nothing to fear. Between yawns, Cheryl complained that she was hungry so, afterward, we were taken to a large kitchen and fed some dry tasteless food. When we finished eating, we were taken to the infirmary and put to bed.

We were finally left alone to ourselves and it really did feel like we were completely abandoned in that pitch black space. Cheryl groped her way to my bed and crawled in with me. She spoke for the first time since we got here, 'Apple, them was boogeywomen?'

I smiled in the darkness for two reasons. I hadn't thought to call them that and she had been thinking the same thing I had. 'No, I don't think so. They didn't eat us,' I said to reassure her.

For a minute, she was silent. 'They didn't like us?'

'I don't know.'

After more silence, she asked, 'Apple, we will go home in the morning time?'

'I don't think so, Cheryl.'

'But I want to.'

'So do I,' I said. By now, Cheryl had laid her head down and I could hear the breathing she used for sleeping. I lay there for a while, thinking, wondering.

* * *

I wasn't really thinking about anything when I noticed my arms and hands. They were tanned a deep, golden brown. A lot of pure white people tanned just like this. Poor Cheryl. She would never be able to disguise her brown skin as just a tan. People would always know that she was part Indian. It seemed to me that what I'd read and what I'd heard indicated that Métis and Indians were inclined to be alcoholics. I guess that was because they were a weak people. Oh, they were put down more than anyone else, but then, didn't they deserve it? Anyways, I could pass for a pure white person. I could say I was part French and part Irish. If I had to, I could even change the spelling of my name. Raintree looked like one of those Indian names but if I changed the spelling to Raintry, that could pass for Irish. And when I grew up, I wouldn't be poor; I'd be rich. Being a half-breed meant being poor and dirty. It meant being weak and having to drink. It meant being ugly and stupid. It meant living off white people. And giving your children to white people to look after. It meant that kids like me had to take what kids like the DeRosiers gave, and none of that was good. Well, I wasn't going to live like a half-breed. When I got free of this place, when I got free from being a foster child, then I would live just like a real white person.

Then a question came to mind. What about Cheryl? How was I going to pass for a white person when I had a Métis sister? Especially when she was so proud of what she was? I loved her. I could never cut myself off from her completely. And she wouldn't go along with what I planned. I would never even be able to tell her what I planned. I sat there thinking but the problem wouldn't be resolved. Well, I had a long time to figure that one out. For sure, she would never turn out to be like the rest of the Métis people. She and maybe Mrs MacAdams were special people. Cheryl was already a whole lot smarter than all the rest of the kids in her class and that counted for a lot. I sighed, stood up, and stretched. Now I felt ready to face whatever the DeRosiers had in store for me. One day I would be free of them. One day . . .

* * *

I entered the house which now seemed so empty, so cold. I decided I would pack all of Cheryl's things away in a big trunk, even her clothes. That way I'd always have a part of her. And being able to touch her belongings would strengthen that feeling.

I opened the door to Cheryl's room and the first thing I noticed was an empty whiskey bottle. I hadn't really noticed it before when I had gone into her room, to look for addresses or names. But there it stood on Cheryl's dresser, mocking me. Suddenly, I was filled with a deep hatred of what it had once contained. I grabbed it by the neck, raised it high, and brought it down, smashing it against the edge of the dresser. Again and again, I brought it down, until it was smashed into a million pieces. I was screaming, 'I hate you! I hate you! I hate you!'

My tears came flooding out and I continued screaming, 'I hate you for what you've done to my sister! I hate you for what you've done to my parents! I hate you for what you've done to my people! Our people!'

I threw myself on Cheryl's bed, letting all my pent-up tears pour out. I pounded my fists into the bed, allowing my emotions to tumble out. I felt a frenzied rage at how alcohol had torn our lives apart, had torn apart the lives of our people. I felt angry for having done so many wrong things at so many wrong times. And I felt self-pity because I would no longer have Cheryl with me.

'Oh, Cheryl, why did you have to go and kill yourself? All those people at the funeral, they loved you so much. Didn't they count? I loved you so much. Didn't that count? Didn't it matter to you? You had so much going for you. You didn't have to kill yourself, Cheryl! Why? Why?'

I writhed on the bed as if I were in physical pain. At times I would become still, but not for long. Stronger emotions would come crashing down on me and I would toss and turn again, trying to exorcise the painful anguish from within. I pounded my fists into the bed, again and again, in frustration. 'If only . . .' Those words repeated themselves over and over in my head. But it was too late. Cheryl's death was final.

When I had spent the last of my tears, I sat on the edge of the bed and surveyed the mess I had made in the room. The floor had scattered fragments of the whiskey bottle all over it. Cheryl's pillow was soaked with my tears. I looked again at the floor. If only I could smash the problem of alcoholism as easily as I had that bottle.

Temporarily void of all emotion, I systematically began to clean the room. I put the Kleenex tissues into the garbage container. I began picking up the larger pieces of glass. I grabbed one piece a little too savagely and it cut my hand. I looked at the blood oozing out in a thin red line.

'Still after more blood, are you? Well, you cut down my sister, my parents, my people. But no more. I'll see to it. Somehow. Some way.'

When I had finished cleaning Cheryl's room, I sat down again on Cheryl's bed. I wondered where to start, not wanting to start. Then I remembered all of Cheryl's papers, the journals she had kept. There were two boxes under her bed and I began going through them. The first was full of newspaper clippings, but I wanted her journals. They were in the other box.

I began looking through them. The last entry she had made was in January 1972. That was the month I had been raped. I looked for a 1970 journal. It was this one that I was most interested in, because that was when I had first lost touch with Cheryl.

The entries for January indicated she had started the search for our parents. February had occasional references to her continued search. There was more in March.

I see more and more of what April sees, broken people with broken houses and broken furniture. The ones I see on Main Street, the ones who give us our public image, the ones I see puking all over public sidewalks, battling it out with each other, their blood smearing up city-owned property, women selling what's left of themselves for a cheap bottle of wine. No wonder April ran. She was horrified that this was her legacy. She disowned it and now she's trapped in that life of glitter and tinsel, still going nowhere. Charitable organizations! What a load of crap. Surrounded by a lot of people, business-wise but empty. Just like the Main Street bums.

The more I see of these streets, the more I wonder if April isn't right. Just maybe. Better to live that empty life than live out on the streets. What if I do find our parents? Sometimes I can't help it, I feel like April does, I despise these people, these gutter-creatures. They are losers. But there is a reason why they are the way they are. Everything they once had has been taken from them. And the white bureaucracy has helped create the image of parasitic natives. But sometimes I do wonder if these people don't accept defeat too easily, like a dog with his tail between his legs, on his back, his throat forever exposed.

April, 1970—*Happy Birthday, April. What do you give the person who has everything? I can give peace of mind with a few lies.*

May, 1970—*Struck paydirt with a new address on Austin. The place is rented by a woman named Josie Pohequitas. I knock on the door and it is opened by this little, bent, old woman who is stoned out of her mind. But happy as hell. I have figured out by now, it's better to see these people at certain times of the day. You have to be late enough, so they can start getting over last night's drunk and early enough, so they're not whacked out of it yet. I ask if she knows Henry or Alice Raintree.*

'Henri, Henri Raintree?' She says in a French-type accent.

'Yes, I'm his daughter and I've been looking for him,' I say in a pleasant, polite voice.

'Ah, yes, mais oui, we're good friends, you know. Come in. Here, sit down, here. He comes to our place when the snows are gone. He goes north for winters. He is welcome here. He stays. Sometimes, we have big party. Sometimes, we have big fight. Then he goes. But he always come back, Henri does. He

will come back. You come back in a couple of weeks. You will see. He will be here then.'

I'm tickled a deeper shade of brown, you might say. I tell the toothless woman with her toothless smile that I will be back.

June, 1970—*I knock at this door again, having been here a few times with no luck and expecting none this time.*

'Ah, Cheryl, it's you again. Come in, come in,' her face lights up into a big grin, still toothless.

'Henri, Henri, come out here and see the surprise that is here for you. Hurry up, Henri,' her voice is high-pitched and squeaky. She never pronounces the 'h's.

An old, grey-haired man comes walking out of the kitchen. He is trying to keep his balance, curiosity is piercing through his drunken haze. I assume that Josie has told him about me but still it's a few minutes before he realizes it's me.

My smile disappears but a smile slowly appears on that leathery, unshaven face.

'No, no, it can't be. Not my little daughter, Cheryl. My little baby. You're all grown up now.'

He chuckles and staggers a little closer to me. He makes a visible effort to draw himself up, but he has drunk too much already and the feat is beyond him. His clothes are worn, dirty, and dishevelled. Tears of happiness and perhaps awakened guilt pour from his watery eyes.

The woman, Josie, is beaming with pride as if this 'joyful' reunion were all her doing.

'It's like a miracle. It's like a miracle,' she cackles over and over again, watching father and daughter facing each other. I am rooted to the very spot, absorbing the true picture of my father. I make no effort to move towards him. This goes unnoticed and the old man approaches me.

'I cannot believe that we are standing here, face to face, at long last. At long, long last,' the decrepit, old man says.

I stand quietly, hiding the horror which is boiling inside of me. I hadn't known what to expect. But it wasn't this, this bent, wasted human form in front of me. My father! I am horrified and repulsed; by him; by the cackling, prune-faced woman; by the others who have crawled out of the kitchen to watch all this 'happiness', all of them with stupid grins on their faces; by the surrounding decay; by the hopelessness. The cancer from the houses I've been to has spread into this house, too. To destroy.

All my dreams to rebuild the spirit of a once proud nation are destroyed in this instant. I study the pitiful creature in front of me. My father! A gutter-creature!

The imagination of my childhood has played a horrible, rotten trick on me. All these years, until this very moment, I envisioned him as a tall, straight, handsome man. In the olden days he would have been a warrior if he had been all Indian. I had made something out of him that he wasn't, never was.

Now I just want to turn and run away, pretend this isn't happening, that I have never laid eyes on him. Pretend I was an orphan. I should have listened to April.

Awkwardly, he hugs me. I smell the foul stink of liquor on him. Hell, he probably sweats liquor out of his pores. I close my eyes so no one will see what's in them. I hold my breath against the gutter smell. Seems like ages before he releases me. When he does, he turns to the others and says, 'Don't just stand there, bring her a drink. Now we have something to celebrate. I found my little girl after all these years. Tell me, Cheryl, where is your sister? Where is April? I missed you both so much. Ah, here we are.'

He hands me a beer and wipes his tears and runny nose on the sleeve of his shirt. I don't answer. I just think, 'April is far away from you and she'll never know what you are, you, you gutter-creature!'

Gratefully, I swallow some beer. Disgust, hatred, shame . . . yes, for the first time in my life, I feel shame. How do I describe the feeling? I swallow more beer.

I stay for the rest of the day in spite of my desire to flee. I stay because I want to know about Mom. But I want Dad sober when I ask him about Mom. Funny, I can still refer to him as Dad. I drink away the hours and pass the dizzy, nauseous sensations, laughing stupidly with them. Josie puts me to bed, just in time, on a battered couch in the living room.

Next morning. I wait patiently for Dad to get up. It is almost noon. He comes into the kitchen. He looked in rough shape last night but now he looks worse, with his weak, flabby arms showing because he's in a torn, greyish undershirt. His dark-coloured baggy pants are held up by suspenders that are frayed to the breaking point and all twisted. I get coffee for Dad. Josie is busy puttering around the kitchen. No one talks, the only noises come from Dad slurping his coffee.

Finally, I ask him, 'Dad, could we talk?' Sounds like I'm shouting. I lower my voice. 'I want to talk about Mom. How is she? Do you see her?'

Dad makes a gesture as if he doesn't want to talk about her right now but I persist. 'Please, Dad. Tell me about Mom. Where is she?'

Tears come to his eyes again. He says simply, 'She died last July.'

'Died? Mom died?' I ask, not believing. I then figure out that Mom was in poor health when we were kids and that's why she died. I wish I could have seen her. Poor, dear mother. Maybe that's why Dad turned to booze. He misses her so much he can't live without her. I can forgive that, retract all the bad thoughts about him.

But Dad speaks again. 'I may as well tell you everything.' He sighs and lapses into another long silence.

I try to make it shorter by urging him to continue. 'Tell me what, Dad?'

'Your mother took her own life. She killed herself,' he says at last. 'She left a letter for me but I had gone up north early that year. I have a nephew in Dauphin. I stop in there sometimes. They sent the letter there. She jumped off the Louise Bridge last July. I took the letter to the RCMP and they checked with

the Winnipeg police. *They had found a body and everything matched your Mama. She was not happy with her life. Once she lost you girls and Anna died, she knew she would never get you girls back again. Those visits were too hard on her. So she stopped going. She tried to kill herself before, once, a long time ago.'*

I digest what he says. '. . . too hard on her?' What about April and me? In those foster homes? Okay, only one was real bad and April suffered most of that one. But I suffered for April. And the other ones? Those people weren't our flesh and blood. They weren't even our race. I remember now, those promises you made us, promises we believed, all the waiting for you to take us back home, all the loyalty we gave you—all for nothing.

'Who's Anna?' I'm angry but I don't want to fight. I want information.

Dad looks at me, surprised. 'You don't know about Anna? Oh, of course not. You were just a baby yourself when she died. April must remember her. Maybe not. She was just little too, and Anna wasn't with us very long. She was your baby sister. But she was a sick baby. They should have kept her in the hospital longer, but, no, they sent her home too early and she died. They blamed your Mama and me. That was their excuse for taking you girls away from us. No, my girl, your Mama was not a happy woman.'

'Why didn't you come to see us when we were kids?' I ask in a soft voice, afraid of an honest answer.

There is another long pause. 'I went up north for a long time. I was never here to visit you again,' he says as if that's a good enough reason. 'No, your Mama did not want you girls to see the way she was. She was too ashamed. She couldn't face you again. They shouldn't have taken you away from us. The baby was just sick, that's all.' Dad drifts off into silence again.

Dad asks me to come back and see him tomorrow. I say I will. I do. Josie says Dad left that morning to see some friends of his for a few days. Here I thought he would be impatiently waiting for me. Ha! What a joke!

I sat on the bed with the journal clutched to me. This was the second mention of Anna. I'd been thinking of Anna after Cheryl had told me about her. Baby Anna. I remembered that's what I had called her. Recollections of my mother rocking a baby had come back, much clearer. I'd always had vague pictures in mind but I'd never realized the baby was our own sister. Baby Anna. She'd been with us for just a fraction of our lives. But she was sick and had to go to the hospital. And now, here, in Cheryl's journal were Dad's words saying the same thing. Baby Anna. Such a small part of our lives. Yet she had changed our lives the most.

This was exactly how Cheryl felt when she found Dad. After all that he told her, she still went back to see him the next day. She was still loyal to him. How was it she had the natural family instinct? I had instincts only for self-preservation, pushing anyone away from me who might hurt me. I was a loner. Only recently, had I let Roger in. Then Nancy and her mother, hugging me that night, giving me all that they had felt for Cheryl. Before Roger, who else besides Cheryl had hugged me and meant it? Well, maybe Mrs Dion. I remembered wishing many times that I could be as affectionate as Cheryl. That meeting with Dad, maybe it destroyed her self-image. Strange, though, since she had seen that side of native life before. I wondered what sort of image she had built up about our parents? Was it that image of long ago that had sustained her, given her hope?

February 18, 1971—So. A son is born to me. It should have been a very special day for him. A day when his aunt and grandparents and all his relatives rejoiced. Instead, it's just him and me. What's that joke I read? If he had known what was going to be in store for him, he would have cried a whole lot louder?

February 22, 1971—Having pondered over what to call you, my dear son, I've decided on Henry Liberty Raintree. May you grow up to be all that your grandfather is not.

A son? Cheryl had a son? I felt anger and bewilderment. Not at Cheryl or anyone else. The anger was for me. For being the way I was. Because it had caused Cheryl to feel so alienated from me that she couldn't share the most important event in her life with me. Henry Liberty Raintree. Then I smiled. A part of Cheryl still lived. After a while, I continued reading.

March 10, 1971—Nancy is babysitting and I'm free for a while. Feels great to be let out. Henry Lee's been so cranky lately. On top of that, we've got to move cause kids aren't allowed. Landlord's just a bigot, always looking down his nose at me when I pay the rent. I thought Henry Lee would change my life for the better but I can see I thought wrong. Must say I do feel good about this watering hole. Don't think Nancy will mind my coming home late. She'll understand.

April 8, 1971—Sure am glad Nancy's Mom is letting Henry Lee stay at her place. I'm not so tied down anymore. She sure gives him some good mothering. I don't think motherhood was meant for me. I'd rather be out partying than sitting at home changing dirty diapers.

June, 1971—Nancy's Mom is keeping Henry Lee for me for good now. Do I feel guilty? Only when I'm sober. And I try very hard to see that doesn't happen. I give her money all the time, so I'm sure she doesn't mind. Wish I had a mother like that.

October, 1971—Today Dad says he doesn't know where he is going to stay because he can't pay his rent. I know what he wants so I give him forty bucks. His eyes bulge. Usually I only give him ten or twenty.

At Decarlos with Nancy. The gang is all here, too. Already we got suckers to pay for our drinks. It's cheap coming here. I give my money to Dad so he can go get tanked and I come here and get mine free. I have to laugh at dumb jokes, let these guys run their hands up my legs. They think they're going to get more later, but I can avoid that.

Mark DeSoto. Now if all these guys were like Mark . . . but they're not. Nancy says Mark's ol' lady, Sylvia, is going to have it in for me if I hang around with Mark. He's over there at another table. He comes to say hello. I ignore him. He was supposed to call during the week and didn't. The suckers at my table are really playing up to me tonight. Got to go say hi to Marie.

I'm walking back to my table and I hear this shrill voice. 'Hey, squaw, I don't share my man with no one. You hear me? Especially no squaw.'

Sylvia comes into my path and stops. I stop. I look her in the eye. 'What's your problem, sweetheart? Can't hang on to your guy? And I ain't no squaw, I'm a half-breed.' I feel ridiculous and powerful at the same time. I know what I'm capable of. I give her my coldest stare. I know I've won this round. She can't match my gaze. The 'blond bomb-shell' jabs a finger into my shoulder, telling me what she's going to do to me. I twist around slightly and bring my fist into the side of her face, not real hard but hard enough to back her off. The dumb broad trips over a chair and sprawls on the floor. Everyone laughs, hoping for a fight. I step over her and continue on my way.

'You're going to pay for this, Cheryl.'

'Yeah? Well you'd better give it your best shot, Sylvia.'

Mark struts over to my table. My precious companions scatter. He sits down and grins. 'So you're my prize,' I say to him sarcastically. But the evening ends with Mark in my bed.

Mark moves in. Nancy moves out. Landlord requests that we remove ourselves after the first party. I find a cheap place on Elgin.

November, 1971—*I'm working. Mark is working the streets. We're always broke. I sell all the furniture, except the typewriter. I wonder why April gave it to me? She's the one with the writing talent. I give it to Nancy for safekeeping, so Mark won't sell it.*

We're stone broke. Mark owes everyone so we can't hit anyone up for a loan. Mark says to me, 'You know that guy who comes to Neptune's and he always looks the chicks over. Well he's loaded and sometimes I sit and talk to him.'

'I know who you mean. What about him? You're going to borrow some money from him?'

'He never lends money. But sometimes he sees a chick he likes and asks me if I can arrange a meeting. So, I go to her and if she's interested we share the money he pays, see?'

'You mean you're some kind of pimp?'

'Not a pimp, Cheryl. I just do two people a favour and I get some money out of it. We need money now, bad, and I know he's got the hots for you. I just thought you might consider it, just this once.'

'You're asking me to go to bed with another man?'

'Well, it's not like there's any feelings between you. Just think of it as a business transaction. I told him you were a very special girl and he's willing to pay more for you. Come on, Cheryl, one hour's work and you could make fifty bucks. I'll try to get more.'

'Forget it.' I'm bloody mad.

'I ain't no prostitute.' I storm out of the house. A week later. We're still broke. I'm drinking at Neptune's. I'm almost drunk. Mark comes over. This sucker who's been buying me drinks leaves quickly. Funny the power Mark has. 'Cheryl, please, we gotta get some money. The landlord today said he'd give us another twenty-four hours and no more.'

'Is he kinky?' I'm just dirt. Who cares if he's kinky.

Later, I'm back at Neptune's. We have our rent money now, plus some. I have a drink. Another one. Another one. My parents deserted me, April has left me, Mark . . . is a good for nothing woman user. Make that last word, abuser. I have another drink. And another one. Let Mark use me. I don't care. Let April sit in her fancy white palace. I just don't care any more.

January, 1972—*I'm an old pro now. I'm working the streets full time. I avoid the pigs by picking johns that are obviously not pigs. Well, they're pigs, too, but in another way. Mark arranges a lot of meetings, too. I've gotten into other things I bet Mrs Semple never heard of in her old 'syndrome speech'. I'm still broke. First thing Dad says when I see him is, 'Cheryl, I need twenty for groceries.'*

'I don't have any.'

He goes into a rage. 'What do ya mean, you don't have any? You got enough to go drinking but you can't spare your poor Pa any? Did that bum you're shacked up with tell you not to give me any more? You're just as bad as your ol' lady was, you know that? A lazy no good for nothing. Running around all the time, living with bums. I need some money. I need groceries and I got to pay the rent. Now I got nothing, just cause you couldn't hang onto a simple job.'

I tell him he's worse. I swear at him. I tell him what I think of him, that he's a parasite, a gutter-creature. I tell him it's his fault Mom killed herself. The tears spring to his eyes. I leave him. Let him stew in his guilt. I sure as hell stew in mine.

At home, Mark comes in. I'm angry and still brooding. Mark is angry. I'm supposed to be at Neptune's. We need money real bad. He yells. I yell. He beats me. I'm used to it. He avoids hitting my face. He has learned it's not good business. He leaves.

I walk along Main Street. This is where I belong. With the other gutter-creatures. I enter a hotel. I don't know which one. The word 'Beverage' is all I see. I need a drink. A couple of drinks. The depression is bitterly deep. The booze doesn't help this time. I'm back on the street. I'm drunk. I want to run in front of a car. The guy who was buying my drinks comes with me. What a creep. We head to my place on Elgin. We take a short-cut down a back lane. The creep wants to fondle me and kiss me. He can't wait. 'Back off, you ugly old man. I'm no whore, you know?' I don't know why I say that, but I repeat it. I can scarcely keep my balance. It's like there are two of me, one watching, one doing. 'I wanna kiss you. You know what you are. So don't pretend with me, I paid for you.'

'You stink. Leave me alone, you filthy pig!' I slur the words. He gives me a push. I slam into the wall and fall into a sitting position. My legs have given out. They're sprawled out in front of me, like they don't want to go on, any more. I close my eyes. I like the sensation of everything spinning around at full speed. I half open my eyes. I watch the man. He's looking real scared. He turns and runs, clumsily, boozily. I smile and shut my eyes again.

I come to. I'm still lying around with my legs out there in front of me, still going nowhere. I notice the garbage cans and garbage bags on either side of me. 'Hello there!' I says to them. 'I've come home. At long, long last.' I chuckle to myself. I hiccup. I chuckle some more. I think in the morning the garbage men will take us all away, me and my friends. I giggle. I try to get up. I can't. So I stay put. Every once in a while I chuckle to myself. And hum a tuneless song.

I wake up. April holding my hand. I can't see her but it's April. I squeeze her hand.

For a long time, I sat very still, thinking. Then I looked at my watch. And sighed. It was three a.m. I knew what I had to do. I knew now, why it had been so important for me to return to Nancy's place. I'd have to wait until morning. I paced around the room and finally returned to the journals. I put them back in the box and set them on the floor. Then I laid on Cheryl's bed, on top of the covers, still clothed. With my hands under my head, I stared up at the ceiling. The clock downstairs was abnormally loud and so, so slow. A few hours more and I could be on my way to Nancy's place to Henry Lee.

For the moment, I thought of Cheryl. Memories came back, memories of her voice, the memory of her reciting her powerful message at the Pow Wow. Why, oh why didn't she talk to me? Why couldn't we have talked to each other? And would it have helped? At times I was overwhelmed with her memories and tears would trickle down the sides of my face.

The next morning I woke up, dismayed that I had fallen asleep. Then I was dismayed to find it was still too early to go to Nancy's place. The sun was just beginning to rise, spreading orange yellowish hues across the skies. I went downstairs to make coffee and freshen up. My eyes felt swollen. Again the house seemed so empty, cold, lifeless. With my cup of coffee in hand, I opened the front door and stood looking out at the still empty street. The birds were just beginning to sing their morning praises to their Creator. It had rained during the night. Everything was wet. The smell of wet earth was invigorating, so clean. I stood there breathing deeply when I noticed there was a letter in the mailbox. I thought of leaving it for the moment, but didn't. The moment I saw it was Cheryl's handwriting, my heart started to pound. I tore it open and sat down, heedless of the damp step.

Dear April,

By the time you get this, I will have done what I had to do. I have said goodbye to my son, Henry Liberty. I couldn't bring myself to tell you about him before. Now I know you will do what is right where he is concerned. I also know that Mary and Nancy will do as you wish. They're taking care of Henry Lee. All my life, I wanted us to be a real family, together, normal. I couldn't even mother my own baby!

Do not feel sorrow or guilt over my death. Man thinks he can control Nature. Man is wrong. The Great Spirit has made Nature stronger than man by putting into each of us a part of Nature. We all have the instinct to survive. If that instinct is gone, then we die.

April, there should be at least a little joy in living and when there is no joy, then we become the living dead. And I can't live this living death any longer. To drink myself to sleep, day in and day out.

April, you have strength. Dream my dreams for me. Make them come true for me. Be proud of what you are, of what you and Henry Lee are. I belong with our Mother.

Love to you and Henry Lee,
Cheryl

An hour later, I was at Nancy's place once again. She opened the door for me, as if she had been expecting me right at that precise moment. I followed her down the hall to the kitchen. Sitting at the table, was a small boy eating some cereal. He looked up at me as I walked into the room. He smiled, the same kind of smile I had seen a long time ago, on his mother's face when she was that age, the age of innocence.

Nancy began explaining, but I stopped her. I told her I understood everything. As I stared at Henry Liberty, I remembered that during the night, I had used the words, 'my people, our people', and meant them. The denial had been lifted from my spirit. It was tragic that it had taken Cheryl's death to bring me to accept my identity.

But no. Cheryl had once said, 'All life dies to give new life.'

Cheryl had died. But for Henry Liberty and me, there would be a tomorrow. And it would be better. I would strive for it. For my sister and her son. For my parents. For my people.

Yin Chin

For Sharon Lee, whose real name is Sky, and Jim Wong Chu

she is tough,
she is verbose,
she has lived a thousand lives

she is sweet,
she is not,
she is blossoming
and dying every moment

a flower
unsweetened by rain
untarnished by simpering
uncuckolded by men
not coquettish enough
for say the gals
who make a career of shopping
at the Pacific Centre Mall

PACIFIC CENTRE, my gawd
do North Americans never tire
of claiming the centre
of the universe, the pacific and
everywhere else . . .

I am weary
of North Americans
so I listen to SKY.

Standing in the crowded dining hall, coffee in hand, my face is drawn to a
noisy group of Chinese youth; I mentally cancel them out. No place to sit—
no place meaning there aren't any Indians in the room. It is a reflexive action
on my part to assume that any company that isn't Indian company is generally unacceptable, but there it was, the absence of Indians not chairs determined the absence of a space for me. The soft of heart, guilt-ridden liberals
might argue defensively that that sweeping judgement is not different from
any other generalization made about us. So be it; after all it is not their

humanity I am calling to question. It is mine. Along with that thought dances another. I have lived in this city in the same neighbourhood as Chinese people for twenty-two years now and don't know a single Chinese person.

It scares me just a little. It wasn't always that way. The memory of a skinny little waif drops into the frame of moving pictures rolling across my mind. Unabashed she stands next to the door of Mad Sam's market across from Powell Street grounds surveying 'chinamen' with accusatory eyes. Once a month on Saturday the process repeated itself; the little girl of noble heart studied the old men. Not once in all her childhood years had she ever seen an old man steal a little kid. She gave up, not because she became convinced that the accusation was unfounded, but because she got too big to worry about it.

'Cun-a-muck-ah-you-da-puppy-shaw, that's Chinee for how are you,' and the old pa'pa-y-ah would laugh. 'Don't wander around town or the old Chinamen will get you, steal you' . . . 'Chinkee, chinkee chinamen went down town, turned around the corner and his pants fell down' and other such truck had been buried somewhere in the caverns of the useless information file tucked in the basement of her mind, but the shape of her social life was frighteningly influenced by those absurd sounds. The movie was just starting to lag and the literary theme of the pictures was coming into focus when a small breath of air, a gentle touch of a small woman's hand invited me to sit. How embarrassing. I'd been gaping and gawking at a table-load of Hans long enough for my coffee to cool.

It didn't take long. Invariably, when people of colour get together they discuss white people. They are the butt of our jokes, the fountain of our bitterness and pain, and the infinite well-spring of every dilemma life ever presented to us. The humour eases the pain, but always whites figure front and centre of our joint communication. If I had a dollar for every word ever said about them instead of to them I'd be the richest welfare bum in the country. No wonder they suffer from inflated egoism.

I sat at the table-load of Chinese people and toward the end of the hour I wanted to tell them about Mad Sam's, Powell Street, and old men. I didn't. Wisely, I think now. Our sense of humour was different then. In the face of a crass white world we had erased so much of ourselves and sketched so many cartoon characters of white people over-top the emptiness inside, that it would have been too much for us to face that we really did feel just like them. I sat at that table more than a dozen times but not once did it occur to any of us that we were friends. Eventually, the usual march of a relentless clock, my hasty departure from college the following semester, and my failure to return for fifteen years took its toll—now even their names escape me.

Last Saturday (seems like a hundred years later) was different. The table-load of people was Asian/Native. We laughed at ourselves and spoke very seriously about our writing. We really believe we are writers, someone had said, and the room shook with the hysteria of it all. We ran on and on about our growth and development and not once did the white man ever enter the room. It just seemed all too incredible that a dozen Hans and Natives could sit and discuss all things under heaven, including racism, and not talk about white people. It only took a half-dozen revolutions in the Third World, seventeen riots in America, one hundred demonstrations against racism in Canada, and thirty-seven dead Native youth in my life to become. (For grammar fanatics I am aware that the preceding is not 'gutt Inklish'.) I could have told them about the waif but it didn't seem relevant. We had crossed a millennium of bridges the rivers of which were swollen with the floodwaters of dark humanity's tenacious struggle to extricate themselves from oppression and we knew it.

We were born during the first sword wound that the Third World swung at imperialism. We were children of that wound, invincible, conscious, and movin' on up. We could laugh because we were no longer a joke. But somewhere along the line we forgot to tell the others, the thousands of our folks that still tell their kids about old chinamen.

It's Tuesday and I'm circling the block at Gore and Powell trying to find a parking space, windows open, driving like I belong here. A sharp 'Don't come near me, why you bother me?' jars me loose. An old Chinese woman swings a ratty old umbrella at a Native man who is pushing her, cursing her, and otherwise giving her a hard time. I lean toward the passenger side and shout at him from the safety of my car: 'Leave her alone, asshole.'

'Shut-up you f'ck'n' rag-head.' I jump out of the car, without bothering to park it—no one honks, they just stare at me. He sees my face and my cowichan, bends deeply and says very sarcastically that he didn't know I was a squaw. Well, I am no pacifist; I admit, I belted him, gave him what for and the coward left. I helped the old woman across the street, then returned to park my car. She was still there where I left her, shaking, so I stopped to try and quell her fear.

She wasn't afraid. She was ashamed of her own people, men who had passed her by, walking around her or crossing the street to avoid trying to rescue her from the taunts of one of my people. The world raged around inside me while she copiously described every Chinese man who had seen her and kept walking. I listened to her in silence and thought of me and old Sam again.

Mad Sam was a pioneer of discount foods. Slightly over-ripe bananas (great for peanut butter bannock sandwiches), bruised apples, and day-old bread were always available at half the cost of Safeway and we shopped there regularly for years. I am not sure if he sold meat, in any case we never bought meat; we were fish-eaters then. I doubt very much that Sam knew we called him 'Mad' but I know now the mad was intended for the low prices and the crowds in his little store, not him. In the fifties, there were store owners that concerned themselves with their customers, established relationships with them, exchanged gossip, and shared a few laughs. Sam was good to us.

If you press your nose up against the window to the left of the door you can still see me standing there, ghostlike skinny brown body with huge eyes riveted on the street and Powell Street grounds. Sometimes my eyes take a slow shift from left to right, right to left. I'm watchin' ol' chinamen, makin' sure they don't grab little kids. Once a month for several years I assume my post and keep my private vigil. No one in the street seems to know what I'm doing or why, but it doesn't matter. The object of my vigil is not appreciation but catchin' the old chinamen in the act.

My nose is pressed up against the window pane, the cold circles the end of my flattened nose; it feels good. Outside, the window pane was freckled with crystal water drops; inside, it was smooth and dry, but for a little wisp of fog from my breath. Round 'o's of water splotched onto the clear glass. Not perfectly round, but just the right amount of roundness that allows you to call them 'o's. Each 'o' was different as on the page at school when you first print 'o's for the teacher. On the paper are lots of them. They are all kind of wobbly and different, but still 'o's.

I could see the rain-distorted street scene at the park through the round 'o's of water. There are no flowers or grass in this park. No elaborate floral themes or landscape designs, just a dozen or so benches around a wasteland of gravel, sand, and comfrey root—weeds—and a softball backstop at one end. What a bloody long time ago that was, mama.

Blat. A raindrop hit the window, scrunching up the park bench I was looking at. The round 'o' of rain made the park bench wiggle toward my corner of the store. I giggled.

'Mad Sam's . . . Mad Sam's . . . Mad Sam's?' What began as a senseless repetition of a household phrase ended as a question. She knew that Mad Sam was a chinaman . . . Chinee, the old people called them . . . but, then, the old people can't speak 'goot Inklish'—know what I mean? But what in the world made him mad? I breathed at the window. It fogged up. The only kind of mad I know is when everyone runs aroun' hollering and kicking up dust.

I rocked back and forth while my finger traced out a large circle which my hand had cleared. Two old men on the bench across the street broke my thoughts of Sam's madness. One of them rose. He was wearing one of those grey tweed wool hats that people think of as English and associate with sports cars. He had a cane, a light beige cane. He half bent at the waist before he left the bench, turned and, with his arms stretched out from his shoulders and flailing back and forth a few times, accentuated his words to the other man seated there.

It would have looked funny if pa'pa-y-ah had done it, or ol' Mike, but I was acutely aware that this was a chinaman. Ol' chinamen are not funny. They are serious and the words of the world echoed violently in my ears . . . 'don't wander off or the ol' chinamen will get you and eat you.' I pouted about the fact that mama had never warned me about them. 'She doesn't care.'

A woman with a black car coat and a white pill-box hat disturbed the scene. Screek, the door of her old Buick opened. Squeak, slam, it banged shut. There is something humorously inelegant about a white lady with spiked heels, tight skirt, and a pill-box hat cranking up a '39 Buick. Thanx, mama, for having me soon enough to have seen it.

Gawd, I am so glad I remember this: there she be, blonde as all get out, slightly hippy, heaving her bare leg, that is partially constrained by her skirt, onto the bumper of her car, and cranking at the whatever had to be cranked to make the damn thing go. All of this wonderfulness came squiggling through a little puddle of clear rain. The Buick finally took off and from the tail end of its departure I could see the little old man still shuffling his way across the street. Funny, all the cars stopped for him. Odd, the little Chinese boy talked to him, unafraid.

Shuffle, shuffle, plunk of his cane, shuffle, shuffle, plunk; on he trudged. The breath from the corner near my window came out in shorter and louder gasps. It punctuated the window with an on-again, off-again choo-choo rhythm of clarity. Breath and fog, shuffle, shuffle, plunk, breath and fog. BOOM! And the old man's face was right on mine. My scream was indelicate. Mad Sam and mama came running.

'Whatsa matter?'

'Whah iss it,' from Sam and mama respectively.

Half hesitating I pointed out the window. 'The chinaman was looking at me.' I could see that that was not the right answer. Mama's eyes yelled 'for pete's sake' and her cheeks shone red with shame, not embarrassment, shame. Sam's face was clear. Definably hurt. Not the kind of hurt that shows when adults burn themselves or something but the kind of hurt you can sometimes see in the eyes of people who have been cheated. The total picture spelled something I could not define.

Grandmothers you said if I was ever caught doing nothing you would take me away for all eternity. . . . The silence was thick, cloying, and paralyzing. It stopped my rain and stilled my emotion. It deafened my ears to the rain. I could not look out to see if the old man was still there. No grannies came to spare me.

My eyes fell unseeing on a parsnip just exactly in front of my face. They rested there not to stray until everyone stopped looking at my treacherous little body and resumed talking about whatever they were talking about before I had brought the world to a momentary halt with my astounding stupidity. What surprises me now is that they did eventually carry on as though nothing was wrong.

The floor swayed beneath me, while I tried hard to make it swallow me and carry out my wish, but I didn't quite make it. A hand loaded with a pear in front of my face jarred my eyes loose from the parsnip.

'Here,' the small, pained smile on Sam's face stilled the floor but the memory remained a moving moment in my life.

The old woman was holding my hands saying she felt better now. All that time, I did not speak or think about what she said. I just nodded my head back and forth and relived my memory of Mad Sam's.

'How unkind of the world to school us in ignorance' was all I said, and I made my way back to the car.

Sojourner's Truth

From inside my box, an ugly thought occurs to me. I know what hell is—actually, I knew it all along, but in my haste to barrel along and live, I had not thought about it until just now. Hell just might be seeing all the ugly shit people put each other through from the clean and honest perspective of the spirit that no longer knows how to lie and twist the truth.

Can you imagine, there you are watching some maniac jerk his wife or kids around, pulling arms out of their rightful places in sockets and you walk on minding your own business, only this time you don't feel like just shuffling along and ignoring it. Your spirit cries out for humanity, but all you get to do is weep and remember that you didn't care when your soul was housed in living meat. You could have struck a blow at violence against women and children, but the little whisper from your living soul was drowned by the reality of all that flesh.

In its final resting pose your soul knows that all the maxims that guided your hypocrisy are just so much balderdash. 'Spare the rod and spoil the child.' 'Don't let her get away with it.' Whoever heard of such a ridiculous proposition! 'Don't drop the apples, they bruise easily' is more like it. Pictures of all the lickings I laid on Emma and the kids file through my mind. In my newly dead state I try to rationalize one more time: if you don't subject the kid to a certain amount of brain rot, the kid is apt to object to even a minimum of authoritarian discipline. Hell is seeing the lie in all your excuses.

My thoughts come to an abrupt halt. I know that I am in the box and must get out. How convenient: the very moment you realize you must get out, there you are outside, watching everyone from the most advantageous viewpoint. They are all gathered around the box. Those that talk are whispering as though they might interrupt the soul of me; others are in tears. The kids are playing. Why everyone gathers around the boxes housing the bodies of the dead is beyond me, though. The truth of me has long left the box.

The truth of me is a little unnerved by the realization that there are not as many living bodies gathered around my box as I expected. I face it, though. What the hell did I expect? I didn't do anything to inspire anyone to show up and grieve my departure, permanent though it is. (At least there aren't any Chinamen.)

Oh God, there are a hundred thousand Chinamen living in this city and I cannot count even one of them as a human being who will miss me. I weep. No tears, just the kind of pain of the inner self that goes with the action; the sort of hot, wracking emptiness, but without the tears to cool it off. There aren't any Indians or Blacks. *Oh God, there aren't even many white people here.* I lived for seventy years moving around in a sea of almost a million people and only fifty show up to bury my body and bid my spirit adieu.

'It's a crying shame, he wasn't that old.' Thanks, Mike, but it really isn't a shame. Death is natural, but then we are inclined to add shame to all that is natural. The naked body and spirit is a deep source of shame to the mortal beings crawling about the earth. Life does look a little different from the vantage point of death.

A ripple of pleasure overtakes me as Emma speaks. 'You know he didn't take care of himself.' It is the worst she could come up with and still wear a mask of polite mourning. Hate jumps out at me and for a moment the essence of me is seared by it. A storm of hidden knowledge, secret pain, leaps at my soul, accusing, huge in its condemnation of my treatment of her as wife. I can see where it all comes from: the mind-bending brutality, the intimidation, the violence, the erasure of her soul—the screaming soul she denied. *Oh God, the living body of me scarred and twisted the very soul of Emma.*

In a corner, my brother and sister are secretly plotting for the spoils of my bodily being. Jerks. My spirit rolls back to my own plotting for the spoils of my parents before they were properly laid to rest. The twisting begins again, the terrible, unbearable heat of deceit in life burns my soul in death.

Oh God, I cry, *Don't do this to yourselves.* No one hears me. It is a little confusing being dead. You feel more alive than ever, except no one knows you are there. No soul present actually misses me, most particularly not Emma. She is relieved.

Shit. And mountains of it appear from nowhere. Shit loads tumbling down from above me. A wall of crap. *I don't believe this.* The spirit of me is swept up in this sheet of rank-smelling human feces. *What's going on here?* We hit the water together, the shit and the truth of me. The water is filthy without the help of the crap. Rushing along, spreading itself out, and running for the vast bankless river of salt, the crud holds my truth in a vice-grip of gut-wrenching stink. *What the hell is this all about?* The water ejects me at the exit of the river just next to an old man sitting on a park bench reading a newspaper.

I remember it now. Three million metric tonnes of untreated sewage dumped into the Fraser River, protested, of course, by a few crazies—college rejects, calling themselves eco-something or others. *Oh God. I wish I had been one of them.*

Hey, you oughta be reading that with a little more soul, old man. The polluting happened before I died so my words are wasted, but the truth is, it still goes on.

On the wings of a snow white dove, my truth sails across the vast expanse of weeping earth and choking fauna and my soul mutters helplessly to the wreckage below: *Jesus, I didn't know.*

'Oh yes, but you didn't seek.' From out of the blue, he appears on the tip of the dove's other wing, looking just as normal as can be. He can't be normal, though—he must be just as dead as me. The dove dips and drops us both in a mountainous wasteland—earth brutalized by a flurry of murderous chainsaws that massacred her treasured children. Not satisfied, man consigned the weak, the unusable seedlings and brush to a widow's pyre.

Didn't seek? I repeat dumbly.

'Yes, you know, seek and ye shall find,' and he fades away.

WAIT.

No presence, just a soft chuckle and a clean voice: 'You silly fellow, you cannot command another man's soul here.'

Oh Lord.

'That's another thing, the whole business of lords has no roots in heavenly reality.' At first I think he is kidding. But after I listen to it, I realize the whole notion of lords in heaven is ridiculous. It could not have been contrived by ethereal souls.

From inside the stone walls of Parliament, the House of Lords drivels nonsense while their lying souls convince their mouths that the bullshit they are peddling is true. I can't believe that I ever had faith in these fools. It's embarrassing. 'Apartheid is not a question for us to address,' some wigged lord with South African investments is saying. *I'll bet not. After all, you're the white guys.* I would laugh, but the truth stops me and there in the kitchen of my own neighbourhood is Mike, being disgusted by all the uppity Blacks 'who had a lotta nerve shooting us', and the body of me is agreeing. The blood of Soweto runs thick in the kitchen. The screaming pain of children being shot fills me. It muffles the stupid words uttered by pompous arrogance, and soils forever my truth.

A child, heartsick and ashamed, appears in the school yard with my grandson, who leads the others in cruel taunts against the solitary child.

Oh don't. Jesus don't.

'I never did. I always maintained that all children are a great offering to life.' There he is again and the truth of his African heritage is written on his soul.

Actually, I was talking to my grandson.

'His name is not Jesus,' and he disappears.

Is this all there is? Endless pictures of the whole suffering world? The wind carries my longings to the mouth of a poet whose words are secretly laughed at. *Oh God*, and a vast sense of nothingness sweeps over me. The nothingness is unmoving, cloying in its inertia. It suspends my soul in a terrifying void. It ends like it began, suddenly and of its own will. Nothingness is scary, but still it offers temporary relief from the tearless weeping. Since I came to this God-forsaken place, I have laughed but once.

In the meadow where the void jerks to a halt, children are playing, chasing illusive butterflies. Peace rests within me. Laughter delights their little bodies, captures the heart of the grasses, and the trees chatter, echoing the sensuous happiness of childhood. The sun whispers gently and its light plays about on the skin of the earth's young. Grass, trees, and little children are swollen with peace and joy. It is the first moment of rest for my soul.

'Growth is joyous. The knife that inhibits growth is the sword of death,' the grasses breathe in blessed refrain.

The children disappear and a plane carrying defoliants flies overhead spraying the meadow below in preparation for clear-cutting the forest at the edge of the meadow. The horror of the whir from the airplane's engine slaps the peace from my soul.

Jesus, when does it all end?

'Be clear. When does what all end?' (*Jesus, I am getting tired of this guy. Every rhetorical or philosophical remark prefaced by his name calls him forth.*)

'You won't be so tired when your novitiate is over. I don't have to answer forever, you know.' I did not know that there are no private thoughts in heaven. Jesus smiles.

Well, the butchery?

'Ah,' and he leaves. The earth sighs to the sun, 'It ends when the body of people stop hiding from the truth of the spirit.' It seems too simple.

'It is simple. Why are you, of all people, doubting that?' she asks. And suddenly, I need the comfort of Emma's long suffering presence . . .

*   *   *

'Hallo-oo, how are you?' and the lilt in Mike's voice veils his discomfort at seeing Emma again. He doesn't want to know how Emma is. His deception is an ugly sight. Deception has got to be hell's inner face. A deluge of scenes of deception bombards my truth: verbal garbage, physical garbage, and most criminal of all, food garbage—all deceptively rationalized as respectable by the bodies of humanity that race across my view. The soul of people takes the shape of their deception, and the eyes of my essence ache with the unbearability of the sight.

Jesus. What is going on?

'Well, this is heaven and here you are, dead, looking at life through the honest eyes of your soul.'

Well, if this is heaven, what is hell?

'You already know the answer to that one. Perhaps you want to know more about how it all works. You see, heaven is simply the sky. At the point of mortal departure, your spirit gets to walk the wing tips of the wind witnessing the reality of your life. The soul is not blind, however. In death the truth is not dressed in the deceptive clothes of mortal flesh. The soul is incapable of rationalization.'

You mean I have to watch over and over, everything I have just seen?

'That is about it, but for a minor exception.'

What do you get to see—the same thing?

And he laughs. The sound comes from deep within the earth, rich and resonant. It spreads out thick and joyous. The winds catch the laughter and layer the seas and grasses with it. Embarrassed, I try digging around inside for guilt to hide my shame. Only shame blossoms, relentless in its flowering. I yearn for the agony of guilt to absolve me. I fall over in a foolish, prostrate position of remorse, but guilt does not come.

Oh Jesus, can't I even enjoy the comfort of guilt?

'Oh no. Heaven is not like that. Here, there is but pleasure and pain. You see, if pain were experienced with the absolving comfort of guilt, it would be impure. Guilt is an intellectual contrivance that reduces the pain the spirit needs to experience if it is to alter the actions of the body. In that sense, guilt is the ultimate deception—hell. The spirit resides in heaven; it knows not hell.'

Holy mother of Jesus. I can't go through this for all eternity.

'Yes you can. People do it all the time.' She said it without sympathy—just a matter of fact, eternal reality.

'Hello mom,' Jesus purrs.

'Jesus, how nice for our paths to cross.'

Christ, this is insane. I balk at the bizarre meeting between mother and son, two thousand years dead. In my mortal life the idea of Mary as Jesus' mother ended with his birth.

'You called?' Jesus interrupts my thoughts.

I meant God, really.

His voice swells with magnificent urgency: 'Man in his opportunist desire to ease life and deceive himself that the torment of others is no concern of his distorts the natural world of the spirit. Man creates a vision of heaven and hell for himself that he might justify his selfishness and appease his conscience while outraging human and natural life. God, good, all began as the 'great offering' of one's life to the world. But now, it is a catch-all word for every kind of desperate anguish living mortals wish to hide from. The offering is disempowered, destroyed, and its meaning lost to humanity by the distortion of godliness. God has become the mantle for the greatest human atrocity—war.'

Horseshit, I snap, and it begins again, the crap, the children, the hunger of humanity.

Oh Jesus. I want to go back to my box and rest.

'You can't. It has been buried. Heaven is the sky and you cannot return to the earth. How long did you think eternity was?' Jesus leaves and the terror of having to walk the winds witnessing my life's trials without the comfort of his company follows his departure. The memory of my mortal life, cold nights warmed by Emma's yielding flesh, fill me with desire. *Emma, help me.* Below my shameless begging stands Emma, staring hard at the window of her quiet living room. She hears nor sees a thing. She is busy making a decision.

'He seems like a nice fellow. Not like the last,' she whispers silently to herself, not even according me my name or the title of husband. 'Ah courtship, if only love could grow from the sweet seed of courtship to the lovely flower marriage was intended to be.' The inside of her new love lays itself bare to me. While the man's body anxiously occupies my chair and waits for her reply, his damaged soul shouts his truth at mine. I try to warn her but know she hears not a word. Alone at fifty-six, afraid, desperate for affection, Emma says 'yes.'

In the beginning he is sweet, as though he has not fully awakened to the realization that the courtship is over. For a while there is laughter in Emma's little house. But, as men are wont to do from time to time, he screws up at work. The boss gives him 'what for' and he comes home, full to the brim with another man's anger and his own humiliation.

Like a replay of my own mortality, the beer follows, then drunken, impotent raging about the boss, and wild, unreasonable demands on Emma. She is slow to move on his drunken commands. (Sabotage, I had surmised as a living person, and quite correctly. What woman jumps happily to a drunken husband's command?)

Then the fists fly. The thud of human meat battered by the hammer that can be a man's hand. The tears, the screams, the agony of his perverse triumph over the lively body that he alone has reduced to limp life. And my wasted soul stretches itself over her body in a futile attempt to protect my Emma from this other man's fists.

Inside the body of Emma a black emotion rises and spirals to the centre of her being. The soul of me catches in the madness of her emotion, captivated by her bleakly intense struggle to convert her outrage to despair. A crazy cacophony of raw passion carries me to that magical place where all feelings begin. A single crystal teardrop, alone in a fit of rage, rests peacefully. In shocked disbelief, my truth stares at the perfect droplet.

Jesus . . .

'But it is beautiful, isn't it?' His voice brings momentary relief from the desperation that lingers in the clarity of the tear.

Is this all there is left, just one tear, one tear to account for her entire life?

'Imagine, if you will, that she can hear the mutterings of her innermost self and rise up. Imagine the great flood that this little tear could become in the tide of her resistance. Bear witness, my friend.'

Jesus fades and compassion rises in the soul of me. My soul envelops the tear. I plead for its life, praying for it to swell and to multiply. Softly murmuring, I cajole the tear to grow. *Not twice, Emma. I am dead. Surely you must know that I should never have lived thus, comfortable with your suffering. Emma, hear the words whispered to thee by thy self, thy perfect self. Abide by thy perfect right to be.*

I stretch my truth throughout her body, grow small around the tear, my soul rhythmically undulating with my fervent desire for her salvation. My love reaches its purest moment. Spent, my passion drapes itself in a perfect circle around the lonely tear. I feel her body rise. I hear the resounding 'no' from every cell of her flesh. In my death watch, there is great rejoicing. The knife in her hand drives through the sleeping man's heart. The blood mesmerizes her and then the wall of tears drives me outside herself.

But more my spirit knows. Police and courts are next. Emma sits in wordless teary repose, my own madness her defence. 'Not twice.' The very words of my soul she repeats to her counsellor. From my sky perch I am compelled to watch. Jesus came first among the throng that gather. Curious, I ask why his presence.

'This is the very thing to which I am called, the judging of the meek and courageous by the lords of violence.'

Nine Black boys gather next to us, giggling and shuffling and watching by turns.

Who are they?

'The Scottsboro boys. You must remember them.'

How could I forget. The boys hung for a rape they were much too innocent to commit. The madness of racism runs sour and acrid in my soul. I, coward that I was, sanctioned the dirty deed. Sympathy, simpering and jelly soft, obscures my outrage.

It must have been terrible for them to come here.

'Not at all. They have enjoyed themselves immensely since being freed from the prison of racial violence. Why, they have participated in every glorious riot, in every movement of Black resistance from Birmingham in 1948 to Soweto, just a short time ago. They have had their vengeance.'

Is there then only freedom in death?

'Quite the contrary. When the slave is no longer a slave, what you have left is an ex-master. If the master insists on protecting his position with weapons, the slaves will have to covet the gun.'

The congregation includes the strangest people.

Who is the funny-looking little fellow who speaks a strange language?

'Why that's Vladimir Ilyich Ulyanov, you probably know him as Lenin.'

But he is an atheist.

'Heaven is the one place that does not discriminate.'

The congregation swells its ranks with the champions of the meek and poor: those who so loved the world that they sacrificed their selves that justice to earth and people might prevail. Marx, Fred Hampton, Jackson, Krupskaya, Gwarth-Es-La and his standard bearer . . .

These people are all rebels.

'Yes, they are all in their own way like myself.'

I am no rebel.

'Ah, but you unlocked the door to Emma's rebellion.'

The court case drags on in its usual ceremony of arrogant rigidity and stupid exactitude of language without sentiment. My life with her is dragged forward couched carefully in legal mumbo-jumbo. Her character is attested to by women who assure the world that Emma was a kind and devoted wife to a brutal first husband. Even our children testify that they and their mother had been abused. Emma rises to her own defence. She refuses to deny that her hand held the knife that stabbed her second husband, but she confesses no guilt.

'I am a Christian woman. This is supposed to be a Christian country. Jesus himself forbade the abuse of the meek, but he did not deny our sacred right to resist abuse. "Where ye shall have no justice, ye shall have no peace." The man that would batter his wife is less than a serpent. I was born three months ago; until that day, I wandered the world a slave . . .'

'Oh, ain't she a woman? . . . Ain't she a woman?' and the tall reedy body of an old Black woman waltzes and sways to the music of her own words.

Who are you?

'Why, I'm Sojourner Truth. An' Emma an' me was born on the same day. I was delivered from slavery at fifty-six years ol' and so was she.'

'I should have killed that first brute,' Emma says, 'but he died on me. And this lawyer sitting here doesn't know what he is about. Didn't know what I was doing? No one who feels the plunge of a blade through the human heart can ever testify that they did not know what they were doing. I knew I stabbed him. I knew it would send him to his maker. But I am guilty of no crime. I did not kill a man; I stabbed a snake.'

The judge looks aghast. She feels her own emotion rising, contemplates quitting herself of the case, but a voice whispers from within that the jury, not she, would be pronouncing the verdict on Emma. She remains riveted to her throne. She counsels the jury that she must resolve some legal questions before they can retire to decide Emma's fate, and she buys time for her own troubled soul.

In the week that follows, the congregation remains vigilant. There is a hub-bub of discussion about the possibilities that lay ahead for woman and earth should Emma win. Joy hangs in the air, visible as Thoreau's lily. Even the old woman next to me, grim-faced most of the time, chuckles now and then.

What is your name?

'Emily.'

Carr, the artist?

'Hmph.'

I am honoured, I pule.

'I would rather you be enjoyed.'

The week draws to a close and the judge counsels the jury. 'The defendant takes precedence over her own counsel. Indeed, according to Benjamin Franklin, Thomas Jefferson, and the "defender of the constitution", Daniel Webster, the founding fathers of this United States of America intended the values of this country to reflect those of the New Testament. The jury is to decide the fate of Emma in accordance with the book of Revelations and the word of Jesus. There is no doubt that Emma slew her second husband, but the law governing America, and finally Emma, is the law of Christ.'

The jury retires, armed with twelve New Testaments. And the heavenly congregation replies in blessed song:

> Praise her soul, she saw the light
> The truth of this sojourner,
> has been seen at last.
> Praise her soul, she saw the light.

Tomson Highway b. 1951

CREE

From *The Rez Sisters*

*[In the van, driving down the highway to Toronto, at night. The women have
intimate conversations, one on one, while the rest are asleep or seated at the
other end of the van. Annie is driving. Emily sits beside her listening to her
Walkman, while Marie-Adele is 'leaning' over Annie's shoulder from her
place in the middle seat. Veronique sits beside Marie-Adele, sleeping. Pelajia
and Philomena are in the very back seat with Zhaboonigan between them.]*

MARIE-ADELE: Nee, Annie, not so fast. *[Pause. Annie slows down.]* So. You
   couldn't get Ellen and Ray*mond* to come along. I'd like to meet this Ray-
   mond some day.

ANNIE: *[Angrily insisting on the correct pronunciation.]* Ray*mond*! Ellen says
   he's got a whole library full of cassette tapes.

MARIE-ADELE: Annie. You ever think about getting married again?

ANNIE: Not really. I can hear the band at the Silver Dollar already.

MARIE-ADELE: Do you still think about . . . Eugene?

ANNIE: What're you talkin' about? Of course, I think about him, he's my
   brother-in-law, ain't he?

MARIE-ADELE: He made his choice.

ANNIE: Yeah. He picked you.

MARIE-ADELE: Annie. I never stole him off you.

ANNIE: Drop dead. Shit! I forgot to bring that blouse. I mean. In case I sing.
   Shit!

MARIE-ADELE: If I'm gone and Eugene if he start drinkin' again. I see you
   going for him.

ANNIE: Why would I bother? I had my chance twenty years ago. Christ!

MARIE-ADELE: Twenty years ago, I was there.

ANNIE: Why should I want fourteen kids for?

MARIE-ADELE: That's exactly what I'm scared of. I don't want them kids to be
   split up. You come near Eugene you start drinking messing things up me
   not here I come back and don't matter where you are . . .

ANNIE: I don't want him. I don't want him. I don't want him. I don't want
   him. I don't want him.

EMILY: Put us all in the fuckin' ditch!

PELAJIA: Hey, watch your language up there.

ANNIE: Shit! I don't care. There's nothing more to say about it. Why don't you
   take your pills and go to sleep. *[Pelajia and Philomena begin talking.]*

PHILOMENA: September 8 again.

PELAJIA: Hmmm? What about September 8?

PHILOMENA: You don't remember?
PELAJIA: What?

[Annie and Emily, at the front of the van with Annie driving, are laughing and singing, 'I'm a little Indian who loves fry bread.' From time to time, they sneak each other a sip of this little bottle of whiskey Annie has hidden away inside her purse.]

> I'm a little Indian who loves fry bread,
> Early in the morning and when I go to bed;
> Some folks say I'm crazy in the head,
> Cuz I'm a little Indian who loves fry bread.
>
> Now, some folks say I've put on a pound or two,
> My jeans don't fit the way they used to do;
> But I don't care, let the people talk,
> Cuz if I don't get my fry bread, you'll hear me squawk.

ANNIE: So tell me. What's it like to go to a big bar like . . . I mean like . . . the Silver Dollar.
EMILY: Lotta Nishnawbs.*
ANNIE: *[Disappointed.]* Yeah? Is the music good?
EMILY: Country rock.
ANNIE: *[Screams gleefully.]* Yee-haw! Maybe the band will ask me up to sing, eh? I'll sing something fast.
EMILY: You would, too.
ANNIE: *[Sings real fast.]* 'Well, it's 40 below and I don't give a fuck, got a heater in my truck and I'm off to the rodeo. Woof!' Something like that.
EMILY: Yup. That's pretty fast.
ANNIE: Hey. Maybe Fritz the Katz will be there. Never know. Might get laid, too, eh? Remember Room 20 at the Anchor Inn? Oh, that Fritz! Sure like singin' with him. Crazy about the way . . .
EMILY: *[Starts singing Patsy Cline's famous 'Crazy . . . crazy for feelin' so lonely . . .' all the way through Annie's next speech.]*
ANNIE: . . . he stands there with his guitar and his ten-gallon hat. Is that what you call them hats? You know the kind you wear kind of off to the side like this? That's what he does. And then he winks at me. *[Sings.]* 'Crazy . . .' Oooh, I love, just love the way the lights go woosh woosh in your eyes and kinda' wash all over your body. Me standing there shuffling my feet side to side, dressed real nice and going *[Sings.]* 'Oooh darlin' . . .' with my mike in my hand just so. Oh! And the sound of that band behind me. And Fritz. *[Sings.]* 'Crazy, crazy for feelin' so lonely . . .'
EMILY: Yeah. You look good on stage.
ANNIE: Yeah?

* Indians. (Ojibway)

EMILY: How come you're so keen on that guy anyway?

ANNIE: Sure Veronique St. Pierre isn't just pretending to be asleep back there?

[Emily and Marie-Adele check Veronique in the middle seat.]

MARIE-ADELE: Nah. Out like a lamp.

EMILY: Hey! We'll get her drunk at the Silver Dollar and leave her passed out under some table. Take two beers to do that.

ANNIE: Hey. Too bad Big Joey had to come back from Toronto before we got there, eh?

EMILY: Man! That dude's got buns on him like no other buns on the face of God's entire creation. Whooo! Not to mention a dick that's bigger than a goddamn breadbox. *[Annie screams gleefully.]* How about Fritz? What's his look like?

ANNIE: *[After an awkward pause.]* He's Jewish, you know.

EMILY: *[Laughing raucously.]* World's first Jewish country singer!

ANNIE: Don't laugh. Those Jews make a lot of money, you know.

EMILY: Not all of them.

ANNIE: Fritz buys me jeans and things. I'm gonna be one of them Jewish princesses.

EMILY: What's wrong with being an Indian princess?

ANNIE: Aw, these white guys. They're nicer to their women. Not like Indian guys. Screw you, drink all your money, and leave you flat on your ass.

EMILY: Yeah, right. Apple Indian Annie. Red on the outside. White on the inside.

ANNIE: Emily!

EMILY: Keep your eye on the road.

ANNIE: Good ol' highway 69.

EMILY: Hey. Ever 69 with Fritz?

MARIE-ADELE: Neee.

ANNIE: White guys don't make you do things to them. You just lie there and they do it all for you. Ellen's real happy with her Ray*mond*. You can tell the way she sounds on the phone. Maybe someday I'll just take off with a guy like Fritz.

EMILY: Then what? Never come back to the rez? *[Annie is cornered. Emily then slaps her playfully on the arm.]* Hey. Know what? *[Sings.]*

> When I die, I may not go to heaven,
> I don't know if they let Indians in;
> If they don't, just let me go to Wasy, lord,
> Cuz Wasy is as close as I've been.

ANNIE: Lots of white people at this Silver Dollar?

EMILY: Sometimes. Depends.

ANNIE: How much for beer there?

EMILY: Same as up here. Nah! Don't need money, Annie Cook. You just gotta know how to handle men. Like me and the Rez Sisters down in Frisco.

ANNIE: Yeah?
EMILY: I'll take care of them.
ANNIE: Maybe we can find a party, eh? Maybe with the band.
EMILY: Whoa! Slow down, Annie Cook! Easy on the gas!
MARIE-ADELE: Annie! *[Pow. Black-out. They have a flat tire.]*

[The flat tire. Everything now happens in complete darkness.]

VERONIQUE: Bingo!
PHILOMENA: What was that? What happened?
ANNIE: I don't know. Something just went 'poof'!
EMILY: All right. Everybody out. We got a fuckin' flat.

[They all climb out of the van.]

VERONIQUE: Oh my god! We'll never get to the bingo.
ZHABOONIGAN: Pee pee.
PELAJIA: I can't fix a flat tire.
ANNIE: Emily can.
PELAJIA: Get the jack. Spare tire.
ANNIE: Philomena's wearing one.
ZHABOONIGAN: Pee pee.
PHILOMENA: This is all your fault, Annie Cook.
MARIE-ADELE: It's in the back.
ANNIE: So what do we do?
PELAJIA: What's the matter with Zha?
PHILOMENA: Gotta make pee pee.
VERONIQUE: I knew there was something wrong with this van the moment I set eyes on it. I should have taken the bus.
PHILOMENA: Oh shut up. Quack, quack, quack.
ANNIE: Don't look at me. It's not my fault the tires are all bald.
PHILOMENA: Nobody's blaming you.
ANNIE: But you just did.
PHILOMENA: Quack, quack, quack.
VERONIQUE: Where are we?
ANNIE: The Lost Channel. This is where you get off.
VERONIQUE: *[Groans.]* Ohhh!
EMILY: Yeah, right.
PHILOMENA: Shhh!
PELAJIA: Jack's not working too well.
EMILY: Okay. Everybody. Positions.
VERONIQUE: Not me. My heart will collapse.
EMILY: You wanna play bingo?
VERONIQUE: *[Groans.]* Ohhh!
ANNIE: Hurry up! Hurry up!
EMILY: Okay. One, two, three lift.

[Everybody lifts and groans.]

PELAJIA: Put the jack in there.

[All lift, except Marie-Adele and Zha, who wander off into the moonlit darkness. Dim light on them.]

ZHABOONIGAN: Ever dark.
MARIE-ADELE: You'll be fine, Zhaboonigan.

[Suddenly, a nighthawk—Nanabush, now in dark feathers—appears, darting in the night.]

ZHABOONIGAN: The birdies!
MARIE-ADELE: Yes, a birdie.
ZHABOONIGAN: Black wings!

[Marie-Adele begins talking to the bird, almost as if she were talking to herself. Quietly, at first, but gradually—as the bird begins attacking her—growing more and more hysterical, until she is shrieking, flailing, and thrashing about insanely.]

MARIE-ADELE: Who are you? What do you want? My children? Eugene? No! Oh no! Me? Not yet. Not yet. Give me time. Please. Don't. Please don't. Awus! Get away from me. Eugene! Awus! You fucking bird! Awus! Awus! Awus! Awus! Awus! *[And she has a total hysterical breakdown.]*

[Zhaboonigan, at first, attempts to scare the bird off by running and flailing her arms at it. Until the bird knocks her down and she lies there on the ground, watching in helpless astonishment and abject terror. Underneath Marie-Adele's screams, she mumbles to herself, sobbing.]

ZHABOONIGAN: One, two, three, four, five, six, seven . . . Nicky Ricky Ben Mark . . . eight, nine, ten, eleven, twelve . . . *[Until the other women come running. Total darkness again.]*
EMILY: What the . . .
ANNIE: Marie-Adele!
PELAJIA: Stop her! Stop her!
VERONIQUE: What's happening?
PHILOMENA: Marie Adele. Now, now . . . come . . . come . . .
EMILY: *[In the background.]* Stop that fucking screaming will ya, Marie-Adele!
PHILOMENA: Emily. There's no need to talk to her like that now.
PELAJIA: Help us get her in the van.
PHILOMENA: Come . . . come, Marie-Adele . . . everything's fine . . . you'll be fine . . . come . . . shhh . . . shhh . . .

[And they ease Marie-Adele back into the van. Once all is beginning to settle down again:]

PELAJIA: Everything okay now?

PHILOMENA: Yes. She's fine now.

PELAJIA: Emily, take over.

VERONIQUE: Yes. I don't trust that Annie Cook. Not for one minute.

EMILY: All set?

MARIE-ADELE: What time is it?

PELAJIA: Twenty after four.

ANNIE: Oh! We're over two hours behind schedule. Hurry up. Hurry up.

VERONIQUE: I'll be exhausted for the bingo tomorrow night. Maybe I should just take fifteen cards.

EMILY: You can rest your heart. And your mouth. All day tomorrow. All set? *[And she starts up the van. The van lights come back on.]*

[The dialogues resume. Marie-Adele now sits in the front with Emily, who is driving. Zhaboonigan sits between them. Pelajia and Philomena are now in the middle seat, Annie and Veronique in the back.]

EMILY: You scared the shit out of me out there. *[Silence.]* Don't do that again. *[Silence.]* Feeling better now? *[Silence.]*

MARIE-ADELE: I could be really mad, just raging mad just wanna tear his eyes out with my nails when he walks in the door and my whole body just goes 'k-k-k-k' . . . . He doesn't talk, when something goes wrong with him, he doesn't talk, shuts me out, just disappears. Last night he didn't come home. Again, it happened. I couldn't sleep. You feel so ugly. He walks in this morning. Wanted to be alone, he said. The curve of his back, his breath on my neck, 'Adele, ki-sa-gee-ee-tin oo-ma',* making love, always in Indian, only. When we still could. I can't even have him inside me any-more. It's still growing there. The cancer. Pelajia, een-pay-seek-see-yan.**

PELAJIA: You know one time, I knew this couple where one of them was dying and the other one was angry at her for dying. And she was mad because he was gonna be here when she wasn't and she had so much left to do. And she'd lie there in bed and tell him to do this and do that and he'd say 'Okay, okay.' And then he'd go into the kitchen and say to me, 'She's so this and she's so that and she's so damned difficult.' And I watched all this going on. That house didn't have room for two such angry people. But you know, I said to her, 'You gotta have faith in him and you gotta have faith in life. He loves you very much but there's only so much he can do. He's only human.' There's only so much Eugene can understand, Marie-Adele. He's only human.

EMILY: Fuckin' right. Me and the Rez Sisters, okay? Cruisin' down the coast highway one night. Hum of the engine between my thighs. Rose. That's Rosabella Baez, leader of the pack. We were real close, me and her. She

---

* Adele, I love you. (Cree)
** Pelajia, I'm scared to death. (Cree)

was always thinkin' real deep. And talkin' about bein' a woman. An Indian woman. And suicide. And alcohol and despair and how fuckin' hard it is to be an Indian in this country. *[Marie-Adele shushes her gently.]* No goddamn future for them, she'd say. And why, why, why? Always carryin' on like that. Chris'sakes. She was pretty heavy into the drugs. Guess we all were. We had a fight. Cruisin' down the coast highway that night. Rose in the middle. Me and Pussy Commanda off to the side. Big eighteen-wheeler come along real fast and me and Pussy Commanda get out of the way. But not Rose. She stayed in the middle. Went head-on into that truck like a fly splat against a windshield. I swear to this day I can still feel the spray of her blood against my neck. I drove on. Straight into daylight. Never looked back. Had enough gas money on me to take me far as Salt Lake City. Pawned my bike off and bought me a bus ticket back to Wasy. When I got to Chicago, that's when I got up the nerve to wash my lover's dried blood from off my neck. I loved that woman, Marie-Adele, I loved her like no man's ever loved a woman. But she's gone. I never wanna go back to San Francisco. No way, man.

MARIE-ADELE: *[Comforting the crying Emily.]* You should get some rest. Let Annie take over.

EMILY: I'll be fine. You go to sleep. Wake you up when we get to Toronto.

[Emily puts her Walkman on and starts to sing along quietly to 'Blue Kentucky Girl' by Emmylou Harris with its 'I swear I love you . . .' while Marie-Adele leans her head against the 'window' and falls asleep.]

[After a few moments, Zhaboonigan, who has been dozing off between Emily and Marie-Adele in the front seat, pokes her head up and starts to sing along off-key. Then she starts to play with Emily's hair.]

EMILY: *[Shrugging Zhaboonigan's hand off.]* Don't bug me. My favourite part's comin' up.

[Initiated by Zhaboonigan, they start playing 'slap'. The game escalates to the point where Emily almost bangs Zhaboonigan over the head with her elbow.]

EMILY: Yeah, right. You little retard. *[Mad at this, Zhaboonigan hits Emily in the stomach.]* Don't hit me there, you little . . . Hey, man, like ummm . . . I'm sorry, Zha.

ZHABOONIGAN: Sorry.

EMILY: *[Emily feels her belly thoughtfully. After a brief silence:]* You gonna have kids someday, Zha?

ZHABOONIGAN: Ummm . . . buy one.

EMILY: Holy! Well, kids were all right. Aw geez, Zha, that man treated me real bad. Ever been tied to a bed post with your arms up like this? Whoa! *[Grabbing the steering wheel.]* Maybe you should drive.

ZHABOONIGAN: Scary.

EMILY: Aw, don't be scared. Fuck.

ZHABOONIGAN: Fuck.

EMILY: Zhaboonigan Peterson! Your ma'll give me a black eye.

[Zhaboonigan turns her head toward the back seat, where Veronique sits sleeping, and says one more time, really loud.]

ZHABOONIGAN: Fuck!

EMILY: Shhh! Look, Zha. You don't let any man bother you while we're down in T.O. You just stick close to me.

ZHABOONIGAN: Yup.

EMILY: We're sisters, right? Gimme five. *[They slap hands.]* All right. Bingo!!!

[Instantly, the house lights come on full blast. The Bingo Master—the most beautiful man in the world—comes running up centre aisle, cordless mike in hand, dressed to kill: tails, rhinestones, and all. The entire theatre is now the bingo palace. We are in: Toronto!!!!]

BINGO MASTER: Welcome, ladies and gentlemen, to the biggest bingo the world has ever seen! Yes, ladies and gentlemen, tonight, we have a very, very special treat for you. Tonight, ladies and gentlemen, you will be witness to events of such gargantuan proportions, such cataclysmic ramifications, such masterly and magnificent manifestations that your minds will reel, your eyes will nictitate, and your hearts will palpitate erratically.

Because tonight, ladies and gentlemen, you will see the biggest, yes, ladies and gentlemen, the very biggest prizes ever known to man, woman, beast, or appliance. And the jackpot tonight? The jackpot, ladies and gentlemen, is surely the biggest, the largest, the hugest, and most monstrous jackpot ever conceived of in the entire history of monstrous jackpots as we know them. $500,000! Yes, ladies and gentlemen, $500,000 can be yours this very night! That's half a million—A HALF MILLION SMACKEROOS!!! IF you play the game right.

And all you have to do, ladies and gentlemen, is reach into your programs and extract the single bingo card placed therein. Yes, ladies and gentlemen, the single bingo card placed therein, which bingo card will entitle you to one chance at winning the warm-up game for a prize of $20. $20! And all you have to do is poke holes in that single bingo card. Yes, ladies and gentlemen, just poke holes in that single bingo card and bend the numbers backward as the numbers are called. And don't forget the free hole in the middle of the card. Twenty dollars, ladies and gentlemen, that's one line in any direction. That means, of course, ladies and gentlemen, that the first person to form one line, just one straight line in any direction on their card, will be the very lucky winner of the $20 prize. $20! Are you ready, ladies and gentlemen? Are you ready? Then let the game begin! Under the G 56. Etc. . . .

[The audience plays bingo, with the seven women, who have moved slowly

into the audience during the Bingo Master's speech, playing along. Until somebody in the audience shouts, 'Bingo!']

BINGO MASTER: Hold your cards, ladies and gentlemen, bingo has been called.

[The Bingo Master and the assistant stage manager check the numbers and the prize money is paid out.]

BINGO MASTER: And now for the game you've all been waiting for, ladies and gentlemen. Now for the big game. Yes, ladies and gentlemen, get ready for THE BIGGEST BINGO IN THE WORLD! For the grand jackpot prize of $500,000! Full house, ladies and gentlemen, full house! Are you ready? Are you ready? Then let the game begin!

[The house lights go out. And the only lights now are on the bingo balls bouncing around the bingo machine—an eery, surreal sort of glow—and on the seven women who are now playing bingo with a vengeance on centre stage, behind the Bingo Master, where a long bingo table has magically appeared with Zhaboonigan at the table's centre banging a crucifix Veronique has brought along for good luck. The scene is lit so that it looks like 'The Last Supper'.]

[The women face the audience. The bingo table is covered with all the necessary accoutrements: bags of potato chips, cans of pop, ashtrays (some of the women are smoking), etc. The Bingo Master calls out number after number—but not the B 14—with the women improvising responses. These responses—Philomena has 27 cards!—grow more and more raucous: 'B 14? Annie Cook? One more number to go! The B 14! Where is that B 14? Gimme that B 14! Where the fuck is that B 14?!!! etc. Until the women have all risen from the table and come running downstage, attacking the bingo machine and throwing the Bingo Master out of the way. The women grab the bingo machine with shouts of: 'Throw this fucking machine into the lake! It's no damn good!' etc. And they go running down centre aisle with it and out of the theatre. Bingo cards are flying like confetti. Total madness and mayhem. The music is going crazy.]

[And out of this chaos emerges the calm, silent image of Marie-Adele waltzing romantically in the arms of the Bingo Master. The Bingo Master says 'Bingo' into her ear. And the Bingo Master changes, with sudden bird-like movements, into the nighthawk, Nanabush in dark feathers. Marie-Adele meets Nanabush.]
[During this next speech, the other women, one by one, take their positions around Marie-Adele's porch, some kneeling, some standing. The stage area, by means of 'lighting magic', slowly returns to its Wasaychigan Hill appearance.]

MARIE-ADELE: U-wi-nuk u-wa? U-wi-nuk u-wa? Eugene? Neee. U-wi-nuk ma-a oo-ma kee-tha? Ka. Kee-tha i-chi-goo-ma so that's who you are . . . at rest upon the rock . . . the master of the game . . . the game . . . it's me . . . nee-tha . . . come . . . come . . . don't be afraid . . . as-tum . . . come . . . to . . . me . . . ever soft wings . . . beautiful soft . . . soft . . . dark wings . . . here . . . take me . . . as-tum . . . as-tum . . . pee-na-sin . . . wings . . . here . . . take me . . . take . . . me . . . with . . . pee-na-sin . . .*

[As Nanabush escorts Marie-Adele into the spirit world, Zhaboonigan, uttering a cry, makes a last desperate attempt to go with them. But Emily rushes after and catches her at the very last split second. And the six remaining women begin to sing the Ojibway funeral song. By the beginning of the funeral song, we are back at the Wasaychigan Hill Indian Reserve, at Marie-Adele's grave.]

---

* **Marie-Adele**: Who are you? Who are you? Eugene? Nee. Then who are you really? Oh. It's you, so that's who you are . . . at rest upon the rock . . . the master of the game . . . the game . . . it's me . . . me . . . come . . . come . . . don't be afraid . . . come . . . come . . . to . . me . . . ever soft wings . . . beautiful soft . . . soft . . . dark wings . . . here . . . take me . . . come . . . come . . . come and get me . . . wings . . . here . . . take me . . . take . . . me . . . with . . . come and get me . . . (Cree)

The Lover Snake

The magazine photograph is of a Sikh. A male Sikh. Male Sikhs wear turbans. It's a tradition that goes back many, many generations, so it is said. You can always tell a Sikh when you see one by the turban he wears. Most, as I recall, also wear beards like this one in the photograph does. Fine beards. A fine-boned people. This particular Sikh, the man in the photograph, has, pictured with him, the uppermost portion of a large snake slithering down over the front and centre of the bright orange turban he wears, the reptile's diamond-shaped head, with its distended eyes, hovering just centimetres over the man's forehead, its flickering tongue slicing air between his eyes. This is the photograph in the magazine.

Dahljeet has always worn a turban, as I remember. In fact, he has an entire closet full of them at his home in Vancouver. Dahljeet is a Sikh.

Now Dahljeet and I have been friends for many years. An unusual alliance, people would observe from time to time. And between us, Dahljeet and me, we would agree that the friendship was an unusual friendship. I mean, there he was, very much an Indian and here I was, also very much an Indian. Only, we were such totally different kinds of Indian. Worlds apart. So different, it was laughable. And we'd laugh. North Cree hunter ambles down the slope of Robson Street beside north Indian maharajah. An odd pair. To be sure.

And yet, we became close, Dahljeet and I. More than friends, more than brothers, more than lovers, even. It was almost as if, in the midst of certain totally unexpected moments in time we spent together, there would arrive from somewhere a certain buzzing half-sound, a certain inner ringing as perfect in pitch and purity as the tone from a tuning fork. It was beautiful. We met when we were both just short of twenty years of age.

Dahljeet would talk of elephant parades at magnificent royal weddings in the heat and dust of not-so-long-ago north India and of dark women in rainbow-coloured saris, draped in silver and gold and diamonds at summer places in the mountains and at winter places away from mountains. He had stories, too, of cobras that I remember particularly well.

And me? Well, I would talk to him of pure white snow and of rivers that never run dry and of ice-cold lakes from which you could drink by simply dipping your hand through crystal surfaces and cupping and lifting water to your mouth. I talked—not to be outdone by his stories of elephant parades and gold-sprinkled saris—of vast herds of caribou in spring-time, a sea of rolling, shifting, swaying antlers before my hunter father's keen, watchful eye. And of moccasins and belts covered with the most fanciful patterns and designs in glass beads. My sister, Marie-Adele, in particular, I'd confide to Dahljeet, is an artist at the art of applying beadwork to the smoked hide of young caribou. He owned twenty-seven turbans, my friend said in reply, and, later that afternoon, he showed me these twenty-seven turbans in his closet at his home in Vancouver: the colours were fantastic!

There are no snakes where I was born, so Weesageechak, that half-crazed little Cree Indian clown whom no one's ever seen, though he's lived ten thousand years and more among us, I told Dahljeet, this particular Weesageechak, well, he's never seen a snake or done anything with one or ridden one or cooked one and eaten one. He would have danced with one if he'd met one, I laughed. No. No snakes in far north Saskatchewan . . . which made his stories of maharajahs and cobras, yes, cobras in particular, that much more fascinating. I was electrified!

They say, in north India, according to my friend, Dahljeet—he of the twenty-seven multi-coloured turbans and the fine, dark beard—that cobras mate at a certain time in their lives, the male with the female, and that they then sustain this relationship for the rest of their lives, as a couple—unlike sled dogs and caribou and men and women. And there comes a time when the occasional cobra will get killed by some over-zealous hunter, some nervous little man. And when this happens, the surviving cobra, the mate of the snake just killed, will find that man, the killer of his mate, will hunt him down even if it should take him thirty years and more, even if he should have to travel from the pale yellow dust of Punjab province to the border of Nepal or even to North America somewhere, perhaps Vancouver—he will travel there, this other cobra, somehow, even in the realm of the dream world, and he will find that man and he will kill that man, that over-zealous hunter, that nervous little man. Then, and only then, will that cobra, the lover snake, lie down and die.

Many, many years later, Dahljeet and I ceased to be friends. Something happened. Something died inside of me. I haven't seen him in many years;

he and I, we've lost touch. I understand that he lives still in Vancouver and has become even more the academic, the scholar, the thinker he so much was back then, that he teaches at one of the universities, so I've learned only recently, lecturing on the teachings of some obscure Eastern philosopher whose work relies to a great degree on the inner workings of myth and legend. I, on the other hand, now make my home in northwestern Ontario, working in the field of radio broadcasting and helping as much as I can—as poet, writer, thinker after my own fashion—to revive the breathing, the singing, and the shrieking of that half-crazed little Cree clown, Weesageechak, that essential spirit many had thought was on his way to dying, to leaving forever these snow-white landscapes so precious to us all. Now that we're over thirty years of age, we've lost touch, Dahljeet and I. This is the way of things, they say, the natural course of events in the lives of friendships, of love.

But I refuse that explanation. For me, it is a pale, flimsy story, of no consequence, no fantastic substance. I hold, instead, this magazine photograph in front of me and I gaze into it and I wonder if that isn't Dahljeet there in his brilliant orange turban and his fine, dark beard. And the snake? The cobra, the lover snake, come to lay claim to his over-zealous hunter, his nervous little man. And kill him . . . kill . . . kill . . .

Dahljeet and I, we are no longer friends.

Alootook Ipellie b. 1951

INUIT

Summit with Sedna, the Mother of Sea Beasts

As a shaman, I had many occasions to visit Sedna, the Mother of Sea Beasts. Making spirit journeys to her home at the bottom of the sea was often perilous. But these journeys were done out of great sense of duty to my people when hard times beset them.

One winter, a great famine was affecting a number of camps in our region of the Arctic. I was curious to know if other regions were having the same problem. So I made a spirit journey in order to contact all my fellow shamans. Indeed, the great famine was not restricted to our area.

A decision was immediately made what we, as a collective of shamans, could do to reverse our bad fortune. This was before I found out that our respective shamanic powers had greatly diminished in recent months. Sedna, in her moodiness, was directing her vengeance toward all shamans by not granting their pleas to release the sea beasts. I began to question my fellow shamans about the type of encounters they recently had with the Goddess of the Sea.

Unbelievably, what I found out from my peers could well go down in history as a 'sexual misconduct' that had the potential to wipe out the Inuit nation from the face of the earth. It was the kind of news I could not have fathomed in my lifetime.

From the beginning of winter, Sedna had apparently been making sexual advances to the visiting spirits of the shamans. Although she was well-acquainted with certain sea animals she controlled, she had never been able to have an orgasm no matter how hard she tried. In her last act of desperation, she had begun to solicit for sexual favours before she could release the sea beasts to the Inuit living in the natural world.

My peers didn't really have any choice but to feel obliged to fulfil her requests fearing that their failure to convince Sedna to release the sea beasts might brand them incapable in the eyes of their people. Being seen as a weak shaman would not only diminish their economic well-being, but most certainly wipe out their prestige among their fellow Inuit. As hard as they tried to use their sexual experience to their advantage, they had all failed the ultimate test.

Sedna, feeling miserable and sexually bankrupt, had decided to withhold all the sea beasts until a shaman, any old shaman, succeeded in releasing her sexual tensions.

After having heard this unbelievable story, I spent some time trying to figure out a way to break the impasse. Our people's predicament became a desperate situation calling for once-in-a-lifetime encounter with the Goddess of the Sea. Being one of the most powerful shamans living in the Arctic, I was selected by my peers to prepare a summit with Sedna.

It took me a week to go back and study all of my shamanic rituals and taboos that had worked before. Then I had to come up with a new technique which might change the course of our misfortune.

My plan called for all shamans of the Arctic Kingdom to get together for a combined spirit journey to the bottom of the sea. Each shaman was asked to invite their respective spirit helpers which would be collectively molded to create a giant malevolent creature, a hundred times larger than a normal human being. This new creature would also possess spiritual powers equivalent to a hundred spirit souls.

From the very beginning, I knew it was quite unusual planning to confront Sedna in such an unorthodox manner. We had never before gone out of our way to try to make her submit to our demands. Our fool-proof method was always to plead with her to release the animals. So it was with some apprehension that we proceeded to try our luck.

Moments after darkness descended over our camp, the ecstatic journey began. I started with a song which I had constructed for this particular journey in order to evoke my spirit helpers as well as those of my peers. It was one of the most complicated seances I had yet tried.

Finally, after having expended a vast amount of emotional energy through my songs and chants, I was successful in summoning all the spirit helpers to one spot. The next step was to make the earth move open so that we could enter it and proceed to find our way to Sedna's abode. Before we ever got close to its vicinity, we had to pass through abysses, fire, and ice, and then face Sedna's Sea Dogs which always guard the entrance to her home.

Moments after successfully passing the Sea Dogs, we got a glimpse of Sedna swimming into her huge bedroom. I motioned my helpers to wait behind as planned so that I could confront Sedna one on one and try to find my bearings with her.

She lay there on her bed, which was well covered with seaweed. Her long, unkempt hair had become quite dirty. By the look of her distraught eyes and downturned mouth, I had the inkling she was still sexually frustrated.

As was always the case in my past encounters with her, I immediately started to comb and braid her hair while pleading with her to release the sea beasts. She was perfectly willing to—under one condition. I wanted to know what it was. What I then heard was a long, drawn-out preamble to her life-long sexual history, or lack of it.

It had all started when she was still a little girl living in the natural world a few years before she became a Goddess of the Sea. Her father had sexually abused her many times, and when they occurred, they lasted for hours on end. It was because of this prolonged abuse that she became emotionally, mentally, and physically doomed to sexual impotency—unable to ever again have an orgasm no matter how hard or what method she tried.

In a last-ditch effort to turn her misfortune around, she had begun to relegate her best hopes to the visiting spirits of the shamans from the entire Arctic Kingdom. When an attempted bribe failed with each spirit, she would try again with another. This sordid affair continued for the whole winter. And now, she was asking me to do the unthinkable. I was perverted by her desperate words.

It was at this moment that I turned and left the bedroom as if I had given up and was returning to the natural world. Sedna started to sob like a little, trembling child. I understood that nothing would make her more sad than another opportunity lost for sexual fulfilment.

My only alternative was to release our version of 'Frankenstein' to confront Sedna. Frankenstein crawled into Sedna's bedroom. Sensing the presence of unusual energy around her, Sedna sat up, moving like a cobra, and turned her head to look over her shoulder.

What she saw in front of her was a giant of a monster, more fearsome than any creature she had ever encountered at the bottom of the sea. Frankenstein stood up and towered over the tiny body of Sedna. Sedna shrieked the hell out of her lungs. She begged the monster to stand back, extending her webbed hands toward the monster's eyes which were streaked with crimson and glowing like gold.

Frankenstein started a special chant I had composed for him. It was designed to put Sedna under a trance. This would allow her to have an ecstatic dream—a sensual trip she had never taken in her lifetime. After all, Sedna had become, over the passing of many years, an almost senseless soul, unable to express intimacy in light of her impotency.

During her forced-sensual dream, Sedna finally met her match. It was her male equivalent, Andes, a God of the Sea, who presided over all the sea beasts on the other side of the universe. In her dream of dreams, Sedna finally had a sexual encounter measurable in ecstatic terms only attainable in the world of Gods and Goddesses.

In her state of heightened sexual ecstasy, Sedna released a perpetual explosion of orgasmic juices. In the same instance, during her virgin joy, she released all the sea beasts who immediately proceeded to travel with impunity to the hungry Arctic world.

It was beautiful to see the lovely beasts, swimming torpedo-like, toward the breathing holes on the sea ice. It was wonderful to experience the same excitement as the unleashing of bottled tension Sedna was going through for the first time in her long vocation.

It was also the first time in the history of the Arctic Kingdom that all of its shamans had worked together to avert an almost certain threat of extinction of its people from the face of the earth. From this day on, the Inuit were assured survival as a vibrant force in what was oftentimes an inhospitable Arctic world.

And, perhaps more importantly for me, in the eyes of my people, my reputation as a powerful shaman remained perfectly intact.

Waking Up

Waking up
Just as I have
In the last one hundred years
Barely ahead of the trickling-in of dawn

But this time there was a difference

A rude wakening
Had to blink a few times
To make sure the image stayed the same
After each opening of my lids

Then pinched both my cheeks
Slapped them slightly
To neutralize the tinge of pain
Spreading it around more evenly
So they would survive the ordeal

Stood up and looked down at my naked feet
Wanting to be re-assured
That they were indeed firmly planted
On the earth-bound moss

Affirmation was there for the taking
If only I could find it
Within this misty soul

Turned around in despair
Hoping to see familiar faces
Afraid of what I might see
In the pre-dawn shadows
I became terrified of whatever
I had just turned away from
Scared of the unknown

Premature arrival of Armageddon
Just like being trapped in a nightmare
Running slightly ahead of certain death
The passage of time lasting forever

Who said waking up
Each morning was a blessing from god
For having survived another night

And again face the un-doing
Of your consciousness

Life is like night and day
Painted in black and white
Graphic as ever
Does it mean we are headed for paradise
Or doomed to oblivion

That's the beauty of our lives
It is what keeps us going forward
Wondering
Wondering what is next to come
Around the next bend
Beyond the next horizon
By experiencing the unravelling of events
Within the edge of our vision
And in the universe of our minds

Waking up
From what was literally
A nomadic life the night before
To a lifestyle where Inuit hunters
Spend all their precious time
Sitting in front of a computer
Pushing predetermined buttons and keys
That allow them to launch
Rocket-powered harpoon missiles
Arrows and fish-spears

These are the days of return to innocence
Since the fish birds and animals
Never get to encounter
Their predatory enemies anymore

The Arctic has become a class-less society
Since the tools of the twenty-first century
Have finally arrived

No pride nor dignity in that
And I am saddened
Since I cannot show off my skills any more
To my loved ones
As well as to those who are accustomed
To being impressed
By my prowess as a great hunter

Waking up
Not needing to go outdoors to meet nature
As I was able to only yesterday

Damn

I had to work hard for my living
And I could also reward myself
With a triumphant kill
After having witnessed
The frightened eyes of

The bountiful bull caribou
The majestic polar bear
The sleek-backed ringed seal
The lumbering girth of a walrus
The feathered friend of a waterfowl
The slippery skin of an arctic char
And the welcome sight of a beluga whale

Waking up
Sitting in front of a damn computer
Breathing only used oxygen
Remembering my glory days
As a powerful shaman

Lament my friends and enemies
Lament for the enlightened days of yesterday
Lament for the husky who is forced to retire
Lament for the beautiful Arctic landscape
Which will never again be seen with naked eyes
Lament for the salty sea
For it will no more hug me and my kayak
Lament for the sun and the moon
For they will no more show off their shine
Lament for the northern lights
For they will no more find human heads
To play ball with
Lament for the great spirit
Which takes care of the natural world
For its time has come to an end

Waking up
With a slap in the face

My preference is to go back to yesterday
And begin all over again

Tonight
I will think twice about going to sleep
I will be afraid of
Waking up

Journey Toward Possibilities

Nothing should be left to an invaded
people except their eyes for weeping.*

Like Mary
My mother and father created
An Immaculate Conception
Well almost
Who in his right mind would think
He was immaculate
There are plenty of souls out there
Who will make such a confession
Woebegone to this vulnerable world
Nothing immaculate in what I
See hear feel taste or smell
But I have always expected immaculateness
Ever since being able to comprehend
My fellow man's outpourings
But as these years pass by
My great disappointment is still endless
Man's penchant for immaculate discovery
In human beings will always fail miserably
Simply because he is doomed to a
Finite failure
Civilization in its very nature is violent
And we are but a small portion
Of its victims
Although it can be said that
Because of man's violent nature
We as a distinct entity
Have survived obliteration
For now

---

* Prussian chancellor, Prince Otto Von Bismarck, late nineteenth century.

Manipulation has played a central role
Within our side of the world
The circumpolar world

But to manipulate men,
to propel them towards goals
which you—the social reformers—
see, but they may not, is to
deny their human essence,
to treat them as objects without
will of their own, and therefore
to degrade them.*

Our homelands have been stamped
With these very words
For as long as dominators
Of dominant societies
Have dominated us
Unfortunately for the foreseeable future
These very words will remain
Comfortably cemented

Unless a new era dawns
In our circumpolar world
A yearning not quite like any
Other hunger is growing
Along with a desire
To break away from the grasp
Of colonialism
So we may once again squire dignity
Within our hearts and minds
And replenish our souls with pride
Until we are given back our
Lost pride and dignity
We shall drape indignation
On all those who
Enjoy our friendliness
And the splendour of our homelands
Until these chains tied
Around our will are removed forever
We as a collective
Will continue to be denied
Our freedom

---

* Sir Isaiah Berlin, Fellow of All Souls, Oxford University.

Allow us to imagine that
Wonderful state of mind
When ecstasy runneth over
Our goose pimples
In the final realization
Of our greatest desire
To be freed from
Our dominators' cage
The hand that may well
Secure our sacred freedom
Is contained in the
Embodiment of a new
Arctic Policy
For our circumpolar world
Our greatest hopes
Have found a perfect
Gilded foundation
On which to build a protective structure
For our people's continued existence
As a distinct entity
In this global cultural mosaic
Since many of our cherished dreams
Still fade unfulfilled
We are as determined as ever
To embark on a journey
Toward possibilities
For our people
And our homelands

Godspeed

Walking Both Sides of an Invisible Border

It is never easy
Walking with an invisible border
Separating my left and right foot

I feel like an illegitimate child
Forsaken by my parents
At least I can claim innocence
Since I did not ask to come
Into this world

Walking on both sides of this
Invisible border
Each and every day
And for the rest of my life
Is like having been
Sentenced to a torture chamber
Without having committed a crime

Understanding the history of humanity
I am not the least surprised
This is happening to me
A non-entity
During this population explosion
In a minuscule world

I did not ask to be born an Inuk
Nor did I ask to be forced
To learn an alien culture
With an alien language
But I lucked out on fate
Which I am able to undo

I have resorted to fancy dancing
In order to survive each day
No wonder I have earned
The dubious reputation of being
The world's premier choreographer
Of distinctive dance steps
That allow me to avoid
Potential personal paranoia
On both sides of this invisible border

Sometimes this border becomes so wide
That I am unable to take another step
My feet being too far apart

When my crotch begins to tear apart
I am forced to invent
A brand new dance step
The premier choreographer
Saving the day once more

Destiny acted itself out
Deciding for me where I would come from
And what I would become

So I am left to fend for myself
Walking in two different worlds
Trying my best to make sense
Of two opposing cultures
Which are unable to integrate
Lest they swallow one another whole

Each and every day
Is a fighting day
A war of raw nerves
And to show for my efforts
I have a fair share of wins and losses

When will all this end
This senseless battle
Between my left and right foot

When will the invisible border
Cease to be

Margo Kane b. 1951

SAULTEAUX/CREE

Moonlodge

[NOTE: All characters are played by one woman. As audience enters there is the warm, inviting, playful sound of women's voices in Cree and English around a fire. Agnes enters with a suitcase.]

AGNES: Millie? Are you in there? *[Peeks in door.]* Oh, excuse me—I'm looking for—you are here. Am I late? Thank goodness. Where should I sit? *[Makes her way inside the lodge.]* Ooops, sorry! *[Sits.]* There . . . O.K.

It was Millie who invited me to the lodge. Her round face, sparkle in her eye—her smile, always teasing. And long, thick black braids—tight, neat braids. I trust her like a sister or my mother. Her hands, always busy, darting here—and fluttering like a bird—*[Struggling with a sudden memory.]* the bird that got caught in my house when I was a child.
[She stands and relives memory.] The bird . . . in my house . . . the screen door snaps shut . . . there's a whirr and a flutter. It's a bird! Mom!

MOM: Something's gonna happen! Agnes! Open the door! I'll get the broom!
[Mom swipes at the bird and hits Agnes accidentally.] Oops, sorry! *[She laughs.]* And the bird crashes into the kitchen window where it bangs and flutters. *[Her hands fly up either side of her face to show the bird crashing into the kitchen window.]* The tea towel! *[Still laughing, she swipes at the ceiling, opens the door.]* And the bird flies out into the yard.

AGNES: *[Hugs mother.]* She was laughing . . . and I hung onto her skirt, my head against her belly.
[Piecing more memory together.] I was making frybread, standing on a stool in front of the stove . . . *[Tends frybread with spatula.]* . . . for a big dinner!

How will we feed everyone? We barely have enough food to last till the next cheque. Auntie Edna always says, 'The Creator will provide.'
[Draws cross in the air with a spatula while intoning . . .] My father can beat your father at domino-o-o-s.

Auntie Edna! Tansi! *[Opens door, takes large bowl.]* Macaroni salad. *[Wrinkles nose distastefully.]* My favourite! Would you like some tea? *[Brings her a cup.]*

Auntie Edna always smelled like powder and lipstick. Her hair was . . . curly and whirly . . .

[Remembers.] Uncle Alvin! *[Moves to hanging drum.]* Before dinner, Uncle Alvin sang . . . in Indian . . . I didn't know what he was singing. We were sitting on the floor . . . the food was on . . . cardboard? . . . on the floor . . . it was full . . . the room was full of people and food! Meat and

berries and macaroni salad and . . . frybread. I made the frybread. Uncle
Alvin was singing.

I poured the tea for the grownups after dinner. Their voices got louder
and louder and my father's was right along with them. He was tall, head-
scarf . . . *[Imitating.]* They been takin from us for a long time and now
we're takin their welfare cheques.

FATHER: I'm not gonna take this lyin down!

AGNES: Us kids, we beat it outta there! *[Runs out of the house.]*

We played down by the creek until it was too dark to play any more. We
played . . . One bannock, two bannock, etc. . . . . *[Peeking.]* 100 bannock!
[Sneaks directly to Annie's hiding spot.] I see you Annie!

ANNIE: *[Whining.]* No you don't.

AGNES: Last one home's a mud guppie! *[Agnes races for home.]* Home free!
Annie's a mud guppie!

[Laughing, she collapses on ground and looks up at the sky.] It was late.
The moon took her light behind the clouds. Some dogs were yappin in the
distance. Us kids, ssshhh! *[Signals kids to follow her.]* We crept onto the
porch and peeked in through the screen door. Few people sittin. My father.
He's still talkin! His head snaps to attention. Us kids freeze. He comes
towards the door and stops. He sniffs. *[She sniffs the air like an animal.]*
Eiyiyiy!! We tackled his legs and tried to pull him over. He dragged us
around the room!

FATHER: *[Collapsing on the ground.]* Ahhh. My little army. They can take me
but they'll never take us all.

AGNES: *[Realizing.]* My father was taken away soon after by some men. And
then the welfare came to take us.

Mom, there's two cars pulling up. The priest—and some white people.
Mom! *[Runs in house and hides behind Mom.]*

MOM: They're my kids! No you don't!

AGNES: *[Fighting.]* No! Mom! Let me go! No! *[She falls to floor.]*

MOM: They're my kids! *[Trying to grab kids.]* Eddie! You take care of your
brother. Robbie, don't cry. Don't hurt her! Sarah stay close to your sister.
Annie it'll be okay. Agnes I'll come for you soon.

AGNES: My fists are bruised as they crash against the car window, where I
bang and flutter. *[Agnes beats the car window with her fists and open
hands alternately as she silently screams* Momma! *She freezes with hands
still on window either side of her face in the same motif as the bird against
the kitchen window.]*

AGNES: The last time I saw my mother, she was runnin down the road after
the car.

[She steels herself against the pain of abandonment.] They moved us
from foster home to foster home. They took brothers from sisters and sisters from sisters, until I sat all alone in the car just looking out the window.

I remember moving and moving until I didn't know where I was or
where I was going or where I came from.

I had to share beds with all kinds of children. And dinner tables filled with strangers. *[Sits on suitcase and folds hands.]* I had to say grace all by myself.

God is good . . . *[Corrects herself.]* . . . great. God is good. Let us thank him for our food.

[Sing-songie without feeling.] Come Lord Jesus be our guest. And let this food to us be blessed. Amen.

[Sarcastic.] For what we are about to receive. May the Lord make us truly thankful. *[She is slapped.]*

[Retreats with suitcase.] I remember moving and moving.

Finally I came to live with a woman named Aunt Sophie.

[Opens suitcase and dresses in Sophie's scarf, sweater, and shopping satchel.]

Now Aunt Sophie was a very large woman with a very large voice. She was a very practical and sensible woman.

SOPHIE: Now Agnes, if you're going shopping with me today button up your coat. I won't have you catching your death. And get that hair out of your eyes or I'll scalp you. Now stand up straight. Put your shoulders back. Come along.

AGNES: And off we'd go for our weekly shopping. Aunt Sophie knew everybody.

SOPHIE: Well, hello Mrs Rosenberg. How are you feeling today dear? You're still looking a little peaked. Really. I think I maybe should give you my doctor's number because I don't know if yours is doing the best for you dear. Trust me. Ohhh! I've been busier than a one-armed paperhanger. Agnes and I are going shopping today for her first brassiere. You know she's at that age!

AGNES: I hated everyone knowing our business!

SOPHIE: Well, hello Mr Weitzel and how are you today dear? Oh, I hope these aren't the same cabbages you sold me last week. I think you owe me this one. You know the last ones you sold me, when I opened them up to make cabbage rolls I found them crawling with maggots. Believe me! *[Weitzel makes a pass at her.]* Oh, Mr Weitzel!

AGNES: Mr Weitzel had a son named Solomon and I loved to watch him work. I felt kinda sorry for Solomon. He had spectacles and really scrawny arms. When he lifted the banana boxes I just wanted to run and help him!

[Agnes moons over Solomon.] Aunt Sophie! *[Searches the store.]* Oh my God! Aunt Sophie's heading towards the Moonies selling flowers on the street corner. Oh my God!

SOPHIE: Children, now listen to me. I'll give you a quarter to call your parents. They're probably worried sick about you. Look at you. Standing on street corners, givin up your education and job and everything. And for what? You think that Reverend Sun-in-the-Moon would be standing on the street corner for you? Hmmm?

AGNES: And the Moonies just stood there smiling and lovebombing everyone that went by.

[Takes off Sophie's clothes and packs for Brownie camp.] Aunt Sophie knew a lot about a lot of things but she didn't know a thing about Brownies. When my girlfriend Lynnette asked me to join Brownies I had to explain to Aunt Sophie.

Well, there is all kinds of Brownies. There's elves and fairies and gnomes and pixies and sprites and imps and kelpies . . . and they help people. And if you're a Brownie you get badges for making your bed and cleaning your room and helping your mom. And Brownies live in the woods so we get to go to camp and take nature walks and learn about trees and flowers and birds and . . . and . . . things and sing campfire songs.

SOPHIE: I think it's very important that you get in touch with your tribal heritage!

AGNES: Tribal heritage? I just want to go to Brownies! *[Takes suitcase to Brownies, dresses in headband and feather from inside it, sits on it in cartoon Indian pose—arms and legs crossed.]*

It was at Brownies that I learned my first Indian song. *[Gets hanging drum.]* And I got to lead the campfire songs because I had a very strong voice. *[Earnestly drums in Hollywood tom-tom tradition.]*

My Paddle

My paddle keen and bright
flashing with silver
follow the wild goose flight
dip, dip and swing
dip, dip and swing

And the Brown Owl, Mrs Corscadden smiles at me and then signals all the girls to join in.

dip, dip and swing her back
flashing with silver
swift as the wild goose flight
dip, dip and swing
dip, dip and swing
dip, dip and swing

[Stands and grins at audience.]

The next song I'm going to sing is Land Of The Silver Birch.

Land of the silver birch
home of the beaver
where still the mighty moose
wanders at will

blue lake and rocky shore
I will return once more
boom diddy boom boom

boom diddy boom boom
boom diddy boom boom

I loved camp.

There were no Indians in my neighbourhood. The only Indians I saw were on television. I remember the Walt Disney Injuns. They were big, fat redmen with flat noses. 'Ugh! Me wantum smokum peacepipe.' And pretty little princesses named Princess Minni-Haha. And cartoon Injuns that danced the rain dance. *[She whoops and dances.]*

And I remember some of the popular songs on the radio. *[She becomes a country singer.]* Okay all you Injuns out there. This one's for you. Whoo! Whoo! Whoo! *[Starts tom-tom beat.]*

Kawliga

Kawliga was a wooden Indian
Standing by the door
He fell in love with an Indian maid
over in the antique store

Kawliga
Just stood there and never let it show
so she could never answer yes or no

He always wore his Sunday feathers
and held a tommyhawk
The maiden wore her beads and braids
and hoped some day he'd talk

Kawliga
too stubborn to ever show a sign
because his heart was made of knotty pine

CHORUS:
Poor ol' Kawliga
he never got a kiss
Poor ol' Kawliga
he don't know what he missed
Is it any wonder
that his face is red
Kawliga that poor ol' wooden head

Another song that struck a chord in my red soul was the story of Running Bear and Little White Dove who couldn't be together because their tribes were at war.

[Music up/Running Bear. She imitates a cartoon Running Bear doing a war dance.]

Running Bear

On the banks of the river
stood Running Bear, young Indian brave
on the other side of the river
stood his lovely Indian maid

[She poses on standing suitcase as Little White Dove.]

Little White Dove was her name
such a lovely sight to see

All the women were either subservient or sexy. I preferred sexy! *[Is dancing seductively flaunting and pouting.]* And the women always followed their men ten paces behind.

But their tribes fought with each other
so their love could never be

Hollywood version. Lots of leg. *[Chorus line kicks.]*

Running Bear loved Little White Dove
with a love as big as the sky

Fringed mini-skirts. Lots of skin. *[More chorus line kicks.]*

Running Bear loved Little White Dove
with a love that couldn't die

Savage tragedy! *[Melodramatic pose. Dives onto floor and does frog stroke.]*

He couldn't swim the raging river
'Cause the river was too wide

[Continues swimming various strokes.] Because his name was Running Bear and not Swimming Bear!

He couldn't reach Little White Dove
waiting on the other side

[She shades her eyes.] And Indians always looked like this because if they looked like this *[Covers them]* they couldn't see anything.

In the moonlight he could see her
blowing kisses across the waves
her heart was beating faster
waiting there for her brave

[Much shimmy with breasts and shoulders.] Primitive, primal, savage, supernatural love. *[Music is fading.]*
[Music out.] Indian!

I was one of the few brown faces in school and then Indians were bussed in. Real Indians! Marvin was tall and handsome. His hair was long and wild. All us girls would hang near him waiting to catch his eye. Then he'd turn and flash his famous smile and we'd all melt. I had a crush on him. Even some of the white girls had crushes on him. But I never talked to him. He scared me. I knew he could see the Indian in me. He looked right in and touched it with his eyes. He knew me but I didn't know him. He came from a remote reserve that I knew nothing about. I didn't belong to his world. He didn't fit into the system and eventually he quit school. *[Hangs up drums.]*

Somehow I managed to graduate from high school and everyone was talking about California and San Francisco and Haight-Ashbury and love-ins. It sounded so . . . groovy! And they were all taking their backpacks and hitchhiking . . . all over. There was a bigger world outside of my Aunt Sophie's. *[Packs up feather and headband, takes out flower and psyche-delic scarf and ties scarf around waist.]*

Aunt Sophie . . . she'd never let me go. Well I'm old enough. I've saved up my money. I'll leave her a note. I'll send her a postcard from some-where. I'll phone her from a telephone booth on the highway.

[Placing call.] Hello Aunt Sophie? Yes it's me. No, I'm not going shop-ping with you today. No, I'm going on a trip. I'm hitchhiking. Aunt Sophie. Aunt Sophie, please don't cry. Please, Aunt Sophie. I'm not run-ning away. I'll call you. I'll phone collect. Aunt Sophie, listen. I love you very much. *[She hangs up and begins to sing.]*

Big Yellow Taxi

Don't it always seem to go
That you don't know what you've got
til it's gone

You pave Paradise
put up a parking lot
doooo doo doo doo doo
doooo doo doo doo doo

[While singing she has put flower in her hair and picked up suitcase.]
Bye Aunt Sophie!
[She begins to hitchhike still singing and dancing 'The Jerk' and then 'The Hitchhiker'.]
Thanks!

My first ride was—well . . . the ashtray was overflowing with butts and ashes and there was a film on the window and he had nicotine stains all over his fingers and teeth. And he kept staring at me. But he bought me lunch.

Well, it was really groovy that you gave me a ride. Thanks for the lunch.

But you know I just remembered that my Aunt Delores lives down this way! And it would be really awful if I didn't stop to visit her. These people over here said they would give me a ride. Can you believe it? Miracles! Take care of yourself. Peace. *[Gives him the peace sign and walks away, suitcase in hand.]*

He was playing footsie with me under the table and when he looked at me he wasn't looking at my face if you know what I mean!

There's a gas station down the way. For sure I'll get a ride somewhere.

Oh my God! Harley Davidsons! A whole herd of Harley Davidsons! So much chrome . . . chrome mirrors, chrome pipes, musta cost a mint! Chrome everywhere! Electric colours—fluorescent orange and yellow flames! *[Lowers herself slowly onto the bike suitcase.]* Baby blue metallic! California plates! It's the most incredible, fabulous, outta sight, outta m-i-n-d . . . *[Sees Marlon in front of bike.]*

Hi! Is this your bike? Oh. It's the most incredible bike I've ever seen. I've never been on a bike before. I just had to . . . I just couldn't help myself! *[Gets off the bike.]*

There was this guy and he had a white t-shirt stretched over his tight muscles, cigarette pack under the sleeve and tight jeans and big biker boots. Over his shoulder he carried a black leather jacket and he shifted from hip to hip. He looked like Marlon Brando.

BIKER: 'Charlie, Charlie!'

AGNES: He even sounded like Marlon Brando.

BIKER: 'You were my brother. You shouldda taken care of me!'

AGNES: Are you from California? I see you have California plates. Do you live there? Oh, you're so lucky! Oh God! You know I would do anything to ride on a bike.

I'm just hanging on his every word. He's very cool. Where are you going?

BIKER: 'Charlie! Charlie! I couldda been a contender!'

AGNES: Wow! Santa Fe. Is that on the way to California? I've heard it's really beautiful. It would be great to go there. Then he says . . .

BIKER: Uhhh. You . . . *[Thumb points to her.]* Me . . . *[Points to himself.]* Uhh . . . *[He waves hand between them.]* Eh? *[Points with thumb over shoulder to bike.]*

AGNES: Then he asks me to go along!

[Music up—'Born To Be Wild'. She leaps onto bike, tries to jumpstart it. It rumbles on the second try. She lipsyncs to first verse.]

Born To Be Wild

Get your motor runnin
head out on the highway
lookin for adventure
in whatever comes our way

And here I am riding down the highway on a Harley Davidson. I can just hear Aunt Sophie!

SOPHIE: Hooligans! Riff-raff! No self-respecting girl would be caught dead tearing around the countryside with such . . . neanderthals!

AGNES: Oh Aunt Sophie! You don't know how to live!

[Music up high and she rides away, her skirt flying. She sits backwards, her skirt always billowing and she is smiling and laughing. She sits side saddle the wind blowing her hair all over. She picks up her scarf end and it flies full against her face as she rides. She continues on under the music alternating the billowing from side to side.

She gets off bike and joins a party. She drinks from a bottle, takes a joint, and chokes on the toke. Finishes beer and heaves the empty bottle away. Music fades out. She is high and intoxicated.]

That first night we rumbled into the campground at dusk. I look across the fire to see Marlon beckoning to me. I'm alone with Marlon under the starry sky.

[She rises shyly and moves slowing to biker. She begins to sing 'On The Street Where You Live' in a high soprano. She puts her hand out and he kisses it and sweeps her into a waltz.]

On The Street Where You Live

> I have often walked down these streets before
> but the pavement always stayed beneath my feet before
> All at once am I several stories high
> knowing I'm on the street where you live

[She extends her hand and he grabs her and drags her around the stage and pushes her onto the ground. She is startled and grabs the scarf/shawl to keep herself covered. They struggle for the scarf pulling it back and forth.]

> And ohhhh, the towering feeling
> just to know somehow you are near
> that overpowering feeling
> that any second you might suddenly appear

[In one strong movement he pulls the scarf off and throws it away. In another he pushes her back on the ground and abruptly separates her legs.]

> People stop and stare
> They don't bother me

Wait a minute, you're crushing me! *[She struggles.]*

> for there's nowhere else on earth
> that I would rather be

No!

> Let the world go by

Noooooo!

[She freezes. Her head and shoulders just off the floor, her arms tense and stretched out in the air. She sings with the last of her strength at her highest pitch.]

> I don't care if I
> can be found
> on the street
> where
> you
> live!

[She collapses and reaches for the discarded scarf. Very frightened she slowly and painfully moves away from him.]

Somehow I made it all the way to Sante Fe.

[Throws flower away, picks up suitcase, and leaves.]

Sante Fe is the oldest place I've ever seen. I get to the centre of town and there's this little park—plaza they call it. And there's Indians everywhere. They're sitting in doorways and on sidewalks and on blankets full of silver jewellery and weavings and other knick knacks. As Aunt Sophie would say, *[Sophie's voice]* 'You know, peddling their wares. It's good they're getting something for their handicrafts. Lord knows they need jobs!' And the art galleries are full of Indian paintings.

SOPHIE: And they're being sold in the hotels, no less. Is this art or something?

AGNES: And this one woman catches my eye and she's surrounded by the most gorgeous pottery in oranges and browns—very traditional I'm told. And this one piece is at least a foot high. It's this pueblo woman with all these babies hanging off her.

Oh, it's so beautiful! Did you make it? The Storyteller? The Storyteller.

And there's these blue cowboy boots in front of me and these long legs. And there's this Indian man standing under a huge cowboy hat. He's got long braids and a big silver and turquoise belt buckle. And then he turns and strolls away.

Do you know him?

There was something about him. *[She begins to follow him.]* Every time he turned around I pretended I was looking in a store window. I didn't know what to say. Oh my God. He's getting into his truck. I'm going to lose him. I'll head him off at the pass. *[She hitchhikes. The truck stops and she climbs in.]*

Thank you very much. My name is Turtle Dove. Well, my real name is Agnes. So what's your name? Lance.

He had this beautiful brown face with high cheekbones, deep brown pools for eyes, and this big pearly, Colgate smile.

You know, I've never seen blue cowboy boots before. You look like you just got off a horse. *[Pause.]* I'm from Canada. So, where are you from? South Dakota. Oh, I know where that is. It's north of here isn't it? *[Pause.]*

Which tribe are you from? I know all about the Sioux. Television. *[Pause.]* What was Custer's famous last words at the Little Battle of Bighorn? These Siouxs are killing me! *[She kills herself laughing. He doesn't enjoy the joke.]*

I see this feather hanging from the rearview mirror.

What kind of feather is this? Eagle! Where did you get it?

Then Lance tells me it was given to him. You can't buy eagle feathers. They have to be given to you. The eagle is a very sacred bird, a messenger. You can't go out and shoot an eagle for its feathers. The eagle will leave them for you.

[Pause.] I'd sure like to have one some day.

So I ask Lance where he's driving to and he says he's meeting some of his brothers down the road.

LANCE: The revolution has already begun—always been there smouldering, waiting for the spark. That spark could be you! I see Alcatraz and Wounded Knee wherever our red brothers and sisters take a stand. When are you gonna get up on your hind legs and fight? I'm not going to take this lying down. They've been takin from us for a long time now you're takin their welfare cheques! Hmmmm?

AGNES: He says that a lot of his brothers will be at the Powwow. Powwow.

What's a Powwow? *[Powwow drum up.]*

It was like a scene out of the movies. Tall teepees standing in the dusk surrounded by a huge encampment of tents and campers, trucks and jeeps and old station wagons loaded with kids. I've never seen so many Indians in one place! Some are covered in feathers and furs with sleigh bells around their ankles that jingle as they walk. Old men walk by in coloured shirts hung with ribbons and grannies in kerchiefs and flower-print dresses. Some men look like cowboys . . . boots and stetsons. They lean against vans and half-tons joking and teasing each other—in a language I don't understand. I notice the people moving towards the sound of the drumming and I don't remember Lance after that. *[Powwow music up higher.]*

I am standing in a huge dance arbour surrounded by bleachers full of Indians. Around the dance floor sit at least a dozen big drums surrounded by singers and their families and friends. The announcer's banter rises above the drumming.

ANNOUNCER: Hooo-yah! Powwow time! Intertribal! Heeeeeyah! Everybody dance! Hokah! Hokah! Hokah! Hey!

AGNES: *[Begins to dance.]* The dancers move around and around in a slow circle. The whole arbour is a sea of rippling fringes and feathers and beads. *[She continues her attempt to dance watching those around her.]*

The old people are so dignified. The women carry shawls over their arms. Feather fans salute the sky. *[She dances on the spot saluting the sky.]*

Children imitate little birds, strutting and hopping. Some are so serious! *[She dances as the little boys and then the little girls.]*

Grass dancers! Long fringes sway like meadow grasses in the wind. *[She dances.]*

Painted traditional men parade in their bustles of eagle feathers. They carry staffs and eagle wings. *[She dances.]*

Acrobatic young men show off feather bustles like huge prairie chickens, strutting and twirling! *[She dances.]*

Young women, fancy dancers! Their braids hung with otter and weasel fur. Their beaded moccasins are a blur as they prance and kick and twirl. Their shawls fly around their shoulders. *[She dances and ends with pow-wow music.]*

I could have danced all night!

Lance finds me later that night in a crowd around the Black Lodge Singers. Sleep? Do you have a tent? Oh. Are there snakes around here? The back of the truck would be perfect.

[She lies down.] Is that a coyote?

[Lights fade. She sings closing song dreamily, sitting up and looking around. Then lies down and sleeps.]

[Waking up, yawning and stretching.] Mmmm! Coffee! Lance. Lance!

[She sees Millie.] At the camp next to us a woman pours steaming coffee into mugs and hands them around. Her long braids swing, a child clings to her skirt.

[She is caught staring.] Good morning! Coffee? Oh yes, thank you.

MILLIE: Help yourself to some cream and sugar.

[Noticing mess.] Damn dogs! Rooting around in the garbage!

What do you call a dog with no legs? What's the use of calling him. He won't come anyway!

My name is Millie. Agnes. So what are you Agnes? Stoney? Cree? You don't know!? Your first powwow? Ohhhh. You better watch out for them singers. My husband is a singer.

Hey! Remember that song you used to sing when you were first courting me. Aaah!

Okay, then I'll sing it! *[She finds drum.]* Back then he had all his teeth. He could still see his belt buckle. *[She sings and drums.]*

> Oh, yes I love you honey dear
> I don't care if you're married sixteen times
> I'll get you yeah!
> ah yeah hah yeah
> yeah hah hah yeah

Oh I have a very good memory. *[Hangs up drum.]* Would you like some frybread?

It used to be my job to make frybread for the big dinners. I had a stool in front of the stove at—home. . . . *[Retreating.]* I've gotta go. Excuse me. I'll be back later. *[As memory floods in.]*

[She leaves, eating frybread thoughtfully as she goes. As she finishes eating she looks around at craft tables in front of her. Spies a bracelet and picks it up.]

Jewellery! Oooh!

How much is this? *[Replaces it quickly.]* It's very beautiful.

There's this guy at one of the tables dressed like an Indian, sort of. He's got all kinds of beads and claws and stuff hanging off him and his hair is in scrawny braids—but it's blond! Well, Aunt Sophie always says, 'Never judge a man until you've walked a mile in his moccasins!'

Indian Tarot cards? Sacred dog? Sacred eagle? Sacred bat! Your card? *[Reading.]* Peter Many Painted Ponies. Shaman for any occasion. Ceremonies, Sundances, Vision Questing, Rebirthing, and Past Life Regression. Thanks. See ya.

Lance! There's this white guy sellin Medicine things and he's dressed like an Indian! Lance is preening in the truck mirror and doesn't even look at me.

LANCE: Probably a member of the famous Wannabee tribe.

AGNES: Wannabee?

LANCE: Cherokee, Pawnee, Comanche, Wannabee.

AGNES: Wannabee? I met a red-haired woman who said she was Cherokee but she looked like Edna Feinstein who lived down the street. Wannabee. *[Understanding.]* And this blonde woman who called herself Yellow Moon Rising.

And when they found out I was Indian, I had more friends than you could shake a stick at.

WOMEN: Ohhh, so you're an Injun? You don't look Injun. What tribe are you? Well, where're you from? Canada? Ohhhh, so you must be Eskimo.

If you're an Indian what's the colour of North on the Sacred Medicine Wheel? What's your Indian name? You're sure you're an Indian?

Do you have a totem animal? You should go to the sweat lodge to get one! My totem animal is a black panther.

I don't tell everyone this but I'm a pipe-carrier as well and I'm training to be a Medicine-Woman.

AGNES: *[Backs away.]* Medicine? I got to talk to Millie.

MILLIE: Hmmm? Medicine. There's all kinds of medicine for all kinds of people. Could you hand me that box please? *[Packing.]* We're packin up now, so we can get an early start on the trail. *[Gently.]* You look confused. Your medicine will come from your own people.

AGNES: My own people? *[Under her breath.]* But I don't remember who they are.

MILLIE: *[Still packing.]* Where are you headed next? Do you know where you're going? I don't think so. What are you looking for?

AGNES: I didn't know I was looking for anything.

MILLIE: Have you ever looked for your family? Maybe that's what you should be looking for. *[Handing present to her.]* Here, I want you to have this.

This is a special little feather. We call it an eagle plume. You see I've attached it to a beaded rosette. Just tie it into your hair when you're dancing.

AGNES: *[She is overwhelmed.]* A feather. An eagle feather. Thank you Millie! *[Puts feather in hair.]*

MILLIE: You know the eagles watch over all things. They can soar high above the earth close to the Creator Spirit. They bless our ceremonies when they soar overhead. They keep watch for us—keep us on the right road.

Well, you know where to find me. When you're in my neck of the woods just ask around. I'm the only Millie there. Come and stay awhile. I'll be expecting you.

AGNES: *[Quietly.]* Bye Millie. *[Sound of wind is heard.]*

It is miles outside of Santa Fe that I stand in the desert mountains. I stare, transfixed, at ancient cave dwellings carved out of a huge mesa. I crawl through stone chambers and climb stone stairways to the mesa top. The ruins of an old village surround a grassy plaza. I stand all alone breathing in the warm desert wind. I am high above the plains and valleys that stretch for miles and miles. I can see what those ancient people must have seen—the mauve and rose-coloured landscape as the sun begins to hug the horizon. And I am running across that open plaza, climbing through stone buildings, tracing pathways into deep stone wells to sit quiet and hushed on stone benches, feeling the cool earth inside the hot stone village. And I wonder what became of these people. Where did they move to? And why did they leave?

I climb down into a nearby canyon. The moon offers her light to brighten my way. The wind whips the dust into tiny tornadoes. A tumbleweed whirls across my path. No water runs in the dry creek bed. Nothing green grows. Only twisted bushes cling to canyon walls. It feels like something has died here and been blown away and I want to go home.

[She picks up drum and sits on the floor in front of a fire. Sound of women's Cree and English voices.]

It was Millie who pointed me in the right direction.

Outside the wind rustles in the tree leaves. The smell of fresh pine boughs under me. The sparks and ashes from the fire drift up and out the smoke-hole of the teepee of the Moonlodge. I see my grandmothers and sisters and daughters all around me. Millie finishes her preparations and looks at me across the fire.

MILLIE: *[Offers her drum.]* Welcome, my girl. Welcome to the circle. We are grateful and thank the Higher Power that you are here.

AGNES: *[Begins to drum softly.]* I have this dream. A woman gives me a cage with a white bird in it. I don't trust her but I say, 'Thank you very much.' And I back away. I am moving so I get into my car full of my possessions and place the cage on the front seat between me and my big Indian friend. As I drive down the road the bird keeps escaping and my friend shoves it back into the cage but it keeps squeezing out between the bars and both of us are trying to keep it in. And it's growing and its wings are flapping in my face and around my head. I can't see where I'm driving! And my window is open a few inches and it grabs the window with its claws and it's the size of an albatross and its beak is out the window gasping for air. If it doesn't get enough air it's gonna die. And I freak out and stop the car. I wrap the bird in my jacket and hold it very close. Ssshhh.

[She sings same song that she fell asleep to after Powwow dancing, as lullaby which soars as lights fade to black.]

Duncan Mercredi b. 1951

INNINEW/CREE

could be anyone but i call him syd

syd smokes dope most any night he can
he'll visit acquaintances on sundays
taking the back alleys for emphasis
trying to look suspicious
no use wasting the neighborhood watch
syd used to roll drunks for a living
course most of the drunks he knew were friends
syd would feel guilty and treat them the next day
with their money
syd smokes dope most any night he can
says it don't affect him none
just can't remember what year it is
and if he's a hyphenated canadian
syd he tried going traditional once
but he thought the four day grace period
was cruel and unusual punishment
so syd went back to being catholic
only cost a few our fathers and hail marys
the rosary some one had left at some church
downtown it was syd who had gone in to warm up
was a cold bitchin' day remember last
syd he'd forget sometimes but he never forgot
where i lived
or he'd phone
then he'd stroll up the walk and i'd watch
houses around ours would suddenly wake
windows would have eyes
and syd smokes dope most any night he can
he'd turn and face the street and bow
then lift his arms to show he was unarmed
nothing had been lifted
syd didn't like being hyphenated
didn't like smoking dope
he was sorry he rolled friends
he hoped god wasn't too upset
that he asked the creator not to judge him
syd smokes dope most any night he can
doesn't anymore

he wanders the back alleys he used to live
seeking the memories he left bleeding
as they begged for mercy
crying as syd lifted the little money they had left
watching it stagger away with syd
knowing where to find tomorrow's release from demons
that appeared the same time syd did
syd smokes dope most every night he can
now he doesn't sleep
haunted by past losers crying for spare change
wondering if he knew them
syd doesn't smoke most nights now
he doesn't need to   his visions are his own now

statue

oh bent naked mis-shapen spokesman of god
with nothing to cover your shame
but half built circles to hide you from the cold
faced away from the river that gave your kookum life
now discarded by your descendants
with some ill-conceived notion of greatness
oh bastard child of the prairies
whipped and beaten by time and myth
placed on a pedestal made of leather and bones
bleached white by the prairie wind and sun
gaunt body holding grotesque head
writhing in pain
forever and ever
in mind's eye we see lies that were told
revealed now in your anguish
staring in vain at the doors in front of you
they remain closed
but one of you sits in the queen's house
shoulder to shoulder
with one like them that draped the noose around your neck
a brother of the wind
rejecting the past
as though you were pre-ordained to serve your enemies
oh discarded child of the prairies
the wind carries your message
but no one hears the agony of defeat
the weight of years lost standing naked

ridicule heavy on your twisted shoulders
insane he spoke to spirits
but we understood
oh abused man of god
the tears have not stopped
your sons have discarded the leather and tobacco
trading them for a bible and collar
that binds you to a vengeful god
leaving your children to wander for a century
still seeking their place
while hiding a part of themselves
savages
you too lived inside leather houses
you slept on buffalo robes
now the pain of rejection by two nations
is etched in your body
mis-shapen man of the prairies
you hold your head high
on a false pedestal
your circle is incomplete
what was your dream

god shrugged and turned his back

famine begets hunger distended bellies beget tears
children dance the devil's tune
blood spills and another butterfly dies
silenced rivers criss-cross by humming wires
fish float belly up
and i feel the poison in my blood
burning forests clear cuts scar the land
blue waters turn red then black
suicidal whales hit the beaches
awash in oil a bird dies
broken treaties broken bodies
money pays for guns not food
people shoot at people who could be brothers
pieces of cloth stitched together
another star's light fades from the sky
a sister lives in fear of the night
children selling bodies
for a bit of pain killer
other men decide our futures

as we stand outside the gate
watching brothers pocket their seven pieces of silver
riots death dreams rising into the sky on smoke
jesus came down to listen to the wolf sing
and found him dying
smeared on his body a message
thou shalt not kill
jesus raised his arms to the sky
and cried why hast thou forsaken me
the priest smiled his smile
as god shrugged and turned his back

big bear

i walked where big bear danced
i feel his joy in the wind
that carries his messages
from the past
i danced where big bear danced
his dance steps an imprint on the land
his face a shadow that calls to me
the wind whispering his name
i sleep where big bear sleeps
a prisoner with no walls to hold him
he remained a prisoner
so he danced in his mind
when he heard the steel doors slam
he journeyed on the breeze
that caressed him in his cell
he sang his songs in silence
i walk where big bear danced
i heard his prayer
i felt his pain
i am his anger
big bear still dances
on the ground where i walk

kiskisin (i remember)

images
like photographs
of a river
still
silent
flashing from time to time
in my mind
and just before sleep you would appear
woman
shoulders slumped in weariness
hands immersed in water
coal oil lamp
with feeble light
casting shadows
hiding tears
images
woman
silently rocking in a chair
body buried in a shawl
kookum
when no one was around
did you speak to spirits
images sounds
when ni-mama laughed
she was dancing
but those photographs are rare
images
i recall wandering into the house
my father in the kitchen
stopping me
shut out from women things
secrets
but i wanted to see
only to make me wait
till the cry
then they would pout
at the snare wire hanging on the ceiling
images
these powerful women
saying
the rabbit got away
but we caught the baby
see a girl

then they'd laugh
at my confusion
even ni-mama weakly
from the bed
covered in sweat
shoulders slumped in weariness
images
kookum
gently blowing on the baby's face
i asked why
she would say
this way she will always remember me
images
watching the land receding
ni-papa
at the rear of the boat
steering
into the waves
getting larger
i would shake
and he'd say
do not fear the lake
images
kookum gently blowing on my face
ni-mama
looking north
towards her home
she was the stranger
but i remember her gently blowing
on my daughter's face

Daniel David Moses b. 1952

DELAWARE

The Sunbather's Fear of the Moon

Now that I'm out walking alone, old Bone
face looks jealous of the blood ruddiness
of my skin. Just let her try to scrape it
away and she will see it takes more than
petty metal to get to me, she'll see

how useless a good cool staring-down is
against skin this tough and crusty. And she
should identify with that. What the pale
fool won't understand quite as easily
is that my shine's not a reflected light

because it's always noon inside my chest
where day has a home the size of a fist.
I'm flushed with the heat of its love and of
the pleasures it brings through its bright
probing fingers and tongues. It's made me so

young I can go it alone. I don't need
that shine she gives to the land so wanly
old Boneface must know it can't cut the dark,
can't make it bleed anymore than I did
by day. The bit of bright blood I shed soaked,

as her light does, into the mud. Might be
red rain subterraneously. Or stars
for the troglodytes to see. It doesn't
matter. I refuse to shatter and set.
Let Boneface put on her idiot gape.

Inukshuk

You were built from the stones,
they say, positioned
alone against the sky

here so they might take
you for something human

checking the migrations.
That's how you manage this,
standing upright despite
the blue wind that snow is,
this close to Polaris.

Still, the wind worries
you some. It's your niches
which ought to be empty.
Nothing but lichen grows
there usually. Now

they're home to dreams. Most come
from the south, a few from
further north—but what flows
out of their mouths comes from
no direction you know.

They keep singing about
the Great Blue Whale the world
is; how it swims through space
having nightmares about
hunters who only hunt

their brothers—each after
the other's snow-white face.
How beautiful frozen
flesh is! Like ivory,
like carved bone, like the light

of Polaris in hand.
So it goes on and on,
the hunting refrain. Dead
silence would be better,
the Pole star overhead.

The wind agrees, at least
wants to stop up each niche.
How long can you stand it
—that song, the cold, the stones
that no longer hold you

up now that they hold you
down? Soon the migrations
recommence. How steady
are you? Dreams, so they say,
also sing on the wing.

The Persistence of Songs

The people feed from the river and conceive songs.
But the strangers with the dead heads march towards the long
edges of their own blades. They see a thundering
fog along the horned horizon and turn around
to stalk the rising sun. They find four lanterns made
of skin arrayed along the river, the people
still feasting within. The strangers feed off their own
anger, flooding the river with blood. The four songs,
who are the children, go dumb and their white dogs mad
before the people have the strangers rounded up.

They bind them with skin from the fog and throw them in;
then, they wait for the river to heal. They try
to feast again. They pray to the children. By noon
the river grows an old skin and the children fade.
In the cold mud the strangers congeal. A fog
bleeds from the river, drowns the lanterns and stops up
the ears of the people with a dull, three-note song.
The strangers are praising honed edges and the white
meat of their own bodies. They curse the sun and vow
the moon turns so perfectly round they will square it.

They lurch up through the river's dull skin and begin
the marching again. The people search in the skin
for reflected light, the sunset or a lantern,
then assume the skin as mourning. The procession
the people enter tracks the moon through fog, cuts it
into quarters. And black dogs track the procession.
They feed off their own hunger and conceive a song
in praise of a perfect horizon made of meat.
That song fades; but, the four songs, who are the children,
return with horned heads. They feed from ears and edges.

The Line

This is not the poem, this line
I'm feeding you. And the thought
that this line is not the poem
is not it either. Instead
the thought of what this line is
not is the weight that sinks it
in. And though this image of
that thought as a weight is quite
a neat figure of speech, you
know what it's not—though it did
this time let the line smoothly
arc to this spot, and now lets
it reach down to one other,
one further rhyme—the music
of which almost does measure
up, the way it keeps the line
stirring through the dampening
air. Oh, you know you can hear
the lure in that. As you know
you've known from the start the self
referring this line's doing
was a hook—a sharp, twisted
bit of wit that made you look
and see how clear it is no
part of this line or its gear
could be the poem. Still it cast
and kept the line reeling out
till now at last the hook's on
to itself and about to
tie this line I'm feeding you
up with a knot. Referring
to itself has got the line
and us nowhere. So clever's
not what the poem is about
either. We're left hanging there
while something like a snout starts
nudging at your ear, nibbling
near my mouth—and it's likely
it's the poem about to take
the bait. From the inside ought
to be a great way to learn
what the poem is. And we'll use
this line when the poem's drawn it

taut and fine as breath to tell
what we know, where we are and
where we'll go—unless the line
breaks. How would it feel, knowing,
at last, what the poem really
is, to lack the line to speak?

Cry

a chorale

Someone is crying in the woods.

Someone is crying.

Can you hear it? Can you hear that high, almost animal note?

What makes a throat that tight?

What makes that note go on and on?

Is that what you call *keening*?

—meaning *loss*. Loss.

What could be lost in these woods?

What could be gone?

I mean other than us, here in these walls of logs, holding each other close to the fire.

I mean other than you there in the city.

You're not the one who's crying.

Neither am I.

The cry in our ears comes from out there.

Out there in the woods.

Out there in the winter.

The bare trees.

The crusted snow.

The sun so pale and low that the moon throws more light on the trails

Throws more light on the wails?

No, neither you nor I could cry like that, could weep.

What could be lost in those woods?

What could be gone?

That note goes on and on and keeps me from sleep

and I wonder if someone young or old, beautiful or beloved, has been separated from the family.

Is that why the cry wanders aimlessly among the trees,

looking under logs, into thickets, for fallen bodies,

a child,

a grandmother?

A child sings a song, in its own crying, about what is to come.

I know that's true, even though you and I lie here together, intent upon the silence and the crying in the woods.

I have heard children cry.

And I was once a child myself, a while ago.

I know I'm not supposed to know that.

I know that we're lost, holding each other close.

And I don't really know it, do I?

It's only something I hear underneath that note that goes on and on.

It's only a dream,

a hallucination.

Hold me close as I listen to that voice.

Hold me tight.

Let me feel you, muscles and skin, heart and breath.

Be real for me.

Real.

Or maybe what I don't really feel, don't really know underneath that voice, is an old woman, that grandmother, gone off into the cold night, intent upon finding her own end, or then again merely distracted unto death.

There is, in her breathing that has gone on so long, ninety some years, something I want to know.

I am so sentimental.

It is an old story, an old song, a voice I know no longer belongs in this world.

An old woman who has seen so much cannot be in touch with what's happening now.

She even knew that.

She even believed it's best left unsaid.

My life? What do you want to know about my life for? My life doesn't matter. I'm just an old woman. If you knew what I know it would only get you into trouble. It won't do you any good, grandchild.

And of course, perhaps she smiled, leaving us here in these walls.

Whoever it is, is lost, does not belong to us.

We know where we are, here by the fire, away from the cold.

It is not our child who is lost.

It is not our grandmother who is old.

We would know if it were. We would know.

We know those people so well.

We have their pictures.

We have their papers.

We know what their stories are.

We will get a letter later.

Or make a visit on a holiday.

We will hear their voices then.

Their voices are not like that one.

To whom does it belong, that crying in the woods?

That note that goes on and on in our ears?

Are there fallen bodies under logs, in the thickets?

This high, almost animal note—why won't it go away?

Why won't it die?

Why does it have to stay here in my ears?

What is it that keeps it there in the trees?

What can live in a winter that cold?

Can you tell me? Can you?

What doth thrive in that dark?

I'm afraid of sleep, with that note in my ears.

I'm afraid of nightmares.

I'm afraid of snow, blowing into the shapes of bodies.

I'm afraid of that note, blowing the snow.

I'm afraid of the snow, blowing away, leaving bones.

And you thought they were birch trees!

Hip bones here, thigh bones there, wish bone, wish bone, anywhere.

The eternally hopeful grin of a skull.

It's hunger. Hunger's out there.

That's where that note comes from.

Hunger so great, it has eaten the meat off the fallen bodies.

It has eaten its own hungry meat off its own hungry bones.

And is still not satisfied.

A stomach consuming itself. Ulcer.

It has died of hunger and it cannot rest.

It is a ghost, a demon of hunger.

It is frost.

It carries icicles for knives and it is not alone as it waits for us.

The edges of snowflakes.

It waits for us to come outside.

They also are sharp.

It knows we will.

And now even the frost bites.

It waits for us to gather wood.

On and on it goes.

It knows we need to eat. It knows it well.

It is not alone.

It waits for us to come out for food.

It is not alone.

How much will we take?

It waits with the trees.

They mistake us for the winter.

They mistake us for the cold.

Each tree shivers in the wind, sheltering the dead of a family.

We have eaten the meat off their bones.

The grandmother's eyes.

The child's fingers.

No.

That's why we are alone here.

No no no no.

Why there is no crying in the woods.

No.

No one is crying in the woods.

No one.

Listen. You can hear it, can't you?

The silence.

The silence.

THE END

Hotel Centrale, Rotterdam

I am awake between stiff
sheets tonight in room thirty
four, listening to the heat

tick through the radiator,
seeing a television

pour out news of the war,
the war in the air, the war
in the Gulf. The walls vibrate
with video light. This is
no room for sleep anymore.

There is no room for dreams.
The shooting stars on the screen
are as real as a rain
of fire can be, falling
on some other city. And

here I have a star's eye view
—the glide toward the intended
target, the blink of a bridge
into nothing. Do I want
to see that again? I do.

Who am I now? Where? I want
to be in that blue leather
armchair down in the lobby,
talking with the people there
about the stories we're in

this city to tell. But now
they're using their several
tongues to question the news and
I want none of that, want not
to fall for it again. I

am trying to fall asleep.
Those people keep on asking
all night through. *Where are the wives?*
How much is lost? Just what is
the story? In that, a small

glory—like that glow, say, down
below, as my overnight
flight ended, a greenhouse bright
as day, a dream suspended
in the blue and frost of dawn.

Report on Her Remains

The Micmac woman's body has been disinterred and her
severed hands are being transported by air for identification
in Washington. In a refrigerated drawer in South Dakota a
thirty eight caliber bullet floats, an icy glimmer within her
skull. A similar glimmer comes off her fingernails. In the
box passing above the Mississippi her hands are rustling,
the nails growing, the fingers unfolding, refolding, pale
wings migrating toward the Atlantic.

Her body sleeps the sleep of the abandoned. Its marrow
refuses to condense. Her blood searches for the pine ridge
under which the shallow grave is. It finds only turquoise left
over from the last wind and leather so softly cured it wel-
comes starlight through. The leather's stained with sweat
and semen, but even these relics fade.

Her hands remember only the last jet of breath, the warm
gun butt, and the dream of power. They try to dream it
again, the dream of black soil flooding and drowning the
prairie, of the sky clearing with light like the shine of warm
blood, of the woman perching on the palm of a flying stone.
But that dream imploded when the woman died. Through
their own glimmer her hands dream the remnants, dream of
men with no faces swimming a storm of hot powder; their
heads oiled and hands sharp as shovels, they dig up and
burn the Dead to ash in the steely air.

Through the sinking light her body feels a sound. Her
hands have escaped the box and her bones the wrappings of
skin. They swing on their tendons, chiming.

Some Grand River Blues

Look. The land ends up
in stubble every
October. The sky
today may feel as

empty. But just be
like the river—bend

and reflect it. Those
blues already show

through the skin inside
your elbow—and flow
back to the heart. Why
let a few passing

Canada geese up
set you? Just remind
yourself how the land
also renews. Don't

despair just because
they're already too
high to hear. Your heart
started beating with

their wings the moment
you got sight of them
—but that's no reason
to fear it will still

when they disappear.
Look away now. Let
loose. See? The river's
bending like a bruise.

Party Favour

When you bared your china
coloured shoulder, telling

the whole room how a steel
pin had been popped in, how

thin a feel the air had
then, the naked scar blushed

deep enough to kiss. It
seemed the only part of

you in the smoky mix
of your party to keep

up modesty, a mouth
shaped spot holding shut while

the rest of your flesh spoke
out, dancing loudly and

alone in the middle
of the room. Only at

the end of the night were
you quiet, did that spot

seem to speak through the kiss
on the cheek and embrace

each of the last few to
take leave of you received.

Descending to the slick
street where flooded gutters

and darkness chilled my feet
and music and an orange

glow seeped out of your bay
window—I thought it had

a magic lantern sort
of look—I felt how close

in those inebriate
hours comradery

came to love. As close as
healing did to your wound.

Ruby Slipperjack b. 1952

OJIBWA

Blueberry Days

SUMMER 1962

I stretch out with a big yawn and wriggle my toes. Tony shoves an elbow in my face. Jane throws a leg over me and I lay still while I unclasp a safety pin off my sweater. Slowly, I press the pin against Jane's skin above her knee until she pulls her leg away and turns over. Maggie's snoring softly on the other side of Tony.

I lift my head. We're laying like driftwood on a colourful rocky shore, our blankets have been long since kicked off. I smell wood smoke and fresh air comes through the open door. Dogs are barking somewhere and flies are buzzing around inside the house. Everyone's still asleep. I shall be the first one up again this morning. Mom is very happy in the mornings when everything is quiet. I like it best when there are just the two of us by the fire. Sometimes, Mom leaves in the canoe to check our fishnet and comes back before anyone is up. She likes to sneak off by herself in the early morning.

I'm hungry. I can't smell what's sizzling out there but it sure sounds good. Slowly, I climb over Jane and onto the floor. From the half dozen pairs of socks on the floor I pull on a pair and slip into a pair of running shoes. I run out the door; three steps and off the open porch, barely making it over the dog's head, and off to the outhouse. The outhouse stands about fifty yards in the bushes behind the cabin. What's that noise? Scratching. I peer around the corner of the outhouse. There's a dog digging behind the toilet. I grab a stick and throw it at him. 'Get out of here. Go away!' I watch him slink off into the bushes.

Coming out at a run, I pause to listen to a bird chirping in the bushes beside me, 'Cee-oh-dee, cee-oh-dee.'

I ask, 'C.O.D.? What did you order in the catalogue, silly bird?' I run back behind the cabin, past Mom who kneels beside the cooking fire. I grab a towel and soap from the block of wood and skip over the stepping stones to my special rock to wash my face by the lake. My rock shifts to one side but I know it well. Maggie tried to get my rock one morning. She went off balance when it moved and then, splash, into the water. I laughed for days.

I breathe in the fresh air and hold my face to the warm sun. Oh, it smells so good. The water glistens and sparkles in the sunlight. Today is going to be a nice day again. I hop back onto the grass and drop the towel and soap back on the wood for the next person. I flop down beside Mom. She breaks off a piece of hot soft bannock, puts in a couple of pieces of salt pork she has fried, and hands it to me. Then she hands me another piece of bannock with butter and jam on it.

The flies are driving Mom crazy. She swats them and covers up the food. She also keeps a long stick beside her to keep the dogs away. They wiggle and crawl close to her, hoping for a taste of the morning meal. Jumbo, the black pup, had a long, long tail, until we decided he'd go crazy in the head if it were left that long. So we chopped off about six inches. It's stubby at the end now, but decent in length. The beige female by the door is very gentle. She used to be my father's favourite lead sled dog. She's Jumbo's mother. Her name is Rosiak. They're loose because the flies would get at them if we left them tied up and they're also a lot cleaner now. They can roll in the grass and swim and splash in the water with us. Like us, they get a dose of mosquito repellent around their ears.

Raised voices break out in the house. Mom sighs. Annie and Vera are up and at it again. I wonder if they fight like that when they're not home? Seems like a long time ago since we got out of school for the summer. I miss school. I miss the smell of crayons, paper, plasticine. Mom pokes me, 'Gee, you're always daydreaming! Go get the pan of water I asked you to get.'

In the cabin I watch Annie while I grab the pan from under the water pail shelf by the door. I fill it up from the lake and put it over the dying fire. It will be warm by the time everyone's finished eating. By now, the others are coming out of the house, racing for the outhouse. I smile. I won't be waiting in line this morning.

I sit again with my back comfortably against the tree, knees up. Jumbo comes over and licks my face. Eesh. His tail practically throws his whole back end from side to side. He's going to lose another couple of inches if he's not careful. 'Hey Mom, I heard a bird this morning saying, "C.O.D., C.O.D." He thinks he ordered a C.O.D. from the catalogue,' I giggle.

Mom says, 'Well, I hope he realizes he has to pay for it before he can take it home.'

I laugh again. Annie comes running from the outhouse and asks, 'What are you laughing at?'

Mom answers, 'Oh, about a bird that ordered a C.O.D.'

Annie gives me a look that says I'm strange, shakes her head as she picks up the towel and soap.

Mom and Barbara are cleaning up inside the cabin and the quilts and blankets are already hung on the hanging pole behind the cabin for airing. I jump up and run inside. Mom is packing our lunch in a cardboard box while Barbara fills another box with cups, mugs, and cans. We're going to the portage about three miles away to go blueberry picking. I carry things to the lake where Barbara and Vera have already turned the canoe over and lowered it into the water. Boy, that canoe looks great. A fresh coat of green paint. Mom worked on that last week. I wish I could ride in that canoe, but I usually walk on the railway tracks with the others every time we go to the big portage.

Finally, everyone's ready. The door's locked and I watch them get in the canoe. Barbara gets in, then Cora, Brian, Tony, and Annie. Vera smiles at me, 'All right, get in. I'll walk this time.'

I glance at Mom. She nods. I step into the canoe and sit down beside Annie. She is absorbed in folding her soft, delicate turquoise scarf on her knee. I reach over and touch the material before she tucks the scarf into her pocket. This is my first canoe ride this summer.

Mom gets in and pushes the canoe away. We wave to the others on shore. I know exactly what Mom will say next because she always says the same thing: don't run on the railway tracks and watch out for the trains. Then we paddle away. The water is sparkling and dancing in the sun.

With me paddling in the middle, Mom at the front, and Barbara at the back, we glide across the water pretty fast. I love the feel of water against my paddle and get into the rhythm of pushing the whirlpools created by Mom's paddle. I daydream while I paddle. The pains in my arms come and go in waves but I know if I slack off, I would get a poke from behind. Seagulls circle gracefully above; they screech occasionally. It is so quiet on the lake that we can still hear noises from the village we're leaving behind.

Cora, who's about three years old, sleeps at Barbara's feet behind me. Brian sits in front of Annie and drags a triangular-shaped board for a boat. Tony sits behind Mom. Mom has that thick scarf over her head again. I don't know how she can stand the heat with that thing on. Once in a while Mom remarks on the beaver-chewed poplar sticks that drift along the shoreline or points out a dry tree that would be good firewood in the fall.

We have left the third island behind us now so we should be there soon. There's the point now. A breeze is coming up too. I hope the waves aren't too high by the time we come back. Well I'll be walking home with Jane and Maggie anyway.

Finally, we slow down at the channel going into the portage. We're going to check our fishnet first. I rest my arms while they manoeuvre the canoe for Mom to fish the net cord up with her paddle. Mom pulls us along the net, lifting it to view the width. There's a good sized pike, some suckers, and two pickerel. Mom is good at taking the fish out of the tangled net. She drops the end of the net back into the water and I watch it sink down in a straight line.

We start paddling again, softly this time, into the marshy bay where the portage is. The water lilies are so beautiful. As we pass by, the yellow and white flowers among the lily pads bob in the slight waves. I can smell perfume.

Silently, we check out each hidden bay and dark shadow. This is a moose-feeding area and there are always lots of moose tracks here.

Finally, we come to the end of the long bay to the portage and there's Jumbo, in a whirl of tail and excitement, prancing about.

Vera and Jane emerge from the bush to pull our canoe in. I step out of the canoe and hold it for Annie to step out. We run up the pathway to join Maggie in the shade on the soft moss. Mom calls us for tea and to hand out our containers for the blueberries.

After much shoving and pushing and squeals of laughter, we amble toward the railway tracks where the berries hang in thick clumps. The heat shimmers off the steel tracks. It is very hot here. I can feel the sweat on my neck already.

I step carefully around the bushes and rocks. On blueberry picking days at least two snakes will get their heads bashed in. The paddle for that job is brought up with the bucket for the berries. Sure enough, a yell and commotion on the other side of the tracks, 'There. There it goes!' Maggie is yelling as everyone runs to help. Barbara has the paddle. I sink behind the bush, hoping no one will notice I'm not around. I don't understand why the sight of a snake could be such a bad omen that it has to be killed immediately to ward off the bad luck. I continue picking. Last summer, I'd made the mistake of saying that I had almost stepped on a snake at the corner of the cabin. Everyone stared at me, then dashed out the door. Later, I heard them yell. I felt awful. I saw them carry the dead snake at the end of a stick and throw it into the camp fire. Afterwards, every time I went near the fire, I kept thinking that I might see the bones of the snake, or, perhaps, the head with eyes if it didn't burn. I shudder. It's not that I love snakes but killing them like that because they're messengers of the devil is scary.

It's so hot and that sun just beats down on my head. I've been daydreaming again and my cup is only half full. The other girls are already dumping theirs into the large bucket that Mom and Barbara keep in the shade. Vera drops a handful of berries into my cup as she passes. I like Vera. Her shiny, curly, brown hair is so beautiful in the sun. I didn't comb my long, straight, black hair this morning.

I kick at an anthill to see how fast the ants will scatter. I remember the day Barbara, Vera, and Annie came home laughing after they had gone blueberry picking along the tracks. Railroad section men in a motor car had stopped to chat and Annie stepped on an anthill while they were talking. Next thing she knew, she had ants up her pants. 'What's the matter?' one of the men asked. Then, trying to be helpful, he advised, 'Take your pants off and give it a shake!' Yeah, right.

I'm hungry. It seems like hours and my neck is stiff. I've filled my cup so many times, I've lost count. Mom is very pleased and Barbara hasn't even said anything. I can see smoke and hear pots banging. They're making lunch by the lake on the other side of the railway tracks. That's the camping end of the portage. It's too swampy on this side. I hope we can swim before we eat. I see the others drift towards the fire. I'm done.

Mom smiles at me when I empty my cup and head for the lake. I'm thirsty more than anything else. A train's coming, the third one since we've been here. The men in the caboose always wave at us when they go by. Must be nice to ride in a train all day.

The girls are jumping off the boulder to my left. I drop my cup, kick off my runners, and flop into the water. Clothes and all, of course. We never bother taking off our clothes when we go swimming on blueberry-picking days. We take off our underthings and wash them and the clothes on us at the same time, while we're in the water. Also, we scrub our hair. That, I don't like. When my long hair gets wet, I have a big clump of pulled-out hair by the time Mom combs out the tangles. In a little while, the clothes we're not wearing are hung up to dry. The rest dries on us, keeping us cool until the sun has us dry and hot again.

The girls are still in the water, swimming with bloated tops on the back of their necks. Jane looks like a humpbacked muskrat. I'm always afraid a bloodsucker might get into my blouse. Barbara comes down to the lake, yelling, 'Tony, Brian, come out now!' The boys scramble up the sloping rock, one brown body, one white. Their pants are piled on a rock with their shoes and shirts. They're not allowed to get their jeans wet, they take too long to dry. I pull myself out of the water. Lunch is ready and we all troop to the fire, dripping wet and splashing each other.

Hot bannock, fried slices of bologna, and a cup of tea. And, of course, blueberry jam for bannock dunking. After a while we are smiling with blue teeth, black mouths, and sparkling eyes, laughing at each other. We head back up the trail with our containers. We have already wandered half a mile to get the best berries. Jumbo follows me. He moves from shade to shade at each place I stop, but then he wanders off. I've been here for quite a while. I'll look for a different spot. It's quite rocky here, so I think I'll go across the tracks to where Mom is. More shade there.

As I come around a clump of bush, Jane looks up with a smile. 'You going across?' she asks.

'Yep,' I answer and hop onto the rock where she had her foot. Her other foot is on a small boulder a couple of feet away. She squats with her dress tucked under each knee, picking the berries with one hand and holding her cup with the other. Does she even notice the huge mound of anthill directly behind her? Each time she rocks back on her heels to look up at me, her behind gets closer to it. I point to the anthill. 'You're trying not to step on that?'

She glances behind and says, 'That's an anthill. Some ants are black and some are small. Some can be quite big too.'

I nod, not quite sure about the conversation, and jump onto another rock, going around her.

Jumbo's tail sticks out wagging from behind a rock. Sure enough, a chipmunk chatters and scampers onto the rock above Jane. It turns to give Jumbo a parting shot before it plunges into the thick weeds and grass in front of Jane.

Well, nothing could have saved that girl! Jumbo comes sailing over that rock with large, flopping ears, looking like a giant, black, ugly bird. He pounces on the ground in front of Jane. Jane gasps, waves her arms to get her balance. She looks like she's trying to fly. Then she grabs a branch and thinks she's safe. Jumbo's back end whips around and smacks her across the face with what's left of his tail. Almost in slow motion, Jane sinks down right in the middle of that anthill. Then she comes to life! She shoots out of that anthill. Some of the ants probably land on the nearby trees, as she flails away at her dress. Bounding and panting, Jumbo passes me and heads down the hill. I can't remember if Jane has made any noise the whole time. I disappear behind a boulder and stumble to the tracks with my chest and throat bursting. There, I finally clamp my mouth with both hands and let my laughter out of my chest like a deflating balloon.

I had learned how to keep from laughing when I had been caught in situations where I couldn't laugh. Like the time our storekeeper served each customer with a smile, despite the fact that one eye was almost swollen shut from a mosquito bite. For me, that was torture. Mom's expression never changed. Or there was the time our minister gave a sermon from his open Bible, held upside down for quite a long time before he noticed it. Again, for me, that was murder. Mom's expression never changed. Then there was the time at church and that John, one of the elder men, was a little tipsy and he toppled over backwards, chair and all, and went down with a mighty crash. All we could see were his feet sticking up. Oh, I would have died then, if I hadn't noticed that Mom was silently shaking with laughter, too.

I'm getting tired. I seem to be by myself, too. I don't see anyone anywhere. I don't like to be alone . . . I start thinking about bears. I've filled my cup. I'd better go. I see a snake and jump so fast I stagger and slip down the slope. My feet finally come to rest on the gravel beside the railway tracks. My cup tumbles down the slope. I almost cry when I see the empty cup at my feet. Mom is standing on top of the ridge about ten yards from where I was.

'What's the matter? Are you okay?' she asks.

I nod my head. She has been there all this time. I stand there blinking away my tears.

'Once,' she says, looking at me, 'Wess could fill his cup every two minutes, 'til one day, he tripped in front of me and out rolled a wad of moss he had been using to stuff his cup over halfway full.'

I started to laugh, and she turns away to continue with her picking.

The rest of the afternoon goes quickly. Toward evening, we drift back to the fire. Supper smells delicious—fried fish with onions, mashed potatoes, canned corn, and, of course, the hot bannock and blueberry jam washed down with camp-fire tea. We talk and laugh with our backs against the trees. Mom is telling a story again. The horseflies bite and drive us crazy because they fly around and around and around our heads. Too bad they don't get dizzy and crash into trees and things. I smile at the thought and then see Barbara glaring at me. Whatever Mom had been saying wasn't supposed to be funny. I put my head down and concentrate on finishing my supper.

After supper, Vera and I wash the dishes by the lake, while Jane and Maggie dry them. It's nice to be with Vera. She is always laughing. We begin carrying our things back to the other side of the tracks, down the portage path to the canoe. Rosiak has just emerged from the shade beside the canoe, yawning and stretching, licking her chops. The bay is absolutely calm. With the birds twirping and flies buzzing, it is so peaceful. 'Get out of the way, will you?' Barbara marches by me with her arms stretched down by buckets full of berries.

I'm so tired after my full meal, I hate the thought of walking the three miles back home. But at least my arms won't feel like they're falling off; only my legs will.

Finally, we push the canoe away from the shore. Jane, Maggie, and I, with Jumbo and Rosiak, straggle back up the path. Then, Jane pipes up, 'Hey, let's see if we can get there before they do! It's not so hot now.'

So, we walk and run for the first mile through two rock cuts. One more to go. Then just around the bend, we'll be at the edge of the village.

It seems like ages that we've been walking. Another train's coming. The dogs won't waste any time getting off the tracks. I hope it's not a cattle train . . . they stink. We wait by the shade of a large pine tree. A small path runs through here. This is called the 'little portage' but it's a miserable looking place at each end.

The train whistle is loud. We turn our faces to the wind as the train rattles by. Again, we wave to the man in the caboose.

After the last half mile, we take the path that leads to our cabin by the lake. The dogs are already gone, probably fast asleep by the doorstep by now. We run all the way to the cabin. There, the dogs are lying in the shade of the tree. Jumbo is cleaning his paws; good idea, he's got tar on them. He'll get clobbered for sure if he puts one dirty paw on our wood floor.

There's the canoe, with paddles flashing in the evening sun. The lake is very still and smooth, like a huge mirror. We splash water on our faces while we sit by the lake. I lean back onto the cool grass to catch my breath.

We'll all have a good sleep tonight. Tomorrow, we'll be going to the general store to trade in our berries. I hope Mom buys bananas and tomorrow is Wednesday, the day the way-freight comes to unload groceries for the general store. I lay on the grass with my eyes closed, smelling the earth and wild flowers beside me.

Louise Halfe b. 1953

CREE

Pāhkahkos

Flying Skeleton
I used to wonder where
You kept yourself.
I'd hear you rattle about
Scraping your bones

I opened a door
You grinned at me
Your hollow mouth
Stared through my heart
With empty eyes.

You lifted your boney hands
To greet me and I
Ran without a tongue.

You jumped on my back
Clinging to my neck you hugged
My mound of flesh.

For a thousand years you were
The heavy bones
The companions who would not leave.

You knocked your skull
On my head
I felt your boney feet.
I dragged and dragged
I couldn't carry
Your burden more.
I pried you loose
Bone after bone.

We stood, skull to face
Pāhkahkos, your many bones
Exposed
I, lighter than I could stand.

I fed you the drink of healing
You ran skeleton fingers
Down your face and onto mine.

I gave you a prayer cloth
I wove a blanket of forgiveness
You covered us both, skeleton and flesh.

I gave you the smoke of truth
You lit your Pipe to life
You lifted it to your ghostly mouth,
To mine.

My *Pāhkahkos* companion,
My dancing Skeleton
My dancing friend.

We carry our bundles
Side by side
Bones and flesh.

She Told Me

She always told me
to take a willow branch
and gently whip the spirits
out of the house
calling, calling

Āstam we are leaving
āstam do not stay.

She always told me
to put the food away at night
to cover the dishes
or the spirits
would crackle and dance
whistle in our ears
and drive us mad.

I obeyed.

She always told me
never to eat the guts of
animals while I was pregnant
or the baby would be born
with a rope around the neck.

I yearned for the guts.

She always told me
never to walk over men
while I was in my moon
or they would die from my power.

I thought that was the idea.

She always told me
that *Nōhkom*, the medicine bag
had given her three cigarettes.
That's why the lizards
walked around inside her head.

I watched the flicker of her tongue.

Body Politics

Mama said,

Real woman
don't steal
from the sky and wear clouds
on their eyelids.

Real woman
eat rabbit well-done
not left half-raw
on their mouth.

Real woman
have lots of meat
on their bones.
They're not starving,
hobbled horses
with bony, grinding hips.

Real woman caress
with featherstone hands
not with falcon fingernails
that have never worked.

When she was finished talking
she clicked her teeth
lifted her arse
and farted
at the passing
city women.

Fog Inside Mama

I'm going to take you home, Mama.

Yes, to that log shack where Papa skinned beaver
on the dirt floor.

The grass is tall. There'll be lots of mosquitoes.

Yes, Mama, the old fridge is still there and no, there's no
lightning going through to make it breathe.

The windows are broken and the barn swallows have built
their nest where the stovepipe used to smoke.

Oh Mama don't, Papa hasn't walked on that land, not for
years. Not since the last time he crushed your ribs on that
fridge.

He's on skid row somewhere.

It's safe. All we have are the old ghosts drifting
through the clouds of our heads.

Yes, Mama. I remember the tadpoles from the slough swishing
inside my red fireman's boots. They were my favorite boots.
I slept in them, I never took them off till those little
swimming snakes squished inside.

Your bones are tired and I can't find the road. I've got a
fly in my eye and it's making the rain fall from my nose.

Yes, I remember the lard pail hanging from my stomach
with a belt of twine. I'd pick so fast trying to beat Papa,
the berries drummed. Only
I never won. Papa, he picked twigs and bugs and insisted that
he had won the race.

What was that Mama?

Oh yeah, for school I had your bannock and fried rabbit.
I'd eat it *kīmōc* in the bathroom so the white kids
wouldn't laugh at me. Oh, it was good. So good.

You want some tea and a cigarette?

Yes, we're almost there.

I can see the old shack, the outhouse, the chicken coop,
the jalopy.

Yes, Mama we're going home. No more hiding.

Stones

Men
day hang dere balls
all over da place.

what I didn't no
is day
whack dem
fundle dem
squeeze dem
dalk to dem
whisper to dem
scream at dem
beg dem
pray to dem
g ah sh
even
swear at dem

I no dese
cuz I followed dem

at dat place
where day use ghost berries
nd buff alow sticks
nd play in da
buff a low mud
nd day use dat
stick
nd whack dem
berries
into
dem
gopher holes

dere all ways drying
to put dem
dere balls everywhere
why
I evin saw dem
at dem dere
dinner dables
coloured balls
wit a big long broom
boking,
rolling,
nd smacking dem
all together
into
six holes
in dat dable.

g ah sh
wit all dat whacking
day shoold of come
a long dime ago
nd be satisfied.

but no
dere still
jiggling dem
between dere legs
drying to find
different hole
to put dem in.

dem balls by now

should be so heavee
day make dere walk
hard
liddle bit
like dem
African elephants
I saw on
DV

Idylwyld Crow

Rushing home
into the dark
I drive by
a moving scarecrow.

Red cap
perched on
grey corn-husk hair
toothless mouth
jutting jaw.

Can't help but stop
and offer her a ride.
In broken English
she tells me she lives in
Kilburn.

Pulls out her blue
hospital card with
her address
explaining all the while

She's been out
buying the cheapest
stale bread in town
somewhere in Idylwyld.

A Saulteaux,
a dark crow,
feeding her children
crumbs in the city light.

My Ledders

dear pope
i no, i no, you dired of my ledders
i couldn't let dis one go
i dought you could do somedin 'bout it.
years ago you stopped *nōhkom* and *nimosōm*
from prayin in da sweatlodge and sundance,
drummin, singin and dancin.
you even stopped dem from Indian speakin
and storydellin.
well you must have some kind of bower
cuz da govment sure listen.

well, pope
last night on DV
i watched some whitemen
sweat in da lodge, and at
dinner dime on da radio
i heard dat man dell us
dat some darafist was havin a retreat
and to register.
what dat mean, i not sure
anyway he is buildin' a sweatlodge.
i never hear anybody before on da radio
dell da whole world dat.
i sure suprise and kinda made me mad.

i wonder if you could dell da govment
to make dem laws dat stop dat
whiteman from dakin our *isistāwina*
cuz i dell you pope
i don't dink you like it
if i dook you
gold cup and wine
pass it 'round our circles
cuz i don't have you drainin
from doze schools.
i haven't married you jeesuz
and i don't kneel to him,
cuz he ain't my god.

dese men, pope, don't know what
tobacco mean, what suffer mean,

alls dey no is you jeesuz die for dem
dey don't no what fastin' mean
dey jist dake and gobble our *mātotsān*
as if dey own it.
dey don't no what it mean to dake
from da earth and give somedin' back
i so dired of all dis *kimoti*, pope
deach your children.
eat your jeezuz body.
drink his blood.
dell dem to go back to dere own deachings,
pope.

for Omeasoo

I lift my wrist
suck out marrow
blow into my daughter.
I spoon the spill
into her lips.

I lift my mother's finger,
add *Nōhkom*'s ashes,
and stir.

My daughter dances
a leaf twirling
on the wind.

She blows the baritone
a gosling calling,
Kīwētinohk.
She delivers
dried meat and croissants
to *Nōhkomāk.*

She is a rainbow,
the give-away feast
of our blood.
She bleeds.

The Heat of My Grandmothers

The old man calls my *Nōhkomāk*
a bunch of bitches, *pisikwātisiw.*

Yes, I took painted warriors:
molded their sinew thighs,
into my flesh.
Our spirits moaned, laughing between
teepee poles reaching the heavens,
stars leaping against the breathing hide.

I was fourteen winters when I was told
my first husband was the elder's choice.
That winter in our teepee
the smoke couldn't hide
the fragrance
of muskeg tea
and juniper
we mixed between our bodies.
The second winter two calves
dropped to the earth.

My first husband's bones
I found beneath the autumn buffalo,
his arrows in the meat. My moccasins heavy,
I swayed the roundness of my body
wailed till the buffalo sweat
melted his skin into
the prairie grass.

My second husband of three winters
I received at a give-away between
the Blackfoot and Cree. He kissed
the valleys of my buttocks, licked
the paths of my swollen breast. He,
antelope of clouds. I,
wider than his open mouth.

I found him after a skirmish with
the white meat, a bullet between his eyes.
I was winter in my spring. My braids
greyer than the passing snow. I called
magpie, crow, and raven to clean
his body cradled in the trees.

My third husband took my calves and
gave them to the black robes. His
eyes bluer than mountain rivers, hands
took half the hide I made for travois. He'd
flicker his eyelashes; Monarchs in my sleep,
while I dreamt of babies hungry and
frightened behind cold fences.

Ten babies. Six of prairie blood, four
of meeting rivers. A beaded rainbow,
each child suckled by my wind-bitten nipples
their fathers loved.

Monique Mojica b. 1954

KUNA/RAPPAHANNOCK

From *Princess Pocahontas and the Blue Spots*

[Alejandra enters as beauty pageant host.]

HOST: Good evening, ladies and gentlemen, and children of all ages, and welcome to the 498th annual—count them, that's nearly 500 years of the
North American Indian Beauty Pageant. This is George Pepe Flaco
Columbus Cartier da Gama Smith, but you can call me Bob, coming to
you live from the Indian Princess Hall of Fame. *[Crosses centre.]* Our first
contestant in the Miss North American Indian Beauty Pageant, from her
home in the deep green forest on the other side of the mountain, by the
shores of the silver sea—Princess Buttered-on-Both-Sides!!

*[Host begins to 'oooo' the first line from the 'Indian Love Call' which is
echoed by Princess Buttered-on-Both-Sides as she enters dressed in a white
'buckskin' dress and carrying an oversized ear of corn.]*
*[As she weaves through the audience she offers them handfuls of Cornnuts
(from the plastic bag she bought them in).]*

PRINCESS B: Corn . . . Corn . . . Corn . . . Corn . . . *[The music is a mixture of
Hollywood 'tom-toms', the 'Indian Love Call', 'The good, the bad and the
ugly', and the 'Mazola' commercial.]*
PRINCESS B: *[To audience.]* Excuse me, which way is east? *[After a member
of the audience answers.]* Many, many thanks.

*[Princess Buttered-on-Both-Sides tosses Cornnuts to the four directions and
places her ear to the earth, then rises, arms and face lifted to the heavens.]*

PRINCESS B: *[Pointing to the ear of corn.]* Corn. *[Pointing to herself.]* Maid-
en. For the talent segment of the Miss North American Indian Beauty
Pageant, I shall dance for you in savage splendour the dance of the sacri-
ficial corn maiden, and proceed to hurl myself over the precipice all for
the loss of my one true love, CAPTAIN JOHN WHITEMAN. *[Swoons.]*

*[Music starts up—the corn celebration production number from the movie
Rose Marie played on pan pipes with vocalized cartoon sound effects.
Princess Buttered-on-Both-Sides performs a Hollywood 'Injun dance'.]*

PRINCESS B: *[Teetering on the edge of the 'precipice' or stage.]* OH, that's
Niagara Falls down there, but I just can't live without him! *[Teeters but is
saved by the music beginning again. Princess Buttered-on-Both-Sides
dances again, removes the buckskin dress and runs to the edge of the
precipice once more. She jumps.]* GERONIMOOOOOOOOO!!!!!

* * *

PRINCESS B: Live from Tee Pee Town, it's Princess Pocahontas and the Blue Spots!

ALEJANDRA: *[As the 'Blue Spots'.]* Shoo bee, doo bee, wa!

MONIQUE: *[À la Marilyn Monroe.]* Way ya hiya! *[Princess descends pyramid and they sing.]*

MONIQUE: *[Singing with a drawling Country and Western feel.]*

> Captain Whiteman, I would pledge my life to you
> Captain Whiteman, I would defy my father too.
> I pledge to aid and to save,
> I'll protect you to my grave.
> Oh Captain Whiteman, you're the cheese in my fondue.

> Captain Whiteman, for you I will convert,
> Captain Whiteman, all my pagan gods are dirt.
> If I'm savage don't despise me,
> 'Cause I'll let you civilize me.
> Oh Captain Whiteman, I'm your buckskin-clad dessert.

> Although you may be hairy,
> I love you so-oo,
> You're the cutest guy I'll ever see.
> You smell a little funny,
> But don't you worry, honey,
> Come live with me in my tee pee.

> Captain Whiteman, I'm a little Indian maid,
> Captain Whiteman, with long ebony braids.
> Please don't let my dark complexion
> Inhibit your affection.
> Be my muffin, I'll be your marmalade.
> Be my muffin, I'll be your marmalade.
> Be my muffin, I'll be your marmalade.
> Way ya hey yo.

ALEJANDRA: *[Before song ends, Alejandra, as the 'Blue Spots', runs up centre aisle, screaming]* ¡Capitán! ¡Capitán! !No te vayas, Capitán! Don't leave me!

PRINCESS B: May you always walk in beauty, my dear sister.

Now, was that not spiritual? Many, many thanks, you have made my heart soar like the noble rabbit. My heart, your heart bunny heart, one heart. Um hmm. I would like us to be friends, real good friends, you know what I mean? I mean like blood brothers, and blood sisters.

Um hm.

I have many names. My first name was Matoaka. Some people call me Lady Rebecca, but everyone knows the little Indian Princess Pocahontas, who saved the life of Captain John Smith. *[Four gestures, once with no words, once with sounds]:* (1) NO! *[Hands over head, on knees.]* He's so brave his eyes are so blue, his hair is so blond and I like the way he walks. (2) DON'T! mash his brain out. I don't want to see his brains all running down the side of this stone. (3) STOP! I think I love him. (4) Oooh he's so cute. *[Removes Princess dress, stands downstage right.]*

MONIQUE: Where was her mother?

ALEJANDRA: *[As Troubadour, complete with Robin Hood hat, singing.]*

In 1607 the English came sailing across the ocean—
In the name of their virgin queen, they called this land Virginia-O.

[Monique joins.]

In the gloom and silence of the dark and imprenetrable forest—
They might all have died if it had not been for the Indian Princess
   Pocahontas-O.

Her father was a stern, old chief, Powhatan was his name-O
Sweet and pretty was Pocahontas
As he was ugly and cruel-O.

Then into her village strode a man with steps so brave and sure
Said he in a deep voice like a God's
'My name is Captain John Smith-O'.

[Chorus.]

Heigh-ho wiggle-waggle wigwam wampum,
   roly-poly papoose tom-tom,
      tomahawk squaw.

MONIQUE: *[As Lady Rebecca.]* How cam'st I here? I know how to walk, I know how to stand, I know how to incline my head, how to bow. My heart is on the ground!

MONIQUE AND TROUBADOUR:

The fiendish red men they did deem that John Smith
   he must die-O
      They placed his head upon a stone,
         and raised their tomahawks high-O.

Then from the crowd there rushed a girl, the
   maiden Pocahontas
      Shielding his head with her own,
         crying save him, save the Paleface-O.

[Chorus.]

Heigh-ho wiggle-waggle wigwam wampum,
   roly-poly papoose tom-tom,
      tomahawk squaw.

LADY REBECCA: *[Crosses to wall right, swings out larger-than-life gilded portrait frame which contains Lady Rebecca's Elizabethan ruff and cuffs and her velvet hat with ostrich plume.]* How cam'st I to be caught, stuck, girdled? I'll tell you—Captain John Smith:

'You did promise Powhatan that what was yours should be his, and be the like to you; you called him father. And fear you here I should call you father? I tell you then, I will, and you shall call me child, and so I will be forever and ever your countryman. They did tell us always (that) you were dead, and I knew no other until I came to Plymouth. Yet Powhatan did seek to know the truth, because your countrymen will lie much.'

TROUBADOUR: *[Singing.]*

> When Pocahontas went to see her friend John Smith in
> Jamestown—
>> She'd run and cartwheel with the boys,
>> though she be naked underneath it-O.
>
> John Smith said of the Indian girls 'I could have done
> what I listed'-O
>> 'All these nymphs more tormented me,
>> crying "love you not me? Love you not me?"'

[During these verses Lady Rebecca caresses clothing in frame.]

LADY REBECCA: Now see you here I wear the clothes of an Englishwoman and will disturb you less when I walk. Here, I am Princess and Non Pareil of Virginia. I am Lady Rebecca. For me the Queen holds audience. Treachery, Captain, I was kidnapped!

TROUBADOUR:

> There chanced to be in Jamestown a planter named
> John Rolfe-O
>> His heart was touched by Pocahontas
>> he claimed her for his bride-y-O.

LADY REBECCA: John, my husband, is a businessman, a merchant, and a tobacco planter. I know how to grow tobacco, it is our sacred tobacco plant.

TROUBADOUR: *[Singing.]* Yo sangro por ti . . . *[Continues under Apostle's Creed; live voice and drum layered over taped voices.]*

LADY REBECCA: *[Fitting neck and wrists into collar and cuffs; fanning herself with ostrich plume fan.]* I believe in God the Father Almighty, maker of Heaven and Earth, and in Jesus Christ his own son our Lord, who was conceived of the Holy Ghost, born of the Virgin Mary, suffered under Pontius Pilate, was crucified, died, and was buried. He descended into hell. I believe in the Holy Ghost, the holy Catholic Church, the communion of saints, the forgiveness of sins, the resurrection of the body and the life everlasting. Amen.

I provided John Rolfe with the seeds to create his hybrid tobacco plants and I provided him with a son, and created a hybrid people. I have such a nice fan to hide my face and fan myself in these hot, heavy clothes.

What owe I to my father? Waited I not one year in Jamestown, a prisoner? One year before sent he my brothers to seek me. 'If my father had loved me, he would not value me less than old swords, guns, or axes: therefore I shall still dwell with the Englishmen who love me.'

Can I still remember how to plant corn? I'll stay. Never, never go back where anyone might know Matoaka. My name is Lady Rebecca forever and always. I am a Christian Englishwoman!

TROUBADOUR:

> Alas for our dear lady, English climate did not suit
> her—
>> She never saw Virginia again,
>> she met her end at Gravesend.

LADY REBECCA: Says John, my husband: For the good of God, for the good of the country, for the good of the plantation, it is righteous and it is good. No mark, no trail, no footprint, no way home. It is enough that the child liveth!

TROUBADOUR: *[Joined by Monique.]*

> And so here ends the legend of the Princess
> Pocahontas—
>> Fa la la la lay, fa la la la la LELF—
>> if you want any more, make it up yourself.

> *[Chorus.]*

> Heigh-ho wiggle-waggle wigwam wampum,
> roly-poly papoose tom-tom
>> tomahawk squaw.

* * *

ALEJANDRA: *[Singing with guitar while Monique sheds shawl, kerchief, and calico dress and hangs them on the tree. The buckskin yoke remains on.]* In the middle of my dream I came face to face and the copper hand reached to touch my back. I awakened sad, cold, confused, for the journey had been long and far . . . avec Marie, Margaret, et Madelaine . . . avec Marie, Margaret, et Madelaine . . . avec Marie, Margaret, et Madelaine, Madelaine . . . avec Marie, Margaret, et Madelaine.

ALEJANDRA: Princess, Princess!

MONIQUE: Princess, Princess!

[Princess Buttered-on-Both-Sides as the Cigar Store Squaw crosses centre with an oversized bunch of cigars.]

PRINCESS B: *[Offering cigars.]* UGH! I used to have this job, standing out in front of the tobacco store, but I didn't like the crowd. Besides, do you think anyone would talk to me? Not even chit chat. Do you think anyone would bring me a dozen roses, or an orchid corsage? No. Do you know what they gave me? Cigars. Do you know, the other day, somebody actually lit a match on me. Do you want to know where? So humiliating.

But I want it all! I want to be free to express myself! *[Sets cigars down at tree.]* I wanna be the girl next door! *[Removes buckskin yoke in exasperation.]* I wanna have lots and lots of blonde hair—great big blonde hair. I wanna be—Doris Day, Farrah Fawcett, Darryl Hannah—Oh, you know the one—Christie Brinkley! *[Hums 'Uptown Girl' while putting on white buckskin mini-dress.]* I wanna be a cover girl, a beauty queen, Miss America, Miss North American Indian! That's it!

According to the 'Walk In Beauty Seminar' it's very, very important to have the right look. *[Notices dress; screams.]* O.K. for the talent segment, but for the evening gown competition? The Finals? It's a rag! A rag! *[Pulls out pouch of buckskin dress to reveal a shimmering evening gown of the tackiest sort, and velcros it onto dress.]* Ahhh! Isn't this a devastating gown? I designed it myself. So, here I am a finalist in the Miss North American Indian Beauty Pageant! Think of it! Little me from in front of the tobacco store, fighting for DEMOCRACY!

HELLO WORLD!!

ALEJANDRA: *[Enters up left as beauty pageant host.]* And now, the moment you've all been waiting for . . . the winner of the 498th annual Miss North American Indian Beauty Pageant, from her woodland paradise . . . Miss Congeniality . . .

PRINCESS BUTTERED-ON-BOTH-SIDES!!!!

PRINCESS B: *[Screaming; jumps up and down flat footed as Host presents her with her oversized corn 'bouquet' and 'crowns' her with a tablita style headdress covered with small ears of corn which light up. She begins her triumphant walk down the runway, weeping and blowing kisses, while Host throws popcorn at her feet and sings Debbie Boone's 'You Light Up My Life'. When Princess reaches upstage centre, she strikes the pose of the Statue of Liberty, and the ears of corn on her headdress are illuminated in full.]*

Thank you, thank you . . . Oh! I can't believe it! I love you all . . . You have made my heart soar like a rabbit . . . I'll never forget this moment! *[She unplugs herself; corn lights go out. Exits upstage left.]*

* * *

[Lights snap to bright—sudden transition to mundane, urban environment.]

MONIQUE: *[Ramp left.]* It's International Women's Day—No, I didn't go to the march. *[Cross to centre; footprints in sand.]* So many years of trying to fit into feminist shoes. O.K., I'm trying on the shoes; but they're not the same as the shoes in the display case. The shoes I'm trying on must be crafted to fit these wide, square, brown feet. I must be able to feel the earth through their soles.

So, it's International Women's Day, and here I am. Now, I'd like you to take a good look—*[Turns.]* I don't want to be mistaken for a crowd of Native women. I am one. And I do not represent all Native women. I am one. *[Crosses to tree upstage right; brings basin and pitcher centre.]* And since it can get kinda lonely here, I've brought some friends, sisters, guerrilleras—the women word-warriors, to help. *[Pours water; Alejandra approaches, kneels by basin, they wet each other's faces, hair, and arms, purifying. With a cupped handful of water each, they sprinkle stage in opposite circles.]*

MONIQUE: *[Upstage left.]* Gloria Andalzua!

ALEJANDRA: *[Singing softly, under.]*

Una nación no sera conquistada . . .
     hasta que los corazónes de sus mujeres
          caigan a la tierra.

MONIQUE: 'What I want is the freedom to carve and chisel my own face, to staunch the bleeding with ashes, to fashion my own gods out of my entrails.' *[Dips hand in basin again, sprinkles water to stage right.]*

Diane Burns describes that to hold a brown-skinned lover means: *[Face to face, they wash each other's chests over heart.]* '. . . we embrace and rub the wounds together.' She also says: 'This ain't no stoic look, this is my face.' *[Dips hand in basin again, sprinkles half circle.]*

The Kayapo woman, of the Rain Forest, who stands *[up centre]* painted, bare to the waist, holding a baby by the hand, and confronts the riot squad in the capital of Brazil *[Walks downstage right.]* and says: *[Gesturing with arm; punctuating.]* I am here to speak for my brother and my brother-in-law. Where are your sisters to cry out for you? I am enraged with you! You steal our land! I am calling upon you! I throw my words in your faces!!!! *[Drum kicks in loudly, a 'call to arms'; song begins in Spanish to an Andean rhythm and evolves into a round dance—a '49' (contemporary native song with English words).]*

ALEJANDRA: Una nación no sera conquistada hasta que los corazónes de sus mujeres caigan a la tierra.

BOTH: Una nación no sera conquistada hasta que los corazónes de sus mujeres caigan a la tierra.

ALEJANDRA: No importa que los guerreros sean valientes o que sus armas sean poderosas.

MONIQUE: A nation is not conquered until the hearts of its women are on the ground.

BOTH: Then, it is done, no matter how brave its warriors, nor how strong its weapons.

[Blind faith leaps in the dark.]

BLACKOUT

Marilyn Dumont b. 1955

CREE/MÉTIS

The White Judges

We lived in an old schoolhouse, one large room that my father
converted into two storeys with a plank staircase leading to the
second floor. A single window on the south wall created a space
that was dimly lit even at midday. All nine kids and the
occasional friend slept upstairs like cadets in rows of shared
double beds, ate downstairs in the kitchen near the gas stove and
watched TV near the airtight heater in the adjacent room. Our
floors were worn linoleum and scatter rugs, our walls high and
bare except for the family photos whose frames were crowded
with siblings waiting to come of age, marry or leave. At supper
eleven of us would stare down a pot of moose stew, bannock and
tea, while outside the white judges sat encircling our house.

And they waited to judge

waited till we ate tripe
watched us inhale its wild vapour
sliced and steaming on our plates,
watched us welcome it into our being,
sink our teeth into its rubbery texture
chew and roll each wet and tentacled piece
swallow its gamey juices
until we had become it and it had become us.

Or waited till the cardboard boxes
were anonymously dropped at our door, spilling with clothes
waited till we ran swiftly away from the windows and doors
to the farthest room for fear of being seen
and dared one another to
'open it'
'no you open it'
'no you'
someone would open it
cautiously pulling out a shirt
that would be tried on
then passed around till somebody claimed it by fit
then sixteen or eighteen hands would be pulling out

skirts, pants, jackets, dresses from a box transformed now
into the Sears catalogue.

Or the white judges would wait till twilight
and my father and older brothers
would drag a bloodstained canvas
heavy with meat from the truck onto our lawn, and
my mother would lift and lay it in place
like a dead relative,
praying, coaxing and thanking it
then she'd cut the thick hair and skin back
till it lay in folds beside it like carpet

carving off firm chunks
until the marble bone shone out of the red-blue flesh
long into the truck-headlight-night she'd carve
talking in Cree to my father and in English to my brothers
long into the dark their voices talking us to sleep
while our bellies rested in the meat days ahead.

Or wait till the guitars came out
and the furniture was pushed up against the walls
and we'd polish the linoleum with our dancing
till our socks had holes.

Or wait till a fight broke out
and the night would settle in our bones
and we'd ache with shame
for having heard or spoken
that which sits at the edge of our light side
that which comes but we wished it hadn't
like 'settlement' relatives who would arrive at Christmas and
leave at Easter.

Squaw Poems

peyak

'hey squaw!'

   Her ears stung and she shook, fearful of the other words
like fists that would follow. For a moment, her spirit drained like

water from a basin. But she breathed and drew inside her fierce
face and screamed till his image disappeared like vapour.

niso

Indian women know all too well the power of the word *squaw*.
I first heard it from my mother, who used it in anger against
another Indian woman. 'That black squaw,' she rasped. As a young
girl, I held the image of that woman in my mind and she became
the measure of what I should never be.

nisto

I learned I should never be seen drunk in public, nor should I
dress provocatively, because these would be irrefutable signs. So
as a teenager I avoided red lipstick, never wore my skirts too
short or too tight, never chose shoes that looked the least
'hooker-like.' I never moved in ways that might be interpreted as
loose. Instead, I became what Jean Rhys phrased, 'aggressively
respectable.' I'd be so god-damned respectable that white people
would feel slovenly in my presence.

newo

squaw is to whore
          as
Indian maiden is to virgin

squaw is to whore
          as
Indian princess is to lady

niyanan

I would become the Indian princess, not the squaw dragging
her soul after laundry, meals, needy kids and abusive husbands.
These were my choices. I could react naturally, spontaneously to
my puberty, my newly discovered sexuality or I could be mindful
of the squaw whose presence hounded my every choice.

nikotwasik

squawman:

a man who is seen with lives with laughs with   a squaw.

'squawman'

a man is a man is a whiteman until

he is a squaw he is a squaw he is a squawman

Let the Ponies Out

oh papa, to have you drift up, some part of you drift up through
    water through
fresh water into the teal plate of sky soaking foothills, papa,
to have your breath leave, escape you, escape the
weight of bone, muscle and organ, escape you, to rise up, to loft,
till you are all breath filling the room, rising, escaping the white,
    the white
sheets, airborne, taken in a gust of wind and unbridled ponies,
    let the ponies
out, I would open that gate if I could find it, if there was one
to let you go, to drift up into, out, out
of this experiment into the dome of all breath and wind and
reappear in the sound of the first year's thunder with
Chigayow cutting the clouds over your eyes expanding, wafting,
    wings
of a bird over fields, fat ponies, spruce, birch and poplar, circling
wider than that tight square sanitized whiteness
you breathe in, if you could just stop breathing you could
escape, go anywhere, blow, tumble in the prairie grass,
bloom in the face of crocuses
appear in the smell of cedar dust off a saw
in the smell of thick leather
in the whistling sounds of the trees
in the far off sound of a chainsaw or someone chopping wood
in the smooth curve of a felt hat, in unbridled ponies

Horse-Fly Blue

'. . . d'you believe in god?,' I ask

                              he says, he 'doesn't
                              know,
                              care'
'But,' I say,

'can't you see that this sky
is the colour of the Greek Mediterranean,
and won't last?'

          although I've never seen the Mediterranean
          I have faith

'Can't you see that this light,'

               'what light?' he says

is the same as all those other afternoons when
the light was receding like
our hairlines, when it shone through
our winter skin and we
awoke from a long nap and
it was light all the time we were sleeping?

'Doesn't this light remind you of all those other times
you looked up from your reading
and weren't expecting to see
change and nothing
did change except the way
you looked, the way you met the light,
greeted it at the door as a friend
or smiled at it from a distance as your lover?

Can't you see that the sky is
horse-fly blue?
I swear I've seen this light before;
before I was born,
I knew the colour of the sky.
When I was five
the yard I played in
had a sky this colour,' I say   'what colour?' he says.

Not Just a Platform for My Dance

this land is not
just a place to set my house my car my fence

this land is not
just a plot to bury my dead my seed

this land is
my tongue   my eyes   my mouth

this headstrong grass and relenting willow
these flat-footed fields and applauding leaves
these frank winds and electric sky

are my prayer
they are my medicine
and they become my song

this land is not
just a platform for my dance

Letter to Sir John A. Macdonald

Dear John: I'm still here and halfbreed,
after all these years
you're dead, funny thing,
that railway you wanted so badly,
there was talk a year ago
of shutting it down
and part of it was shut down,
the dayliner at least,
'from sea to shining sea,'
and you know, John,
after all that shuffling us around to suit the settlers,
we're still here and Metis.

We're still here
after Meech Lake and
one no-good-for-nothin-Indian
holdin-up-the-train,
stalling the 'Cabin syllables /Nouns of settlement,
/. . . steel syntax [and] /The long sentence of its exploitation'[1]
and John, that goddamned railroad never made this a great nation,
cause the railway shut down
and this country is still quarreling over unity,
and Riel is dead
but he just keeps coming back

---

[1] F.R. Scott, 'Laurentian Shield'

in all the Bill Wilsons yet to speak out of turn or favour
because you know as well as I
that we were railroaded
by some steel tracks that didn't last
and some settlers who wouldn't settle
and it's funny we're still here and callin ourselves halfbreed.

The Devil's Language

1. I have since reconsidered Eliot
   and the Great White way of writing English
   standard that is
   the great white way
   has measured, judged and assessed me   all my life
   by its
   lily white words
   its picket fence sentences
   and manicured paragraphs
   one wrong sound and you're shelved in the Native Literature section
   resistance writing
   a mad Indian
   unpredictable
   on the war path
   native ethnic protest
   the Great White way could silence us all
   if we let it
   it's had its hand over my mouth since my first day of school
   since Dick and Jane, ABC's and fingernail checks
   syntactic laws: use the wrong order or
   register and you're a dumb Indian
   dumb, drunk or violent
   my father doesn't read or write
   the King's English says he's
   dumb but he speaks Cree
   how many of you speak Cree?
   correct Cree not correct English
   grammatically correct Cree
   is there one?

2. is there a Received Pronunciation of Cree, is there
   a Modern Cree Usage?
   the Chief's Cree not the King's English

as if violating God the Father and standard English
is like talking back(wards)

as if speaking the devil's language is
talking back
back(words)
back to your mother's sound, your mother's tongue, your mother's
language
back to that clearing in the bush
in the tall black spruce

3. near the sound of horses and wind
   where you sat on her knee in a canvas tent
   and she fed you bannock and tea
   and syllables
   that echo in your mind now, now
   that you can't make the sound
   of that voice that rocks you and sings you to sleep
   in the devil's language.

Circle the Wagons

There it is again, the circle, that goddamned circle, as if we thought
in circles, judged things on the merit of their circularity, as if all we
ate was bologna and bannock, drank Tetley tea, so many times 'we
are' the circle, the medicine wheel, the moon, the womb, and
sacred hoops, you'd think we were one big tribe, is there nothing
more than the circle in the deep structure of native literature? Are
my eyes circles yet? Yet I feel compelled to incorporate something
circular into the text, plot, or narrative structure because if it's linear then that proves that I'm a ghost and that native culture really
has vanished and what is all this fuss about appropriation anyway?
Are my eyes round yet? There are times when I feel that if I don't
have a circle or the number four or legend in my poetry, I am lost,
just a fading urban Indian caught in all the trappings of Doc Mar-
tens, cappuccinos and foreign films but there it is again orbiting,
lunar, hoops encompassing your thoughts and canonizing mine,
there it is again, circle the wagons. . . .

Armand Garnet Ruffo b. 1955

OJIBWAY

From *Grey Owl: The Mystery of Archie Belaney*

Annie Espaniel, 1923

He comes in all serious,
sits down at the table beside me and
says he's organizing an Indian War Dance
for Queen Victoria Day.
Me, I smile to myself when he tells me this
and look at the long face he makes.
So I say Archie, What's an Indian War Dance? None
of us Indian people have had one of those recently.
For Archie that's OK.
He's going to take care of everything.
He'll show everybody
what they're supposed to do.

Of course he needs my help to make a special suit.
You can't have an Indian War Dance without a costume.
I agree, and he brings home some brown material
and red ribbons from the lumber company store.
He draws me a pattern and I make it up for him.
When I'm finished he paints on little arrows,
adds animal teeth and bones.
He does a good job.
It's when he makes a drum out of a cheese box
that I have to shake my head.

Why I Write

So I can live in the past,
earn a living,
protect the beaver,
publicize conservation,
attract attention,
sell 35,000 copies in 3 months,
give 138 lectures in 88 days,
travel over 4350 miles,
wear feathers,
wear make-up,

play Indian—no
be Indian,
get to go to pow wows,
get to tour Britain,
meet the King & Queen,
become famous,
become alcoholic,
leave a legacy,
lose a wife,
be lonely.

Archie Belaney, 1930–31

The current is faster than I expect.
Suddenly my articles break into demand.
Letters of congratulations come flying
in from across Britain and the United States
(few from Canada which I find disconcerting).
Strangers want to visit me.
Reporters want to interview me.
They announce that I'm the first
to promote conservation:
the beaver,
the forests, the
Indian
way of life.

I begin by signing my name Grey Owl,
and saying I was adopted by the Ojibway,
and that for 15 years I spoke nothing but Indian;
then, before I know it, I have Apache blood.
Finally I'm calling myself an Indian writer.

Fast, it all happens so fast.
At first I'm hesitant.
I'm unsure of the name, the sound of it.
(Although, do I not prefer traveling at night?
Did I not hoot like an owl in Bisco?)
I think of the risk, those who know me.
There are Belaneys in Brandon.
My wife Angele in Temagami—
who knew me when I still carried an accent—
not to mention all those folks in northern Ontario.

But the thrust of self-promotion is upon me,
and head first into it, I hear myself

convincing myself that nobody's going to listen
to an immigrant ex-trapper from England,
promote an indigenous philosophy for Canada.
And if this is the only way
to get Canadians to listen,
then I'll do it, and more
if I have to. I'll be
what I have to be.
Without hesitation.

* * *

This is my wife Gertie, an Iroquois Chief's daughter,
21 years old. Tall, slim & very strong.
A woman of great courage & a true partner.
Well-educated, talks perfect English; everybody likes her.
—Archie Belaney in a letter to Aunt Ada, 1926

How Do You Know?

Because she's the one who tells her father
she'll be gone for the day
joins you
and never returns.

Because she knows how to let the past go,
and encourages you to do the same,
to open yourself as you would your cabin door
to the medicine winds of spring.

Because she has wings, transparent bright wings,
that you want so much to hold and tame
you sit up nights watching her sleep
your arms aching with emptiness.

Because she lets you call her beautiful Insect
even though she carries her share
and doesn't complain
she's not used to snowshoeing 70 miles.

Because she cooks so deadly you're afraid to eat.
Drinks and plays cards.
Argues fiercely
and goes for your revolver
to shoot up your moosejuice party.
Stabs you
with your own skinning knife,
then cries hysterically seeing you hurt.

Because this is the woman who somersaults your life
who can't bear to watch you club beaver to death.
Who makes you see, as she sees,
the suffering you inflict.

How do you know
she's the woman? Because:
She's the only one who beats you to the draw,
and walks out on you.

Poem For Duncan Campbell Scott

(Canadian poet who 'had a long and distinguished career
in the Department of Indian Affairs, retiring in 1932.'
The Penguin Book of Canadian Verse)

Who is this black coat and tie?
Christian severity etched in the lines
he draws from his mouth. Clearly a noble man
who believes in work and mission. See
how he rises from the red velvet chair,
rises out of the boat with the two Union Jacks
fluttering like birds of prey
and makes his way towards our tents.
This man looks as if he could walk on water
and for our benefit probably would,
if he could.

He says he comes from Ottawa way, Odawa country,
comes to talk treaty and annuity and destiny,
to make the inevitable less painful,
bearing gifts that must be had.
Notice how he speaks aloud and forthright:
        This or Nothing.
        Beware! Without title to the land
        under the Crown you have no legal right
        to be here.
Speaks as though what has been long decided wasn't.
As though he wasn't merely carrying out his duty
to God and King. But sincerely felt.

Some whisper this man lives in a house of many rooms,
has a cook and a maid and even a gardener

to cut his grass and water his flowers.
Some don't care, they don't like the look of him.
They say he asks many questions but
doesn't want to listen. Asks
much about yesterday, little about today
and acts as if he knows tomorrow.
Others don't like the way he's always busy writing
stuff in the notebook he carries. Him,
he calls it poetry
and says it will make us who are doomed
live forever.

Creating a Country

They came to North America in search of a new life,
clinging to their few possessions, hungry for prosperity.
They'd had enough poverty and suffering to last a lifetime.
And so they believed with all their hearts
that if they laboured they would all become barons
in a classless society. Patriots were thus born
on both sides of the border. But the process of creating
a country took much longer than most ever imagined.
For there were a myriad of unforeseen obstacles
in this formidable new land. Like mosquitoes and Indians.
Undaunted, the pioneering spirit persisted.

In Canada, Susanna Moodie arrived to take notes.
After writing anti-slavery tracts in England,
she thought it only natural to document the burden
of roughing it in the bush. Susanna shied away
from both mosquitoes and Indians. One day, however,
quite by accident, she met a young Mohawk
whom she thought handsome and for a period flirted
with the notion of what it would be like to be swept away
by him. But she soon tired of such thoughts and nothing ever
became of it. Later she would say neither Indians nor mosquitoes
make good company. She did make it perfectly clear
that she bore no grudge. She believed everything has a place.

Just as she believed her place was across the ocean,
but she too had heard stories of golden opportunities.
Lies! She could be heard screaming. Nothing but lies!
Susanna also believed she was turning life into art

and creating the first semblance of culture
in a godforsaken land.
It was her only compensation.
When she spoke about her life her eyes rolled in her head
like a ship leaving port. She never gave up the dream
of returning home. Dreamed so hard
that even on her death bed she never stopped
talking to herself.

South of the border, Lt. Col. George Armstrong Custer
never once worried about mosquitoes.
It's said that he too was interested in culture
and for this reason carried a gun.
He was a soldier, not an artist, and made no pretence
about it. Custer rarely wrote and never spoke
unless formally addressed. Yet, he was a passionate man
who dreamed the same dream every night.
He fancied that he had discovered the final solution.
Each night he rounded up all the buffalo
in what is now Montana and shot every last one of them.

As a son of European peasantry, he had heard stories
about what it was like to go hungry.
He also knew Indians could starve
just like white people. As a patriot,
he believed his solution was perfectly reasonable.
He also believed American politicians
would see to it that both the buffalo and the Indian
would find a new home
on the American nickel.

Susanna Moodie never met General Golden Hair (as Custer
was affectionately called), she never liked Americans anyway.
She was an old lady of 73 when he died young on the plains
of Little Bighorn trying to live out his dream.
They say that Custer was singing,
'The Girl I Left Behind Me' the day he headed west.
We know he wasn't singing to Susanna Moodie.
We also know that after hearing what the U.S. Cavalry
was doing south of the border, Susanna thought
about the anti-slavery tracts she had written years before
and, for a brief moment, about what had ever become
of her young Mohawk,
if he fared any better.

Hospital Visit

Bringing apples, plums and pears for someone else
I pass grey heads in white rooms
scanning the corridor for a sign of recognition.
The disinfected hospital enters the mind
through the nostrils.
We greet.
There was a time when his fingers
were like tree roots—shake firmly
keep a firm grip, man to man.
Our eyes meet picking up the slack that age
accumulates like loose skin.

Between us there is much to add and subtract.
Precision cannot be shucked casually
like a shrug or a glance.
It is demanded by the creases in our face, in our life.
Like beadwork our stories are suspended
and must be gathered with care.
What is evident is that soon your body breaks,
a cramp in the neck, in the back and that
is just the beginning. Oh, of course there is always
the temporary relief—firm massaging hands
naked thighs—but it never lasts long enough.

Story: There are two young men hunched and drumming.
A ritual of feathers in their hair.
There is no other sound. The beat is hard
and steady and lasts long into the night.
Come the black and white of morning
the fire between them is transparent. No longer
are there sparks shooting their animal eye sharpness.
Only the outline of the drummers remain.
They become something else:
another life
another story.

Again I see you in a forest among the pines.
The setting seems to change little, if at all.
This time perhaps it is winter, a northern winter,
dogs howling, wind and snow cold.
On the trapline or delivering the Queen's mail
strength is your ally. Endurance keeps you
going and some kind of dedication, to exactly what

I am uncertain. Straining
through moments of silence you find difficulty
in expressing yourself.
Sitting next to the bed, wrapped in a blanket,
you say they suggested you change
your name, give up your identity.
So you did (or so everyone thought).
They said that you could probably make it
in the system.
So what if you couldn't read or write.
You would succeed
at all costs.

Perched fourteen floors up you wait
as if in a swaying watchtower. For you
traffic smudges are fires on a forest horizon,
soot a hot exhaust. Will your bush sense, your sixth
sense, somehow get you through?
You are the crew-boss. Your name is called.
The clouds are setting in like a prayer.
You say be thankful they hold rain. Your crew
laughs while you remain quiet
thinking about your work and the vague notion
of equality among men.
There is no time for idleness
you grab a shovel.

What does it mean to you, I wonder,
to lie between cold hospital sheets
for the first and last time and know it.
The trail, a life once stripped of the non-essentials
buried somewhere deep inside you.
I wonder if there will be a flood
in the operating room? I mean
after the surgeons make the first incision.
Will they be suddenly plunging their hands
into icy river water?
Will there be a snow storm?
Tell me.

Admittance: Visiting hours 2:00-9:00.
A nurse stands in the doorway.
I will not tell her
of a memory filled with rivers and lakes.
I cannot explain the calluses worn into your hands
or the stoop of your shoulders. Halfway through the knot

of a portage the blackflies descend. The cut
of the tumpline across the forehead.
One thing is for certain: I cannot remain.
Forests cover footprints; the city covers me.

Proclamation: From now on let us hold to the ways
of the young and the wise.
Let us savour the smoke,
and drink hard for the last time,
dance beside the railroad tracks,
toss knives and then swim in clean water.
We will speak
of our dreams and share everything
we always wanted.
We will laugh like children eating fruit.

The Season

In a week or so
we will be travelling
these days
it is the season
and it feels good
to be on the move
because before we know it
we've returned
and settled into a stationary existence
of boardrooms and timetables
where we'll find ourselves
pretending
we never had
a loon
          a deer or even a whale
locked inside us
          and wanting out

Poetry

makes me
want to write poetry,
exotic disease I guess,
          butterfly palpitations
bursting across the kitchen table
fragrance of sweetgrass
and wild mint wafting into the room,
          jasmine tea
          for two
suddenly on the boil,
          whistling intimacy,
warming what is inside,
perfection of nipple, im-
perfection of heart,
arc of arm,
shape of (tender?) greeting,
(bitter?) farewell,
extended from toe to thigh to infinity.

nothing to do with
I can do better
nothing like that, this honest desire
that kicks
like a new born calf
jumping up and disappearing
into its own geography.

Richard Wagamese b. 1955

OJIBWAY

From *Keeper'n Me*

I'm used to it now having been back five years but that first day I wondered where the hell I was landing once we approached the reserve. First there was a big sign on the side of the road with about a hundred bullet holes in it that said: YOU ARE ENTERING THE WHITE DOG INDIAN RESERVE. NO ADMITTANCE. VISITORS REPORT TO THE BAND OFFICE. NO ACCESS WITHOUT PERMISSION.

Then about a quarter mile after that was a sign that read: KEEWATIN'S GENERAL STORE! WHERE NO STOCK ISN'T A PROBLEM! GOOD FOOD! GET GAS! NO LINEUPS! BIG ED KEEWATIN PROP.

We rounded the final curve into the townsite and I swear it looked like something outta a foreign documentary. Houses were perched on toppa rocky outcroppings and they all looked about ready to tumble down. There wasn't any siding on a lotta them and it looked like most were just sitting there on the land with no basements, plumbing or furnaces. They were all about a quarter mile apart and there was a lotta dead-looking automobiles parked everywhere. Reminded me of what Lonnie described the Detroit ghettos to be like. There was scruffy kids running around everywhere, shirtless and wearing rolled-down black gumboots, and the occasional old person walking around lookin' tired and glum. Out back of all the houses was a big lake and there were lotsa shaky-lookin' docks around with boats tied up to them. There was a big red brick schoolhouse and a few modern houses all hunched together close by and further away was a buncha aluminum trailers too. First thing I noticed was the missing power and telephone poles, and I saw someone behind one of the houses walking up from the dock with a five-gallon pail with water slopping over the sides. There were outdoor johnnies behind the houses too and I worried about how I was gonna get the slivers outta my ass. It was the only time in my life I ever thought constipation might be a blessing. Everyone looked up as the cab pulled in and by the time we pulled up in front of the store there were about fifty Indians all heading towards us. Kinda reminded me of those movies I used to watch as a kid. One minute they weren't there and the next minute they were everywhere. It was true after all. Indians did just pop outta nowhere.

They were all craning their necks real good trying to get a glimpse of who it was behind the tinted glass, and it gave me a chance to check out the locals and try to see any faces I recognized from the pictures Stanley'd sent. Seeing all those brown faces craning and squinty-eyed reminded me of something you see in *National Geographic* and I laughed while I handed the cabbie his dough. I could hear them chattering in Ojibway, laughing and rustling around. When I opened the door they all stepped back in one motion like a gumbooted chorus line.

The silence was deafening. As soon as I flung one lime green spangly platform-shoed leg out the door there was a loud gasp all around the cab. And when I stepped out there was about fifty heads all leaning in gazing at my yellow balloon-sleeved shirt and you could hear the sounds of a few dozen sniffers catching a whiff of my fifty-dollar scent. Four or five sets of hands were scrunching up my Afro and I could hear giggles from the kids as everyone was pressing closer and closer towards me. When the cab pulled away in a flurry of gravel, they surrounded me. It was true after all. Indians did love to surround you.

There was another loud gasp when I took off my shades and smiled all around.

'S'app'nin'? I said, bobbing my head and reaching out for hands to shake.

'Ho-leeee!' someone said.

'Wow!'

'Ever look like Stanley!'

'Ever, eh?'

'Ho-leeee!' said about three together.

Just about then a tall guy with a long ponytail reached through the crowd all excited like and started pushing people back amidst grumbling and something that sounded like cussing. When he made it up to me he stopped and looked at me with shiny eyes and kinda reaching out with his arms then pulling back, reaching out and pulling back. Finally, tears started pouring down his face. Everyone got real quiet all of a sudden and when I looked at this guy it was almost like looking into a mirror except for there being a ponytail where the Afro should have been and a definite absence of funky threads. He stared at me for what seemed an eternity with all kindsa things working across his face, and when he spoke it was a whisper.

'Garnet,' he said. 'Garnet. Garnet. Garnet.'

He reached out and touched me finally, one soft little grab of the shoulder, and then he collapsed into my arms sobbing like a kid while everyone around us moved in a little closer too.

'Twenty-two years,' he said, sobbing. 'Twenty-two years, my brother. Twenty-two years.'

I was crying by this time too and all the faces around me went kinda outta focus through the tears but I could tell we weren't the only ones breaking down and I remember thinking I wasn't exactly being downtown cool, but right then it didn't really matter. Holding my brother in my arms was unlike anything I'd ever felt, and as we cried I could feel that lifelong feeling of wind whistling through my guts getting quieter and quieter.

He looked up finally, threw his arm around my shoulder and turned to the crowd.

'This is my ... my ... my brother,' he said, choking up and sniffling. 'The one that disappeared. He's home.'

People started coming up and shaking my hand and smiling and touching me and there were tears everywhere as I heard the names of aunts and uncles and cousins and just plain White Dog folk for the first time. Stanley stood off to the side looking over at me and smiling, smiling and smiling. After a while they all moved away and started looking me over again.

'Ho-lee!' said a voice.

'Wow!'

'Sure he's a Raven?' someone asked. 'Looks like a walkin' fishin' lure or somethin'!'

'Yeah, that hair's a good reminder to the kids 'bout foolin' round with the electrical!'

'An' what's that smell? Smell like that should have fruit flies all around his head!'

'Damndest-lookin' Indyun I ever saw! Looks kinda like that singer we seen on TV that time. What's 'is name now? James Brown? Yeah. We got us one James Brown-lookin' Indian here!'

'Come on,' Stanley said once people started moving away. 'There's a buncha people up at my house been feelin' kinda down 'cause they figured you weren't comin'. Seein' you's gonna make 'em all feel a whole lot better. You okay?'

'Yeah,' I said. 'Least, I think so. It's kinda weird, man.'

'Yeah,' he said, 'I guess so. Wanted to ease you in slow but you weren't on the bus. What happened?'

'Nothin', man,' I said. 'Don't matter.'

'Least you're here now,' he said. 'That's all we wanted. Took a long time to find you.'

'Tell me about it,' I said. 'Tell me about it.'

They been comin' for our kids long time now. Nothin' new. Not for us. They been comin' on the sly for years. I always thought it was us Indyuns s'posed to do all the sneakin' and creepin' around. but those white people, boy, they got us beat when it come to sneakin' through the bushes. Maybe we taught 'em too much. Heh, heh, heh.

The boy's story's not much diff'rent from what we seen around here for a long time. Sure, in them movies us Indyuns are always runnin' off with children and raisin' them up savage. Give 'em funny-soundin' names like Found on the Prairie, Buffalo Dog or somethin'. I always figured they shoulda called 'em Wind in His Pants, Plenty Bingos, Busts Up Laughing or Sneaks Off Necking. Somethin' really Indyun. Heh, heh, heh. But in the real world it's the white people kept on sneakin' off with our kids. Guess they figured they were doin' us a favour. Gonna give them kids the benefit of good white teachin', raise them up proper. Only thing they did was create a whole new kinda Indyun. We used to call them Apples before we really knew what was happenin'. Called 'em Apples on accounta they're red on the outside and white on the inside. It was a cruel joke on accounta it was never their fault. Only those not livin' with respect use that term now.

But we lost a generation here. In the beginning it was the missionary schools. Residential schools they called them. Me I was there. They come and got me when I was five and took me and a handful of others. The boy's mother was one of them. They took us and cut off our hair, dressed us in baggy clothes so we all looked the same, told us our way of livin' and prayin' was wrong and evil. Got beat up for speakin' Indyun. If we did that we'd all burn in hell they told us. Me I figured I was already brown why not burn the rest of the way, so I ran away. Came back here. Lots of others stayed though. Lots never ever came back and them that did were real diff'rent. Got the Indyun all scraped off their insides. Like bein' Indyun was fungus or somethin'. They scraped it all off and never put nothin' there to replace it but a bunch of fear and hurt. Seen lotsa kids walkin' around like old people after a while. Them schools were the beginning of how we started losin' our way as a people.

Then they came with their Children's Aid Society. Said our way was wrong and kids weren't gettin' what they needed, so they took 'em away. Put 'em in homes that weren't Indyun. Some got shipped off long ways. Never made it back yet. Disappeared. Got raised up all white but still carryin' brown skin. Hmmpfh. See, us we know you can't make a beaver from a bear. Nature don't work that way. Always gotta be what the Creator made you to be. Biggest right we all got as human bein's is the right to know who we are. Right to be who we are. But them they never see that. Always thinkin' they know what's best for people. But it's not their fault. When you quit lookin' around at nature you quit learnin' the natural way. The world gets to be somethin' you gotta control so you're always fightin' it. Us we never fight the world. We look around lots, find its rhythm, its heartbeat, and learn to walk that way. Concrete ain't got no rhythm, and steel never learned to breathe. You spend time in the bush and on the land, you learn the way of the bush and the way of the land. The natural way. Way of the universe. Spend time surrounded by concrete and steel, you learn their way too, I guess.

Back when I was a boy there was still a strong bunch of us livin' the old way. Lot of us crossed over since then and with those of us who's left maybe only a handful still practisin' the old way. Rest are Catholic and some other whiteman way. S'okay though. They're still our people no matter how they pray on accounta prayin's the most important thing anyway. Long as there's some kinda prayer there's some kinda hope. But there's not many of us old traditional people left walkin' around. Not many for the young ones to come to no more. That's why you hear more English than Anishanabe around here. Same other places too. Other tribes, other Indyuns. S'why it's so important for old guys like me to be passin' on what we know. I'm not talkin' about bringin' back the buffalo hunt or goin' back to the wigwam. I'm talkin' about passin' on the spirit of all those things. If you got the spirit of the old way in you, well, you can handle most anythin' this new world got to throw around. The spirit of that life's our traditions. Things like respect, honesty, kindness and sharin'. Those are our traditions. Livin' that old tribal way taught peo-

ple those things. That they needed each other just to survive. Same as now. Lookin' around at nature taught the old ones that. Nature's fulla respect, honesty, kindness and sharin'. S'way of the world, I guess.

But lotsa our people think that just learnin' the culture's gonna be their salvation. Gonna make 'em Indyun. Lotsa young ones out there learnin' how to beat the pow-wow drum and sing songs. Learnin' the dances and movin' around on the pow-wow trail ev'ry summer. Lotsa people growin' hair and goin' to see ceremony. Think they're more Indyun that way. S'good to see. But there's still lotsa people out there still drinkin', beatin' each other up, raisin' their kids mean. All kindsa things. That's not our way. So just doin' the culture things don't make you no Indyun. Lotsa white people doin' our culture too now and they're never gonna be Indyun. Always just gonna be lookin' like people that can't dance. Heh, heh, heh.

What I'm tryin' to say is tradition gives strength to the culture. Makes it alive. Gotta know why you dance 'steada just how. It's tradition that makes you Indyun. Sing and dance forever but if you're not practisin' tradition day by day you're not really bein' Indyun. Old man told me one time he said, the very last time you got up in the mornin' and said a quiet prayer of thanks for the day you been given was the very last time you were an Indyun. Then he said, the very last time you got handed some food and bowed your head and said a prayer of thanks and asked for the strength you got from that food to be used to help someone around you, well, that was the very last time you were an Indyun too. And he told me he said, the very last time you did somethin' for someone without bein' asked, bein' thanked or tellin' about it was the very last time you were an Indyun. See, it's all respect, kindness, honesty and sharin'. Built right in. Do that all the time and boy, you just dance and sing up a real storm next time. Heh, heh, heh.

That's what we gotta pass on. 'Cause tradition'll keep you goin' when you're livin' it. Us we need to remember these things. Keep 'em alive inside me. Live 'em so they stay strong. Lotsa kids comin' back nowadays really need to be shown. Tough thing to do when the kids are forty-four, twenty-five or whatever.

Nowadays the whiteman comes in lotsa diff'rent ways. Oh, they still come with their schools and their foster homes, but we got some of our own teachers and social workers now, so kinda gettin' better there. But they still come for the kids. They come with their TV, money, big inventions and ideas. They come with big promises 'bout livin' in the world, with their politics and their welfare. They come with their rap music, break dancin' and funny ways of dressin'. All kinds of shiny things. Kids get all excited, funny in the head 'bout things, wanna go chasin' after all that stuff. Tradition? Ah, it's just borin' stuff for old guys like me can't rap dance. Somethin' you gotta do when you ain't got no other choice. That's how they come nowadays. On the sly. Harder for kids to come back from these things than from them schools or foster homes sometimes.

That's why we gotta pass it on. Always gotta be someone around who

*knows. Always gotta be someone around to catch 'em when they land here all
owl-eyed and scared, askin' questions, tryin' to find if they belong here still.
If they wanna stick around. Always gotta be someone who knows the kindness
built into tradition. Ease 'em back slow. Got the Indyun all scraped offa their
insides, carryin' 'round big hurts an' bruises. Poke around too much you hurt
'em an' they run away. So you bring 'em back from the inside out. Nothin' in
this world ever grew from the outside in. That's why I help the boy understand. He learned 'bout respect before he ever learned to sing or dance.
Learned to be kind and share before he learned to tan a hide or how to hunt.
Learned to be honest before I let him be a storyteller. Learned about bein'
Indyun, about himself. That way he'll survive anything.*

*He looked funny enough when he got here wearin' all those strange things
and havin' a head of hair looked like a cat been through the dryer, smellin'
like fruit and talkin' funny. Guess if he could survive walkin' around lookin'
and smellin' like that, learnin' to live an' learn off the land was gonna be
simple. Heh, heh, heh.*

The first thing most people notice about us Indians is how we're laughing
most of the time. It doesn't really matter whether we're all dressed in traditional finery or in bush jackets and gumboots, seems like a smile and big
roaring guffaw is everywhere with us. Used to be that non-Indians thought
we were just simple. You know, typical kinda goofy-grinning lackeys riding
out to get shot offa our horses by the wagon train folks. Or standing around
on a corner in some city bumming smokes an' change but yukking it up anyway. But the more they stick around the more they realize that Indians have
a real good sense of humour and it's that humour more than anything that's
allowed them to survive all the crap that history threw their way. Keeper says
laughin's about as Indian as bannock and lard. Most of the teaching legends
are filled with humour on accounta Keeper says when people are laughing
they're really listening hard to what you're saying. Guess the old people figured that was the best way to pass on learning. Once you stop to remember
what it was you were laughing at you remember the whole story, and that's
how the teachings were passed on. Guess if it was thirty below and I was
hunched around some little fire in a wigwam I'd wanna be laughing too
instead of listening to some big deep talk.

Teasing's big around here too. You get lotta teasing from people on
accounta teasing's really a way of showing affection for someone and like me
at first, a lotta people have a hard time figuring that out. Get all insulted and
run away. But once you figure that out it's a lotta fun being around a bunch
of Indians.

When Stanley and me got to his cabin that first day I was expecting a big
warm family kind of scene like on 'The Waltons'. I figured there'd be a big
spread on the table, maybe a little wine, music and a party happening. Instead
there was about ten people sitting around drinking tea they were pouring out
of a big black old-fashioned metal pot on a pot-bellied stove in the middle of

the room. There weren't any decorations or anything unless you can call six or seven pairs of wool socks hung over the stove pipes decorations.

They all looked up as we walked in. The silence was deafening.

'Ho! Whatchu got there, Stanley?' said a big gap-toothed guy with a brush-cut. 'Not Halloween yet, is it?'

'Ho-wah!' said a large fat woman with gumboots, a kerchief around her head and smoking a pipe. 'Thought he was coming from T'rana, not Disney-land!'

'Reee-leee!' said another woman. 'Who'd you say adopted him? Liber-ace?'

'Ahh, he's just dressed fer huntin',' said an old man with so many wrinkles he looked like he was folded up wet and left overnight. 'Wanna make sure he don't get mistook fer no deer.'

'Deer? Maybe get mistook for the northern lights but sure ain't nobody gonna be thinkin' he's a deer no matter how dark it gets,' said a tall spindly woman busy pouring herself another tea.

Stanley eased me into the centre of the room with his hand on my shoulder and I could feel the pressure of it getting a little firmer the more nervous I got. Like he wanted to hold me from bolting for the door, which was exact-ly the thought going through my mind at the time. He smiled at me and waved at a large round woman leaning in the doorway and staring real hard at us both.

'Your sister,' was all he said. Or at least I think that's all he said because I got swept up in her big brown arms and disappeared for about five minutes. I could feel her breathing deeper and deeper as she hugged me and when she finally let me surface for air she was crying real quiet and smiling at the same time. She was a lot wider than me, but it's kinda spooky when you look at someone you swear you've never seen before and you can see your own eyes looking back at you. I didn't doubt for a minute that this woman was my sis-ter.

'Hi, bro,' she said. 'I'm Jane. Do you remember me at all?'

'No,' I said real quiet. 'No, I don't think I do.'

'S'okay,' she said. 'S'okay. I remember you real good. Little bigger than before but I remember you, all right.'

'Ahh, get the hell outta the way, Jane, and let us meet this boy kept us wait-in' three days and twenty years anyway!' said an energetic little guy. 'How you doin', T'rana? I'm yer uncle Buddy.'

Well, they all lined up and for the next half hour or so I was introduced to my uncles Gilbert, Archie and Joe, aunties Myrna and Ella, Chief Isaac McDonald and wife, Bertha, and the wrinkled-up old guy who said his name was Keeper and who left right away with Buddy.

Two things really got my attention that day. The first was the way they just seemed to treat me like I was someone they'd always known. Like the twen-ty years didn't matter to them or the way I was dressed, the Afro or anything. It was like I was already a part of their lives and let's get on with it all. The second thing was the absence of my mother and my other brother, Jackie. Of all the things I was scared of, meeting my mother after all that time was the biggest and I wondered why she wasn't there. Anyway, after all the introductions were over everybody just visited with each other and it was like the excitement was over and life was back to normal for them. Me, I was pretty confused.

Paul Seesequasis b. 1958

CREE

The Republic of Tricksterism

We were urban mixed-bloods. Shopping malls and beer parlours were our sacred grounds, reaching adolescence in the 70s, the Sex Pistols and the Clash provided the tribal drums. Fallen between the seams and exiled from the reserves we were the prisoners of bureaucratic apartheid, of red tape and parliamentary decrees.

Our tribal links were obscure, our colonial banishment confirmed by the Indian Act. White bureaucrats and tribal politicians alike were our oppressors. 'We are heading toward self-government,' proclaimed Tobe, the Grand Chief of the Fermentation of Saskatchewan Indian Nations (FSIN) as he shook the hand of then Saskatchewan Premier Allan Blakeney.

In his hands Tobe, the Grand Chief, held a paper promising tens-of-millions of dollars, but that money and power were destined only for a select few. The Grand Chief's vision was obscured by power and long-legged blondes. He denounced Indian women who had married white men, while at the same time blonde secretaries and assistants crossed their legs in his plush office at the FSIN.

Mary Seesequasis, aka Ogresko, was born on Beardy's reserve on January 20, 1934. The first child of Sam Seesequasis, of Beardy's reserve, and Mary Rose Nahtowenhow, of the Sturgeon Lake band. Sam, my *nimosom*, danced through life with gentleness and humour and became a leader in the community. Mary Rose, my *nohkom*, was large and became a bear when she laughed. She hunted rabbits, decapitated chickens, and farted in the direction of bureaucrats and posers.

They made love, had nine children, and seven lived to adulthood.

The grand-chief-to-be and his family lived downwind from my grandmother's farts. He was born the same day as my mother but their lives were destined to take far different paths. Tobe was born mixed-blood, his father Cree, his mother white. But the irony and humour of being mixed-race was lost on Tobe. He would grow up as mixed-race pure-blood, purer than thou and given to exaggerating the quantity of his half cup of tribal blood. Tobe lived in denial of his white parentage.

Being the same age, Tobe and my mother played together as children, they fell asleep infused with dreams of *Wesakaychuk* and *Pakakos*, they hid under the covers from the wetigoes and the hairy hearts.

But The Indian Act enabled Tobe to imagine himself the pure-blood. With Indian father and white mother he was allowed to stay on the reserve. In 1950 my mother met and fell in love with a white man, Dennis Ogresko, and because she was in love with a white man and she was *hisqueau*, a woman, she had to leave the reserve.

The hairy hearts ran amuck in 1950s Saskatchewan. Cannibal spirits plagued the small towns and hid in the grain elevators. It was open season on squaws, wagonburners, and breeds. By courageously proclaiming brown-white love my parents challenged the humourless segregational values of the time.

Unable to hide on the reserve they weathered taunts and jeers with laughter. That love could exist between races offended all the pure-bred breeders; and in making love Dennis and Mary parented two cross-breed mutts, my brother and I.

We experienced childhood between the seams, spending summers on the reserve, winters in the city. We played without leashes, without pedigree we learned to live with our genetic-mixture coats and our lack of papers. We lived in a no-man's land between Indian and white. At school we quickly learned to stick together to avoid the beatings of the pure bred-breeders. We found delight in the repulsion others felt for us. We pissed on the city trees, marked our traditional urban territories, and barked ferociously at the white poodles.

It was the 1960s and my mother, now a registered nurse, worked in the Community Clinic in Prince Albert where she healed the urban orphans and mixed-bloods who were now entering the cities in increasing numbers.

Tobe, the mixed-blood/full-blood too had grown up. He became a tribal politician, a Chief of the reserve and a wearer of suits and ties. His hair was short and his speeches were long. He spoke of self-government and economic development but his mind was on attending conferences and getting laid in hotels.

With enthusiasm he joined Wild Jean's Indian Affairs Bandwagon and Wild West Show and with conferences here and there and blondes to his left and right, it was the modern-day chief's delight. Tobe sold his Pontiac—*the Poor Old Nechee'd Thought It Was A Cadillac*—and actually bought a real Cadillac, and a blonde chauffeur. But while Tobe played the colonial game a revolution was brewing in Prince Albert.

Uncle Morris was a *rigoureau*; a mixed-blood shape-shifter. He often came to visit our home on the east side, the poor side, of the city. My uncle was a co-founder of the Metis Association of Alberta in the 1930s, and an urban activist who cut through the lies of white bureaucrats and tribal politicians alike. His mission was to liberate the urban reserves from the cannibal spirits and the hairy hearts. He told my mother of his vision and Mary laughed and agreed to help him. Uncle Morris wanted to take over the Prince Albert Friendship Centre and remove the metal detectors from the door. Those detectors beeped a warning anytime someone without a status card tried to walk in.

Malcolm spoke passionately about uniting all urban skins, mixed or full.

'Burn your status cards!' he proclaimed, 'and throw away your colonial pedigree papers. Don't let the white man define us. Let's define ourselves.'

Uncle Morris knew how to respond to taunts and jeers with trickery. When he laughed he became a bear and his joyous chuckles reverberated from deep within. My mother would prepare dinner and then we would sit, expectedly, waiting to hear of his latest exploits.

As a *rigoureau* Morris was hated by the hairy hearts and the cannibal spirits. They envied his power, his ability to turn into a dog, a bear, or almost any kind of rodent he chose. I remember once his turning into a red squirrel, jumping from his chair and scurrying around the kitchen floor while my parents cried with laughter and said 'Enough! Enough!'

From Morris I learned to see the evil spirits around me. I saw them in the frowns and looks of scorn us mixed-bloods received on the streets. I felt the disapproving glares of the police, farmers, tribal politicians and store owners. They were everywhere in the city and their numbers were increasing.

The cannibal spirits and the hairy hearts ruled the cities and reserves. They fed on both Indians and whites. 'There just aren't enough of us *rigoureau*'s left to stop them,' uncle once told me. 'These evil spirits,' he explained, 'feed on souls that are empty, rub against their bodies and penetrate the skin. Sometimes a person can repell them if they are strong enough or if they can call on a *rigoureau* to drive the spirit away. But most people succumb and the cannibal spirits continue in their goal to create a world of hate. A world in which they can proliferate.'

Morris would often go to the clinic where my mother worked to watch and to offer humour to those who were forgetting how to laugh. He played the compassionate trickster, upsetting the plans of the cannibal spirits, and frustrating the violent emotions of the hairy hearts. Many a body was purged of poison.

Then, one day, Uncle Morris went missing. Search parties were organized and the mixed-bloods and urban orphans looked everywhere but it was the squirrels, the rodent friend of the *rigoureau*, who led us to him. He had been dumped into a grain chute and his body was badly beaten. We lowered ropes and a canvas stretcher. My mother was among those selected to gently retrieve his body from that dark cavern.

While the crows cawed mournfully and the stray dogs howled their lament, our procession carried Morris back to our house. He was laid in the guest room and a group of women healers worked with him. They washed his bruised body, set his broken bones, removed all the grains that had been shoved down his throat and nostrils, and, after a few days, his heart began to beat again.

Time passed and Morris cracked a smile and we rejoiced, knowing he would live. 'My spirit has tasted life again though parts of my body probably never will,' he confessed. True he was now paralysed from the waist down. We pooled our meagre resources and had made for him a cedar wood wheelchair with wheels of rounded stone. Being confined to a wheelchair didn't slow Morris down. Rather he called for a gathering of mixed-bloods and urban orphans.

I remember that day. We met at an old skating rink. Long benches had been set up for the occasion. The building was packed. Uncle Morris's life history was in that building and each person had a story to tell. Some kindness, some help from trouble, some funny story. There were trappers from the north, none more than three feet tall, with bristled faces and wooden pipes. I remember how they stamped their fur-covered feet in applause when Morris was wheeled into the arena. There were *kokums*, grandmothers, with shawls wrapped tightly around their heads and their aged but strong fingers beading leather. There were young street girls who took the day off from work. I recall the smell of perfume, their make-up, and the candy they gave to the children who ran up and down the aisles. And there were nurses, construction workers, loggers, teachers, drunks, and others and they had all come to hear my uncle.

'The main cannibal spirit has arrived in town,' Morris roared in his bear voice. There was silence in the hall. 'He has come for me. I have frightened him and he seeks to destroy me with violence.'

'Shame!' cried the audience.

'He has come in the guise of an Indian. A Chief. A person you know well. He is Chief Tobe, the plains warrior wearer of chokers and ties, the politician without humour. The one whose ideas are short and his speeches are long.'

The crowd laughed.

'You remember Tobe. He speaks of purity and his heart is cold. He has chased the mixed-bloods from the reserves and he has created a world of urban orphans. I shall trick him with humour. With your help we will create a story. A myth. That is something that cannot be destroyed by violence. It will annoy him immensely because we will create a world he cannot shatter with hate, for it exists here,' Morris said, pointing to his head.

Uncle told of his plan to establish the Republic of Tricksterism, a place where humour rules and hatred is banished, where love's freedom to go anywhere is proclaimed. 'Our headquarters will be the Indian Friendship Centre which, as you know, has been controlled by the hairy hearts. We don't seek permanence for our republic but a moment of time that lasts forever.'

We cheered and with Morris's wheelchair at the head, we marched downtown on our mission of liberation. We marched into the Friendship Centre as the hairy hearts, panic-stricken, climbed out the back windows. They left in a rush, not having the time to shred their Indian Affairs hit list of their sacred status card membership rolls. We took their defining documents, turned them upside-down, and wallpapered the building. The children, myself included, were given crayons and told to draw freely. We created a world of merging colours, a world without paint-by-numbers.

The Republic of Tricksterism was proclaimed. All skins are equal was the first constitutional decree and a pair of red drawers became the new flag. Skins from the street came in to help the social workers heal themselves and tribal lawyers were deprogrammed.

Chief Tobe was soon in a fury. He roared with anger and dark clouds pelted the city with hail. He smashed his fists on the ground and the streets cracked and the sewers overflowed. He called loudly and the poisoned souls congregated outside the offices of the Prince Albert Regional Tribal Council to hear his message of hate. The Tribal Council was in an uproar, they passed resolutions and sent ultimatums to the Republic of Tricksterism demanding they abdicate power. 'We are the Chiefs!' they proclaimed. 'The big white men in Ottawa say so.' 'Ah—go on,' replied the Republic of Tricksterism. When even memos from the Minister of Indian Affairs failed to dislodge the trickster-upstarts, Tobe went into action.

A hundred tribal goons were summoned. They were armed with baseball bats, dog repellent and mace. 'We shall disperse these mixed-bloods. These defilers of our traditions. These people without status!' The goons chanted their approval in unison. The Tribal Council Chiefs smiled, patted their beer bellies, and licked their fat lips in anticipation.

The assault came at dawn. Calling in the mounties, who in honour of the chiefs donned full regalia and did a musical ride, Tobe, the goons and the mounties marched in a column toward the Friendship Centre. But the urban animals, the squirrels, raccoons and foxes, ran out ahead of the approaching army and barked out a warning to the citizens of the Republic of Tricksterism.

'We must avert bloodshed,' Morris observed to the citizens. 'Violence is the tool of fools. It is with humour and irreverence that us urban animals must survive. Let them have their building back, let them issue their proclamations with dead trees, let them have their dubious titles like national chief, let them become the media stars. We'll find our humour back on the streets.'

And so it came to be that Tobe and his goons recaptured the Prince Albert Friendship Centre without bloodshed. 'These mixed-bloods are cowards,' Tobe proclaimed, in disappointment.

Uncle Morris was captured by the tribal goons and brought before the Prince Albert Regional Tribal Council. 'He must be punished as an example,' proclaimed Tobe. 'He has committed blasphemy and challenged our noble and sacred institutions.'

'Spare him!' yelled the urban orphans and mixed-bloods but, as always, the chiefs were deaf to the sounds of the streets. On a Sunday, surrounded by a procession of goons, Morris was forced to wheel his chair to the highest hill in Prince Albert.

There he was nailed to a metal medicine wheel, his arms and legs spread in the four directions. Morris died soon after and his body was taken by the goons and buried in an unmarked grave. The mixed-bloods and urban orphans mourned. Crows flew high and cawed his name to the clouds. A wake was held and for four days the memory fires burned from street corner garbage cans. On the fifth day the crows told the people that my uncle had been resurrected but that he had come back as a termite.

The urban people rejoiced and Morris, in his new life form, moved into the regional Indian Affairs building and gnawed at the bureaucrats' desks until they dissolved into sawdust. Meanwhile Tobe, sporting the retaking of the Friendship Centre as another dishonourable feather in his war bonnet, ran for national leader of the FSIN and won the big chief position at that fermenting organization.

'Who better to speak the politicians' garble? Who better to hide the truth between platitudes of self-government and economic development than Tobe?' proclaimed the FSIN in their press release announcing his victory.

Then, one day, despite the opposition of the FSIN, C-31 became law. At the stroke of a bureaucratic pen, status was restored to those long denied, a government decree pronouncing the end of a hundred years' damage. 'Hallelujah, we're Indians,' responded the mixed-bloods. Our hearts soared like drunken eagles. We donned our chicken feather headdresses, our squirrel tail bustles, and fancy-danced around the Midtown Plaza.

My mother, a full-blood Cree woman, could only laugh at the gesture. Meanwhile in the FSIN offices Tobe, the mixed-blood/pure-blood, and his Indiancrats, were having a bad day. They grumbled, drank double shots of rye, and hit their blonde secretaries.

But C-31 was only a temporary irritation for Tobe. His vision remained focused on careerism and playing the colonial card game. He wore blinkers whenever he entered the city to avoid seeing the urban orphans. He talked about first nations as if the cities did not exist. He became bloated with his power and gained weight by the hour. As the Honourable Heap Big Chief he increased his salary and his belly respectively. Mary Seesequasis moved to Saskatoon and worked at the 20th Street Community Clinic where she administered to the mixed bloods: the whores, dykes, queers, street people, everyone. My uncle's words, 'We are not victims. We are survivors,' was the motto she lived by. Tobe also was a survivor but in a more dangerous game. My mother saw the Indian Act as a bad joke. Tobe embraced it as a career. His sense of humour was lost in the shuffle of colonial cards and his heart was hardened by the cannibal spirits.

Meanwhile Uncle Morris, having completed his job in Prince Albert, found his way into a chief's pocket and made it to Ottawa. Rumour has it that even today he has led an army of termites into a certain national chief's organization where he is currently munching away at the legs of that chief's chair.

Thom E. Hawke b. 1959

ANISHNAHBE

Lasalle, Quebec

Hate's ugly scab ripped off last night
A hail of rocks pounded our chevy
Grandmother screamed, her window shattered
Did they not see the elderly, the children, the infirm?

Neighbour, I did not know you hated me so
I didn't mean to inconvenience you
Perhaps you weren't aware of our histories, perhaps,
you just don't care

Hate's soldiers, protected by the police,
shrieked in a cacophony of contempt.
Grandfather's been hit, his cheek bleeding
Did they not see the fear in our eyes, the sadness of our scorn

Neighbour, I did not know your malice ran so deep
I didn't mean to try your patience
Perhaps you don't understand endurance, perhaps a two hours drive
is your test of time.

Lock and Load

The fetid stench of death drifted past my door
beckoning, beckoning for me to play
Let's rock and roll said the warrior
unconditional resolve, unrepenting fate
Decidedly, my fingers grasped the freshly cleaned A-K

Over the mantel hung Grandfather's hunting rifle
Clashing myriads of images flashed
THE HUNT, THE CHASE, THE KILL
    THE HUNT, THE CHASE, THE KILL
Who were we? Did it matter now?

Children, oh sweet children, Mommy will take you . . . someplace,
someplace safe? We kissed.
Closing the door, I clicked my weapon to full auto
Down the road, my ancestors were also buried

Apologies to Elijah Harper

Kanehsatake, March for Peace and Justice

Attended the march for freedom
The speeches, singing, dancing, the heat
We revelled in clenched fist unity
Trigger fingers taut, the police flinched

A half mile down the road, warriors, women, children nervously
watched the unity throng
A short distance lengthened by the width of a rifle barrel
A short distance strengthened by power of mind
A short distance

The national MP readied himself . . . a feather appears
Media jostled and squirmed. Click! Hey! Mister Harper?
Security quelled the scrum. Sit, the king speaks

We sweat, everyone adrift to the oratory
Will I make my tee off time, tomorrow?

The Death of John Wayne

The wind blew in gusts in desperation as John (Cowboy) Wayne brazenly swaggered in the Beothuck encampment. Cowboy Wayne, rock farmer and part-time Indian agent brought news of impending government relief.

A multitude of leather garbed Beothuck warriors quickly encircled Cowboy Wayne and hurriedly escorted him to the great council house of their leader and undisputed chief, TON O BUCKS.

Having been trained at numerous Indian cross cultural workshops Mr Wayne was quick to offer the mighty chief obligatory salutations and gifts of little or no intrinsic value.

With a sweeping hand gesture, TON O BUCKS motioned for the rugged cowboy hero to sit on a soft pile of cedar boughs ceremoniously placed by the raging council fire.

Upon taking place the gathered assemblage of Beothuck warriors women and children followed his lead and quietly seated themselves awaiting the beginning of the policy consultation process.

Effortlessly, Mr Wayne rose from the cross-legged sitting position then addressed the seemingly enraptured audience. TON O BUCKS, listen here and listen tight, I offer your people self determination and justice.

A resounding gasp lofted from the Beothuck mass indicating a twinge of displeasure with the harsh manner Cowboy Wayne disrespectfully spoke to their chief and tribal leader.

Sensing metaphysical reaction of Beothuck negativity which the Cowboy quickly dismissed as pent-up post colonial guilt, he promised the Beothuck cultural restoration, self-government, money, and more money.

Hours later the great chief responded to the Cowboy's offer of municipal government and financial compensation. He spoke of freedom, justice, and the native way.

The chief vehemently felt that the new deal was the final opportunity for the Beothuck to determine their own destiny. Little did the assembled know that TON O BUCKS was on the same payroll as John.

Confidently armed with the knowledge that TON O BUCKS was loyally hemmed in his back pocket, Cowboy Wayne proceeded to patronize the assembled mob with the point his government knew what was right for the Beothuck.

Suddenly breaking free from the ranks of the Beothuck throng a young warrior emerged accusing TON O BUCKS of treason and John of administering termination policies.

With the emergence of the young Beothuck warrior, John became visibly distraught. He soon took the defensive and pleaded for cooler heads and support for his just and reasonable offer.

Removing a feather from his Chief's head, the young warrior began inciting the frenzied Beothuck mass to join him in the sacred chant of war and victory.

Chanting feverishly, a crescendo of rhythm emanated from the Beothuck mob, as the young warrior commanded his people to remove the Cowboy from his place of ceremony and throw him in the raging council fire.

Completely without escape, John (Cowboy) Wayne begged for mercy. Hearing his pleas the young Beothuck warrior doused the Cowboy hero with flammable bear oil and lit a match.

Joseph A. Dandurand b. 196?

SALISH/NOOKSACK

Salmon Queen

She died.

Went like the wind.

Into the water she dove
till her nose brushed
lightly against the soft
underworld.

She became the Salmon Queen.

A beautiful lady who never
spoke loudly.

Her children chase the water-bugs
and they dance their spring
celebration:

their tails going
side to side
side to side.

The moon calls out to all
night people:

the owl
the mice
the coyote
come to the water
and watch the queen
as she prepares
to mate.

Her eyes close and she
accepts the treacherous male:

his teeth biting her soft
flesh.

The eggs spread and mix
with his milky life.

The moon smiles
the owl blinks
the mice run
and the coyote
chews hungrily
on the dying queen

Swimming the Cannon River

sleepy

eyes heavy

forgot to keep
my balance

fell into
the unforgiving
river

panic

followed by
release

slept
till they
pulled me
out

visions
of ghosts
and demons
never came

found
myself
swimming
with the
fish
i was to
catch

Lorne Joseph Simon 1960–94

MICMAC

From *Stones and Switches*

THE SECOND COMING

'I was just getting ready to check my net,' Skoltch hollered at Megwadesk, as they stamped the mud off their boots and hung their jackets, 'when I heard you yelling! Gisúlk, Máli! I thought somebody was killing you! The way you were going on, I almost ran into the house to get my rifle! And then to find out it was just my dog—well, I didn't know who to throw into the ditch—the dog for playing with you or you for screaming like it was the end of the world! Nisgam nuduid, I'd hate to see you in a war! Here! Take a seat!'

'Boys oh boys, I'm telling you,' Megwadesk replied, 'if that bitch comes at me again, eh, I'm gonna slit its throat from ear to ear! Cut its damn head right off!'

Megwadesk kept his navy-blue cap on. He scratched his left arm through his shirt. It felt swollen but he could not tell for sure.

'How are you, anyway? Did it bite you anywhere?' Skoltch asked.

Megwadesk rolled up the sleeve and they looked at his arm. It didn't appear to be cut anywhere but it was swollen. Skoltch offered to bind it up but Megwadesk insisted that he was fine.

'Well at least have something to drink!' Skoltch said. 'What will it be? Tea or coffee?'

'Tea, if you got some,' Megwadesk replied.

'Sure we got tea, boy! We got bologna, too!' Skoltch bellowed. Megwadesk noticed a large scab on Skoltch's brow and he guessed rightly where it came from.

'You know what the Maliseets say about us, don't you? "What's a Micmac breakfast? Tea and bologna!"'

Skoltch laughed at his joke as he struck a match and lit a kerosine lamp. Beside the lamp stood a jar of pickled babycorn. Megwadesk could hear Skoltch's wife snoring through the open bedroom door. Skoltch poured some water from a bucket into a kettle and set the kettle on the stove.

He put a cigarette in his mouth and added, 'Say, you sure looked woebegone checking your net a few days ago! Your jaw just about dropped to the water! Whoa, there! I almost told my son to reach over with a bucket to catch your jaw before you lost it in the water! But you caught it in time! Nisgam nuduid! You had your empty net pulled out of the river and up over your head and you kept looking this way and that, and up and down, and shaking your head, and staring! Ho! I told my son, "Get your handkerchief out because he's going to start bawling any minute now!" Ho, boy, you sure were a sight!'

That's Skoltch all right, Megwadesk noted. *He gets a little lucky 'n' he loses no time 'tall getting up there on his high horse 'n' he forgets how to talk to people in a sensible way! He's got to shout at the top of his lungs, eh, like he's talking to his lessers 'n' he's got to exaggerate everything, too, eh!*

'Since then, though, I haven't seen you check your net!' Skoltch shouted as he stood by the counter, his arms crossed over his chest. It seemed he forgot the cigarette. The tip of it constantly bobbed up and down as he spoke. 'Is this your seventh day, or what? You've made the world and you've set the lamps in the sky, right, and now it's time to rest, huh! Ah, ha, ha! Or is your girlfriend keeping you in bed? What is it? Too much of that and you'll soon start to waste away! You won't want to do anything else! That's what my father told me! Gisúlk, Nisgam, he should have knowed! He got ten kids out of my Mum alone! That's before he took off to Cape Breton to start another brood! And, you know, come to think of it, that old geezer must have been right! He never did do much else! I had to learn fishing from my uncle! That's where my son is now—with my uncle. They went out to the breakwaters yesterday to spear eels! I miss my boy already! Anyway, he'll learn from the best—he'll be learning from Uncle Noel! Like I said, Dad could talk fishing but I never seen him so much as bait a hook or haul a minnow! So don't tell me your new little lady is getting you to be like he was! Whoa, there, big fella! Ho!'

Skoltch had acquired his nickname, which meant frog, because of his double chin. It was so enormous it seemed pendulous. The great width of his mouth and the thin, flat lips that lined it further enhanced his resemblance to a frog. The size of his mouth had never pleased Skoltch. In his youth he had spent many hours before the looking glass puckering his lips, trying to make his mouth smaller. Years later, he hit upon the idea of letting his facial hair grow to cover up his mouth but there must have been only a thimbleful of French blood in him. His beard was sparse.

'I should say it's your woman who's keeping you in bed,' Megwadesk replied. 'You don't see me check my net, eh, 'cause you don't get up early 'nough no more.'

And Megwadesk slyly winked and quickly pointed by jutting out his bottom lip to Skoltch's bedroom door. Skoltch's wife kept snoring. Skoltch laughed heartily. Any comment ascribing virility to him, easily flattered him. Between hoots of laughter, Skoltch blushed and cried, 'Nooo!' in a faint attempt to put the matter into sober perspective. At length, Skoltch regained composure.

'Nugú!' Skoltch announced, his face red. 'Let's not talk about our better halves no more, huh!'

'Oh, come on.' Megwadesk pretended disappointment.

'No, no, no! We'll save those stories for when we're out of ear shot! You're an eager young buck and all that, I know, so there are things you want to learn from an old nabéw like me! Ho, I can tell you stuff! But in due time, boy! In due time!'

Skoltch took a match out of the matchbox, struck it, and lit his cigarette. He inhaled peacefully. Skoltch's compressed eyes gleamed and dimples formed in his fleshy round face as he stood looking at the stove, impatient to hear another protest—another, 'Oh, come on'—certain that Megwadesk had not taken his injunction to heart. Skoltch was reluctant to leave so soon, the laudable subject of his manly ardour, but he had felt it was only proper to show some degree of modesty, which was why he had feigned insistence on waiving the matter. Now he stood grinning at the steaming kettle, a suitable epic about his virility set to course from his mouth, just waiting for another protest and a chance to roar with bogus reluctance, 'Well, all right! If you insist! I'll tell you a little something I know about women!'

Megwadesk, however, missed his chance to humour Skoltch. He shrugged his shoulders and said, 'Whatever you say.'

Skoltch found something suspect in this sudden indifference. To make matters worse, Megwadesk made Skoltch positively hostile by pointing out the sizable scab over his left brow and asking, 'Is that cut on your head from a rock, eh? Are they still throwing rocks from the bridge?'

'Do you really care to know?' Skoltch growled. Then he sucked on his cigarette three times.

Megwadesk was taken aback. After a long pause, Megwadesk said, hoping to break the hostile silence, 'I heard you're going to get a new sail-boat.'

Skoltch ignored the question and said, 'Well, if you really want to know, I did get hit with a rock! Now what do you want?'

'What do you mean?' Megwadesk asked. He thought Skoltch was asking him what he wanted that information for but that made no sense.

'What do you want? Why are you here?'

'Oh, that! I'm here to find out what's been going on at the bridge, eh. I haven't gone past it 'tall in six days now.'

'Humph! Don't look like you'll be going past it any time soon either, so why are you worried?'

'I'm thinking of going to ykdánug, spearing eels, eh. Ain't had no luck 'tall this far upriver for too many days.'

'Spearing eels, eh! I should head out there one of these nights, too, just to do some spearing with my boy! Nisgam! Kids sure grow up fast, eh?'

Skoltch didn't expect an answer. He was still feeling surly. He took a deep drag from his cigarette and then he said, 'Yeah, I'm looking at a twenty-footer with a twenty-four foot mast!'

'A twenty-footer!' Megwadesk said, with the proper measure of wonder in his inflection. 'Man oh man, that'll hold quite a load, eh, an' with a good breeze them wardens'll never catch you 'tall!'

Nobody owned a twenty-foot-long boat in Messkíg. Sixteen-foot sail-boats, mostly scows equipped with centre-boards, were standard. Still, Megwadesk was not spontaneously expressing his surprise for he had already heard about the details of Skoltch's proposed purchase some time ago. Skoltch, however, found his visitor's calculated response flattering. 'It's lapped hardwood!' Skoltch said. 'It's a fancy sloop, a real cutter, complete with a jib and a centre-board as deep as I am tall! I can set three nets if I want to! It'll easily hold that much catch! A twenty-foot cutter with high gunwales! Nisgam! That's a lot of space!'

'Man oh man, that'll be a wonder,' agreed Megwadesk.

Skoltch smiled indulgently and then, for the sake of modesty, he redirected the conversation again, deciding it was time to offer some friendly advice.

'Well, anyway,' he said, 'if you're going to ykdánug just make sure to go past the bridge by night, if you wanna avoid trouble! Even a mere stub of a mast'll slip you by fast enough! But then you have to hope the wardens don't see you, either! Jumping Moses, it's like we're a bunch of criminals, eh! It's like we're the newcomers instead, huh! Can't touch the animals! Can't touch the fish! Nisgam! We can't even touch the trees! You see a good stand of ash, perfect for axe-handles, and you go take a couple down—one or two, that's all—and some milky-eyed madman's gonna run out with his rifle and tell you to get away from his trees! Everything's theirs now! Gisúlk, Máli!'

'Pretty soon they'll be telling us we can't keep time by the moon 'cause that's gonna be theirs too! You know what really gets me, though, is how they point the finger at us when the fish stocks go down! Isn't that something, huh? They've had them great big boats fishing off the Grand Banks and shipping millions and millions of tons out to every corner of the world since before the time of Christopher Columbus! When they blame us, it sounds like this to me: like one kid, who has taken and eaten most of the cookies in the cookie jar, blaming a smaller kid for eating all the cookies just because that smaller kid took one cookie, which so happened to be the last one! See? For thousands of years we've been taking that one cookie every year, but when all that's left is our one cookie and we still take it like usual, well, we get called gluttons! And a lot worse things, too! Anyway, it's boiling! You like your tea strong?'

'Éq! Black as crow's butt, eh,' Megwadesk answered.

'Six tea bags, then! I like mine strong too! One, two, three, four, five, six, and pick up sticks! Or, around here, pick up switches! There we go! Hey, look at that!'

Megwadesk looked out the window above the counter. Hazy sunlight filtered through the clouds.

'You can stop shaking in your boots now, boy, 'cause it looks like it's gonna clear, after all!' Skoltch roared, as if Megwadesk had fled like a child to the security of Skoltch's house in fear of the storm.

'I didn't even notice 'tall that the thundering had stopped, eh,' Megwadesk said.

'Oh, I know you didn't! But I did! I noticed right away—as soon as that last rod of lightning flashed four miles away! Nadóq, I said to myself, it's over now—that last one sounded like no more than a fart! It's over all right! I'll set the teapot right here on the table!'

As he put the teapot down, there followed a faint flash and several seconds later, another distant rumble.

'Humph!' was all Skoltch voiced. He took the butt out of his mouth and squashed it in a clay ashtray and he turned to the cabinets.

While Skoltch thrust his meaty arms into the cabinets to retrieve two cups and two saucers, a bowl of sugar, and a bag of home-made doughnuts, Megwadesk thought about the storm. Storms, especially very windy ones, used to be explained by his people as the doings of Wejúsyn, a giant bird, whose great beating wings moved the air. This, in turn, made him think again about the man in white and about spirit stories. Spirits, as far as he was concerned, were nothing more than tricks of nature, tricks that people misunderstood.

He had been mulling over this idea for several weeks but he could not share it with anyone. It was still too fuzzy in his head. He felt he had to bring together many examples before he could say clearly what it was he meant. And he knew that to talk about any idea before it had fully matured in his head was the worst thing to do, because people wouldn't understand it and they would only muddy up the water some more. Besides, Mimi often got impatient with his speculations. Megwadesk had learned that, with most people, it was best to skirt around an idea first just to see how they felt about things by slightly touching on the question.

Megwadesk thought about how he enjoyed talking to Mr Severman because the preacher enjoyed talking about things that most people considered foolish, strange or dangerous. During their talks once, Megwadesk had told Mr Severman that maybe what people sometimes called goodness was just the outcome of weakness and, to his surprise, the preacher had answered, 'William Blake, the prophet-poet of England, would have agreed with you, my friend. He wrote that people who bridle their desires can do so because their appetites are naturally small to begin with. No virtue in temperance from that perspective—is there?'

Skoltch set the cups and saucers, and the sugar and doughnuts, on the table. Then he opened a drawer and took out two spoons and set those on the table as well.

'Help yourself!' Skoltch ordered. 'I don't put up with timidity in my house! Go on, boy! I'm not serving anyone! If you can't fend for yourself, you'll starve—that's all!'

'Thank you,' Megwadesk answered, as he poured the tea into his cup. He drank it black.

'Oquetédud! This is a man's tea, eh, a Micmac's tea, all right!'

'Oh, yes!' Skoltch answered and he sat and poured himself a cup too, adding three heaping spoons of sugar.

The two men quietly sipped their tea for several minutes.

Skoltch pushed the doughnuts to his guest and said, 'Here! Try some! They're good!'

Megwadesk took a doughnut and swallowed a bite and then washed it down with tea. Skoltch dipped his doughnut into his tea and chewed on it. Megwadesk noticed the rain had stopped. He looked out the window to the east and saw a pair of rainbows, one fainter than the other. The rainbows reminded him of a promise of some kind—he couldn't remember exactly what it had been about—a promise anyway—that God had made to Noah after the flood.

Suddenly Megwadesk asked, 'Do you believe in that Bible stuff, eh? You know, all the miracles like Jesus raising the dead?'

'Sure, I believe in Jesus,' Skoltch answered, not at all surprised by the question. He had been expecting something like this from Megwadesk. For such an uncanny fisherman, Skoltch thought, Megwadesk still asked the foolish questions of a youth.

'Can you believe in a god who'll make everybody rise stark naked 'n' all rotted on judgement day, eh?' Megwadesk continued. The growing sunlight made him bold. He could voice his secret horrors now.

'Sure, sure,' Skoltch answered with forced impatience. He was pleased actually, for this opportunity to wax philosophical. A conversation with Megwadesk was always good for that. 'But you shouldn't worry about them details! Let the white people worry about all that stuff! Nisgam gejidoq! We didn't have nothing to do with his murder! As far as I see it, on judgement day Jesus will come down on a cloud and he'll go to all the reserves first and tell all the Indians to just keep right on fishing, that's all! Then he'll get back on his cloud again and fly off to Trenton and go deal with the white people there, and everywhere else there's whites—and, by God, they'll pay for killing him all right, and for killing all the land and all the rivers and all the fish and leaving none for us! Amudj! They'll pay! Jesus was a fisherman! And don't you forget it! He knew where to set his nets, too—even better than you, I'm sure! He understands us! So don't you worry!'

Skoltch's comments annoyed Megwadesk. He told Skoltch, 'You make Jesus sound like Glúskeb almost, eh, the way he'll help us and all.'

'Well, they're cousins, I think,' Skoltch declared. 'Or maybe step-brothers! I forget right now how it was my dad put it! My dad was only good for stories, you know! But anyway, Glúskeb took care of us for a long time till he got tired, 'cause we were always making trouble for him, going to war with all kinds of tribes and everything like that! Gisúlk, Máli! So Glúskeb needed a rest! Before he left, he called his cousin, Jesus, and told him to come on over and take care of us for a while! Sort of like babysit, I guess! So Jesus said, no problem, jínym! Remember, Malsum still had to be watched or else that devil would take over the world again! So Glúskeb knew somebody like Jesus had to be here while he went out west to sleep a bit!

'But Jesus was kinda lazy, see! He liked his wine too much, I think! Anyway, he stayed home and only sent his messengers to look after us! That's the priests and stuff! But you know how messengers are! Glúskeb never could leave anything up to his messengers, loon and rabbit! Nisgam gejidoq! If he did, they would make a mess of things! Éq! Bana total mess! So it's the same with these messengers from Jesus! Instead of just taking care of us and baptizing us and giving us decent burials, these priests turned around and invited all kinds of other people with them, see! Bana foolishness!

'So judgement day's going to come around just after Glúskeb wakes up and just before he gets back here! Glúskeb is going to shoot his arrow ahead of him and it'll land in the Minas Basin, see, to tell Jesus he can pack up his stuff and get ready to go back to his home! And Jesus'll get scared, see, 'cause he's let his messengers make a big mess of things here, and it's really all his fault 'cause he's been so lazy, see! Gisúlk, éq! That's when he'll come around on his cloud and tell us to keep right on fishing and then he'll take all the other people together, even the dead ones—he'll call them right up from their Loyalist graves and all—and tell them, "Listen here," Jesus will say, "either you go back with me or you go to hell!"

'Of course, you know how stubborn white people are! Many of 'em'll stand around their farms with their shotguns in their hands! Nisgam! They'll be just ready to kill Jesus all over again, if he so much as steps near their potato gardens! So poor Jesus'll have no choice but to send Satan after them! Satan'll come out of the water with his red cape and red whip and flog the laggards! Some clever ones'll manage to run away and hide in the swamps, though! Then Glúskeb'll come back and if there's any left over—shotgun or not—he'll take them by the scruff of their necks and throw them across the ocean, and tell them to stay there! They can hide from Jesus and Satan but they won't be able to hide from Glúskeb, that's for sure!'

Megwadesk did not find the story helpful. In his mind, either one believed in the old ways or one believed in the white man's Christian ways and yet there were many stories around which were a blend of the two.

'I've heard stories where Glúskeb and Jesus had contests and Glúskeb always won, eh,' Megwadesk said. 'First time I heard this one, though.'

'Oh, yeah, Glúskeb always wins!' Skoltch said very seriously. 'Dad told me them stories, too! Oh, there's hundreds of them! One time, some white guy came around here and wrote a couple down, but the old timers pulled his leg! Instead of telling him all the Glúskeb stories, they told him fairy tales, with Indians in them though, just to see if he'd write those down, too, and call them legends! Nisgam! And he did! So that's how much some people know! Ho! We're always pulling people's legs—and looking pretty serious when we're at it, too! But, anyway, about this Jesus and stuff! Meantime we got to go to church and all that just like a kid has to listen to a baby-sitter! But don't worry about all that judgement day stuff! It's just for white people really! That's why the priests are always going on about it, because they're guilty and they know it and it's always on their minds, bugging them like! So they go on and on about it! Me and you, we're okay and we'll keep right on fishing, either way! Personally, I wouldn't blink an eye if judgement day happened this afternoon!'

Skoltch coughed and then fell silent. His voice was hoarse from all the shouting. Talking down to people was exhausting sometimes.

'Oh, I'm not scared of that stuff, either. Don't get me wrong, eh,' said Megwadesk. 'I'm just curious 'bout what you think, that's all. But you don't really believe that silly story, eh? That's the matter with our people!'

'What's the matter? What're you talking about? Don't you know a good story when you hear one?'

'Too many of our stories are like that, that's all.'

'Like what?'

'They're just like wishes that we keep holding tight to, eh, an' after a while alls we got's is wishes.'

'What do you mean, "wishes"? I'm telling you what my elders told me! It's like a story the prophets tell! It talks about what's gonna happen one day!'

'An' I say instead of wishing the white people'll just disappear one day and we'll all live happily ever after, we gotta start dealing with the facts, eh. Geez, we keep acting like we can just go on ignoring the real world, like we don't have to change someday 'n' start picking up ways of surviving in the white world!'

'That's not—'

'Sure it is! Sure, that's what it's about! Boys oh boys, just look at the story they tell about Old Set-Ból coming back to haunt the priest. They just wish the old priest could be scared by something the way he can scare the people, eh, so they make this story up 'n' it makes 'em feel good—like it really happened. That's like justice for them. But, really, eh, it's just a fill-in for justice. It's all really 'bout wishful thinking, and nothing 'tall else! Nisgam nuduid, why do you think people believe in spirits and witches for, eh? It's 'cause they feel like they got no real power. So they need this magic power. If they can't get back at the whites for stealing all the land, then they'll say that the spirits like Jesus or Glúskeb or whatever'll get back at them one day! That's no different than anything else, either! If you do something wrong to another fellow in Messkíg, 'n' you get away with it, like you don't pay a fine or go to jail or nothing, eh, then that fellow'll tell himself, *Well, maybe I can't do nothing but the spirits'll get 'im back 'cause what goes 'round comes 'round.* Then he'll feel a little better. See what I mean? All these stories 'bout spirits 'n' medicine 'n' stuff is just a way of keeping our blinders on! We don't even see half—'

'So that's all you see in them stories, huh?' Skoltch cut in. 'Then it's you who don't even see half of what them stories are for! First off, let me tell you that I don't act like I don't have to deal with the white world! I have to deal with them people all the time and some of them are real nice but lots of times they get away with things like throwing rocks at people and stealing land left and right! Okay, then! This story I told you tells me that we're not like them! We never went across the ocean and stole their land and told them they couldn't do this or they couldn't do that! So who's right? We're right! Now if we're right, does it mean that we should forget about our honest ways just because we're in a weaker position now? No, sir! I don't think so! Like I said in the story, we keep right on fishing and living the way God wants us to! We don't just turn around and be like them, stealing land, hurting people, taking kids away from their parents, breaking up families, destroying all the trees, being greedy, greedy, greedy! If they're right, then I'd rather be wrong! You see now what you missed in that story?'

'Well, let me put it 'nother way—' Megwadesk said but just then, the door opened and a brutal-looking middle-aged man with a twisted nose, a chipped eyebrow and a lopsided grin swaggered in. His hair was dishevelled and there were branches stuck to his clothing in a manner that hunters sometimes wore to camouflage themselves in the woods.

'Here to see godmother Molly!' the fellow demanded, banging the door shut behind him. Megwadesk glared at him. Even from seeing only his back, he knew it was Rancid.

Connie Fife b. 1961

CREE

Communications class

if i drop out of your educational system
do not fool yourself that i have fallen
off the face of the earth and
am just another statistical write-off.
this act will cause you embarrassment and
i am familiar with the feeling of
being caught turning red in the face
tomorrow if you do not find me, again,
dozing during another one of your lectures
do not think firstly that i have disappeared
amongst sheets of paper shelved in
a reference library. . . .
instead picture me wide awake at 3:00 a.m.
throwing ink upon blank white squares
creating with your own language
a universal formula for change.

Stains

I

stained ochre earth mourned her past
    remembered woman's footsteps across
forest floor   down hillsides into eye
of opening where women gathered
in sanctuary   before the bloodlet
there was song   before the slaughter
the laughter of children rested
amongst tall pine   before the raped woman
housed entire nations within her ribcage
    from this place she became mountain
    transformed to trickster
    returned to mountain's face
earth and woman recall masked men
    their lies   the distortion
    touch of dead fingers on living flesh

the moment the violation began
death followed daughters mutilation   stood
bathed in sunlight   claws embedded in vulva
he tore away at her beauty   devoured her
entrails   thirsted for more in his
frenzied cannibalism of woman's heart
      not satisfied he sought out
the youngest   still the hunger continued
      the feeding became a feast
yellow moon wailed stone mourned   cried
out to the night for the madness to cease
      implored that the banquet table be
destroyed that the masks fall away
      that the monster be starved
instead the constellations wept and buried
womanhood   in   starlit   tears

                    II

beneath her soles lay crushed bone
      ash and dust held together by earth
blood riddled thoughts hurried skyward
      she does not remember that once she loved
      cannot find the memory in
      which she loved others
her face emerged in the water   she answered
in garbled profanity scarlet   princess squaw
      eyes filled with hate stared back
challenged her to live or die in this windswept
valley   urged her to give in give up
      surrender to the sharp taloned beast
clenched fists beat her to forget   discard
      passion   mutilate womans landscape
destroy lineage empty memory filled basket
where heart sits on her knees she pounded her
reflection turned fingers of rage into chokehold
      forced hand down throat   tore out
entire history then threw her grandmothers
against jagged rock   when her voice cried out
she ground it into the dark stain   stood
back while the river of blood spread then
deepened   her flailing arms weakened as the
current overcame her screams   lungs caved in
      resistance succumbed to her monsters
      resilience died embraced by defeat

determination vanished under the
cover of turbulent clouds
she looked around for the final time only
to bear witness to her land being consumed
    by fire

III

imprints
deep
imbedded in earth
story
a journey across twinned mountain
twinned heart
reminders of all life found in this
plush forest of self
woman within man
man inside woman
twinned spirit
a gathering in the hillsides of a country where woman
life
creation
are seen as one
a time when two spirits
one body and the beginning are remembered
ancient woman dance
ancient woman thought
ancient woman language
fire inside minds eye
voice housed within ribcage of all beings who
walk this forest floor
shape changer
she/he
past and future sheltered by memory
war is foreign
not an option
twinned stone knows
understands
called woman home
brought her to this opening
old woman
young woman
heart upon heart
vision upon vision
history gathered amongst tall cedar

aware of heralding change
determined to emerge whole
unfaltered
steadfast
story woman was never homeward bound
thought woman does not need to return
woman language not lost
twinned heart never disappeared
plush green hillsides bathed in sunlight
know this

Dream

last night you drummed me Azania
i heard her shores and felt her lap against my heart
beating
        beating
                deep into the night
you brought me to the edge of her forests into
a clearing down into the opening   i walked towards
women gathered in a circle   renewal of spirits   a
dance to celebrate your survival   a dance of masks
you drummed me Azania on a taut skin
the colour of my own   down from the mountains your
voices travelled on bolts of lightning   touching
down on moist earth
beating
     beating
                and you raise your arms to the sky
your chanting grows stronger as your bodies move to
and fro   colliding with the old women you honour
through your struggle
beating
     beating
                and your hands touch one another
                touch the earth
                touch me
last night you drummed me Azania deep into the night
taking me to her hills and a circle of women whose
outstretched arms embraced me and
     beating
     beating

your spirit met mine and
we celebrated
beating
   beating
      you drummed me Azania

dedicated to Thato Bereng

Driftwoodwoman

buried under a mountain of her own victimization
grabbing at sun covered by her distorted thought
caught by her reflection in a cracked mirror
veiled in drifting spiderwebs
unable to hear the voice of spiderwoman
unyielding to the rhythm of thoughtwoman
a prisoner by her own conviction
beyond her cement walls
a gathering of women tend the fire
calling her home
calling her home

Drew Hayden Taylor b. 1962

OJIBWAY

Pretty Like a White Boy:
The Adventures of a Blue Eyed Ojibway

In this big, huge world, with all its billions and billions of people, it's safe to say that everybody will eventually come across personalities and individuals that will touch them in some peculiar yet poignant way. Individuals that in some way represent and help define who you are. I'm no different, mine was Kermit the Frog. Not just because Natives have a long tradition of savouring frogs' legs, but because of his music. If you all may remember, Kermit is quite famous for his rendition of 'It's Not Easy Being Green'. I can relate. If I could sing, my song would be 'It's Not Easy Having Blue Eyes in a Brown Eyed Village'.

Yes, I'm afraid it's true. The author happens to be a card-carrying Indian. Once you get past the aforementioned eyes, the fair skin, light brown hair, and noticeable lack of cheekbones, there lies the heart and spirit of an Ojibway storyteller. Honest Injun, or as the more politically correct term may be, honest aboriginal.

You see, I'm the product of a white father I never knew, and an Ojibway woman who evidently couldn't run fast enough. As a kid I knew I looked a bit different. But, then again, all kids are paranoid when it comes to their peers. I had a fairly happy childhood, frolicking through the bullrushes. But there were certain things that, even then, made me notice my unusual appearance. Whenever we played cowboys and Indians, guess who had to be the bad guy, the cowboy.

It wasn't until I left the Reserve for the big bad city, that I became more aware of the role people expected me to play, and the fact that physically I didn't fit in. Everybody seemed to have this preconceived idea of how every Indian looked and acted. One guy, on my first day of college, asked me what kind of horse I preferred. I didn't have the heart to tell him 'hobby'.

I've often tried to be philosophical about the whole thing. I have both white and red blood in me, I guess that makes me pink. I am a 'Pink' man. Try to imagine this, I'm walking around on any typical Reserve in Canada, my head held high, proudly announcing to everyone 'I am a Pink Man'. It's a good thing I ran track in school.

My pinkness is constantly being pointed out to me over and over and over again. 'You don't look Indian?' 'You're not Indian, are you?' 'Really?!?' I got questions like that from both white and Native people, for a while I debated having my status card tattooed on my forehead.

And like most insecure people and specially a blue-eyed Native writer, I went through a particularly severe identity crisis at one point. In fact, I admit it, one depressing spring evening, I died my hair black. Pitch black.

The reason for such a dramatic act, you may ask? Show Business. You see, for the last eight years or so, I've worked in various capacities in the performing arts, and as a result I'd always get calls to be an extra or even try out for an important role in some Native oriented movie. This anonymous voice would phone, having been given my number, and ask if I would be interested in trying out for a movie. Being a naturally ambitious, curious, and greedy young man, I would always readily agree, stardom flashing in my eyes and hunger pains from my wallet.

A few days later I would show up for the audition, and that was always an experience. What kind of experience you may ask? Picture this, the picture calls for the casting of seventeenth-century Mohawk warriors living in a traditional longhouse. The casting director calls the name 'Drew Hayden Taylor' and I enter.

The casting director, the producer, and the film's director look up from the table and see my face, blue eyes flashing in anticipation. I once was described as a slightly chubby beachboy. But even beachboys have tans. Anyway, there would be a quick flush of confusion, a recheck of the papers, and a hesitant 'Mr Taylor?' Then they would ask if I was at the right audition. It was always the same. By the way, I never got any of the parts I tried for, except for a few anonymous crowd shots. Politics tells me it's because of the way I look, reality tells me it's probably because I can't act. I'm not sure which is better.

It's not just film people either. Recently I've become quite involved in Theatre, Native theatre to be exact. And one cold October day I was happily attending the Toronto leg of a province-wide tour of my first play, *Toronto at Dreamer's Rock*. The place was sold out, the audience very receptive and the performance was wonderful. Ironically one of the actors was also half white.

The director later told me he had been talking with the actor's father, an older non-Native type chap. Evidently he had asked a few questions about me, and how I did my research. This made the director curious and he asked about the father's interest. He replied, 'He's got an amazing grasp of the Native situation for a white person.'

Not all these incidents are work-related either. One time a friend and I were coming out of a rather upscale bar (we were out YUPPIE watching) and managed to catch a cab. We thanked the cab driver for being so comfortably close on such a cold night, he shrugged and nonchalantly talked about knowing what bars to drive around. 'If you're not careful, all you'll get is drunk Indians.' I hiccuped.

Another time this cab driver droned on and on about the government. He started out by criticizing Mulroney, and eventually to his handling of the Oka crisis. This perked up my ears, until he said 'If it were me, I'd have teargassed the place by the second day. No more problem.' He got a dime tip. A few incidents like this and I'm convinced I'd make a great undercover agent for one of the Native political organizations.

But then again, even Native people have been known to look at me with a fair amount of suspicion. Many years ago when I was a young man, I was working on a documentary on Native culture up in the wilds of Northern Ontario. We were at an isolated cabin filming a trapper woman and her kids. This one particular nine-year-old girl seemed to take a shine to me. She followed me around for two days both annoying me and endearing herself to me. But she absolutely refused to believe that I was Indian. The whole film crew tried to tell her but to no avail. She was certain I was white.

Then one day as I was loading up the car with film equipment, she asked me if I wanted some tea. Being in a hurry I declined the tea. She immediately smiled with victory crying out, 'See, you're not Indian, all Indians drink tea!'

Frustrated and a little hurt I whipped out my Status card and thrust it at her. Now there I was, standing in a Northern Ontario winter, showing my Status card to a nine-year-old non-status Indian girl who had no idea what one was. Looking back, this may not have been one of my brighter moves.

But I must admit, it was a Native woman that boiled everything down in one simple sentence. You may know that woman, Marianne Jones from 'The Beachcombers' television series. We were working on a film together out west and we got to gossiping. Eventually we got around to talking about our respective villages. Hers on the Queen Charlotte Islands, or Haida Gwaii as the Haida call them, and mine in central Ontario.

Eventually childhood on the Reserve was being discussed and I made a comment about the way I look. She studied me for a moment, smiled, and said 'Do you know what the old women in my village would call you?' Hesitant but curious, I shook my head. 'They'd say you were pretty like a white boy.' To this day I'm still not sure if I like that.

Now some may argue that I am simply a Métis with a Status card. I disagree, I failed French in grade 11. And the Métis as everyone knows have their own separate and honourable culture, particularly in western Canada. And of course I am well aware that I am not the only person with my physical characteristics.

I remember once looking at a video tape of a drum group, shot on a Reserve up near Manitoulin Island. I noticed one of the drummers seemed quite fairhaired, almost blond. I mentioned this to my girlfriend of the time and she shrugged saying, 'Well, that's to be expected. The highway runs right through the Reserve.'

Perhaps I'm being too critical. There's a lot to be said for both cultures. For example, on the left hand, you have the Native respect for Elders. They understand the concept of wisdom and insight coming with age.

On the white hand, there's Italian food. I mean I really love my mother and family but seriously, does anything really beat good Veal Scallopini? Most of my aboriginal friends share my fondness for this particular brand of food. Wasn't there a warrior at Oka named Lasagna? I found it ironic, though curiously logical, that Columbus was Italian. A connection I wonder?

Also Native people have this wonderful respect and love for the land. They believe they are part of it, a mere chain in the cycle of existence. Now as many of you know, this conflicts with the accepted Judeo-Christian, i.e., western view of land management. I even believe somewhere in the first chapters of the Bible it says something about God giving man dominion over Nature. Check it out, Genesis 4:?, 'Thou shalt clear cut.' So I grew up understanding that everything around me is important and alive. My Native heritage gave me that.

And again, on the white hand, there's breast implants. Darn clever them white people. That's something Indians would never have invented, seriously. We're not ambitious enough. We just take what the Creator decides to give us, but no, not the white man. Just imagine it, some serious looking white man, and let's face it people, we know it was a man who invented them, don't we? So just imagine some serious looking white doctor sitting around in his laboratory muttering to himself, 'Big tits, big tits, hmmm, how do I make big tits?' If it was an Indian, it would be 'Big tits, big tits, white women sure got big tits' and leave it at that.

So where does that leave me on the big philosophical scoreboard, what exactly are my choices again; Indian—respect for elders, love of the land. White people—food and big tits. In order to live in both cultures I guess I'd have to find an Indian woman with big tits who lives with her grandmother in a cabin out in the woods and can make Fettuccini Alfredo on a wood stove.

Now let me make this clear, I'm not writing this for sympathy, or out of anger, or even some need for self-glorification. I am just setting the facts straight. For as you read this, a new Nation is born. This is a declaration of independence, my declaration of independence.

I've spent too many years explaining who and what I am repeatedly, so as of this moment, I officially secede from both races. I plan to start my own separate nation. Because I am half Ojibway, and half Caucasian, we will be called the Occasions. And I, of course, since I'm founding the new nation, will be a Special Occasion.

James Tyman b. 1964

MÉTIS

From *Inside Out*

I was alone in the house one Saturday afternoon when I got the impulse to enter my parents' bedroom. I knew they kept our old report cards there, and I wanted to see the kinds of things the teachers used to write about my two older brothers. I didn't think they'd had as much trouble in school as I was having, but I thought comparing my behaviour with theirs might help me understand why I acted the way I did.

I was fumbling through some papers when I came across a large brown envelope marked 'Saskatchewan Social Services Department'. My head went light. There was a letter with 'Adopt Indian Métis' in dark blue letters across the top. I must be a Métis Indian, I thought. I wondered what tribe that was. I knew we had Sioux Indians all around us on the reserves. But where was the Métis reserve? I read on: 'Born in Ile-à-la-Crosse, Saskatchewan'. Where the hell was that? My mom said I was born in Saskatoon. The letter gave those two bits of vital information: the rest was details of meetings for parents to attend in Regina. I read it three times. There was no hint of who I was, no name. But its impact on me was staggering.

Up until then I'd felt very close to my mother and father. Now I felt alienated; it was a mixture of love and hate, and my resentment was building. I wanted to know who my biological mom was, but who could I ask? My adopted mother? I couldn't figure out why they'd never told me anything.

It took a few days for me to realize I should look in the encyclopedia for a map of Saskatchewan and find out where Ile-à-la-Crosse was. I flashed through the index. There it was! 'Ile-à-la-Crosse, G-5'. I put one finger on G and the other on 5. Ile-à-la-Crosse was 200 miles northwest of Saskatoon. One road went there, and according to the map that's where it ended. Ile-à-la-Crosse was the end of the road, the end of civilization. I shut the encyclopedia. I was more confused than ever. I was alone in the house, so I went back to the drawer which contained my past.

I looked through the letters from the Social Services Department. Again there were meetings for my parents to attend, and one letter listing all the diseases I'd contracted. It was a long list. I tried to remember being so sick. There were no names on these letters, just 'the subject'.

'I'm a subject,' I smiled to myself. Then I finally found some news: 'Kenny Howard Martin was placed with William and Cecile Tyman on September 17th, 1967. His new name will be James Kenneth Tyman.' I felt a heat rush. That was it! Now I know who I am. I have another family. But where are they?

My mind flashed back to the day I walked into the Tymans' house, the time I hid up in the crawl space, the time my sister showed me how to ride a bike in the dusty street out front, which was now paved. I remembered the first bike the Tymans gave me: it was red and had training wheels. I smiled at that thought. I used to spend hours roaring around the house, almost running into my mom's afternoon visitors. I remembered all the questions the kids asked about my 'real' family. Now I could tell them where I was born. I sat on the back fence mulling over my memories. They were pleasant, the ones about growing up in this house.

When Mom and Dad came home I watched them as they talked about their day's accomplishments at the new house. I wondered why they had taken me. I wondered why I had been put up for adoption. I wondered, more than anything, why I hadn't been told anything. That question was always with me. I'd say, 'This is the day I ask what's going on.' But I didn't know how to approach them. I thought, 'If they didn't want to talk about it, then maybe I shouldn't bring it up.' That was my reasoning. What it was, really, was my means of escaping what I concluded would be some pretty painful memories. Why else couldn't I remember a thing?

My emotions were in turmoil that summer. I felt cheated by a mother I didn't even know. I felt deserted. I felt angry because the Tymans hadn't told me the truth. I felt resentment toward people who gave me a hard time about who I was. What did they know? 'No one cares about me!' I shouted out one day. 'So I don't care about anyone!' I was walking through Valley Centre Park, just below where my parents were constructing the house. I looked up and saw them working away. 'Why you guys?' I asked myself.

I felt alienated from the Tymans and 'their relatives', as I put it. I felt awkward at family gatherings. I stuck out like a sore thumb in family pictures. I wanted to talk, to ask questions. But I didn't want to rock the boat. The family members were in a jubilant mood most of the time, building their new home. It was my father's dream house. I didn't want to bring up such a sensitive subject and disrupt the harmony of the family. I kept it inside. My conflicting emotions were eating me up like a cancer.

* * *

The Regina Correctional Centre was the most unfeeling, violent, and desperate place I had ever come across. You didn't need a master's degree in sociology to see the desperation and hatred in people's faces. The jail was divided into four 'units', all connected. The first one you encounter is the oldest and the most violent unit in all of Saskatchewan's correctional system. Knifings are common. Beatings come the same way as the afternoon soap operas: regularly and on time. Inmates mutilate themselves with razors, or with nails smuggled from the carpentry shop, or just by banging their heads against the wall till either they're dead or they've knocked themselves unconscious. Extortion is as common as insects. The smell of sweat, feces, urine, and dried blood fills my nostrils, clouding my already perplexed mind and emotions.

The unit I'm supposed to head for is Unit Four C and D. When I ask a harmless-looking guy about it, he smiles smugly. I figure out why when I walk into Unit Four C and D: it's for first-timers, 'fish', virgins. I'm ushered to the back of Unit Four, where there are four bunk beds set up for overflow inmates. As I walk along I notice most of the inmates are younger than me, like that snot-nosed Howard. I'm shown my bunk and start going through the kit I was issued in the shower room: one very used towel, one comb, one toothbrush and toothpaste, one razor and shaving lotion, and a complete change of clothes. Other inmates come to check me out. Some of the bolder ones stop and chat. One kid of sixteen, his forearms a maze of criss-crossing scars, is very talkative. Within minutes I know his age, his home town, his place of birth, his grandma's ailments, his charges, and his release date. Finally he stops verbalizing long enough to ask me my name. I'm in no mood to talk to him. For one thing he's white, and white people are at the bottom of the social ladder in here. I'm not about to make friends with one of them. It could come back to haunt me.

After his performance, along comes an Indian of the same age and size. He's quick to point out that the honkies watch their step in here: 'It's not like the street for them racist fuckers,' followed by raucous laughter. I nod. This is different, I'm thinking. The honkies are the oppressed minority in here. Yep, this is a different world, all right.

I was quickly accepted among the inmates. I was a solid guy, good people, a bro to my fellow Indians who made up 75 per cent of the unit's population. But the young white kid, Kelvin, was the range's punching bag. Everyone made snide remarks to him about his baby face, or the fact that he was going to get fucked in the ass if he was ever sent to main population, or that he didn't have enough guts to kill himself when he slashed up. He was offered assistance if he ever wanted to try it again.

'I'll slash your wrists for ya! Make sure you bleed to death this time, honky!'

'Come to my cell next time. I'll hang you and fuck you!'

It was always followed by loud, coarse laughter. I'd been expecting raw behaviour, but the racism was blatant. 'You stinking honky!' would erupt from a card game where both whites and Indians were playing. I'd wait for a fight, some retaliation from the honky. There was none. The white race was definitely on egg shells in Four C and D.

Unit Four C and D had its own gym time slot, its own weight room time slot, even its own time to pick up fresh clothing. It was the administration's way of keeping the first-timers away from the harder and more damaging influences of the repeat offenders and career criminals. I noticed the fear it struck among first-timers when a guard threatened to move them into the general population if they didn't comply with unit rules and the orders. It worked on me, for a while.

We had our own gym period four nights a week, and that gave me a chance to play floor hockey. I received thunderous cheers from the Indian congregation whenever I rammed a white person into the wall, the floor, the net, or up three rows into the bleachers. I was blowing off steam. I was always seething.

I couldn't put my finger on it, but once my blood was pumping in a game I'd become obsessed with hurtling my 220 pound frame at anyone on the opposite team. The guards watched in delight when one inmate tried to harm another. That was acceptable. But I had to even the odds a few times, so I'd ram Indian boys into the walls, too, so the guards couldn't label me a racist.

I was assigned a job within a week of my arrival. I was to work in the carpentry shop. It started at eight-thirty and ended at three-forty-five, with one hour off for lunch and two regulated, fifteen-minute coffee breaks. I was expecting stiff commands and harsh work. I thought of the beatings the guards could give you. I thought of the possibility of being shanked or piped. I thought of the rumours of prison rape. I had those fears when I walked in, but after a week I drew my own conclusions. A lot of the stuff you hear about jail does happen in the Regina Correctional Centre. But for some strange reason I had the impression that I'd learn a trade, start a new life. I'd been tried, convicted, and sentenced; now I thought the system was going to train me, give me parole and push me in the direction of a new life. I must have still been on acid when I was thinking up that scenario.

I walked to work on a cold January morning with thoughts of learning to be a carpenter, a new beginning. I waited eagerly for the shop boss to give me instructions, or a work project. I waited. And I waited. I spent two weeks waiting. Finally I resigned myself to making sure the other inmates had coffee and keeping the coffee area clean. After that I'd lean back in a chair, pull my baseball cap over my eyes, and catch a few winks.

* * *

The shop boss was a man in his later years who was obviously just waiting to retire—no hassles, no confrontations, just do what's necessary. I found a lot of staff with this attitude. Others were there only to aggravate you, to frustrate you, to make sure you hated every goddamn day you were there. Jail is full of bitter men, and that type of bull just ferments the bitterness inside a man. I guess it's their version of rehabilitation.

My shop boss was a walking ghost. He never said more than was necessary. He never rose from his desk unless it was necessary. One day he called me over to look at my progress report. He had filled in 'good work habits'; I never did a thing in there. He had filled in 'follows orders well'; he had never spoken to me in the three weeks I'd been there. Then near the bottom he had me down as a 'sloppy dresser'. I looked at him for an explanation, but he was busy staring into space. I shrugged and signed my name, confirming that I was a good worker who could follow orders but I needed guidance in dressing myself.

I got tired of the monotonous routine of the carpentry shop, so I put in a request to see the counsellor. I went to see him about the same time I had my progress report. He was interested in getting me paroled, and asked me about it. I told him maybe. I was learning from other inmates that when you're only doing ten months you're supposed to be solid and say, 'I'll do my time.' I'd have to do the entire ten months on parole, or do seven months in jail and be released with no restrictions. The more I thought of that, the easier it became to think, 'Fuck your parole. I'll do my time.' Eventually I said it, too.

'Well, Jim, I'll contact your local police and get their opinion.' I snorted with laughter. 'You don't think that's a good idea?'

'They've come to the jail twice since I've been here, trying to get me to confess to crimes I've never heard about. I don't think they'll be keeping open arms for my return.'

'Oh, I don't know. Well, I'll still see.' The counsellor always talked with a cocky grin on his face. 'If not, how about CTR?'

'What's that?'

'Community Training Residence. It's a halfway house for guys who aren't quite ready to be released from custody. The house enables you to look for work, and if you're planning to go to school, they'll let you live there. Do you have your grade twelve?'

'Yeah.'

'That's a change. How did you get it?'

'Going to school. How else?'

'Most guys don't have grade twelve. Even fewer got it by graduating from school. You're one of the rare ones.'

'I'm honoured,' I said. 'Now how about getting me a job where I can use all my worthy talents, instead of sitting on my ass waiting to die.'

'I'll have to see. What do you want to do?'

'Anything where I can keep busy. I hate doing nothing. I thought jail was a place where they busted your ass, or trained you for something.'

'If you were in the pen you could get training,' he said. 'But this is a provincial institution, and there are no funds for it.'

'Next time I'll make sure to tell the judge to give me pen time, so I can become a mechanic or something.'

'You plan on coming back?'

'No, but if they're going to throw you in jail, they might as well give you something to hope for. You know, there are guys on our range asking other inmates for money so they can get their General Education Diploma. The province would rather spend thousands of dollars keeping you inside than give you $20 to help you write your grade twelve final.'

'Write to the premier. See what he says.'

'Ah, fuck you too.'

His smirk disappeared. 'Watch yourself, Tyman. I could charge you and . . .'

'Don't be so ignorant. You're supposed to be a counsellor. Why don't you write to the premier and tell him a few things?'

He stared hard at me for a moment, then changed the subject. 'Let's talk about your history.'

I sighed. It was no use trying to explain anything to him. He wasn't going to listen.

One afternoon I started banging on the barred gate that separated the counsellor's office from the main prison. Then I rang the bell until he came out, red-faced, to demand an explanation.

'I want a job! I want a job where I can work and sweat and feel like I'm doing something useful!'

'Have you heard of requests?'

'Don't give me that bullshit!' I didn't flinch under his threatening gaze. 'You're right here and I'm right here, so fire me or transfer me to another job. I want to work, Christian! There are guys here who don't want to work and you're forcing them to work, so don't give me the run-around about no jobs to be had.'

'Okay, you're fired until further notice!' He turned and stalked back to his office, slamming the door.

Things could have been worse. At least now I could sleep in and watch television all day. And the counsellor eventually did get me a job working in the greenhouse, planting flowers and vegetables that would later be transplanted into the gardens around the jail. There was only one problem: he didn't inform me when I was supposed to start. So one day I found myself being escorted to kangaroo court, the committee that handled internal discipline in the institution. Failing to report for work placement was the infraction.

'The counsellor didn't tell me I had to report for work today,' I pleaded to the discipline panel members.

'According to him, he informed you yesterday. Why didn't you report?'

'I'm telling you, he never let me know.'

'Have a seat outside for a minute.'

I sat in the hall, expecting that the counsellor would be phoned and he would explain that he had made a note to phone the unit and had simply forgotten. They did phone him, but he confirmed his earlier report. I was speechless. The counsellor had got his revenge on me for disturbing his afternoon. I had heard they did this type of stuff, but I didn't believe it till now. I was told that I could be charged with lying to staff members, but would be given a warning this time.

'Five days remission will be placed over your head,' said the Assistant Deputy Director, 'The Five', as he was called; I don't know why. It was just part of prison slang. 'Further charges will result in your losing five days, plus new sanctions brought up at that time.'

The next morning I walked to the greenhouse in plenty of time, sure that the counsellor was just giving me another bogus job to shut my mouth for a while. I sat with the other inmates on the detail: two brothers who were doing two years less a day each for robbing a man on a busy Regina street, a quiet burnt-out Indian who obviously measured your gas tank with his lungs, and Larose the comedian, who kept everyone's ribs sore with his remarks about guards, politicians, churches, and of course white people.

I was pleased with the work. 'That damn counsellor came through,' I thought to myself. I was pleased that I was doing something useful. We planted onions, tomatoes, flowers, and even some marijuana, but that was quickly discovered by the greenhouse boss. He surprised me by not firing the lot of us; he just told us to plant it in a better place next time.

Our shop boss was a good man. He kept us busy, and he'd sneak fresh pineapple from the kitchen for us every Friday afternoon. He talked to you as if you weren't an inmate but simply another human being. He was retiring in a year, but unlike the carpentry shop boss he wouldn't let you sit on your ass even if you were tired. If you didn't follow his rules, you were fired. He wasn't one to do meaningless work, either. He told us at coffee break one day how he'd just had a beef with the administration over some work project he concluded was absurd.

'They want to fire me, good for them,' he said. 'I'm getting out of here next year anyway. They can take their job and stuff it! What do you say to that, Larose?'

'Hail Messiah. You have spoken. It will be written.'

I had one friend in there, an Indian from Meadow Lake who was doing two years less a day, the maximum for a provincial jail. He had forty-three breaking and entering charges against him, so they gave him a break and ran every other charge concurrent after he received two years for the first. We went outside when the snow melted and played horseshoes or walked the track together. My first impression was that he was a hardcore racist, but after talking to him for a while I learned that I was the one who really was not informed. It was like meeting Lorne all over again, the Indian back at Bert Fox Composite High School who'd told me to get some Indian bros and quit hanging around with honkies. 'Maybe you'll see what the truth really is,' Lorne had said, and now, finally, I was ready to hear it. I had learned about Indians from white people. I hadn't bothered to question their analysis because I was afraid of rejection. After talking to Herbie about Indian people and their beliefs, I found that I was myself a hardcore racist. I felt disgusted with myself, remembering all the snide remarks I had made over the years about Indian people. They weren't a bunch of bloodthirsty savages. They were my own people. I hated my own people. My own people hated white people. I didn't know who I was or where I was going.

'You're an apple, Tyman,' Herbie was quick to point out.

I wanted to ask him if he knew any Martins from Ile-à-la-Crosse. I thought that could be what I was looking for—the past I couldn't recall, a sense of identity, of who I really was. You can't take someone's past away and expect him not to miss it, or not to look for it. It was eating at my insides. Finally I did ask him, and he replied, 'There's lots of Martins up there. Why? You related to them?'

'Uh, no. I just knew a couple. I was wondering if there were quite a few of them up there, that's all.' I never told people I was adopted unless they saw my family, and then it became obvious. It was sure to prompt a horde of questions I couldn't answer. I wanted to avoid that lost feeling I had when someone asked me, 'Who are you?'

I had been there two months when the counsellor sent word up to the unit that he wanted to see me. I went to his office. He had his smirk in place. 'Jim, how about going to CTR?'

'When?' I felt excited. I could get out on the street and see people.

'You're appealing your sentence, aren't you?'

I was appealing the sentence for the simple reason that it got me out of jail for a day. 'I go up in two weeks. Why?'

'We can't do anything till your court appearance is dealt with.'

'Oh.'

'I see what you mean about the police in your town.' He broke formation and looked serious. 'They object strongly to your release there. They say you're a menace.'

'Parole is out of the question, then.'

'I would say so. Your mother says she can't control you, and the community would rather see you on TV than on the street, if you know what I mean. The best alternative is to get you to the halfway house in Regina.'

I told him that would be fine with me. He handed me an application and told me he'd be in touch. Three days later he told me I was accepted, but I had to wait for the court decision concerning my appeal.

March 14th was the date of my appeal. It was beginning to cause me sleepless nights. I was more than a little upset with my sentence after learning that other inmates were doing only six months for their third break and enter.

I had made contact with a lawyer who ran a small organization of work projects for ex-cons and who in fact had been a con himself before taking hold of his life and becoming a lawyer. I wanted to ask him how he'd done it, but when he was interviewing me he never once looked at me. He'd ask questions and scribble down my replies. He left telling me not to worry, I'd win my appeal. I didn't see him again till I walked into appeal court.

I sat through the whole session. Everyone who went up got some time knocked off his original sentence. My lawyer was also representing three others, and he was doing a whale of a job. Hell, I thought, if I was one of the judges I'd probably be giving his clients money and a place to live, let alone a lighter sentence. Finally it was my turn to enter the little box below the judges' podium.

'Your Lordships, James Tyman has just recently turned nineteen years old. This is his first incarceration. James has informed me that he was a meat-cutter for nine months, and hopes to go to school to continue his training. James is also a talented football player and has received offers to try out with the Saskatoon Hilltops organization. As you can see, Mr Tyman's release date is set for the end of July. I have been in contact with the organization to find out their starting dates for training camp. As a rookie, Mr Tyman would have to report at the beginning of July, since that is the date set for newcomers. I would also like to point out to your Lordships that the usual sentence for first-timers on a breaking and entering charge is from three to six months. I feel Mr Tyman's sentence is harsh, and would ask the court for compassion in light of these facts. Thank you.'

I felt this had all been rehearsed before I got here, including my lawyer's bullshit about the Saskatoon Hilltops. The three judges looked at each other, they nodded, and I was told to stand up. 'Mr Tyman, the court is merciful and understanding. Your nine-month sentence for breaking and entering will be reduced to six months. Dismissed.'

I walked down the narrow flight of stairs to the holding cells where a jubilant bunch of cons were celebrating their good fortune. I could hear them behind the steel door, slapping each other on the back and planning their futures. I guess it was then that I realized where I really was. I saw two names carved into the wall, and recognized both of them right away. One had just received a life sentence for killing a local prostitute; the other had just received a life sentence in a well-publicized trial for the murder of a university professor. This was the real thing.

I told the counsellor about my victory in court. 'Really!' He had a look of astonishment. 'Well, I'll get hold of CTR and we'll get you out of here as fast as possible. How's that?'

I walked onto the range shouting, 'Justice has been done! We live in a free society where fairness and honesty are put on a pedestal! We the people should be . . .'

'Ah, shut the fuck up!' an Indian from Alberta spoke up.

'Just because you're dogging it, doesn't mean I am,' I said. 'So go lock yourself in your drum and write poetry.'

He gave me a half smile. 'You won your appeal, I take it.'

'Justice has been done!' I raised my hands in true preacher fashion and walked down the range, telling everyone my new release date.

My enthusiastic entrance did not in the least impress Gord Farrow, our little general. He was one of the regular guards, and his sole purpose was to ensure that before he got off his shift someone would be pulling his hair out in frustration over some act he had pulled. He looked daggers at me as I went singing around the range, telling everyone that the justice system was fair and honest. He was going to carry the flame of his own justice and deliver the message from the correctional centre.

It was Saturday morning two days after I came back from my appeal when Farrow came barging into my cell. 'Tyman! You're locked up for sleeping in!' I rolled over and sighed. I knew my release was soon and I didn't want to screw it up because of one man's ignorance. I closed my eyes and made myself relax.

But Farrow wasn't done with me. The following week I slept late. I jumped to my feet, throwing my clothes on. I raced to the gate. It was open from 8:20 to 8:30 to let us out for work. I got there at 8:28, but according to Farrow I was too late. He placed me on charge for sleeping in. He was giggling when he slammed the gate, and still giggling when he handed me the charge sheet. 'Justice has been done, Tyman. Justice has been done.' I was placed on room confinement till the disciplinary panel could hear my case the next day.

I almost hooked that five-foot-eight-inch bag of hot wind. But my instincts told me I was headed for a world of trouble if I laced this guy. We did have one guard who was more than willing to take you on. It was simple: you wanted a fight, he would oblige, and there would be no administration problems after. He had a handful of black belts, and he never smiled unless he was belittling you. General Farrow was just the opposite: he insulted you and degraded you till you swore at him or, like Kelvin finally did one day, took a swing at him. Then he'd scoot like a spooked mouse to his office and dial for help. Soon the goon squad would come and haul your carcass to the hole, all because this guy had an attitude problem.

I walked to kangaroo court resigned to say nothing, for the simple reason that it did no good.

'Three days remission lost.' The Five put on his best threatening face for me. 'I suggest you get up in the morning from now on.'

One day I had a few choice comments for Farrow, who threatened to move me off the unit and into main population. I laughed at him, and that made him madder. Then he turned to answer the phone ringing in his office.

'The counsellor wants to see you, Tyman,' he spat.

'Well, Jim,' said the counsellor, 'you go to CTR tomorrow.'

The halfway house was located in a lower-class area of Regina between Alberta and Broad Streets, two blocks from the YMCA. I didn't know it at the time, but a few of my old schoolmates were boozing it up and dealing with drugs a block and a half away. It was convenient.

The first person I saw was the former owner of the café from my home town, the same café where my parents used to take us after church. She was the cook at the halfway house. She recognized me right away, and was visibly surprised to see me in a house for cons.

'You were such a good boy, Jimmy,' she said in her heavy Greek accent. 'Your papa was such a good man, and your mama was such a nice lady. Jimmy, Jimmy, you stay outta trouble.'

I was confined to the house the first night, as per policy, but the second day I awoke with a sense of excitement and expectancy. I was allowed out for the entire day to look for work. I never looked for work those first two days. I just walked the Cornwall Centre mall in downtown Regina. It felt odd to see all these people, and not some desperate cons. All I could think about was jail and what my fellow cons were doing back in The Hill. Now that I was out, I knew I was different from other people. I'd come from a place few have been, and fewer know what it is really all about. 'Come on Jim,' I kept telling myself. 'You were only there three months. Forget it and start fresh.' But I kept thinking that everyone knew I was a criminal. They wouldn't give me a chance.

When I did look for work my old fears were there instead of my new ones. I was met with cold stares or stunned expressions when I asked for work. 'Well, I don't know, really. How about filling out this application and we'll give you a call?' I knew what they were thinking. Being an ex-con wasn't my problem. My problem was that I was an Indian.

I contacted my old chum Terry who was living with his mother. I felt companionship with him more than ever now. We understood each other. We talked briefly about my incarceration, but it was more of a silent conversation. I mentioned the racism and he nodded his understanding. I mentioned the bulls, and he nodded. He mentioned the filth, and I nodded.

Jordan Wheeler b. 1964

MÉTIS

A Mountain Legend

The school bus drove into a small summer camp at the base of a towering mountain. Boys and girls between the ages of eight and twelve, who had signed up for the three-day camping trip, poured out of the bus. Following instructions from counsellors, they began hurriedly preparing their camp as the sunset dripped over the rock walls towering above them. For many, it was their first time away from the city, which they could still see far off in the distance. Tents were put up and sleeping bags unrolled before the last of the twilight rays gave way to the darkness of night.

Roasting marshmallows around a large campfire, the young campers listened intently to stories told by the counsellors. Behind the eager campers, the caretaker of the camp sat on the ground, himself listening to the stories.

As the night grew old, the younger children wearily found their way to the tents, so that by midnight only the twelve-year-olds remained around the fire with one counsellor and the caretaker. Their supply of stories seemingly exhausted, they sat in silence watching the glowing embers of the once fiery blaze shrink into red-hot ash.

'The moon is rising,' announced the caretaker in a low, even voice. All eyes looked up to the glow surrounding the jagged peaks of the mountain. The blackness of the rock formed an eerie silhouette against the gently lit sky.

The caretaker's name was McNabb. He had lived close to the mountain all his life and knew many of the stories the mountain had seen. He threw his long, black braided hair over his shoulders, drew the collar of his faded jean jacket up against the crisp mountain air, and spoke.

'There is a legend about this mountain once told by the mountain itself,' he said, paused for a moment, then continued. 'People claim that long ago it told of a young boy who tried to climb up to an eagle's nest which rested somewhere among the many cliffs. He was from a small camp about a day's journey from here and when he was twelve years old, he thought he was ready to become a warrior. His father disagreed, saying he was too young and too small. But the boy was stubborn and one morning before dawn he sneaked out of his family's teepee and set off on foot toward the mountain. There were no horses in North America in his time. They were brought later by the Europeans.

'It took most of the day for him to reach the mountain. The next morning, he set out to find an eagle and seek a vision from the mighty bird, as that was the first step in becoming a warrior. But as he was climbing up the rock cliffs to a nest, he fell to his death, releasing a terrible cry that echoed from the mountain far out across the land. The legend says the boy's spirit still wanders the mountain today.'

A coyote howled in the distance and the campers jumped.

'Is it true?' asked one of the boys, with worry and fear in his voice.

'Some people say so, and they also say you can still hear his scream every once in a while.'

All around the dying fire, eyes were straining up at the menacing rock peaks. The caretaker McNabb, however, wasn't looking at the mountain, he was watching one of the young campers. He was an Indian boy, smaller than the others, with short braided hair that fell down his back. The boy was gazing up at the mountain, his curiosity obviously blended with fear. Turning his head, his eyes met those of McNabb. For a fleeting moment, they locked stares, then McNabb relaxed, a knowing expression spreading over his face, while the boy continued to stare at him, wide-eyed and nervous.

There were small discussions around the fire, debating the story's truth before the counsellor told them it was time for sleep. Both tired and excited, they retreated to their tent and crawled into their sleeping bags.

The boy Jason lay in a tent he shared with two other boys, who lay talking in the dark. As Jason waited for the heat of his body to warm his sleeping bag, he thought of that long ago boy. He felt a closeness to him and imagined himself in his place.

'Hey Jason, why don't you climb up that mountain tomorrow morning and try to catch an eagle?' It was Ralph, who was against the far wall of the tent on the other side of Barry.

'Why?' asked Jason.

'You're Indian aren't you? Don't you want to become a warrior?'

True, Jason was Indian, bu the knew nothing of becoming a warrior. He had spent all his life in the city. All he knew of his heritage was what his grandmother told him from time to time, which wasn't much. He had been to three pow wows in his life, all at a large hall not far from his house, but he never learned very much. His time was spent eating hot dogs, drinking pop, and watching the older boys play pool in the adjoining rooms. Little as he knew though, he wanted Ralph and Barry to think he knew a lot.

'No. It's not time for me to be a warrior yet,' he told them.

'Why not?' Barry asked.

'It just isn't, that's all,' Jason said, not knowing a better answer.

'You're chicken, you couldn't climb that mountain if you tried,' Ralph charged.

'I'm not chicken! I could climb that mountain, no problem. It just isn't time yet.'

'You're chicken,' Ralph said again.

'Go to sleep!' boomed a voice across the campground.

Ralph gave out three chicken clucks and rolled over to sleep.

Jason lay there in mild anger. He hated being called a chicken and if the counsellor hadn't shouted at that moment, he would have given Ralph a swift punch. But Ralph was right, the mountain did scare him.

With his anger subsiding, he drifted into a haunting sleep, filled with dreams. Dreams the wind swept through the camp, gently spreading the mountain spirit's stories throughout. A coyote's piercing howl echoed down the rocky cliffs, making Jason flinch in his sleep.

The following morning, Ralph, Barry, and Jason were the first ones up. As they emerged from the tent into the chilled morning air, their attention was immediately grasped by the huge rock peaks looming high above. Ralph's searching eyes spanned the mountain. A light blanket of mist enveloped its lower reaches.

Pointing up he said, 'See that ledge up there?' Jason and Barry followed Ralph's arm to a cliff along one of the rock walls just above the tree line. 'I bet you can't get to it,' he dared Jason.

'I could so,' Jason responded.

'Prove it,' Ralph said.

Jason was trapped and he knew it. If he said no, he would be admitting he was scared. And there was another challenge in Ralph's voice, unsaid, but Jason heard it. Ralph was daring him to prove himself an Indian. Jason had lived his whole life in a city on cement ground and among concrete mountains where climbing was easy as walking up stairs or pressing an elevator button. To prove to Ralph and himself that he was Indian, Jason had to climb to that ledge. He knew that mountain climbing could end a life. And there were wild animals he might have to deal with. How was he supposed to react? How would he react? He was afraid. He didn't want to go. But if he didn't?

'What's the matter?' Ralph taunted. 'Indian scared?'

At that point, Jason decided he would face the mountain and he would reach that ledge. 'Okay,' he conceded.

At first, the climbing was easy, but his progress became slow and clumsy as he got higher up. Struggling over uneven ground and through trees, he came across a large flat rock. In need of a rest, he sat down and looked down at the campground he had left right after breakfast an hour ago. He could see bodies scurrying about. If they hadn't noticed by now that he was missing, he thought, no doubt they would soon.

Looking up, he could just see the ledge above the tree line. It wasn't much further, he thought. He could get to it, wave down at the camp to show he had made it, and be back in time for lunch. Raising himself up, he started to climb again, marching through the trees and up the steep slope, over the rough terrain.

A few moments later he heard a loud howl that seemed to come from somewhere above. At first, he thought it was a coyote, but it sounded more like a human. Nervously, he kept going.

In the camp, Ralph and Barry were getting ready to help prepare lunch. McNabb was starting a fire not far away. They, too, heard the howl.

'I never knew coyotes did that during the day,' Ralph said to Barry.

Overhearing them, McNabb responded. 'That was no coyote.'

Half an hour later, Jason stood just above the tree line. The ledge, his goal, was thirty feet above, but what lay ahead was treacherous climbing, nearly straight up the rock wall. He scrutinized the rock face, planned his route and began to pick his way up the last stretch.

The mountain saw the boy encroaching and whispered a warning to the wind sweeping strongly down its face as it remembered a similar event long ago. Jason felt the wind grow stronger, driving high-pitched sound into his ears. Gripping the rock harder, he pulled himself up a bit at a time. The wind seemed to be pushing him back. But he felt something else, too, something urging him on.

When he was about twenty feet up the rock face, with his feet firmly on a small ledge, he chanced a look down between his legs. He could see that if he slipped, he would plummet straight down for that twenty feet and after hitting the rocks below, he would tumble a great distance further. He knew it would spell death and for a split second, he considered going back down. But once again he felt an outside force pushing him to go on. It gave him comfort and courage. His face reddened, his heart pounded, and beads of sweat poured from him as he inched his way higher. Straight above, an eagle flew in great circles, slowly moving closer to Jason and the ledge.

Far down the mountain the search for Jason was well underway, but the counsellors had no way of knowing where he was, as Ralph and Barry hadn't told. McNabb also knew where Jason was, but he, too, remained silent.

An eight-year-old girl in the camp lay quietly in her tent, staring up through the screen window at the sky. The search for Jason had been tiring and she had come back for a rest. She was watching a cloud slowly change shape when a large black bird flew by high above. Out of curiosity, she unzipped the tent door and went outside to get a better look. She watched the bird fly in smaller and smaller circles, getting closer and closer to the mountain. She took her eyes off the bird for a moment to look at the huge rock wall, and there, high above the trees and only a few feet below a ledge, she saw the boy climbing. Right away she knew the boy was in danger. After hesitating for a moment, she ran to tell a counsellor.

Jason paused from climbing, just a few feet before the ledge. He was exhausted and the insides of his hands were raw, the skin having been scraped off by the rough rock. The ledge was so close. He pulled himself up to it, placing his feet inside a crack in the rock for support. Reaching over the edge, he swept one arm along the ledge, found another spot for his feet, hoisted his body up, rolled onto the ledge and got to his feet. There, an arm's length away on the ledge, were two young eagles in a large nest. For several minutes he just remained there looking at the baby eagles. He had never seen an eagle's nest before. He was so interested in the two young eagles he didn't notice the mother eagle circling high overhead, nor did he hear her swoop down towards him and her nest. She landed in front of him, spread her wings, and let out a loud screech. Jason was so terrified, he instinctively jumped and in doing so, lost his balance. Both feet stepped out into air as he grabbed the rock.

His hands clung desperately to the ledge as the sharp rock dug into his skin. He looked down and saw his feet dangling in the air. The wind swung him, making it impossible to get his feet back on the rock where they had been moments earlier. A coyote howled and Jason's terror grew. Again he looked down at the rocks below. Tears began streaming down his face. He didn't want to die. He wished he had never accepted Ralph's dare. He could picture them coming up the mountain, finding his dead body among the rocks, and crying over him. He began crying out loud and heard it echoing off the rock. Or he thought it was an echo. He stopped and listened. There was more crying, but not from him. Again he felt the presence of something or someone else. The wind swirled in and whispered to Jason the mountain's legend.

Though running swiftly, the boy Muskawashee had paced himself expertly for the day's journey. He would arrive at the base of the mountain far earlier than he had expected and would have plenty of daylight left to catch his supper and find a spot for a good night's sleep. Though small and having seen only twelve summers, his young body was strong. He would be able to reach the mountain in only two runs, pausing in between to catch a rabbit for lunch.

As his powerful legs moved him gracefully across the prairie, he thought back to the conversation with his father the day before. He had explained how most of his friends were already in preparation for manhood and he felt he was ready also. He did not want to wait for the next summer.

When some of his friends came back later that day from a successful buffalo hunt, he decided he would go to the mountain alone and seek a vision from the eagle.

He knew he would have to rise before the sun to get out of camp without being seen.

When he reached the base of the mountain, the sun was still well above the horizon. He sat down in a sheltered area for a rest. He decided this was where he would sleep for the night.

After a few minutes, he got up and made himself a trap for a rabbit and planted it. After laying the trap, he wandered off to look for some berries to eat while preparing his mind for the following day when he would climb the mountain. After some time, he returned to his trap and found a rabbit in it. He skinned it with a well-sharpened stone knife he had brought with him, and built a fire to cook his meal. He would keep the fire burning all night to keep away the wild animals while he slept.

Finishing his meal, he thanked the creator for his food and safe journey and prayed for good fortune in his quest for a vision. Then he lay down in the soft moss and fell asleep to the music of the coyote's howls and the whispering wind.

The next morning, he awoke to the sun's warming shine. The still-smouldering fire added an aroma of burnt wood to the fresh air. He again prayed to the creator for good fortune in his quest for a vision and for a safe journey up the mountain. When he finished, he looked up, high above, and saw eagles flying to and from a rock ledge. This would be his goal.

Half an hour later, he stood where the trees stopped growing and the bare rock began. His powerful body had moved steadily through the trees even though he wasn't used to uphill running. Without resting, he continued his climb, knowing he would have to be careful ahead. The mountain could be dangerous and its spirit could be evil.

As he pulled himself up the face of the rock, he heard the mountain spirit warning him to stay away. Its voice was the whispering wind, which grew stronger and seemed to be trying to push him back. With determination, Muskawashee climbed. High above, the powerful eagle circled its nest.

Just five feet below the ledge, Muskawashee paused. He was dripping with perspiration from fighting the wind and the mountain. Though scared, he would not let fear overcome him. His desire for manhood was stronger. His hands were hurting and covered in blood from the climb, but he reached out again. After several scrabbling attempts, he was able to grab hold of the ledge and pull himself up onto the narrow, flat edge. Eye to eye with two baby eagles, he stopped. He felt great pride and relief in having reached his goal and stood there savouring those feelings. He didn't hear the approach of the mother eagle. As she landed on the ledge in front of him, she let out a loud screech and spread her wings wide. Muskawashee was startled, stepped back and lost his footing. A gust of wind shoved him further and he could feel his body in the air as he tried to get a foot back on the rock. He grabbed the edge, but his arms were trembling and he could not pull himself back up. His fingers ached and began slipping from the edge. Knowing he would soon fall, he began whimpering. He looked up, into the eyes of the eagle. One day, he thought to himself, he would be back.

His fingers let go and he fell, releasing a loud terrifying scream that echoed from the mountain, far out across the land, and down through time.

McNabb and one of the counsellors left the camp when the eight-year-old girl told them what she had seen. Both experienced hikers and mountain-climbers, they were able to cover the distance in a third of the time it took Jason. When they heard the scream they quickened their pace. Minutes later, they reached the edge of the tree line and looked up at the ledge.

Jason, who had been hanging there for several minutes, also heard the scream and looked down into the eyes of Muskawashee as he fell. Jason felt the tension in his fingers, but sensed there were greater forces keeping him hanging there, perhaps the mountain itself was hanging on to him. Whatever it was, Jason remained high above McNabb and the counsellor, who were watching from the tree line. The wind died down and the eagle stepped back, making room for him on the ledge. Jason hoisted a foot back onto the ledge and tried again to haul himself onto the shelf.

Suddenly, he saw Muskawashee standing on the ledge, extending a hand down to him. Jason grabbed his hand and Muskawashee pulled. The two boys faced one another, looking into each other's eyes. The descendant gaining pride in being Indian, and the ancestor completing the quest he had begun hundreds of years earlier. A powerful swirl of wind swept Muskawashee away, leaving Jason alone before the eagle's nest. Jason reached down and picked up a feather out of the nest.

Below him stood the counsellor and McNabb. They had witnessed Jason's rescue.

'Who was that other kid up there?' asked the counsellor in disbelief.

McNabb smiled and answered. 'Muskawashee. He will wander this mountain no more.' Then, unravelling a long line of heavy rope he said, 'Come on, let's get Jason down.'

kateri akiwenzie-damm b. 1965

ANISHNAABE

kegedonce

i thought about you all last night
now here you are
when my eyes are cloudy
and my tongue is swollen
giving me words as if tomorrow depends on them
you say
nniichkiwenh this morning i heard a bird's voice calling to the sun
and i was that bird
i was a swallow swooping into forest
then i was that forest turning my leaves towards the warmth and light
i say nothing
then you sing me your swallow song until my words are loosened
and come pouring out like a dammed river bursting in spring
i say
words are heavy with meaning
they are the true survivors
echoing into infinity when we have become bones cradled by the earth
you say
we belong to them and they belong to us
i say to you
words are my manitouwan my conjurors
with their magic the spider can be set in her web
the old people can live in the memory of generations
people from every direction can be made kin
the world can be recreated out of a fistful of clay
then
i pour my words over you smoothly
you give your words to me in song
i throw my words like poisoned arrows
but you steal the venom and give me back to myself
together we are healed with words
so we open our ears and take the scales from our eyes
letting our words shine like silver in the sun
together we are different yet one
speaking a language of true people

> then you say in my voice
> we are joined to each other as we are joined to this land
> and i say in your tongue
> i do not know how we came to this spot
> but maybe it is enough to know that we are here
> we are safe
> and we are together

the resurrection of desire

the craft of devotion
is the passion of saints idiots lovers
and abusers of every kind
those whose heads of filled reflections and suffering
float slowly downstream
while their lips move as if in prayer
counting branches waving from the shore

homeless
forgotten sailors
swept in a tidal wave of their own creation
destroyers of flesh
worshippers of forever
mapping the way to heaven
across feet and hands and heads and torsos
rejecting the beautiful mortifications that haunt the minds of perverts
the guilt of sinners three scalps hanging from their belts
starkly insanely lovely

delicate in flight these wingless birds
transform into sweet bloody joyous messiahs
noiselessly stripping themselves of flesh
to the envy of those who sing of pain and make love in the dark

manitouwan oh manitouwan
earthy earthly exalted exiles
where is the raven
or those strange ancient monsters of the waterways
who would drag an innocent to that other world
where death sleeps

tell us
what ceremony or madness will safeguard their return?

words for winter

i cannot touch you
but i know how you dream
about a country
where snow falls in sacred secret places

i picture you
          standing out
against the whiteness
          tall
breathing life into the air around you
while the world rushes headlong

  i sigh
cloaking myself in the darkness of a january night
    watching the snow fly
safe from the howling storm outside

Grandmother, Grandfather

i carry a picture of you
in my head
i carry your blood in my heart
like a secret
i carry a cross
since you went away

i lost your words
i lost the sound of your voice

my skin is made of spirits
at night i feel them dance
my hair is a thousand feathered arrows
my face a dull moon

i carry a picture of you in my head

Why This Woman

(For Jo-Anna and Pietra Anna)

why this earth
in solemn patterns
turns
why this sun
circles nightly
casting shadows across the sinking front porch
swing
why this woman
in holy wonder
repeats the human story
why this child
grows in beauty
laughs and cries
lives
turning never escaping
this simple narrative spins us
into reflections
versions of each other

turning turning
we watch
as brightly shines the moon

Gregory Scofield b. 1966

MÉTIS

Nothing Sacred

Excavate:	uproot a granny gets a new resting place pay five bucks to view her in a plexiglass tomb
New Age Movement:	b & e our healing lodge making off with our medicine bird so much for your exhausted Buddha on the altar
Fashion:	Pocahontas makes Vogue in that two-piece buckskin trim your fantasy with fringe and beads feathers tacky
Tourist Traps:	only place to get a genuine Wong & Sons totem pole deciphering clan designs extra
Read All About It:	Pigeon Park Indians make Premier an honorary drinking chum big powwow scheduled after party
For Now:	steal our spotlight his high profile mixing promises and Lysol

Âyahkwêw's Lodge

for Garry G.

êkwa êkosi, nikîwêhtatânân ôhi mistatimwak
and gave them to our women
who in turn

gave them to our men.
That night a baby was born in camp,
eyes clenched shut,
fist in his mouth.

In the lodge
there was an old woman
who had woken in the night
to a lightless presence.
She was instructed
to make offerings,
bring water and blood
from the sacred woman's belly.

These she took to *Âyahkwêw*.

In the blood
a twinning spirit was seen.
The water
was marked by thunder.
Âyahkwêw prepared the rattle,
placing inside
the child's umbilical cord.

At dawn, the time of prayer
they brought the child
to our lodge to be named—
and so we named him twice,
Mistatim-awâsis /
He Who Calls *Piyesîwak-iskwêw*.

êkwa êkosi, nikîwêhtatânân ôhi mistatimwak: And so, we brought these horses home
Âyahkwêw: loosely translated as a person who has both male and female spirits; also
    known as Two-Spirited
Mistatim-awâsis: Horse-child
Piyesîwak-iskwêw: Thunder-woman

Promises

not always did I have an aversion
to shiny objects, convenient arrangements

beneath the buffalo robe

snuggle into him   temporary
the famine his doeskin fingers snail
across my lips of strawberry pleasure

beneath the buffalo robe

spread my arms, my legs
I offer moose tongue and berries
generations he devours in seconds

beneath the buffalo robe

I don't get sweet-talked easy
his hands know what to do
in the dark / light of day

beneath the buffalo robe

promises he whispers   temporary
the taste his foreign tongue snakes
through ravines, over valleys

beneath the buffalo robe

each kiss
history
lolls on the tip of my tongue

Cycle (of the black lizard)

It was a priest
who made him act that way
so shy he wouldn't say shit
if his mouth was full of it.
At least that's what his
old lady said
each time her face got smashed
with his drunk fist.
The last time
he just pushed her around
then passed out.
Later, her *kôhkum* said
a lizard crawled inside his mouth
and laid eggs.

It was a black lizard, she said
the kind who eat the insides
feasting slowly
until their young are hatched.
Already his tongue was gone
from so much confessing.
Other boys at the boarding school
never talked out loud
for fear the lizard
would creep into their beds.
At first it just moved around
inside his head
manoeuvring serpentine
like a bad dream.

Then one night
his brain caved in & oozed out
his ears, nose and mouth.

It was his mouth
that caused him so much trouble.
In there was rotten teeth
and stink breath
made by that gluttonous lizard.
Morning Mass
he swallowed hard to rid the slime
but nighttime it just returned
and slithered around.

Another boy, only older
had the same trouble.
Recess
they eyed each other's dirty holes
and spit, spit, spit.
Once they got caught
and had to scrub the stairs—
and neither said shit about it.

At school, the teacher
noticed his kids had dull eyes
and never spoke or laughed.
The girl was ten
and developed for her age.
When asked in class to tell an Indian story
she went crimson in her face

and cried.
Every few days
her brother got sent
to the principal's office.
They thought he was just naturally rough,
like all Indians.
What they didn't know
was in her pee-hole, his mouth
a lizard crawled around
leaving eggs
during the Lord's prayer.

---

kôhkum: grandmother

How Many White People Noticed
(and recounted the scene over dinner)

Outside the Dodson
the scene wasn't as disturbing
as seeing a wino
plunge twelve stories or
hearing the fatal crack
of a human skull
upon impact.
Still, by the way she landed
she must have went down
like a ton of bricks.

At first
I thought she was a goner.
Then I saw
her fingers twitch.
'She's had it, eh?' some drunk said,
wobbling down beside her.
'You her old man?' I asked,
moving in
so he couldn't cop a free feel.

A crowd assembled, mostly drunks
from other boozecans
along 100 block.
9-1-1 said turn her on her side,
clear her mouth, tilt her head back,

talk calmly, wait.
Brushing back her hair I saw
she was in her early twenties.
Her face was smooth
and free of bruises—
I could tell
she didn't put up with any shit.

Finally the paramedics arrived.
Having checked her vital signs
and finding them satisfactory
they shook her so roughly
she opened her eyes.
'How much have you had
to drink today?'
'Hey, how much have you had
to drink today?'
'HOW MUCH HAVE YOU HAD
TO DRINK TODAY?'

Her eyes floated over
and discovered me slowly.
'My boy's in care,' she slurrred,
grabbing my hand,
'I gotta see my worker.'

Across the street
a businessman sat in his car
watching the entire scene.
Only after she was up
and staggering towards Pigeon Park
did he leave, grinning
as smart as
the clatter of china, the clinking
of knives on crystal,
always the knives, I thought
their goddamn knives.

Warrior Mask

This face
wasn't always
a concrete mask

littered in neon
to be spit, frowned
or pissed on.

In puberty
my *Âyahkwêw* eyes
followed strangers
and saw the black junk
squishing
around inside.

The face
came one night
when a grandfather
worked his medicine
in a dream.

'*Sâwanohk*,' he said
softly, mixing pollen and spit
he covered the right side
completely and
gave me summer songs
to sing.

A black line divided.

'*Pahkisimotâhk*,' he continued
grinding charcoal, spitting
and mixing and
marked four black dots
on the left.

'*Â*' he clapped,
'your path to the spirits.'
'*nikamow*,' *itêw*, '*nikamow*.'

Âyahkwêw: loosely translated as a person who has both male and female spirits; also
    known as Two-Spirited
Sâwanohk: south
Pahkisimotâhk: west
Â: exclamation or acknowledgement
'*nikamow*,' *itêw*, '*nikamow*': 'Sing,' he said, 'sing.'

Eden Robinson b. 1968

HAISLA/HEILTSUK

Terminal Avenue

His brother once held a peeled orange slice up against the sun. When the light shone through it, the slice became a brilliant amber: the setting sun is this colour, ripe orange.

The uniforms of the five advancing Peace Officers are robin's egg blue, but the slanting light catches their visors and sets their faces aflame.

In his memory, the water of the Douglas Channel is a hard blue, baked to a glassy translucence by the August sun. The mountains in the distance form a crown; *Gabiswa*, the mountain in the centre, is the same shade of blue as his lover's veins.

She raises her arms to sweep her hair from her face. Her breasts lift. In the cool morning air, her nipples harden to knobby raspberries. Her eyes are widening in indignation: he once saw that shade of blue in a dragonfly's wing, but this is another thing he will keep secret.

Say nothing, his mother said, without moving her lips, careful not to attract attention. They waited in their car in silence after that. His father and mother were in the front seat, stiff.

Blood plastered his father's hair to his skull; blood leaked down his father's blank face. In the flashing lights of the patrol car, the blood looked black and moved like honey.

A rocket has entered the event horizon of a black hole. To an observer who is watching this from a safe distance, the rocket trapped here, in the black hole's inescapable halo of gravity, will appear to stop.

To an astronaut in the rocket, however, gravity is a rack that stretches his body like taffy, thinner and thinner, until there is nothing left but x-rays.

In full body-armour, the five Peace Officers are sexless and anonymous. With their visors down, they look like old-fashioned astronauts. The landscape they move across is the Surreycentral Skytrain station, but if they remove their body-armour, it may as well be the moon.

The Peace Officers begin to match strides until they move like a machine. This is an intimidation tactic that works, is working on him even though he knows what it is. He finds himself frozen. He can't move, even as they roll towards him, a train on invisible tracks.

Once, when his brother dared him, he jumped off the high diving tower. He wasn't really scared until he stepped away from the platform. In that moment, he realized he couldn't change his mind.

You stupid shit, his brother said, when he surfaced.

In his dreams, everything is the same, except there is no water in the swimming pool and he crashes into the concrete like a dropped pumpkin.

He thinks of his brother, who is so perfect he wasn't born, but chiselled from stone. There is nothing he can do against that brown Apollo's face, nothing he can say, that will justify his inaction. Kevin would know what to do, with doom coming towards him in formation.

But Kevin is dead. He walked through their mother's door one day, wearing the robin's egg blue uniform of the great enemy, and his mother struck him down. She summoned the ghost of their father and put him in the room, sat him beside her, bloody and stunned. Against this Kevin said, I can stop it, Mom. I have the power to change things now.

She turned away, then the family turned away. Kevin looked at him, pleading, before he left her house and never came back, disappeared. Wil closed his eyes, a dark, secret joy welling in him, to watch his brother fall: Kevin never made the little mistakes in his life, never so much as sprouted a pimple. He made up for it though by doing the unforgivable.

Wil wonders if his brother knows what is happening. If, in fact, he isn't one of the Peace Officers, filled himself with secret joy.

His lover will wait for him tonight. Ironically, she will be wearing a complete Peace Officer's uniform, bought at great expense on the black market, and very, very illegal. She will wait at the door of her club, *Terminal Avenue*, and she will frisk clients that she knows will enjoy it. She will have the playroom ready, with its great wooden beams stuck through with hooks and cages, with its expensive equipment built for the exclusive purpose of causing pain. On a steel cart, her toys will be spread out as neatly as surgical instruments.

When he walks through the door, she likes to have her bouncers, also dressed as Peace Officers, hurl him against the wall. They let him struggle before they handcuff him. The uniforms are slippery as rubber. He can't get a grip on them. The uniforms are padded with the latest in wonderfabric so no matter how hard he punches them, he can't hurt them. They will drag him into the back and stripsearch him in front of clients who pay for the privilege of watching. He stands under a spotlight that shines an impersonal cone of light from the ceiling. The rest of the room is darkened. He can see reflections of glasses, red-eyed cigarettes, the glint of ice clinking against glass, shadows shifting. He can hear zippers coming undone, low moans. He can smell the cum when he's hit into passivity.

He wanted to cut his hair, but she wouldn't let him, said she'd never speak to him again if he did. She likes it when the bouncers grab him by his hair and drag him to the exploratory table in the centre of the room. She says she likes the way it veils his face when he's kneeling.

In the playroom though, she changes. He couldn't hurt her the way she wanted him to; she was tiring of him. He whipped her half-heartedly until she told the bouncer to do it properly.

A man walked in, one day, in a robin's egg blue uniform, and Wil froze. When he could breathe, when he could think again, he found her watching him, thoughtful.

She borrowed the man's uniform, and lay on the table, her face blank and smooth and round as a basketball under the visor. He put a painstick against the left nipple. It darkened and bruised. Her screams were muffled by the helmet. Her bouncers whispered things to her as they pinned her to the table, and he hurt her. When she begged him to stop, he placed the painstick against her right nipple.

He kept going until he was shaking so hard he had to stop.

That's enough for tonight, she said, breathless, wrapping her arms around him, telling the bouncers to leave when he started to cry. My poor virgin. It's not pain so much as it is a cleansing.

Is it, he'd asked her, one of those whiteguilt things?

She'd laughed, kissed him. Rocked him and forgave him, on the evening he discovered that it wasn't just easy to do terrible things to another person: It could give pleasure. It could give power.

She said she'd kill him if he told anyone what happened in the playroom. She has a reputation and is vaguely ashamed of her secret weakness. He wouldn't tell, not ever. He is addicted to her pain.

To distinguish it from real uniforms, her uniform has an inverted black triangle on the left side, just over her heart: Asocialism, she says with a laugh, and he doesn't get it. She won't explain it, her blue eyes black with desire as her pupils widened suddenly like a cat's.

The uniforms advancing on him, however, are clean and pure and real.

Wil wanted to be an astronaut. He bought the books, he watched the movies and he dreamed. He did well in Physics, Math, and Sciences, and his mother bragged, He's got my brains.

He was so dedicated, he would test himself, just like the astronauts on TV. He locked himself in his closet once with nothing but a bag of potato chips and a bottle of pop. He wanted to see if he could spend time in a small space, alone and deprived. It was July and they had no air conditioning. He fainted in the heat, dreamed that he was floating over the Earth on his way to Mars, weightless.

Kevin found him, dragged him from the closet, and laughed at him.

You stupid shit, he said. Don't you know anything?

When his father slid off the hood leaving a snail's trail of blood, Kevin ran out of the car.

Stop it! Kevin screamed, his face contorted in the headlight's beam. Shadows loomed over him, but he was undaunted. Stop it!

Kevin threw himself on their Dad and saved his life.

Wil stayed with their father in the hospital, never left his side. He was there when the Peace Officers came and took their father's statement. When they closed the door in his face and he heard his father screaming. The nurses took him away and he let them. Wil watched his father withdraw into himself after that, never quite healing.

He knew the names of all the constellations, the distances of the stars, the equations that would launch a ship to reach them. He knew how to stay alive in any conditions, except when someone didn't want to stay alive.

No one was surprised when his father shot himself.

At the funeral potlatch, his mother split his father's ceremonial regalia between Wil and Kevin. She gave Kevin his father's frontlet. He placed it immediately on his head and danced. The room became still, the family shocked at his lack of tact. When Kevin stopped dancing, she gave Wil his father's button blanket. The dark wool held his smell. Wil knew then that he would never be an astronaut. He didn't have a backup dream and drifted through school, coasting on a reputation of *Brain* he'd stopped trying to earn.

Kevin, on the other hand, ran away and joined the Mohawk Warriors. He was at Oka on August 16 when the bombs rained down and the last Canadian reserve was Adjusted.

Wil expected him to come back broken. He was ready with patience, with forgiveness. Kevin came back a Peace Officer.

Why? his aunts, his uncles, cousins, and friends said.

How could you? his mother said.

Wil said nothing. When his brother looked up, Wil knew the truth, even if Kevin didn't. There were things that adjusted to rapid change—pigeons, dogs, rats, cockroaches. Then there were things that didn't—panda bears, whales, flamingos, Atlantic cod, salmon, owls.

Kevin would survive the Adjustment. Kevin had found a way to come through it and be better for it. He instinctively felt the changes coming and adapted. I, on the other hand, he thought, am going the way of the dodo bird.

There are rumours in the neighbourhood. No one from the Vancouver Urban Reserve #2 can get into *Terminal Avenue*. They don't have the money or the connections. Whispers follow him, anyway, but no one will ask him to his face. He suspects that his mother suspects. He has been careful, but he sees the questions in her eyes when he leaves for work. Someday she'll ask him what he really does and he'll lie to her.

To allay suspicion, he smuggles cigarettes and sweetgrass from the downtown core to Surreycentral. This is useful, makes him friends, adds a kick to his evening train ride. He finds that he needs these kicks. Has a morbid fear of becoming dead like his father, talking and breathing and eating, but frightened into vacancy, a living blankness.

His identity card that gets him to the downtown core says *Occupation: Waiter*. He pins it to his jacket so that no one will mistake him for a terrorist and shoot him.

He is not really alive until he steps past the industrial black doors of his lover's club. Until that moment, he is living inside his head, lost in memories. He knows that he is a novelty item, a real living Indian: that is why his prices are so inflated. He knows there will come a time when he is yesterday's condom.

He walks past the club's facade, the elegant dining rooms filled with the glittering people who watch the screens or dance across the dimly-lit ballroom-sized floor. He descends the stairs where his lover waits for him with her games and her toys, where they do things that aren't sanctioned by the Purity laws, where he gets hurt and gives hurt.

He is greeted by his high priestess. He enters her temple of discipline and submits. When the pain becomes too much, he hallucinates. There is no preparing for that moment when reality shifts and he is free.

They have formed a circle around him. Another standard intimidation tactic. The Peace Officer facing him is waiting for him to talk. He stares up at it. This will be different from the club. He is about to become an example.

Wilson Wilson? the Officer says. The voice sounds male but is altered by computers so it won't be recognizable.

He smiles. The name is one of his mother's little jokes, a little defiance. He has hated her for it all his life, but now he doesn't mind. He is in a forgiving mood. *Yes, that's me.*

In the silence that stretches, Wil realizes that he always believed this moment would come. That he has been preparing himself for it. The smiling-faced lies from the TV haven't fooled him, or anyone else. After the Uprisings, it was only a matter of time before someone decided to solve the Indian problem once and for all.

The Peace Officer raises his club and brings it down.

His father held a potlatch before they left Kitamaat, before they came to Vancouver to earn a living, after the aluminum smelter closed.

They had to hold it in secret, so they hired three large seiners for the family and rode to Monkey Beach. They left in their old beat-up speedboat, early in the morning, when the Douglas Channel was calm and flat, before the winds blew in from the ocean, turning the water choppy. The seine boats fell far behind them, heavy with people. Kevin begged and begged to steer and his father laughingly gave in.

Wil knelt on the bow and held his arms open, wishing he could take off his lifejacket. In four hours they will land on Monkey Beach and will set up for the potlatch where they will dance and sing and say good-bye. His father will cook salmon around fires, roasted the old-fashioned way: split down the centre and splayed open like butterflies, thin sticks of cedar woven through the skin to hold the fish open, the sticks planted in the sand; as the flesh darkens the juice runs down and hisses on the fire. The smell will permeate the beach. Camouflage nets will be set up all over the beach so they won't be spotted by planes. Family will lounge under them as if they were beach umbrellas. The more daring of the family will dash into the water, which is still glacier-cold and shocking.

This will happen when they land in four hours, but Wil chooses to remember the boat ride with his mother resting in his father's arm when Wil comes back from the bow and sits beside them. She is wearing a blue scarf and black sunglasses and red lipstick. She can't stop smiling even though they are going to leave home soon. She looks like a movie star. His father has his hair slicked back, and it makes him look like an otter. He kisses her, and she kisses him back.

Kevin is so excited he raises one arm and makes the Mohawk salute they see on TV all the time. He loses control of the boat, and they swerve violently. His father cuffs Kevin and takes the wheel.

The sun rises as they pass Costi Island, and the water sparkles and shifts. The sky hardens into a deep summer blue.

The wind and the noise of the engine prevent them from talking. His father begins to sing. Wil doesn't understand the words, couldn't pronounce them if he tried. He can see that his father is happy. Maybe he's drunk on the excitement of the day, on the way that his wife touches him, tenderly. He gives Wil the wheel.

His father puts on his button blanket, rests it solemnly on his shoulders. He balances on the boat with the ease of someone who's spent all his life on the water. He does a twirl, when he reaches the bow of the speedboat and the button blanket opens, a navy lotus. The abalone buttons sparkle when they catch the light. She's laughing as he poses. He dances, suddenly inspired, exuberant.

Later he will understand what his father is doing, the rules he is breaking, the risks he is taking, and the price he will pay on a deserted road, when the siren goes off and the lights flash and they are pulled over.

At the time though, Wil is whiteknuckled, afraid to move the boat in a wrong way and toss his father overboard. He is also embarrassed, wishing his father were more reserved. Wishing he was being normal instead of dancing, a whirling shadow against the sun, blocking his view of the Channel.

This is the moment he chooses to be in, the place he goes to when the club flattens him to the Surreycentral tiles. He holds himself there, in the boat with his brother, his father, his mother. The sun on the water makes pale northern lights flicker against everyone's faces, and the smell of the water is clean and salty, and the boat's spray is cool against his skin.

Philip Kevin Paul b. 1971

W̲SA'NEC'

Belly Button

My mother was careful
about what she ate
when it was my turn

inside her. It was already me
well before she had problems
getting up out of chairs.
Already me before I had elbows
to poke her with,
her hand on her tight skin
waiting for my next move.

It was my presence in her,
my nearly unstoppable growing,
that made her breasts tender,
her tailbone sore,
made her hungry
and ill. So many times

she has spelled out the odds
I was up against.
Her joke about my arrival,
the pill in my tiny fist.

When I was old enough to be
curious, I asked her
about the small round hole in my tummy.

She said, *That's your belly button,*
it used to be your mouth.

Still Falling

Below the burial ground, K̲ENNES
has taken to its winter form, the echo
of its rhythm stumbling hard
into this ceremony of grief.

KENNES is the name of the stream
and the name of the whale
that died in the mouth.
I say the word and I can see
the whale that beached itself there
and the ancient man who found it,
the fresh water of the stream
falling around this enormous, slow-
breathing creature; the whale feeling
its own weight
for the first time.
I am standing with the man just briefly
as he says, 'KENNES', and looks into the water fall,
then at the whale
washed up on the shore at low tide.

The winter has always been hard on us.

But when a family stands here together,
we know just what family is—
look how we hold on
to each other as we see
the casket sink into the ground,
my uncle's body
inside. Each of us holds a corner of this story,
though some of us have no hands
to speak of.

It's true,
when I feel helpless
I am the only one
who feels this grief:

KENNES is the name
of the stream and the name of the whale
that died in the mouth.
I say the word and I can see
the whale that beached itself there
and the ancient man who found it,
the fresh water of the stream
falling around this enormous, slow-
breathing creature. The whale feeling
its own weight
for the first time.

How long had whales returned here
before this one? How long had people
come to witness their return?
To see them chase the young salmon
into the small bay,
nearly to the foot of the falls.

The body of a whale is like any body,
the canoe for an ancient spirit. The water,
like time, moving to the same edge for so long.

Still,

I feel as though I am witnessing the first
whale to wash ashore here.
My father's last living brother.

Uncle,
our last handshake in Saanich, this
shovel full of dark earth
on your grave.

Richard Van Camp b. 1971

DOGRIB

From *The Lesser Blessed*

KISS

I smoked up a lot after that first night. Sometimes it was in the potato field, other times it was at Johnny's apartment. We had to be careful of Donny. He was a bandit.

'Hey, chief,' he said as he walked into the kitchen. 'I got a quarter that says you don't have hair on your nuts.'

'What?' I asked in disbelief. Johnny was in the bathroom so it was just Donny and me. Van Halen was playing on the stereo and it was a Friday.

'You heard me, chief,' he said. 'We on, or are you a baldy?'

'Hey, Donny,' I said, motioning towards the swear jar, 'you better cool it. You're headed for a burn out.'

'Whatever,' he sneered as he sat across from me. 'Wanna play some cards? I know crib, rummy, crazy eights, crazy eight countdown. You know crazy eight countdown? Here, I'll show you.'

Just as he was about to start dealing, I noticed a small hole in his left hand. It wasn't big. It looked like a dent.

'Hey,' I asked and touched his hand. 'What happened?'

'Oh,' he said.

'Scoop?'

Donny looked down and covered the hole. He said in a whisper, 'A man at one of my mom's parties put a cigarette out on my hand.'

'Oh, man, I'm sorry—'

Johnny came around the corner tucking in his shirt.

'Donny,' he pleaded, 'I told you no more cards. Did you do your homework?'

'Awww, it's stupid,' he answered. 'As if I'm going to use that stuff anyway.'

'Come on, Donny,' he answered, 'your report card said—'

'Dad said I didn't have to if I didn't want to.'

Johnny stood over him and started pointing. He raised his voice. 'You don't listen to him, okay? You listen to me. The only thing you have to worry about right now is how you're gonna raise those marks!'

Donny's face started to darken and he folded his arms.

'Understand?' Johnny asked.

Donny didn't answer, and I got embarrassed for him.

'Jeeeez,' Donny said. 'Okay then . . .'

'I know it sucks but you gotta do it,' Johnny said. 'Dad's coming soon. We're almost out of this shit town. Now go in your room and do some homework, okay?'

'But I want to talk with Larry,' he answered.

I smiled.

'Larry's gonna be here for a while. You do that homework and you can talk to him after.'

'Yeah?' he asked.

'Yeah,' I answered.

Donny got up and walked into his room. 'Turn the music down,' he called over his shoulder.

Johnny got up and went into the living room. He turned the music down and came back. 'Man, what am I gonna do about that kid? Did you see his teeth? They're already yellow.'

I was still in shock over Donny's hand. 'How bad is it at school?' I asked.

'Pretty bad. I got his report card and he's got a lot of C's and a few D's. I went and talked to his teacher and she said he's a wise guy in class who likes to fight.'

'Hmmm,' I said. 'What does your mom think?'

'Mom doesn't give a shit,' Johnny answered. I kept my mouth shut.

Johnny put his hands together like he was praying and exhaled loudly. He closed his eyes and I watched him.

'How's your coffee?' he said after a minute.

'Donkey piss,' I said. 'Weak.'

'Yeah, yeah, we're running low.'

Johnny's hair had fallen over his forehead. He was handsome, but in a lost sort of way. He could grow a beard if he wanted to and some days he didn't shave. Sometimes when we were stoned I'd see him staring at me with those glittering blue eyes of his.

'If I could perform the autopsy on him,' I thought, 'I'd steal his eyes.'

I got up and went to the stereo. 'Hey! Let's write a song. We'll call it "Hickey Juice".'

'Yeah,' he called back, 'the first line will be, "She's a little bitch with a capital B!"'

I shook my head and smiled. We were listening to Van Halen. The synthesizer and drums were pounding 'I'll Wait until Your Love Comes Down'. I turned it up just a bit while Johnny fired up the hot knives on the stove in the kitchen. He peeked around the corner and smiled. 'Landlord's gonna shit!'

'Piss on 'im!' I yelled. I was on the couch, having another coffee. I was downing coffee about five times a day. The cool thing about Johnny's place was they drank coffee out of glass mugs. I always felt like a trucker on Highway 5, taking a break in some diner in South Dakota, taking sips from my glass mug, having a smoke, my rough scraggy beard on my face, my wallet thick with fifties.

I started thinking about Juliet. I really had this thing for her—I'm talking twelve cylinders of love! I mean, my nipples became fire ants at the thought of her: red, hard and venomous. I could close my eyes and see her, and when

I did it was like somebody pulled my heart a little. She got grounded for what happened at the party and tonight was her first night of freedom. I know. I marked it on my calendar.

Johnny told me tons about his past. He had a slew of pictures of pretty girls. Mostly he went for brunettes. In lots of the pictures, they had purple hickeys on their necks and bottles in their hands. I was always hoping that he'd open up about Juliet and tell me more about what she was like, what she did, how she did it. I had brought this best of Iron Maiden tape over that I had mixed. Man, the music felt good. 'Wasted Years' was blaring now, and if it weren't for Donny, we'd have had it cranked even higher. Johnny came around the corner from the kitchen and gave me thumbs-up. I joined him and inhaled the hash. No hooter this time. Just me and the smoke.

'Yeah,' I thought, 'the day I saw Juliet Hope was the day I felt my pubic hair grow.' I could still close my eyes and see her on the bed. I looked at Johnny, who was at the table rolling a fatty.

'You know, Lare, I had this girl once, her name was Lisa Beatty. What a fuck doll. This one time we were fooling around and she gave me a hickey. I told her not to do it again, and she did. She gave me another one and I got her back. I gave her hickeys on her ass. I did a big J on one cheek and a big B on the other. She was a lifeguard at the swimming pool in Hay River, and she had this bathing suit that was green and white. When she dove into the water, you could see the J and B—and I wasn't the only one who noticed!'

'Wow!' I said, 'Now that's a story!'

'Yeah,' he smiled, 'that's Hay River for you. She was smooth, brother, smooth.'

'Wasted Years' ended; 'Power Slave' began. We paused to listen to the guitars. The glasses on the table were shaking as I inhaled some more.

I sat down next to Johnny and put my hand on his shoulder. He looked at me and I smiled. I had never really said anything to him about helping me out, and now it seemed like I could say it without sounding like a pansy. 'Thanks for taking care of Jazz, man.'

Johnny smiled back. 'No prob.' He thought about it as he rolled. 'Listen, Lare, I gotta teach you some new moves.'

'Yeah?' I asked. 'Yeah, you better. I don't know how to fight.'

'The next time you smoke someone it better be three hits: you hitting them, the shit hitting their shorts and the ambulance hitting ninety!'

I laughed.

'Stand up and put your arms on my shoulders.'

I did.

He whipped his arms over mine and slapped them around my back. He pulled up while he kneed me in the gut.

'Ugh,' I grunted and hit the floor.

'Lare,' he laughed, 'you gotta block it.'

I struggled up and rested on bent knees. I guess he could see that I was mad because he sat down again and straightened his hair with his hands. I could smell the Right Guard in his scalp. He had showed me that if you sprayed your head with it for a long time, you could do cartwheels and your hair wouldn't move. Rubbing my gut, I stared at him.

'So tell me about being fool blood,' he said.

I sat down. 'Whattaya wanta know?'

He got up and handed me a cigarette. He was saving the joints till later.

'Well, what tribe are you? Chip? Cree?'

'Dogrib.'

'I thought they were from around Yellowknife.'

I got a little nervous. 'Yeah.'

'What's the scoop?'

'Well, Jed told me that our tribe came from a woman who gave birth to six puppies.' I eyed him while I said that because I knew some people would laugh. He didn't, so I continued.

'Well, she had to live by herself in the woods so she could raise her pups. One day she left her hut so she could check her snares, and when she came home she could see human footprints in the snow and ashes.'

'No shit,' Johnny said.

'Yeah . . . so one day she went out like she was going to check her snares but she snuck back and watched her hut. She could hear her pups yapping like this: Yap! Yap! Then she could hear them laughing like children. After a while she could hear kids running around the hut and choo! Out from the hut run six kids, all naked.'

'Whoah!' Johnny said.

'Yeah! So she watches them and they're playing in the snow all laughing and having a great time. She runs out of the bush and chases them back into the hut. They all make a run for the bag she used to leave them in. Three make it and turn back to pups. A girl and two boys don't. She catches them. They stay human and they're the first Dogribs. She raised them to be beautiful hunters with strong medicine.'

'Hunh. Wait a minute,' Johnny interrupted. 'What happened to the three that made it back to the bag?'

'Humph. I don't know. Jed never told me that part.'

'Better find out.'

We were quiet for a bit. Then he spoke.

'Lare, that's something. That's really something. You're a storyteller, man. Your voice even changed when you talked.'

'Yeah?' I asked, proud of the moment and the revelation. That was the first time I had told the story and I liked how it felt.

'Larry?' Johnny said. 'Do you drink?'

'Oh,' I said, 'I had a bet going with my dad that I wouldn't touch a drop of liquor until I turned eighteen. He said he'd give me a hundred bucks if I make it.'

'Where is your dad?' he asked.

'Oh . . . uh, I don't know. He and my mom split up. It was a bad scene.'

'Yeah,' he said, 'I know what you mean. Shit city, hey?'

'Hunh,' I agreed. 'How come you?'

'Long story, man. It sucks the cockaruski.'

'Aaah, come on.'

'I'll say this,' he said. 'I have a feeling if I picked up a bottle, I'd never put it down.'

I nodded. 'Deep.'

'It's casual, man. You only bet a hundred dollars with your old man?'

'I was nine when I made that bet. At the time, a hundred bucks was a hunk of a hunk.'

'Sounds good. I should get that deal going with Donny.'

Johnny lit a joint and handed it to me, looking at my lips. I got nervous, so I asked, 'What do you think of Miss Sauvé's tits?'

'Don't matter to me,' he winked. 'The kind of fucking I do, you don't need tits.'

I started to laugh, and he pointed to my lips.

'Time for a shave.'

'What?'

'Time for a shave there, muskrat mouth. You look like Charles Manson.'

'You figure?'

'Yeah, look. Juliet's coming over in a bit. You better shave before she gets here. Maybe she'll bring a friend. Go in the bathroom and shave that fuzz off your lip.'

'I never shaved before.'

'Well, it ain't that hard. Go on!'

I felt the whiskers on my lip and agreed. I walked to his bathroom. 'Use my electric!' he yelled. I locked the door and saw dirty towels, toothpaste spitting out of the tube and yellowed Q-Tips lying on the counter.

The doors under the sink were hard to open so I yanked. They gave. It was the weirdest thing; behind some blue Tampax boxes and rolls of toilet paper, I saw some bottles. I moved the boxes aside, and there were two big-ass bottles of Golden Wedding.

'Holy shit,' I whispered. What if Donny got a hold of these?

I thought of Johnny saying, 'That's one woman you'll never want to meet' about his mom. Looking at those two bottles, I suddenly knew why.

'House of Pain' began on the stereo. I was a bit nervous because of what I had found. I shut the cupboard door and continued with my search. I couldn't find an electric razor, so I used a pink one lying on the side of the tub. I could hear the buzzer go off in the hallway. That meant that someone was downstairs in the lobby and wanted to come up. I ran the water and squirted some shaving cream into my hand. I put the lather on my lips, under my nose, on my cheek and in my sideburns. I grabbed the razor. Resting it on my chin, I yanked up, just like in the movies, and sliced my nostril.

'Shit!' I hissed. I started bleeding in the cream. I pushed down on the blade the next time for traction and I screamed some more. Shit! What was I doing wrong? The next time, I pulled the razor down my lip. That seemed to be smoother. I shaved my sideburns too, and then I dried my face on a white towel, leaving a blur of blood behind. I looked into the mirror. My upper lip was red and blotchy, and it was swelling up like a worm about ready to burst. My sideburns itched and my face was starting to feel like it was on fire. I put some after-shave on. My face burned even more, and I whimpered like a puppy. The music stopped, and I heard Johnny start it up again. I looked at myself again in the mirror.

'Shit,' I said. 'Juliet.'

I didn't want her to see me bleeding to death so I knocked on Donny's door. 'Enter,' he said. I did.

Donny's room was pretty barren. All he had was a box spring, a mattress and a lamp. He was sitting on the carpet, drawing.

'Whatcha doing?'

'What's it look like, chief?' he said, holding up his picture.

It was bizarre. There was a kid holding a gun and he was smiling; in the background there were five dogs lying dead, with a hundred lines behind them saying the same thing: 'Stab the dog stab the dog stab the dog.'

'Whatdaya think, chief?' His eyes were looking into me for a reaction, so I told the truth.

'Pretty grim.'

He snatched it back. 'Yeah, what do you know?'

As I looked around, I realized he had drawings hung up all over. In the bare closet he had drawn on the wall. There were men and women crying and there were fallen-down scarecrows, thousands of them. He had tried to write swear words, but they all came out like, 'Fok FoK fOK.'

'Shit, man, you psycho?'

'Gotta be, it's a fuckin' war zone,' he said.

'You're rude.'

'I guess,' he said and looked down.

'It snowed,' I offered.

'Big deal. Snow melts.'

'No,' I said, 'you should be playing outside.'

'And freeze?'

We were quiet.

'You know,' I tried. 'I was reading that playing Mozart helps plants grow.'

He went back to drawing. 'Fuck Mozart.'

'Sol later, man,' I said.

'Yeah, sol, chief.'

Aha! At least somebody knew some Raven Talk.

I walked down the hallway, and the synthesizer shot Van Halen's '1984' into my veins. I got piss shivers. I heard the clink of bottles and laughter. I went around the corner and there she was, Juliet.

But she was with Jazz! Jakka Jazz! The biggest asshole in the universe! The Leonard of all Leonards! I looked at Johnny, but Juliet and him were hugging and kissing, slopping their tongues all over each other. Johnny had his hands in her hair and she was grabbing him back.

'Were you pushing or pulling in there?' Jazz asked me. Johnny's giving him a lickin' hadn't changed anything at all.

'What?' I slurred. That music was too loud. I could see Juliet laughing at me and my fat lips. I could see Johnny squinting at me, and I felt humiliated. Everyone was laughing and I hated it. I could see Juliet's ass in those black pants that I loved. I could see Jazz and his smug skinny-ass face. He was drinking out of my favourite glass mug and he had beer in it. I could see Johnny giving me the knee and I could hear the hoofs on the pavement again and I could hear the puppy being torn to pieces and dogs roaring. The whole damn world was turning up the volume. I could see the nurses who made me look in the mirror and me screaming when I saw the skin peeling from my cousins as the people pulled the blankets off; and my father doing it—my father fucking, the teeth of the hammer sinking into his soft eyes and me yelling, 'I send you to hell, Daddy, I send you to hell!'

'I said!' Jazz reached out and pinched my nose. 'Were you pushing or pulling in the bathroom—'

I punched Jazz so damn hard his feet touched the ceiling. He hit the floor rolling and I landed on top of him. I was yelling so loud I couldn't hear the music. Johnny pulled me off him after a bit. I guess he knew Jazz had it coming. I felt like I had water in my lungs. I couldn't breathe. I just couldn't take it. I tried to put my fist through Jazz so hard that I heard something snap. After that, I blacked out.

Next thing I knew, I was on the couch. Johnny and Juliet were looking at me. Juliet's eyes were huge as she put a blanket over me.

'Holy shit, Larry,' she said. 'If you were Mexican you'd be Rocky!'

'Larry, holy fuck.' Johnny shook his head and offered me a smoke. 'You didn't have to do that, man. You busted his nose!'

I waved the smoke away and looked at Juliet. I savoured her hair. It looked like a fire on a mountain rolling down the forest. She was chewing gum: Bub-blicious. I could smell that it was strawberry flavour. I wanted that gum so bad. I saw the glint of her teeth and I wanted her. Big time.

'Gimme gum,' I said, and she gave it to me. She stuck it in my mouth and I bit soft. Johnny took her other hand and led her away. I watched them as they went around the corner. I heard a door close. The music had changed. This time it was Power Station: 'Get it on! Bang a gong!'

I got up and sat at the kitchen table. I was looking at my swollen knuckles. The blood from Jazz's nose had caked on them and turned choco-late brown. There was blood on my white socks. I could see cigarette butts in an ashtray, one with Juliet's lipstick on it. I picked it up. It was a small butt and I lit it. I placed my lips where she had placed hers. I puckered and swal-lowed deep. I burned my thumb and lip; I coughed and hacked. The music had ended, so I put Van Halen back on. I turned it low and sat down. I looked out the window and tried pretty hard not to look at my reflection. When I heard the bed bang chang against the wall, I turned up the system as loud as it would go.

I had it bad for Juliet. I wanted her for my secret, my prayer. I wanted her as my sweet violence of seeds and metal. I wanted to spill candles with her, to hold hands and walk around in gumboots with her. I wanted to do anything and everything with her. I mean, if she were in a coma, I'd make sure the nurses played her favourite music over and over so she'd come back to life and thank me.

I was looking at the floor, past my bloody socks, and I saw those burns in the linoleum floor, the ones that looked like scorched blurred eyes. Except this time it wasn't the ceiling they were staring at; it was me. They were studying me and I wondered what they were seeing, what they were thinking.

I sat back on the couch, and all I could do was think of when I was younger. I looked around the living room. There was a couch like this one in the old house, but ours was green. The music was blasting then, too. My dad stood over my mom. He had called me out of my room. He was holding the yellow broom. He was speaking French. He had learned it in the residential schools. He never talked about what had happened there, but he always talked French when he drank.

My mom was passed out on the couch. A couch like this one. This was back when she used to drink. She had gone to residential schools, too. She was passed out, in her bathrobe. My father took the broomstick and started laughing. He spread her legs and with the yellow broomstick—

I shot awake.

'Fuck fuck fuck,' I said, 'No!'

I purposely made myself remember the lake in Rae. One time before the accident, I was hanging out with my cousins there. We used to play in the sand way down the beach. We'd take some toys down and build houses. We'd also sniff gas. I wasn't too crazy about it at first, but after seeing my dad do the bad thing to my aunt, it took the shakes away. I could feel the heat on my back from the sun. Every now and then we'd stop to eat or take a leak. Me and my cousin Franky were good pals, even though he was demented. He was the guy who told me that if you touch gasoline to a cat's asshole, the cat'd jump ten feet into the air. He was the guy who taught me about bennies.

He'd say, 'Close your eyes, Larry. Close them tight. Now face the sun, that's right. Face it and feel the bennies bouncing off you.'

I'd close my eyes so tight my forehead would stretch, and after a while I'd relax and, sure enough, I could feel bennies bouncing off me. They'd hit one area and the warmth would spread. It was glorious. I began to shout, 'Hey! Hey Franky! I feel them! I feel them!'

One time we were taking leaks and facing the sun. We could feel the bennies bouncing off us and we were yelling, 'Bennies! Bennies! Bennies!' but soon I was the only one who was yelling, and when I opened my eyes, there was Franky pointing at my feet.

'Cousin,' he whispered, 'you're pissing blood.'

I was.

That's all I remember.

I woke up when Johnny led Juliet to the door. She was putting on her running shoes and her damn sweater was inside out. Why didn't she just goddamned advertise on the blue channel: 'Hello! I just got plowed!'

She had her damn socks off and I could see her tiny toes. I wanted to run over there and bite her ass! Johnny kissed her and told her he'd call her. She hugged him and whispered something to him. He laughed. After she left, he came over and sat next to me. His hair was messed up and he didn't look too happy either.

'Lare,' he asked, 'what's in your hair?'

I didn't answer. I just looked at him. I knew he was gonna give me a lecture.

'Let's go for a walk,' he said.

FLOATERS

Fort Simmer braces for two things in winter. The first is the cold. The second is the Floaters. Floaters are the town drunks who stagger around the community at all hours of the night. Hobo Jungle is where they camp. But when it's cold out, they come into town to pass out in the alleys, or in the hotel lobby or at the taxi stand. Some throw bricks through the windows of the Bay so they can be charged and shipped off to Yellowknife where they can hibernate and clean up. They are the lost, and Johnny and I walked among them. The ice popped and cracked under our feet and we shimmied like we were wearing kimonos.

Johnny took me out to the back roads of town, by the landslide. We passed two men, one of whom shuffled slow with his head down; the other jumped around him, shadowboxing in old tennis shoes and a bright yellow sweater. His big belly bounced up and down, and he strutted up to us, away from his brother.

'I'm a boxer!' he said and raised his fists. His breath rose above him and plumed like a baby Hiroshima.

The other man was trying to say something in his raspy voice. He was drunk. I could smell the men downwind. They reeked of sweet Lysol and sour fish. The raspy man's voice was haunting, as if he were a face screaming without a throat.

'Have you ever walked in the footsteps of Jesus?' he asked. I could see his long nose, which slid across his face like a snake off its trail. It had been broken many times. His eyes were black, as black as the eyes of a corpse. They were lifeless, staring at me.

'No,' I said.

Rasp Man shambled closer and raised his hands like the lord of the cross. 'Have you ever walked in the footsteps of Satan?' he whispered. I stepped back instinctively. I did not want to touch the man or breathe the air around him.

'Great!' Johnny said and came between the Boxer and his brother. He handed the Boxer a smoke. The man stopped his fists long enough to accept it. Johnny lit it for him. Rasp Man floated towards them. I couldn't see his feet move. He just floated. I heard a quiet thanks that sounded like a death prayer and both men shook Johnny's hand. Johnny said something to them and they continued on their way towards town. Johnny put his hands in his pockets and walked over to me.

'Fuckin' chronics,' he whispered.

I was cold and shivering. We started following the brothers towards the town lights. There were pockets of snow on the roads and the ice had glassed over in a thick skin. When the Floaters walked on the ice, it cracked, sounding like panes of glass.

'You really did it tonight, buddy,' Johnny said, changing his tone. 'Now you're in. Now you gotta learn the rules of fighting. When you broke Jazz's nose—and you owe me one for wiping up the blood—you got brought into a circle. This circle is one for fighters, like Buddy X up there,' he motioned with his head.

The bigger man was shadowboxing his fists about his brother's head without making contact. He was quick. His belly bounced and bounced. Rasp Man cackled back and started to call and cough loudly. It was a scene of shadow puppets, almost as if we were watching an ape and a lizard meet in an arena. Rasp Man raised his arms again and the Boxer held him.

Johnny snorted and lit up a smoke. 'Pretty soon the word is gonna be out that you're a scrapper. The next time you're at a party and someone's looking for a fight they might grab you. You're fair game now. You're in.'

He took a puff and passed the cigarette to me. I was smiling inside: I was in.

'This here's unspoken. I'm only gonna say it once. If you get into a fight and you get hurt bad, stay down. Just stay down and cover your head. Whoever it is that's scrapping you will take that as a surrender. It works 99 per cent of the time. If they're drunk, you just run your Indian ass the hell out of there, 'cause drunks like to keep kicking. If they're stoned, they'll usually stop when you cover your head. You got that?'

I took a drag and handed the smoke back to him. 'Yeah,' I said, 'go on.'

The brothers stopped up ahead. They were arguing. The Boxer started to yell and Johnny and I stopped to watch. There weren't any streetlights where we were, but the men were close enough to the Bay that we could make out their silhouettes. The Boxer planted his feet in the cold gravel. The raspy brother tried to walk away, but was grabbed and shaken by the Boxer. Johnny continued to talk, keeping a watchful eye on the two men.

'Larry,' he said, 'if I have to listen to my mom fuck one more guy, I don't know what I'm gonna do.'

He went silent, and I felt sad.

'Johnny,' I said. 'I didn't know . . .'

'Well, shit,' he said, blowing smoke in my face, 'now you got the hunger; you'll probably want to start screwing anything that walks. I'll tell you something, Lare, and this is coming to you straight. Sex is a drug; once you start, you can't stop. Sometimes it's downright ugly what people will do to get it.'

'Man, I know that,' I said, thinking of my father.

Up ahead, Rasp Man was trying to get free of the Boxer. His hands fluttered like the wings of a shot chicken. The Boxer yelled into his face and shook him again. In the distance, from where I stood, they looked like lovers in an incredible dance.

Johnny continued with his grim message. 'You wanna start screwing someone, you talk to Dean Meddows. His mom works at the hospital as a nurse. She knows all the girls in this town that have the dose. She tells Dean every name. I know it's bad—you can just close your mouth—but this is a shit town and she's just looking out for her own. I had Juliet checked out. She's okay. You think you'll remember that before you wet your wick? You pay Dean five bucks and he'll give you a list of all the chicks who got the clap.'

'Yeah,' I said, watching the brothers. Johnny took a long drag and handed me the smoke. 'What else?'

The Boxer threw his brother on the ground and proceeded to smash his sneakers into him. The younger man began to scream. I started to run towards them, but Johnny grabbed my jean jacket and held me with sudden tank force.

'Never fuck a friend,' he said, looking into my eyes. 'That's the golden rule.'

I looked back towards the two men. 'They're ghosts, Johnny.'

'Wha?'

'Nobody's told them they died.' I took a big swallow. 'Nobody told them they're dead.'

Birthmark

(For Trevor Evans)

I remember the panic on my younger brother's face, Roger, when he saw my scars. He came back to town from College for Christmas break. 'Jesus, Rich, what happened?' he asked. I could have told him the truth but I told him it was a birthmark.

'But you weren't born with it,' he said. 'Tell me the truth. How did it happen?'

'It's just like Dr Hoffman said,' I answered. 'Sometimes birthmarks come to you later on in life. Sometimes people get them when they're in their thirties, sometimes in their forties.'

'Well can't they give you something for it?'

'Sure. They could give me acid and burn it off, or they can use a sander and obliterate the skin leaving a bigger scar.'

He winced. 'Man that would hurt.'

'Exactly.'

'So what are you gonna do? It looks like a hickey or something.'

'Well it was first diagnosed as skin cancer and then . . .'

'Cancer!'

'Yeah, skin cancer,' I emphasized. 'And then it was diagnosed as juvenile warts.'

'Well whatchagonna do?' he asked.

'Don't know,' I answered. I could tell he was disgusted with my scar, so I started to tease. 'It changes shape! It changes color!'

'Hey!' My brother threw his hands at me and walked away.

'It's alive!' I teased and started to giggle—something I've been guilty of even as a child. I could never keep a straight face in the darkest moments: Indian humor I'm told.

He shot around as if to stop the game in its tracks. 'We'll kill it, Richard, just kill it.'

I stood there long after he had gone into the house and I ran my finger over the coarse skin. It felt like something scaly, something warm and scaly that had burrowed in my neck, leaving its husk exposed for all to stare at. The scar itself is located at the base of my neck, above the collar bone.

'Just kill it.'

I wish I could.

I guess a long time ago, when Fort Smith used to be a boom town during World War Two, there was this gentleman named Mr Twisted Finger. He rented out his house to the best poker players in the Northwest Territories. His house was smack dab in the middle of Indian Village. Nobody got into any scraps in his house because everyone respected him. It was not uncommon for the games to last for days. Sometimes players would get so feverish in their game, they would throw their truck keys on the table or a pair of moccasins or a moose-hide jacket or their best pair of shit-kickers. Mr Twisted Finger watched on, making his money from an entrance fee, and his five daughters, who were rumored to be the best cooks in town, would sell stew and bannock—even in the throws of a good game the players would sometimes call 'time-out' and share a meal. Like I said, it was a good time and a lot of people made some good money in that house; however, a lot of hard-working trappers lost a season's worth of furs in a few hours. There was no drinking allowed in Mr Twisted Finger's house, and that was just fine with everyone who came to play.

Well I guess one night there was a knock on the door, it was a Friday, payday. Mr Twisted Finger opened the door and saw a tall stranger waiting for him out in the yard. It was winter out and the stranger was all dressed in black. He wore gloves and had long hair. He could have been a Half-breed, sometimes it's hard to tell. The stranger made no move to come into the house until invited, and even then he didn't speak.

Mr Twisted Finger barred him before he went into the house and said, 'Buddy, that'll be four dollars to play in my house.'

Mr Twisted Finger used to be one of the best trappers in the South Slave area but he wrecked his knees one year by having a tree buck on him when it fell. He told the men after that night that when the stranger gave him the money, and when his hands touched the stranger's glove all that stiffness he had been feeling went away. It was like someone breathed a puff of warm air in his knees and he walked the stranger into his house with his arm wrapped around him.

'Gentlemen!' he called out, 'this here stranger's gonna join you at the poker table, so make him comfortable.'

As he was saying this, I guess, everybody smelt something mighty high, like out-house shit on a hot humid day. Everybody covered their noses and asked Mr Twisted Finger if it was a good idea to let the stranger into the house. Mr Twisted Finger said he couldn't smell anything, and when the stranger pulled out a wad of cash as big as his fist nobody seemed to be able to smell anything either.

They played what was called 'bullshit poker'. I don't know if you know what that is and I don't either, but that's what they used to play, and right away that stranger started to lose. Everybody tried to talk to him, as that was the custom. They wanted to know where he was from, if he was in the army, if he was a drifter trying to make a little money, or if he was related to any-one in town. They were just being polite—no harm in that—especially if you're taking all his money! But he couldn't answer; and all through the games, he kept his long black jacket on, and his gloves too.

All five of Mr Twisted Finger's girls were hovering around the handsome stranger hoping to catch his eye. They offered him stew and bannock, but I guess he was mute, couldn't speak. That was fine enough and he was los-ing—which makes it finer still, he can't complain—and he lost and lost. Finally, after about eight straight hours and a lot of money circulating that table, the stranger was broke. Mr Twisted Finger had been watching him all night and put his hand on the stranger's shoulder to bid him a polite farewell, but when he touched the stranger's long black coat he said it was like some-one blew ice in his knees.

'Sir,' he said as he winced, 'I'm going to have to ask you to leave. There's about three guys here who want to take your seat at the table.'

The stranger calmly stood up and began to smile. He bent over the table and shook everybody's hand and started to laugh—I mean he started to laugh really loud, and I guess the men who had taken all of his money smiled and laughed with him. Soon everyone started to get a little scared. They hadn't heard anything from him the whole night, and here he was laughing right in their faces!

After he shook their hands, he started to walk out of the house, and one of the girls who was just finished making a fresh pot of stew came in from the kitchen and said good night to him, but as she did, she dropped her pot all over the floor and called out, 'Look.'

Everybody stood up and rushed over, and from under the stranger's coat, before he went out the door, dragged a cow's tail.

Everybody in the house recoiled and the stranger started to laugh again as everybody threw the still warm money back on the table.

But it was too late, I guess. The deal was made.

The next day they could see that in the tracks of the stranger's cowboy boots, there were holes cut into the feet right where the toes should have been and in those tracks were hooves.

Well that there story was told to me by Red Kettle Woman, as they called her. She told this to me before she passed away.

But I didn't want to hear that story. I didn't even know anything about Mr Twisted Finger's house—that was before I was born. I had wanted to know about her scar, the one that I kept seeing every time her scarf slipped or loosened as she was getting into the Handi-Bus for bingo. I'm the town driver. Anyways, I kept asking her and asking her, 'Red Kettle Woman, could you tell me how you got them scars?' She kept telling me I didn't want to know.

I would bring her gifts: silver spoons for her collection, Labrador tea, or Kinniknick leaves which she liked to smoke. I brought her lots of stuff, just for that story, and then she told me.

She told me about Mr Twisted Finger's house and poker games. I guess one night, one of Mr Twisted Finger's girls was really sick and he hired her for the night because it was a payday and he knew it would be mighty busy— that's when people felt the luckiest—and that girl that seen the tail, that was Red Kettle Woman who seen it and pointed it out.

She said when she dropped the stew, some of it splashed her body and that's how she got those scars.

Funny thing though, the day she died, which was Mother's Day, 1991, that was the day I got my scar. At first I ignored it, but then people started to ask about it when I'd go swimming down at the rapids, or if I'd take off my shirt when I was tarring roofs for Johnny Vogt. I just tell them I got kissed by the devil—that shuts them up and it's better I don't tell them the truth. I ain't never gonna tell this story to anyone, not even my younger brother. I don't want to give anyone what I got, and it's better that part of Fort Smith's history die with me.

Nope, I ain't gonna tell this story to no one. Ever . . .

Notes on Authors

TRADITIONAL ORATURE FROM THE SOUTHERN FIRST NATIONS
While the majority of pieces collected here are writings by Native authors, the cultural roots of this literature are in traditional orature. The term 'orature' is chosen as a parallel term to that of 'literature'. 'Orature' indicates that body of knowledge usually termed 'oral literature'. The latter term is problematic, including as it does the term 'literature', with its implications of reading and books, and the term 'oral', with implications of the spoken and heard. 'Oral literature' seems a debased version of a true, written, literature. The term 'orature' allows this body of knowledge its own validity.

It is tempting to emphasize authenticity in a consideration of traditional material, but this is generally counter-productive. If 'authentic' implies without change through white contact, there is no such account of traditional cultures from southern Canada. The first considered white accounts of Native cultures long post-dated the first contact.

We have used early versions of poems and songs as they were recorded, usually by amateur folklorists, to suggest the cultural and aesthetic roots of this collection. All the examples here come from John Robert Colombo's *Songs of the Indians*, which provides interesting notes and comments about the material, both general and specific. The verse forms and word usage more likely reflect English literary values than Native ones, but their provenance gives them clear historical positions. They are also of interest as demonstrations of various cultural tensions.

As an example, here are some comments made by the famous American folklorist and collector Charles G. Leland, in *The Algonquin Legends of New England*, on a piece provided by Mrs W. Wallace Brown of Calais, Maine.

> The old woman ended this story by saying abruptly, 'Don't know any more. Guess they all eat up by *mooin*' (the bear). She said it was only a fragment. 'If you could have heard her repeat this,' adds Mrs Brown, 'in pieces, stopping to explain what the characters said, and describing how they looked, and anon singing it again, you would have got the *inner sense* of a wonderfully weird tale. The woman's feet-covering and the man's dress *like* a rainbow, yet not one, which made their bodies invisible, seemed to exercise her imagination strangely; and these were to her the most important part of the story.' The fragment is part of a very old myth; I regret to say a very obscure one. The poem, 'declared to be very ancient', is given here as 'Fragment of a Passamaquoddy song'.

The section given here from 'Traditional History of the Confederacy of Six Nations' is a different example of the problem of authenticity. As Colombo notes, 'This official version of the oral tradition was prepared by a Committee of the Chiefs at the Six Nations Reserve, Grand River, at the turn of the century.' Like the material presented by traditional storytellers today, it has the authenticity of all oral material which is reaffirmed through its transmission within a cultural tradition.

TRADITIONAL SONGS FROM THE INUIT
Much of the note on traditional orature from the Southern First Nations can be applied here, with the exception that the records are much later. Once again taken from a collection by John Robert Colombo, *Poems of the Inuit* (1981), his primary source was Knud Ramsmussen but all of his sources were twentieth-century. Thus one might assume that the combination of the greater isolation of the Inuit and of developments in scientific ethnography should make for greater accuracy. By the same token, the Inuit's absence from the white culture which had had centuries to influence other First Nations by the time of the collecting of their traditional material made the Inuit that much more difficult for white explorers to begin to comprehend. Thus, it once again would be best to assume that accuracy is not to be found but to see these as samples of a recording process which comments on both cultures involved.

KATERI AKIWENZIE-DAMM Anishnaabe, b. 1965
kateri akiwenzie-damm is a 'mixed-blood' member of the Chippewas of Nawash First Nation, based on the Cape Croker Reserve on the Saugeen Peninsula in southwestern Ontario. She received her Bachelor's degree from York University and her Master's degree from the University of Ottawa. She works as a communications consultant with First Nations groups and she also teaches at the En'owkin International School of Writing in Penticton, British Columbia.

'I write because I need to write; because for me writing is ceremony. It is a spiritual practice, a way of connecting with others, a way of contributing back to my community and to all of creation. It is a form of activism, a creative, positive, giving, true way to maintain who we are as indigenous people, as Anishnaabe, and to protest against colonization in its many forms. It is a way to share, to reaffirm kinship, to connect with the sacredness of creation. I write because I believe love is medicine, love is the strongest power in creation, and writing is a way of expressing and experiencing this.'

akiwenzie-damm's critical writing has appeared in *The Journal of Canadian Studies* (1996) and *Looking at the Words of Our People: First Nations Analysis of Literature* (1993). Her poetry has appeared in many journals, anthologies, and audio recordings, including *Rampike* (1997), *Sweetgrass Surrounds Her* (1997), *Returning the Gift* (1994), and *Your Silence Will Not Protect You* (1989). Her collected work is represented in *my heart is a stray bullet* (1993).

ANNHARTE Anishnabe, b. 1942
Born in 1942 to an Anishnabe mother and an Irish father, Marie Annharte Baker was raised in Winnipeg, where she could see the hard life of the streets.

She describes herself as a cultural worker who wants to produce 'films, plays, and books that celebrate cultural survival after five hundred years of resistance to settler lit(ter) (not literature).'

Baker's publications include two books of poetry, *Being On The Moon* (1990) and *Coyote Columbus Cafe* (1994), and a play, *ALTERNATIVE: The Only Native Alternative* (1994). Her writing shows her concern with 'the smallest stories; stories in our everyday conversations (wrongfully dismissed as gossip), stories of how we survived and resisted (cheeky stories), and, of course, the "lost stories" (stories of men, women, and children who are lost or outcast to their own people, the ones who have "no voice" but speak to us in dreams or haunt our every waking moment with their shocking statistics).'

Baker was a co-founder of the Regina Aboriginal Writers group. Her broader interests include the writings of Women of Colour and the forms of street poetry, dub poetry, and rap.

She has a son who is also a writer.

JEANNETTE C. ARMSTRONG Okanagan, b. 1948
Born on the Penticton Indian Reserve in British Columbia, Jeannette Christine Armstrong is a fluent speaker of the Okaganan language and a student of her community's traditional teachings.

'The Native people of this land developed a lifestyle through a unique worldview. I believe its underlying values and structures are important contributions to the pool of knowledge and critical factors in reversing and reshaping a worldview whose values foster an attitude of self-destruction.'

Armstrong holds a Bachelor of Fine Arts degree from the University of Victoria and is recognized as a visual artist as well as an activist and author. Her publications include two children's books, the ground-breaking novel *Slash* (1987), the collection of poems *Breath Tracks* (1991), and the book of essays *Looking at the Words of Our People: First Nations Analysis of Literature* (1993), which she edited.

'I write because it is a way to contribute to the vast dialogue of the human spirit in its course through time. It is a way to reach others I may never meet in person now and in the future. I appreciate voices from the past like Pauline Johnson and my own great aunt, Mourning Dove. They are windows into a time and place I can never experience directly myself. I write because oral literature is now extremely vulnerable.'

Armstrong is the Director of the En'owkin International School of Writing in Penticton, British Columbia, which offers Canada's only creative writing program designed for Native people. She has also served on her community's traditional council, and she consults with international councils and working groups on the wide variety of issues of concern to indigenous cultures.

SIMON ARNAVIAPIK Inuit, b. 1915
Simon Arnaviapik is from Pond Inlet, Northwest Territories. This selection is a good example of the personal-experience narrative, usually one of the first

types of written literature produced by a culture. It is of particular interest in a situation such as the Native one, in which an indigenous culture meets an invading one which perceives the indigenous as exotic. Thus, Arnaviapik's story might be seen as describing Inuit life 'from the inside'.

This piece was originally published in *Inuktitut* magazine in 1974 but is here taken from the anthology *Paper Stays Put*, edited by Robin Gedalof (McGrath).

BETH BRANT (DEGONWADONTI) Mohawk, b. 1941
Beth Brant is a Bay of Quinte Mohawk from Tyendinaga Mohawk Territory in Ontario. 'I come from a long line of storytellers and I feel that my written words are just another form of translating the language of the oral.

'I started writing when I turned forty. It was a gift brought to me by Eagle. In these ten years I have been writing, I am always conscious that I am writing for my own People. That is my audience. That is who the stories are about and for. And if non-Natives pick up a book of mine and learn about the effects of racism and colonialism on Native Peoples and then take that within themselves to make change, that is a good thing.'

Brant has a firm sense of the integration of her life and work. Her personal biography describes her as 'born May 6, 1941—a Taurus with Scorpio rising', 'a mother and grandmother' who 'lives with her partner of twenty years, Denise Dorsz'. Brant states, 'All of my writing identifies as Native, lesbian, and working class.' She is the author of two books of short stories—*Mohawk Trail* (1985) and *Food & Spirits* (1991)—and of *Writing as Witness: Essay and Talk* (1994). She is the editor of *A Gathering of Spirit* (1984), an anthology of writing and art by Native women. Her latest publication is *I'll Sing Till the Day I Die: Conversations with Tyendinaga Elders* (1995).

Brant is also known as a generous teacher of creative writing.

JOSEPH BRANT (THAYENDANEGEA) Mohawk, *c.* 1742–1807
Joseph Brant was born in what is now Ohio in either 1742 or 1743. He was with Sir William Johnson as early as his expedition against Fort Niagara in the Seven Years' War (1759) and as Johnson's protégé was sent in 1761 to Moor's Indian Charity School for two years. In the following years he acted as an interpreter for Johnson, his successor Guy Johnson, and for missionaries.

A Loyalist, after the outbreak of the American Revolution he chose to lead Native forces as a war chief against the Americans. Following the Revolution he worked to create a new confederacy of Native peoples to block American expansion westward.

In 1784 Brant led a group of Mohawk Loyalists to a settlement on the Grand River (named Brant's ford in 1827, now Brantford) in what is now Ontario. The land was a grant given by the British in compensation for loss of land in the United States, and for support to the British cause. Brant's activities have had long-standing repercussions. His decision that the Native future must be tied to developing white methods of agriculture and his attempt to lease land to whites to gain working capital resulted in extended conflict with both Native people and the government. He died in Burlington, Ontario.

Brant is better known as a figure in literature than as an author. His Christianity, his Loyalism, his statesmanship, and his military reputation have made him a perfect subject for depiction as a 'noble savage'. These portraits range from the nineteenth-century closet drama *Thayendanegea*, by J.B. Mackenzie, to the television mini-series *Divided Loyalties*. Still, Brant devoted significant energy to his words as a statesman, as is typical of Native politicians, from the oratory of the pre-contact culture to the essays and speeches of Native leaders today. These examples of his writing embrace sophisticated rhetorical principles, with a forthright commitment to the power of language. In his later years, Brant also worked to translate the Bible into Mohawk.

JOHN OJIJATEKHA ('BURNING FLOWER') BRANT-SERO Mohawk, 1867–1914

John Brant-Sero was born on the Six Nations Reserve in Ontario, his mother a descendant of Joseph Brant, his father a Bay of Quinte Mohawk, the two great traditions of the Mohawk Loyalist heritage. He went to the reserve school, to the Mohawk Institute to study carpentry, and, finally, he took a business course.

Among Brant-Sero's various occupations, he was translator to the curator of the Archaeological Museum in Toronto. His history, however, suggests his vocation was as an actor and recitalist. He toured in North America and Europe, following the path later pursued more notably by Pauline Johnson. A promotional brochure depicts him in a suit, his hair flowing, under the caption: 'The only Canadian Mohawk Indian now before the English public in a Concert & Lecture Tour.' Most of Brant-Sero's extant material suggests his role as second vice-president of the Ontario Historical Society. Such prominent journals as *Man* and the *Journal of American Folklore* record his comments on specific points of Native history.

This selection is representative of Brant-Sero, with its apparent 'humility' that still asserts his importance as a cultural figure, the representative Native Loyalist, and, as this suggests, the political descendant of Joseph Brant. The imperial tone to his record of his South African experience, and the significant absence of concern for either the Boers or the Native peoples of South Africa, seem relevant here. Brant-Sero's comments show concern for inequities in the treatment of Native peoples, but his focus is never far from himself.

MARIA CAMPBELL Métis, b. 1940

Maria Campbell describes herself as a storyteller, which is the role she plays in *Stories of the Road Allowance People* (1995), her versions of traditional Métis tales. *Halfbreed* (1973), her first publication, is an autobiography that describes the situation of the contemporary Métis. *Little Badger and the Fire Spirit* (1977), *Riel's People* (1978), and *People of the Buffalo* (1978) were written in response to needs expressed by her grandchildren. *The Book of Jessica* (1989), which includes the play she co-authored with Linda Griffiths, documents the difficulties of such cross-cultural projects.

Campbell has been writer-in-residence at the Banff School of Fine Arts and at the universities of Alberta and Regina. She also works extensively in film and video and helps run the Gabriel Crossings Foundation, a Native arts school dedicated to the preservation of traditional culture and the arts. Campbell is currently on the faculty of the University of Saskatchewan.

The storyteller was not only a skilled entertainer, but he/she was also an historian, a teacher and healer as well. Stories could not be told just any old time—each group had their specific time, i.e., some were winter stories, others were only told in the summer or spring. . . . Stories are precious to all Aboriginal people, but to the Métis they are the greatest inheritance of all. Land you can't give away because it doesn't belong to you. And it is not 'it' anyway, 'she' is your Mother. . . . No one ever told a story that was not his/her own, and if they did, it was only if the story had been given to them or if the story was purchased by way of trade. Even then, the storyteller would begin the story by telling how he/she came by it, and the name of the original creator would be given. The storyteller who had been given the story could not pass it on to anyone else without permission or prior consent.

HAROLD CARDINAL Cree, b. 1945

Harold Cardinal was born in High Prairie, Alberta. In the late sixties, when the social activism of youth became a major force in North America, Cardinal was one of a number of young Native people who introduced their own agenda. In 1966, with Duke Redbird and Tony Mandamin, Cardinal set up the Canadian Indian Youth Council which, among other things, was intended to become a Native arm of the Company of Young Canadians (a voluntary government agency focused on social, economic, and community development).

In 1968, Cardinal became the youngest elected president of the Indian Association of Alberta. In office until 1977, he became a national spokesperson on a variety of Native issues. Although a provincial leader, he was probably the best-known Native to appear in the media throughout Canada in this period. His comments on the maintenance of Native culture and religions, and on issues of special status, received wide attention.

His first book, *The Unjust Society* (1969), was titled in response to one of Prime Minister Pierre Trudeau's most famous catch-phrases, 'the just society'. Although at times attacked for the level of its polemic, *The Unjust Society* became the most significant book produced on Native rights in Canada. Its influence on other Native people and on government might be questioned, but its impact on the Canadian public cannot be.

Cardinal also participated in drafting a reply by Alberta Natives to a government white paper. This 'Red Paper', *Citizens Plus*, was part of a general exploration of Native possibilities in Canada. Cardinal has also worked with Indian Affairs as the first Native to be appointed Alberta regional director, as a consultant to band councils, as chief of his home reserve, the Sucker Creek band, and as vice-chief for the prairie region under the Assembly of First Nations in 1983.

The selection here is taken from Cardinal's second book, *The Rebirth of Canadian Indians* (1977). Taken together, Cardinal's books can be seen as the best of Native writing before 1980.

GEORGE COPWAY (KAHGEGAGAHBOWH) Ojibway, 1818–69

George Copway, Kahgegagahbowh (He Who Stands Forever), was born near what is now Trenton, Ontario, the son of 'a medicine man', one of the chiefs of the Rice Lake Indian Village.

His father was converted by Native Methodist missionaries in 1827, and his mother soon after. George converted in 1830, at the age of twelve, and began work as a teacher in 1834. He was sent to Jacksonville, Illinois, in 1836, to study for two years at the Ebenezer Methodist Seminary. He became an ordained minister and travelled with his English wife as a missionary to Native tribes in both the United States and Canada. When two Native bands in Canada accused him of embezzlement, the Methodists expelled him, and in 1846 he returned to the United States where he became a successful lecturer and author.

Copway translated part of the Bible into Ojibway, but his major literary achievement was his autobiography, *The Life, History, and Travels of Kahge-ga-gah-bowh* (1847), from which this selection is taken. It was the first book in English written by a Canadian Native person.

Copway also wrote *The Traditional History and Characteristic Sketches of the Ojibwa Nation* (1850), and *Running Sketches of Men and Places in England, France, Germany, Belgium and Scotland* (1851), an account of his European travels, and he edited the short-lived weekly *Copway's American Indian* (1851).

Copway had prominent supporters in the United States, including James Fenimore Cooper, Washington Irving, Henry Wadsworth Longfellow, Francis Parkman, and Henry Rowe Schoolcraft. His books were popular successes, with his autobiography published in six editions. That book's anti-paganism and passionate faith in conversion seem obsessive today, but Copway's attacks on British and American Native policy, and his imaginative proposals on land rights, were decidedly progressive.

BETH CUTHAND Cree, b. 1949

Born in La Ronge, Saskatchewan, Beth Cuthand grew up there and in Alberta. She attended the University of Regina and the University of Saskatchewan, where she received a Bachelor of Arts degree in sociology;

she then earned a Master of Fine Arts degree in creative writing from the University of Arizona. She has been a teacher at a variety of Native institutions, including the Gabriel Dumont Institute, the Saskatchewan Indian Institute of Technology, the Saskatchewan Indian Federated College, and the En'owkin International School of Writing in Penticton, British Columbia. Her columns and stories have appeared in *UBCIC News*, *Indian World*, *Saskatchewan Indian*, *From the Pipe*, and *Tomorrow File*. She has also been an editor for *Saskatchewan Indian Magazine* and the Institute for the Development of Indian Government.

Cuthand has edited a number of books, including Maria Campbell's *Stories of the Road Allowance People*, Ruby Slipperjack's *Silent Words*, and the anthologies *Gatherings V*, with William George, and *Re-inventing the Enemy's Language*, with Joy Harjo and others. She wrote and produced twenty-five scripts for CBC radio's *Our Native Land*, as well as scripts for various television programs, including *The Story of George* and the documentaries *Indians and the Constitution* and *Indian Government Today*. In addition, she co-wrote a made-for-television movie, *The New Kid*. She has published poetry and short stories in a number of periodicals and anthologies, as well as in her own books, *Horse Dance to Emerald Mountain* (1987) and *Voices in the Waterfall* (1989; second expanded edition, 1992).

JOSEPH A. DANDURAND Salish/Nooksack, b. 196?

Joseph Dandurand is a poet and playwright from the Kwantlin Reservation of the Fort Langley band in British Columbia.

He received a Diploma in Performing Arts from Algonquin College and a Bachelor of Arts in Theatre and Direction from the University of Ottawa. His produced plays include *Crackers and Soup* (One Crow's Theatre, 1994), *No Totem for My Story* (Native Earth Performing Arts, 1995), and *Where Two Rivers Meet* (The Theatre Centre, 1995).

Dandurand's poems have appeared in *Voices from Home*, *Gatherings*, and *The Upside Down Raven* and are collected in *I Touched the Coyote's Tongue* (1994) and *burning for the dead and scratching for the poor* (1995).

MARILYN DUMONT Cree/Métis, b. 1955

Marilyn Dumont was born in Olds, Alberta on 15 March 1955. As a descendant of Gabriel Dumont, she is clear about the delicate balance between the traditions of the Métis people and those of the various First Nations. In one of her poems she encounters a 'full-blood' who responds to her as if 'he's leather and I'm naugahyde.'

Dumont earned a Master of Fine Arts degree from the University of British Columbia and has a diverse background in film and video production, as well as in education. Her first book, *A Really Good Brown Girl* (1996), received wide acclaim. *Globe and Mail* writer Judith Fitzgerald said the collection 'immediately turns readers into willing captives witnessing a preternaturally gifted artist in possession of a world-class bag of poetic tricks.'

In her writing, Dumont uses a variety of forms, which detail the tensions she feels in her positions within and between cultures; as she observes, '*Cree Language Structures* and *Common Errors in English* book-end my life.'

CONNIE FIFE Cree, b. 1961

Originally from Saskatchewan, Connie Fife has been published in many anthologies and was writer-in-residence at the En'owkin International School of Writing in Penticton, British Columbia. Her poetry collection, *Beneath the Naked Sun* (1992), features supportive comments by Chrystos, Joy Harjo, and Beth Brant. The latter asserts, 'Connie Fife has made music out of the chaos and pain of being indigenous and lesbian in a culture that respects neither. I feel honoured to hold this book in my hands.'

As editor of an Aboriginal women's issue of *Fireweed* and of the anthology *The Colour of Resistance*, Fife sees herself as very much a part of a larger movement. In the introduction to the anthology she states:

> Whether oral or visual, Indigenous literature has always existed throughout the Americas. Our collective memory remains intact regardless of any attempt to separate us from its origins. No matter the authors or their skills in the written word, European writers have failed miserably at conveying the essence behind our words; they have failed to transport the life we find in language onto the page. This is our struggle as Native writers, as women who inherently know the nature of birth: to bring to life a language that is at times lifeless.

Fife lives with her son in Vancouver, where she works for the Urban Native Youth Association. She is preparing her next collection of poetry, tentatively titled *Speaking Through Jagged Rock*. In her biography entry for *Piece of My Heart: A Lesbian of Colour Anthology*, Fife says, 'I am a Cree woman who writes in the hope that my words find their mark. I offer them healing, pain, and ways of making radical change in a confused world. Meegwatch to my sisters. They know who they are.'

RON GEYSHICK Ojibway, 1942–97

Ron Geyshick was a healer and guide from the Lac La Croix Reserve in northern Ontario, on the United States border.

> A few years ago, I started to write down stories I've gathered over time, say a little over thirty years. I told them to schoolchildren and people who wanted to know about my own struggling ways. At the school, kids asked me for the same stories year after year, so I started writing things down to help me remember. . . . Based on what I've heard from my grandmother, my dad and my grandfather, and lots of other elders. . . . In these stories I can almost hear their voices. I sat around with them for hours, listening, and sometimes I didn't understand much at all. Not until years later did I get the meaning, but I liked to visit them and help out, and they helped me

a lot. Some of these stories are my own, things I've discovered myself because I wanted to know.

Te Bwe Win (Truth) was published in 1989.

RICHARD G. GREEN Mohawk, b. 1940
Richard Green was born in Grand River Territory, 'commonly known as the Six Nations Indian Reserve', in Ontario. He attended school in that province and in New York State. Since 1972, his stories, articles, and cartoons about North American Indian people have appeared in Native periodicals and literary anthologies in both the United States and Canada.

'I write just about anything except poetry, lyrics, and three-act plays. This includes legislation, legal and commercial writing, and writing for all media, including entertainment media. . . . I think Onkwehonwe people have much to contribute and teach. While we have not been invited to this table until recently, we are now able to share some of our knowledge as caretakers of North America. This information is needed not only to fortify our own people, but also to teach those who are not indigenous to our homeland. It is up to us writers to communicate the natural law that governs Turtle Island.'

Green's publications include *The Last Raven: A Collection of Short Stories by a Mohawk Author* (1991) and *Sing, Like a Hermit Thrush* (1995), a novel for young adults.

In addition to his career as a writer, Green is also a publisher in his community and a teacher of Native Studies at Mohawk College in Brantford, Ontario.

ALMA GREENE Mohawk, 1896–1984
Alma Greene, Gah-wonh-nos-doh (Forbidden Voice), was a Mohawk of the Turtle clan, a clan mother and a medicine woman who championed Longhouse traditions. She lived on the Grand River Lands of the Six Nations all her life.

I dreamed once that I went to the door of a longhouse here on the reserve. It was not, of course, the Mohawk longhouse, thanks to Joseph Brant. But it was one of the others where the Indians hold their own ceremonies.

When I got there the door would not open. I tried again and again, but it seemed as though something was pushing against it, holding it closed.

So I went around to the side, to a window, and looked in. There was the faithkeeper, crouched in horror in a corner. And the rest of the longhouse was filled with a serpent, as big around as a seven-inch pipe, lying from one end of the room to the other.

That's one dream I think has already come true.

'A New Clan Mother', *Forbidden Voice*

LOUISE HALFE Cree, b. 1953
Louise Bernice Halfe, whose Cree name in English is Sky Dancer, was born in the town of Two Hills in northern Alberta. She grew up a member of the

Saddle Lake Reserve ('My parents were nomads who worked for the Ukrainian farmers and in the sugar beet fields when I was a youngster . . .') and she attended the Blue Quills Residential School. She has a degree in social work from the University of Regina, as well as training in drug and addiction counselling.

'I was living in a tepee with my lover in the mountains when Grandfather came in a dream. He was the one who lifted these fingers and said "Read, write", lips moving quietly across the syllabics. . . . How could I write when I could barely articulate and identify the pain that controlled my fears? . . . In order to accept the gift of writing, to earn it, to honour it, I turned to my community, ceremony, and ritual. . . . My war party doesn't differ from my ancestors'. Living a nomadic life with lance, bow and arrow, gathering bundles, takes the same precision, thoughtfulness, determination, and discipline. The issues are the same: adversity and joy, unity and harmony, life and death.'

Halfe's first collection of poetry, *Bear Bones & Feathers* (1994), 'focuses on prayer, song, stories of my Grandparents, life on the reserve, residential school, and mixed relationships.' The book was nominated for the Saskatchewan Writers Guild's First Book Award and it won the 1996 Milton Acorn People's Poetry Award.

'I write because I love. I write for the survival of self, my children, my family, my community, and for the Earth. I write to help keep our stories, our truths, our language alive.'

THOM E. HAWKE Anishnahbe, b. 1959

Allen Deleary, an Ojibway, supplied us with this information about Mr Hawke:

'Born into the life of the nomadic ironworker family, T. Hawke swiftly adjusted to the basics of urban Indian conceptuality, pathfinding his way through the roots of Indian bureaucracies, programs, services, and assorted First Nations establishments. Nowadays, Hawke sightings are confined to his perch behind a computer . . . writing, or he can be seen performing live with the band 7th Fire.'

Here is Hawke's advice on storytelling/writing: 'Do not be afraid to formulate and express opinions. The ability to convey one's thoughts, ideas, and feelings is a magical process. Lighten the dark, darken the light, question the colours, make the world see through your eyes just for a moment.'

TOMSON HIGHWAY Cree, b. 1951

Tomson Highway was born in December 1951 on his father's trapline, in a tent on an island in Maria Lake, one hundred miles north of his home reserve at Brochet in the far northwest of Manitoba. The eleventh of twelve children, his early years were spent there, travelling by sled and canoe, hunting and fishing, speaking only Cree.

At six years of age, he was sent to a Roman Catholic boarding school in The Pas, Manitoba, where he learned English and started playing the piano.

At that time he was able to visit with his family only two months each summer. At fifteen, he moved again, to Winnipeg, to attend high school.

He next spent two years studying piano at the University of Manitoba's Faculty of Music, followed by a year studying to be a concert pianist with William Aide in London, England. He returned to Canada to complete his Honours Bachelor of Music degree (1975) at the University of Western Ontario and to spend another year completing English courses necessary for a Bachelor of Arts degree (1976). During this time he met and worked with James Reaney and saw his first Michel Tremblay play. The works of these artists, who find their subject matter in their own communities, became touchstones for Highway.

He spent the next seven years working in his own community with culture and recreation programs for Native people on reserves, in friendship centres, in prisons, on the streets, and in bars, familiarizing himself with the networkings of Native lives and politics in Canada.

At the age of thirty, Highway began writing plays and working with the Native theatre community with De-Ba-Jeh-Mu-Jig Theatre on Manitoulin Island, Northern Delights in Sioux Lookout, and Native Earth Performing Arts in Toronto. With these companies he wrote words and/or music and produced and/or performed in theatre works such as *The Rez Sisters* (1986), *Aria* (1987), *New Song . . . New Dance* (1988), *The Sage, the Dancer, and the Fool* (1989), and *Dry Lips Oughta Move to Kapuskasing* (1989). *The Sage, the Dancer, and the Fool*, in its second production, and *Aria* were both nominated for Dora Mavor Moore Awards, and both *The Rez Sisters* and *Dry Lips* won Dora awards for best new play. *The Rez Sisters* also garnered a Chalmers Award. *The Rez Sisters* and *Dry Lips* have been published by Fifth House (1989 and 1990, respectively).

Highway's plays emphasize a Trickster figure, derived from the Native storytelling traditions, who is emblematic of indigenous humour and spirit in the face of both historical and existential dilemmas.

Highway also directs, composes, and writes for film, as well as working to encourage literacy and the development of literature in all the languages Native people use. He is concerned that Canada's culture may lose the unique contributions of the living Cree, Ojibwa, and Inuit languages. He hopes his work in English can teach his audience 'something new and something terribly relevant and beautiful about the particular landscape that they too have become inhabitants of'. His ambition in life is to 'make the "rez" cool and to show and celebrate what funky folk Canada's Indian people really are'.

ALOOTOOK IPELLIE Inuit, b. 1951
Alootook Ipellie was born in a camp on the north shore of Frobisher Bay in the Northwest Territories on 11 August 1951: 'I grew up in the Arctic as a semi-nomad with my family. And then we were forced to settle in a community of other Inuit families. So I spent most of my adolescence in Iqaluit during a period of Inuit cultural upheaval. . . . It was a trying period because

most families were struggling to adjust to community living that festered with new social problems mainly associated with alcohol abuse and the generation gap. . . . I went through school wanting to write about what I had seen and what I could do to help my people cope with their problems.'

Ipellie was educated in Iqaluit, Yellowknife, and Ottawa, where he still lives. He has worked for the CBC as an announcer/producer and for the magazines *Inuit Today, Inuit, the Magazine of the Inuit Circumpolar Conference*, and *Nunatsiaq News* as a writer, artist, and editor. From 1989 to 1993 he was Project Co-ordinator of the Baffin Writers' Project. Ipellie now works as a freelance editor and he also edits *KIVIOQ, Inuit Fiction Magazine*.

'I've always thought writing and storytelling were means of exploring some parts of truth about human nature, and that stories need to be told or written in order to understand ourselves better. They are essentially tools we use to help express our 'silent voice' within our conscious or unconscious minds. . . . Writing and storytelling allow us to escape our own predicaments in this physical world and free our minds to go beyond it. . . . [They] should sometimes educate but always, always entertain.'

Ipellie's art is featured in the Inuit anthology *Paper Stays Put* (1981) and his writing and art are collected in *Arctic Dreams and Nightmares* (1993). He has completed a number of works as yet unpublished, including a novel, *Akavik, the Manchurian David Bowie*. He is also preparing a collection of his cartoons.

RITA JOE Micmac, b. 1932
Born on 15 March 1932 in Whycocomogh, Cape Breton, Nova Scotia, Rita Joe spent her childhood with foster families. At the age of twelve, she recalls: 'I put myself into the Indian Residential School in Shubenacadie. That school plays an important part in my life, along with Native upbringing by many mothers.' After completing high school, she pursued a business educational program in typing, and completed a twelve-week course on reading and writing Micmac at the University College of Cape Breton.

Joe now lives on the Eskasoni Reserve in Cape Breton. The widowed mother of ten children, two adopted, and now a grandmother as well, she is active in the education of Native children, both within her family and throughout the country. She is also involved in the education of the world at large on the subject of Native culture. She talks to a broad range of groups, from university students to Brownies and Boy Scouts: 'My education is my people—I have a front seat to see and feel their needs, the major one being that we, too, live with ideal productiveness.'

In 1974, Joe entered and won a competition held by the Nova Scotia Writers Federation: 'The surprise had even more meaning to it; I remember thinking at the time, now my people will think, "If she can do it, so can I." ' Thus, for Joe, to be a Native writer is a significant responsibility: 'The label is deeprooted and the stroke of a Native pen does wonders, especially for the coming generation.'

Joe's first book, *Poems of Rita Joe* (1978), consists of twenty-six untitled poems, for the most part brief, some with Micmac translations. Her second book, *Song of Eskasoni: More Poems of Rita Joe* (1988), has no full translations but features Micmac lines and phrases. The book's editor, Lee Maracle, sees an inner force to this combination of cultures: 'Her Micmac spirit—her love of the land—peers through her strong sense of Christendom and dominates her sense of spirituality.' Since 1988 Joe has published another poetry collection, *Lnu and Indians We're Called* (1991) and, with the assistance of Lynn Henry, *Song of Rita Joe: Autobiography of a Mi'kmaq Poet* (1996).

The hallmark of Joe's poetry, in form and content, is simplicity: 'The attitude I have in writing is a positive outlook on life. Sure, we all have a hard time sometime or other, but we cannot dwell on the negativeness forever; at times I get discouraged but do not let it get to me.'

The politics of Joe's poems, while subtle, is always an important element. In response to the Oka crisis, for example, she declared, ' "This is my country!" yet my country was doing things I never for a moment thought they would do to my people. I know there are two sides to any story, but I have to side with my people here.' Lee Maracle has stated, 'Rita Joe's poems pen for the reader that most important love of all—the love of people in their quest for a just society.' Joe's statement on the appropriation of voice is typical in its rejection of confrontation and its assertion of the positive over the negative: 'If we consider our Native culture important, we the Native people must put it down on paper our way. . . . If I get too sentimental in my choice of words, excuse me. I have to call attention to the gentle people of Canada. My song is gentle, bear with me.'

EMILY PAULINE JOHNSON (TEKAHIONWAKE) Mohawk, 1861–1913

E. Pauline Johnson's place in Canadian literature was always political. Born on the Six Nations Reserve, the daughter of a Mohawk chief, George Henry Martin Johnson, and his English wife, Emily Susanna Howells, at a time when Canadian culture was mainly imperialist, her family connections established her as both Native aristocracy and Loyalist descendant. Her pro-British proclamations continued the allegiance of her illustrious ancestors, such as her grandfather, John Smoke Johnson, a hero of the War of 1812.

Johnson originally performed to support her poetry, but she became one of Canada's most prominent recitalists. She was an ethereal, enigmatic love figure in her stage persona of the Indian princess, and the oral traditions gave her the status of a bard or orator. And Johnson, usually appearing in buckskin and beads, had the obvious theatrical aid of a good costume.

During the period of her greatest success Johnson wrote in three genres. Her poetry covers a range of subjects but focuses on the patriotic or pastoral 'Indian'. Almost all are short lyrics and narratives. Her short prose narratives often have a moral direction. Her *Legends of Vancouver* (1911) is a collection of mythic narratives as told by Chief Capilano.

Johnson's work combines genre writing, with all of its popular appeal, with substantial comments on the position of Native peoples in her society. This combination causes A. LaVonne Brown Ruoff to consider Johnson a late but typical example of the Victorian woman writer. Johnson's adventure stories, many collected in *The Shagganappi* (1913), constitute a clear moral agenda. In their publication in *The Boy's World*, a prominent American example of 'muscular Christianity', they provide a constant recitation of the moral character of Native peoples and, in particular, their civilization, as shown particularly in 'We-hro's Sacrifice'. Johnson's stories for another periodical from the same publisher, *Mother's Magazine*, show that she grasped the didactic potential of her venue and produced material which is, as Ruoff notes, both pro-Native and feminist. Perhaps the best example is 'My Mother', which emphasizes the matriarchal elements of Mohawk society.

Johnson always possessed clear perceptions of her racial position. In his introduction to *The Shagganappi*, Ernest Thompson Seton quotes her: 'There are those who think they pay me a compliment in saying that I am just like a white woman. My aim, my joy, my pride is to sing the glories of my own people.' Another quotation by Seton shows Johnson's romantic histrionics but also her recognition of her symbolic position: 'Oh, why have our people forced on me the name of Pauline Johnson?' she said. 'Was not my Indian name good enough? Do you think you help us by bidding us to forget our blood? by teaching us to cast off all memory of our high ideals and our glorious past? I am an Indian. My pen and my life I devote to the memory of my own people. Forget that I was Pauline Johnson, but remember always that I was Tekahionwake, the Mohawk that humbly aspired to be the saga singer of her people, the bard of the noblest folk the world has ever seen, the sad historian of her own heroic race.'

Johnson used the 'noble savage' archetype implied by the words 'saga singer' and 'bard' to argue against the racist assumption of the dying Native society, which 'sad historian' implies, and to create a space in popular literature for Native issues, presented from a specifically Native perspective. This is no small achievement.

BASIL H. JOHNSTON Ojibwa, b. 1929

Basil Johnston was born on the Parry Island Reserve and received his education at Cape Croker Public School, the Spanish Residential School, Loyola College (Montreal), and the Ontario College of Education. Johnston has spoken on and has taught Ojibwa history, language, and culture in a variety of settings, from university conferences to public schools. His writing includes translations, language primers, satire, autobiography, fiction, essays, poems, reviews, and material for children. His publications include *Ojibway Heritage* (1976), *How the Birds Got Their Colours* (1978), *Moose Meat and Wild Rice* (1978), *Indian School Days* (1988), and *The Manitous: The Spiritual World of the Ojibway* (1995). He has also worked in film and television.

Johnston is now retired from the Department of Ethnology of the Royal

Ontario Museum, which published a number of his collections of Ojibwa tales. He is a member of the Order of Ontario.

MARGO KANE Saulteaux/Cree, b. 1951
Margo Kane is an interdisciplinary artist who has worked as a storyteller, actor, singer, dancer, choreographer, director, video and installation artist, producer, and teacher.

'I write only because I felt it necessary to develop and perform work that meant something to me. Waiting and hoping for scripts in the seventies, I finally began to work towards my own script development process. I wanted to perform scripts that spoke to my humanity both as a Native contemporary woman and as an artist.

'I began experimenting with style and technique using storytelling methods learned from formal Western theatre and drawing on my experiences of storytelling in the Native community, formal and informal events, from stories around the campfire to witnessing various ceremonial "performances" in the West Coast Bighouses.'

Kane's best-known piece, *Moonlodge* (1990), was first produced by Native Earth Performing Arts. Other performances include her first one-woman show, *Reflections in the Medicine Wheel*, which was created for Expo 86; *O Elijah, We've Always Been Here*; *Childhood Burial*; *Memories Springing/Waters Singing*; *I Walk, I Remember*; and *Confessions of An Indian/Cowboy*.

Kane travels with her performances into both rural and urban Native communities across Canada. Her commitment is to produce work that is not only socially relevant but empowering as well.

LENORE KEESHIG-TOBIAS Anishnabe, b. 1949
Lenore Keeshig-Tobias is a member of the Chippewas of the Nawash First Nation, which is 'situated on unceded territory surrounded by the province of Ontario' on the Bruce Peninsula, commonly known as the Cape Croker Reserve. She received her Bachelor of Fine Arts degree from York University in North York, Ontario. Keeshig-Tobias is a storyteller, culture worker, mother, and grandmother. She has served as the founding chair of the Racial Minority Writers Committee of The Writers Union of Canada and has worked as editor of *The Ontario Indian*, *Sweetgrass*, and *The Magazine to Re-establish the Trickster*. She currently serves as an education trustee for the Nawash First Nation.

'I write for the enjoyment of language, and, when necessary, out of a sense of responsibility to "speak up" or "speak out". I write mostly about the experiences of Anishnabe children, and poetry. My writing (whatever genre) is always related to my identity as a Native person, whether or not it is marked by themes or with language specifically identifying Anishnabe culture and heritage.

'Storytelling has always been part of our family life, not just as a heritage in the traditional stories, but as a necessary function in our individual life circle. Some of these stories are not flattering, but nevertheless will be told time and again—reflections of the Trickster-Teacher, and of what not to do.'

Keeshig-Tobias's most recent publications are *Bird Talk* (1991) and *Emma and the Tree* (1996), bilingual children's books in Anishnabemowin (Ojibway) and in English, both illustrated by her daughter Polly. *Bird Talk* won the 1993 Living the Dream Book Award (an award that commemorates the life and work of Dr Martin Luther King Jr).

WAYNE KEON Ojibway, b. 1946
Born on 12 December 1946 in the Ottawa Valley of Ontario, Wayne Keon grew up with a strong sense of Native heritage in an extended-family setting about forty miles west of Pembroke: 'Everyone was about two generations away from the reserve but still involved in hunting, fishing, and trapping.'

Keon attended high school in Elliot Lake, where his father, Orville, worked for Denison Mines. Wayne also worked in the mines during summer holidays, and a developing interest in the financial side of mining led him to take business administration courses at the Northern Institute of Technology in Kirkland Lake. Keon now lives in Toronto, where he is an internal auditor for the mining conglomerate Rio Algom.

Keon's writing career began when his father gave him some poetry to submit to a school newspaper. Thinking it unlikely that a father's work would be published in a school paper, Wayne presented the poems under his own name. When he admitted the hoax, he was forced to come up with his own material to prove himself.

One result was *Sweetgrass* (1972), a collection of poetry by Wayne, his father, and his brother Ronald, which featured sketches by Wayne as well. Wayne and Orville then published a novel, *Thunderbirds of the Ottawa* (1977) and Wayne went on to publish poetry in various periodicals, including *NeWest Review*, *Canadian Forum*, *Queen's Quarterly*, *Exile*, and *The Malahat Review*. In the nineties he has published three collections of poetry, *Sweetgrass II* (1990), *Storm dancer* (1993), and *My Sweet Maize* (1997).

'We, my father and my brother and myself, have never taken the traditional Native storytelling as fact, the way some storytellers see it as living history. I take as background all that I know of the traditional values and spiritual heritage of all Native peoples.' Keon feels such connections are treated differently in a Native context: 'It's a funny thing to grow up in a Native home because there's so much that is different from a regular Canadian home. I don't ever recall having an argument with any member of my family about a case of ownership. I used to get really confused when a non-Native friend would shout, "This is mine!" I guess that all came because in the past the subsistence of a Native group required interdependency.'

Keon is a careful reader of contemporary poetry in general, and notes his appreciation of bill bissett in one of his poems: 'bill bissett is a writer that I've read a lot of, perhaps because bill has quite an interest in Native peoples' culture and spiritual values.' Keon does not automatically reject a white writer's use of such material: 'It depends on how you do it. I belong to the

Pan American Indian Association. You don't have to be a Native to join, you just aspire to the same spiritual creed. I guess it's a bit like how I relate to my ancestry. I don't have any aspiration to live the life my mother did on the traplines. That was a hard life, too hard. Yet I still have the values my mother and my aunts and uncles held.'

THOMAS KING Cherokee, b. 1943

Thomas King's mother is Greek and his father Cherokee and he was born in California, but his practice as a Native writer is much more complicated than this heritage suggests. In 1980 he arrived at the University of Lethbridge in Alberta to teach Native studies. There he combined his extensive knowledge of Native American literary traditions, as shown in his doctoral dissertation from the University of Utah, with various explorations of Native life in Alberta. One of his comments about his writing is especially revealing: 'I write about Natives because it's the subject matter I know and enjoy. I know it has something to do with who I am, but I can't quantify it in any way.'

King, who now teaches Native literature and creative writing at the University of Guelph, produced his first book as an academic editor—*The Native in Literature: Canadian and Comparative Perspectives* (1987). His second book was *All My Relations: An Anthology of Contemporary Canadian Native Fiction* (1990). Since then he has published a children's book, *A Coyote Columbus Story* (1992), and a collection of short fiction, *One Good Story, That One* (1993). However, he has made his greatest mark through his novels.

Medicine River (1990) shows his flair for humorous anecdote and his unusual combination of irony and sensitivity in his portrayal of the Native cultures he encountered in Alberta. In the 1993 film produced from the novel, King maintained this sensibility in his screenplay and enhanced it by his own appearance in the movie, playing a slow-moving, sardonic basketball player. His second novel, *Green Grass, Running Water* (1993), features a postmodern structure constantly informed by Native oral tradition and theology. The comic fun is still there, but within a portrait of politics and cosmology that is near overwhelming. *Green Grass, Running Water* sets a standard seldom equalled by novelists in any culture.

Green Grass, Running Water has received attention given to few Canadian writers, with notices in a variety of mainstream American periodicals. Since its publication, King has gone on to develop his talents in yet other directions, writing television scripts for *North of Sixty* and a series of film treatments and radio dramas. His radio series *The Dead Dog Cafe Comedy Hour* exemplifies his ability to recognize the potential of a creative medium. The miniature scale of the setting of Dead Dog, a small reserve cafe with a one-man radio station visited by a writer (King as himself), seems almost the antithesis of the epic comedy in *Green Grass, Running Water*.

JOHN McLEOD Mississauga, b. 1949

John McLeod writes: 'I was born 29 November 1949 in Oakville, Ontario. Ever since then, I've lived in what is now known as The City of Mississauga (correctly pronounced Miss-is-aw-gee). I am a Mississauga Tribesman by birth, a Treaty Indian and a member of the Alderville Band by law.

'"The Shivering Tree" is my first published work. [McLeod's stories and cartoons have appeared in Native journals like the *Ontario Indian* and the *Toronto Native Times* since the early seventies.] It's a quasi-traditional work, a working together of old traditional tales and a few small products of my own imagination.

'That, I believe, is what storytelling (I told the story before I wrote it) is all about.

'My play, *Diary of a Crazy Boy*, enjoyed a healthy run in Toronto. It was produced by Native Earth and published by *Theatrum*.

'Currently, I live with my long-suffering but redoubtable mother. I'm a cranky, bookish bachelor whose hobbies include Canadian military history (there's a strong military streak in my family. I'm a son, nephew, and grandson of war veterans), studies of espionage, and paleontology. I'm also a collector of Yardbird recordings. (Make that re-recordings in view of my financial situation.)

'I don't own a working typewriter.'

LEE MARACLE Métis/Salish, b. 1950
Lee Maracle was born in North Vancouver, the daughter of a Salish father and a Métis mother.

Despite not finishing high school, she has become a prolific essayist, poet, and writer of both short and long prose fiction. 'The difficulty for me has been mastering a language different from my own, without having my own. Most of us learned English from parents who spoke English in translation. Many of our parents had been to residential school and thus did not speak the old language any better than the average five-year-old speaks English.'

Maracle has read widely in history, her own people's in particular. She has also studied sociology and creative writing at Simon Fraser University in British Columbia.

With her first publication, *I Am Woman* (1988), Maracle defined her way of writing as 'oratory'. 'As orators, we are not short on vocabulary . . . . Our best orators, in English or their own language, are those who have struggled with the language unencumbered by the tedious commas and colons of the English language.'

Maracle's other publications include *Bobbi Lee: Indian Rebel* (1990), *Sojourner's Truth and Other Stories* (1990), *Oratory: Coming to Theory* (1990), *Sun Dogs* (1991), and *Ravensong* (1993). She is also a co-editor of and a contributor to *Telling It: Women and Language Across Cultures* (1990).

MARTIN MARTIN Inuit, 1889–1976   SUSAN MARTIN Inuit, b. 1897
Martin Martin, born at Oka, Labrador, and Susan Martin, born at Hebron, Labrador, are part of a very specific environment. The Labrador coast has been used by whites as fishing grounds for centuries. A few remained on the

shore to become known as 'settlers'. The population has remained small, and devoted to its own traditional ways—trapping and fishing—thus giving rise to the Canadian anomaly of a long-standing, isolated, subsistence-based white population.

As a result, there has been intermarriage and a general intermingling between Inuit, white, and Innu and Naskapi for a long time. Although the identities of the cultures have remained separate, and although there has been significant racial tension at times, there has also been an acceptance of the rights of tenure of all these populations, often stated in opposition to new-comers, and specifically to Newfoundlanders and Québécois.

These two reminiscences are taken from the Labrador magazine *Them Days*, which includes a multitude of personal experience narratives from all of the cultures. In its accounts of mixed-race lives from this unusual 'melting pot', it provides insights unseen in the records of other Canadian areas. It also, like various magazines and newspapers which represent other First Nations, shows the 'literary' responses from Native cultures at a time when there was no literary culture which included them.

DUNCAN MERCREDI Inninew/Cree, b. 1951
Born in Grand Rapids, Manitoba on 17 August 1951, Mercredi moved at the age of sixteen to Cranberry Portage to finish high school. After graduation he worked for twenty years in construction, much of the time as a surveyor, throughout Manitoba. He recalls the many instances of overt and covert racism he encountered during that time, including the simple surprise that a Native man might be employed with a white survey crew. On one occasion his foreman related a comment by a farmer who had been observing Mercre-di working: 'That little Japanese guy sure has good eyesight.'

Mercredi is now a researcher with the federal government, but he is also a prolific and committed writer. He recalls the influence of the stories told by his *kookum* [grandmother]: 'I always thought how incredible she was that she could take me places and experience events that she had stored away in her mind and heart.' Although his grandmother gave Mercredi the desire to write, he did not pursue writing until his late thirties: 'After meeting Maria Camp-bell, Jordan Wheeler, Lee Maracle, and other writers of First Nation ances-try, I began writing with a passion as I felt the need for others, meaning "white society"—or is it mainstream society?—to experience what I have and in my words.'

Mercredi has published *Spirit of the wolf: raise your voice: poems* (1990), *Dreams of the wolf in the city: poems* (1992), and *Wolf and shadows: poems* (1995). His next book, *The Duke of Windsor—Wolf Sings the Blues*, is tenta-tively scheduled for publication in early 1998.

MONIQUE MOJICA Kuna/Rappahannock, b. 1954
Monique Mojica was born and raised in New York City, the daughter of a the-atrical family; both her mother and an aunt are long-time members of the

illustrious Spiderwoman Theatre. Mojica migrated to Toronto, Ontario, as a founding member of Native Earth Performing Arts. She has worked in theatre and film there, particularly with Native Earth, The Centre for Indigenous Theatre, and Nightwood Theatre, as an actor, director, and writer.

In collaboration with Native Earth Performing Arts, she produced *Double Take A Second Look* (1983) and *Give Them A Carrot (For As Long As The Sun Is Green)* (1985). She also collaborated with the Inuit actor Makka Kleist to produce *Sea Cows* (1985–7). Her acting roles have included the title character in the play *Jessica*, Ariel in *The Tempest*, and Marie-Adele in *The Rez Sisters*.

It is as an actor that Mojica found her way to writing. Her play *Princess Pocahontas and the Blue Spots* (1991) resulted from a recognition that stories important enough to tell as performance also need to be written down, documented, saved. The ephemeral quality of performance, particularly of texts developed in the collective process, threatens truths that need to be told. She still sees herself working as part of a community, 'not as an isolated writer.'

Mojica's other dramatic work includes *Birdwoman and the Suffragettes: A Story of Sacajawea*, a play for radio (1991), and *A Fast Growing Mould Bitter as Shame* (1994).

DANIEL DAVID MOSES Delaware, b. 1952
Daniel David Moses recalls his childhood on a farm on the Six Nations lands along the Grand River, near Brantford, in southern Ontario: 'I grew up nominally Anglican in a community of various Christian sects and of the Longhouse, the Iroquoian traditional religious and political system. These form the largely unarticulated base of my understanding of the world.'

Moses often asserts the importance of his Delaware heritage, in opposition to various assumptions that he belongs to other tribal groups more common in southern Ontario. Part of this is pride in heritage, but it also reflects a concern for precision, something clear in all of his work, but most obvious in his poetry.

This devotion to craft is related to Moses's education, first an Honours Bachelor of Fine Arts degree from York University and then a Master of Fine Arts degree from the University of British Columbia, where he won the Creative Writing Department's prize for playwriting in 1977. Part of his learning was also in Native literatures; during his undergraduate years he worked three summers for the Department of Indian Affairs on an annotated bibliography of books by or about Native peoples.

Moses returned to Toronto in 1979 where he worked part-time, including a stint as an assistant immigration officer at Pearson Airport. After 1986 he devoted all of his time to writing. The results were periodical and anthology publications; his plays *Coyote City* (produced in 1988), *The Dreaming Beauty* (produced in 1990), *Big Buck City* (produced in 1991), *Almighty Voice and His Wife* (produced in 1991), and *The Indian Medicine Shows* (produced in 1996);

and a collection of poems, *The White Line* (1990). As well, he has read at a variety of events in Canada, the United States, and Europe. Recently he has had extensive experience as writer-in-residence in locations across Canada.

Moses's first book was *Delicate Bodies* (1980), a collection of poems. He recalls that writing poetry was a purposeful choice, to reflect his perception of his stage of development: 'I felt (and now believe I was wise to feel) that lyric poetry was the only form in which I could combine the techniques of writing with the only thing I could claim to know as truth, my own experience. I told myself in poetry I would perfect my technique while I gave myself time to grow up.' Moses now sees this 'growing up' as also a return to certain perceptions traditional to his culture. He recalls his early years as 'being educated to have—let's call it—a western mind, to balance being a good Judaeo-Christian with being scientific.'

When he came to write *Coyote City* Moses blended these facets with what he terms a 'ghost story'. He recalls that Native actors found it much easier to accept the reality of such spirits than others. Moses associates this with their unconscious understanding of the Trickster and his ambivalent nature. Questions of Native mythology are often central to Moses's prose and drama. His poetry represents a comparable rejection of easy answers, as in his analysis of letters in the poem 'Paper':

> It's too bad if anyone imagines
> words have ever bled when the clean blackness
> of letters on this paper should imply
> that it's easy to live. You can't deny
> the truth of salutation or address—
> there is nothing but white between the lines.

BEATRICE MOSIONIER Métis, b. 1949
Born on 27 August 1949 in St Boniface, Manitoba, Beatrice Mosionier (formerly Culleton) was the youngest of four children of Louis and Mary Clara Mosionier. At the age of three, she was taken by the Children's Aid Society of Winnipeg to grow up in foster homes, away from her family and her people, with the exception of several years when she lived in one foster home with one of her older sisters. Two of her sisters committed suicide.

Her first novel, *In Search of April Raintree* (1983), based largely on her life experience, was welcomed by the Native community as part of its healing process and was reissued in 1984 as *April Raintree*. Mosionier has also worked in Native publishing; has written books for children, *Spirit of the White Bison* (1985) and *Christopher's Folly* (1996); and has scripted *Walker* (1991), a short film for the National Film Board.

PHILIP KEVIN PAUL WSA'NEC', b. 1971
'After writing "Still Falling", which is really a thought in progress, I began defining what I called "The Weight",' recalls Philip Kevin Paul. 'Since so

much has been taken away from my people in the last 150 years, most that was good about W̲SA'NEC' seems only to be a memory. My grandfathers and grandmothers on both sides heard the stories of W̲SA'NEC' in sadness, because their parents lived in the generation that truly made the transition from one way of life to another. Thankfully, my grandparents lived in and remembered the old ways, but they also remembered (without knowing it, I think) the sadness that the stories were told in. That sadness, or weight, has been passed from one generation to the next along with each story. As the sadness gets farther from its original generation, the weight of it gets heavier, because it becomes less comprehensible. To my generation, the weight is very heavy, but to the generations behind me, it is crushing.'

Philip Kevin Paul received a degree in writing and English from Camosun College and the University of Victoria, British Columbia. At Camosun he won awards in creative writing and in English. One of his plays has been given a staged reading at Kaleidoscope Theatre in Victoria and he did a report for the Institute of Ocean Sciences on correlations between Saanich place names and modern scientific research. His work, both creative and technical, has been published in *The Bound With Glue Review*, *Gatherings*, *Breathing Fire*, and *BC Studies*. He was a contributor to *Our Ancestors* and *The Reef Net Technology of the Salt Water People*.

'Though I have a somewhat limited vocabulary in my own language, I grew up hearing my language, especially when referring to the ideas that do not translate into English. All the poems, in the collection of poems that I am working on, are based on the discovery of a map hidden within the language itself (meaning my language, SENC'OTEN). Since writing will never be central to my life, but will be used to express what *is* central, many of my poems could be considered translations; I am trying to express the feeling of a tradition that has always contained me.'

DUKE REDBIRD Chippewa, b. 1939
Duke Redbird was born 18 March 1939 on the Saugeen Reserve on the Bruce Peninsula, near Owen Sound, Ontario.

Redbird is a former President of the Ontario Métis and Non-Status Indian Association, former Director of Land Claims Research and former Vice-President of the Native Council of Canada. He has worked with all levels of government and the private sector to meet the needs of Indians in the fields of education, alcohol and drug abuse, economic development, housing, tourism, culture, the arts, and health care.

In the seventies he performed his poetry to audiences throughout Canada and the United States. In 1977 a multi-media musical based on his poetry was performed in the presences of Their Royal Highnesses Queen Elizabeth II and the Duke of Edinburgh during Silver Jubilee celebrations in Ottawa. In the following year Redbird received his Master's degree from York University.

A respected poet and scholar, Redbird's work has been widely published and in 1981 he published a collection of poems: *Loveshine and Redwine*. In 1985 he was recognized by the Native Council of Canada for his contributions to Aboriginal peoples. In the same year he represented Canada at the Valmiki World Poetry Festival in Delhi, India, and in June 1989, a commissioned work was read for the opening of the Canadian Museum of Civilization in Hull, Quebec.

Redbird continues to write poetry and paint canvasses and original works of art on pine carvings that reflect his love of the wilderness.

Each event of Redbird's life is a stage in the development of his own Native consciousness and in his efforts to develop the Native awareness of all Canadians. *We Are Métis* was yet another step. Written as an interdisciplinary thesis at York University, it is part of the recent renaissance of the Métis, asserting themselves as a nation within Native cultures in Canada.

In addition to writing, Redbird currently is an Arts and Entertainment reporter for CityPulse News in Toronto.

EDEN ROBINSON Haisla/Heiltsuk, b. 1968
Eden Robinson was born on the Kitamaat Reserve of the Haisla Nation's traditional lands in the rainforests of northern British Columbia. She earned a Bachelor's degree from the University of Victoria and a Master's degree from the University of British Columbia, both in creative writing.

Robinson's first collection, *Traplines* (1996), was well received. An admitted fan of Stephen King, she describes the collection's four stories about adolescents confined by their age and class as 'dark fairy tales'. 'I love grim stories. They just make your own life seem so much better.'

About her second book, *Monkey Beach* (1997), a novel set in her home community, she has said, 'It's a tougher book for me to write because I'm not hiding behind these flamboyant psychopaths. None of the characters are bad. They're just reacting like everyone else to situations of loss and death. . . .

'It's a balance between my artistic freedom and the privacy of the community I come from. That's a scary balance for me. I find it hard. I want to get it right before I do it. It really feels rude in some ways to write about people who can't write back at you.'

HARRY ROBINSON Okanagan, 1900–90
Harry Robinson was born on 8 October 1900 in Oyama, near Kelowna, in the Okanagan Valley of British Columbia where his mother's family were seasonal farm workers. They soon moved back to the Similkameen Valley near Keremeos. Robinson's early years were spent primarily with his aged grandmother, one of many elders and storytellers who influenced him. This was his education, as he spent only five months in school, at the age of thirteen, and did not learn to read and write until he became an adult. A ranch hand from the age of seventeen, Robinson was twenty-four when he married a rancher.

By the mid-fifties he owned four ranches, but when his wife died in 1971 he sold everything and moved to a small bungalow. He died in 1990.

Wendy Wickwire provides this information in her introduction to *Write It On Your Heart: The Epic World of an Okanagan Storyteller* (1989), which she compiled from twelve years of interviews with Robinson. Since then she has produced another collection, *Nature Power: In the Spirit of an Okanagan Storyteller* (1992).

Robinson's purpose as a writer was to create a record: 'I'm going to disappear and there'll be no more telling stories.' For him, this was only part of a general deterioration of his way of life: 'I think way back is better than now. Old days lots of fish.'

As Robinson grew older, he found that even his Native listeners were unable to understand the Okanagan language, so he decided to tell his stories in English. Wickwire chose to present the stories in lines of text rather than in run-on prose: 'I searched for a presentational style to capture the nuance of the oral tradition—the emphasis on certain phrases, intentional repetition, and dramatic rhythms and pauses. I have, therefore, set the stories in lines which mirror as closely as possible Harry's rhythms of speech. Harry's stories are really performed events, rather than fixed objects on a page.' Wickwire made no other changes except to regularize the pronouns.

Wickwire recorded more than a hundred stories but she acknowledges that the selection was Robinson's and that the choice might have been shaped by his sense of what a young white female would want to, or perhaps should, hear. Still, she tried to present a 'cross-section' in her collections.

'Captive in an English Circus' is not altogether representative of Robinson's writings, as the majority of these writings are in some sense animal stories, many of which folklorists label 'pourquoi tales', narratives explaining how an element of nature came to have a certain form. Only 'Captive in an English Circus' and three other poems are in the section of the first book that Wickwire titled 'World Unsettled: The Age of the White Man'.

This separation is Wickwire's, however, as Robinson, like storytellers of many traditional cultures, distinguished subject matter, not historical veracity. Wickwire comments, 'All the stories are considered true stories. . . . Stories describe either situations experienced personally or they describe situations passed on by others who similarly experienced them, however long ago. In the case of the latter, Harry simply explains, "This is the way I heard the stories so I tell it that way."' Robinson perceived himself as not an author but a transmitter.

Wickwire notes that 'Captive in an English Circus' is the only story in the first collection that has no displays of ' "power", no transformations, no dying and coming back to life, no spiritual healing by Indian doctors, and no *shoo-MISH* [guardian spirit].' The story shows the maintenance of Okanagan culture, and yet the absence of such power suggests the community can no longer be strong in the face of white control. This perhaps represents Robinson's feeling of loss, which led him to tell these stories.

ARMAND GARNET RUFFO Ojibway, b. 1955

Armand Garnet Ruffo was born in northern Ontario and holds a Master's degree in literature and creative writing from the University of Windsor and an Honours degree in English literature from the University of Ottawa. He presently teaches Native literature at Carleton University and has previously taught creative writing at both the Banff Centre for the Arts and the En'owkin International School of Writing in Penticton, British Columbia.

Strongly influenced by his Ojibway heritage, his first collection of poetry, *Opening In The Sky* (1994), reveals an abiding interest in the complexities of aboriginal identity in a multicultural society. His second book, a creative poetic biography, *Grey Owl: The Mystery of Archie Belaney* (1997), further 'raises difficult questions about voice and identity, aboriginal culture, human rights, and the environment.' In addition, he has written plays, stories, and essays, which continue to appear in literary periodicals and anthologies both in Canada and the United States.

BUFFY SAINTE-MARIE Cree, b. 1941

Buffy Sainte-Marie was born on the Pay-e-pot reserve in the Qu'Appelle Valley of Saskatchewan. She was raised by foster parents in Maine and Massachusetts. Her foster mother was part Micmac, but Sainte-Marie recalls all her childhood environments as being 'very white'. She was adopted by the Cree at a powwow when she was eighteen.

Sainte-Marie has had significant successes as a singer and songwriter from her early twenties. One of her best-known songs, 'Until It's Time For You To Go', has been recorded in seven languages by more than one hundred artists, from Elvis Presley to the Boston Pops. Sainte-Marie has published hundreds of other songs, which have been recorded in sixteen languages. One early song, 'The Universal Soldier', written in a Toronto folk club, became one of the anthems of the peace movement and it continues to be sung in that context. Regardless of her successes, Sainte-Marie found it difficult to book performances in the United States in the seventies and eighties, apparently because of her political activities. Thus, at a time when she was drawing an audience of 90,000 in Paris, she appeared only on reserves in the United States.

Many of Sainte-Marie's songs, such as 'Now That the Buffalo's Gone' and 'My Country 'Tis of Thy People You're Dying', focus directly on Native causes. She recorded an album for the American Indian Movement and has donated much of her royalties to a foundation she created for Native education, the Nihewan Foundation.

Today, Sainte-Marie lives in Hawaii but she continues to compose and perform throughout North America and has become a leader in the use of computer and Internet technology in both music and design. Many of her songs have been composed for films; for example, 'Up Where We Belong', recorded for the Hollywood movie *An Officer and a Gentleman*, won an Academy Award for best song in 1982.

For five-and-a-half years she was a regular performer on the children's television program *Sesame Street*, where her main activity was to increase awareness of Native cultures. She saw this as part of a general transition in her public persona from despair to pride. In 1978 she commented: 'I began to have this feeling that a lot of people were coming to see me just to watch this Indian cry, and I didn't accept that for a minute. I looked around at my culture and said, what do Indian people need? We need a sense of our own joy, our own beauty, our own dignity, our own life and laughter.'

Sainte-Marie was awarded the Order of Canada in 1997.

GREGORY SCOFIELD Métis, b. 1966

Gregory Scofield was born in Maple Ridge, British Columbia, of Cree, Scottish, English, and French ancestry. He spent much of his childhood in the 'bush', the northern parts of Manitoba, Saskatchewan, and the Yukon. He found public school 'extremely disastrous' and left at the age of fifteen, later completing grade eleven at Vancouver's Native Education Centre before enrolling as a mature student in the Native Human Justice Program of the University of Regina's Gabriel Dumont Institute. He returned to the West Coast in 1988 and began working with young offenders. In 1993 he attended the Native Youth Worker Training Program at the Vancouver Community College and is now an alcohol and drug counsellor and outreach worker.

'I am called a poet—a political poet, an angry poet, a Métis poet, an ex-street-involved poet, a gay poet—yet I think of myself as a community worker, a teller of stories, a singer of songs. . . . My voice is the voice of many communities, the voice of ancient speakers, the voice of contemporary nomads—though always it is the voice of my "Grandmothers and Grandfathers", a voice that sings one small song in a community of powerful singers.

'I am pleased to say that I've never received formal education to write—and have written three books to date.'

Those books are *The Gathering: Stones for the Medicine Wheel* (1993), *Native Canadiana: Songs from the Urban Rez* (1996), and *Sakihtowin-Maskihkiy Ekwa Peyak Nikamowin/Love Medicine and One Song* (1997).

PAUL SEESEQUASIS Cree, b. 1958

Paul Seesequasis was born in Melfort, Saskatchewan, into a family that blended Plains Cree and Dakota with Ukrainian and German ancestry. 'I like the idea of mixed blood existing between cultures and not being easy to place. That hybrid existence is the direct result of the meeting of different people and it can create new imaginings of self, which I think are reflected in my writing. I'm fascinated with the creative potential of miscegenation. My identity as a Native person is real in terms of family and lived memory, but not in any pan-tribal or pan-spiritual sense. My grandfather and my mother are the two Indian people who have had the greatest impact on my life and I can't remember either of them ever talking about "being Indian". They are simply people who dance through life with humour and gentleness.

'I want my writing to deal with transformation and crossing boundaries. I hope my writing contains a "trickster spirit" in that it challenges the reader as much as it entertains them. . . . I think we are entering a new nomadic age where, especially in the urban wilderness, there are cross-breeding, cross-gender, and cross-culture things happening. Nothing is pure and the only two constants are love and change. In these new meetings I think the trickster can thrive.'

Seesequasis's stories and essays have appeared in *All American* (1997) and the Banff Centre's *10 Years of Arts Journalism*. He worked as an editor for *Aboriginal Voices Magazine* and is now working for 7th Generation Books in Toronto.

LORNE JOSEPH SIMON Micmac, 1960–94

Lorne Simon died in a car accident on 8 October 1994. He was heading home from his Bachelor of Education studies at the University of New Brunswick to the place where he was born, Big Cove Reserve. Fluent in Micmac, Simon had been well-educated in traditional culture but had also attended the En'owkin International School of Writing in Penticton, British Columbia and in 1992 he was its top graduate. *Stones and Switches* was about to become the first publication by Theytus of a book by an En'owkin graduate.

Stones and Switches is dedicated 'With love to my mother, Sarah, who told me the story—and knows better than I do what really happened to Meg-wadesk.' In the book, Jeannette Armstrong quotes from a letter the author sent to her:

> You recently spoke to the public on the excitement you felt about the work Native writers will be doing in the future in reclaiming and revitalizing our past and our cultural heritage. I feel that I am part of this. . . . Currently there are hardly any Micmac writers who are vigorously taking part in this effort, yet I am sure that I will be setting an example and that others will follow. What I am doing is a ripple emanating from a pearl thrown into the pool of talent. Keep throwing pearls into the pool, for they are not wasted.

RUBY SLIPPERJACK Ojibwa, b. 1952

A member of the Eabametoong First Nation, Ruby Slipperjack was born on a trapline near White Water Lake north of Armstrong, Ontario. She received her education in Collins, Ontario, in Sault Ste Marie at the Shingwauk Residential School, and in Thunder Bay. She received her Bachelor of Arts, Bachelor of Education, and Master of Education degrees from Lakehead University.

Slipperjack's novels *Honour the Sun* (1987) and *Silent Words* (1992) depict Ojibwa life in transition, through the eyes of child narrators. 'I write . . . to offer my children an insight into life as it was in my own childhood. I was born and raised in the lands of my ancestors and grew up in a traditional and cultural upbringing with its teachings and discipline as had been passed down for generations past. I cannot teach my children these things in the city . . . .

The traditional oral storytelling sessions were very much a part of my life and I have attempted to extend this knowledge and the wisdom of the teachings into the content of my novels.'

An assistant professor at Lakehead University, Slipperjack co-ordinates the Faculty of Education's Native Teacher Education Program.

CATHERINE SONEEGOH SUTTON Ojibway, 1822–65

Catherine Soneegoh Sutton, whose Ojibway name was Nah-nee-bah-wee-quay (Upright Woman), was born near the Credit River. When she was two, her family moved to the Credit Indian village, a Methodist settlement. In 1837 she went to England with her aunt, the wife of Peter Jones, the first Native Canadian to be ordained.

After attending school in England for a year, Sutton returned to Canada and in 1839 married an English immigrant, William Sutton. They served as Methodist missionaries in various venues, including a model farm near Sault Ste Marie in 1852 and two years later a mission in Michigan.

The Nawash band of Owen Sound had ceded them land in 1845, but when they returned to Owen Sound in 1857 the land had been laid out for sale. Sutton was first refused a share of the Nawash band's annuities for having married a white man and being absent from the country, and then was not allowed to purchase the land because she was an Indian.

Through a series of lectures in Canada and the United States, Sutton was able to raise money for a journey to England where she petitioned the Queen. As a result, she was able to return to Canada and buy back some of the land. She continued actively to pursue Native rights until her death in 1865.

This selection is from an entry in her journal, held in the Grey County and Owen Sound Museum. It is taken here from *Native Literature in Canada* (1990), by Penny Petrone, who surmises that it is a copy of a letter written in response to an editorial in the periodical *The Leader*. The entry is dated 8 September 1864.

MARY AUGUSTA TAPPAGE Shuswap, 1888–*c*. 1978

Mary Augusta Tappage, known to her community as Augusta, was born at Soda Creek in British Columbia's Cariboo country, 11 February 1888. Her background was Shuswap and Métis.

At the age of four, Augusta was sent to a Catholic mission school near Williams Lake. Her memories of that period are typical of students from residential schools: 'If we were heard speaking Shuswap, we were punished. We were made to write on the board one hundred times, "I will not speak Indian any more". . . . And now we are supposed to remember our language and our skills because they are almost lost. Well, they're going to be hard to get back because the new generations are not that interested.' Augusta left school at thirteen and returned to the reservation at Soda Creek. In 1903 she married George Evans, a non-status Shuswap, and so she lost her own Indian status.

Augusta's working life was spent homesteading and subsistence farming on Deep Creek, near her birthplace. The education of her sons reflects her non-status position: 'My two boys, Joseph and George, they never went to school. Taxpayers' children couldn't go to the Mission. Well, I didn't care about that. But there was no other school close by, so I taught them myself. Yes, I guess they can read and reckon as good as most folk can. I taught them myself.'

After the deaths of her husband and eldest son, Augusta worked cooking and cleaning for various families. She acted as informal foster mother to many young people. Like many other Native people of her generation, Augusta committed great energy to cultural education, to keep Shuswap, which is not a written language, alive.

DREW HAYDEN TAYLOR Ojibway, b. 1962

Drew Taylor, from the Curve Lake Reserve near Peterborough, Ontario, is known for his humour: 'My mother says I was eleven pounds twelve ounces when I was born. That's probably why I'm an only child.'

After receiving an Honours Diploma in Broadcasting from Seneca College in 1982, Taylor worked in media journalism and contributed to documentaries on Native culture. He also 'spent time working in the television mines, writing scripts for *The Beachcombers*, *Street Legal*, and *North of Sixty*.

Taylor's work in theatre earned him a Chalmers Award for *Toronto at Dreamer's Rock* (1989), a Canadian Author's Association Award for *The Bootlegger Blues* (1990), a Dora Mavor Moore Award for *Only Drunks and Children Tell the Truth* (1995), and the 1996 University of Alaska Anchorage Native Playwriting Contest for *The Baby Blues*.

His publications include *Toronto at Dreamer's Rock/Education is Our Right* (1990), *The Bootlegger Blues* (1991), *Someday* (1993), and *Funny, You Don't Look Like One: Observations from a Blue-Eyed Ojibway* (1996), a collection of his humorous commentaries.

'I have written practically everything under the sun, in one form or another, except for a novel or poetry. Maybe someday I'll combine the two and write a poetic novel.'

ANTHONY APAKARK THRASHER Inuit, 1937–89

Anthony Thrasher began life as a nomadic Inuk in the small community of Paulatuk. At the age of six, he was sent to Aklavik, to a residential school, as what he later called 'a Grade 1 captive' of a Roman Catholic mission. He recalled the joys of his summers when he felt a full participant in hunting, fishing, and all aspects of traditional life, and then the severe shock each fall when the nuns would harshly reintroduce him to the rules of school.

When Thrasher was twelve, his father had a stroke and Thrasher was discharged from the school to help the family. He worked at first in traditional pursuits but at seventeen went to Tuktoyaktuk to work on the construction of military stations for the Distant Early Warning Line. He realized this was part of a

general change in the North and at nineteen went south to take a course in driving machines. 'Half of the population of Aklavik was relying on government
hand-outs. It was either that, or join the white construction gangs, or starve.'

In Edmonton, Thrasher was amazed by everything from traffic lights to
prostitution. Alcohol became a major problem for Thrasher and for the other
Inuit new to the South. When he got back to the North he was able to get
work in the creation of the new town of Inuvik.

At the beginning, Thrasher's criminal record suggests a series of petty misunderstandings. Many, if not all, of the convictions were alcohol-related. At
twenty-seven he was sent to an alcoholic rehabilitation centre. This only
helped for a time. He soon returned to alcohol. He described this period as
'anybody's riverbank pal'. Now sniffing glue and nail-polish remover, he
returned to the rehabilitation centre, but it had no long-term effect. In jail, he
tried unsuccessfully to hang himself. Then he was charged with murder, for
the death of a man he couldn't remember even meeting.

Given seven years for manslaughter, Thrasher was sent to the Prince Albert
Penitentiary, where he felt, from both the other inmates and the guards, 'the
ever-present danger.' The worst thing was trying to deal with the racism—of
whites, 'niggers', and 'Indians': 'As an Eskimo, I was in the middle.'

Thrasher records other terrors of prison life, from drugs through suicides.
He tried to record his own experiences but found it impossible. Instead, he
turned to education, as both student and lecturer, and began to speak about
his culture to southern Native groups. A transfer to minimum-security camp
on Vancouver Island followed, but drugs and alcohol led to a fight and he was
sent next to the British Columbia Penitentiary. He was soon transferred to a
hospital for the criminally insane. Although eventually released, Thrasher
never succeeded in regaining control of his life. He died in 1989.

Thrasher's autobiography, *Thrasher: Skid Row Eskimo* (1976), was written
at various times. At the urging of his lawyer, Thrasher's 'collaborators',
Gerry Deagle and Alan Mettrick, collated 'what was essentially a loose-
leafed diary into narrative form'. The result is a combination of two stories
common to Native biographies: the nostalgic recall of traditional life, most
common in Inuit narratives, and the decay through alcohol and institutional
racism, more often seen in the stories of southern Native peoples.

MARION TUU'LUQ Inuit, b. 1910
Marion Tuu'luq, born in Chantrey Inlet, Northwest Territories, lived a traditional nomadic life before she moved to Baker Lake in 1961. She married
twice and had sixteen children. Beginning with small scenes sewn on fabric,
she became part of the burst of development in Inuit art at Baker Lake in the
early seventies.

Tuu'luq's achievements as an artist, a creator of wallhangings, drawings,
and prints, are remarkable. She has had various two-person shows with her
artist husband, Luke Anguhadluq, and has participated in group shows of
Inuit art in Winnipeg, Ottawa, Vancouver, and New York. Her work was

included in the Inuit Masterworks exhibit at the McMichael Canadian Collection in Kleinburg, Ontario in 1983 and in the show, 'Contemporary Indian and Inuit Art of Canada', at the United Nations in New York in 1983. One of her wallhangings was included in the 1974 World Crafts Council show, 'In Praise of Hands'. She was elected a member of the Royal Academy of Arts in 1978 and the University of Alberta awarded her an Honorary Doctorate of Laws in 1990.

'A Story of Starvation', which first appeared in *Inuit Today* in 1977, is a true and not unusual story, notable for its strong sense of pacing and of what might be called a narrator's feel for the order of things. The diction is subtle and appropriate, particularly in the brief dialogue included. Recorded by Susan Tagoona as orature, not literature, it shows the creativity possible in what folklorists call the 'personal experience narrative'.

JAMES TYMAN Métis, b. 1964

James Tyman, born in Ile-à-la-Cross, Saskatchewan, has few memories of his early years as Kenny Howard Martin in Saskatoon. He was later told that as a result of his parents' alcoholism and abuse of him and his seven older siblings, he was taken away by Saskatchewan Social Services at the age of four and began a new life in Fort Qu'Appelle, in a white foster family, with the new name of James Tyman.

The recollections of his early years, recorded in his autobiography *Inside Out: An Autobiography by a Native Canadian* (1990), are similar to those of other Natives growing up in a white environment. He felt alienated, both from the strange Natives in the street and from the kind yet self-evidently different family at home.

When he began to go to school at Lebret, the racist stories he heard about 'Indians' created more confusion. But perhaps the greatest problem was social: Tyman recalls the antagonistic white and Native groups as 'the white racists and the warriors', and found his friends among the few who belonged to neither.

In high school, Tyman had a degree of success as a football player, but any sense of belonging was destroyed when his adoptive father died: 'I don't care if I was adopted, he was truly my father. And this is wrong. We weren't finished. I'm only seventeen! I want a father. First they took me away from one, and now I've lost another.'

After high school, Tyman recalls, 'Our crimes were bizarre and senseless.' Much of *Inside Out* recalls drugs, alcohol, and racist police. The selection presented here is of one jail spell in this period.

Tyman's sense of self became a product of his prison and street experience: 'I'd been a good Indian, a scummy Indian, an apple, and now a racist Indian.' He moved to Saskatoon to trace his roots but ended up involved with pimping and more drugs, and he nearly suicided. The end of his autobiography records the discovery of his birth mother, a one-time encounter, which led only to a reassertion 'of who was really my real mom: Cecile Tyman'. His next encounter with alcohol led to another stay in jail, where he began to write. The author profile in *Inside Out* records that he hopes to study for a law or journalism degree.

RICHARD VAN CAMP Dogrib, b. 1971

Richard Van Camp was born in Fort Smith, Northwest Territories, which he calls 'the greatest town in the whole wide world'. The multiculturalism and general sense of community found there are central to his work: 'Dogribs are rare here. My being born outnumbered and having friends from every spectrum of the rainbow has given me the gift of, I believe, an open mind and an open heart. I write about Northerners, people who have decided to spend their lives and their love up north.'

Van Camp says, 'I write everything from poetry to children's stories to graphic scripts to transcriptions of elders' stories to novels.' The creation of a children's book, *The Man Called Raven*, with illustrations by George Littlechild, has led him to pursue other co-operative ventures and he is now working on an anthology of First Nations storytellers. The first in his *Four Directions*, a series of novels set in the Northwest Territories, is *The Lesser Blessed* (1996), to be followed in 1998 by *Come a Little Death*.

Van Camp was educated at the En'owkin International School of Writing in Penticton, British Columbia and at the University of Victoria, but he describes his desire to become a writer as rooted in his friendship with Lorne Simon: 'I became a writer the day I heard he died. When I write now I feel him around me. We still talk, Lorne and I. I know he guides my hand. He taught me more about writing than any school. Writing is about feeling. It's about gut. It's raw. It's sexy. It's impact.'

In 1997 Van Camp received the Canadian Authors Association Air Canada Award, presented annually to young writers of 'outstanding promise'.

RICHARD WAGAMESE Ojibway, b. 1955

Richard Wagamese comes from the Wabaseemoong First Nation in northwestern Ontario. *Keeper'n Me* (1994) is his first novel, to be followed in 1997 by a second, *A Quality of Light*.

Wagamese has worked extensively as a journalist, broadcaster, television producer, and writer. Among his achievements are the Native American Press Association Award for best local columns in 1989 and the National Newspaper Award for his columns in the *Calgary Herald* in 1991. In these columns he ranged from autobiographical reflections on drug and alcohol abuse and prison experience to commentary on both historical and contemporary Native people and issues. A noteworthy element was the 'Eagle Feather', which he awarded at the end of each column to a person or group, Native or non-Native, that he felt had made a positive contribution to the Native community. Many of his columns are now collected in *The Terrible Summer* (1996).

Unlike the irony of *Keeper'n Me*, Wagamese's columns are direct, unflinching, and very serious. A good example of this sensibility is a piece (not included in the collection) on imprisoned Native activist Leonard Peltier published in the American periodical *News from Indian Country* (1991):

> Peltier is dangerous. He's dangerous because he represents an image of Native Pride, Native solidarity and Native fortitude. . . . To free him is tantamount to admitting wrongdoing and recognizing the solidarity of Native groups across North America who have fought long and hard to see justice implemented.

EMMA LEE WARRIOR Peigan, b. 1941

Emma Lee Warrior grew up on the Peigan Reserve in southern Alberta, close to the American border, a member of the North Peigan (Blackfoot) band. She attended a boarding school there. 'But with all the rules and restrictions, it might as well not have been anywhere near home.' Warrior writes to overcome the effects of that early repression. 'I find great freedom in writing. I find myself.'

Warrior's stories and poems have appeared in *Wicazo Sa*, *A Gathering of Spirit*, *Harper's Anthology of Twentieth Century Native American Poetry*, and *Canadian Fiction Magazine*. She acquired a Master of Arts degree from the University of Washington. She continued to live in the state of Washington, writing and training to be a counsellor. However, she remains tied to her home community. 'That landscape is within me.'

JORDAN WHEELER Métis, b. 1964

Jordan Wheeler was born in Victoria of Cree, Ojibway, Irish, English, Scottish, and French descent. Educated at St John's Ravenscourt School, Winnipeg, he began writing at the age of seventeen. Three of his stories were published in an anthology, *Achimoona* (1985). *Brothers In Arms* (1989) is a collection of three novellas about Native brothers. Wheeler now lives in Winnipeg where he works in video, film, and popular theatre, writing plays with inner-city youth. He states that he feels a particular closeness to the Touchwood Hills area of Saskatchewan.

ALEXANDER WOLFE Saulteaux, b. 1927

Alexander Wolfe was born on the Sakimay Reserve in south central Saskatchewan during the Depression. His early education took place at a boarding school operated by the United Church of Canada. In 1950, he moved to the Turtle Mountains of North Dakota, where his family had originated. In 1964 he participated in President Johnson's Great Society Community Action Program and earned his high school diploma and a teacher's aide certificate in pre-school education.

> To be responsible for retelling the stories of the grandfathers today, the *Anishnaybay* must renew their commitment to the oral tradition. At the same time, we must turn to a written tradition and use it to support, not destroy, our oral tradition. The structure of our society in the days when the

grandfathers were still with us was very different from what we have today. Information and instruction were transmitted to us orally, in story form, by our old people. Listening and absorbing what was told required great lengths of time. The use of the mind and memory were important; this is why the stories were told over and over again. The environment of that time held nothing to distract the listener and storyteller.

Today many things distract the listener and disrupt the storytelling. Radio, television, video, and printed material take precedence in the everyday lives of many children, and even the adults, in our present society. We are ceasing to be storytellers and listeners, and in so doing we are losing that great virtue called patience, so strongly emphasized by the grandfathers. If we are to preserve the stories that contain our history we must restore the art, practice, and principles of oral storytelling. We must also commit our oral history to written form. That written form, however, must still comply with the wishes and aspirations of the grandfathers, now long gone from our numbers.

Index